Treat this book with care and respect.

It should become part of your personal and professional library. It will serve you well at any number of points during your professional career.

RISK AND INSURANCE

4th Edition

Mark R. Greene
Professor of Insurance
The University of Georgia

F33

Published by
SOUTH-WESTERN PUBLISHING CO.

CINCINNATI WEST CHICAGO, ILL. DALLAS PELHAM MANOR, N.Y.
PALO ALTO, CALIF. BRIGHTON, ENGLAND

ISBN: 0-538-06330-0
Library of Congress Catalog Card No.: 76-9708

1 2 3 4 5 H 1 0 9 8 7
Printed in the United States of America

PREFACE

Since the first edition of this text appeared in 1962, many important changes have occurred in the field of risk and insurance, which were reflected in subsequent editions in 1968 and 1973. This fourth edition continues the task of presenting as modern a picture of risk and insurance as possible. New developments such as increased government participation in and regulation of insurance, new versions of basic insurance contracts, the developing no-fault insurance law, and the changing international scene are incorporated. Tables and charts have been updated. Several chapters have been rewritten and reorganized for greater clarity and improved coverage of the material.

A basic concept has been retained in this text: to recognize that one book in risk and insurance is the maximum number that most college students will ever study. Nearly all fields of insurance have been covered, and basic problems caused by risk in our world have been emphasized before posing solutions. In this way it is hoped that analysis of insurance will be more meaningful to the student than would be possible by factual discussion of insurance contracts without any analysis of the problems which established the basic need for such contracts. Emphasis has also been placed on teaching how contracts may be analyzed so that the student may apply this knowledge to new policies as they are developed.

The original goals in writing the book have been preserved: (1) to cover basic ideas, problems, and principles found in all types of modern insurance and other methods of handling risk; (2) to emphasize the fundamental unifying elements of risk and insurance; and (3) to stimulate thought about the problems of risk and insurance through questions at the end of the text which often cannot be answered by short factual statements taken directly from text material.

Two types of supplementary materials have been developed to enhance the usefulness of this text as a learning device: (1) A new and separate study guide for use by the student has been written by Dr. James S. Trieschmann, of The University of Georgia. (2) The instructor's manual has been completely reworked. It contains objective test material applicable to each chapter along with notes on each end-of-chapter question appearing in the text. The instructor's manual also contains other teaching suggestions for the book.

There are many who should be thanked for their kind assistance and inspiration to the author in preparing this fourth edition. Gratitude is expressed to those teachers who gave generously of their time in writing letters of helpful suggestions for needed changes and corrections in the book. It is felt that orporation of these suggestions into the manuscript has improved the book many ways. The result should make the material more meaningful to students in the quest for a scientific study of risk and insurance.

Finally, I would like to extend special thanks to Carol Corina who is mainly responsible for typing revisions, proofreading, and making changes to rid the manuscript of phraseology which could be interpreted as reflecting male chauvinistic bias. The author accepts the final responsibility for any remaining evidence of such bias.

Mark R. Greene
Athens, Georgia

CONTENTS

Chapter *One*

CONCEPTS IN RISK AND INSURANCE

Risk, defined as uncertainty as to loss, is universal in that it poses a problem to individuals in nearly every walk of life. Students, householders, business people, employees, travelers, investors, and farmers all must face risk and develop ways of handling it. If a cost or a loss is certain to occur, it may be planned for in advance and treated as a definite and known expense. It is when there is uncertainty about the occurrence of a cost or loss that risk becomes an important problem.

To illustrate the universality of risk, consider briefly the ways in which risk becomes a problem to the average business firm. First, there is risk of loss of the firm's assets and earning power through destruction or loss of its plant or other property by fire, windstorm, or other events. These perils or events may or may not occur, but the possibility of their occurrence and subsequent effects cannot be ignored by the prudent manager in any firm.

Second, the business faces risks of loss from unintentional acts which cause loss to others, resulting in legal liability for such loss. Third, the business faces market risks. The manager may misjudge the desires of consumers by manufacturing goods which can be sold only at a loss. Bad debt losses, losses by advertising in inappropriate media, and losses through selection of improper marketing channels may also occur.

Fourth, the business faces production risks. Losses may occur by breakdown of machinery, improper quality control, poor weather, inefficient labor, or use of faulty materials. Fifth, the business faces social risks. Events such as strikes, riots, civil commotion, laws which hinder business operations, currency inflation, and political events which restrict business activity may all cause loss.

Sixth, the business faces financial risks. Sales slowdowns may reduce cash flow thereby preventing repayment of debt and resulting in possible bankruptcy. Investments may turn sour. Loans needed to keep the business operating may be turned down, causing the firm to use credit sources whose terms or interest charges may be onerous.

It is not surprising that most people try to avoid risk as much as possible or to reduce its negative consequences. Unfortunately not all risk can be minimized or avoided. In order to make progress in maximizing insulation from the adverse effects of risk, we must study the subject scientifically, learn more about the specific nature of the different types of risk, and find ways to deal with risk more effectively.

RISK DEFINED

In common parlance, the word *risk* is used in many different ways, variously referring to general uncertainty, doubt, an insured object, or chance of loss. In this book risk is defined in two ways: objectively and subjectively. *Objective risk*, or statistical risk, applicable mainly to groups of objects exposed to loss, refers to the variation that occurs when actual losses differ from expected losses. It may be measured statistically by some concept in variation, such as the standard deviation. *Subjective risk*, on the other hand, refers to the mental state of an individual who experiences uncertainty or doubt or worry as to the outcome of a given event. Both definitions of risk are concerned with events which may or may not produce economic loss or an involuntary parting of value.

The economic loss can take many forms, such as the loss of property by physical perils such as fire, tornado, or explosion. It can take the form of premature death of a key person in a business enterprise or of a family breadwinner. It can result from a lawsuit to recover damages for some negligent act. Whatever its form, the risk of economic loss is something most people wish to avoid. Hence, it becomes especially important to have a clear understanding of its nature.

To illustrate, consider an event whose probability of occurrence (i.e., long-run chance of occurrence) is known to one person, but unknown to another. For example, *A* is an experienced poker player and knows that the probability of drawing an ace for a straight on the next round is very low because *A* has observed that three aces have already been dealt. *B*, on the other hand, also trying to fill a straight, has failed to notice this fact and is faced with considerable uncertainty as to what to do. The true probability of either player drawing the ace is the same, but each has a different attitude toward the possibility because of different degrees of knowledge. *A* realizes that if faced with this identical situation a large number of times, the chance of drawing the needed card is very low. *A* is a coldly calculating player, whose primary influence is knowledge of the odds and the length of time to be played. We can say the type of risk with which this player is dealing is measurable and can be objectively determined; *A* is dealing with objective risk. *B*'s behavior is based on other things, such as faith in good luck, bluffing ability, and feelings at the time. We can say that the type of risk with which *B* is dealing is subjectively determined—subjective risk.

Objective Risk

Objective risk, then, may be defined as the relative variation of actual from probable loss. In this book we will be concerned mainly with the range of variability of economic losses about some long-run average (most probable) loss in a group large enough to analyze significantly in a statistical sense. For example, an insurer, from observing past data, finds that in a group of 100,000 houses there are on the average 100 losses from fire each year. The insurer is naturally concerned with the problem of whether the actual number of losses experienced will be exactly 100, or some other number, such as 95 or 105. If he can be 95% sure that the range will not exceed the bounds of 95–105, one rate may be quoted. On the other hand, if the range is likely to be 80–120 losses, a higher rate may be quoted because the objective risk is higher. The probable variation of actual losses from the average or probable loss or range is one measure of objective risk of the insurer. It may be expressed as follows:

$$\text{Objective Risk} = \frac{\text{Probable Variation of Actual from Probable Losses}}{\text{Probable Losses}}$$

Subjective Risk

A subjective risk may be defined as a psychological uncertainty which stems from the individual's mental attitudes or state of mind.[1] Generally subjective risk has been measured by means of different psychological tests, but no widely accepted or uniform tests of proven reliability and validity have been developed.[2] Thus, although we recognize different degrees of risk-taking willingness in persons, it is difficult to measure these attitudes scientifically and to predict risk-taking behavior, such as insurance-buying behavior, from tests of risk-taking attitudes. In Chapter 2, the concept of economic utility is discussed as one means of quantifying subjective risk and rationalizing insurance-buying behavior.

A significant reason for studying subjective risk is the influence it has on decision making when the decision maker is interpreting objective risk. One risk manager may determine that some given level of objective risk is "high" while another may simultaneously interpret this level as being "low." These different interpretations depend on the subjective attitudes of the decision maker toward risk. Thus, it is not enough to know only the degree of objective risk; the risk attitudes of the decision maker who will act on the basis of this knowledge must be known. A person who knows that there is only one chance in a million that a loss will occur may still experience worry and doubt, and thus would buy insurance, while another would not. It depends upon an individual's outlook toward risk.

Various studies have been made to learn more about the factors which influence subjective risk. The change in individual decisions regarding risk as a result of exposures to group discussion is the subject of a large psychological literature.[3] In general, psychologists have demonstrated that group discussion

[1] Some writers have used the word "uncertainty" to be synonymous with subjective risk, as defined here.

[2] Paul Slovic, "Convergent Validation of Risk-Taking Measures," *Journal of Abnormal and Social Psychology*, Vol. 65 (1962), pp. 68-71.

[3] Russell P. Clark, III, "Risk Taking in Groups: A Social Psychological Analysis," *Journal of Risk and Insurance*, Vol. 41 No. 1 (March, 1974), pp. 75-92.

tends to cause the decision maker to assume more risk after group discussion than before. It has been shown that age and sex influence risk attitudes, with women being more conservative than men and older people being more conservative than young people.[4] It has also been shown that there is a tendency for people to overestimate low likelihoods and underestimate large likelihoods.[5] Thus, due to mental attitudes toward risk, a poker player might disregard extremely low probabilities of success and take gambles unwarranted by the size of the pot. Similarly, a person facing a substantial probability of loss of an automobile through collision might refuse insurance.

DEGREE OF RISK

What is meant by a high degree of risk or a low degree of risk? The answer depends on whether we are speaking of subjective risk or objective risk. A high degree of subjective risk may be said to exist when a person experiences great mental uncertainty or doubt as to the frequency of occurrence of some event which may cause a loss and as to the amount or severity of this possible loss. Generally, high subjective risk produces very conservative conduct and low subjective risk tends to produce less conservative conduct.

Objective risk, on the other hand, may be said to vary according to the ratio of probable variation of actual from probable loss. If a loss has already occurred, the probable variation is zero and, thus, objective risk is also zero. Similarly, if the loss is impossible to happen, the probable variation is zero and the objective risk is zero.

For example, assume that Jack Smith goes into his basement one morning and smells smoke. His house is on fire. He realizes suddenly that he has not purchased fire insurance, so right after phoning the fire department he phones his insurance agent and says, "Cover me." The agent says, "Sorry, Jack, we can't insure a burning building." Did the agent refuse because the risk was too high? Not at all. In this case, there is no risk at all, for there is no uncertainty as to loss. The loss has already occurred. Furthermore, there is very little risk that more damage will occur before the firemen arrive. The agent cannot bind the insurer in such a situation. As obvious as this example may seem, there are many similar cases each year where individuals seek insurance on an event that is almost certain to cause loss. They have failed to recognize that risk must be dealt with in advance of the event, when the loss is still unknown and uncertain.

RISK AND PROBABILITY

It is necessary to distinguish carefully between risk and probability. Many elementary mistakes in risk management occur because of failure to recognize

[4] N. Kass, "Risk in Decision Making as a Function of Age, Sex, and Probability Preference," *Child Development*, Vol. 35 (1964), pp. 577-582.

[5] M. D. Preston, and P. C. Baratta, "An Experimental Study of the Auction Value of an Uncertain Income," *American Journal of Psychology*, Vol. 161 (1948), pp. 183-193.

the difference between these two concepts. *Probability* refers to the long-run chance of occurrence, or relative frequency of some event. Insurers are particularly interested in the probability or chance of loss, or more accurately, the probability that some peril will occur and cause a loss to one of a group of insured objects. Actually, probability has little meaning if applied to the chance of occurrence of a single event. Probability has meaning, then, only when applied to the chance of occurrence of a large number of events.

Risk, as differentiated from probability, is a concept in relative variation. We are referring here particularly to objective risk. As stated above, objective risk can be measured meaningfully only in terms of a group large enough to analyze in a statistical sense. If the group of objects is too small, the range of probable variation is so large as to be virtually infinite as far as the insurer is concerned. It may be, for example, that there are 1,000,000 persons age 25 and it is predicted from past experience that 3,000 of them will die in a given time period. The probability of loss is thus .003. Mary Smith may be interested in the risk that she will be among the 3,000 who are supposed to die. An insurer who has 10,000 persons covered under life insurance contracts may be interested in the risk that some number *other* than the probable number, 30, will die within the given time period. Clearly, the probability of death is the same, no matter from whose viewpoint one is speaking. The risk, however, is quite different for the insurer and the insured.

The reason that the risk is different is understood, almost intuitively, by recognizing that the law of large numbers is operating in the case of the insurer, but not in the case of the individual insured. The *law of large numbers,* a basic law of mathematics, says that as the number of exposure units increases, the more certain it is that actual loss experience will equal probable loss experience. Hence, the risk diminishes as the number of exposure units increases. The individual seldom has a sufficient number of exposure units to reduce the risk significantly through the operation of the law of large numbers. This individual may join with others, however, and obtain this advantage. Basically, the insurance mechanism is the device through which such grouping can be effectively accomplished.

OBJECTIVE RISK AND THE LAW OF LARGE NUMBERS

The law of large numbers has great practical value to an insurer who can reduce objective risk to the vanishing point in some cases by securing an ever larger number of units in the insured group.

Effect of Numbers Exposed on Objective Risk

To illustrate the effect of the number exposed on objective risk, assume that an insurer has only 100 automobiles in an insured group and that the probability of collision loss is .20 per year. On the average, then, the insurer can expect 20 collisions per year. However, with only 100 autos, the variation from the average may be quite large. In fact, it can be demonstrated that under certain mathematical assumptions there is a chance of about 1 in 3 that the number of collisions will exceed the average by 4, and there is about a 5% chance that collisions will exceed the average by 8. A variation of 8 from the average number 20 is 40% (8/20). The insurer may not wish to accept this much risk. However, if the number of insured autos is increased to 900, the risk is such that there would be only a 5% chance that actual losses would exceed the average losses by as much as 24. Since for 900 autos the average losses would be 180, a variation of 24 amounts to a 13⅓% variation, or one third of the variation experienced with 100 autos. The results may be summarized as shown below.

Probability of collision loss = 20%

	100 autos	900 autos
Objective Risk $= \dfrac{\text{Probable Variation in Losses}}{\text{Probable Losses}}$	$\dfrac{8}{20} = 40\%$	$\dfrac{24}{180} = 13\tfrac{1}{3}\%$

By increasing the number in the insured group nine times, the risk was reduced to a third of its former level. This illustrates a fundamental point. Under given mathematical assumptions, other factors remaining the same, *objective risk varies inversely with the square root of the number of exposures*. In the case above, the square root of the number of exposure units increased from 10 in the first case to 30 in the second case (three times), while risk declined to one third of its former level.

Effect of Probability on Objective Risk

In the previous example it was assumed that the underlying probability of loss did not change. We may now inquire what would happen to objective risk if the probability of loss is varied, but the number of exposure units remained the same.

What is the relationship of objective risk to probability? One might first believe that the higher the probability, the higher the risk. However, this is not the case. Rather, the opposite is true because as probability increases, the variation of average losses from probable losses tends to decrease, assuming a constant number of insured exposure units.

To illustrate, assume that there are two employers, *A* and *B*, each with 10,000 employees, and it is desired to insure these employers against the peril of occupational injuries to workers. Employer *A* is in a "safe" occupation, and the probability of disabling injury in *A*'s plant is .01. Employer *B* is in a "dangerous" occupation, and the probability of disabling injury in *B*'s plant is .25. In the long run, Employer *A* may expect 100 disabling injuries per year, compared with 2,500 for Employer *B*. There is about a 95% chance that the probable variation in injuries in *A*'s plant will not exceed 20, while in *B*'s plant the probable variation will not exceed 87. Thus, objective risk in *A*'s situation is 20/100 or 20%, compared with 87/2,500 or 3.5% for *B*. In this example, although *B*'s objective risk is only about 17% (3.5/20 = .175) that of *A*'s, *B's* probability of loss is much larger.[6] The principle thus emerges: *Objective risk varies inversely with probability for any constant number of exposure units*. This law is a corollary of the law of large numbers, noted above.

We may now summarize the two most important applications of the law of large numbers as it affects objective risk:

1. As the number of exposure units increases in an insured group, objective risk decreases. Specifically, objective risk varies inversely with the square root of the number of exposure units, other things remaining the same.
2. As the probability of loss increases, objective risk decreases. In general, the rate of decrease in objective risk is less than proportionate to the rate of increase in probability of loss.

From this analysis, the student may erroneously conclude that an insurer would always charge a lower premium as the probability of loss rises because of the reduced risk. Such, of course, is not the case. Basically, it is the probability of loss that governs the amount of premium charged in a given situation. However, if an insurer had so few in an insured group that it would not be possible to determine just what the losses might be—i.e., objective risk is high—the insurer would tend to assume the worst and make a charge for coverage based on the worst possible result. In effect, the insurer makes a charge both for risk as well as for expected losses. In the event that the insurer is able to attract a sufficiently large group of insureds, thus reducing or eliminating objective risk, the charge for risk greatly diminishes.

Frequently, an insurer is asked to offer coverage on a single exposure unit. In such an event, the law of large numbers is of no help to the insurer, who must rely on subjective judgment and quote a rate based on subjective attitudes toward the risk. In such a situation, the risk may properly be termed subjective risk.

[6] Assuming certain mathematical properties in the distribution of losses. See Chapter 2 for a fuller elaboration. Alternate definitions of objective risk are of course possible. For example, Fikry Gahin and Jerry L. Jorgensen have defined risk in the formula

$$R = \frac{1 + X(\sqrt{N} - 1)}{\sqrt{N}}$$

where R is the risk coefficient, N is the number of exposure units, and X is the loss ratio expected in a given type of loss exposure. The loss ratio is an estimate of probability. Thus, under this definition, it follows from the formula that risk varies inversely with the square root of the number of exposure units, but directly with loss probability. The concept of objective risk treated in this book considers risk to vary inversely with probability, because it is felt that as an event becomes more certain to happen, there is less risk and the loss-producing event becomes progressively less susceptible to coverage through insurance (see Chapter 3). The converse is true when the probability of loss decreases. Gahin and Jorgensen's formula gives a more logical view of subjective risk, since most people probably tend to worry more as probability of loss rises and to worry less when it falls. Fikry Gahin and Jerry L. Jorgensen, "The Theory of Risk and Insurance—An Alternate Approach" (A paper given to the Risk Theory Seminar of the American Risk and Insurance Association, St. Louis, 1971).

THE BURDEN OF RISK

To some, the idea of risk bearing and risk assumption is tantalizing, an element which makes life more interesting. What these individuals have in mind mostly is the uncertainty of making a profit or a gain, and not the uncertainty of incurring disastrous losses. In this book, we will be dealing with the latter type of uncertainty. Recognizing that risk assumption carries with it the possibility of losses as well as gains, most individuals constantly seek ways of avoiding the former in as efficient a manner as possible, without destroying the possibility of gain.

How does risk create an economic burden? It does so in several ways. In the first place, risk necessitates the setting aside of a reserve fund to meet losses if and when they do occur. Such a reserve fund, if it were not used for this purpose, could be employed in other ways, presumably at greater advantage than as a demand deposit, or as an investment at low interest rates in a form readily convertible into cash.

Secondly, the existence of risk not only raises the cost to society of certain services, but may also deprive society altogether of services "too risky" to warrant the investment of savings. There is, in general, a shortage of "risk capital" in all nations, with most investors preferring greater or lesser degrees of safety. This attitude was epitomized by a saying attributed to Mark Twain, who commented that he was more interested in the return *of* his money than he was in the return *on* his money. In other words, the riskier the venture, the greater the return that must be promised to investors; hence, the more costly that particular service is to society. And if risk is too great, the service may be withdrawn altogether.

An additional burden of risk is the mental unrest that accompanies risk. One of the greatest human drives is to achieve security. A feeling of security seems necessary before society can work efficiently and perform creative achievements. As long as a society is forced to spend a major share of its energies fighting its enemies or struggling against the elements for survival, it is classed as a relatively primitive society. The same generalization applies to an individual. This perhaps explains why people struggle hard to achieve an advanced civilization and to cultivate a secure atmosphere in which creativity can be expressed and wherein relative abundance can be established.

Two examples will illustrate the burden of risk in society. In 1975, a spokesman from the American Medical Association commented that without medical malpractice insurance, many physicians would refuse to practice medicine. The comment arose from publicity given to reports that many insurers planned to withdraw malpractice coverage from the market because of heavy losses and inadequate rates. Thus, the inability to transfer risk to others threatened the reduction of vital medical services, because physicians perceived significant risk of loss from legal suits by patients over the medical treatment received. In another example, the quantity and quality of business services rendered in high-crime areas of large cities has markedly deteriorated because of the risk of loss due to robbery, burglary, and theft.

RISK, HAZARD, AND PERIL

Many persons commonly employ the terms "risky," "hazardous," and "perilous" synonymously. For clarity in thinking, however, the meaning of these words should be carefully distinguished.

A *peril* may be defined as a contingency which may cause a loss, and a *hazard* is that condition which introduces or increases the probability of loss from a peril. Both of these terms are more closely related to probability than they are to risk. For example, one of the perils that can cause loss to an auto is collision. A condition that makes the occurrence of collisions more likely is an icy street. The icy street is the hazard and the collision is the peril. In winter, the *probability* of collisions is higher owing to the existence of icy streets. In such a situation, the risk of loss is not necessarily any higher or lower, since we have defined risk as the uncertainty that underlying probability will work out in practice.

TYPES OF HAZARDS

In the preceding paragraph, a hazard was defined as a condition which introduces or increases the probability of loss from a peril. This definition might also be expanded to include conditions that make the loss more severe, once the peril has occurred and has caused a loss. What are the various types of hazards which not only increase the probability of loss but also increase the severity of loss once it occurs? Although there have been many classifications used, there seem to be only three basic types of hazards: physical, moral, and morale.

Physical Hazard

A *physical hazard* is a condition stemming from the physical characteristics of an object that increases the probability and severity of loss from given perils. Physical hazards include such phenomena as the existence of dry forests (hazard to fire), earth faults (hazard to earthquakes), and icebergs (hazard to ocean shipping). Such hazards may or may not be within human control. Many hazards to fire, for example, can be controlled, such as by placing restrictions upon building camp fires in forests during the dry season. Some hazards, however, cannot be controlled—little can be done to prevent or to control air masses which produce ocean storms.

Moral Hazard

A *moral hazard* stems from the mental attitude of the insured. Because of indifference to loss or owing to an outright desire for the loss to occur, the individual either brings about personal loss or intentionally does nothing to prevent its occurrence or to alleviate its severity.

Moral hazards are typified by individuals with known records of dishonesty or indifference. Moral hazards may exist in situations where excessive amounts of fire insurance are requested on "white elephant" properties, properties no longer profitable and where an incentive might exist to "sell the building to the fire insurance company." Every underwriter knows that fire losses are more frequent in depression periods, for example. During the depression of the 1930's, life insurers had such a substantial rise in the frequency of claims for disability income that the coverage had to be withdrawn almost completely.

Morale Hazard

Even though an individual does not consciously want a loss, nevertheless there may be a subconscious desire for a loss with the result that losses tend to be higher among a group with this mental attitude. The *morale hazard* includes such hazards as the mental attitude that characterizes an accident-prone person. This type of individual does not appear to cause deliberately the accidents that frequently happen, but the psychologist would probably diagnose the cause of excessive and repeated accidents as a subconscious mental desire to gain attention.

The morale hazard also includes a situation, which insurers are trained to recognize almost instinctively, where those who are in a position to have a loss and who need protection against it, tend to be the only ones in a larger group who apply for protection. Thus, those in the low areas of flood zones may be the only applicants for flood insurance. Among applicants for group health insurance, there is a tendency for those in poor health to be overly represented in the group. Insurers refer to such a situation as *adverse selection* and, of course, take all sorts of precautions against it. Without such precautions, the loss tends to become certain, and hence uninsurable.

PURE RISK VERSUS SPECULATIVE RISK

A distinction has been made between pure risk and speculative risk which further clarifies the nature of risk.[7] In *pure risk,* there is uncertainty as to whether the destruction of an object will occur; a pure risk can only produce loss, should the peril occur. Examples of pure risk include the uncertainty of loss of one's property by fire, flood, windstorm, or other peril, or the uncertainty of total disability caused by accident or illness. In *speculative risk,* there is uncertainty about an event under consideration that could produce either a profit or a loss, such as a business venture or a gambling transaction. The distinction is significant because usually the pure risk is insurable, while the speculative risk is normally handled by methods other than insurance.

Pure risks may be further classified according to the major types of economic losses or perils which they concern. Two major types of such losses may be recognized: personal and property. *Personal losses* include all those directly affecting an individual's life or health. Examples include loss of life,

[7] Albert H. Mowbray and Ralph H. Blanchard, *Insurance* (5th ed.; New York: McGraw-Hill Book Company, Inc., 1961), p. 6.

hospitalization expense, loss of income due to disability, and medical expenses. *Property losses* include all those directly affecting an individual's property or income. Examples include fire, flood, windstorm, and liability for negligent conduct.

Insurers do assume speculative risks in some cases. Examples may be found in both underwriting and in investment operations. In underwriting, for example, speculative risk is sometimes assumed in the issuance of variable annuities, or in sales of mutual funds and term life insurance combinations. Some insurers offer guarantees to insureds that after a stated period of years the value of their mutual fund or variable annuities will not be less than the total of the premium payments, regardless of what has happened to the current market value of the underlying securities. Insurers also assume some speculative risks by investing part of their assets in common stocks. Normally, however, insurers tend to shy away from assuming speculative risks.

Speculative risks may be illustrated by price risks. A price risk is the risk that price may decline before an inventory can be sold at a reasonable profit. If an insurer agreed to cover a merchant seeking protection against price decline, the insurer would, in effect, become a business partner with the insured and would be asked to assume serious risks at a set price but without the corresponding opportunity to share in the profits if there should be any. Without an intimate knowledge of the business, the insurer would have little basis on which to make probability estimates of the expected gain or loss. Normally the insurer would have no opportunity to obtain the required knowledge for its protection. For these and other reasons, specialized ways of handling risks other than through insurance have been recognized or developed for speculative risk.

HANDLING OBJECTIVE RISK

Individuals cannot reduce their objective risk unless they control a large enough number of exposure units. Obviously it is impossible for most people to meet this condition. After all, each has but one life. Most people own no more than one house; and even if two or three autos are owned, this is an insufficient number to allow the law of large numbers to work.

The question arises then, "What alternatives are there for handling objective risk?" For convenience, the ways of handling risk may be grouped under the following headings:

1. Assuming the risk.
2. Combining the objects subject to risk into a large enough group to enable accurate prediction of the loss. This method includes the insurance mechanism.
3. Transferring or shifting the risk to another individual.
4. Utilizing loss-prevention activities.
5. Avoidance of the risk.

Risk Assumption

Risk assumption (also called risk retention) is perhaps the most widely used of all ways to handle risk. Most people go through life assuming a wide variety of risks, perhaps not realizing they are even doing so. The limitation of funds usually prevents one from using other methods except for those risks where the severity of loss, should it occur, is burdensome.

Laying aside a fund in a bank to meet some possible loss is not self-insurance, but is really assumption of risk. Many persons erroneously believe that they have used insurance in such a case. Insurance, however, is not possible unless a large enough number of exposure units can be grouped, and most individuals cannot meet this requirement. An example will make it clear why the setting aside of a rainy day fund is not insurance. If a person saves $1,000 in the bank to pay for a hospital bill, this person has no way of knowing whether or not this fund is adequate. A single period of hospitalization could easily exhaust the savings, and a second period of hospitalization might occur before the savings could be restored. Thus, the risk of loss of savings due to an illness requiring hospitalization has not actually been reduced. However, a properly drawn insurance plan, in which the risk of loss is effectively transferred to another, will take care of an indefinite number of hospitalizations.

Combination of Objects Subject to Risk

The method of *combination* is the system of handling risk that usually involves the use of large numbers. As pointed out previously, when sufficiently large numbers are grouped, the actual loss experience over a period of time will closely approximate the probable loss experience. To the extent that this is true, risk has been greatly reduced or even eliminated for all concerned.

One of the clearest illustrations of the combination method of reducing risk is found in the practices of early Chinese merchants. These merchants took periodic trips inland to gather merchantable products for sale on the coast. In traveling down the Yangtze River, the merchants would gather above the rapids and redistribute their cargoes so that each boat had a small portion of the other merchants' cargo aboard. Thus, if one boat were lost in the rapids, no one merchant would have suffered a total loss. This simple cooperative scheme saved many traders from ruin and increased the profits of all.

Commercial insurance companies utilize the combination method as the basis of their insuring operations. These companies simply persuade a large number of individuals, known as *insureds* or *assureds,* to pool their individual risks in a large group, and in that manner reduce or eliminate their risks. Under ideal conditions, the insurer has little or no objective risk. The risk simply disappears because risk is defined as the uncertainty of loss surrounding an *individual* object. When all of the individual objects are pooled into one group, the risk is no longer present, providing certain other requirements are met. This process may be compared to an alliance of a group of nations to ward off attack. Individually, each nation may have substantial risk, but in a group the risk to each is reduced.

A commercial insurer is not the only social or economic institution which can employ the combination method of handling risk. Large business organizations frequently have a sufficiently large group of insurable objects so that they can accurately predict loss experience. For example, a firm may make a study of automobile collision losses to determine for a given period of time just what losses may be expected from a large fleet of autos owned by the concern. From these data the firm makes careful estimates of the funds needed to meet these losses and lays aside funds for this purpose. It does this with relative certainty that, within narrow limits, the fund so set up will actually equal the losses to be suffered. This method of handling risk has been termed *self-insurance* and is to be distinguished from the practice of laying aside a rainy day fund to meet some emergency with no assurance that the fund will be adequate if the emergency should occur and cause a loss. This latter plan has been called *noninsurance* and is actually assumption of the risk.[8]

The method of combination also has been used to meet various types of *uninsurable risks*,[9] such as the risk of losing one's markets due to product obsolescence, of loss due to labor strikes or actions of competitors. The wave of business mergers in recent years has been attributed in part to the desire to reduce such market risk.[10] Thus, two or more firms may combine into one for the purpose of securing a more diversified product line, so that in the event the sale of one product is unprofitable, another might compensate for it. The uncertainty of loss from one unprofitable line is thus reduced.

Risk Transfer or Shifting

In the *transfer*, or *shifting*, method, one individual pays another to assume a risk that the transferor desires to escape. The risk bearer agrees to assume the risk for a price. The risk of loss is often the same to the transferee as it was to the transferor. The risk bearer (transferee), however, may have superior knowledge concerning the probability of loss, and thus may be in a better financial position to assume the risk than the transferor. Nevertheless, the risk still exists.

It is easy to confuse the transfer method of handling risk with the combination method. The essential difference between the two lies in the fact that in the transfer method, the risk is not necessarily reduced or eliminated; whereas in the combination method, the risk is actually greatly reduced or perhaps almost completely eliminated.

Examples of risk transfer are found in many phases of business activity. A furniture retailer may not wish to stock large quantities of furniture for fear that prices may fall before the stock can be sold, or for fear that the stock will be unsalable due to style changes. The retailer therefore buys only limited quantities of goods at a time, thus forcing a wholesaler to carry sufficient inventories to meet demand. The wholesaler in this case is the bearer of risk of loss due to price changes. The risk of loss is not necessarily reduced to the wholesaler.

[8] M. R. Greene, "Risk Management," *Best's Insurance News, Fire and Casualty Edition* (July, 1955), p. 116.

[9] See Chapter 3 for a discussion of these risks.

[10] Federal Trade Commission, *Report of Corporate Mergers and Acquisitions* (May, 1955), pp. 103-143.

Such risk of loss must be charged for ultimately in the form of higher prices than would prevail if the retailer bought in large quantities. The wholesaler may attempt in turn to shift the risk backward to the manufacturer.

Insurance companies themselves often operate as transferees of risk, rather than utilize the combination method, simply because it is impossible to obtain a sufficiently large number of exposure units in order to allow the law of large numbers to operate. If Lloyd's of London accepts an insurance contract covering the loss to the hands of a famous pianist, they are acting in the capacity of risk transferees, not as agents to pool the risks of large numbers of pianists. In commercial insurance operations it is often difficult to tell just where the combination method ends and the transfer method begins, for there are many instances in which an insurance concern has an insufficient number of exposure units to obtain extremely accurate predictions of loss experience. To the extent that the loss cannot be predicted accurately, the insurance company owners act as transferees. Again, the risk is not necessarily reduced.

Other examples of the transfer method of handling risk are bankruptcy and leasing. A person or a business may voluntarily enter bankruptcy, thus shifting to creditors the losses which might otherwise be borne by the bankrupt person. A person who leases or rents property rather than owns it shifts to the lessor the ownership risk. The cost of shifting the risk is contained in the rental payments, which must be high enough to compensate the lessor for the costs as well as for the risk of owning the property.

Loss-Prevention Activities

It is sometimes erroneously believed that loss prevention is "good insurance." Loss prevention is not insurance, but it does usually reduce the degree of subjective risk. Thus, people may worry less when they are riding in a large automobile, which is considered less susceptible to crushing during a collision. However, loss prevention may actually increase the degree of objective risk because it may reduce the probability of loss. The less probable an event is, the greater the relative dispersion of actual loss to expected loss. Even though probable losses are reduced, risk may yet be present since there is still the *possibility* that there may be substantial deviations from underlying probability.

Of course, risk of loss is eliminated if loss-prevention activities reduce the probability of loss to 0. One may eliminate the risk of having an auto accident by eliminating the possibility of exposure; that is, by never riding in a car or venturing upon a street where autos travel. If a surefire vaccine against arthritis were discovered and universally applied, there would be no risk of becoming ill from this source because the vaccine would have reduced to 0 the probability of having the disease. Thus, risk may be eliminated by first eliminating the possibility of loss.

Risk Avoidance

Closely related to loss prevention is the method of *avoidance* of the possibility of loss in the first place, thus avoiding risk. The method of avoidance is widely used, particularly by those with a high aversion toward risk. Thus, a person may not enter a certain business at all, and avoid the risk of losing capital in that business. A person may not use airplanes and thus avoid the risk of dying in an airplane crash. Insurance companies may avoid underwriting a certain line of insurance, and thus avoid the risk of loss in that line.

HANDLING SUBJECTIVE RISK

The preceding discussion of ways of handling risk refers mainly to objective risk. What about ways of handling subjective risk?

Each individual is faced with psychological uncertainty in dealing with risks (1) which can be insured or otherwise reduced or transferred by one or more of the methods outlined above, and (2) which cannot be insured or otherwise handled by any formal methods. Even insurance companies are often faced with underwriting decisions in which the law of large numbers is of no particular assistance, due to such factors as an inadequate number of exposed objects. In this case, the insurer must also deal with subjective risk.

As noted above, subjective risk deals with an attitude of mind toward uncertainty. Analysis of subjective risk is a very complex subject, and there is no general agreement as to how it should be measured or even what it really is. One can appreciate the importance of studying subjective risk, however, by studying several examples illustrating different mental attitudes toward risk in different situations.

Insurer *A* is offered an opportunity to insure a certain peril, but refuses, while Insurer *B* accepts; or alternatively, Insurer *A* quotes a much higher premium for the same peril than Insurer *B*. In each case, there is no obvious explanation other than the fact that Insurer *A* is conservative. Banker *A* refuses a loan proposition which Banker *B* accepts easily and under equivalent conditions. Student *B* graduates and accepts a position at a low initial salary but offering an opportunity for a large income for a few who succeed in the company; Student *A* graduates and accepts a position at a higher and more secure salary than *B*'s position paid, but under conditions which limit opportunities for advancement. Consumer *A* is offered certain types of goods over the telephone, but refuses to buy; Consumer *B*, offered the same goods, buys even without full information. Doctor *A* refuses to try out a new drug or a new surgical method even though Doctor *B* has been using the same drug or surgical method successfully. Business person *A* insures his plant against fire even though the premium may be very high, while Business person *B*, a neighbor operating under similar conditions, refuses the insurance.

In all of the above examples, *A* can be described as apparently perceiving a higher degree of risk in the given situation and behaving more conservatively than *B*.[11] *A* tends to be a risk averter and *B*, a risk taker. What set of psychological, sociological, or economic factors has produced these differences? Once

[11] It is possible, of course, for individuals to perceive high risk and still behave in an unconservative manner.

identified, can attitudes toward risk be measured and resulting human behavior predicted? What is the role of increased knowledge or fear and worry upon behavior in uncertain situations?

Psychologists have studied reactions to subjective risk other than economic, such as physical or social risk attitudes. However, the ways in which attitudes toward economic risk differ from attitudes toward physical or social risk are relatively unexplored. It is known that these attitudes may differ in the same person. A person willing to take great physical risks (for example, undertake a dangerous occupation) may be very conservative when it comes to assuming economic risk. It is not known how consistent individuals are in their attitudes toward subjective risk over time; that is, if a person avoids an economic risk today, will that person be likely to behave the same way tomorrow, or next month, or next year?

Experiments have been performed to measure subjective risk, and attempts have been made (mostly unsuccessful) to predict human behavior in uncertain situations by developing risk profiles of these mental attitudes. For example, in one experiment a group of students was given a written test to measure their outlook on risk. The students were divided into two subgroups, those whose scores indicated they were relatively willing to take risks and those whose scores indicated they were relatively unwilling to take risks. Another test was then given to the students to determine what odds they would require before entering into a certain gambling situation. It was found that students most willing to take risks on the first test were also likely to take the longest odds in a gambling game. Would it be possible to predict other risk-taking behavior, such as insurance buying behavior, by such methods? Early experiments along these lines lead to no definite conclusion, but evidence gathered to date indicates that as we learn more about subjective risk, important progress in the science of predicting human behavior may be expected.

One technique that has been developed to explain and help predict insurance buying behavior is that of utility analysis. One experimenter reported considerable success in predicting business decisions by knowing one's attitude toward financial risk, as measured by utility analysis. In the experiment, about 100 business executives were given tests to measure how willing they were to make risky investment decisions. It was found that subjective attitudes varied widely and willingness to take risk tended to vary according to the amount of money the executives were used to dealing with personally, not according to the amount of money available to the business as a whole.[12]

Perhaps the major way of handling subjective risk is through knowledge and training. A risk-averting person may be more willing to accept risk once there is a better understanding of the uncertainties because with better knowledge one is likely to perceive less risk in the situation. A risk-taking person may be willing to assume even greater risks as knowledge increases. As insurers get more experience in a given line, very often they become willing to insure risks

[12] Ralph O. Swalm, "Utility Theory Insights Into Risk Taking," *Harvard Business Review* (November-December, 1966), pp. 123-138.

they formerly rejected and at reduced premiums. An example is the area of nuclear explosion, formerly uninsurable, and now insurable by private insurers through pooling arrangements because of an enlarged body of knowledge and experience in the field. Lack of knowledge can produce worry and fear in the insurance buyer whose subjective risk and willingness to pay a high price for coverage are thereby heightened. At the same time, the insurer whose knowledge is greater is generally willing to accept the risk and is able to charge a higher premium because of the high subjective risk in the mind of the insurance buyer.

SUMMARY

1. Risk is defined as the uncertainty as to the occurrence of an event.
2. Objective risk is defined as the relative variation of actual from probable loss.
3. Subjective risk is defined as that type of psychological uncertainty which stems from individual mental attitudes or state of mind.
4. Probability is the long-run chance of occurrence or relative frequency of some event.
5. Other things being constant, objective risk varies inversely with the square root of the number of objects in the group. Objective risk varies inversely with the probability of loss, given a constant number of objects.
6. In a given situation, objective risk can be high and subjective risk can be low, and vice versa.
7. Since risk imposes an economic burden on society and upon individuals alike, it becomes important that ways of handling risk in a scientific manner be developed.
8. Risk may be handled in several ways: by assumption, by combination, by transfer, by loss-prevention activities, by avoidance, and through increased knowledge. Insurance is primarily an example of the combination method, but insurance companies utilize the other methods as well.

QUESTIONS FOR REVIEW AND DISCUSSION

1. Is it ever possible that a condition which could be a hazard in one case is a peril in another case? Give some examples.
2. Is there any point in studying risk management as a science when the state of our knowledge of future events will always remain uncertain? Why?
3. What words, if any, should be substituted for *risk* or *risky* in the following statements to make them accurate? Why?
   (a) When children play with fire in a dry forest, a high degree of *risk* is present.
   (b) An icy highway is a *risk* factor in driving safety.
   (c) To underwrite this *risk* (building) is dangerous.
   (d) Flood is a *risk* we won't take.
   (e) You don't have a large enough group of people to enable us to reduce the *risk* sufficiently to handle this on a group basis.
4. A certain investor took great pleasure in playing the stock market, especially in highly speculative issues. The investor expressed the feeling that it was the risk which gave the most fun.
   (a) Do you think this feeling is genuine?
   (b) Would you suggest an alternative explanation for the pleasure that many take in gambling?

5. What type of hazard is illustrated in each of the following situations?
   (a) An accident-prone driver.
   (b) A known embezzler applying for a job as cashier.
   (c) The owner of several lumber mills that have burned over the years precisely when lumber prices declined sharply.
   (d) A teen-age driver.
   (e) A tinder-dry forest.
   (f) A retail liquor dealer in a poor neighborhood.
   (g) A northern shipping route in winter.
6. (a) Differentiate between pure risk and speculative risk. Why is such a distinction important? Explain.
   (b) In what way is insurance related, if at all, to speculative risk?
7. (a) Distinguish between assuming the risk and self-insuring the risk.
   (b) In what basic way are these two concepts different?
8. What economic institutions other than insurance companies have used the combination method of handling risk? Explain.
9. In what sense is a business merger a risk-handling device? Explain.
10. It has been said that our defense expenditures are actually insurance premiums against the peril of war. Is this true? Why? If not, how would you classify such costs?
11. If the number of exposure units increases four times, what may be said to happen to the degree of objective risk? Explain, giving the basic principle illustrated.
12. It is stated in the text that the insurance premium varies both with probability and with risk. Which of these elements presumably becomes more important as probability of loss rises? Why? Which becomes more important as the number of exposure units declines? Why?
13. An automobile insurer decided to set auto insurance rates on youthful drivers only after scores had been taken on an "attitudes toward risk" test. Drivers with five years' experience were grouped into four classes in accordance with their test scores; and claim costs were developed based on the number of years' experience with each class. It was found that if Group 1 costs were labelled 100%, then Group 2 costs were 148%, Group 3 costs were 199%, and Group 4 costs, 231%. It was concluded that the "attitudes toward risk test" was a useful device to differentiate between drivers and to predict total claim costs of each group.
   (a) In what way is the "attitudes toward risk" test similar in concept to a measurement for subjective risk? Explain.
   (b) Would you prefer the use of such a test in classifying automobile drivers to a classification system which employed such variables as age, sex, geographical location, and type of vehicle? Why, or why not?
14. Think of a recent article or service you have purchased in which subjective risk may have influenced your decision to choose this service or article rather than another. What evidence does your purchase provide in indicating whether or not you tend to be a risk taker or a risk averter? Discuss.
15. A writer commented, "The growing burden of malpractice insurance is already forcing a number of doctors to retire early or consider moving to states where rates are lower. It is also making it increasingly difficult for young physicians to set up practice. . . . Hospitals are struggling to meet their rising malpractice premiums by passing costs along to the patient. . . . Many physicians and hospital administrators are now demanding additional X-rays and laboratory tests to document the need for treatment in case the patient sues." In what ways does the above quotation illustrate the burden of risk to society? Discuss.

Chapter *Two*

PROBABILITY, RISK, AND INSURANCE

Probability analysis and the law of large numbers constitute the scientific basis for insurance rate-making and for understanding the science of insurance generally. There is some evidence that strict adherence to some of the mathematical principles underlying insurance have not always been observed, with unfortunate financial results for the insurance industry. In this chapter we shall describe some of these scientific fundamentals in as nontechnical a manner as possible. Major consideration is given to:

1. Basic rules and assumptions of probability analysis.
2. The concept of expected value.
3. The law of large numbers, including the question of how large the number of exposure units must be for a given accuracy.
4. Why individuals are willing to pay an insurance premium which is more than the expected value of the loss.
5. How one determines the importance of risk through utility analysis.

PROBABILITY

Laypersons often define probability in a very simple manner such as "the chance of occurrence of an event" or the "long-run chance of occurrence." Intuitively, most people understand that a "probable" event is one which is most likely to occur. However, such definitions are not very useful in analyzing and solving a scientific problem because they are too vague. Before we can employ probability in a useful manner, a more refined definition is necessary. Certain terms must be introduced and explained.

Definition

Our definition of probability begins with the concept of a sample space and an event. Imagine a set, S, of possible events or outcomes of a given description. Such a set might consist of a listing of the number of collisions of all automobiles registered in a certain state during a given year. We refer to this set as the *sample space* of the events in which we are interested. Other sample spaces might consist of all the deaths among individuals aged 21 in the United States, or the sinking of all ships of a certain description while traveling on the North Atlantic route.

Next, consider a smaller segment of the total set, which we may call E, a *subset* of S. In automobile insurance, this subset might describe the number of collisions involving all high-performance automobiles—those with an extra powerful engine in relation to the weight of the car. The total set S describes the probability of a collision of automobiles in a certain state in a given time period. We wish to know what the probability is that there will be a collision of a high-performance car. To determine the probability, we shall assign a number called a *weight* to each individual event in the set S. This weight might be assigned according to some empirical evidence concerning our past knowledge of the likelihood of loss among automobiles, such as the region in which the automobile is driven or the type of driver. Let the expression $W(S)$ be the sum of all weights in the set S, and $W(E)$ represent the sum of all weights in the subset E. Then the probability p that a high-performance auto will be involved in a collision would be represented by the expression

$$p(E) = \frac{W(E)}{W(S)}$$

If it is presumed that all the simple events in the set S are equally likely, this formula may be reduced to a simple ratio of the number of outcomes in the subset E to the total number of outcomes in the set S, or simply,

$$p(E) = \frac{E}{S}$$

Alternatively, we can express the probability q, that there will be no loss to a high-performance automobile, as

$$q(E) = \frac{S - E}{S}$$

To illustrate, assume that set S consists of 10,000 automobiles, 1,000 of which are high-performance cars and 9,000 of which are not. A weight of two may be assigned to high-performance cars because it is found that they are twice as likely to suffer a collision as other cars due to the way in which they are driven. A weight of one is assigned to all other cars. The probability that there will be a collision to a high-performance car is by our definition:

$$\begin{aligned} p(E) &= \frac{W(E)}{W(S)} \\ &= \frac{2 \times 1{,}000}{(2 \times 1{,}000 + (1 \times 9{,}000)} \\ &= \frac{2{,}000}{11{,}000} = \frac{2}{11} \end{aligned}$$

If all events received equal weight,

$$p(E) = \frac{E}{S} = \frac{1{,}000}{10{,}000} = \frac{1}{10} \qquad q(E) = \frac{S - E}{S} = \frac{10{,}000 - 1{,}000}{10{,}000} = \frac{9{,}000}{10{,}000} = \frac{9}{10}$$

Thus, there is a 2/11 probability that there will be a loss to a high-performance car (and a corresponding probability of 9/11 that there will be no such loss) when different weights are applied to different types of events contained in the set. If equal weights are assigned to all events in the set, or sample space, the probability of loss to a high-performance car turns out to be 1/10 (and the probability of no such loss is therefore 9/10). The significance of weights is illustrated by these examples. It is through changing of weights that the insurance underwriter can accurately reflect his evaluation of the probability of occurrence of various events.

Description of Events

The preceding definition of probability involves the assumption that one of the events in the set S is bound to occur. Furthermore, it is assumed that the events are described in such a way as to be *mutually exclusive,* which means that both events cannot happen at once. For example, the events "loss to a high-performance car" and "loss to any car" are not mutually exclusive since any car may also include a high-performance car. The two events could happen simultaneously. The quantity expressed as $W(E)$ in the formula on page 20 refers to events which are mutually exclusive.

As another example, consider the probability of death. The events "a person dies" and "a person lives" are mutually exclusive and they exhaust all possibilities. A person either lives or dies; one cannot do both at once. Assuming equal likelihood of events, it is proper to state that the probability of death can be expressed as a simple fraction of the number of people dying during a given time period out of some total number living at the beginning of the period. For example, if there are 100,000 people living at the beginning of the year and 2,000 die, the probability of death for that group would be 2% and the probability of survival is therefore 98%. On the other hand, if we were told that out of 100,000 people, 2,000 catch the flu and 5,000 catch colds, we cannot say that 7% catch either a cold or the flu because the events are not mutually exclusive. It is possible (and very likely) that there are people who catch a cold and also catch the flu. Unless we know this number, we cannot determine the total probability of catching either a cold or the flu. This leads us to the following basic rule, referred to as the *additive rule:*

> The total probability of occurrence of two or more mutually exclusive events is the sum of the respective probabilities of the separate events.

If the events are not mutually exclusive, other methods of defining the probabilities must be formulated.

As an example of the additive rule, assume that there is a well-mixed deck of playing cards, and we wish to calculate the probability of drawing either an ace or a king on a single draw. Since there are four aces and four kings, the probability of drawing an ace would be 4/52 or 1/13, and the probability of drawing a king would be 1/13. We are assuming that it is just as likely to draw an ace or a king as any other card, since the deck is well mixed. Under the additive rule the total probability of drawing either an ace or a king is, therefore, 2/13. We know that it is impossible to draw a card marked ace-king, since there is no such card in the set. The event "draw a card which is not an ace" is mutually exclusive with the event "draw a card which is an ace." We must have one event or the other—never both—on a single draw. As another example in coin tossing, the event "flip a head" is mutually exclusive with the event "flip a tail." The probability of flipping either a head or a tail is 1/2 + 1/2, or 1. It is assumed that it is impossible for any other event to occur, such as "flip and the coin stands on end." Therefore, the sum of the probabilities of each separate event in a set is always one, as shown below.

Positive Weights

It is assumed in probability theory that all assignments of weights to individual events in a set will be positive. Since probability is expressed as a ratio of events in a subset to events in the total set, it can be seen that the probabilities of all events when added together must equal 1. If an event is certain to happen, its probability will be 1; if the event cannot happen, its probability is 0. It follows that the sum of p, the probability that an event will occur, and q, the probability that it will not occur, equals 1.

In summary, we may say that there are three axioms upon which the definition of probability is built. These are:

1. Probability is a number between 0 and 1 that is assigned to an event.
2. The sum of the probabilities assigned to a set of mutually exclusive and collectively exhaustive events must equal 1.
3. The probability of an event which is composed of a group of mutually exclusive events in a set is the sum of the individual probabilities.

Probability Is Approximate

Only in rare instances can it be said that probability is known absolutely. For example, in drawing balls from an urn containing six red balls and four white balls mixed at random, it can be said that the probability of drawing a white ball is .4.

$$p(\text{white ball}) = \frac{W(E)}{W(S)} = \frac{E}{S} = \frac{4}{10} = .4$$

In reality such precision is seldom possible, however, because it is difficult to determine precisely just how many lives will be lost out of a group, what percentage of autos will be wrecked in a given year, or what proportion of total employees will steal. What is done is to observe how many lives are lost out of a sufficiently large group, how many cars are wrecked, and how many employees steal. These losses are then expressed as a percentage of the total number of exposure units in order to obtain an *empirical* estimate of probability.

From an empirical standpoint, probability may be looked upon as the long-run frequency of events, expressed as a percentage. If an event happens w times out of a possible number of cases, n, the empirical probability may be expressed as the fraction w/n. It should be recognized, however, that this fraction represents historical data. Its use in predicting future events is necessarily limited to an approximation unless the past exactly repeats itself, which is most unlikely. It should also be recognized that because the probability is, say, 3/4 that a given event will happen, this does not imply that we can expect the event to happen exactly three out of four times in a small number of cases. If n is small, there may be large variations from the probable number of events. It is only as n approaches infinity that the fraction w/n can express the empirical probability with precision. This observation, termed the law of large numbers, is further discussed on page 29.

Independent Events

A concept of great importance in probability and in its application to insurance is that of *independent events*. Two events are said to be independent when the outcome of one event in a group of possible events does not affect our assessment of the probability of the next event. For example, flipping a coin and obtaining a head should not affect our assessment of the probability of securing heads on the next flip. Even if we have obtained 10 heads in a row, our assessment of the outcome of the next flip should not change since there is nothing to persuade us that the probability of heads on the next flip is any different from the probability on prior flips—that is, it is still 50%. The coin has no memory and is not impelled to make up for past results.

An example of events which are *not* independent is that of drawing balls from an urn without replacing each ball after each draw. Thus, if there are five white balls and five red balls in an urn, the probability of drawing a white ball on the first draw is 5/10. If a white ball is drawn but not replaced, the probability of drawing a white ball on the second draw is now 4/9. The result on the first draw affected our assessment of the probability on the second draw.

An example in insurance in which exposures will not produce independent losses would be the case of insuring a group of employees against illness, after it has been determined that two or three employees have contacted typhoid. The fact that typhoid is spreading affects our assessment of the probability of further losses; the losses are certainly not independent of one another.

Independent Trials

Just as two or more events in a given set may be independent of one another, the outcomes of a succession of experiments may be considered independent of one another. In such a case the sample space is defined in terms of successive *trials,* and the outcomes are the various results that can occur in such trials. For example, consider a coin-flipping experiment in which we flip two coins twice. The sample space may be defined as Heads, Heads; Heads, Tails; Tails, Heads; Tails, Tails. Thus, there are four possible "events" in these two trials. We may assign a probability of 1/4 to each event. If we are interested in the event of all outcomes in which heads appear, the probability we would assign to this event would be 3/4.

Randomness

Events are said to occur at random when equal probabilities are assigned to each event in the sample space. If we are just as likely to draw one ball from an urn as any other ball, we may say that our selection is random. If the balls were marked in some way or were not mixed thoroughly, the trials might not be random since perhaps the balls on top would have different characteristics than the balls at the bottom.

If an insurance company agreed to insure everyone who passed by a certain street corner, would it have a random selection from a set comprising all the people in that city? Decidedly not, since during the daytime, men and children would probably not be properly represented and those who were unemployed might be overrepresented. There is not an equal probability that *any* person may be selected. Similarly, if an insurance company is considering applications for life insurance that are given voluntarily without prior solicitation, can it consider that these applications constitute a random selection from a set comprising the insurable population? No, because those who have a tendency to be in poor health would be more likely to apply than those who are in good health.

Significance in Insurance of Randomness and Independence of Events

Randomness and independence of events are of crucial importance in insurance. Underwriters make every attempt to classify exposure units into groups in which the losses may be considered independent random events. In this way a uniform charge to each member of the group can be easily justified, since each member knows that the loss is just as likely to happen to him as to any other. If the probability of personal loss were less than to the others, an insured would be unwilling to pay the same premium as all the rest.

Another result of randomness in insured groups is that a loss is just as likely as not to be suffered twice by the same insured. If a person is struck by an automobile this month and if automobile accidents are randomly distributed, the person has the same chance of being struck again next month as this month. Thus, it may be false reasoning to assume that if one has suffered a loss, it will not happen personally again for a long time.

Compound Probability

If two or more independent events may happen simultaneously or in sequence, the probability that all events will occur is the product of their separate probabilities.

To illustrate, suppose we wish to know the probability of obtaining two heads in a row in a coin-flipping experiment. Since the events are assumed to be independent, the joint probability is $1/2 \times 1/2 = 1/4$. Similarly, if the probability of *A* living to age 65 is 3/4 and the probability of his wife to age 65 is 4/5, the probability of *both A* and his wife living to age 65 is $3/4 \times 4/5 = 3/5$, always assuming independence.

The events "living to age 65" and "not living to 65" are mutually exclusive.[1] The probability of *A not* living to 65 is $1 - 3/4$, or 1/4; similarly, for *A*'s wife the probability of *not* living to 65 is $1 - 4/5$, or 1/5. Therefore, the separate compound probabilities are additive, as demonstrated below:

Event	*Probability*
Both *A* and wife live to 65	$3/4 \times 4/5 = 12/20$
A lives to 65, wife does not	$3/4 \times 1/5 = 3/20$
A does not live to 65, wife does	$1/4 \times 4/5 = 4/20$
Neither *A* nor wife lives to 65	$1/4 \times 1/5 = 1/20$
	$20/20 = 1$

There are four possible events, each pair of which is mutually exclusive. Only one of these four events is possible. The total probability is therefore 1.

The application of compound probability in insurance may be seen in a contract known as the joint and last survivorship annuity. In this contract an insurer writes an annuity on two lives, usually a husband and wife, and promises to pay an income to the two individuals as long as either one is alive. Thus, the probability of survival of two lives jointly becomes important.

Repeated Events

If we know the probability is p that an event will happen in a single trial, then the probability that the event will *not* happen can be stated by the equation $q = 1 - p$. We can calculate the probability that the event will happen r times in n independent trials by means of the binomial formula.[2] The binomial formula

[1] If the events are not mutually exclusive, other rules of probability are available to aid in the task of assigning probability values to the events.

[2] The binominal formula is: Probability of r successes in n trials equals

$$\frac{n!}{r!(n-r)!}\, p^r q^{n-r}$$

The expression $n!$ is read "n factorial." The word "factorial" refers to a successive multiplication of the numbers n, $n - 1$, $n - 2$ . . . 0! Thus, 4! means $4 \times 3 \times 2 \times 1$, or 24. 0! is conventionally defined to be 1. Tables of binomial probabilities are generally available for obtaining the values in the above formula for small values of n (150 or less). For larger values of n, other formulas, such as the Poisson or normal density functions, are used as an approximation.

uses the rules of compound events and the additive property of mutually exclusive events discussed on page 21.

It is of importance in insurance to estimate the probability of certain numbers of losses in an insured group. If there are 10,000 automobiles being insured, the binomial formula (or other approximating formulas) may be used to calculate the chance of 10 losses, 100 losses, 200 losses, or any other number of losses, providing we know both p and q. Similarly, if there are 100 exposure units, such as houses, and we know from past experience that the separate probability of loss of any one house by fire each year is .01, reference to a binomial table tells us that the probability is:

	.37	that the number of houses that burn will be none
	.37	" " " " " " " " " one
	.19	" " " " " " " " " two
	.06	" " " " " " " " " three
	.01	" " " " " " " " " four or more
Total	1.00	

The above schedule is a sample of a *probability,* or a *frequency distribution,* in this case, a theoretical probability distribution known as the *binomial distribution*. It is only one of the many types of probability distributions used in insurance, but one of the most important. In order to use the binomial formula, assume the following conditions:

1. There are two possible events, or outcomes, which are mutually exclusive.
2. The probability of each event is known, or can be estimated.
3. Since each event is independent of all other events, the probability of each event does not change from trial to trial, but is constant throughout the entire process. Because the probability of occurrence is known, and there are only two events, we also automatically know the probability that the event will *not* occur (one minus the probability that it will occur).

It can be seen that if a series of repeated events follows the Bernoulli process[3] (that is, meets the above conditions), the insurer will have a powerful tool for predicting the frequency of losses. Even when all the conditions above are not met perfectly, the binomial theorem is extremely useful in making educated guesses as to the frequency of losses. For example, in insurance the true probability of loss is never known exactly, since even for large numbers of exposure units, there will be some variation. Yet, a mathematical model helps the insurer make estimates that otherwise would be made without much guidance.

Conditional Probability

An example of the use of mathematical models to assist a person in estimating future losses is the concept of conditional probability. *Conditional probability* is defined as the probability of occurrence of some event, given that

[3] The events in the binominal process are called Bernoulli trials, after Jacob Bernoulli, who was one of the first mathematicians to formalize this theorem.

another event has already occurred. We are thus concerned with the probability of two events which are not independent of each other. In the example referred to on page 26, suppose the insurer wishes to estimate the probability of three or more fires, *given that a fire does occur*. The probability that a fire will occur is 1 minus the probability that there will be no fires, or 1 − .37, or .63. The probability that there will be three or more fires is .07, (.06 + .01) by the additive rule. Therefore, if a fire occurs the probability that it will involve three or more houses is .07/.63 or 1/9, or .11.[4] An insurer now has an estimate of what the loss severity might be, if there is any loss at all. It is of considerable help to the insurer to be able to make some reasonable estimate of the maximum probable loss.

Expected Value

The *expected value* of an event is determined by preparing a schedule of possible outcomes and weighting each outcome by its probability. The results are then added and the expected value of the event is obtained.

In the preceding example relating to house fires, assume that the average dollar loss per fire is $1,000. The insurer might reason as follows: since there is a .37 chance of one loss, the expected value or cost of this loss is $370. If the loss occurs, the insurer must pay $1,000; but the insurer is not at all positive that the loss will occur. Therefore, the insurer assigns a probability to the loss, and the result is that the probability of one loss is weighed and evaluated at $370. Similarly, the expected cost of two losses is .19 × $2,000, or $380; three losses, .06 × $3,000, or $180, etc. Such calculations are used in making estimates of total losses, and provisions are made for charging each insured an appropriate premium. In the binomial distribution, the total of all the expected losses is the number of trials, or events, times the expected long-run frequency (.01 in the above example) times the money outlay per loss. If there are 10 houses, each fire in which causes an average loss of $1,000, theoretically, the total expected cost of the losses is 10 × .01 × $1,000, or $100. Of course, if the insurer had only 10 houses, it could not be determined that $100 is the proper premium, because of insufficient exposure. In addition, the insurer would have to make an adjustment for the costs of doing business.

Expected value enters into our daily life in many significant ways. For example, suppose a contractor is asked to build a house. If all goes well and no unusual conditions arise, it is figured that the contractor will earn $1,000 profit on the contract with a probability of .9. There is, however, a .1 probability that an unplanned amount, such as $1,000, may be spent on extra excavation if soil conditions are poor. Thus, the expected value of the contract is $900 − $100, or $800, as shown in the following table.

[4] In formula,

$$\frac{\text{Probability Of Event One } (E_1)}{\text{given Event Two } (E_2)} = \frac{P(E_1)}{P(E_2)} = \frac{.07}{.63} = .11$$

where E_1 = Probability that the loss will be 3 or more houses, if there is any loss at all (.06 + .01), and E_2 = Total Probability that there is any loss at all (.37 + .19 + .06 + .01 = .63).

Probability	Outcome	Expected Value
.9	+$1,000	+$900
.1	−$1,000	−$100
1.0		$800

The contractor may consider the opportunity of building this house along with several other opportunities for the employment of capital. Other things being equal, the contractor will probably accept the proposition that offers the highest expected value. The builder might also be willing to pay up to $100 as a sort of insurance premium to someone to assume the risk of loss in case soil conditions are poor. In this way the contractor may feel that plans can be made with greater certainty.

Expected value considerations must often be modified in making a decision because a decision maker may not want to run *any* probability of a very large loss, even though the probability of gain may be large enough to offset it. For example, the contractor may not be willing to accept the contract under any conditions if there is a .90 probability of making $10,000, but a .1 probability of losing $20,000, even though the expected value of the contract is $9,000 − $2,000, or $7,000. This may be true because the contractor could not afford a $20,000 loss if it should occur.[5] The analytical tool necessary to treat this problem is the concept of *utility*, which is discussed later in this chapter.

RISKS OF THE INSURER

Under the somewhat unrealistic conditions imposed by the binomial distribution, the probability of having *exactly* one house burn in a consideration of only 100 houses is .37. There is a probability of .26 that two or more houses will burn. This is true even though the long-run probability (mathematical expectation) of loss is exactly one house. Thus, we can begin to see why an insurer must be concerned primarily with large numbers of exposures. With only a few exposures, the insurer cannot be at all certain that the mathematical expectation of loss will be realized in practice. The risk may be defined as the uncertainty attached to the proposition that actual losses equal probable losses.

While consideration of the binomial model is an interesting theoretical tool in explaining some basic results in risk and insurance, in the real world the assumptions of this system do not usually hold, or hold only imperfectly. For example, in the real world, we do not know in advance what the true p, probability of loss, is; but we must estimate it. This estimate involves statistical errors. Not only are there risks introduced by these errors, for a given period, but the insurer is also faced with the problem that the underlying probability is

[5] See Robert Schlaifer, *Probability and Statistics for Business Decisions* (New York: McGraw-Hill Book Company, Inc., 1961), Chapter 2, for a discussion of the concept of expected value and utility in decision making. In addition, Samuel Goldberg, *Probability: An Introduction* (New York: Prentice-Hall, Inc., 1960), Chapter 5 has an excellent discussion of the binomial distribution and its applications, including decision making under uncertainty.

constantly shifting. It may be .01 in one time period, .005 in another time period, and .015 in another time period. Calculations of the estimated probability are invariably made for a past time period; but the insurance contract must cover a future period, and there are frequent changes, such as changing legal conditions, inflation, and changed attitudes toward loss, which must be judged individually.

In the real world, the insurer cannot be certain that losses are indeed independent events. The probability of loss in a binomial distribution is assumed to remain constant for each trial. However, in a group of insured exposure units, the probability may change after one or two losses have been experienced because loss-prevention measures may be introduced, or people may become more careful than they were before the loss.

Another reason why the assumptions of the binomial model do not usually hold in the real world is that there may not be a sufficient number in an insured group so that the mathematical expectation of loss will be realized with the required degree of certainty.

All of the various ways in which the underlying assumptions of probability estimates may not be realized in practice may be said to constitute the *risks of the insurer*. It is sometimes argued that the insurer has no risk since a sufficient number of exposure units can be combined to make losses nearly perfectly predictable. This is a gross oversimplification of the real situation, as the previous discussion has indicated. Even if objective risk could be eliminated, subjective risk exists. One of the basic reasons why insurance is a science is the necessity of devoting great study to the ways in which the insurer's risks may be met successfully in practice. Many tools of analysis from other disciplines are used to help reduce the insurer's risks. For example, in life insurance, a medical analysis of the physical condition of the applicants for insurance helps ensure that those accepted are, as nearly as can be determined, homogeneous in nature, and not subject to nonrandom influences which would distort the loss experience on which premiums are based. Many important concepts from mathematics are used in reducing the insurer's risk. As we have seen, the theoretical binomial distribution and other distributions, such as the Poisson and the normal, are used. Some of the implications of the normal distribution are explored below.

The Law of Large Numbers

The law of large numbers tells us that if we do not know the underlying probability of occurrence of certain events, we can estimate it more and more precisely by increasing the number of our observations in a sampling process. The average value of a very large number of observations will approximate very closely the true average of the population from which the observations were taken. This result arises from what is known as the *central limit theorem*. According to this theorem, if we extract sample observations from a population of events, the mean of the samples will be distributed normally and the value of this sample mean will approach the mean of the population as the number of samples increases. This is true even if the population of events itself is not distributed normally. The statistical error caused by using sample observations rather than the total population (which is never known anyway) may be estimated by a measure known as the standard deviation around the sample mean. The error varies inversely with the square root of the sample size. As the sample size increases to infinity, the error approaches zero.

The law of large numbers constitutes a fundamental theoretical basis for the insurance function. As large bodies of appropriate statistics on losses are gathered and analyzed, the insurer may predict loss experience with considerable accuracy. In the field of life insurance, for example, data on the frequency of death in various societies are summarized in mortality tables and are widely employed as the basis for the life insurance premium.

Normal Distribution

As mentioned above, it can be shown that if losses in a sample are random and independent, they will be distributed approximately normally.[6] What is meant by being "distributed approximately normally"? Figure 2–1 illustrates graphically the general shape of a normal, or bell-shaped, distribution. In a normal distribution the frequency of occurrence of the measured events is distributed symmetrically in the general shape of a bell about the mean value.[7] In Figure 2–1 the frequency of occurrence, or probability of loss, is shown on the vertical axis, and the number of losses appears on the horizontal axis. If there are 100 exposure units, each of which has a probability of occurrence of loss of .30, the mean number of losses is 30. The probability that exactly 30 losses will occur is .09; that exactly 26 losses will occur is .06; that exactly 25 losses will occur is .05; etc. Summing all the probabilities in this manner will result in a total probability of one, since the events are mutually exclusive and collectively exhaustive and independent. Note that the number of losses on the graph starts with 20, since the probability that less than 20 losses will occur, when the expected number of losses is 30, is very small, actually, .0089. Similarly, the number of losses ends around 40, since it is very unlikely, with probability .0125, that more losses than this number will occur. In theory, it is possible to have 100 losses out of the total number of 100 exposure units, and so the vertical bars would never reach the horizontal axis. The bars would be so close to it after the limits shown, however, that for all practical purposes the probability of having a loss of less than 20 or more than 40 can be ignored.

The significance of the fact that losses are normally distributed is that we can calculate within known tolerances, the probability that losses will fall within a certain range of their mean number. This will be explained by an example. Before the example is given, however, we must review what is meant by a statistical measure of dispersion known as standard deviation.

[6] For a mathematical proof of this, see E. Parzen, *Modern Probability Theory and Its Applications* (New York: John Wiley, 1960), pp.239-245.

[7] There are other distributions which fit this description too. The precise meaning of a normal curve must be given by a somewhat complex mathematical formula. To avoid explaining this formula, an explanation is given in terms of the binomial, which, as has been noted, is closely approximated by the normal curve.

OCCURRENCE OF 30 LOSSES, BINOMIALLY DISTRIBUTED, WITH PROBABILITY OF .30 OUT OF 100 EXPOSURES

Figure 2-1

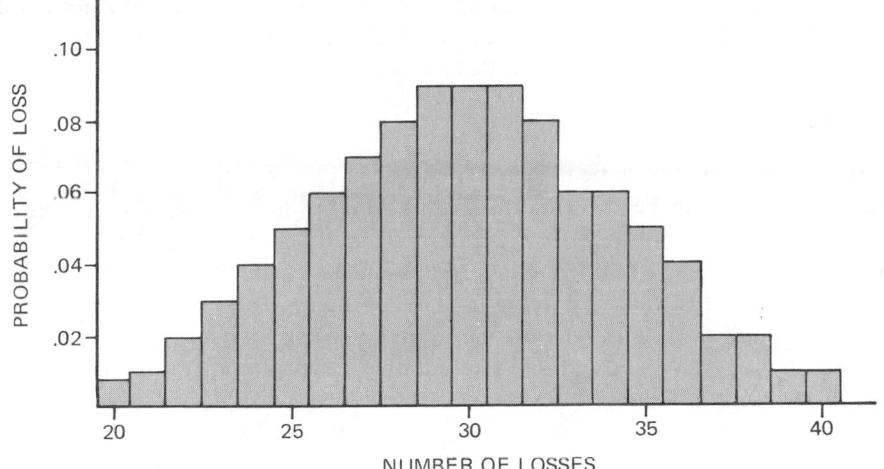

Standard Deviation

Standard deviation is a number which measures how close a group of individual measurements are to their average value. For example, if a group of 10 trees is such that individual tree heights range from 6 to 100 feet, but the average tree height is 50 feet, we would find that the dispersion of individual tree heights is rather great. The trees range in height from 6 to 100 feet and to say that the "average height of the trees is 50 feet" is not very descriptive of the height of these trees. For example, in comparing the above group of trees with another group of 10 trees, which range in height from 45 to 55 feet, but whose average height is 50 feet, one naturally seeks a way to state precisely just how the two groups differ. The concept of standard deviation is probably the most important statistical tool used to accomplish this purpose. By comparing the standard deviation of the heights of the two groups of trees, one can indicate precisely how much variation in height occurs. It is possible to state, for example, that the height of three fourths of all the trees falls within one standard deviation of the mean height in one group, and that only 10% of the trees fall within one standard deviation of the mean height of the other group. With such a statement, we have a much more accurate description of the average height of the two groups of trees.

Standard deviation is thus a gauge of the dispersion of measurements about the mean. If, for example, the standard deviation is 20 feet, we might say that the "scatter" of heights about the mean is, on the average, 40% (20/50 = .40) in the range of one standard deviation, 80% in the range of two standard deviations, etc.[8] When standard deviation is expressed as a percent of the mean, as above, statisticians call the result the *coefficient of variation,* which is one way to characterize the concept of mathematical risk to the insurer. It is, in fact, the method of measuring objective risk used in Chapter 1. If losses from a group of exposure units have a low coefficient of variation, there is less risk associated with this group of exposures than with another group with a high coefficient of variation, since the insurer can say with greater certainty just what the financial outlay is likely to be.

Confidence Intervals

What conclusions can be drawn if the losses are normally distributed? In the normal curve it can be demonstrated that roughly 68% of all losses will fall within a range of one standard deviation from their mean number; approximately 95% will fall within two standard deviations of the mean; and about 99% will fall within three standard deviations of the mean. If we know the standard deviation of a distribution, we are able to make *confidence interval* statements. For example, we can say with 68% confidence (or probability) that our events will fall within one standard deviation of the mean, with 95% probability that our events will fall within two standard deviations of the mean, etc.

Figure 2–1 illustrates a binomial distribution, which although similar in shape to a normal distribution, is not actually a normal distribution.[9] However, since the normal distribution is a good approximation of the binomial distribution, we can employ the principles which apply to the normal distribution to illustrate the nature of confidence interval statements. In Figure 2–1 the expected number of losses out of an insured group of 100 units is 30. The standard deviation is approximately 4.6 losses.[10] Thus, the probability is .68 that the actual number of losses will be within the range of about 26–34 (approximately one standard deviation range); .95 that the actual number of losses will be in the range 21–39 (approximately a two standard deviation range); and .99 that the actual number of losses will be in the range 16–44. Due to rounding, these figures are only approximate.

[8] To obtain the standard deviation of a group of measurements, first find the average value by adding the values of all individual items and dividing by the total number of items. Each individual value is then subtracted from this average and the resulting figure is squared. These squared differences are added and the result is divided by the number of items. We then have the mean of the squared deviations, which is known as the variance. The square root of the variance is the standard deviation. *Example:* Find the standard deviation of five numbers, 0, 1, 2, 3, 4. *Solution:* Mean is 2. Sum of squared deviations from mean is 10. Average of squared deviations is 2, the variance. Standard deviation is 1.414 (the square root of 2).

[9] A normal distribution is continuous in nature, while the binomial distribution is defined in such a way that each trial must be counted separately as an integer, and is called a discrete distribution. It is for this reason that the range of standard deviations must be expressed in whole numbers.

[10] Actually the standard deviation is 4.58, obtained by a mathematical shortcut. The binomial distribution is given by the quantity np (number of trials times the long-run probability), or in this case, (100) (.30), or 30. The standard deviation of a binomial distribution is secured from the formula: $\sqrt{np(1-p)}$, or in this case, $\sqrt{(100)(.30)(.70)} = 4.58$.

With only 100 exposures and with a probability of .30, the insurer cannot be too sure just how the losses will occur. The insurer expects 30, but cannot be more than 95% confident that the loss experience will be even within the range of roughly 21–39, a variation of 30% from the mean (9/30). This is a rather wide dispersion and might not satisfy the insurer's standards of accuracy. A 95% confidence interval may be satisfactory, but the insurer may want this interval to be somewhat narrower than that stated above.

Number of Exposures Required for a Given Accuracy

A question of considerable interest, both to the commercial insurer and the would-be self-insurer, is how large an exposure (that is, how many individual exposure units) is necessary before a given degree of accuracy can be achieved in obtaining an actual loss frequency that is sufficently close to the expected loss frequency. As the number of exposure units becomes indefinitely large, the actual loss frequency will approach the expected true loss frequency; but it is never possible for a single insurer, whether a commercial insurer or a self-insurer, to group together an indefinitely large number of exposures. Undoubtedly many individuals are under the mistaken assumption that they are in a position to self-insure if they have under their own control, say, 10 automobiles. These persons think that certainly it would be unusual for more than one or two automobiles to be lost in a given time period, or that no more than one damage suit would befall them. That this position is a dangerous one will be illustrated.

The question arises, How much error is introduced when the insured group is not sufficiently large? More precisely, an insurer might wish to ask, "How many exposure units must be grouped together in order to be 95% sure that the number of actual losses will differ from expected losses by no more than 5%?" It is assumed that the expected losses for a very large population of exposures are known, or can be estimated from industry-wide data, or can be determined subjectively. Essentially, the insurer wishes to know how stable its loss experience will be, i.e., how much objective risk must be accepted for a given number of exposure units. Certain mathematical and statistical laws help provide an answer to this question. While the assumptions required by these laws may not always hold in the real world, they enable the insurer to make an approximation which will be of considerable help in making a sound decision. The required assumption is that the losses occur in the manner assumed by the binomial theorem. In other words, each loss occurs independently of each other loss, and the probability of loss is constant from occurrence to occurrence. Stated in mathematical terms, the losses are to be viewed as Bernoulli trials.

A simple mathematical formula is available which will enable the insurer to estimate the number of exposures required for a given degree of accuracy. Unless mathematical tools such as the one given below are used with great caution and are interpreted by experienced persons, wrong conclusions may often be reached. The formula is given only as an illustration of how such tools can be of help in guiding an insurer to reduce its risk. The formula is based on the assumption that losses in an insured population are distributed normally.[11] The formula concerns only the occurrence of a loss, and not the evaluation of the *size* of the loss, which is an entirely different problem beyond the scope of this book. The formula is based on the knowledge that the normal distribution is an approximation of the binomial distribution, and that known percentages of losses will fall within one, two, three, or more standard deviations from the mean. The formula[12] is

$$N = \frac{s^2 p(1-p)}{e^2}$$

where: N is the number of exposure units sufficient for a given degree of accuracy.

e is the degree of accuracy required, expressed as a ratio of actual losses to the total number in the sample.

s is the number of standard deviations of the distribution. The value of s tells us with what level of confidence we can state our results. Thus, if s is 1, we know with 68% confidence that losses will be as predicted by the formula; if s is 2, we have 95% confidence, etc.

As an example, suppose in the above case, where our probability of loss is .30 (not an unusual probability in certain areas for collision of automobiles), we want to be 95% certain that the actual loss ratio (number of losses divided by total number of insured units) will not differ from the expected loss ratio of .30 by more than two percentage points, that is, .02. In other words, we want to know how many units there must be in our insured group in order to be 95% certain that the number of losses out of each 100 units will fall in the range 28–32. Substitution in the formula, $\frac{s^2 p(1-p)}{e^2}$ yields $\frac{2^2(.3)(.7)}{(.02)^2}$, or 2,100 exposure units. The value of s is 2 in this case because of our requirement of a 95% confidence interval statement—we know that 95% of all losses will fall within a range of two standard deviations of the mean.

We may demonstrate the logic of the above result by working backward. The formula tells us that 2,100 automobiles are necessary for us to be 95% confident that our losses will not vary by more than 2% of the number exposed, or by more than 42 losses (.02 × 2,100). If losses are normal, we may expect a mean loss of 630 (.30 × 2,100) and a standard deviation of 21 (by the formula given in footnote 10, page 32), i.e., $\sqrt{np(1-p)}$, or $\sqrt{2{,}100\ (.3)(.7)} = 21$. Two standard deviations is, thus, 42 (2 × 21), which is the variation in the number of losses permitted by our assumptions. Other examples given below may be verified in this same manner.

[11] Of course, there is no guarantee that losses will necessarily be distributed normally. Statistical tests can establish the existence or nonexistence of a normal distribution of past loss histories, on which assumptions can be made concerning a given future expectation for a loss experience. If the tests of a binomial distribution are met, however, losses will be approximately normally distributed.

[12] See Parzen, *op. cit.*, pp. 228-232, for the mathematical derivation of a similar formula.

As another example, suppose we are satisfied with an accuracy of .05 for the value of *e*. In this case, the formula yields $\frac{2^2(.3)(.7)}{(.05)^2}$ or 336 exposure units. If we are satisfied with an accuracy of .10, we would need only $\frac{2^2(.3)(.7)}{(.10)^2}$ or 84 exposure units. If we wished to be 99% sure that our loss frequency will not differ from the expected loss frequency by more than .02, we would need $\frac{3^2(.3)(.7)}{(.02)^2}$ or 4,725 exposure units.

In the preceding illustration, the probability of loss was very large. In many fields of insurance it is somewhat unusual to experience such large probabilities. It is much more common for the probability of loss to be about 5% or less. If the probability of loss is only 5%, the insurer will undoubtedly wish to insist on a higher standard of accuracy than was true in the preceding case. Thus, .03 might be satisfactory when the expected loss ratio is .30, because a deviation of .03 from a mean of .30 represents only a 10% error (.03/.30 = .10). If the basic probability is only .05, however, an error of .03 in the above formula becomes a deviation of 60% away from the expected loss ratio (.03/.05 = .60). Hence, the insurer may say that if the expected loss ratio is .05, the standard of accuracy will be .005, or 10% away from the expected loss ratio. Substitution of .005 for *e* in the above general formula yields, at a 95% confidence level, $\frac{2^2(.05)(.95)}{(.005)^2}$ or 7,600 exposure units as the minimum number necessary.

In life insurance it is interesting to observe that at a young age, such as 20, the probability of loss is less than .002. If a life insurer is to be 95% confident that its actual number of deaths among all insured lives, age 20, is to be within .0002 (again, 10% away from the expected loss ratio) of its expected death rate, it must insure $\frac{2^2(.002)(.998)}{(.0002)^2}$ or 199,600 lives.

The formula produces a very large number of lives required for the degree of risk acceptable, but the example illustrates a fundamental truth about insurer risk: when the probability of loss is small, the insurer needs a larger number of exposure units for the degree of risk which is acceptable than is commonly recognized. Mathematical formulas such as the ones used in these examples can assist the insurer considerably in making estimates of the degree of risk assumed with given numbers in an exposure group.

Such formulas as given above offer a way for an insurer to consider simultaneously the interrelationships of numbers of exposure units, probability of loss, errors in prediction, and confidence levels of future estimates of loss. Once any three of these variables are ascertained, the fourth may be found. Using the formulas, a commercial insurer may, for example, discover that a much larger penetration of an insurance market is necessary to reduce the risk to acceptable levels. A decision to withdraw from a given market or to spend additional sums in promotional efforts may thus be made with greater intelligence. Again, a self-insurer's firm may be running risks of catastrophic loss because there are too few exposure units for loss stability. If the self-insurer decides to continue self-insurance anyway, it should be recognized that the probability of expected losses will be that the firm's self-insurance fund will be depleted in the forthcoming year. Management can thus decide whether to increase the self-insurance fund, purchase commercial insurance, or continue to run the risk.

Credibility Tables

The use of a mathematical model in determining the number of exposure units needed to achieve a given degree of loss stability is also important in preparing credibility tables. *Credibility tables* indicate the degree of reliability that a rate maker can ascribe to loss experience on existing exposure units. For example, if a rate maker is to raise or lower an insurance rate, based on higher or lower loss ratios observed in the past year among an insured group, an important question which must be answered is, "Is this insured group enough to produce a credible rate?" Mathematical and statistical techniques are very useful in this regard (see Chapter 26).

RISKS OF THE INDIVIDUAL

The basic risk to an individual is the uncertainty which exists as to whether the loss will be a personal one. An insured may know that the probability of loss is small, but there is no way of knowing where or on whom the lightning may strike. If the *possibility* of a serious loss exists, even though its *probability* is small, the individual will generally seek some way of avoiding this possibility.

From the preceding discussion, it was seen that rarely will a private individual have a sufficient number of exposure units to achieve a high degree of accuracy in statistical predictions as to loss. We may say that for the individual, risk is very high indeed. Hence, to avoid this risk insurance may be purchased or other methods may be sought. Of course, an individual may not really care whether a loss occurs or not, since the amount of money involved may be very small in relation to existing wealth. An individual may be unwilling to buy insurance against the occurrence of a small loss, such as fire insurance on a woodshed, even if the coverage is very inexpensive. Yet the insured may be willing to buy insurance on a new automobile, even if the mathematical expectation of loss is less than the premium to be paid, simply because there is unwillingness to expose to loss an investment which is relatively large when compared with total wealth.

For example, suppose that there is a 2% probability that collision will completely destroy a person's automobile. The owner of a \$1,000 auto may realize that the expected value of the loss is .02 × \$1,000, or \$20. Yet the owner may find that collision insurance would cost \$40 because the insurer must charge enough to pay for all expected losses plus the costs of doing business. Should the owner insure? If a \$1,000 auto represents a large portion of this person's total wealth, insurance will likely be purchased. If, however, the person is wealthy and has several other vehicles more valuable than this one, insurance may not be purchased. This situation suggests a very important fundamental principle of insurance. *Due to the element of risk, an individual may be willing to pay more to avoid a loss than the true expected value of this loss*. In fact, if it were not for this phenomenon, insurance could not exist. The insurer must always charge more for service than the expected value of the loss. If an individual acted solely according to the criterion of expected loss, insurance might never be bought, assuming, of course, that the expected value of the loss is known. In many cases, however, the expected value of the loss is not known. Nevertheless, risk is a burden on society and most individuals are willing to pay money to avoid it.

UTILITY ANALYSIS OF INSURANCE CONSUMPTION

Subjective risk stems from mental attitudes toward uncertainty. If people tend to act according to their mental attitudes, and if we could measure these mental attitudes, presumably we would have a valuable tool with which to predict human behavior in given situations. In particular, we might be able to predict risk behavior such as insurance buying by knowing more about mental attitudes toward risk. One concept which has been employed to measure mental attitudes toward risk is that of utility.

Utility is the subjective value an individual ascribes to commodities, services, or other things of personal worth. Such utility value summarizes all psychological, economic, and sociological factors into one net figure. Economists have long used the concept of utility to explain price and demand in the market. If a basket of groceries and a table radio each have the same total utility to the buyer, presumably the prices of these two commodities will be equal in a free market, and the buyer is indifferent as to which commodity to choose. In the same way, if the probability of winning a certain sum of money is equated in the mind of the consumer with the price of a lottery ticket, presumably the consumer is indifferent about the two choices. If the price of the ticket is reduced slightly, perhaps the consumer will decide to gamble and will purchase the ticket. The utility of goods and services is not necessarily related to cost of production. Hence, the seller can get a profit over cost by raising the value of a commodity in the mind of the consumer through such techniques as advertising.

In order to explain the fact that increasing the quantities of goods for sale tends to depress price, economists have relied heavily on the concept of diminishing marginal utility.

Marginal Utility

Marginal utility refers to the subjective value to the consumer of the last unit of a commodity purchased. It is presumed that the value of each additional unit of a good has less value to the consumer (although the price is the same) than the unit of a good immediately preceding it. As more and more goods are purchased, a point is reached where the price of the article will not be worth its cost to the user. Thus, the consumer will buy no more goods at that price. Following this reasoning, the loss of a marginal unit of a good is considered less serious to a rich person than to a poor person, who will therefore have a greater reason to insure against loss than a rich person.

Measuring Utility

The question arises as to how utility analysis can be practically employed to study buying decisions in insurance. First, a way must be found to measure the utility of each buyer—that is, the buyer's attitude toward risk. For example, we have stated that a large loss is considered more serious than a small loss, but how do we determine how much more serious? Friedman and Savage have outlined a method for determing this value.[13] Essentially, this method involves determination of the point at which an individual is indifferent between two alternatives, a certain sum of money on one hand and an uncertain, but larger sum of money on the other. The method may be outlined as follows:

1. Select any two amounts, say $500 and $1,000, and assign an arbitrary value of utility of 0 and 1, respectively.
2. Select any intermediate amount, say $600. Find its utility.
3. Ask whether the individual would be indifferent between a certain income of $600 or a *p*th probability of $500, and a *q*th probability of $1,000. Find the value of *p* so that the individual would be indifferent. For example, see if the person would be indifferent between $600 and a 1/10 chance at $500 and a 9/10 chance at $1,000 (if the latter is preferred, reduce the odds). Say the value of *p* turns out to be 2/5. This means that the individual is indifferent between a certain income of $600 and a 2/5 chance of $500 and a 3/5 chance at $1,000. The actuarial value of the chance is $200 plus $600, or $800. But the person would just as soon have a certain amount of $600 than an uncertain amount whose expected value is $800 because of the individual's particular set of values and outlook on uncertainty.
4. The value of the utility, because of our arbitrary initial assignments, is .6, arrived at as follows:

   $$U\ (600) = 2/5\ U\ (500) + 3/5\ U\ (1{,}000)$$
   $$U\ (600) = 2/5\ (0) + 3/5\ (1) = .6$$

   where U ($) = a person's utility assignment to a given sum of money.
5. Repeat the experiment for every value between $500 and $1,000.
6. To get utilities for values outside the range of $500–$1000, proceed as follows: Offer the consumer a chance, *p*, of $500 and a chance, *q*, of say $10,000 and a certainty of $1,000, varying *p* until the consumer is indifferent between the two. Say *p* is 4/5. This means that the consumer is indifferent between the certain amount of $1,000 and an uncertain amount of $400 (4/5 × $500) plus $2,000 (1/5 × $10,000) or $2,400. A utility of 1 has been assigned to an amount of $1,000 and 0 to $500; so,

   $$\begin{aligned} 4/5\ U\ (500) + 1/5\ U\ (10{,}000) &= U\ (1{,}000) \\ 4/5\ (0) + 1/5\ U\ (10{,}000) &= 1 \\ 1/5\ U\ (10{,}000) &= 1 \\ U\ (10{,}000) &= 5 \end{aligned}$$

[13] Milton Friedman and L. J. Savage, "The Utility Analysis of Choices Involving Risk," *Journal of Political Economy,* Vol. LVI (1948), pp. 279-304, and reprinted in American Economics Association, *Readings in Price Theory* (Homewood, Ill.: Richard D. Irwin, Inc., 1952).

SAMPLE CONTINUOUS VALUE GRAPH UTILITY ANALYSIS

Figure 2-2

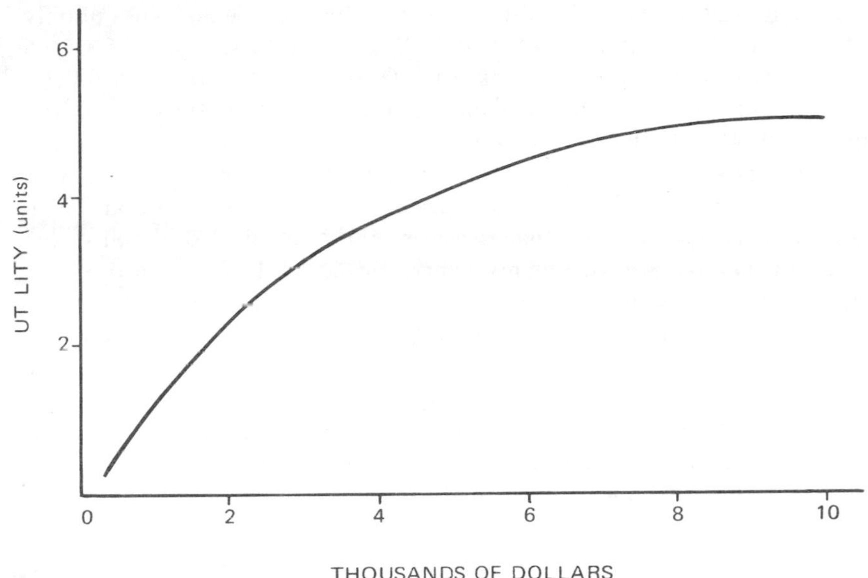

Graphically, the continuous values might appear as shown in Figure 2–2. If an individual were "linear" in money, the utility curve in Figure 2–2 would be represented by a straight line instead of a curved line. However, it is believed that relatively few individuals have such an outlook on risk, for this would mean that a person would be completely indifferent between a certain amount of money such as $1,000 and a .01 chance of receiving $100,000. Few persons would pay $1,000 for a 1% chance of winning $100,000. If the argument above is true, utility analysis must be taken into consideration in any decision involving risk, such as insurance.

To illustrate, in a specific way the application of utility to an insurance buying decision, assume that Smith's outlook on risk has been measured by the process above and can be summarized as follows:

Possible Monetary Outcome If Fire Occurs	Utility Points Assigned
−$50,000	−2,000
− 10,000	− 300
− 5,000	− 60
− 1,000	− 10
− 500	− 3
0	0
+ 500	+ 3

Apparently Smith is not an extremely rich person because a serious loss of \$50,000 means far more personally than a loss of more modest proportions, such as \$10,000. A loss of \$50,000 would mean a loss of utility of 2,000 points, whereas a loss of \$10,000, one fifth as much as before, means a loss of only 300 points, 15% of the utility loss of \$50,000. Similarly, a loss of only \$500 means a loss of utility of only 3 points. A loss of \$500 is 5% of the loss of \$10,000. The loss of utility assigned to \$500, 3 points, is only 1% of the utility loss of the 300 points which were assigned to \$10,000.

Now suppose that, for a premium of \$1,000, Smith can insure against a loss of \$50,000, whose probability of occurrence is .01. Smith knows that the probability of loss is only 1% and that therefore the long-run likelihood of loss, if exposed to this loss for very many years, would likely cost, on the average, \$500. Should the insurance be purchased? According to Smith's utility curve, a loss of \$50,000 means a loss of 2,000 utility points. In the long run a loss of 1% could be expected, or 20 points. In other words, the mathematical expectation of utility loss is 20 points. However, only 10 utility points to a premium outlay of \$1,000 is assigned. Accordingly, *Smith should in fact purchase insurance on all risks until the utility of the premium outlay equals the expected utility of the loss*. This rule can be illustrated in the following table:

(1) Monetary Outcome If Fire Occurs	(2) Utility Points Assigned	(3) Probability of Occurrence	(4) Expected Value of Utility Lost by Fire (2) × (3)	(5) Insurance Premium		(6) Loss in Utility Points by Paying Premiums [from (2)]
				(As a Percent)	In Dollars	
−\$50,000	−2,000	.01	−20	2	\$1,000	−10
− 10,000	− 300	.05	−15	10	1,000	−10
− 1,000	− 10	.10	− 1	20	200	− 1
− 500	− 3	.20	− .6	40	200	− 1
− 200	− 1	.30	− .3	60	120	− .6

According to the table above, Smith should insure losses in the amounts above \$1,000, but not below \$1,000. Below \$1,000, the insurance premium is too high since the utility loss by paying premiums exceeds the expected value of the utility loss of fire. For example, Smith is asked to pay \$200 for insuring against a loss of \$500 whose probability of occurrence is .2. The loss of utility by paying this amount is a certain amount, namely, one point. The expected value of the utility loss by fire, however, is only .6 points. This result occurs because the insurer is assumed to charge premiums at a rate which is twice the expected value of the loss in order to cover its operating expenses. At the same time it will be observed that Smith is more nearly linear in money as the possible loss approaches 0.

In summary, the concept of diminishing marginal utility explains why a person would often be willing to pay more for insurance to avoid loss than the true expected value of the loss.

Some support for the utility hypothesis in explaining insurance buying behavior is found in certain psychological experiments where it has been shown that people tend to overestimate small probabilities and to underestimate large probabilities of loss or gain. A dividing line of approximately .20 was established in one experiment conducted by Preston and Baratta[14] as being the point below which subjects tended to overestimate the true probability of loss. Since most probabilities involving insurance are quite small, it can be seen that there may be a tendency for individuals to believe that the true probability of loss (and consequent loss in expected utility) is larger than it really is. Hence, the cost of insurance appears relatively small to such persons.

Friedman and Savage[15] noted that some persons will purchase insurance and yet, in a seemingly inconsistent manner, will also enter into gambles. If a person's utility curve were shaped as the curve in Figure 2–2, that person would not gamble since the expected marginal utility of the gain would be less than the marginal utility of the stake. Accordingly, Friedman and Savage hypothesized that it is possible for a person's utility curve to appear as an elongated "S", first increasing at a decreasing rate, then at an increasing rate, and finally again increasing at a decreasing rate as his wealth or income rises. If a person's income or wealth is at one of the points at which the rate of change in utility begins to increase at an increasing rate, presumably this person would be willing to gamble since above this level of wealth the expected gain in utility from winning would be worth more personally than the utility lost by paying the stake. Graphically this person's utility curve appears in Figure 2–3.

In reading the chart, assume that Jones's current wealth is $20,000, giving a utility value of 17 points. Jones is presented with a gamble in which there is a chance to increase his wealth to $30,000 for a stake of $3,000. The chart shows that the utility lost by paying the stake is one point, while the utility of the gain is 13 points. The utility of the gain is 13 times the utility of the stake. Presumably Jones will enter into the gamble if the probability of winning exceeds 1/13. Suppose the probability of winning is .10. The expected utility points from the gain is 1.3 (.10 × 13), while the utility lost by paying the stake is 1. These results occur even though in dollars Jones is apparently willing to pay $3,000 for the chance of winning $10,000, which is three times the expected value of the game.

Let us assume that Jones is also asked to pay a premium of $3,000 to purchase insurance against a possible loss which will reduce his wealth from $20,000 to $10,000. The utility curve shows that the total utility would decline from 17 to 2, or 15 points, while the loss in utility from paying the premium would be 1 point. Presumably Jones would purchase the insurance if the probability of loss exceeds 1/15. If the insurance premium is 10%, for example, the

[14] M. G. Preston, and P. Baratta, "An Experimental Study of the Auction Value of an Uncertain Outcome," *American Journal of Psychology,* Vol. 61 (1948), pp. 183-193.

[15] Friedman and Savage, *op. cit.*

HYPOTHETICAL UTILITY CURVE OF AN INDIVIDUAL WITH WEALTH OF $20,000 **Figure 2-3**

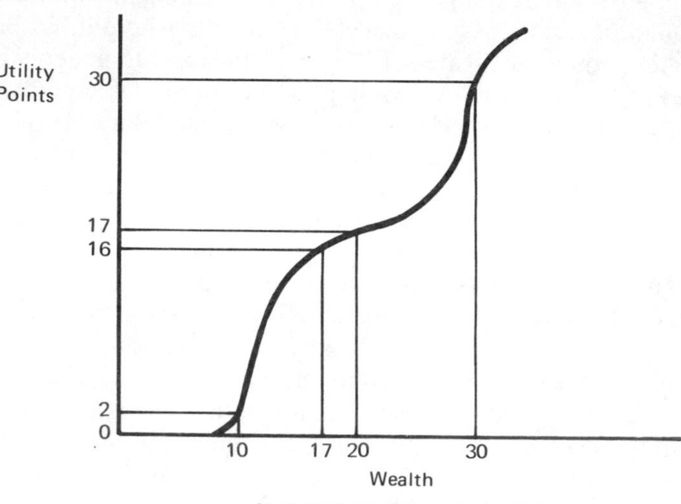

expected loss in utility by running the risk is 1.5 points (.10 × 15), while the utility lost by paying the premium is one point.

Thus, Jones might be willing to buy insurance and still enter into a gamble. Even though this might seem inconsistent conduct, the particular shape of Jones's utility curve for money explains why Jones does so. As Friedman and Savage point out, many persons do buy insurance and gamble at the same time. In a psychological experiment to test the Friedman and Savage hypothesis, Mosteller and Nogee[16] showed that players in a gambling situation appear to have utility curves closely resembling the curve shown for Jones.

It may be observed that above a certain level of wealth ($30,000) Jones's utility curve again becomes convex from above, indicating a dislike of risk above this point. This would appear to suggest why most wealthy persons become conservative with their money and are in fact large purchasers of insurance.

SUMMARY

1. The basic theorems of probability are of great importance in insurance, especially in rate-making, financial management, and contractual provision formulation. They are of crucial importance in protecting the solvency of the insurer by enabling more accurate predictions of losses, especially when empirical data are scanty and educated guesses must be made as to the course of future

[16] F. Mosteller and P. Nogee, "An Experimental Measurement of Utility," *The Journal of Political Economy* (October, 1951). pp. 371-404.

events. They give guidance to the underwriter in determining what constitutes an adequate number of exposure units in order to achieve financial stability. Probability theory is also an important guide to the would-be self-insurer in assessing the nature of a risk.

2. Probability is defined as the long-run frequency of certain events expressed as a percentage of the total number of possible events in a sample space, each of which has been assigned some number called a weight to reflect its relative importance in the total. Probability is a number between 0 and 1 assigned to an event.
3. When events in a sample space are defined to be mutually exclusive, the total probability of occurrence of two or more events is the sum of the respective probabilities of the separate events. This is called the additive rule in probability. The sum of such probabilities cannot exceed 1, and cannot be less than 0.
4. An important assumption in insurable events is that the events are independent and random. Independence means that the probability of one event does not affect the assessment of probability of the next event in a sample space. Randomness means that each event in a sample space is just as likely to occur as any other event. Insurers try to classify exposure units in such a way that occurrence of losses will be independent and random.
5. If two or more independent events may happen simultaneously or in sequence, the probability that all events will occur is the product of their separate probabilities. Known as the rule of compound probability, this statement underlies the more complicated methods of determining the probability of occurrence of a given number of events out of a larger number of events in the sample space, a device most useful to the insurer who is interested in the probability of occurrence of more than one loss.
6. The concept of expected value is basic to probability calculations. Expected value of an event or a series of events is calculated by preparing a schedule of possible outcomes, multiplying each outcome by its probability, and summing.
7. Conditional probability is the probability that some described event will occur, given that some other event has also occurred. The concept of conditional probability is especially useful in judging the severity of possible losses, if there is any loss at all.
8. The chief risks of the insurer are: (a) the uncertainties involved in estimating the probability of an event, (b) the uncertainties involved in determining that the events to be insured are independent and random, or that they conform to other mathematical assumptions, and (c) the fact that the insurer may not have a sufficient number of exposures to predict losses with a required degree of certainty. The coefficient of variation is one way to characterize the objective risk of the insurer in obtaining a sufficient number of exposure units for mathematical accuracy.
9. The chief risk of the insured is the uncertainty attached to whether or not a given loss will occur. Since this risk is generally very large due to the inability of the average insured to obtain a sufficient number of exposure units to obtain accurate predictions as to occurrence of losses, ways are sought to reduce risk through insurance and other means. It is not the probability of loss which causes difficulty, but rather the uncertainty as to whether an individual will be among those who are expected to suffer loss. Losses

which are certain can be prepared for in advance by those affected. It is the uncertain loss which requires refined methods of handling.

10. The concept of utility is an important tool in explaining the economic growth of the insurance mechanism as a way of handling risk. Without the idea of utility, it would be difficult to explain why anyone would pay $20 for insurance against a loss of $10,000, whose expected value (10,000 × the probability of occurrence) is .001 of $10,000, or $10. The answer lies in the fact that to most people the potential loss of $10,000 is so great that they are willing to pay far more than $10 to avoid the possibility of losing this much.

QUESTIONS FOR REVIEW AND DISCUSSION

1. (a) Referring to the example on page 26, calculate the probability that if a fire should occur at all, the number of fires will be one.
(b) What is the value of the concept of conditional probability to an insurer?

2. A jar contains 1,000 marbles—300 red, 300 white, and 400 blue.
(a) If the marbles are mixed and drawn at random, what is the probability of drawing a blue marble?
(b) What is the probability of drawing *either* a blue or a white marble?
(c) What is the probability of drawing two blue marbles in a row?
(d) What law of probability is illustrated by examples (b) and (c)?

3. In spinning a roulette wheel, it is said that the wheel has no memory. This means that if there are one half black numbers and one half red numbers each color alternated, each color has an equal chance of coming up each spin.
(a) What is the probability of getting a red number after 10 black numbers in 10 successive spins? after five successive spins have been black?
(b) How do you account for the fact that the same color might appear 10 times in succession? Discuss.

4. A common misunderstanding of the law of large numbers or the law of averages is that the longer one goes without an accident, the more likely it is that his turn is coming up. Why is this a misunderstanding of the law of large numbers?

5. A person flips a coin 100 times and obtains 35 heads. It is reasoned that if the coin is flipped another 100 times the individual will get about 65 heads to make up for the failure to get 50 heads during the first 100 flips. Accordingly, the coin is flipped another 100 times but only 40 heads are obtained. The flipper reasons that since the first set of flips was off by 15 heads, and the flips are now off by 25 from the expected 100, the law of averages is not working. Do you agree? Why?

6. A student decides to gamble on a game of cards in a casino with a probability of winning one in four. The student reasons that there is a better chance of winning if he plays a long time than if he plays a short time, on the grounds that losses can be compensated for by betting more heavily after a series of losses. Advise.

7. A famous French mathematician, D'Alembert, argued the following: Flip two coins. There is a possibility of getting 0, 1, or 2 heads, each with equal probability. Therefore, the probability of getting one head is 1/3 and not 1/2 as commonly believed. What important element in the analysis of probability did D'Alembert ignore?

8. An insurer is asked to insure under a group policy the lives of the passengers on a large ship, but refuses on the grounds that the events are not distributed randomly. Explain the insurer's attitude. Is it logical?

9. An underwriter argues that if the probability of a house burning by fire is .02 and the probability of its being damaged by windstorm is .03, the probability that it will be damaged by either fire or windstorm is .05. Is this true? Why?

10. An insurer is asked to write a contract covering two automobiles in a family. There is a 1 in 10 probability that the father will have an accident and a 1 in 5 probability that the son will have an automobile accident.
(a) What is the probability that both will have an accident?
(b) What assumptions underlie your answer?

11. From Figure 2–1,
(a) Indicate the probability that exactly 30 losses will occur; 40 losses will occur.
(b) Verify that if one takes each number of losses from 20 to 40 and multiplies each by its separate probability of occurrence, the result is 30.
(c) What is another name for the result that out of 100 exposure units, 30 losses are the most probable.

12. In Figure 2–1, verify that approximately 68% of the losses fall within a range of 26–34 (one standard deviation of the mean) and 95% of the losses fall within a range of 22–38 (two standard deviations of the mean).

13. The text states, "The statistical error caused by using sample observations rather than the total population . . . may be estimated by a measure known as the standard deviation around the sample mean. This error varies inversely with the square root of the sample size." This implies that the standard deviation of a population of events may be estimated by dividing the standard deviation of the means of the sample observations by the square root of the sample size. Suppose that in some samples of observations an insurer estimates the following distribution of average automobile collision losses:

Number of Policies	Average Dollars of Loss	Total Loss
300	$ 0	$ 0
50	40	2,000
40	100	4,000
10	1,000	10,000
400		$16,000

(a) Verify that the mean and standard deviation of the above loss distribution is $40 and $156.84, respectively.
(b) What is the best estimate of the standard deviation of the population of losses from which this sample is drawn?
(c) Verify that the insurer may be "95% confident" that average losses will range between $24.32 and $55.68, and "99% confident" that average losses will range between $16.48 and $63.52.
(d) If the sample size is increased to 1,600 (4 times its original level) but the mean is the same, what would you expect to happen to the estimated standard deviation of the population of losses? Explain.
(e) Upon what mathematical assumptions do your answers to (b) through (d) rest? Explain.

14. An industrial concern owns 300 automobiles which are scattered throughout the United States and used by its salespeople. From past data the firm's insurance manager knows that 12% of these autos are involved in a collision each year, with an average loss of $500. In the past, commercial insurance has been carried. The question is

being raised as to the feasibility of self-insurance, but the insurance manager questions its advisability on the grounds that variations of losses in a given year could cause an unusual amount of profit fluctuation in certain territories. The manager would be willing to self-insure, however, if it could be demonstrated that there is only a 5% probability that the actual loss frequency would vary from the expected loss frequency by more than 3%.
(a) Does the firm have a sufficient number of automobiles to guarantee the result asked for by the insurance manager, assuming that the firm's automobile collisions are normally distributed? Show that your answer is correct.
(b) Answer (a) on the basis that the firm is satisfied with an accuracy of .06.
(c) Find the degree of accuracy, in loss frequency, which 300 automobiles will produce under the assumptions of a two-standard-deviation confidence interval and a normal distribution of losses.
(d) How much dispersion from the expected loss frequency is represented by this degree of accuracy.

15. A firm is considering the advisability of self-insuring bodily injury liability. In this field, the firm's expected loss frequency is only .04; but the severity of losses, once they occur, is such that the average amount of claim is $10,000. The firm is insistent that before self-insurance can be attempted it must be true that there is a 95% probability that the actual loss frequency will not differ from the expected losses by more than .004. How many automobiles must the firm have to self-insure its bodily injury liability risk?

16. (a) Is it generally true, in your opinion, that a wealthy individual can afford not to insure more often than a poor person?
(b) What theoretical argument would support this position? Explain.

17. You are given an opportunity to purchase a ticket on a horse whose probability of winning $20 is 50%.
(a) How much would you pay for the ticket? How much would you pay if the winning ticket (whose probability of payoff is still 50%) paid $10? $1,000? $10,000? $1,000,000? In each case, assume it is your own money you are paying, and that you have this amount of money plus a 10% margin in your bank account.
(b) What has this experiment to do with risk?

18. The text states that "If an individual acted solely according to the criterion of expected loss, insurance might never be bought." Why is this true?

19. A. H. Willett stated:
It must be noticed also that the statement that risk or uncertainty entails a burden upon society by no means implies that society would necessarily be better off if all risk were avoided . . . The fact that capital can obtain the extra reward necessary to induce it to enter a hazardous employment shows that society values so highly the product of industry that it prefers to bear the extra expense rather than content itself with the products of of safe investments. . . .
(a) To what extent, if any, does insurance encourage investment in hazardous enterprises through reduction of risk?
(b) How is investment in hazardous enterprises of benefit to society?

20. "Uncertainty is a form of disutility that no one will voluntarily incur unless something is to be gained by so doing." Do you agree? Explain.

Chapter *Three*

HOW INSURANCE HANDLES RISK

Insurance is one of the major risk-handling methods. Insurance has grown rapidly and constitutes a major social and economic force. However, there are definite limitations to its use. Not every risk is insurable, due to legal, physical, and moral hazards, as well as other factors. The cost of insurance sometimes outweighs its economic value to the user. Finally there are certain social and economic cost considerations in determining the extent to which insurance can serve in handling risk. These and other questions are analyzed in this chapter.

THE GROWTH OF INSURANCE

The insurance industry has enjoyed one of the more enviable records of long-term growth of any of the financial institutions. From humble beginnings, it has developed into one of the major industries of the United States, and is regarded as essential to a highly developed industrial nation. In the period 1900 to 1945, the assets of life insurance companies, for example, increased approximately 57-fold, while assets of all banks in the United States increased about 15-fold.[1] This relative gain in the rate of growth has not been maintained in recent years, as shown in Table 3–1, where insurance firms' assets are compared with the major financial institutions. Table 3–1 indicates the size, as measured by assets, of major financial institutions in this country in 1941 and 1974.

From Table 3–1 we can see that the total assets of life insurance companies grew somewhat slower than mutual savings banks and commercial banks over the period 1941–1974, while property and liability insurance companies increased their assets somewhat faster than banks. Insurance companies combined increased their assets 9-fold over the period, compared to a growth of 48-fold for savings and loan associations, and 11-fold for commercial banks.

[1] Calculated from statistical tables given in *Life Insurance Fact Book 1958* (New York: Institute of Life Insurance, 1958) and *Historical Statistics of the United States 1789-1945* (Washington: U. S. Bureau of the Census, 1949), p. 262. These data for banks do not correspond precisely with the data given in Table 3–1, since the former are derived from data from the Comptroller of the Currency, which treats branches as separate banks.

TOTAL ASSETS OF MAJOR FINANCIAL INSTITUTIONS IN THE UNITED STATES, 1941 AND 1974 **Table 3-1**

Institution	Billions of Dollars 1941	Billions of Dollars 1974	Ratio, 1974/1941
Commercial Banks	$79.1	$884.3	11.2
Insurance Carrier			
Life	32.7	258.4	7.9
Property-Liability	5.3	84.0	15.9
Total Insurance	38.0	342.4	9.0
Savings and Loan Associations	6.0	288.0	48.0
Mutual Savings Banks	11.8	108.7	9.2

Sources: *Federal Reserve Bulletin* (February, 1975), pp. A-16, A-32/33. *Insurance Facts 1974. Statistical Abstract of the United States, 1967.* Ratios calculated.

Although insurance companies together have almost as many assets as savings and loan and mutual savings banks combined, it is clear that the latter institutions are growing somewhat faster.

The importance of insurance from the standpoint of premium income may be appreciated by comparing total premiums collected by insurers to disposable personal income. It is estimated in Table 5–1 that 18.7% of disposable personal income in 1974 was spent on insurance of all types. Of this amount, government insurance programs accounted for about 8.7%, and private insurance the remaining 10%. In 1950, private insurers collected about 7.5% of disposable income in insurance premiums.[2] Thus, insurance is gaining both absolutely and relative to total income.

A national survey taken by the Institute of Life Insurance covering the year 1969 shows that 91% of all husband-wife families own one or more life insurance policies. About 80% of the total adult population are covered by life insurance, and 85% by health insurance of some type. Most new life insurance is purchased by the age groups 15–24 and 25–34, which purchased 26% and 39% respectively of all new ordinary life insurance sold in 1973. These age groups are increasing the most rapidly in the United States population, indicating a continuing picture of rapid growth in insurance in the United States in the coming decade.

INSURANCE DEFINED

Insurance may be defined in two major contexts: as an economic or social institution designed to perform certain functions, and as a legal contract between two parties. A definition that relies exclusively on either of these contexts is undesirable because each has something to offer to the person seeking a comprehensive definition. The advantage of the first, the functional definition, is that it is descriptive of the basic way in which insurance reduces

[2] Based on $207 billion of disposable personal income in 1950.

risk by combining a sufficient number of exposure units to make the loss predictable. The functional definition, however, does not contemplate an insurance agreement where no risk *reduction* takes place. Many contracts of insurance exist where the insurer takes on a risk as a transferee and where there is no actual reduction of the risk in society as a whole. The risk is merely taken off the shoulders of one party and placed on the shoulders of a second party, for a consideration.

On the other hand, a strictly legal definition of insurance does not describe the subject in a sufficiently broad way to include those insurance arrangements that are not effected by a private legal contract, as in the case of social security and unemployment insurance. A definition that combines both approaches is needed. The following definition is offered as a basis for discussion.

> *Insurance* is an economic institution that reduces risk by combining under one management a group of objects so situated that the aggregate accidental losses to which the group is subject become predictable within narrow limits. Insurance is usually effected by, and can be said to include, certain legal contracts under which the insurer, for consideration, promises to reimburse the insured or render services in case of certain described accidental losses suffered during the term of the agreement.

This definition stresses how the main economic function performed by insurance, namely risk reduction, is accomplished. The emphasis on the word "usually" is made because not all insurance is effected by means of a legal contract. Thus, this definition is broad enough to contemplate various types of social insurance. Furthermore, this definition will include an insurance agreement in which there is no particular reliance on the law of large numbers as a means of predicting a loss because the definition contemplates an arrangement under which a risk is simply transferred by means of a legal contract.

The definition of insurance given above refers to insurance as an economic institution. The legal status of the insurer is not important, for an insurer can have the status of a chartered insurance company, a private corporation, a group of associated individuals cooperating in an insurance venture informally, or a governmental agency. The definition refers to "accidental losses." Losses which are certain to occur are not insurable. The loss must be due to some chance contingency or unexpected event. An agreement to keep a television set in working condition is not insurance, but a service contract. However, if a service contract covered the contingency of burglary or some other chance event, it might indeed be considered insurance.

REQUISITES OF INSURABLE RISKS

Unfortunately, not all risks are insurable. While insurance relies upon the law of large numbers as a basis for its economical operation, there are many situations that can cause loss where the law of large numbers does not operate satisfactorily. In other situations it may work reasonably well under most instances; in still other cases it works almost ideally. There are many degrees of insurability between the extremes.

A few illustrations will make this clearer. The peacetime use of atomic energy is still in its infancy. Insurers as a class are usually unwilling to cover this type of peril except under rigidly controlled conditions. The reason is, of course, that there has been no opportunity to collect statistics over a sufficient length of time on losses resulting from this peril so that insurers can accurately predict the probable loss experience. At present, loss from atomic energy is insurable only when the insurer can inspect the conditions under which a given insured is using a nuclear reactor and then only if rigid standards of safety are maintained. Even so, each insurer will impose conservative limits of liability.

In the field of life insurance, on the other hand, insurers have gathered reliable statistics over many years and have developed tables of mortality that have proved reliable as estimates of probable loss. Furthermore, life insurance is well accepted—it is relatively easy for the insurer to obtain a large group of exposure units. Here the law of large numbers works so well that for all practical purposes the life insurance company is able to eliminate its risk.

We can classify the requisites of insurable risks under two general headings: requirements from the standpoint of the insurer, and requirements from the standpoint of the insured.

These requirements, as presented below, are not necessarily complete. The requisites refer mainly to pure risks, not speculative risks, and are intended to be suggestive of the type of underwriting standards usually looked upon as basic to the acceptance or rejection of risks as submitted to the insurer. These requirements should not be considered absolute, as iron rules, but rather as guides. They should be viewed as ideal standards, and not necessarily as standards actually attained in practice. In practice, for example, it is not at all uncommon for an insurer to accept a risk even though some of the following requirements are not met, providing the premium compensates the insurer for its risk.

Requisites from the Standpoint of the Insurer

From the standpoint of the insurer, there are several requisites of insurable risks that must be met:

1. The objects must be of sufficient number and quality to allow a reasonably close calculation of probable loss.
2. The loss, should it occur, must be accidental and unintentional in nature from the viewpoint of the insured.
3. The loss, when it occurs, must be capable of being determined and measured.
4. The insured objects should not be subject to simultaneous destruction; i.e., catastrophic hazard should be minimal.

Objects To Be of Sufficient Number and Quality. The objects must be of sufficient number and quality to allow a reasonably close calculation of the probable loss. The probable loss must be subject to advance estimation. If only a few objects are covered, the insurer is subject to the same uncertainties of random experience as the insured. The quality of the objects to be insured must be homogeneous so that reliable statistics of loss can be formulated. The insurer must be able to control its risk. Risk varies inversely with the square root of the number of objects exposed and inversely with changes in the probability of loss. Thus, the insurer attempts to make careful estimates of probability and of the various hazards contributing to loss, and to obtain sufficient numbers of exposed objects so as to reduce its risk to the minimum. It would be improper to group commercial buildings with private residences for purposes of fire insurance since the hazards facing these classes of buildings are entirely different. Furthermore, the physical and social environment of the group should be roughly similar so that no unusual factors are present that would cause losses to one part of the group and not to the other part. Thus, buildings located in a hurricane zone must not be grouped with buildings not found in such a zone.

Loss To Be Accidental and Unintentional. There must be some uncertainty surrounding the loss. Otherwise, there would be no risk. If the risk or uncertainty has already been eliminated, insurance serves no purpose since the main function of insurance is to reduce risk. Thus, if a person is dying from an incurable disease which will cause death within a given time, there is little uncertainty or risk concerning the payment of loss; insurance would not be feasible. Theoretically, the insurer could issue a policy, but the premium would have to be large enough to cover both the expected loss and the insurer's cost of doing business. The cost of such a policy would probably seem prohibitive to the insured.

Because of the requirement that the loss be accidental, insurers normally exclude in all policies any loss caused intentionally by the insured. If the insured knew that the insurer would pay such losses, a moral hazard would be introduced, and there would be a tendency for losses and premiums to rise. If premiums become exceedingly high, so few would purchase insurance that the insurer would no longer have sufficiently large numbers of exposure units to be able to obtain a reliable estimate of future loss. Thus, the first requirement of an insurable risk would not be met.

It has been said that insurance is one commodity that must be purchased before it is needed. Once the fire starts, it is too late to buy fire insurance. While this statement illustrates the requirement that the loss must not be certain to happen, it ignores a basic truth about insurance. This truth is that insurance is not purchased, as such, to recover losses, but is a method of eliminating the uncertainty that exists for each individual as to whether or not the loss will happen personally. Looked upon in this light, insurance performs its chief function during the period before any loss. The insured has the satisfaction and security of knowing that should the insured be the one to have the loss, there will be reimbursement. Yet the insured hopes that the insurance will not be needed. Insurance has been defined as the distribution of losses of the unfortunate few among the fortunate many. Each insured hopes to be among the fortunate many, for seldom does the insurance policy fully compensate the unfortunate few for *all* of their losses. Even if one's house burns and the owner is fully insured, often use of the house cannot be recovered—the additional expenses of providing temporary living arrangements elsewhere, the inconvenience, the depreciation, and, perhaps, the lost income resulting from the fire. Only the uninformed, or perhaps the dishonest, secretly hope for the loss to occur so they can "get something out of their insurance."

Loss To Be Determinable and Measurable. The loss must be definite in time and place. It may seem unnecessary to add this requirement since most losses are easily recognized and most are capable of being measured with reasonable accuracy. It is a real problem to insurers, however, to be able even to recognize certain losses, let alone to measure them. For example, in health insurance, the insurer may agree to pay the insured a monthly income if "he should become so totally disabled as to be unable to perform the duties of his occupation." The question arises, however, as to who will determine whether or not the insured meets this condition. Often it is necessary to take the insured's word. Thus, it may be possible for a dishonest person to feign illness in order to recover under the policy. If this happens, the second requirement, that the loss be unintentional, is not met.

Even if it is clear that a loss has occurred, it may not be so easy to measure it. For example, what is the loss from "pain and suffering," or of an auto accident victim? Often only a jury can decide. What is the loss of cargo on a sunken ship? It often takes a staff of adjusters many months or even years to decide. Suffice it to say that before the burden of risk can be safely assumed, the insurer must set up procedures to determine if loss has actually occurred, and if so, its size.

Loss Not To Be Subject To Catastrophic Hazard. Conditions should not be such that all or most of the objects in the group might suffer loss at the same time and possibly from the same peril. Such simultaneous disaster to insured objects can be illustrated by reference to large fires, floods, and hurricanes that have swept major geographical areas in the past. The history of fire insurance reveals that hardly a major American city has escaped a catastrophic fire sometime in its history. In certain areas hurricanes sometimes flatten entire cities within a matter of minutes. If an insurer is unlucky enough to have on its books a great deal of property situated in such an area, it obviously suffers a loss that was not contemplated when the rates were formulated. Most insurers reduce this possibility by ample dispersion of insured objects.

Requisites from the Standpoint of the Insured

From the standpoint of the insured, the two main requisites of insurable risks are that the potential loss must be severe enough to cause financial hardship and that the probability of loss must not be too high.

Potential Loss Must Warrant Protection. It would seem apparent that most individuals do not normally try to insure some minor contingency, the loss from which they can well afford to bear. There are many instances, however, among individuals who fail to recognize the severity of a potential loss. For example, it is not uncommon to discover that a person has insured against collision an automobile valued at $350, and at the same time carries little or no insurance against the loss of his life, whose value to his dependents may be $100,000 or more.

What is a serious loss to one person may not be serious to another. In general, a person will seek protection against those losses that cannot be comfortably absorbed out of current income or savings. A basic principle of insurance buying, however, is that the most economical use of insurance premiums is first against the serious loss and then against the less serious losses, and not vice versa.

Probability of Loss Not To Be Too High. It may seem contradictory to urge that one of the insured's requirements is that one should not insure against a highly probable loss. The point to remember, however, is that the more probable the loss is, the more certain it is to occur. The more certain it is, the greater the premium will be. A time is ultimately reached when the loss becomes so certain that either the insurer withdraws the protection or the cost of the premium becomes prohibitive, or both.

The basic purpose of insurance is to protect against the improbable loss. It has been estimated that if the chance of loss is greater than 50%, the insurer finds it impossible to offer the protection because the premium becomes too great to be worth it to the insured. The contract becomes one of trading dollars with the insurer, but on an unfavorable basis to the insured, since the insurer must collect more money than is paid out to policyholders in order to cover costs.

TYPES OF RISKS

It is now pertinent to raise the issue of which risks fall into the category of insurable risks and which do not. The following outline includes each type:

I. Insurable risks
   A. Property risks—the uncertainty surrounding the occurrence of loss to property from perils that cause:
      1. Direct loss of the property
      2. Loss of property indirectly
   B. Personal risks—the uncertainty surrounding the occurrence of loss of life or income due to:
      1. Premature death
      2. Physical disability
      3. Old age
      4. Unemployment
   C. Legal liability risks—the uncertainty surrounding the occurrence of loss due to negligent behavior resulting in injury to persons arising out of:
      1. The use of automobiles
      2. The occupancy of buildings
      3. Employment
      4. The manufacture of products
      5. Professional misconduct

II. Risks uninsurable by commercial insurers
   A. Market risks—factors that may result in loss to property or income, such as:
      1. Price changes, seasonal or cyclical
      2. Consumer indifference
      3. Style changes
      4. Competition offered by a better product
   B. Political risks—uncertainty surrounding the occurrence of:
      1. Overthrow of the government or war
      2. Restrictions imposed on free trade
      3. Unreasonable or punitive taxation
      4. Restrictions on free exchange of currencies
   C. Production risks—uncertainties surrounding occurrence of:
      1. Failure of machinery to function economically
      2. Failure to solve technical problems
      3. Exhaustion of raw material resources
      4. Strike, absenteeism, labor unrest

The several types of insurable risks which face the individual will be thoroughly discussed in Parts IV and V.

It should be noted that the uninsurable risks are to be considered generally uninsurable from the viewpoint of a private insurer. Governmental agencies commonly insure political risks such as those arising from war (ocean marine risks during wartime) and currency restrictions (export credit insurance and investment guarantees). There is the possibility that ways and means may be found for private agencies to assume risks considered catastrophic or unpredictable in nature, or to assume speculative risks. Nevertheless, it seems likely that such a development will be slow.

To illustrate the reasons for uninsurable risks, let us use market risks as the first example. Take the case of a manufacturer who wishes to insure that the price of a product will not fall more than 10% during the policy year. Such a risk is subject to the catastrophic loss, since simultaneous loss from this source is possible to all of the firm's products in a depression. Further, the losses are not subject to advance calculation since, in an ever-changing, free, competitive market such as ours, past experience is an inadequate guide to the future. Hence, the insurer would have no realistic basis for computing a premium. Furthermore, in times of rising prices, few would be interested in the coverage; and in times of falling prices, no insurer could afford to take on the risk. The insurer could get no "spread of risks" over which to average out good years with bad years. Again, if such insurance were offered, there would be a tendency for each person to increase output since the possession of a price guarantee would in all probability drive the price downward, thus bringing about the very contingency against which the manufacturer was insured.

Political risks are also beyond the control of the insured for the most part, since losses from this source cannot be estimated accurately nor measured. For example, many war risks are such that one cannot measure the degree to which many types of losses stem from a war or from some other peril. Also, this peril often brings about catastrophic losses. Again, since no two wars are alike and their courses cannot be predicted, there is no way of scientifically calculating a premium.[3]

To the extent that risks are uninsurable, the management of a business firm, or an individual, will employ one or more of the other methods of handling risk discussed on page 11. This subject is explored more thoroughly in Chapter 4.

INSURANCE AND GAMBLING

It is common to confuse insurance with gambling, for to many it is difficult to see clearly why insurance is not gambling. Even legal authorities have not always made a clear distinction between the two, classifying both insurance and gambling contracts under the category of *aleatory contracts*, in which the outcome is subject to an uncertain event.[4] In such contracts it is possible for one party to give up a great deal more than received in the transaction. Aleatory contracts are contrasted with another group, called *commutative contracts,* under which each party gives up approximately equal value in exchange for the promises or acts of the other. Insurance may appear to be a contract under which there is a possibility for the insurance company to pay to a given party a great deal more than it has received in premiums; but this does not mean that insurance is thereby a gambling contract. In fact, from an economic standpoint, gambling and insurance are exact opposites.

Gambling creates a new risk where none existed before, whereas insurance is a method of eliminating or greatly reducing (to one party anyway) an already existing risk. This may be illustrated as follows: Janet said to Jack, "I'll bet you $5,000 to $50 that Dick's house will not catch fire within one year." If Jack takes the bet, a new risk has been created for each person. If the house burns, Jack wins $5,000; but if it does not burn, he loses $50. Before the gamble, neither party had any risk of losing any money from this source, nor, of course, of gaining any. After the gamble, each party becomes subject to a new risk of losing money.

Contrast the preceding incident with the situation in which Dick goes to the fire insurance company and insures his house for $5,000 and the insurer charges a premium of $50. Dick had the risk of having his house destroyed by fire before he entered into the insurance transaction. He has an insurable interest in his house. Afterward he has eliminated the risk of loss from this source in return for a premium of $50. He has exchanged a large *uncertain* loss for a small but *certain* loss, namely, the premium.

INSURANCE AND SPECULATION

Speculation is a transaction under which one party, for a consideration, agrees to assume certain risks, usually in connection with a business venture. A

[3] The student should ask the extent to which each of the types of risks in the outline is insurable, applying the criteria presented in this chapter.

[4] See *Black's Law Dictionary* (4th ed.; St. Paul: West Publishing Co., 1951), p. 94.

good example of speculation is found in the practice known as *hedging*. In hedging, a flour miller, for example, may have purchased grain to grind into flour. The miller realizes, however, that before the grinding can be completed, the price of grain, and consequently that of flour, may have changed, causing either profit or loss. The miller prefers to avoid the price risk and to concentrate on the main business operation—flour milling. Therefore, after buying the grain, the miller enters into an equal and opposite transaction in the grain futures market whereby a speculator, in effect, assumes the price risk.

Although hedging is a complicated process, a simple illustration will clarify the central point. Let us assume that on February 1 our flour miller agrees to deliver flour on June 1, based on the February 1 price of the grain which is $2 a bushel. Ten thousand bushels of grain will be needed to fill the order for flour. Each bushel of grain processed into flour is worth $2.25. Thus, the flour miller expects to earn 25 cents per bushel from the flour milling operations. On February 1, however, the miller has not actually purchased the grain, but expects to do so about May 1. The miller realizes that by May 1, the price of grain may have risen above $2 a bushel, thus causing a reduction in the expected margin. The miller therefore contacts a speculator and *buys* from the speculator 10,000 bushels of grain for delivery in the future at say $2.10 a bushel. This is known as a futures contract. The 10 cent premium, due in part to handling costs of holding grain until the delivery date, is known as the spread.

As May approaches the miller decides to purchase the grain for the flour milling operation. At this time the open market price of grain has indeed risen by 5 cents to $2.05. However, the futures contract value would have normally also gone up 5 cents assuming that the spread has not changed. Thus, the miller is able to sell the futures contract for $2.15, making a profit of 5 cents on this transaction, which just offsets the 5 cents loss suffered by having to pay $2.05 for grain to fill a flour contract based on a price of $2. If the price had gone down instead of up, the transactions described above would be reversed, with the miller losing on the futures contract, but gaining on the cash transaction. Speculators who so willingly accommodated the miller buy and sell futures contracts in the commodity markets just as other speculators buy and sell common stocks.They perform a valuable economic function by permitting the transfer of price risk.[5]

What is the distinction between speculation and insurance? The central purpose of the two types of transactions is very similar, but the actual contracts do not bear any obvious similarity. A speculator is a transferee of risk, and the transferor is usually a business person wishing to pass on a price risk to someone who is more willing and able to bear it. Such a business person then is using the transfer method of handling risk. Normally the risk is a type that insurers are unwilling to handle because it fails to meet the tests of insurability—the risk

[5] For a complete explanation of hedging, see Charles F. Phillips and Delbert J. Duncan, *Marketing Principles and Methods* (6th ed.; Homewood, Ill.: Richard D. Irwin, Inc., 1968), Ch. 20. Several other examples of speculation might have been given. Much of the stock market trading serves speculative purposes. In fact, almost any business situation in which a price risk is involved serves as a potential market for the speculator.

is unpredictable or is subject to catastrophic loss. Perhaps the main difference between insurance and speculation lies in the type of risks that each is designed to handle, and in the resulting differences in contractual arrangements. The main similarity lies in the central purpose behind each transaction.

Let us follow the hedging example through to illustrate these similarities and differences. The futures contract is one to buy or to sell grain (or some other commodity) at a given price and at a given time in the future. The futures contract does not follow the form of an insurance contract, under which one party promises to reimburse another for a loss. Yet the purpose of the futures contract, from the viewpoint of the hedger, is a reimbursement for loss, if any, arising from falling grain prices in the future. The miller has a risk and is shifting it to the speculator by this means.

The speculator's purpose is to agree to take the price risks in the hope of making a net profit out of the sum total of the transactions. In other words, the speculator hopes to "guess right" about price trends a majority of the time. This position is similar to a commercial insurer who accepts risk as a transferee without the benefit of having a large number of exposure units over which to spread operations. Such a commercial insurer may be compared to an underwriter at Lloyd's who agrees to pay a given sum if rain causes a loss to the promoters of a public event.

In summary, from a legal viewpoint, the purpose of the insurance contract and the speculative contract is to transfer risk. The type of contractual arrangement used in each case is entirely different because of the nature of the risk to be handled. Neither of the contracts is a gambling contract because no new risk is created that did not exist before. In most cases, however, insurance transactions have the benefit of the law of large numbers and thus can greatly reduce the risks involved. In speculation, however, the risk is seldom eliminated, but is borne by another person who is presumably better able to handle it because he possesses superior knowledge of the uncertainties involved and perceives less subjective risk than the transferor.

SOCIAL AND ECONOMIC VALUES OF INSURANCE

It has been implied in the foregoing discussion that to distinguish between insurable and uninsurable risk serves a useful purpose. This purpose is that insurance has peculiar advantages as a device to handle risk and so ought to be extended as far as possible, in order to bring about the greatest economic advantage to a given society. In order to establish the validity of this point, some of the social and economic values of insurance are listed below:

1. The amount of accumulated funds needed to meet possible losses is reduced.
2. Cash reserves that insurers accumulate are freed for investment purposes, thus bringing about a better allocation of economic resources and increasing production.
3. Since the supply of investable funds is greater than would be true without insurance, capital is available at a lower cost than would otherwise be true.
4. The entrepreneur with adequate insurance coverage is a better credit risk.

5. Insurers actively engage in loss-prevention activities.
6. Insurance contributes to business and social stability and peace of mind by protecting business firms and the family breadwinner.

Reduction of Accumulated Reserve Funds

Perhaps the greatest social value, and indeed the central economic function, of insurance is to obtain the advantages that flow from reduction of risk. One of the chief economic burdens of risk is the necessity of accumulating funds to meet possible losses. One of the great advantages of the insurance mechanism is that it greatly reduces the total of such reserves which are required for a given economy. Since the insurer can predict losses in advance, it needs to accumulate only enough funds to meet these losses and to cover expenses. If each individual had to set aside such funds, there would be a need for an amount far greater than the insurance company needs because the individual, not knowing precisely how much would be required, would tend to be conservative. For example, in most localities, a $15,000 residence can be insured against fire and perhaps other physical perils for as little as $50 a year. If insurance were not available, the individual would probably feel a need to accumulate funds at a much more rapid rate than $50 a year.

Freeing of Cash Reserves for Investment Purposes

Another aspect of the same advantage described above is the fact that the cash reserves which insurers accumulate are made available for investment. Insurers as a group, and life insurance firms in particular, have become among the largest and most important institutions to collect and distribute the nation's savings. Table 3–2 presents data showing the major sources of long-term capital funds in the U.S. for 1970 and 1975. It may be seen that insurance companies, while contributing a slightly smaller share of the total in 1975 than in 1970, still were one of the major sources of long-term capital in the economy. A substantial part of the contributions of insurance companies is derived from regular savings by individuals through life insurance contracts. The provision of the life insurance mechanism, which encourages individual savings, is a most important contribution of insurance to the savings supply.

From the viewpoint of the individual, the result of the insurance mechanism, then, is to free for investment purposes funds that would otherwise be unavailable for that purpose. Thus, the insurance mechanism encourages new investment. For example, if an individual knows that his family will be protected by life insurance in the event of his premature death, the insured may be more willing to invest his savings in a long-desired project, such as a business venture, without feeling that the family is being robbed of its basic income security. In this way a better allocation of economic resources is achieved.

Availability of Investment Capital at Lower Cost

Since the supply of investable funds is greater than would be true without insurance, capital is available at lower cost than would otherwise be true. Other

SOURCES OF LONG-TERM CAPITAL FUNDS IN THE U.S., 1970 AND 1975

Table 3-2

	Billions of Dollars		Percent of Total	
	1970	1975	1970	1975
Insurance companies				
Life insurance	$ 9.0	$ 17.7		
Property-liability insurance	4.0	5.3		
Subtotal	$ 13.0	$ 23.0	12.5	11.4
Pension funds				
Noninsured	$ 7.8	$ 11.2		
State and local	6.1	11.3		
Subtotal	$ 13.9	$ 22.5	13.4	11.1
Thrift institutions				
Savings and loans	$ 12.5	$ 26.3		
Mutual savings banks	4.2	8.0		
Credit unions	1.6	3.0		
Subtotal	$ 18.3	$ 37.3	17.6	18.4
Investment companies	1.7	.5	1.6	.3
Other intermediaries	2.8	3.3	2.7	1.6
Commercial banks	36.5	67.5	35.1	33.4
Corporations	2.5	9.6	2.4	4.7
Government	10.9	11.4	10.5	5.6
Foreign investors	11.0	14.7	10.6	7.3
Individuals	−6.7	12.5	−6.4	6.2
Total	$103.9	$202.3	100.0	100.0

Source: Bankers Trust Co., *Credit and Capital Markets*, 1975 (New York: Bankers Trust Co., 1975), p. T-1. Percentages calculated.

things being equal, this brings about a higher standard of living since increased investment itself will raise production and cause lower prices than would otherwise be the case. Insurance has another influence in this regard. Because it is an efficient device to reduce risk, investors may be willing to enter fields they would otherwise reject as too risky. Thus, society benefits by increased services and new products, the hallmarks of increased living standards.

Entrepreneur Becomes Better Credit Risk

Another advantage of insurance lies in the importance of insurance to credit. Insurance has been called the basis of our credit system. It follows logically that if insurance reduces the risk of loss from certain sources, it should mean that an entrepreneur is a better credit risk if adequate insurance is carried. One of the earliest known instances of the use of insurance was in connection with credit. This took the form of what was known as a *bottomry contract*, used by the early Romans and Greeks. The bottomry contract provided that if the trader borrowed money to finance an ocean voyage, and an ocean peril caused the vessel to be lost, the money lender would forgive the debt which had been incurred. Naturally, the interest rate charged for the loan was somewhat higher than it would have been without this guarantee, the difference amounting to the premium for insurance.

Today it would be difficult or impossible to borrow money for many business purposes, or for the purchase of a home, without insurance protection that meets the requirements of the lender. One of the most significant things done to restore the confidence of people in banks following their mass closure in 1933 was the establishment of the Federal Deposit Insurance Corporation to insure deposits. Also during the 1930's federal insurance on home loans laid the foundation for a great expansion of long-term credit for home ownership.

Loss-Prevention Activities

Another social and economic value of insurance lies in its loss-prevention activities. While it is not the main function of insurance to reduce loss, but merely to spread losses among members of the insured group, nevertheless insurers are vitally interested in keeping losses at a minimum. Insurers know that if no effort is made in this regard, losses would have a tendency to rise, since it is human nature to relax vigilance when it is known that the loss will be fully paid by the insurer in any case. If the probability of loss rises, premiums must also keep pace; and it is likely that fewer and fewer would be able to afford the insurance. Thus, eventually the offer of insurance would be withdrawn for want of sufficient volume of business. Furthermore, in any given year, a rise in loss payments reduces the profit to the insurer, and so loss prevention provides a direct avenue of increased profit. Insurers have attempted to create an atmosphere in which other loss-prevention organizations can work effectively.

A few illustrations of the work of insurance organizations devoted mainly to loss prevention and control in the field of property and liability insurance are: (1) the investigation of fraudulent insurance claims by the Insurance Crime Prevention Institute; (2) research into the causes and susceptibility to loss on highways by the Insurance Institute for Highway Safety; (3) the recovery of stolen vehicles and other auto theft prevention work by the National Theft Bureau; (4) the development of fire safety standards and public educational programs on fire prevention by the National Fire Protection Association; (5) providing leadership in the field of general safety, including the public information programs on safety by the National Safety Council; (6) furnishing fire protection and engineering counsel for oil producers by the Oil Insurance Association; (7) investigation and testing of building materials to see that fire prevention standards are being met by the Underwriters' Laboratories, Inc.;

and (8) appraisal, reclamation, and disposal of damaged merchandise by the Underwriters Salvage Companies of Chicago and New York. Insurance companies support the activities of loss prevention agencies such as those listed above through an assessment on premiums. In life and health insurance continuous support is given by private insurers to programs aimed at reducing loss by premature death, sickness, and accidents.

Contribution to Business and Social Stability

A final advantage of insurance lies in its contribution to business and social stability. Adequately protected, a business need not face the grim prospect of liquidation following an insured loss. A family need not break up following the death or permanent and total disability of the breadwinner. An unemployed worker usually has a small income to help out until another job can be found. A business venture can be continued without interruption even though a key person or the sole proprietor dies. A family need not lose its life savings following a bank failure. Old-age dependency can be avoided. Loss of a firm's assets by theft can be reimbursed. Whole cities ruined by a hurricane can be rebuilt from the proceeds of insurance.

SOCIAL COSTS OF INSURANCE

No institution can operate without certain costs. These costs are listed below in order that an impartial view of the insurance institution, as a social device, can be obtained:

1. Cost of operating the insurance business.
2. Cost of losses that are intentionally caused.
3. Cost of losses that are exaggerated.

Cost of Operating the Insurance Business

The main social cost of insurance lies in the use of economic resources, mainly labor, to operate the insurance business. The average annual overhead of property insurers accounts for about 33% of their earned premiums but ranges widely depending on the type of insurance. In life insurance, an average of 17% of the premium dollar is absorbed in expenses. The advantages of insurance are not obtained for nothing. They should be weighed against the cost of obtaining the service.

Cost of Losses That Are Intentionally Caused

A second social cost of insurance is attributed to the fact that if it were not for insurance, certain losses would not occur. What is referred to are those losses that are caused intentionally by people in order to collect on their policies. While there are no reliable estimates as to the extent of such losses, it is possible that they are only an extremely small fraction of the total loss payments. Insurers are well aware of this danger and, as we shall later see, take numerous steps to keep it at a minimum, both in underwriting the risk and in effecting loss adjustments.

Cost of Losses That Are Exaggerated

Separate from the costs above, and yet related to them, is another social cost of insurance—the tendency to exaggerate the extent of damage that results from purely unintentional loss occurrences where the loss is insured. There are good studies to illustrate this point. For example, one survey noted a definite indication that loss payments to families insured for accident and sickness claims tend to be higher than the reported losses of uninsured families.[6] This probably is true because part of the extent of loss is within the control of the insured. In other words, once the accident or sickness has occurred, an individual may decide to undergo more expensive medical treatment; or the physician may prescribe it, if it is known that the insurer will bear most or all of the bill.

Another illustration of added costs due to exaggerated losses is seen in the field of legal liability insurance. It is a recognized fact that juries tend to be more generous with an injured plaintiff in a negligence case if it is realized that a liability insurer will be paying whatever judgment is handed down.[7] Another example is found in automobile insurance covering physical damage to the auto. Where it is known that an insurance company is involved, there seems to be an unmistakable tendency for repairers to exaggerate the extent of loss, sometimes in collusion with dishonest insureds.

In weighing the social costs and the social values of insurance, it appears that the advantages far exceed the disadvantages. If this were not true, in a free-market system such as ours, insurance would not be utilized to the extent that it is. Insurance is used because of the great economic services attained thereby. These services cost something, of course; but, like most expenses, insurance premiums are looked upon as essential to the successful operation of a business.

SUMMARY

1. Insurance is an economic institution that reduces risk by combining under one management a group of objects so situated that the aggregate accidental losses to which the group is subject become predictable within narrow limits. Insurance is usually effected by, and can be said to include, certain legal contracts under which the insurer, for consideration, promises to reimburse the insured or render services in case of certain described accidental losses suffered during the term of the agreement.

[6] O. W. Anderson and J. J. Feldman, *Family Medical Costs and Voluntary Health Insurance: A Nationwide Survey* (New York: McGraw-Hill Book Company, Inc., 1956).

[7] An organization of attorneys (The National Association of Claimants' Compensation Attorneys) has been formed for the purpose of devising ways and means of securing larger judgments for injured plaintiffs. Without the existence of almost universal liability insurance covering auto accidents in particular, it is doubtful if such an organization would have been formed.

2. From the standpoint of the insurer, the requisites of insurable risks are four: (a) there must be a sufficient number of homogeneous exposure units to allow a reasonably close calculation of probable future losses; (b) the loss must be accidental and unintentional in nature; (c) the loss must be capable of being determined and measured; and (d) the exposure units must not be subject to simultaneous destruction.
3. From the viewpoint of the insured, the main requirements of insurability are: (a) the loss must be severe enough to warrant protection; and (b) the probability of loss should not be so high as to command a prohibitive premium when compared with the possible size of the loss.
4. Risks facing individuals may be classified into insurable and uninsurable risks. Uninsurable risks include market, political, and production risks.
5. The essential difference between insurance and gambling is that insurance transfers, eliminates, or reduces existing risk, while gambling creates new risk.
6. The main distinction between insurance and speculation is that speculation deals usually with business risk, which is not insurable, but is transferred from one party to another. In insurance, the risk concerns an insurable fortuitous event and employs the combination method to reduce it.
7. There are many social and economic values of insurance, but perhaps the greatest value lies in the reduction of risk in society. The benefits of insurance are achieved at certain social costs, the chief of which is the cost of the economic resources used to operate the insurance business.

QUESTIONS FOR REVIEW AND DISCUSSION

1. A writer on insurance states, "An adequate explanation of insurance must include either the building up of a fund or the transference of risk, but not both." Is this statement in conflict with the position taken in this text? Explain.
2. Why do private insurers generally not insure against strikes? style changes? unemployment? Discuss.
3. If a department store guarantees its merchandise against mechanical failure within a period of five years, does the guarantee constitute insurance?
4. In this chapter, the growth of insurance companies was compared with the growth of banks. Different factors, however, have operated in each case, which might explain the early rapid growth of insurance assets, and the slowing down which was noted later. One of these facts would certainly be the nature of risks faced by each type of institution. Explain and contrast these risks, indicating how they might have accounted for the different rates of growth of the two institutions.
5. After Hurricane Agnes in 1972, which caused serious flood losses in several states, the insurance commissioner of Pennsylvania was quoted as saying: "A lot of people would have been better off if they had tossed a match to their homes before leaving them. At least most of them had fire insurance coverage." Do you agree? Why or why not?
6. *D,* a wealthy investor, feels that the market is such that the price of certain securities will fall in the near future. *D* therefore sells these securities to *A,* who is of the opinion that these securities will not fall in price. Who is the speculator, *D* or *A,* or both? Is such a transaction gambling? Explain.

7. A firm warrants that certain parts in its used automobiles are in good running order and will function properly for a period of one year. If the parts fail, the warranty pays for the replacement. The state insurance department attempted to impose its regulations on this firm because "the company is warranting the mechanical reliability of the mechanical features of the auto and this amounts to insuring the buyer against any defects in those parts." The firm's representatives claimed, on the other hand, that it was warranting only the fact that its inspectors had inspected a particular auto. How would you decide whether this is a proper example of insurance or not? What is your decision? Explain.
8. In a survey among insured persons affected by the tornadoes which struck the U.S. in April, 1974, 83% of those interviewed were satisfied with their loss settlements; 90% said that their claims had been settled by August; 15% said that they thought they should have received more; 27% said that they had been underinsured, but 22% had since increased their coverage.
   (a) Which of the social and economic advantages of insurance does this survey illustrate?
   (b) Judge the effectiveness of the insurance industry's performance in this case.
9. It was reported that in the 960 catastrophes registered in the U.S. in 1974, damages totalling $1.4 billion were incurred, of which $680 million, about half, were insured. Comment, with respect to the social performance of the insurance industry.
10. It has been argued that if it were possible to insure against all risks there would be no justification for our free system of competitive enterprise, one of the fundamental tenets of which is that profits are a reward for risk taking. If risk taking were eliminated, so would be profits. To what extent, in your opinion, is there a danger that the extension of private insurance will threaten our system of free enterprise? Discuss.
11. Suggest some possible ways by which the social costs of insurance can be reduced.
12. Two farmers agree that if either one of their barns were to burn down, the other farmer would help rebuild it. Is this an insurance arrangement? Why, or why not?
13. It is common to hear a person claim to be "insurance poor," yet one seldom hears that one is "savings poor." Is there any justification for either of these complaints? Discuss.
14. A text on industrial organization and management contains the statement: "Insurance should be the last resort, not the first, in meeting business risks. Insurance increases the current cost of doing business and thus narrows the profit margin and makes the product more vulnerable to competition." Evaluate, indicating what elements of truth, as well as what misconceptions, underlie this statement.
15. It has been suggested that the following risks are uninsurable. For each risk, indicate whether you agree or disagree and why.
    (a) Risk of exorbitant demands of a union or prolonged strike.
    (b) Risk of loss through an economic depression.
    (c) Risk that trade secrets of a firm might be stolen, thus causing the firm the loss of potential profits therefrom.
    (d) Risk from loss of a market which is captured by a competitor with a better product.
    (e) Risk that a rezoning or a shift of population will reduce the value of a given location owned by a firm for marketing purposes.

Chapter *Four*

INSURANCE AND RISK MANAGEMENT

The environment in which modern business operates, particularly large industrial units, has become increasingly complex in the 20th century. This increased complexity has been attended by greater need for special attention to dealing with risks facing the enterprise. Most large corporations and many smaller ones employ specialized managers to grapple with the problems of increased risk. Called *risk managers,* or insurance managers, these individuals have developed as important members of the top management team in many companies.

Several factors have contributed to the increased complexity of modern enterprise and have greatly enlarged the risks faced by these enterprises. Among these factors are:

1. The vast growth of world trade and worldwide operations of multinational corporations.
2. Advanced technology which has brought about very complex new products and huge concentrations of values in a single product (e.g., the supersonic airplane).
3. The development of highly integrated business organizations in which failure of one segment may cause shutdowns and losses in other units of the company.
4. Increased social consciousness, which has complicated relationships with government and has required special attention to the problem of complying with new statutes regarding pollution, product standards, legal liability, pricing, and many other aspects of business which were formerly largely unregulated.

This chapter deals with the development of the risk management function in business. We analyze the problem of dealing with risk and insurance from the point of view of the business firm, not the insurance industry. As we shall see, the same problem may be viewed in an entirely different light according to one's perspective, and entirely different solutions to the problem may seem appropriate. For example, answers to problems of whether to self-insure a risk, how large a deductible to choose, whether to form a subsidiary corporation to provide insurance, how many loss-prevention costs to incur, and how to anticipate potential losses may receive very different treatment when given by the business enterprise than when they are proposed by an insurer.

WHAT IS RISK MANAGEMENT?

Risk management may be defined as the function of executive leadership in the handling of specified risks facing the business enterprise. These risks may be insurable by commerical insurers or may be uninsurable commercially. In general, the risk manager deals with pure, not speculative, risk.

There are three concepts of risk management: broad view, narrow view, and intermediate view. In the broad view, the risk manager is seen as an entrepreneur who owns and controls the enterprise and receives the profit or suffers loss, presumably for assumption of business risk. In the narrow view, the risk manager's functions are confined to handling insurable risk, mainly through commercial insurance. The risk manager is the insurance buyer. In the intermediate view, the risk manager's functions go beyond solely buying insurance for the firm, but they do not extend to the responsibility of the entrepreneur for total risk assumption or management. It is the intermediate view of the risk manager's functions which will be developed in this chapter.

THE DEVELOPMENT OF RISK MANAGEMENT

At one time business enterprises paid little attention to the problem of handling pure risks. Insurance policies were purchased on a haphazard basis, with considerable overlapping and duplicated coverage on one hand, and complete gaps in coverage of important exposures on the other. Little control over the cost of losses and insurance premiums was exercised. Many risks were assumed when they should have been insured and vice versa. It was gradually realized that greater attention to this aspect of business management would reap great dividends. Instead of having insurance decisions handled by a busy executive whose primary responsibility lay in another area, management began to assign this responsibility first as a part-time job to such officers as the treasurer, and later as a full-time position.

As the full scope of responsibility for risk management was realized, an insurance department was established, with several people employed. At first, the department manager was usually known as the insurance buyer. Later, the title was changed to insurance manager or risk manager. Many different titles, including insurance buyer, are still used, but the tendency is to reflect the broader nature of the manager's duties and responsibilities. Assistants to the insurance manager, as he is typically called, often include specialists in various branches of insurance, law, statistics, and personnel relations.

Risk managers are now organized into a national association called the Risk and Insurance Management Society (RIMS), formerly the American Society of Insurance Management (ASIM), with over 1,800 member firms. ASIM was established in 1950.

Risk Manager Versus Insurance Agent

It is natural to ask at this point, why is it desirable to have a separate risk manager in the corporation when independent agents or brokers are available to perform this function? Is it not a waste to have two separate persons with identical or overlapping duties and responsibilities? Since the agent has to be paid the same commission whether a risk manager is dealt with, is not the cost of maintaining a risk management function in the enterprise an unnecessary outlay? There are several answers to these questions although full elaboration of them at this point is not necessary.

First, the risk manager and the insurance agent or broker do not perform identical functions, since the job of the risk manager is considerably broader in scope than merely insurance buying. Second, firms have often found from experience that it is difficult to coordinate insurance programs without having someone from inside the firm primarily responsible—an outside broker cannot have the degree of intimate familiarity with internal business affairs necessary for a completely satisfactory performance of the insurance buying function. Third, there is a tendency for independent agents to sell only the policies with which they are familiar or which are easily available to them and to fail to analyze those risks for which they have no standard policies to insure. A risk manager is needed just as a purchasing agent is needed for tangible supplies. Fourth, the responsibility for the protection of corporate property is often considered too important to place in the hands of an outsider. One of the basic duties of a corporate director is to exercise due care in protecting corporate assets against impairment. To expose these assets to loss through failure to effectively supervise their proper insurance might expose the directors to legal liability to the stockholders. If corporate officers do not directly supervise the insurance, they must delegate this responsibility to another, and this person is increasingly being recognized as a full-time employee—the risk manager of the company.

Extent of Use

A detailed examination of the work and responsibility of the risk manager was carried out by ASIM, which sponsored two studies among members in the United States and Canada, one in 1958 and another in 1968.[1] In the 1968 study, approximately 1,700 questionaires were distributed with a 42% response. Respondents represented many types of firms, 53% from manufacturing and 47% from other areas. About 55% of the firms had overseas operations compared with 47% in 1958, attesting to the increasing importance of the risk management function in internationally oriented firms. Gross sales fell in the range of $50 million to $1 billion for two thirds of the respondents, although the total range was $1 million to more than $3 billion of gross sales. Average insurance premiums paid per respondent in 1968 were $2,400,000, which was a little over double the level of the average premium paid per firm in the 1958 study.

Table 4–1 reveals the nature of change in decision-making authority of the risk manager. It may be noted that there is a definite trend toward giving the risk manager greater authority over insurance decisions. For example, the risk

[1] *American Society of Insurance Management Study of the Risk Manager and ASIM* (New York: Woodward and Fondiller, Inc., 1969).

DECISION-MAKING AUTHORITY OF THE RISK MANAGER

Table 4-1

Decision	Percent of Respondents				
	Full Authority		Shared Authority		None
	1958	1968	1958	1968	1968
Whether or not to insure	20	32	78	65	2
Whether to assume risk or self-insure	17	27	79	68	3
Selection or change of broker	22	35	73	54	10
Selection or change of insurer	—	53	—	40	—
Approval of renewals	73	72	17	25	1
When to negotiate rates	80	76	20	19	4
When to seek competitive bids	70	72	27	22	4
What specifications to set up	79	74	17	22	2
Which bid to select	39	42	58	52	4
Whether to buy a deductible or excess plan	32	41	66	55	2
Whether to file claim for small insured losses	50	85	49	12	2
To accept liability loss settlements recommended by insurer	62	58	34	35	4

Source: *American Society of Insurance Management Study of the Risk Manager and ASIM* (New York: Woodward and Fondiller, Inc., 1969).

Note: Figures for 1968 do not add up to 100% due to lack of response to individual questions.

manager makes the final decision on whether or not to insure in 32% of the cases, compared to only 20% ten years previously. In more than half of the cases the risk manager has full authority to select or change the insurer, approve renewals, negotiate rates, seek competitive bids, set up bid specifiations, decide whether or not to file a claim for small insured losses, and accept liability loss settlements recommended by the insurer. The risk manager shares major insurance decisions with top management.

Reflecting the increasing importance of the risk manager is the fact that the risk manager receives compensation well above the average executive at the same level in the organization. The risk manager reports directly to a top financial executive in a company with more than 5,000 employees and sales of over $100 million. Typically this employee is college educated and has an average of 22 years of business experience, 12 years as a risk manager—devoting a major portion of time to risk management activities, although other responsibilities are involved.

Among the responsibilities of the risk manager are the following: insurance selection, risk determination and evaluation, insurance accounting, self-insurance administration, design and administration of group insurance plans and other employee benefit plans, claims handling, loss prevention, and safety administration. Usually the risk manager shares responsibility for these functions.

It may be concluded that the risk management profession is gaining steadily, although a great majority of firms still do not employ a full-time risk or insurance manager or maintain a separate department for this function. Undoubtedly the profession will continue to make gains, particularly as it becomes increasingly evident that while a firm may not employ a risk manager it must still carry out vital functions of risk management.

Why do not more firms have full-time risk managers, if the function is vital to their operations? Among the factors explaining this are the following:

1. The function of risk management pervades the entire operation; to establish a separate department usually requires some reorganization and shifting of responsibilities, a process which is usually resisted by those who presently perform these duties.
2. It is often difficult to separate decisions involving risk and those involved in other functions of business. Thus, the work of the risk manager must overlap the work of other department heads and even the work of top management. For example, safety and loss prevention are the responsibility of each operating manager, and the risk manager may offer helpful advice but usually cannot require that the advice be adopted by an operating division.
3. The areas of responsibility of the risk manager may often be considered too broad for one person; technical assistance is required, and to provide all of the experts needed could result in duplication of effort. For example, it might be considered too expensive for a firm to provide the risk manager with a lawyer, safety engineer, or accountant when these types of personnel are available already in separate departments.

It is perhaps for these reasons that most firms continue to limit most of the risk manager's duties to those more directly concerned with insurance management. In fact, the term "risk manager" has generally not caught on. Rather, the term "insurance manager" or "director of insurance" is used more commonly, being found in about 60% of the cases in the ASIM study referred to previously. The term "risk manager" was found in only 2% of the cases.[2] It should be realized that even though a full-time risk or insurance manager may not be used, the functions still must be performed by one or more persons.

The Need for Better Risk Management

Before examining in detail the functions and responsibilities of the risk or insurance manager, it may be helpful to consider some of the mistakes which have been observed in business when the functions of risk management have not been carried out wisely or well. The discussion below is based on surveys

[2] *Ibid.*, Table 8.

carried out by the author and others mainly among small business firms which have tended to rely on local agents for insurance.[3] Examples of errors in insurance programs and insurance management practices include the following.

Underinsurance. Perhaps the most general error observed was that of failing to insure a reasonable percentage of the potential exposure to loss. Only about half of all firms had coverage equal to 90% or more of the sound value of their buildings. Yet these underinsured firms often had coverage written with clauses requiring insurance of 90% their value. Failure to carry the required percentage would result in coinsurance penalties; that is, in the event of a loss, only a portion of a loss would be recovered by the insured. In 3% or 4% of the cases it was found that the building owner carried no fire insurance at all, 10% carried no fire insurance on inventories, and 18% carried no fire insurance on equipment. Underinsurance was also observed in the field of liability insurance. Inadequate limits were common. In only 9% of the cases was business interruption loss insured. Crime insurance was not carried by 30% of the firms.

Coverage Errors. Many examples were discovered in which firms had rejected the use of clauses, such as coinsurance or deductibles, in which considerable savings in insurance costs would be available to them without significant increase in exposure to loss. Nonconcurrencies in coverage existed in about 6% of the cases. A nonconcurrency exists when more than one policy is purchased containing settlement clauses which conflict with each other and which result in restrictions in effective coverage.

Uneconomic Arrangement of Insurance. Another common error was found to be insuring small loss exposure and underinsuring large loss exposure. For example, nearly a third of the retailers were found to be using a $50 deductible on collision insurance on automobiles, but at the same time carrying inadequate liability limits or leaving serious loss exposures completely uninsured. In over 22% of the cases, there was no liability insurance at all being carried for negligence arising out of business operations.

Organizational Errors. The major error in organization was found to be the usage of more than one agent, with consequent failure to attach responsibility for insurance coverage to one person. This practice greatly increases the chance of gaps in coverage or duplication of insurance. Only a third of the respondents were found to be using one agent. Forty percent of the business people stated that they would not trust their agents with significant facts of their businesses and pertinent personal financial circumstances. Over

[3] Mark R. Greene, *Risk Management in a Catastrophe* (Eugene: University of Oregon, 1962) and Donald Watson and A. G. Homan, *An Analysis of Risk Management Problems of Small Retailers* (Eugene: University of Oregon, 1961). In these studies, 385 small retailers spending between $100 and $2,600 annually for insurance were interviewed. The first study concerned retailers in Roseburg, Oregon, following an explosion which caused major damage to most of the business buildings in town on August 7, 1959. The second study involved a random sample of retailers in three major cities in Oregon. The objective of the studies was to determine how well the insurance management function was being carried out.

three fourths of those interviewed indicated they did not feel insurance salespeople are well enough informed about the risks of their businesses to be able to recommend sound insurance contracts.

Failure to Review Insurance Programs. It was relatively uncommon for the retail firms to have their overall insurance programs reviewed periodically and brought up to date. One store manager had allowed the extended coverage endorsement (providing explosion coverage) to lapse, for a small savings in premium. Within five months the building was destroyed in an explosion of a dynamite truck parked near the building. In another example, it was reported that a large firm has been needlessly paying $37,000 a year in workers' compensation insurance premiums through a misclassification of payroll expense, for work that was not being performed on that particular job.[4] Failure to obtain competitive bids for insurance also is frequent. One small community saved $5,000 a year in its property insurance by obtaining competitive bids; the winning bidder observed that the city had been using an outdated form for its fire and extended coverage insurance and that lower rates applied to the more recently adopted form.

Failure to Adopt Loss-Prevention Techniques. Although it is well known that large savings in insurance are possible by loss-prevention techniques, many firms tend to ignore these possibilities. In one case, adoption of an automatic sprinkler system reduced fire insurance premiums from $11,000 to $1,480 annually, a saving which repaid the cost of the sprinkler system in two years. A program to cut industrial accident rates was installed in one firm, and cut the rate from 9.15 to 2.0 losses per million worker hours, with consequent savings in workers' compensation premiums. Although many small business firms could receive free engineering advice from their state fire insurance rating bureau regarding safety and loss-prevention specifications in the construction of new buildings, most do not take advantage of this service because of ignorance, inertia, or lack of proper advice. Very often the savings in insurance premiums through such advice more than compensate the firm for any increases in building costs occasioned by the loss-prevention measures. This is particularly true when total savings in several lines of insurance (such as crime, fire, business interruption, and liability) are considered.

Responsibilities and Functions

The risk manager has certain general responsibilities, such as overseeing the adequacy of the firm's insurance program and helping to formulate and administer the firm's policy regarding insurance matters. It is the responsibility of the risk manager to see that the firm's profits are not lost because of the occurrence of a peril which could have been insured against or otherwise adequately handled. The insurance manager is expected to keep abreast of

[4] William Guest, "Broker Saves Construction Firm $37,000 on Shea Stadium Job," *Business Insurance* (March 11, 1968), p. 15.

developments in the insurance field and to obtain coverage at the lowest cost compatible with other factors, such as the safety of the insurer and the quality of its service. It is often the responsibility of the insurance manager to see that attention is paid to loss-prevention activities. The manager sees that the firm meets all contractual agreements in its insurance policies; negotiates settlement of insured losses; and is expected to make recommendations to higher management on all aspects of risk management, such as what to insure and what not to insure. It is the job of the insurance manager to keep records of losses and expenses as a guide in making sound recommendations and as a guide to scientific decision making.

Not all risk or insurance managers have complete responsibility for all of the functions listed above. In one survey among 60 large industrial firms, for example, the percentage of firms assigning given responsibilities to their risk managers were: property insurance, 100%; casualty insurance, 100%; insured employee benefits, 60%; loss control and safety, 50%; property preservation, 56%; pension administration, 28%; profit sharing, 8%; and stock purchase plans, 1.6%.[5]

In general, the functions of the risk manager in carrying out the responsibilities assigned are:

1. To recognize exposures to loss. The risk manager must first of all be aware of the possibility of each type of loss. This is a fundamental duty that must precede all other functions.
2. To estimate the frequency and size of loss; that is, to estimate the probability of loss from various sources.
3. To decide the best and most economical method of handling the risk of loss, whether it be by assumption, avoidance, self-insurance, reduction of hazards, transfer, commercial insurance, or some combination of these methods.
4. To administer the programs of risk management, including the tasks of constant reevaluation of the programs, record keeping, and the like.

LOSS ESTIMATION

One of the risk manager's basic responsibilities is the estimation of potential losses which can be guarded against in some way. This function includes recognition of exposures to loss and appraisal of the value of such loss.

Recognition of Exposures

To recognize exposures to loss is the most difficult and complex task of all those facing the risk manager. A modern business enterprise of substantial size offers almost limitless opportunities for loss, and the insurance manager is expected to make an evaluation of all of them. Of course, the insurance manager must be intimately familiar with all phases of the business operations in order to accomplish this task; must be aware of all plans for plant expansion and for entering into new business operations; must work closely with top management and with all heads of departments in order to get a clear insight into these features; and must travel extensively if the business is decentralized

[5] Marshall W. Reavis, III, *Risk Management* (August-September, 1971, pp. 7-11.

geographically. The insurance manager must recognize that there are many types of losses other than those caused directly by physical perils. Examples of such losses are losses from legal liability, from lost profits and fixed charges, from dishonesty of employees, from liability assumed under contract, and from union agreements.

Appraisal of Values

Once the exposure is recognized, the next step is to estimate the size and frequency of the loss. There are countless losses that may happen, but no particular problem would arise if they did. Other losses, however, could bankrupt the firm if they should occur. The risk manager first studies the records of past losses within the firm, if any, and then consults the loss experience of other firms or a commercial insurer.

The risk manager must keep constant surveillance over values of real estate and other property and see that up-to-date appraisals are on hand in order that the severity of loss resulting from the occurrence of a given peril can be accurately estimated. In one firm, a study was made of fire loss in icehouses that were located on leased property with spur-track facilities and that were widely scattered geographically. The maximum original value of each house was $1,500. Since the losses suffered over a period of fifteen years were almost nothing, the firm realized that the probability of loss from fire was not serious and decided to self-insure that particular risk. The risk manager, however, may not be able to obtain accurate estimates of certain possible losses. A good example lies in the difficulty of estimating the size of a lawsuit due to the negligence of some company employee. In such cases the manager must use judgment.

Sometimes rather ingenious methods are devised to estimate the possibility of loss. One formula was developed by a risk manager to measure the exposure to dishonesty losses within a firm. This formula involved the calculation of an index made up of three elements—the cash, inventory, and gross sales. For example, for small firms, the amount of dishonesty insurance required was 20% of cash, 5% of inventory, and 10% of the annual gross sales. This system was developed after an accountant who had only $1,500 of cash as his disposal at any one time was able to steal $187,000 over a period of years.[6]

NONINSURANCE RISK HANDLING

Once the probability of loss has been estimated, the risk manager is in a good position to decide the best method of handling the risk. It is obvious that if the loss would cause no real hardship to the firm, even if it should occur, the risk of loss could well be assumed.

If it is determined that the probability of loss is high, it is likely that insurance would be expensive. In such a case, the risk manager must determine whether to insure in whole or in part, or to self-insure. On this point a great deal

[6] George A. Conner, "Yardstick of Dishonesty Exposure," *The National Insurance Buyer*, Vol. III, No. 6 (November, 1956), p. 42.

of controversy exists. Before this controversy is analyzed, it should be observed that there is a difference between insurance, self-insurance, and risk assumption. *Insurance* refers to the use of a commercial insurer who may be able to reduce the risk greatly by combining a large number of other similar exposure units, or who, for a premium, may accept the risk as a transferee. By *self-insurance,* we refer to a situation where the individual firm meets certain requirements, and then performs essentially all the functions that are usually performed by the commercial insurer. *Risk assumption,* or *noninsurance,* means that the firm does nothing about the risk, but expects to bear any losses out of current working capital and to charge them off to current expense. It is important that the risk manager understand the conditions of each method.

Assumption

Many exposures to loss are so inconsequential that they may properly be ignored. For example, the risk manager may feel that the risk of collision loss to old vehicles is such that it should be entirely assumed. Or the risk manager may assume the first $100 of loss to each vehicle. Such perils as pilferage, breakage of tools or windows, or robbery of vending machines are often assumed because the firm can easily absorb the occasional loss from these sources.

In addition to assuming certain losses, many firms also assume responsibility for certain services necessary to the insurance device. In group health insurance, for example, the firm may handle the claims of employees for illness and accidents. It may see that proper loss forms are filled out, physicians' statements are received in satisfactory form, and other papers are filed in support of the claim. Often the insured can perform such functions more economically than the insurer, and will receive an allowance for it in the premium.

Loss Prevention

Regardless of whether self-insurance is used or commercial insurance is purchased, the risk manager is vitally interested in loss-prevention activities. Ideally the best way to handle risk is to eliminate the possibility of loss where it is economical to do so. While complete achievement of this goal is seldom possible, nevertheless, any degree to which it is achieved results in substantial savings to the insured, not only in lowered insurance premiums, but also in a smoother, more efficient conduct of the business.

Many risk managers are in direct charge of their company's accident-prevention program. Among their varied duties are:

1. Keeping accurate records of all accidents by number, type, cause, and total damage incurred.
2. Maintaining plant safety-inspection programs.
3. Devising ways and means to prevent recurrence of accidents.
4. Keeping top management accident-conscious.
5. Seeing that proper credits are obtained in the insurance premium for loss-prevention measures.

6. Minimizing losses by proper salvage techniques and other action at the time of a loss.
7. Working with company engineers and architects in planning new construction so as to secure the maximum safety and to secure important insurance premium credits when the structure is completed and in use.

An example of what hazard-reduction activities can achieve is provided in a case drawn from aviation manufacture. A plane that was nearly finished caught fire on the assembly line. While a major catastrophe was avoided by quick action of a sprinkler system, still one life was lost, personal injuries were suffered, and property damage amounted to $500,000. Investigation showed that the fire was caused when a short circuit in the electrical system ignited gasoline that was used for testing the fuel system. The testing fuel had become mixed with a "low-flash" highly flammable fuel. As a result, a new testing fuel with a "high-flash" point was adopted and control procedures were tightened. Later on, a nonflammable gas that was nonhazardous and gave substantial production advantages was developed.[7] It is doubtful that anything would have been done about this accident if the firm had not had an individual—an insurance manager—to take action to see that the firm profited from past mistakes.

Transfer

Handling the risk by the transfer method has not been neglected by insurance managers. Transfers of risk may be grouped under two classifications: those involving transfer to an insurance company, and those involving transfer to parties other than an insurance company. The former type is treated later in this chapter as part of managing the insurance program. We shall now be concerned with the latter type.

An interesting example of the transfer method to parties other than insurance companies is found in the use of lease plans. An individual firm may not have a sufficiently large number of automobiles to justify self-insurance. Therefore it may decide that the administrative problems of ownership of vehicles, including the insurance details, can be advantageously transferred to a firm specializing in this business. Accordingly, the firm leases all its autos and thus avoids the problem of auto insurance by transferring the ownership risk to the leasing firm. The firm may lease many other types of property (examples range from floor carpeting to entire buildings) for substantially similar reasons—that of transfer of the ownership risk to specialists. The lessors, of course, may use commercial insurance; but the lessee has handled the risk by transfer.

Avoidance

Outright avoidance of hazards and risk before they are assumed in the first place is another way of handling risk which is closely related to the transfer method. One example of avoidance is to delay taking responsibility for goods

[7] George H. Conncrat, "Risk Abatement," Insurance Series No. 112 (New York: American Management Association, 1956), p. 10.

during their transportation. A trader may have a choice of terms of sale, and may have the seller assume all risks of loss until the goods arrive at the buyer's warehouse. In this way the buyer never assumes the risk and has avoided an insurance problem. A similar illustration of avoidance lies in the common practice of subcontracting. The firm engages a subcontractor to manufacture certain supplies, assuming all risks therefor. Thus, the firm is enabled to escape the responsibility of providing for the risk of loss attendant upon making the goods itself.

SELF-INSURANCE DECISION

In making a decision concerning self-insurance, the risk manager has many factors to consider. The advantages and disadvantages of this method of handling loss follow.

Requirements for Self-Insurance

What are the requirements that should be met before a firm can properly self-insure? Self-insurance will not usually be attempted unless the loss, should it occur, is severe enough to cause financial embarrassment to the insured. In other words, some method other than assumption of the risk is indicated, and the firm is deciding between one of the other methods of risk management. The following conditions are suggestive of the types of situations where self-insurance is possible and feasible:

1. The firm has a sufficient number of objects so situated that they are not subject to simultaneous destruction. The objects are also reasonably homogeneous in nature and value so that calculations as to probable losses will be accurate within a narrow range. If these conditions are present, the firm will be able to predict accurately the size of fund necessary to meet the losses expected.
2. Management is willing to set aside a fund to meet the large and unusual losses. Until the fund is built up, normally a program of outside commercial insurance must be maintained. As the size of the self-insurance fund increases, the amount of outside insurance can be reduced and finally eliminated. It is not satisfactory to have merely a "book" reserve for this purpose, since such a balance sheet transaction would not provide the cash if the loss were to occur. The fund must be actually set aside from operating assets and invested in securities that can be readily convertible into cash should the need arise. If a firm feels that a separate fund is not required, that it can meet any losses out of working capital, then it is not using self-insurance, but is simply assuming the risk, or using noninsurance.
3. The firm must have accurate records or have access to satisfactory statistics to enable it to make good estimates of the expected loss. Otherwise, it is guessing at the size of the necessary fund and has not successfully handled the risk of loss. To increase the accuracy of the calculations, it is wise to use data over as long a period as possible, not merely the last five or ten years. If outside data are used, it is necessary to exercise extreme caution to see that the data employed are applicable to the firm's own experience.
4. The general financial condition of the firm should be satisfactory. There is a tendency for business persons who are in financial difficulties to believe that self-insurance is a good way to save on insurance. While it is often true that the

firm can save money by self-insuring, this is possible only when all of the preceding conditions are met. If a firm is in financial straits, it is unlikely that the necessary fund will be set aside or that if it is set aside it will be of sufficient size to meet the risk. If the firm cannot afford insurance premiums, it is even more unlikely that the firm can afford the loss should it occur, or that the firm can afford to set aside a self-insurance fund.[8]

5. The self-insurance plan requires careful administration and planning. Someone has to be in charge of investing the self-insurance fund, paying claims, inspecting exposures, preventing losses, keeping necessary records, and performing the many other duties connected with any insurance program. If the necesary specialized executive talent is not available, and if the business cannot appreciate the necessity of paying continuing attention to all the details of carry-through, self-insurance will not be a satisfactory solution.

Reasons for Self-Insurance

The central reason for the use of self-insurance is to save money. In general insurance lines, the insurer's expenses may range between 30% and 40% of the premium dollar. It is not realized by some that a substantial part of this, perhaps 10% or 15%, is for the benefit of the insured, directly or indirectly. Such expenses include those for the prevention of losses, for providing certain services to the insured, for reserve funds held for future losses, and for ultimate return to the insured in loss payments, dividends, or both. Even then, the firm may conclude that the services can be provided more cheaply by itself. For example, one firm claimed that, as a result of self-insurance, the annual savings of collision insurance on a fleet of passenger cars and trucks averaged approximately $12,000.[9]

Other reasons for self-insurance include dissatisfaction with the services of the commercial insurer, difficulties in securing favorable rate classifications, and difficulties in securing outside insurance.

Often self-insurance takes place in areas where the peril is deemed to be uninsurable by private commercial insurers. An example is that of strike insurance, which is accomplished through voluntary industry associations in a number of fields, including railroads, airlines, newspapers, and building contracting. Because the strike peril is catastrophic in nature and is usually partially within the control of the insured, it is not generally considered insurable. Yet private firms have organized on a mutual basis to redistribute the cost of work stoppages by adopting rules to overcome the uninsurable features. For example, strike insurance plans usually provide that unless a given percentage, usually 50%, of the firms in the industry are struck, no benefits are payable.

[8] There is an old story to illustrate the conservative approach to this problem. A young man rising in the financial world approached J. P. Morgan for advice. Wishing to impress him about his financial status, the young man asked how much it cost to own a yacht, whereupon the elder Morgan replied, "If you are worried about the cost of owning a yacht, you can't afford to own one." So it is with self-insurance. The risk manager who is in doubt should probably avoid self-insurance.

[9] A. G. Westcott, "Risk Insurance," Insurance Series No. 112 (New York: American Management Association, 1956), p. 13.

This restricts the peril to mean only industrywide strikes over which an individual firm would not have any particular control.

Self-insurance has also taken the form of using large deductibles on commercial policies. In one study of self-insurance practices, for example, nearly a quarter of the 1,100 firms surveyed were found to be assuming losses of $10,000 or more in one or more areas of liability, workers' compensation, and fire insurance.[10] Still other firms adopt self-insurance by forming their own subsidiary insurance company, usually referred to as a captive, which insures the corporate risks and then seeks reinsurance directly from the commercial market. Such reinsurance is often available at rates below those available in the regular market. Captive insurers are widely used in property and liability insurance and are becoming more popular in the field of life insurance. One authority reported that life insurance "captives" cost private insurers an estimated $10 million in premiums in 1967 and 1968.[11] A related form of self-insurance arrangement is the use of the trust to operate a company pension plan rather than using the services of commerical insurers. Thus assets of trusteed pension plans in the United States exceed by a factor of more than 2 to 1 the total assets of pension plans by private insurers.[12]

Why Self-Insurance Is Not Used Generally

In spite of the advantages of self-insurance, most firms continue to employ the services of the commercial insurer for one or more of the following reasons.

1. The firm may decide that even though in the long run self-insurance could result in monetary savings, there are advantages in stabilizing insurance costs and in making this cost predictable each year. The insurance premium constitutes a regular deduction for tax purposes, and also enables management to stabilize profits. Under the self-insurance plan, profits may be higher one year, but drop considerably in the years in which losses occur. If one of these losses occurs in a year which has been generally unprofitable, not only are losses exaggerated that year, but a tax deduction could also be lost due to the limited time within which losses of one year can be carried forward or carried back as an offset to profits in other years.
2. A firm may simply wish to avoid the details involved in managing what may amount to a miniature insurance company within its organization. Management may feel that to do so would amount to fragmentation of executive talent and would constitute a diversion from the central business with which the firm is concerned.
3. The firm may want an outside, disinterested party to settle claims. In the field of credit insurance, for example, oftentimes the insurer can render better, more efficient collection service than the insured. In workers' compensation where

[10] Robert Goshay, *Corporate Self-Insurance and Risk Retention Plans* (Homewood, Ill.: Richard D. Irwin, Inc., 1964).

[11] "Life Captives Threat to Insurers, Contends New Boss of Prudential," *Business Insurance (February 3, 1969), p. 3.*

[12] *Life Insurance Fact Book 1972* (New York: Institute of Life Insurance, 1972), pp. 38-39. In 1971, assets of noninsured pension funds totaled $95.8 billion, compared to $46.4 billion of insurance company controlled assets.

personal bias may influence a claim, there are distinct advantages to having a third party, rather than the firm itself, deal with an injured employee.

4. The firm may want the inspection service of a commercial insurer. Let us say that a firm has steam boilers in which any loss from explosion can be virtually prevented by careful and regular inspections. However, such inspections require a person with a specialized training. It might be uneconomical for the firm to hire a full-time inspector, and an outside inspector may not be available. If, on the other hand, the firm employs the services of a commercial insurer, the insurer will furnish inspection along with the insurance policy at a reasonable cost. Even if the firm maintains an inspection department, it may wish an outside inspection as a check on its own.
5. For reasons relating to its personnel, a firm may desire outside insurance in some lines, even though self-insurance is possible. For the dishonesty peril, the fact that the employee is bonded may itself be a deterrent to wrongdoing. Also, in case of robbery, an employee may feel that it is not necessary to risk his life to save company property if the property is insured in any event. As observed above, in workers' compensation, better employee relations can be maintained if the outside insurer handles the claims. Any disagreements will usually be lodged in the form of complaints against the insurer rather than the firm.
6. The firm may not have a sufficient number of homogeneous exposure units so situated that the aggregate losses to which they are subject can be predicted within sufficiently narrow limits. In other words, the objective risk may be too high. It usually requires a considerably larger number of exposure units than many believe to reduce the objective risk enough to satisfy management that undue risk is not being accepted.
7. The firm may be unwilling to set up an adequate reserve for absorbing uninsured losses, believing that the money can be put to better use within the firm or invested in nonliquid securities. Commercial insurance would be used instead in order to release money that would otherwise be held in reserve funds earning a low interest return. Analysis of this question depends mainly upon the size of the reserve fund required and upon the excess return available to the firm if a fund of this size is released for investment in securities or within the firm itself.

Value of Insurance

Professor David Houston has suggested a method whereby the value of insurance in such a situation can be ascertained.[13] The insurance manager may follow the decision rule: Buy insurance if the expected financial position of the firm at the end of the year is better than would be the case if insurance is not purchased; otherwise, do not buy insurance. The financial result at the end of the year if one buys insurance may be expressed as the existing net worth minus the premium paid plus the investment return earned on the difference between these two amounts. In formula, this may be expressed:

$$(1) \quad FP_b = NW - P + r\,(NW - P)$$

where FP_b = financial position or net worth if one buys insurance

NW = initial net worth invested in the business

[13] David B. Houston, "Risk, Insurance, and Sampling," *Journal of Risk and Insurance* (December, 1964), p. 530.

P = premium paid for insurance; $P/2$ average insured loss per year
r = percentage return available to the firm on funds invested in the business or in nonliquid securities

The financial position at the end of the year of one who does not buy insurance may be expressed as follows:

$$(2)\quad FP_{nb} = NW - \frac{P}{2} + r\left(NW - \frac{P}{2} - F\right) + iF$$

where FP_{nb} = financial position if one does not buy insurance
F = reserve fund which must be set aside for losses because one does not buy insurance
i = interest earned on the reserve fund earned in savings accounts or liquid securities

Other terms in equation (2) remain the same as in equation (1). In words, equation (2) says that the financial position at the end of the year if one does not purchase insurance is arrived at by first subtracting from the initial capital (NW) the average expected loss ($P/2$). To this result we add amounts expressed in the third and fourth terms. The third term expresses the amount earned in the business after removing funds employed for paying losses and for use in the reserve fund. The fourth term expresses the amount of interest received on the reserve fund. In both equations it is assumed that the average loss equals one half the premium paid, which is not entirely unrealistic. The insurance manager will purchase insurance if FP_b is greater than FP_{nb}. The difference between these two amounts is the economic value of insurance to the firm.

To illustrate, assume that a firm with an initial net worth of \$1 million has a piece of heavy equipment valued at \$100,000 and that without insurance a \$100,000 reserve fund is necessary since there is only one piece of equipment and no possibility of predicting average losses through the use of the law of large numbers. Assume further that the reserve fund earns interest at the rate of .04 in savings accounts and .10 if invested in the business. Assume further that insurance is available for 2% or \$2,000 annually. The financial position of the firm at the end of the year if insurance is purchased under these assumptions will be:

$$\begin{aligned}(1)\quad FP_b &= \$1{,}000{,}000 - \$2{,}000 + .10\,(\$1{,}000{,}000 - \$2{,}000)\\ &= \$998{,}000 + \$99{,}800\\ &= \$1{,}097{,}800\end{aligned}$$

If insurance is not purchased and a \$100,000 reserve fund is necessary, the net worth at the end of the year will be:

$$\begin{aligned}(2)\quad FP_{nb} &= \$1{,}000{,}000 - \$2{,}000/2 + .10(\$1{,}000{,}000 - \$2{,}000/2 - \$100{,}000) + .04(\$100{,}000)\\ &= \$999{,}000 + \$89{,}900 + \$4{,}000\\ &= \$1{,}092{,}900\end{aligned}$$

Since the financial position of the firm is improved by \$4,900 by purchasing insurance, ((1) − (2) = \$4,900) the insurance manager is advised to do so. The value of insurance is \$4,900 to this firm under these assumptions.

The value of insurance can be determined more easily by a formula which is derived from (1) and (2) above. This value may be expressed:[14]

$$(3)\quad V = F(r - i) - P(\tfrac{1}{2} + r/2)$$

where V = value of insurance. The other terms are the same as in (1) and (2) above. In the above case, we may substitute in equation (3) the same values used before, obtaining

$$\begin{aligned} V &= \$100{,}000\,(.10 - .04) - \$2{,}000\,(\tfrac{1}{2} + \tfrac{1}{2}\,(.10)) \\ &= \$6{,}000 - \$2{,}000\,(.55) \\ &= \$6{,}000 - \$1{,}100 \\ &= \$4{,}900 \end{aligned}$$

which is the same economic value as making the subtraction (1) − (2).

It is worth noting that equation (3) is very sensitive to the required size of the reserve fund, F, since F is usually large and P is usually small relative to F. Furthermore, the reserve fund can be exhausted with one large loss, while insurance is good for more than one loss, unless it is cancelled or becomes unavailable. This implies that the reserve fund method may contain a fatal weakness; it may become exhausted and a new loss may occur before a new fund can be built up. In such a case, commercial insurance should be purchased until the fund is restored.

Suppose, however, that a firm's equipment of \$100,000 consists of 200 machines each valued at \$500, and it is predicted that the average annual loss is two machines worth \$1,000 with a standard deviation of \$200. Assuming that losses are normally distributed, the firm would have to have a buffer fund of \$600 (three standard deviations) to be 99% certain that its losses would not exceed \$1,600. Using formula (3) above and assuming that the insurance premium is still 2%, or \$2,000, the value of insurance under the same interest assumptions as above is \$600 (.10 − .04) − \$2,000 (½ + ½ (.10)), or \$36 − \$1,100, or − \$1,064. Clearly, commercial insurance would not be used unless the firm had determined that one or more of the other factors listed above offset the negative value of insurance as calculated above.

The illustrations above reveal fairly specifically how a risk manager may determine the economic value of insurance. They do not, however, make any adjustment for the subjective risk. Subjective risk may be crucial to the risk manager's decision. It may be measured by assigning utility values to dollar amounts and then comparing the loss in expected utility by paying the premium to the loss in expected utility by running the risk. In the first illustration, for example, if the insurance premium had exceeded \$10,909, insurance would

[14] The formula given here differs slightly from Houston's original formula.

have had no value.[15] This is the same as saying that the firm would be unwilling to pay $10,909 to avoid a possible loss of $100,000 whose expected value in the long run is $1,000. If the machine were an indispensable part of the firm's operations or if the firm's financial position would be in danger if the loss should occur, the expected loss in utility by running the risk might exceed the loss in utility by paying the premium, and commercial insurance would be advised.

Equation (3) may also be helpful in guiding the insurance manager as to the optimum size of deductible to employ. It may be determined in the above example that if the reserve fund is set at $18,333 or below, and other values remain the same, the insurance will have negative economic value. However, if the firm set the reserve fund at only $18,333 (compared to the asset value of $100,000) and did not buy insurance, it would be running a substantial risk. Therefore the firm could purchase commercial insurance with a large deductible, say $15,000, and reduce the size of the premium substantially. Assume that the premium could be reduced from $2,000 to $500 by accepting a $15,000 deductible, and that a reserve fund of $15,000 is to be set aside. Substituting in equation (3), the insurance manager may determine that in this case the value of insurance is $625 ($15,000(.10 – .04) – $500(.55) = $625). It can be shown that the premium charged could rise to $1,636 before it would not be economical to the firm to purchase coverage.

Evaluation of Self-Insurance

It is clear that the self-insurance decision is not an easy one to make. In most cases, a firm will probably end up with some judicious mixture of self-insurance and commercial insurance in order to optimize economic returns and to minimize risk. The appropriate mix should be studied and reviewed more or less continuously, but frequently this is not done. For example, in Professor Goshay's study of corporate self-insurance, it was reported that loss experience in fire and liability exposures was very unstable among the 1,100 firms studied, but loss experience in workers' compensation was fairly stable. It was found that a majority of the firms using self-insurance also purchased commercial insurance for catastrophic losses. It was concluded that most of the firms using self-insurance had adequate financial capacity and catastrophic protection, but that the firms generally do not consistently evaluate their programs to determine whether savings are being made or other objectives are being reached. The study illustrates the conclusion that self-insurance has not yet reached the point of development where it is feasible for any but a small minority of firms.

COMMERCIAL INSURANCE MANAGEMENT

Commercial insurance is probably the most important and frequently used method of handling risk that is employed by the risk manager. Once the risk

[15] Verification of this is left to the student as an exercise.

STRUCTURE OF RISK ANALYSIS

Figure 4-1

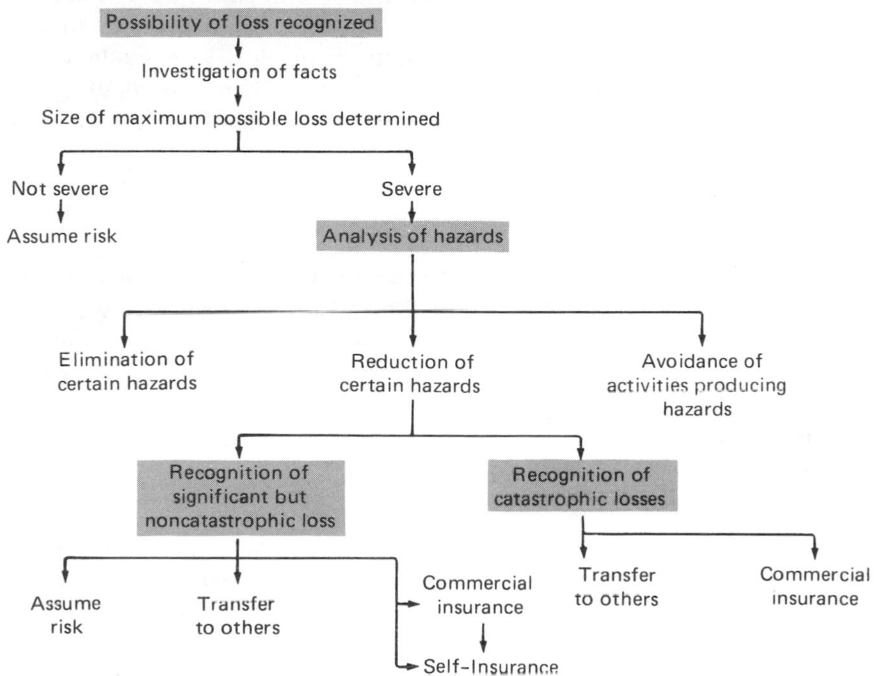

manager has analyzed exposures; determined the probability of loss; taken all loss-preventive measures; and decided what risks not to insure, what to transfer, and what to self-insure, an economical and efficient program of commercial insurance for the remaining risks must be set up.

Figure 4–1 illustrates the functions in risk management discussed so far.

Managing the insurance program involves the following steps, each of which will be briefly elaborated:

1. Deciding which forms of coverage are best suited to the firm's needs.
2. Selecting agents, brokers, and insurers.
3. Negotiating for coverage.
4. Analyzing and selecting methods of reducing insurance costs.
5. Seeing that the terms of insurance contracts are complied with.
6. Handling loss settlements and negotiations with adjustors.
7. Designing and maintaining adequate records of coverage and other data necessary to a sound program of insurance.

Deciding on Form of Coverage

Deciding which forms of insurance are best suited to the firm's needs presents one of the most valuable areas of creativity in which the insurance manager can make a contribution. Often new contract forms, many of which have become standard offerings of the insurance companies, are initiated by the insurance manager. There are literally hundreds of choices available to the risk manager, who must make a selection, usually with guidance from established agents, brokers, or insurers, to meet the firm's particular needs. Each program of insurance should be tailored specifically, since no two situations are exactly alike.

Once the contracts are in force, it is the duty of the insurance manager to verify that the contracts actually state what was intended. Various exclusions, warranties, and conditions must be studied and any necessary changes effected; and management must be advised of the limitations of protection. Rates, premiums, dividends, or discounts must be checked to verify their accuracy. The insurance manager submits any necessary data required under the terms of the insurance contracts. For example, many forms of coverage are subject to an audit at the end of the year and require final data on payrolls, sales, and the like.

Selecting Agents, Brokers, and Insurers

Insurance is purchased through established agents or brokers, or sometimes directly from insurers. Wise selection of agents and brokers can make a great deal of difference in the work of the insurance manager, for it is from these individuals that the insurance manager obtains up-to-date information, expert advice, and skilled aid in negotiation with insurers. The insurance manager cannot hope to be an expert in all lines of insurance. The help of the agent or the broker is needed in handling the many phases of work with commercial insurance. Since the quality and cost of the services of insurers, agents, and brokers vary, the insurance manager must exercise great care in selection of those persons.

Negotiating for Coverage

Negotiating for coverage often is a complicated matter that requires great ingenuity on the part of the insurance manager. The firm may have specialized needs that are not readily solved in the insurance market.[16] Lengthy and complex bargaining sessions may be necessary in order to place the coverage in a satisfactory manner and at a mutually agreeable price. Often it is the insurance manager (frequently with help from an agent or broker) who obtains valuable concessions from insurers in the matter of satisfactory renewal of policies. The task is complicated by the fact that many times it is necessary to cover a given exposure by dealing with a dozen or more separate insurers, each of which takes a fraction of the total risk. Securing uniform coverage of a fire exposure of

[16] The *insurance market* refers to the supply side of the insurance service—the sphere in which price-making forces operate between the insurance seller and the insurance buyer. When it is asked "How is the market for fire insurance?" what is meant is, "Under what terms or conditions is fire insurance available from various sellers?"

perhaps $100 million, not an uncommon exposure among large corporations, is not simple when several insurers are involved.

Analyzing and Selecting Methods of Reducing Insurance Costs

Insurance costs can be reduced in many ways, and the insurance manager must analyze each method with a view of obtaining coverage at the lowest cost compatible with safety and service considerations.

Judicious selection of *deductibles* can be a great cost saver. While deductibles are of many types, essentially they all have one purpose—to control costs and to effect a more efficient method of handling the risk by commercial insurance. Usually the purpose of a deductible is to eliminate from the coverage small losses that are almost certain to occur and, hence, are very expensive to insure. The insurer grants a reduction in the premium for deductibles, and this reduction increases as the size of the deductible rises. However, the insurance purchaser must meet the costs of losses below the deductible, and the sum of these payments may ultimately exceed the savings by accepting the deductible. The job of the risk manager is to select a deductible which maximizes the net savings effected by using this device.

Use of certain contractual provisions can also greatly reduce insurance costs. For example, agreements to employ certain loss-prevention methods, agreements to maintain in force sufficient coverage to equal a stated percentage of total exposed values, and agreements to assume certain administrative responsibilities will all reduce the cost of insurance if these provisions are properly analyzed and applied. As another example, writing a fire insurance contract to exclude from coverage the foundation of a building will reduce premiums without lessening the quality of coverage.

Some insurance costs can be lowered by buying in quantity, and by negotiating a contract to cover a period longer than one year. Insurance costs can often be lowered through competitive bidding. In some cases, such as insurance programs of public agencies, competitive bidding is required. Contrary to what is sometimes believed, not all insurance rates are the same. Some insurers operate more efficiently than others, and it is often only through competitive bidding that the buyer may learn which insurers are the most efficient. Legitimate savings in costs can be realized through better investment policies, automation of record keeping, more careful selection of risks, and more efficient distribution methods. Of course, the insurance manager must take care not to select a low-cost insurer that saves money by refusing to pay proper claims, that gives poor service, or that saves money by failing to set up adequate emergency reserves.

Insurance costs may be lowered by the use of self-insurance or noninsurance for certain risks. Self-insurance need not cover the whole amount of the loss, but only a specified portion. It is not uncommon for some insurance managers to recommend that the firm self-insure, say, the first million dollars of loss, and purchase commercial coverage on the remainder. In this way the economics of self-insurance, if any, can be realized without assuming a risk of catastrophic proportions.

Insurance costs can be reduced by regular reviews to eliminate duplication of coverage, needless endorsements, nonconcurrencies in the contracts, insurance on property no longer owned, insurance on personnel no longer employed, and insurance on buildings or equipment with little or no value.

Finally, insurance costs can be greatly reduced by careful attention to loss-prevention efforts, including recording of the resulting effect of these efforts in reducing exposure to loss (e.g. sprinkler system) or in reducing accident frequency and in communicating these findings to the underwriters so that credits in insurance rates may be granted. This is especially true when insurance contracts come up for renewal or when competitive bidding takes place.

Complying with Terms of Contract

The entire purpose of insurance can be defeated if the firm, knowingly or unknowingly, violates the terms of the contract and thus is unable to collect when a loss occurs. It is the job of the insurance manager to know the contracts thoroughly so that the terms can be complied with before, at the time, and after the loss occurs. For example, the insurance manager must see that necessary permits are granted for extrahazardous operations which might otherwise suspend coverage under the fire insurance policy. Proper methods must be followed to do all that is possible to reduce the size of loss once the insured peril occurs. Otherwise, the firm may lose its coverage. As an illustration, a large corporation once had to pay a substantial liability judgment because it had failed to notify the insurer of the accident until almost a year had passed. The terms of the policy in this case had called for immediate notification of any loss.

Handling Loss Settlements and Negotiations

An important and specilized task of the insurance manager is to represent the employer in the negotiations with the insurer in loss settlements. Often the amount of the loss is not easily determinable. If recent appraisals are not available on the value of a building now totally destroyed, it may take considerable discussion to agree on a settlement. The insurance manager may have to do much research to establish the value, say, of an ocean marine loss, or of a fire loss in a warehouse of goods for which adequate records have not been maintained. The insurance manager normally fills out proof-of-loss forms for employees making claims under group disability policies and sometimes is required to "go to bat" when cases are questioned. The risk manager is the one to decide whether a claim will be filed under the policies, that is, to recognize an insured loss. The terms of many policies are sufficiently complex so that recoverable losses are easily overlooked. This is particularly true under the all-risk forms, wherein any loss that is not specifically excluded is covered.

Designing and Maintaining Adequate Insurance Records

The design and maintenance of proper insurance records is itself a specialized task that may require substantial time and effort on the part of the insurance manager. Typical of the records that will be kept are:

1. Insurance policy premiums and loss recoveries; termination dates by type of contract.
2. List of all automobiles owned, their description and value.
3. Automobile collision losses.
4. Automobile property damage and bodily injury liability cases.
5. List, description, and appraisals of all real property.
6. List, description, and appraisals of major classes of personal property.
7. Number, type, and loss from industrial accidents.
8. Payroll summary for workers' compensation insurance.
9. Status of workers' compensation claims.
10. Fire loss reports, including data on cause and amount of loss.

The reasons for maintaining these and other records include the following: (1) to enable the insurance manager to effect proper renewals of insurance coverage and avoid lapsing of coverage; (2) to furnish the basis for studies of self-insurance, noninsurance, and insurance proposals; (3) to provide material for reports to management concerning the operation of the insurance department; (4) to help control future losses and to enable the risk manager to analyze the cost of losses; (5) to provide data necessary for an advantageous settlement of insured loss claims; and (6) to enable the accounting department to allocate insurance costs among the various divisions or locations. This list is not meant to be comprehensive, but only suggestive of the many purposes served by adequate records.

ADMINISTERING THE RISK MANAGEMENT PROGRAM

On the preceding pages have been outlined the first three of the four major functions of risk management—recognizing the exposures, estimating the probability of loss, and deciding upon the best method of handling the risk. The final function of risk management is that of administering the program. We shall consider two phases of the administration: policy formulation and organization.

Policy Formulation

A *business policy* is defined as a plan, procedure, or rule of action followed for the purpose of securing consistent action over a period of time. Presumably, administrative policies are studied carefully before being put into effect and thus have a distinct advantage over *ad hoc* decisions made on the spur of the moment. It is likely that a policy, once established, remains unchanged as long as the same conditions which gave rise to it continue to exist. An insurance management policy, then, becomes a rule or a course of action that will be followed unless there are good reasons to change it or to make exceptions in a given case. A policy usually is general in nature and allows for discretion in interpreting how the policy is to be carried out.

The advantage of having definite policies to guide insurance management is that once the rule is adopted, executives do not have to take time to restudy recurring problems before making decisions. Furthermore, inconsistent behavior is avoided. All agents and insurers, all parties affected under the contract, receive equal treatment so long as their situations are similar.

Some examples of insurance management policies adopted by one company, a large chemical corporation, are:

1. It is the policy of this company to assume (as a charge against reserves, profits, or surplus) losses resulting from risks considered as not significant in relation to the cash position of the corporation.
2. It is the policy of this company to purchase insurance for risks not assumed.
3. It is the policy of this company to eliminate, or improve, as far as practicable, the conditions and practices which cause insurable losses.[17]

A statement of insurance management policy for a drug manufacturer is:[18]

> It is our policy to assume the risks of property damage, legal liability, and dishonesty in all cases where the exposure is so small or dispersed that a loss would not significantly affect our operations or financial position, and to insure these risks as far as practicable whenever the occurrence of a loss would be significant.

These statements of policy are expressed in general terms, and constitute *major* policies for insurance management. A firm may have hundreds of *minor* policies, dealing with details of handling insurance records, purchasing procedures, and the like.

Organization

How should the insurance department, as it is commonly called, be organized? Where should it fit in the corporate structure? The answer to these questions lies in discovering what responsibilities and duties are placed on the risk manager, and then arranging the work so that the risk manager will have the authority to carry out these duties. It does little good to hold the risk manager responsible for insurance management throughout the corporation, but then give authority over only one phase of the work or confine authority to one plant to the exclusion of others.

Coordination of Risk Management with Other Functions. It is clear that one of the important tasks of the risk manager is to clarify relationships with other executives in the firm. Obviously, these relationships will differ considerably depending upon such factors as the degree of responsibility given to the risk

[17] C. A. Greenley, "Responsibility for Risk Management," Insurance Series No. 111 (New York: American Management Association, 1956), p. 23.

[18] James C. Cristy, "Responsibility for Risk Management," Insurance Series No. 111 (New York: American Management Association, 1956), p. 21.

manager, size of the firm, personalities of the individuals involved, geographical dispersion of the firm's operations, complexity of operations, and other factors. The following discussion assumes that the firm is large enough so that it has assigned the risk management responsibility to one person or department and that this person will seek the assistance of other departments in performing the necessary duties to carry out the responsibilities for coordinating the risk management function throughout the firm.

Accounting. The risk manager works very closely with the accounting department, which is usually in charge of internal systems of control and of budgeting. The accounting department is in a position to furnish the risk manager with estimates of property values, to maintain records of insurance policies, insurance costs, prepaid insurance accounts, and to provide much other valuable information. For example, the internal system of accounting control is of considerable importance in designing a proper insurance system to protect the firm against employee dishonesty. Estimates of future sales and profits are necessary in order to design and install a proper system of insurance protection against business interruption from insurable perils. Finally, detailed information on payroll is necessary in order to make sure that employees are classified properly for purposes of workers' compensation insurance, and that insurance costs are therefore minimized. It can be appreciated, therefore, that the accounting department is almost indispensable to the risk manager.

Finance. Closely related to accounting as an adjunct to the insurance management function is the function of finance in the business firm. The finance manager is often the person to whom the insurance manager reports. The reason for this is that the main job of the insurance manager is to protect the firm's assets against loss or destruction from certain perils, a responsibility that also belongs to the finance manager. If an uninsured peril causes loss to assets, both the finance manager and the insurance manager are directly concerned with the problem of replacement of the asset. The problem of tax management is also of mutual concern to these two executives in such problems as determining the tax advisability of self-insurance, the tax treatment of lost property, and the tax treatment of programs of pensions and group insurance. The problem of credit management is also of mutual concern to the finance and insurance managers. Questions here revolve around such matters as the desirability of insuring open accounts against bad debts, the proper insurance on corporate assets pledged as security for debt, and the planning of bank credit lines to replace working capital lost from destruction of assets which are uninsured as a result of the firm's program of self-insurance.

Production. Since the insurance manager is concerned with accident prevention, insurance of goods in the process of manufacture, and liability exposures in the plant, a close working relationship must be maintained with the production departments in the firm. Assembly line accidents importantly affect workers' compensation insurance costs, and faulty products expose the firm to product liability suits. Use of sprinkler systems and other loss-prevention techniques in the plant may reduce insurance costs, but may also increase production costs; close communication between production and insurance managers is a necessity if the firm's total profits are to be maximized.

Marketing and Transportation. Goods are exposed to serious losses during marketing and distribution, a factor which requires close cooperation between marketing and insurance management. Shipping by financially irresponsible carriers unable to reimburse the firm for their negligence might affect the firm's profits in an important way unless insurance and transportation decisions are coordinated. Misleading advertising of a product might give rise to product liability suits from users of the product. Clauses found in purchase and sale orders often create liability exposures of which the insurance manager should certainly be aware. For example, it is common for a manufactuurer to require a retailer to hold the manufacturer harmless for the legal liability to which it would otherwise be subjected because of a faulty product. Similar requirements are often imposed on the manufacturers by their suppliers. Such clauses should be considered jointly by marketing and insurance personnel.

Personnel. Professor David Ivry conducted a survey of the extent to which insurance managers are involved with programs of employee benefits, such as group insurance, pension programs, profit-sharing plans, supplemental unemployment benefit plans, and the like.[19] He discovered that insurance managers are very heavily involved in these programs, an area often thought of as falling mainly within the purview of the personnel manager or the finance manager, or both. Thus, the insurance manager and the personnel manager have need for close communication and mutual assistance.

Outside Consultants. The specialized services offered by outside consultants in risk management are often-needed adjuncts to a well-rounded program of risk management. For example, independent appraisals of real estate by appraisal firms to establish building values are often more reliable and more accurate than internal appraisals. Internal appraisals often are based on book values and historical cost rather than on replacement costs, the basis employed in insurance settlements. As another example, insurance agents and brokers can often provide specialized knowledge of insurance markets and can be of assistance in locating desirable insurers at minimum costs. University personnel, independent adjusters, attorneys, physicians, and certified public accountants are among the other types of consultants who may also be of value to the corporate enterprise in reviewing risk management programs, evaluating exposures, establishing safety programs, and adjusting claims. Very often, for example, it is desirable to use independent personnel in establishing the amount of damages, once the loss occurs. As we shall see, contracts of insurance are not always clear and leave much room for negotiation in their interpretation, particularly as regards claim settlement. The assistance of attorneys in this regard is often helpful. Attorneys should also be retained to review and approve the legal

[19] David A. Ivry, "The Corporate Insurance Manager and Employee Benefit Plans," *Journal of Risk and Insurance* (March, 1966), pp. 1-17.

language used in purchase and sale agreements, leases, and other contracts so that the liability assumed by the firm will be understood and so that appropriate insurance can be secured, if necessary.

Importance of Centralized Risk Management. In a corporation in which management is decentralized, there are cogent reasons for centralizing certain functions in order to achieve uniformity and the greatest efficiency. Authority for risk and insurance management should definitely be centralized for at least three reasons: (1) to avoid duplication and overlapping of coverage with its resulting wastes; (2) to secure the economies of blanket policies, broader forms, and quantity discounts in insurance purchases; and (3) to secure the services of a full-time, specially trained insurance department that is equipped to handle all insurance questions.

A study by the American Management Association revealed that centralized management of insurance was the practice in two thirds of the companies surveyed. Even when a local unit of a firm had some control over insurance, it was relatively limited control.[20] An organization chart for an insurance department organized under the treasurer's division is given in Figure 4–2. This chart is adapted from typical organizational structures reported in the AMA study.

In reviewing the structure presented in Figure 4–2, one may observe the provision for informal communication between all major departments and the insurance division, and between the major sections of the insurance division. Thus, the insurance manager has communication with the director of pensions, employee benefits manager, safety and loss-prevention division, as well as with other divisions. If the firm has foreign branches, the director of insurance will supervise the insurance programs of these branches. In some firms, the responsibility for safety and loss prevention may fall under this division instead of personnel. In other firms, insurance may be organized under the personnel or accounting divisions.

When the business is large and far-flung, a carefully laid-out plan of organization is even more essential than it is in a small, integrated business enterprise. The insurance manager must establish contacts with operating managers, set up machinery to process claims, devise cost allocation methods, and communicate with insurance and government officials in the various areas where the firm's operations are conducted. It is necessary to travel extensively and to secure the willing cooperation of the many executives relied upon for information.

One firm handled the problem of an organization with decentralized management by means of a committee system. At each plant, key executives were chosen to constitute a committee through which all questions relating to insurance could be channeled to and from the risk manager. Any information required at the plant level could be easily developed through this committee and transmitted to the insurance manager. In this way, management support for insurance problems was achieved.

[20] Albert A. Blum, *Company Organization of Insurance Management* (New York: American Management Association, 1961), p. 31.

AN ORGANIZATIONAL STRUCTURE FOR INSURANCE MANAGEMENT

Figure 4-2

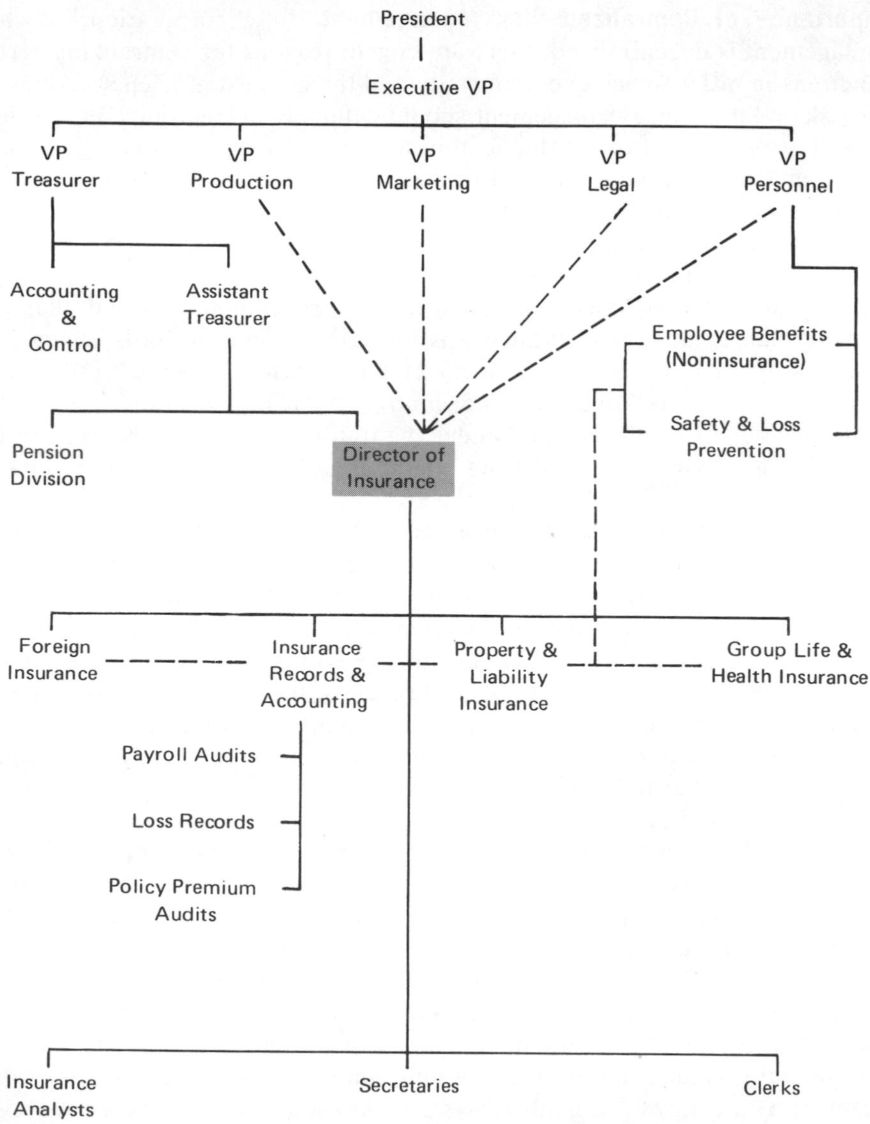

SUMMARY

1. Risk management is the function of executive direction over insurable risks and of devising the best methods of handling such risks. While risk management has been developed most highly as a separate management science in large business enterprises because of increasingly complex problems surrounding the management of these firms, the risk management function should be recognized in all business enterprises as a vital part of administration.
2. The risk manager has certain specific duties: to recognize various exposures to loss, to estimate the frequency and size of these losses, to choose and to implement the best of the various alternative methods of handling the risk, and to administer such programs as loss prevention, record keeping, and reevaluation of exposures to loss.
3. One of the most important duties of the risk manager—supervising the insurance program—has many facets, and the job is such that the specialized and concentrated attention by a full-time executive is usually justified. Use of such an officer, however, does not eliminate the need for the services of an agent or a broker.
4. There are several important ways in which a risk manager can effect savings in insurance costs without destroying the effectiveness of an insurance program. These methods include greater use of deductibles, use of certain contractual provisions, loss-prevention programs, and in some cases, self-insurance. Each of these methods must be used with great care to be effective.
5. Major weaknesses are frequently observed in the performance of the risk management function, particularly when this function is not performed by professional managers. Among the weaknesses are underinsurance, errors in insurance coverage, uneconomic buying of insurance, failure to pinpoint the responsibility for the risk management function, failure to review insurance programs regularly, and failure to utilize loss prevention as a basic device to control insurance and other costs.
6. To be effective, the risk management program must be properly organized and must have realistic policies based on sound insurance principles.
7. An important part of the risk manager's function is to coordinate the firm's activities as they relate to risk management. In particular, the risk manager must work closely with executives in accounting, finance, production, marketing and transportation, personnel, and other departments. Use of outside consultants such as independent appraisers, adjusters, attorneys, physicians, and certified public accountants is often justified in carrying out the risk management function.

QUESTIONS FOR REVIEW AND DISCUSSION

1. Explain each of the three views that has been taken of the job of the risk manager.
2. A risk manager stated that the annual loss to U.S. industry from alcoholism is a great burden—over $10 billion. To illustrate, he cited a study revealing the average sickness payments per alcoholic employee per year in one firm was $2,260, compared to $769 in a control group of nonalcoholic employees. Yet, this loss tends to be hidden because alcoholic

employees attempt to conceal their condition for fear of being discharged or losing their sick pay, hospitalization, extended leaves, promotions, pay raises, or other benefits. He observed that current management policy on alcoholism amounted to a statement that "any employee who can successfully conceal alcoholism will be given continued benefits and promotional opportunities; only those who can no longer conceal it will be fired."

(a) Suggest ways in which alcoholism directly affects insurance programs in industry.

(b) What responsibilities does the risk manager have in combatting this source of loss to the firm?

3. A risk manager has been given the task of deciding whether or not to purchase commercial insurance on a piece of mobile equipment whose replacement cost is $50,000. If the equipment is destroyed or out of commission for a long period, the firm is subject to additional losses of $10,000 due to lost sales. If the equipment is destroyed and is uninsured, a bank loan would be necessary to replace it since the loss could not easily be absorbed in working capital. It is not known how long it would take to arrange such a loan if the equipment had to be replaced. The risk manager finds that funds invested in the business earn an average of 15% and interest on liquid investments available to the firm is 6%. The equipment can be insured for $1,000 annually for its full replacement cost.

(a) Assuming the risk manager wants a reserve fund of $50,000 if the equipment is uninsured, calculate the value of insurance at the price quoted for insurance.

(b) What is the value of insurance if the reserve fund is set at $5,000?

(c) At what insurance premium would the value of insurance be 0 if the reserve fund is $50,000?

(d) Why might the risk manager recommend insurance, even if the price of insurance exceeded the amount you determined in (c) above?

(e) What is the apparent risk attitude of the risk manager who sets the reserve fund at $5,000 as is the case in (b) above? Explain.

4. A risk manager for a large concern read of an experiment whereby a group of problem drivers showed striking improvement in driving efficiency, and lowered accident rates after they had been given a daily dose of 150,000 units of Vitamin A for a certain period. A similar group who had not taken the vitamin showed no improvement over the same period.

(a) What has this experiment to do with the job of the risk manager?

(b) What should the risk manager do, if anything, after reading this article?

5. A chief finance officer stated, "A risk manager is a staff specialist serving both the operating groups and senior management. He is expected to exercise independent judgment, yet operate within corporate policies. If he is doing his job well he soon knows a good deal about every activity of the corporation. While the risk management function is a staff position, the risk manager may get involved, at least as an adviser, in such matters as layouts of plants and selection of equipment, which are line functions."

(a) Can you think of other line functions performed by the risk manager besides those that were mentioned?

(b) How does the quoted statement square with the statement in the text that the risk manager is responsible for the coordination of risk management with other functional executives within the firm?

6. A risk manager stated, "The primary financial consideration in determining the feasibility of self-insurance versus commercial insurance, is to determine which plan provides for a lower cash flow cost after considering income taxes and the cost of capital. Secondarily, which plan offers the most advantageous financing alternative?" (Cash flow cost is defined as the present value of the cash outlay after income taxes.)
   (a) How would you determine the "cash flow cost" of a workers' compensation insurance premium of $1,000 a year for five years if income taxes are 50% and interest is assumed to be 7%? (See the interest table C–2 in Appendix C.)
   (b) How would you determine the cash flow cost of the self-insurance plan for workers' compensation under the following assumptions: gross claim outlays are $600 a year, payable 35% the first year, 30% the second year, and 20%, 10%, and 5% the third, fourth, and fifth years, respectively. Self-insurance administrative costs are $400 annually. Income taxes are 50% and interest assumption is 7%.
   (c) Based on your analysis in (a) and (b) above, which plan should be selected, self-insurance or commercial insurance?
   (d) In what way might the self-insurance plan considered here offer the best "financial alternative"? Explain.
   (e) Why does the risk manager in this case apparently give no consideration to a requirement of a buffer fund against unusual losses? What consideration should enter into the decision other than financial? Discuss.
7. Why is it recommended that the insurance manager have access to the top executives of all major divisions of a business enterprise?
8. A newly appointed insurance manager of a large concern found that the company was carrying insurance on films, projectors, and cameras although the largest single off-premises exposure did not exceed $600. Advertising exhibits off premises were being insured although the most expensive exhibit could be replaced for $2,500. The company also insured some rental houses located on industrial land. Rental income was unimportant, and everyone agreed that the houses would not be replaced even if they were destroyed. Was the company policy based on sound insurance management principles? Why or why not?
9. Is it necessary to have both a full-time insurance manager and an insurance broker or an agent, or are their services overlapping? Discuss.
10. Discuss the pros and cons of using the same insurer year after year regardless of lower insurance costs available elsewhere.
11. Why might self-insurance be undesirable even if savings in direct insurance costs could be demonstrated?
12. Indicate the major problems which the risk manager has in common with executives in each of the following departments of a typical corporation:
   (a) Accounting,
   (b) Finance,
   (c) Production,
   (d) Marketing,
   (e) Transportation,
   (f) Personnel.
13. A speaker stated that the costly failure of the Edsel, a new automobile introduced by the Ford Motor Company, was in reality due to an insurable event for which the risk manager should have planned. The failure of the Edsel car reportedly cost Ford $250 million, and was at least in part due to a sudden change in public taste in car design induced by the first orbiting of the Russian Sputnik in the week

the Edsel was first introduced. The public became more interested in space travel and less interested in the somewhat garish design featured by the Edsel. Comment. Do you believe Ford's risk manager should have been held responsible for insurance against such an event? Why or why not? What, if anything, should the risk manager have done prior to the loss?

14. Work out an algebraic demonstration that equation (3) for the value of insurance in this chapter is derived from equations (1) and (2).

15. The Bon Vivant Company, a canner of soup, was forced into bankruptcy in 1971 due to the financial losses when it had to recall much of its produce from grocers' shelves due to some cases of botulism in persons consuming its product. What action should the insurance manager of the company have taken prior to the loss in order to forestall such a catastrophe?

16. A risk manager stated, "If a risk is to be properly controlled, it must be perceived, and it must be appreciated for probable frequency and possible severity." The writer went on to give two examples as follows: (a) A company brings together in two airplane loads nearly all its dealers and distributors from a certain country. (b) Another company makes a special contract with the government of a foreign country for setting up a factory in that country. Special machinery is to be sent by ship, and customs duty is to be waived if the machinery arrives by a certain date. For each of the situations described above, indicate what losses the companies are exposed to. In your opinion are these risks insurable? If so, what type of insurance should be purchased if any?

17. A risk manager of a discount store chain with a property insurance premium of $200,000, two warehouses, and six retail department stores discovered that his firm was refused special rating for fire insurance because of inadequate water supply, construction deficiencies, and inadequate housekeeping. If these conditions could be corrected, the firm would be able to reduce its fire insurance premiums by up to $95,000 a year. Advise the risk manager as to what action he should take.

18. (a) Verify the statement on page 81 that if the insurance premiums had exceeded $10,909 the insurance would have had no value. (b) Verify the statement on page 82 that the premium could rise to $1,636 before it would not be economical for the firm to purchase insurance.

19. A risk manager determines that he may receive the credits for accepting deductibles as follows: for a deductible of $100, $500 per year savings; for a deductible of $200, $600 savings; and for $300, $700 savings. What calculations should the risk manager make in order to determine which of these deductibles to select? Explain.

Chapter *Five*

INSURANCE AND DISTRIBUTION CHANNELS

In buying aspirin or fresh bananas, the buyer seldom inquires into the nature of the social or economic institutions that were responsible for making these products available, nor is there any compelling reason to do so. When a client engages the services of a lawyer or a patient a doctor, the qualifications of the professional are of as much importance as the needed services, and rightly so, for the two factors cannot be separated. When buying insurance, should the buyer have a knowledge of the nature of the social institutions that provide the service? The position taken in this and the next two chapters is that the buyer should have that knowledge. The nature of the insurer and the type of distribution system employed by it greatly influence both the cost and quality of the insurance service received. If the security of income and property are to be entrusted to an insurer, the buyer should certainly take a close look at the basic characteristics of that insurer.

CONDITIONS FAVORING THE GROWTH OF INSURANCE

Insurance institutions are shaped by the nature of the economic and social environment in which they grow and mature. There are at least four basic conditions necessary before the institution of private insurance can flourish:

1. The economic system should basically be a system of private property.
2. Society should be highly developed and industrialized.
3. Legal relationships should be well organized, known to all, and fairly enforced.
4. There must be an ethical environment for insurance.

The Need for a System of Private Property

Although insurance exists to some extent in countries where the tools of production are owned by the government and where basic economic decisions are made by some central authority, it never assumes great importance as a separate economic device to reduce risk. The government in such countries assumes most of the risks and in a sense acts as one great insurance company.

The Need for a Highly Developed, Industrialized Society

The institution of insurance does not flourish in an economy that is primarily agricultural or is industrially undeveloped. This is true not because risks are entirely absent, but because they are not developed to the degree necessary to support a highly organized system of institutions to handle them. In an agricultural society, individuals have a tendency to be relatively independent, to be willing to assume many more risks than is true in more industrialized societies. Furthermore, people in agricultural societies are not as dependent on money as such, as is true in the more advanced economies. A large part of a farmer's needs may be supplied at home, and thus there would be little trade. A peril that destroys one crop would probably not leave the farmer entirely without food supply because other crops or help from neighbors would supply that need. If a building burns, perhaps neighbors cooperate voluntarily to restore it or to replace it and no dollar remuneration is felt to be necessary.

By contrast, in a highly developed, industrialized society, productive workers are dependent on money income. Their jobs are usually specialized so that the occurrence of some peril which interrupts their income, or destroys accumulated property, is often a serious economic blow. Help from neighbors is usually impossible to obtain in the degree that it might have been available in early times, for individuals cannot take time off from their jobs at will. In the highly developed, industrialized society, standards of living are derived from trading the results of one's labor for the results of others' labor. This exchange involves the shipment of goods long distances, which gives rise to many risks not faced in a nonmanufacturing environment. Consequently, in industrial societies, methods to meet risks must be correspondingly highly developed.

The Need for Well-Organized Legal Relationships

Insurance as an institution flourishes best within a society in which legal relationships are well organized, known to all; and fairly enforced. An impartial system of justice is an absolute essential to a sound program of insurance, for the insurance device must usually be effected by means of a legally enforceable contract. Where political influence, frequent wars or revolutions, or dishonesty of the people upset the judicial system or law enforcement, insurance cannot flourish. While no complete proof of the above statement can be given, it seems intuitively clear that if the insurer could never be sure that its legal rights would be enforced under its contracts, it could not afford to continue in business. As a further example, a war might result in such damage to the monetary system of an economy that an insurance company could not meet its obligations. In Japan, for example, the effect of World War II on the life insurance companies in that country caused their entire reorganization.[1]

[1] M. Suetaka, "Post-War Trend of Life Insurance in Japan," *Journal of the Chartered Life Underwriters* (September, 1950, and June, 1951).

The Need for an Ethical Environment

Professor John D. Long has made a convincing argument that insurance cannot flourish unless the environment in which it operates is characterized by high standards of ethics and morality.[2] Ethical conduct of the people underlies a sound legal and judicial system. Ethical conduct, however, can deteriorate under a number of conditions, such as overpopulation, inflation, or too rapid advances in technology. Some degree of effective regulation of population, inflation, and technology is an additional requirement for a healthy environment for insurance.

Population. Increased population may bring overcrowding in certain areas sooner than expected. Crowding, in turn, engenders rising crime rates, which make insurance at the same time more necessary but more difficult to supply at prices people can pay.

Inflation. Rapid inflation can adversely influence insurance in many ways. Inflation tends to encourage dishonesty and to reduce loss-reduction incentive. Cash values of life insurance cannot be expected to flourish in rapid inflation due to loss in purchasing power of the savings contained in these policies. In property insurance, inflation is reflected in increases in the cost of settling claims above the levels anticipated when rates were established. Insurer attempts to build in an adjustment for inflation in the rate structure are often only partially successful. Thus the supply of insurance tends to diminish. Insurance by its nature is a method by which one plans for the future; a rapidly inflating economy tends to penalize any long-run planning and to encourage a philosophy of "live for today." This in turn tends to dampen the demand for insurance. Thus, inflation may tend to dampen both the supply and demand for insurance. An uncontrolled inflation can eliminate many types of insurance altogether, as was demonstrated in Germany after World War I, and in Japan after World War II.

Technology Advances. Advances in technology, even with the obvious benefits of increased leisure and living standards, may bring about conditions detrimental to insurance. Among these are social unrest, produced in part by lack of education as to what to do with the increased leisure, and an increasing tendency to engage in gambling. More fundamentally, advancing technology which is unaccompanied by other measures to help people use leisure time productively can result in a sense of futility—a lack of faith in one's capability and superiority because "machines have taken over." This further reduces the incentive for advance planning, and with it, the demand for insurance.

Conclusion

It would appear that the message of the preceding remarks is essentially that of "being forewarned is forearmed." Appreciating the potential dangers of

[2] John D. Long, *Ethics, Morality, and Insurance* (Bloomington: Indiana University, 1971).

current trends can produce appropriate countermeasures so that the end result will be favorable.

As we have seen, insurance has grown tremendously in the United States, where a minimum of adverse circumstances has existed. In general, the United States has been characterized by great political stability, fair law enforcement, and a high degree of honesty among its people. Furthermore, it has become rapidly industrialized under a system of free competitive enterprise. All the conditions necessary for the rapid growth of insurance have existed. An understanding of these conditions is helpful in explaining why insurance has not grown rapidly in certain nations such as the Soviet Union, India, China, some European countries, and most South American nations.

The characteristics of insurance institutions in the United States have been, in general, shaped by this favorable environment. However, it may be expected that if the environment deteriorates we may see many changes in insurance institutions in the future. Among these changes might be important moves by the industry to increase the degree of control it exercises over agents, an increase in government regulation of the industry, and an increase in the degree to which governmental institutions increase the supply of insurance in certain areas. A description and analysis of insurers and their marketing systems follows.

THE FIELD OF INSURANCE

Classified by type of coverage, the field of insurance is usually broken down into two areas: personal and property.

Personal Coverages

Personal coverages are those relating directly to the individual. In personal coverage lines, the risk is the possibility that some peril may interrupt the income that is earned by an individual. There are four such perils: death, accidents and sicknesses, unemployment, and old age. Insurance is written on each. Private insurers tend to specialize in the first two coverages, and governmental insurers in the latter two.

Property Coverages

Property coverages are directed against perils that may destroy property. Property insurance is distinguished from personal insurance in that personal insurance covers perils that may prevent one from earning money with which to accumulate property in the future, while property insurance covers property that is already accumulated. Property insurance is used here in the broad sense to include fire, marine, liability, casualty, and surety insurance. Sometimes property insurance is referred to as *general insurance,* while personal insurance is called *life and health insurance*. These terms are used loosely, however, and are not so comprehensive as the other names.

Private and Public Insurance

Insurance institutions in this country have taken two basic forms of ownership: private and public (also called governmental or social insurance).

Private insurance consists of all types of coverage written by privately organized groups, whether they consist of associations of individuals, stockholders, policyholders, or some combination of these. *Public insurance* includes all types of coverage written by governmental bodies—federal, state, and local—or operated by private agencies under governmental supervision.

Voluntary and Involuntary Coverages

Private and public insurance may be further classified into two subgroups: voluntary and involuntary insurance coverages. A great majority of governmental insurance is *involuntary*; that is, it is required by the law that the insurance be purchased by certain groups and under certain conditions. Most private insurance, however, is *voluntary*, although the purchase of certain types of insurance is required by law, for example, automobile liability insurance and workers' compensation insurance in many states.

Figure 5–1 presents the major classifications of insurance with the major types of coverage under each classification. In interpreting the figure, it should be observed that the types of coverage under each heading are meant to be suggestive of each type and not a comprehensive listing, which would take too much space and make the chart too complicated to be useful. In addition, governmental insurance includes coverage offered by both state and federal agencies, and includes areas in which some governmental body merely sponsors or guarantees the coverage that is actually offered by a private agency (such as savings bank life insurance). Involuntary private insurance includes those offerings required to be purchased under certain conditions in some states.

This text will be devoted mostly to the field of private insurance, although some attention will be given to the major types of governmentally sponsored insurance.

IMPORTANCE OF MAJOR LINES OF INSURANCE

In order to give some concept of the relative importance of the major lines of insurance, Table 5–1 shows the estimated premiums received by each type of insurer. As revealed in Table 5–1, government insurers collect about 46% of total insurance premiums and about 57% of total personal insurance premiums. Table 5–1 data are only approximate because no attempt has been made to include every conceivable type of insurance.

It may be seen that the income from property insurance is slightly larger than the income from life insurance among private insurers. For all insurers, however, the total of personal insurance business is nearly four times the level of

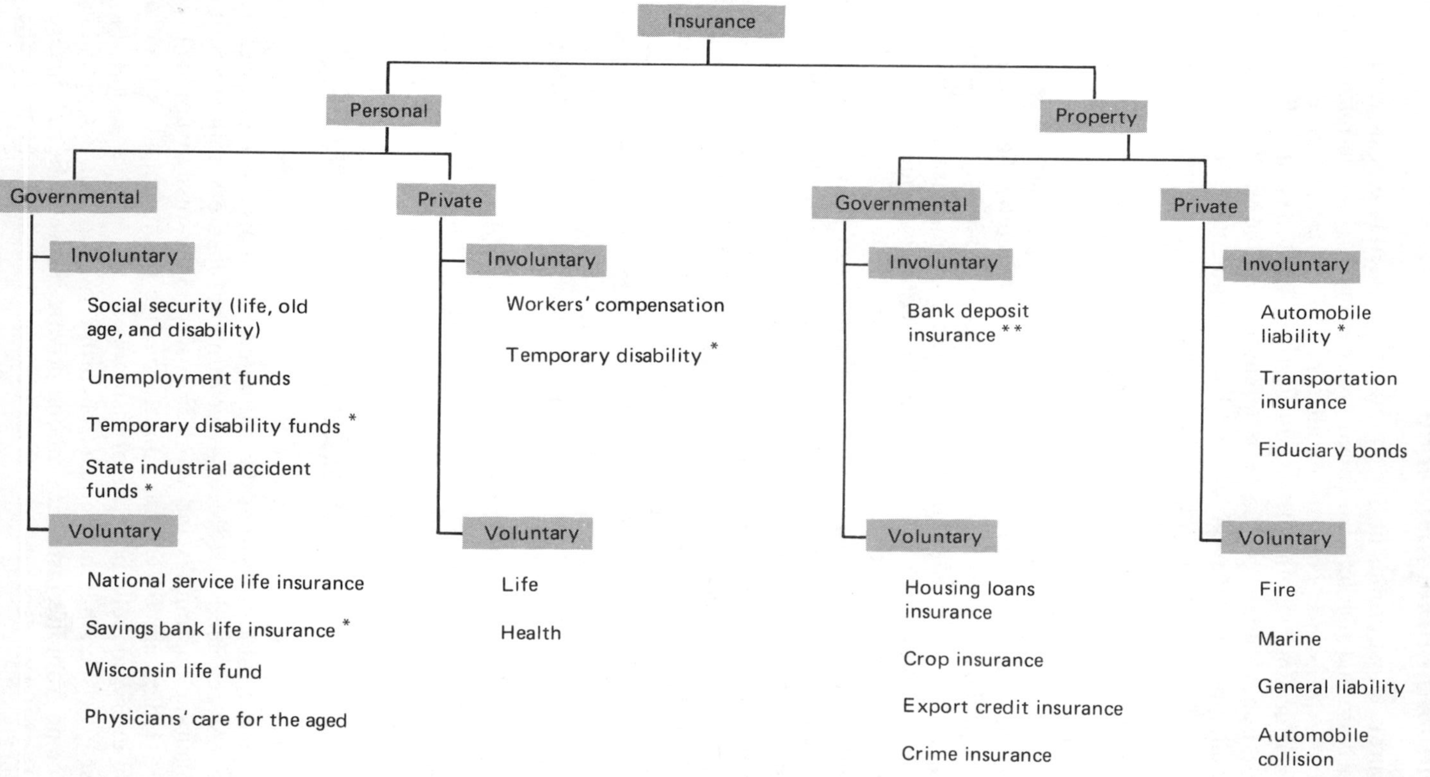
MAJOR CLASSIFICATIONS OF INSURANCE
Figure 5-1
Insurance
Personal
Property
Governmental
Private
Governmental
Private
Involuntary
Social security (life, old age, and disability)
Unemployment funds
Temporary disability funds *
State industrial accident funds *
Voluntary
National service life insurance
Savings bank life insurance *
Wisconsin life fund
Physicians' care for the aged
Involuntary
Workers' compensation
Temporary disability *
Voluntary
Life
Health
Involuntary
Bank deposit insurance **
Voluntary
Housing loans insurance
Crop insurance
Export credit insurance
Crime insurance
Involuntary
Automobile liability *
Transportation insurance
Fiduciary bonds
Voluntary
Fire
Marine
General liability
Automobile collision
* Applicable in only a few states.
** Bank deposit insurance required only in certain types of banks.

ESTIMATED RECENT PREMIUM INCOME IN MAJOR CLASSES OF INSURANCE AND RETIREMENT PROGRAMS

Table 5-1

Insurance Type	Premium Income (Billions of Dollars)	
Private Insurers		
Personal Insurance		
Life insurance and annuities[1]	$33.1	
Health insurance		
Group insurance policies[2]	9.0	
Individual insurance policies[2]	2.7	
Independent plans[2]	1.8	
Workers' compensation[3]	4.8	
Blue Cross-Blue Shield[2]	11.1	
Total personal-private	$62.5	
Property Insurance		
Property-liability policies[3]	$35.8	
Total private premiums		$ 98.3
Government Insurers		
Personal Insurance		
Federal civil service[4]	$ 7.2	
National Service Life Insurance Fund[5]	.9	
Old-age and survivors insurance[6]	48.5	
Disability insurance[4]	6.2	
Railroad Retirement[4]	1.4	
Hospital insurance for the aged[4]	10.8	
Unemployment insurance—federal and state[4]	6.8	
Medical insurance for the aged[6]	1.7	
Total personal-government	$83.3	
Property Insurance		
Crime Insurance (Fed. Ins. Admin.)[7]	$ .06	
FAIR plans[7]	.005	
Loan guaranty insurance[9]	1.63	
Flood insurance[8]	.2	
War risk marine insurance[10]	.004	
Crop insurance	.04	
Total property-government	$1.939	
Total government insurance premiums		85.2
Grand total private and government insurance receipts		$183.5
Percent—private		53.6
Percent—government		46.4
Percent—personal		79.5
Percent—property		20.5
Percent—total insurance premiums to disposable personal income, 1974, of $980 billion		18.7

[1] *Life Insurance Fact Book 1974* (New York: Institute of Life Insurance, 1974), p. 57.
[2] M. S. Mueller, "Private Health Insurance in 1973," *Social Security Bulletin* (February, 1975), p. 32.
[3] *Insurance Facts 1974* (New York: Insurance Information Institute, 1974), p. 11. Includes auto, fire, multiple-peril, marine, surety and fidelity, burglary and theft, crop-hail, boiler and machinery, glass, credit, and aircraft.
[4] *Social Security Bulletin* (March, 1975), p. 21.
[5] U. S. Bureau of the Budget, Appendix to Budget of the U.S. Government, Fiscal Year 1976, p. 837.
[6] *Social Security Bulletin* (March, 1975), p. 25.
[7] U.S. Bureau of Budget, *op. cit.*, p. 501. Reflects total estimated outlays for claims and expenses for 1976.
[8] *Ibid.*, p. 502. Estimate for 1976.
[9] U.S. Bureau of Budget. Estimates for 1973. Includes programs of the Federal Deposit Insurance Corporation, Federal Savings and Loan Insurance Corporation, The Federal Housing Administration, and other loan guaranty programs of the federal government.
[10] U.S. Budget, *op. cit.*, p. 263.

property insurance, measured by premium income. There are sound reasons for this emphasis, for the greatest potential loss facing an individual is the loss of income from the occurrence of given perils.

The great emphasis on personal insurance by governmental insurers accounts for the preponderance of total premiums collected on this type of coverage. It may come as a surprise to some to observe the size of governmental personal insurance. Comparisons over a period of years show the steady growth of government insurance. In various tables developed since this text was first published in 1962, the government share of the total insurance premiums was shown as follows: 1960, 27.3%; 1966, 39.2%, 1971, 42%; 1974, 46%.[3] If this trend continues, government's role in the insurance business will exceed that of all private insurers by about 1980, if not sooner.

Table 5–2 provides some indication of the relative size and growth of the various types of property insurance. Automobile insurance accounts for about 44% of the total property insurance premiums collected by private insurers. Fire, allied fire lines, and multi-peril insurance are second in importance, aggregating 27% of the total. The remaining 29% is accounted for by all other types of property insurance. The great importance of automobile insurance in the field of property coverages is, of course, explained by the tremendous expansion of auto traffic, accompanied by steadily rising loss and premium payments. The fastest growing lines of property and liability insurance are multiple-peril coverages. Glass insurance is declining in volume. In spite of the growth of crime losses in the U.S., burglary and theft insurance is growing very slowly, only 17% in the 10-year period, compared to an average total growth of 153% in property-liability insurance. It is interesting to note that premium income in property-liability insurance in the U.S. increased somewhat faster than the growth of gross national product, which increased 123% over the 10-year period covered in this comparison.

TYPES OF PRIVATE INSURERS

Private insurers are generally classified according to ownership arrangements. Four distinct types are: stock companies, mutual companies, reciprocals, and Lloyds associations.

Stock Companies

A *stock company* is a corporation organized as a profit-making venture in the field of insurance. For those companies organized in the United States, a minimum amount of capital and surplus is prescribed by state law to serve as a fund for the payment of losses and for the protection of policyholders' funds paid in as advance premiums. Stock companies, like all insurers, are organized with authority to conduct certain types of insurance business; and under the so-called multiple-line laws of most states, stock companies can be compared to

[3] Table 5-1 in the 1962, 1968, 1973, and current editions of Mark R. Greene, *Risk and Insurance* (Cincinnati, Ohio: South-Western Publishing Co.).

GROWTH OF MAJOR LINES OF PROPERTY AND LIABILITY INSURANCE, 1964 AND 1974

Table 5-2

(Millions of Dollars)	Net Premiums		Percentage Increase	1974 Percent of Total
	1964	1974 (est.)		
Auto Liability	$ 4,886	$10,775		
Auto Physical Damage	2,508	6,600		
Auto Total	7,394	17,375	135	43.7
Liability, Other	1,110	2,920	163	7.3
Fire & Allied Lines	2,211	3,500	58	8.8
Homeowners Multiple-Peril	1,333	4,000	200	10.0
Commercial Multiple-Peril*	371	3,100	736	7.8
Workers' Compensation	1,868	5,450	192	13.7
Inland Marine	454	1,135	150	2.9
Ocean Marine	248	750	202	1.9
Surety & Fidelity	391	750	92	1.9
Burglary & Theft	111	130	17	.3
Crop-Hail	112	260	132	.6
Boiler & Machinery	102	140	37	.4
Glass	42	34	-19	.1
Credit	n.a.	70	—	.2
Aircraft	n.a.	170	—	.4
Total	$15,747	$39,784	153	100.0

Source: *Insurance Facts 1975* (New York: Insurance Information Institute). Percentages calculated.

* Data for 1974 includes Farmowners Multiple Peril.

deal in all types of insurance, with the exception of life and health insurance. Even this limitation is not imposed in some states.

Stock companies in property insurance normally conduct their operations through the independent agency system. They usually, but not always, operate by setting a fixed rate through rate-making organizations, with the approval of the insurance commissioner of any state in which they are admitted to do business. Some stock companies pay dividends to policyholders on certain types of insurance. Stock companies never issue what are called *assessable policies,* wherein the insured can be assessed an additional premium if the company's loss experience is excessive. The stockholders are expected to bear any losses, and they also reap any profits from the enterprise.

Mutual Companies

Mutual companies are organized under the insurance code of each state as nonprofit corporations owned by policyholders. There are no stockholders. There are no profits as such, since any excess income is either returnable to the policyholder-owners as dividends or is used to reduce premiums. The company is managed by a board of directors elected by policyholders. The bylaws of a mutual may provide for additional assessments to policyholders in the event that funds are insufficient to meet losses and expenses. In most mutuals, however, assessments are not permitted once the company reaches a certain size. Only in very small mutuals are assessments usually provided for. Even then, the assessment is usually limited to one additional annual premium.

There are many types of mutual organizations operating under different laws and with different types of businesses. In any given state it is necessary to examine the insurance code in order to determine the precise nature of the mutual.

Class Mutual. Some organizations, known as *class mutuals,* operate only in a given type of class of insurance, such as farm property, lumber mills, factories, and hardware risks.

Farm Mutual. Where farm property is insured, the group is known as a *farm mutual,* and may be organized under a separate section in the insurance code. Such mutuals insure a large proportion of farm property in some states, primarily because of the specialized nature of the risks. Many farm mutuals operate on the assessment plan, and, in some cases, the assessments are unlimited; each policyholder is bound to a pro rata share of all losses and expenses of the company.

Factory Mutual. A type of class mutual specializing in insuring factories is known as a *factory mutual.* These organizations have been noted for the emphasis that they place on loss-prevention activities. Each member must meet high standards of safety before being accepted into the group. A large advance deposit premium, more than sufficient to meet expected losses, is required; any unneeded portion is returned to the policyholder at the end of the year. The factory mutual generally does not solicit small risks due to the relatively high cost of inspections, engineering services, surveys, and consultations, which are provided by the organization with a view toward preventing the loss before it occurs.

General Writing Mutual. Perhaps the most commonly known mutual in property insurance is the general writing mutual. The *general writing mutual* is one that accepts many different types of insureds; it is not a specialist writing in a certain class. General writing mutuals require an advance premium calculated on about the same basis as that of a stock insurer. In contrast to specialized mutuals, general writing mutuals operate in several states or even internationally. Where an advance premium is required, they usually set the premium to equal that of the stock insurer and contemplate a dividend or a rate reduction if experience warrants it. Many mutuals insist on relatively high underwriting standards, taking only the best risks in order that a dividend will more likely be paid. Some general writing mutuals reduce the initial rate below the stock company level, however, and do not plan on paying any dividends. Some mutuals are both *participating* and *deviating;* that is, they plan to cut the initial rate somewhat below stock company levels, and in addition to pay a dividend, if warranted.

Fraternal Carrier. In the life insurance field, a type of mutual insurer known as a *fraternal* deserves mention. A fraternal benefit society is authorized to do business under a special section of the insurance code providing certain requirements are met. A fraternal is defined as a nonprofit corporation, society, order, or voluntary association, without capital stock, organized and carried on solely for the benefit of its members and their beneficiaries. Fraternals have a lodge system with a ritualistic form of operation and a representative form of government, which provides for the payment of benefits in accordance with definite provisions in the law. A fraternal offers only life and disability insurance contracts. As a charitable, benevolent institution, it is usually exempt from taxation.

Originally fraternals started out as pure assessment companies, charging no advance premium and assessing each member periodically for losses payable under the rules of the society. This proved to be unsound and most fraternals now operate on a full legal reserve basis, similar to other life insurers.

Fraternal organizations underwrite only a small part of the total life insurance in force. At the close of 1975, they had $37 billion of life insurance, or 1.7% of the total life insurance in force. Fraternals have not enjoyed the rate of growth that is characteristic of the industry.

Reciprocals

A *reciprocal,* or *interinsurance exchange* as it is sometimes called, differs from a mutual in the form of legal control and in the capital requirements. In basic concept, both mutuals and reciprocals are formed with the purpose of making the insurance contract available to policyholders "at cost"; that is, there are no profits as such and no stockholders to compensate. In both cases, the policyholders own the company.

In the legal control and capital requirements of reciprocals and mutuals, however, basic differences arise. In a reciprocal, the owner-policyholders will appoint an individual or a corporation known as an *attorney-in-fact* to operate the company. In a mutual, policyholders elect a board of directors to manage the company. A mutual is incorporated with a stated amount of capital and surplus, whereas a reciprocal is unincorporated with no capital as such. Sometimes state laws require that a reciprocal furnish a contingent fund in the form of a deposit with the insurance commissioner for the benefit of the subscribers. Otherwise, the reciprocal organization has no capital other than the advance premiums deposited by the owners.

Reciprocals operate mainly in the field of automobile insurance. The largest is the Farmers Insurance Exchange of Los Angeles, California, which is one of the leading automobile insurers in the country. Most reciprocals, however, tend to be small local associations with poor records of financial stability.

Lloyds Associations

A *Lloyds association* is an organization of individuals joined together to underwrite risks on a cooperative basis. The most important distinguishing characteristic of a Lloyds association is that each person assumes risks personally and does not bind the organization for these obligations. Each underwriter[4] is individually liable for losses on the risks assumed to the fullest extent of personal assets, unless he or she has caused the liability to be limited.

Lloyds associations are similar to reciprocals since in both of these organizations the individual underwriter is an insurer. A Lloyds association, however, is a proprietary organization bent on profit, and the underwriter member is always an individual insurer. A reciprocal is composed of individuals seeking ways to obtain insurance at "cost," and its members are both insurers and insureds at the same time.

Lloyds associations are of two basic types: London Lloyd's and American Lloyds.

London Lloyd's. The Lloyd's of London are among the best known insurers in the world and are in fact one of the earliest known types of insuring operations. It is said to have started as early as 1688 in London, England, as an informal group of merchants taking marine risks while drinking coffee at Lloyd's Coffee House. Their operations are worldwide and they operate extensively in the United States largely in what is known as a *surplus line market*. This market consists of risks that domestic insurers have rejected for one reason or another. Lloyd's business is sold through registered brokers who are given the authority to represent them in this country. In no state except Illinois and Kentucky are Lloyd's of London admitted to do business on any basis except as surplus line insurers.

There are about 6,000 underwriting members of Lloyd's of London who operate through groups known as *syndicates,* each with a manager who acts as a general agent to bind the individual underwriter on various risks offered. The Lloyd's corporation, it should be stressed, is not liable to the policyholder on risks assumed by its members. Nevertheless, the corporation sets up rigid standards of membership, and there has never been a reported instance in which the Lloyd's organization has defaulted on any obligation. There are a number of contingent funds created to back up the promises of the underwriters in event one becomes insolvent.[5]

American Lloyds. American Lloyds are authorized under the insurance laws of some states. Typically the law provides that only certain types of insurance,

[4] The term "underwriter" is said to have originated with Lloyds. The method of assuming risk is for each member to write his or her name *under* the total amount of any one insurance application that the member wants to take. Thus, a member who assumes $1 million of a $10 million marine venture, signs the application for $1 million and thereby assumes $1 million of liability. The member thereby becomes known as an *underwriter.*

[5] Examples are the central guarantee fund of several million pounds held by the corporation, a trust fund deposited in New York for the benefit of American policyholders, underwriting deposits made by individual underwriters, and reserves held by underwriting agents. For a complete statement of the security provisions required by Lloyd's of London, see *Best's Insurance Guide with Key Ratings,* issued annually.

For references on Lloyd's, see C. E. Golding and D. King-Page, *Lloyd's* (New York: McGraw-Hill Book Co., 1952) and "The Risky Future at Lloyd's of London," *Business Week* (October 18, 1969), pp. 102-113.

such as fire, ocean marine, inland transportation, and automobile insurance, may be written by Lloyds groups. The law further states that some minimum number of underwriters, such as 25, is necessary in order to start an association, each member of which must have an individual net worth of a certain amount, such as $20,000. As a protection for policyholders, some laws provide for a minimum deposit, such as the same amount deposited by insurance. The law commonly indicates that the underwriters may not expose themselves to loss in any one risk of an amount in excess of a stated proportion of the cash and invested assets, unless proper reinsurance is effected.

American Lloyds do not enjoy the reputation for financial solvency that is attributed to London Lloyd's. Only 31 American Lloyds organizations were listed in Best's *Key Rating Guide* for 1974. Twenty-nine of these are chartered in Texas, one in New Mexico, and one, the largest, in New York. Only 11 of the organizations received an A+ rating (excellent) from Best. In the past it has been common for members of American Lloyds associations to limit their individual liabilities and otherwise protect themselves against catastrophic claims. Reserves have been inadequate and failures are not uncommon. Some states, such as New York, prohibit the formation of new associations of Lloyds.

Relative Importance of Private Insurers

In the United States there are about 2,900 property and liability and 1,800 life insurance companies (1975). Most of the business, however, is done by relatively few insurers. It is estimated that only about a third of the property and liability insurers operate in all states.

The leading states for property-liability insurers are Illinois (296), Pennsylvania (229), New York (217), and Wisconsin (203), which together have a third of all companies of this type. Iowa (190), Minnesota (183), Texas (183), Ohio (144), and California (100) have domiciled another 800 companies, about 28% of the total. It is worth noting that in 1974 U.S.-based insurers constituted about 45% of the world's insurers (4,685 out of 10,500) and collected about 54% of the total premiums.[6]

The relative importance of the major types of private insurers is presented in Table 5–3.

In the field of life insurance considerable concentration also exists. For example, although there are over 1,800 companies in the U.S., the 500 leading insurers collected nearly 98% of the premiums in 1973. Among these 500, about 44% of the total business was written by 10 large insurers.[7]

During the period 1931–1970, stock insurers suffered a declining share of total property insurance premium volume, while mutuals increased their share by about 90%. Nearly 70% of the property insurance, however, is still written

[6] *Insurance Facts 1974*, pp. 8-9.

[7] The largest life insurers by rank on premiums written in 1973 were: Prudential Life, Metropolitan Life, Equitable Society of New York, Aetna Life, Travelers, New York Life, John Hancock, Connecticut General, Continental Assurance, and Massachusetts Mutual. *Best's Review, Life Ed.*, December, 1974, p. 42.

PERCENT OF PREMIUMS WRITTEN BY PROPERTY-LIABILITY INSURERS BY MAJOR LINES, 1973

Table 5-3

Type of Insurer	Fire	Auto BI	Auto Collision	Workers' Compensation
Stock	71.7	62.4	56.8	72.8
General Writing Mutual	10.6	29.6	29.8	25.9
Factory Mutual	9.5	—	—	—
Other Mutual	.3	—	—	—
Lloyds and Reciprocals	.7	6.0	5.8	—
Reinsurers	7.2	2.0	1.0	1.3
Finance Co.	—	—	6.6	—
Total	100.0	100.0	100.0	100.0

Source: New York Insurance Department, *1973 Loss and Expense Ratios.* Data are based on country-wide premiums for insurers doing business in New York. Percentages calculated.

by stock insurers. Reciprocals and Lloyds associations, while enjoying some growth, still have only a small portion of the total volume. As shown in Table 5–3, the division of total business among different types of insurers varies according to line of business. For example, stock insurers have a smaller-than-normal share of automobile collision coverage because of the greater activity in this line by Lloyds, reciprocals, and finance companies. Lloyds and reciprocals write very little fire insurance, but they are more active in automobile lines.

In the field of life insurance, mutual companies are predominant. In 1973, mutual companies held a little over half of all life insurance in force. Stock companies and miscellaneous types of life insurers held the balance. In 1950, mutual companies enjoyed 70%, and stock companies, 30% of the life insurance in force. It thus appears that in life insurance the mutuals are losing relative to stock insurers, and that in property insurance, the reverse is true.

In each type of insurance—property and life—the minority type of insurer is gaining, but for different reasons. One of the major reasons for the growth of the market share of stock insurers in the life insurance field is the greater relative growth in numbers of stock companies. Stock insurers constituted 91% of the total of 1,815 life insurance companies in the United States in June of 1974. A majority of the stock insurers are small concerns that were formed since 1950. Most of them have been organized in the west south-central region of the United States, particularly in Texas, Louisiana, and Arizona. These three states alone had 707 life insurers in 1973, or one third of all insurers. Other leading states were Illinois, with 92, and Pennsylvania, with 65. Other reasons for the great expansion of stock insurers include the ease with which life insurance companies may be formed in these states, certain tax advantages available to life insurers in reporting investment income, and generous supplies of capital seeking outlets for investment.[8]

On the other hand, the mutual companies in property insurance have grown more rapidly than stock insurers primarily because the mutuals have tended to specialize in the types of insurance (particularly automobile coverages) for which the markets have been growing most rapidly. Furthermore, mutuals have used cost-cutting methods that have made the product available at generally lower rates than those offered by stock insurers.

In summary, the data show that in the field of property insurance, stock companies are most significant, while in life insurance, mutual companies predominate. In both fields, the dominant type of insurer has been losing its relative share of the total market.

Turnover of Insurers

Although the total number of insurance companies has remained fairly level in recent years, turnover among these insurers has been relatively great. One study of property-liability insurers revealed that over the period 1957–1967 there was a 21% reduction in the total number of insurers operating, mainly among mutuals. However, during this period 265 stock insurers disappeared while the total number increased by 47, among a number operating ranging from 790 to 837, indicating a turnover of about 25%. The average percentage of stock insurers disappearing to the average number operating was increasing as follows: 1938–1947, 9.9%; 1948–1957, 31.1%; 1958–1967, 33.7%. Among the stock company exits during the 1958–1967 period, nearly 50% were accounted for by mergers, 20% were voluntarily liquidated, and 24% were forced to liquidate. Disappearances of stock insurers seems to be related to fluctuations in loss ratios, but no authoritative study exists as to why insurers leave the business.[9] In some states failures are more common than in others.[10]

In the field of life insurance, the turnover of insurers has also been large. According to data from the Institute of Life Insurance, over the period 1950–1973 a total of 2,463 insurers were formed and 1,253—about half—were discontinued.[11]

It is possible that some of the turnover among insurers is due to the changing market shares noted above. In life insurance, stock insurance stock insurers are gaining, but not without "growing pains." Many of the life insurer exits can

[8] It should be noted, however, that mutuals, which are much older than stocks as a rule, had about two thirds of the assets of all U.S. life insurance companies. Data are taken from *Life Insurance Fact Book 1974* (New York: Institute of Life Insurance, 1974), pp. 88-89.

[9] Robert E. Nelson, "Property-Liability Company Exits," *Journal of Risk and Insurance,* Vol. 38, No. 3 (September, 1971), pp. 357-366.

[10] According to the *Wall Street Journal*, between 1939 and 1955, nearly 140 insurance companies failed in Texas, more than all other states combined in the same period. Between 1956 and 1957, 51 more companies failed and more are anticipated. Texas has about a third of all insurers chartered in the United States, four times as many as second-ranking New York. Not all companies fail with losses to policyholders, of course, because other insurers take over the business. *Wall Street Journal* (May 2, 1957), p. 20.

[11] *Life Insurance Fact Book 1974*, p. 87.

be traced to undercapitalization of new, small, life insurers.[12] In property-liability insurance, where the failure rate among stock insurers seems to be gaining, competitive pressures with mutuals may have caused some failures. Some insurers may be squeezed out by large competitors with great economic power. Many insurer failures may be traced to inexperience or dishonesty of management. The insurer may have been formed primarily to give profit to the organizers from the sale of stock and not from engaging in insurance.

In spite of the failures, however, the record of longevity among many U.S. insurers is outstanding. Over 200 property-liability insurers have operated for 100 years or more. According to one study, only 6.9% of all insurers in property and liability insurance over the period 1930–1962 failed outright.[13] Insurers are among the oldest companies doing business in the U.S. and include such important firms as Insurance Company of North America chartered in 1792, Aetna Insurance (1819), New England Mutual (1835), Mutual Life of New York (1842), and Massachusetts Mutual (1851).

CHANNELS OF DISTRIBUTION IN INSURANCE

In the field of insurance, there are many arrangements that may be made for the distribution of the insurance contract. These arrangements are comparable to the channels taken by physical goods. For example, life insurance generally takes a short, direct channel, while property insurance normally uses a long, indirect channel with one or more independent middlemen involved. In some fields of property insurance, notably automobile coverage, increasing emphasis has been placed in recent years upon the use of more direct channels. Some of the reasons for these developments will be explained.

Direct Distribution

In the field of life insurance, the distribution channel is usually direct. A salesperson called an agent or underwriter contacts the ultimate consumer and reports directly to the insurer, or to an intermediary, commonly called a *general agent*, who in turn reports to the insurer. The authority of the underwriter or agent is limited; the underwriter cannot be called an independent middleman, since he or she is actually an employee working under contract under the guidance of the insurer or a representative of the insurer.

A general agent, in life insurance, is an individual employed usually at a state or county level to hire, train, and supervise the agents at a lower level. The general agent sometimes collects premiums and remits them to the home office of the insurer. Usually the general agent represents only one insurer, and works on a salary and commission plan, or sometimes on commission only. The general agent is not an independent middleman in the sense that a typical

[12] E. J. Leverett, Jr., "Paid-in Surplus and Capital Requirements of a New Life Insurance Company," *Journal of Risk Insurance* (March, 1971), pp. 15-28.

[13] "Surety and Stability," *Journal of American Insurance*, Vol. 38, No. 11 (November, 1962), p. 17.

wholesaler is, for the general agent does not exercise final control over the issuance and the terms of the contract. The company normally is not bound by the general agent in putting a contract in force. The general agent exercises no control over the amount of the premium, has no investment in inventory, does not own any business written, and has no legal right to exercise any control over policyholders once he or she leaves the employment of the company.

Data reveal that only about half of all persons selling life insurance obtain more than 50% of their income from this activity.[14] The remainder presumably handle, in addition, nonlife policies or perform other types of work. Thus, life insurers do not always enjoy distribution by agents exclusively devoted to their product.

The system of direct distribution has grown up in life insurance because of several basic factors:

1. The need of the insurer to maintain close control over the policy "product."
2. The need of the insurer to exercise control over sales promotion and competition.
3. The infrequent purchase of life insurance.
4. The ability of the agent to make a better living through specialization.

Need for Close Control over Product. The insurer needs to maintain close control over the policy "product" because of its complicated nature, its long duration, and the fiduciary relationship required between the insurer and the insured. A direct channel is appropriate where such close control is desired.

Need for Control over Sales Promotion and Competition. Life insurance is very competitive. The policies of the many companies competing for business are similar in nature. Hence, extra promotion and competition on the basis of superior sales technique of agents often represent the difference between rapid and mediocre rates of growth of a life insurer. The insurer can exercise much greater control over these factors by employing a direct channel of distribution.

Infrequent Purchase of Life Insurance. There are no compelling reasons for life insurance to be offered as one of the many contracts available from a given agent, as is true in property insurance. A buyer usually purchases life insurance infrequently, has infrequent need for claims service, and has little day-to-day contact with the agent regarding endorsements to policies, requests for information, and the like. This is not to imply that the life insurance agent renders no service once the contract has been put in force. The agent stands ready as the local representative to the insured, answers questions, and writes letters to the insurer on behalf of the insured. But this service is not so demanding of the agent's time that a large business operation would be required to provide it. An agent's time is best spent in securing new sales.

Better Living Through Specialization. The life insurance agent has usually found it possible to make a better living by specializing in one field than by taking on many different kinds of insurance. Insurance is a complex subject.

[14] *Life Insurance Fact Book 1974*, p. 98.

Fitting life insurance to an individual's particular needs partakes of a professional service supplied by the agent. Advanced knowledge of the subject is required to render the quality of sales service usually expected. An agent generally does not become an expert in all lines of insurance, but, rather, concentrates in one area. Because the agent usually finds that one company offers all the types of life insurance necessary for clients' needs, and because the agent wishes to avoid the necessity of becoming familiar with the rate manuals and procedures of many companies, the agent usually represents one company only.[15] This situation calls for a direct channel of distribution, for each life insurer can usually distribute its contracts in sufficient volume in a given area at the lowest cost by hiring representatives to cover the area. There is no need for hiring any other middleman to handle the product.

Direct Writing in Property-Liability Insurance. In some lines of property insurance, independent middlemen have been dispensed with and the contract is marketed directly from the insurer to the insured, with or without an intermediary. Small amounts of insurance are sold directly by mail and no agent of any kind is employed; all negotiations are made between the insurance company and the consumer. In most cases, however, the insurer employs a representative called an *exclusive agent* to handle its business, to solicit prospects, to take care of paper work, and, in general, to serve as the insurer's direct contact with the insured. Insurers who employ this type of distribution are called *direct writers*. They include some of the largest automobile insurers in the business.[16] Direct writers have their greatest volume in the field of automobile insurance, but are expanding into other lines, such as residential fire and commercial property insurance. In general, direct writers have been able to sell insurance at lower cost to the final consumer and this, plus a vigorous advertising campaign, has contributed greatly to their success. The lower cost has been achieved largely by stricter underwriting and by paying smaller allowances to the agent for the production and servicing of business. For example, stock insurers writing in New York in 1973 paid an average of 13.9% of premiums to agents as commission and brokerage expense in the area of automobile bodily injury, and 14.1% in auto property damage liability. Leading direct writers, by contrast, paid commissions between 1.1% and 10.7%. Similar differences existed in other lines of insurance.[17]

An explanation of the growth of companies employing direct channels of distribution may be found in some observations about the nature of consumer buying habits in insurance and in other fields. As noted earlier, channels of distribution tend to be fixed in a free-enterprise system according to whether or not they are as efficient as alternative methods. In the tangible-goods field, the postwar experience has noted the growth of discount houses that generally

[15] There is a definite tendency for more and more successful agents to "broker" business through other life insurers and also to branch out into nonlife lines. However, accurate information on the extent to which this has taken place is not available.

[16] Examples are State Farm Mutual, Allstate, Nationwide Mutual, Liberty Mutual, United Service Auto, and Farmers Insurance Group.

[17] *1973 Loss and Expense Ratios* (New York Insurance Department, 1973).

concentrate in the sale of so-called shopping goods, which command a relatively high price, are subject to infrequent purchase, and are substantially standardized in nature. These houses take a considerably lower markup on such goods than is traditional and still make enough profit to justify their existence. They generally offer the consumer little or no credit or other services that are offered by competitors, and they save money in other ways.

In the sale of automobile insurance, a situation similar to that of the discount house exists. The product consists of a fairly standardized policy issued once or twice a year, costing a substantial sum of money and requiring little service except when a claim arises. The traditional allowance to the independent agent is about 15% of the premium dollar. This allowance is granted year after year, even though the agent may do little to earn it after the business is first procured. With the tremendous growth in the number of autos in the United States, a mass market in this field became possible and some insurers saw an opportunity to capture a large amount of it by devising more efficient methods of business development. Accordingly, innovations such as continuous policies, lower agents' commissions, direct billing from the insurer to the consumer, and specialized adjusting offices to handle claims were instituted. These innovators were rewarded with a great relative growth. For example, in 1973, four large direct writers collected about 31% of all the automobile liability insurance premium volume, compared to a negligible amount during the 20 years before.

Indirect Distribution (American Agency System)

The channel of distribution for a majority of property insurance lines is indirect. A system of middlemen, comparable to the wholesaler-retailer system in tangible-goods marketing, is used. This system has been termed the *American Agency System.*

In property insurance, the middleman most comparable to the wholesaler is called the *general agent*, while the retailer is called the *local agent* or *broker*. These terms are not to be confused with those that are applied in the field of life insurance.

General Agent. In property insurance, the general agent usually has a great deal of authority over the distribution of the insurance contract. While the general agent does not "take title" in the same sense that a wholesaler would take title to the inventory purchased from a manufacturer, nevertheless, the general agent has the incidents of ownership that accomplish almost the same purpose as would be accomplished by outright ownership. For example, the general agent can vary the terms of the contract in individual instances; that agent has considerable authority to negotiate the price of the contract, where this is permitted under state laws governing rates; and the general agent has authority over the terms of distribution agreements with local agents. Dealings with the insurer are almost in the nature of banking. The contract of the general agent calls for producing business on the general terms agreed upon and at a given commission rate. The general agent has almost complete control over the business written and looks upon the insurer as a source to pay losses, to be responsible for policyholders' funds, to meet the requirements of insurance commissioners, to effect reinsurance agreements, and the like. The general agent, like a wholesaler, usually represents more than one company.

Local Agent or Broker. The local agent, likewise, is an independent middleman in the property insurance business. Known as the "retailer," the local agent deals with the final consumer of insurance. The local agent may represent from ten to twenty separate insurers and has authority to bind these insurers on most of the contracts that are written. In most cases the local agent is supplied with forms, and has the authority to write a policy and deliver it to the insured. The local agent "owns" the business he or she writes. That is, the local agent has the legal right to access to customer files and to solicit the renewal of policies. The insurer does not have the right to give this renewal information to another agent. If the insurer cancels the agency contract of the local agent, usually the local agent will renew the policies of this insurer with a new insurer, and there is little that the old insurer can do about it. The agent works on a commission basis and has the responsibility of collecting premiums and after retaining the commission, remits the balance to the general agent or to the insurer directly.

The local agent as described above may be contrasted with exclusive agents of direct writers (sometimes called captive agents) and with brokers. Exclusive agents represent only one insurer, not several. The exclusive agent does not own the business written. Generally, the exclusive agent does not handle loss claims or collect premiums, which are billed directly to the insured from the home office of the insurer. The exclusive agent receives a commission, but, as noted previously, this commission is considerably smaller than the commissions allowed independent agents. The main task of the exclusive agent is to sell new business, keep in contact with customers, and serve as a communications link between the insurer and the insured. Brokers operate in a manner similar to local agents, although legally they represent the consumer, not the insurer.

The Branch Office System. Often a given insurer will not use a general agent, but will work directly through local agents, or set up a branch office to deal with local agents. This plan is known as the *branch office system*. It corresponds to a manufacturer's sales branch in the tangible-goods field. This system gives the insurer more control over the distribution of its contracts than when a general agent is employed.

It is significant to note that while the general agent may be replaced, the functions of the general agent are merely transferred to the branch office, perhaps at lower cost. The branch office performs the same general duties performed by the general agent. Of course, only one company, instead of several, is represented in a branch office, and consequently greater specialized attention to the problems of one insurer is possible than is true in a general agency. This same objective is also achieved through the fact that the branch office manager is salaried; hence, greater supervision of his activities is possible than is true under the general agency.

Is the American Agency System Doomed? Naturally those insurers and their agents committed to the traditionally long channel of distribution have become concerned over the future of their business, for the inroads of the direct writers are unmistakably clear. Opinion has been expressed that the agency system is doomed, that it will only be a matter of time until the direct writers take over completely, and that the independent agent will pass from the competitive scene. Before such a radical view is taken, however, the fundamental economic basis of the independent agency system should be examined.

Advantages of the Agency System for the Consumer. The agency system grew because it was needed to distribute the product of insurance efficiently. The agency system is an efficient way for the consumer, particularly the business consumer, to buy insurance. Such an individual might be spending $10,000 a year on 100 or more different insurance policies. To place this volume of business among many insurers by direct negotiation would be a time-consuming and unrewarding task. To keep track of the many involved details and to keep abreast of the technical knowledge needed to place this business intelligently would be nearly impossible without assistance. The point can be further understood by comparing the consumer's problem in buying insurance with the purchasing problems of a food retailer. Such a retailer may stock up to 6,000 separate items. If forced to deal directly with the manufacturer's representatives in securing these goods, there would not be time to conduct business because of the necessity of talking to a continuous stream of manufacturers' salespersons.

The independent agent, who represents many companies and receives a constant flow of information from the insurers, can efficiently supply professional assistance. The consumer receives valuable aid from the agent when a loss occurs. The agent helps the insured file proofs of loss and intervenes on the insured's behalf if a controversy occurs. The agent might be instrumental in helping the insured obtain coverage on risks that might otherwise be turned down by an insurer. Finally, the independent agent helps the insured plan a well-rounded, integrated program of insurance.

Advantages of the Agency System for the Insurer. The agency system evolved also because it is economical for the insurer. Most insurers would find it uneconomical and undesirable to attempt to place a single agent or perhaps two agents in a given territory, as is done by a life insurer, with the expectation that these agents would represent only this insurer for all the business which the insurer hopes to develop in the territory. There are several reasons why this is true.

First, the financial capacity of many insurers is such that they cannot accept all the business offered them from one geographical or industrial location for fear of undue concentration of risks. An insurer would thus turn down business offered it, its agents would lose commissions, and the consumer would have to shop around in order to obtain coverage. Matters are greatly simplified if the agent represents several insurers and can thus obtain markets for all the business developed.

Second, even if the insurer accepted all business offered it, there is doubt that a typical agent could obtain sufficient business in the usual geographical area to justify a salary, or for a suitable living through commissions which are currently allowed on the sale of property insurance. The typical policy premium and commission in property lines are smaller than in life insurance. In addition, competitive factors are such that the total potential volume of business in a community is limited in amount and is divided among at least as many insurers as is true in life insurance.

Third, when an insurer enters a given territory, certain minimum services to the consumer must be offered—claims must be handled, premiums collected, credit extended, and questions of policyholders answered. The insurer is expected to take care of the myriad of details that it could not do directly. Moreover, the insurer could not afford to perform these functions through a salaried representative until the volume of business in a specific area had grown sufficiently large to justify the expense. This is usually not possible, except perhaps in metropolitan areas. Even where the volume of business does increase sufficiently, the insurer is not likely to wish to jeopardize the goodwill of policyholders and agents by switching to a direct-writing system.

Outlook for the Agency System and Direct Writing. Direct writing has tended to grow in areas where there is a mass market for a standardized product that requires little continuous service. Since these conditions do not exist in all areas of insurance, particularly in the industrial market, it is extremely doubtful that direct writers will capture all the market. It is perhaps true that the basic nature of a typical agency contract will be amended to reflect the changed conditions brought on by direct writing. For example, insurers might take over some of the services now performed by agents and brokers, and reduce commission rates accordingly. This has already been done in some areas. It seems unlikely, however, that the independent agency system will be replaced by direct writing unless the property insurance business should become much more greatly concentrated than it is now and unless other basic conditions, now appearing quite unlikely, should come about. As one authority predicted:[18]

> The agency companies are under pressure to cut costs, the direct writers are under pressure to give more service. The end result will probably be, not the demise of either one of the competing marketing systems, but the improvement of each.

SUMMARY

1. A free-enterprise system of economics; a highly developed, industrialized society; and a well-organized, honest, legal system, are among the prerequisites to a flourishing insurance institution.

2. There are two predominant legal forms taken by insurers: stock companies and mutual companies. Property insurance is dominated by stock companies, while life insurance is dominated

[18] Chester M. Kellogg, "Present Insurance Outlook" (An address before the conference of Mutual Casualty Companies, Lake Delton, Wisconsin, June 6, 1956).

by mutuals. In both lines of insurance, however, the minority forms of insurers are gaining. Lloyds and reciprocals, as types of insurers, do a negligible portion of the total insurance business in the United States.

3. As measured by premiums collected, personal insurance (coverages involving the risk of loss of a person's income) is over three times as large as property insurance (coverages involving the risk of loss of a person's property). Governmental insurers account for about 46% of the total insurance premiums collected, with privately organized insurers receiving the remaining 54%.

4. In general, there are two basic methods of distributing the insurance service. The first method—direct distribution—used in life insurance predominantly, involves the use of semi-independent representatives whose authority is limited. The second method—indirect distribution or the American Agency System—following the pattern of distributing tangible consumer goods, involves the use of middlemen who operate independent businesses.

5. While the direct writing method of distribution is gaining in prominence in lines where standardized contracts and large-scale sales are possible, the traditional American Agency System continues to dominate the insurance distribution scene because it enjoys certain basic advantages. Undoubtedly the two systems will exist side by side in the foreseeable future.

QUESTIONS FOR REVIEW AND DISCUSSION

1. Why does insurance flourish better in an industrialized economy than in an agricultural economy? What other conditions seem to be necessary for a healthy growth of insurance? Discuss the reasons, in each case.
2. Benjamin Franklin organized an early fire insurance company called the "Philadelphia Contributionship for Insuring Houses from Loss by Fire." At first it was felt that people would voluntarily join the group, but this proved erroneous. Vigorous solicitation proved necessary. What conditions for the rapid growth of insurance were lacking in Franklin's time?
3. (a) What are the two major types of insurance? Explain the basic logic behind the classification of insurance used in this chapter.
   (b) Which type of insurance is most important from the standpoint of premium income? What reasons would you suggest for the relationship observed?
4. To many, fire insurance is the most important type of all property insurance. This was true before 1940. It is still true today? Explain.
5. The mutual insurer has been called "communistic" in concept because there are no stockholders. Mutual advocates counter this charge with the statement that gain is the motive of the organizers of both stock and mutual companies. Evaluate both of these arguments.
6. (a) Do mutual insurers provide for assessments?
   (b) What advantages and disadvantages are there to the policyholder in being subject to assessments?
7. What motive prompted the formation of factory mutuals?
8. Why do not factory mutuals solicit small risks?
9. What problem exists in fraternals with regard to offering a policy at a fixed premium? Explain.
10. (a) What dangers exist in the reciprocal form of organization?

(b) What is the advantage in the reciprocal form for the policyholder?

11. In both reciprocals and Lloyds associations, individuals are the underwriters. What significant differences exist between individuals in the two forms of organization?

12. Lloyd's of London operate largely in the surplus line market. Explain what is meant by surplus line.

13. Lloyd's of London have a distinguished record of financial stability over many years, a record not shared by American Lloyds. Explain the probable reasons.

14. What trends characterize the respective market share of stocks and mutuals in property and life insurance? Can you suggest any reasons for these trends?

15. Three news items relating to insurer failures were: (1) "S. Mort Zimmerman, one of the nation's most heavily investigated businessmen, and four business associates, including a prominent Florida state legislator, have been indicted on charges relating to their control of State Fire & Casualty Co., a defunct Miami insurance concern." (2) "Allied Reciprocal Insurers, former Peoples Inter-Insurance Exchange . . . is broke. Attorney says company can't meet judgements and calls in Idaho department. . . . The underwriting exhibit of the company showed total of income of $636,777, disbursements of $677,046, incurred losses of $4,274,627, underwriting expenses of $365,482, and total net underwriting losses of $106,326 . . . the only out to pay off outstanding claims will be for the insurance department to assess the policyholders unless some other reciprocal should decide to angel its deficits." (3) "The New York insurance department took over control of Professional Insurance Co. The department said that Professional's capacity was impaired by about $1.6 million. Professional writes primarily professional malpractice insurance. New York has . . . fund that would protect most New York policyholders." What are major reasons for insurer insolvencies, and which would appear to be important in the above cases?

16. In 1975 a writer stated that 150 insurers in Canada were competing for a premium volume of about $3 billion, 40% of which is written by only 20 companies. Certain insurers have either stopped doing business or are considering a pull-out in certain branches or provinces. Which of the various reasons for insurer exits does this statement illustrate? In what ways does the fact that 40% of the business is done by only 20 companies exacerbate the problem? Discuss.

17. Explain the differences between a general agent in property insurance and in life insurance.

18. Why is direct writing typical in life insurance, but the exception in property insurance?

19. Does the American Agency System involve a long channel or a short channel of distribution? Is this system doomed because of the action by direct writers? Discuss.

20. What services to the buyers of insurance are rendered by the retailer?

21. (a) Is the insurance retailer as important to an individual consumer as to large industrial buyer? Explain why or why not.

(b) Is the situation the same for the retailer in the tangible-goods field?

22. What services does the insurance retailer render to the insurance company?

Chapter *Six*

SELECTING AN INSURER

The preceding chapter has dealt with the various forms of legal organization for insurers and has considered the different systems of distribution used by them. The question now arises: How does one go about deciding which type of insurer and which type of distribution system is best?

Perhaps the first reaction in approaching the problem of selecting an insurer is simply to ignore it. This is probably the most common behavior. It is rationalized on the grounds that either there are no important differences in insurers from the viewpoint of the buyer, or that if differences do exist, it is not worth the time, expense, and trouble to make an intelligent analysis of the differences. This type of thinking can be an expensive and sometimes dangerous procedure. As will be explained, not all insurers are alike in matters of insurance costs, financial strength, and the quantity and quality of services. The financial importance of insurance expenses becomes apparent when it is recalled that expenditures for various kinds of insurance in 1974 totalled nearly $184 billion (Table 5–1). This was 18.7% of the $980 billion of personal income in that year. Significant savings through scientific selection of insurers are possible. Paying no attention to the problem at all may result in purchase of insurance from an insolvent insurer. This chapter will attempt to offer certain guides to be used in approaching the problem of insurer selection.

SELECTION OF PROPERTY-LIABILITY INSURERS

From the viewpoint of the buyer, there are four main factors to consider in selecting an insurer:

1. Availability of coverage.
2. Cost of coverage.
3. Financial solvency and stability of the insurer.
4. Quantity and quality of service offered, both by the insurer directly and through the agency system it uses.

In making comparisons on these points, extreme care should be exercised. An insurer that offers a premium lower than that of another insurer may be making up for it by reducing the amount of service, perhaps at the expense of financial strength. Hence, all four factors must be studied before any conclusions are reached.

Availability of Coverage

Before proceeding to make any comparisons of cost, financial strength, or service, the first step in making an intelligent selection of an insurer is to find a group of insurers who are willing to offer comparable contracts to the applicant on terms that are satisfactory. Not all companies offer every insurance facility or every type of insurance contract.[1] If there are only one or two available insurers, the problem is considerably simplified. Furthermore, some insurers refuse, even for an additional premium, to delete or to add certain features that the insured may desire. This may further narrow the field of choice. Finally, contrary to the understanding of most laypersons, some insurers may not be interested in accepting the insured's application at the rate that they are allowed to charge because the insured may not meet minimum underwriting standards or because the particular class of business is not profitable to the underwriter. Thus, drivers under a certain age may not be considered a profitable class of risk and are rejected by some companies. In 1975, medical malpractice insurance became very difficult to obtain at any price due to heavy underwriting losses on this line.

Cost of Coverage

Because insurance contracts and services vary so widely among insurers, it is generally difficult to make precise comparisons of insurance costs. Insurance is a service in which the cost must be estimated in advance by the insurer. Considerable variation among underwriters in these estimates may be expected. In some cases, excess charges for contingency reserves are returned to the insured in dividends or under various types of pricing methods. In other cases, the initial premium is fixed and no dividend or premium adjustment is anticipated. It is very difficult to quantify the many nonprice aspects of insurance. Nevertheless, it is worthwhile to examine several methods of comparing costs and analyzing their limitations. These include:

1. Direct comparison of gross premiums.
2. Comparison of gross premiums less estimated dividends.
3. Comparison of operational efficiency.

In the following discussion it is assumed that no major differences exist in contractual provisions, quality of agency services, financial strength of the

[1] For example, there are only two insurers in the United States that at present offer domestic credit insurance, the type of coverage against failure of debtors to pay their obligations. Unavailablity of crime coverage in some areas has led to the federal government's offering this insurance.

insurer, or other factors of importance to the insurance buyer in making a decision.

Direct Price Comparisons. If there are no dividends or other later premium adjustments to be considered, and all other matters of importance surrounding the insurance transaction approximately are equal, it seems clear that the insured should select the insurance policy with the lowest price. Because of the complexities involved, it often takes courage to accept the lowest price. It is easy for an experienced insurance sales agent to attempt to confuse the price issue by pointing out the many ways in which his particular policy or company differs from that of a competitor. There is no substitute for a careful analysis of the facts by the insured.

One factor which may mislead an insured on the price issue is that of the "loss leader." For example, one insurer might offer the lowest premium in the first year in an attempt to "buy" business, in the same manner as a retailer advertises a loss leader in order to attract people into the store. Then, in later years, after the policyholder is a customer, the premium may be raised, certain services eliminated, loss claims settled on a niggardly basis, contractual provisions restricted upon renewal, or other methods used to make the business more profitable.

Premiums Less Dividends. As mentioned earlier, some insurers deliberately charge a higher premium to allow for contingencies. Thus they anticipate returning any excess to the insured group in the form of a dividend or a premium reduction for the renewal policy. In selecting insurers of this type, the insured must consider estimated dividend schedules, including the timing and the form of the dividend, in deciding whose price is the lowest. In life insurance it is not uncommon to find that premiums of mutual insurers offering participating policies are as much as 20% above the premiums charged by insurers offering policies on a nonparticipating basis. In property insurance, dividends may be given out as a refund of an excess premium, or they may be distributed only if the policy is renewed with the same insurer. It is important to realize that dividends are never guaranteed, only estimated, by the insurer.

Experience suggests that the dividend schedules published by the insurer as typical of what has been paid in the past may vary considerably from actual future experience. These variations cannot be predicted very well and so the insured is always subjected to price uncertainty when purchasing dividend-paying contracts. However, the closer the initial premium is on such a contract to a premium quoted by another insurer without the promise of a dividend, the more certain it is that the insured has little to lose by accepting the dividend-paying policy. At least in that case there is a chance to obtain coverage at a lower final cost if the cost factors of the insurer are favorable.

Operational Efficiency. One method of judging insurance costs is to compare insurers as to their internal operating efficiency in the belief that the most efficient insurer will, in the long run, be the cheapest and best. Internal operating efficiency may be difficult to judge, but some indications may be observed in the loss and expense ratios, and the net underwriting profit. Underwriting profit is equal to 100 minus the sum of the loss and expense ratios.

The expense ratio is the ratio of all expenses to premiums earned. Data on these ratios are published annually for most insurers by line of insurance and lend themselves to easy comparison. Some insurers have been able to reduce expenses greatly through better internal cost control, automation, and reduction in agency commissions. For example, consider the expense ratios published in the field of homeowners multiple-peril insurance for 1973 for the five largest stock insurers doing business in New York:[2]

Insurer 1	48.2
2	40.4
3	37.0
4	36.1
5	33.8

Each insurer wrote more than $100 million of premiums in this field in 1973 nationwide. The range of expense ratios is large, running from a low of 33.8% to a high of 48.2%. The average for all stock insurers in this line in 1973 was reported as 39.8%. Expenses of one insurer were 200%. If the insured is offered an identical premium from Insurer 1 whose expenses are 48.2%, and Insurer 5 whose expenses are 33.8%, the insured may wonder how Insurer 1 can long afford to offer an identical package of product and service. A closer investigation may cause the insured to accept the bid of Insurer 5 unless it is found that Insurer 1 offers more service, more generous claims settlement, or some other distinguishable factor that favorably differentiates its service.

The loss ratio of an insurer is the ratio of losses incurred to premiums earned. The larger this ratio, the greater is the percentage that the insured group receives back out of its premium dollar. It might appear that insurers with high loss ratios would be preferred for this reason. However, the insurer must be able to make an underwriting gain, or its ability to continue in business at all will be impaired. If the high loss ratio threatens the profits of the insurer, it is likely that such a ratio will portend an increase in premiums or a reduction in services in the future. Thus any initial savings to the insured in lower premiums may soon be lost. However, if one insurer has a record showing on the average an 85% loss ratio, a 10% expense ratio, and an underwriting gain of 5%, this may be preferred to another insurer in the same line whose loss ratio is 50%, expense ratio is 45%, and whose underwriting gain is 5%. The first insurer is more likely to be able to offer lower rates, more comprehensive coverage, or both.

We may now review the loss ratio, expense ratio, and net underwriting gains of the five insurers mentioned above in the field of homeowners multiple-peril insurance in 1973:[3]

[2] *1973 Loss and Expense Ratios* (New York Insurance Department, 1973), pp. 24-26.
[3] *Ibid.*

Insurer	Expense Ratio	Loss Ratio	Net Underwriting Profit
1	48.2	49.3	2.5
2	40.4	54.2	5.4
3	37.0	54.4	8.6
4	36.1	57.5	6.4
5	33.8	56.5	9.7

Insurer 5, which had the lowest expense ratio, does not have the highest loss ratio, but it has the largest net underwriting gain of the group. Insurer 1, which had the greatest expense ratio, has the lowest loss ratio of the group. Which insurer has the greatest operational efficiency and is therefore likely to be able to offer insurance service in the most economical manner? One may reason that Insurer 5, in spite of a relatively high loss ratio, has been able to produce the largest net underwriting gain and is therefore in a position to offer lower premiums, broader coverage, or more efficient service during the polcy term than the other insurers. The relatively high loss ratio indicates a greater payback to its policyholders than other insurers. Insurer 1, on the other hand, has relatively large expenses and a low payback. Furthermore, its underwriting gain is the lowest, indicating a lack of cushion to absorb unusual fluctuations in losses or expenses. If the premiums charged by these insurers and other factors are roughly equal, the insured should select Insurer 3, 4, or 5, which have fairly large paybacks and low expenses.

Stocks Versus Mutuals. One may inquire whether an insured is better off financially with a mutual company or a stock company. The main argument for mutuals is that they operate at cost since they are owned by policyholders, while stocks operate at a profit. In spite of the theoretical advantage of mutuals in this regard, an examination of past loss and expense ratios reveals little consistent difference between stocks and mutuals in most lines of insurance.

A fair conclusion seems to be that the particular form of organization does not appear to guarantee to the insured group any major cost advantage or gain in long-run efficiency. Major differences in efficiency seem to stem mainly from savings in distribution costs, in more scientific selection of risks, and in the use of automation to streamline accounting an internal record keeping. Also, it should be recalled that the other major factors, financial strength and quality of services rendered, should be given careful consideration. These factors are discussed below. In other words, before selecting an insurer on the basis of lower costs, one should seek to determine the basic reasons for the lower costs, and then decide if any of these reasons is detrimental.

Financial Solvency and Stability of the Insurer

To obtain insurance at a lower cost at the expense of financial strength in an insurer is obviously foolish. The main item of interest to one in the purchase of insurance is a guarantee of compensation for a covered loss. If bad financial policies, inadequate premiums, or poor underwriting standards endanger the fund that is set aside for losses, a person may find that insurance has been carried for many years to no avail. The loss occurs, but the insurer is bankrupt. This is poor solace for the doubtful advantage of having obtained a lower initial premium.

It is often assumed that, because of the system of state regulation over insurance, financial solvency of the insurer is more or less guaranteed and that the average policyholder has little to fear. While this assumption is no doubt justified in a great majority of cases, there have been and will continue to be failures, with consequent losses to policyholders. It should not be automatically assumed by the insurance buyer that the insurer will necessarily exist when the loss occurs.

Insolvency Funds. The danger of loss from insolvent insurers has been recognized by the recent adoption of laws in nearly all states[4] establishing state insolvency funds. Subject to $100 deductibles and maximum limits of liability, these funds promise to reimburse policyholders for any losses caused by bankrupt insurers. The funds are supported by other insurers operating in a given state.[5] In spite of such protection, careful attention to the financial condition of an insurer is warranted by the thoughtful insurance buyer.

Financial Statement Analysis. Analysis of the financial solidity of an insurer follows the same basic principles common to that type of study of any corporate entity. Conventional financial statement analysis applies, but certain adjustments, to be explained presently, are necessary in order to fit technical insurance concepts into conventional financial analytical molds.

In any corporate balance sheet, the analyst who seeks a guide to financial solvency usually directs attention first to the amount of debt shown in relation to the net worth of the enterprise. Too much debt indicates a possible inability to pay interest and repayment of principal in times of stress, with resulting bankruptcy. Thus, the *net-worth-to-debt ratio* is a common tool of financial statement analysis. Such a ratio is usually calculated over a period of years in order to discover any adverse trends, and it is usually compared with that of similar concerns in order to discover any deviation from average.

For property and liability insurance companies, the net-worth-to-debt ratio is probably the most significant single ratio employed. It is also one of the most widely used ratios. On insurance company balance sheets, the term "net worth" is usually called "policyholders' surplus" and the "debt" becomes the sum of various miscellaneous liabilities. The largest single item of debt on a fire insurer's balance sheet, for example, is called the "unearned premium reserve." One authority, Roger Kenney, insists that for satisfactory strength, the ratio of policyholders' surplus to the unearned premium reserve should be at least 1:1, unless extenuating circumstances exist that would permit a lower

[4] In 1973 only Alabama, Arkansas, and Oklahoma had not passed such legislation.

[5] Harold Krogh, "Insurer Post-Insolvency Guaranty Funds," *Journal of Risk and Insurance*, Vol. 39, No. 3 (September, 1972), pp. 431-450.

ratio.[6] The 1:1 ratio means a margin of safety of 100% of the unearned premium reserve.

What light does the net-worth-to-debt ratio throw upon the financial stability of property and liability insurers? The rationale of the ratio may be explained as follows: Items of debt on the insurer's balance sheet represent amounts which must be returned to policyholders. The two most important items are unearned premium reserves and loss reserves. As the name suggests, unearned premium reserves represent advance premium paid in for protection and not yet earned by the insurer. If the policy is cancelled, these advance premium payments must be returned to the policyholder in cash. Since the policy may be cancelled at any time by the insurer or the insured, the funds must be kept in fairly liquid form and are typically invested in bonds or other negotiable securities or kept in cash. Loss reserves represent estimates of amounts which must be paid out in losses, once the precise amount is reported to the insurer, and are liquidated by actual payment of the loss.

It may be seen that the main items of debt on an insurer's balance sheet represent amounts due to policyholders on a potentially short-term basis. They do not represent long-term debt such as bonds. The assets protecting these obligations must be sufficient at all times and ideally should exceed them by some margin. The 1:1 ratio of net worth to debt suggests that a suitable margin is 100%; that is, for each $1 of debt, there is also $1 of surplus; thus, there should be $2 of assets protecting the debt. Then, in case of business depression or other disruption which reduces the value of the assets, there will still be a sufficient sum to meet the insurer's obligations to its policyholders.

Some analysts believe that a 1:1 margin is too conservative, since the assets are typically invested in liquid securities and may be converted to cash quickly. Furthermore the insurer may use current income to liquidate debt. They believe that the ratio of surplus to debt may safely fall below 1:1 without endangering the position of policyholders. With such a conservative ratio, the capacity of the insurance industry to accept new business is reduced below what it would otherwise be and this tends to hinder the insurance industry in meeting its expanding obligations to the public in offering coverage.

What is the ratio of net worth to debt currently for the property and liability insurance industry? As of 1973, the industry in the United States had about $84 billion of assets, $27 billion of surplus, and $57 billion of obligations to policyholders. Hence the ratio for the industry as a whole was 27:57 or roughly .47:1 instead of 1:1. Apparently industry leaders are less conservative than traditional standards of financial solvency as measured by net worth to debt.

Another standard of financial solvency suggested by Kenney is that the ratio of premiums written to policyholders' surplus should not exceed 2:1. That is, property and liability insurers should not accept more than $2 in new premium volume for each $1 of policyholders' surplus. The rationale for this ratio is that

[6] Roger Kenney, *Fundamentals of Fire and Casualty Insurance Strength* (Dedham, Massachusetts: Kenney Insurance Studies, 1957), p. 37.

new premium volume represents potential liability to policyholders for loss payments and for premium refunds in the event the policies are cancelled. Hence, premium volume becomes a substitute measure for debt. The property and liability insurance industry in the United States wrote $42 billion of premiums in 1973. Since the surplus for the industry as a whole was $27 billion, the premium/surplus ratio of 1.55:1 was slightly more conservative than the Kenney standard of 2:1. In 1974 the U.S. stock market declined sharply, reducing the value of assets held by insurers. This caused the ratio of premiums to surplus to rise to about 2.5:1, producing a ratio above the Kenney standard.

The financial analyst may judge the premium-to-surplus ratio as a measure of financial leverage. Recalling that the combined loss-and-expense ratio is $\frac{\text{Losses + Expenses}}{\text{Premiums Earned}}$, the premium/surplus ratio may be multiplied by the excess of combined loss-of-expense ratio over 100 to find the percentage surplus drain of an insurer in a given year. To illustrate, assume in a given year that an insurer has a premium/surplus ratio of 2:1 and a combined loss-and-expense ratio of 110. This means that the surplus will decline by 2 × 10, or 20%, that year. The larger the premium/surplus ratio, the greater the surplus drain. A ratio of 5 would mean a 50% loss of surplus. This may be demonstrated by an example: suppose the insurer writes $10 million of premiums but has only $2 million of surplus, a ratio of 5:1. Now assume an underwriting loss of 10% of premiums (a combined loss-and-expense ratio of 110). Ten percent of $10 million is $1 million, which is one half of the insurer's surplus of $2 million. It is not uncommon to find insurers with premium/surplus ratios of 5 or 10. Such insurers have unusually high financial leverage, and are financially vulnerable as well to unexpected underwriting losses.

It may be concluded that financial statement ratios are only guides to the determination of insurer solvency and should be used in conjunction with other factors. If the ratio characterizing a given insurer is far out of line with industry averages, the insurance buyer is cautioned to examine that particular insurer in greater detail to seek the reasons for the deviation; if none is apparent, that insurer may be viewed with suspicion as far as its potential solvency is concerned. For example, an insurer with unconservative ratios may be protected by favorable reinsurance arrangements or by guarantees of a parent company. Hence it might be acceptable in spite of these ratios.

To illustrate financial statement analysis as a tool of insurer selection, consider the following case of the United National Insurance Co. of Philadelphia, Pennsylvania, which writes general lines of property-liability insurance: (All data are in thousands of dollars)

Assets, 1970	$2,929	Premiums written, 1970	$1,702
Policyholders' surplus	540	Underwriting loss, 1970	—159
Loss reserves	1,714	Investment income, 1970	169
Unearned premium reserve	604	Underwriting losses, 1966–1970	—510
		Investment income, 1966–1970	618
		Combined loss and expense ratio, 1966-1970	106
		Combined ratio, 1970	111

From these data one may make the following calculations for 1970:

Premiums written/policyholders' surplus	3.15
Policyholders' surplus/total liabilities	.23

Both of the major analytical ratios are less conservative than industry averages by substantial margins (In 1970 industry averages were 1.6 and .53, respectively). The company is using substantial financial leverage which places it in a rather vulnerable position, considering its consistent underwriting losses. Multiplying the premiums/surplus ratio of 3.15 by the average combined loss of .06, one may quickly determine that about 19% of the surplus is being lost annually through underwriting. Without offsetting investment gains, the insurer's solvency would be threatened within about five years. If the underwriting loss of 11% experienced in 1970, equal to 35% of the surplus (3.15 × 11), continues, the insurer would be insolvent within three years without offsetting investment gains. So far, investment gains have been sufficient to offset underwriting losses. Nevertheless, the company has thin margins for unusual contingencies since its surplus is less than a fourth of its liabilities. Best rated the firm C + in 1970, a low rating. (See a discussion of Best's ratings below.)

Best's Ratings. One approach to the problem of how to consider all the relevant factors in judging the financial strength of an insurer is illustrated by the financial ratings given by Best.[7] The ratings attempt to measure five factors that affect the financial stability of an insurer:

1. Underwriting results.
2. Economy of management.
3. Adequacy of reserves for undischarged liabilities of all kinds.
4. Adequacy of policyholders' surplus to absorb unusual shocks.
5. Soundness of investments.

Best's ratings would consider, for example, that even though a given insurer had a high ratio of policyholders' surplus to unearned premium reserves, careless underwriting, extravagant management practices, or unsound investment policies that resulted in asset losses could, within a short time, completely offset its good surplus position.

The great majority of all insurers meet Best's high standards of financial safety.[8] The public has further protection in that it is the duty of the insurance commissioner in most states to examine each insurer for financial solvency at least once every three years.

In summary, it may be stated that there are no simple methods to determine the financial strength of an insurer. No single test of financial strength should be relied upon in evaluating an insurer, but several tests over a period of years should be employed.

[7] See *Best's Insurance Reports,* or a summary of various types of financial data found in *Best's Insurance Guide with Key Ratings.* Each of these annual publications covers over 1,100 property-liability insurance carriers in the United States. Fairly complete financial information about any carrier is available.

[8] Appendixes A and B explain the methods used in compiling Best's ratings.

In a study of 26 insolvent and 26 solvent property-liability insurers during the period 1966–1971, it was found that six ratios were quite effective in predicting financial difficulty. These ratios included the ratio of premiums to surplus, and the combined loss-and-expense ratio. Other effective ratios were the ratio of receivables from agents to total assets, the ratio of the cost of stocks to their market value, the cost of bonds to their market value, and the ratio of loss adjustment expenses and underwriting expenses to net premiums written. Multiple discriminant analysis was used to classify insurers into two groups, solvent or distress. The model was able to classify correctly 49 out of 52 firms included in the study.[9]

Quantity and Quality of Service Offered

Given comparable contracts and equivalent degrees of financial strength, the applicant for insurance is faced essentially with the question, "Do the insurers competing for my business offer coverage at lower cost, and if so, what in the way of service, if anything, is given up in obtaining this lower cost?" As we have seen in the field of property and liability insurance, mutuals, as a group, tend to have lower ratios of expense and loss than do stock companies. Of course, this does not necessarily apply to all mutuals and to all stock companies. Nevertheless, the question of service is a vital one in determining whether any saving in insurance cost is actually a net saving or merely a symptom of the fact that certain functions are not being performed by an insurer who offers coverage at lower premiums.

Various studies have suggested that the quality and quantity of services provided by insurers and their agents often do not live up to expectations. In one study of consumer attitudes toward automobile and homeowners insurance, for example, it was discovered that some type of unfair treatment of the policyholder is the reason most often given for a change of insurer. Respondents complained that agents fail in updating coverage and in presentation of coverage alternatives.[10]

Each insured should consider carefully the quantity and quality of services expected and through careful inquiry attempt to select the agent who will meet these expectations. If the insured has little need for agency services, the other factors in selecting an insurer, such as savings in premiums, may be stressed more highly. A firm with international operations may find that only a few large brokerage firms, those with overseas offices, are suitable.[11] An industrial firm may find only one or two agencies in its locale large enough to provide sufficient

[9] J. S. Trieschmann and George E. Pinches, "A Multivariate Model for Predicting Financially Distressed P-L Insurers," *Journal of Risk and Insurance,* Vol. 40, No. 3 (Sept., 1973), pp. 327-338.

[10] J. D. Cummins, D. M. McGill, H. E. Winklevoss, and R. A. Zelten, *Consumer Attitudes Toward Auto and Homeowners Insurance*, (Philadelphia, Pennsylvania: Wharton School, University of Pennsylvania, 1974), p. 223. See also, Robert E. Osborn, Jr., *The Need for Consumer Orientation in Insurance Marketing*,(Eugene, Oregon: The University of Oregon, 1969).

[11] Large international brokerage firms include Marsh and McLennan, Johnson and Higgins, Alexander and Alexander, Fred S. James, and Frank B. Hall.

contacts with the insurance market, as well as loss-prevention service. A person seeking only a standard fire policy for a personal residence, on the other hand, has less need for investigating agency services.

SELECTION OF LIFE INSURERS

Few thoughtful savers would invest in a business or in the stock of a corporation without a careful investigation beforehand. Comparisons would be made among companies of the same type, and their achievements over a period of years would be analyzed. The advice of established independent brokers would be sought, and in the case of large investments, perhaps an individual study of a corporation, including visits to the plant and interviews with management, would be made. Yet, in buying life insurance, which for many constitutes their only major lifetime savings plan, it is doubtful if in the majority of cases any investigation or analysis takes place. Sizable investments are made over a period of years on the doubtful assumption that "all life insurance companies are alike, so why worry." Apparently the word of the agent that "my company is very sound," is all that is needed to persuade the buyer of the financial worth of the insurer represented.

Study of Financial Data

A study of which is the best life insurer often revolves around deciding between two or three companies whose policies are currently being considered for purchase. It would not be feasible for any but the largest purchasers to make a comprehensive analysis of the 1,800 life insurance companies writing business in the United States today. In the selection process, the same general principles that have been discussed in connection with property and liability insurers, can be applied but with certain differences in emphasis.

Comparison of Contracts

To be certain that one is making a valid comparison between two insurers, one must be sure that the contract desired is the same in each case. It is the problem of determining whether or not the contracts are identical that is probably the most difficult one in the field of life insurance. This problem is less complex in property-liability insurance because, generally, policy standardization has proceeded to a greater extent in that field, and the contracts are of much shorter duration. Furthermore, it is less costly to shift from one insurer to another in property-liability insurance than it is in life insurance. This is true because the first year's acquisition cost in a life insurance policy is heavy, usually exceeding the annual premium. Taking out a life insurance policy one year and dropping it the next is an expensive precedure. This makes a careful selection of the life insurer all the more important. Once it has been determined that the contracts are identical, the factors of cost, financial strength of the insurer, and matters of service can be considered in order to arrive at some decision regarding the best insurer.

Cost

If it is determined that two contracts are sufficiently alike to warrant a comparison of cost, the next step is to compare the gross premiums charged. At this point there is an adjustment that must be made, depending upon whether either of the insurers is offering a participating rate or a nonparticipating rate. The term *participating* refers to the common practice of making an overcharge in the premium with the idea of returning a dividend to the policyholder. Both stock and mutual insurers write participating policies, but the practice is much more common with mutuals. Stock insurers generally offer a *nonparticipating* rate; that is, a rate lower than the participating rate, but at a fixed level. The purpose of the higher participating rate is to provide a margin for contingencies. The insurer in life insurance generally guarantees for life the initial rate charged. Thus, if costs rise, the insurer has no opportunity to increase the premium. By means of charging a higher initial rate than actually required, the insurer can be protected so that if insurance costs rise, the costs can be passed on to the individuals involved through smaller dividends. If insurance costs fall, these same individuals can enjoy larger dividends. In the case of stock insurers writing nonparticipating insurance, it is expected that if insurance costs rise, stockholders will bear any losses, while if insurance costs fall, they will receive the resulting profits.

What are the elements of cost in life insurance? There are three: mortality, interest, and overhead or loading. The insurer with the lowest rate of mortality experience, with the highest rate of interest earned on policyholders' funds over a period of years, and with the lowest cost of doing business will be the lowest cost insurer, *other things being equal.* Unfortunately, it is seldom possible to hold other factors constant.

Mortality. The element of mortality in the cost of life insurance refers to the death rate among policyholders. Since many companies base their life insurance premiums on the same mortality table, one might expect few, if any, differences to arise from this source of cost. It is possible, however, for one insurer to be more restrictive in its underwriting than another and thus experience a lower rate of mortality. Unfortunately, since published figures on mortality experience are not generally available, the average person cannot easily obtain comparisons on this point. It is sometimes possible to obtain information directly from the insurer's actuary about a particular company's mortality rate in a given year compared to the mortality rate assumed in the established mortality table. Since death benefits are of great importance in the company's total outlay, differences in mortality rates can be very significant in judging cost.

Interest. Life insurers as a group earned 6% on invested assets in 1973, excluding assets held in separate accounts.[12] However, returns vary considerably among individual insurers. An insurer earning 7% on its assets is very likely to be able to offer its customers higher cash values, higher dividends, or broader

[12] *Life Insurance Fact Book 1974*, p. 60.

coverage than an insurer earning only 3%. The sum of $100 invested annually at 3% for 10 years accumulates to $1,180. At 7% the $100 accumulates to $1,478, a difference of $298, or nearly 25% more.

Another consideration lies in the major reasons for a higher interest return among certain insurers. An insurer earning only 3% interest return may have most of its assets invested in cash and government bonds. The probable reason for this pattern of investment is that the company may write largely term and group life insurance, which have little or no investment element. Thus, the firm has relatively little need for long-term investment or for emphasizing a larger interest return. The matter of interest return would be of relatively little importance to this firm's major customers. It can be seen that even among recommended companies there are substantial differences in the factors of interest earnings and expense of doing business.

Overhead or Loading. For the year 1973 overhead expenses averaged 16.9% of premiums for all life insurance companies, made up of 7.0% for agents' commissions and 9.9% for other expenses. Variations among individual insurers are wide, although comprehensive data are not available for a thorough analysis of these variations. Some of the differences in expense can be accounted for by differences in distribution efficiency. Some insurers spend substantial sums for the specific selection, training, and supervision of their agency force. Others spend very little. It is logical that, in the long run, the insurer which has the most efficient agency plant can secure business at the lowest cost. For example, higher commissions are needed to attract agents and brokers who receive no training or other aid. Turnover among such agents and brokers is higher, thus necessitating greater hiring costs. Normally the expenses of the firm with the greatest volume of business will be lower than those of firms with relatively small volumes. This is true because the fixed costs can be spread over a larger volume. This factor favors the large insurer. Expenses of insurers employing no agents should be expected to be lower than those of companies with large agency plants. However, there are relatively few life insurers who operate without agents, as pointed out in Chapter 20.

Dividend Comparisons. To aid the prospective policyholder in estimating the cost of life insurance, mutual companies usually publish scales of estimated dividends, based on past performance with respect to the three elements of cost discussed above. The total dividends for say, twenty years, are subtracted from the total premiums to be paid in, and the difference is represented as the cost of the insurance policy. Sometimes the agent subtracts from this figure the cash value of the policy and represents any difference to be the final net cost.

A comparison of projected with actual dividends often reveals considerable variations. For example, Table 6–1 reveals that among ten of the large life insurers in the U.S., insurers' dividends actually paid over the period 1954–1974 were higher than those projected by an average of 30%. The average projected dividend was about 24% of the premiums, while the actual dividend was about 31% of premiums. Table 6–1 shows how insurers ranked on the "net cost" of their policies, based on both projected and actual dividends. Net cost is defined

Table 6-1

DIVIDEND PROJECTIONS AND COSTS OF INSURANCE, 1954-1974, LEADING LIFE INSURERS

	Projected				Actual			
Company	20-Year Premium[1]	20-Year DIV	Net Cost[2]	Net Cost Rank	20-Year DIV	Net Cost	Net Cost Rank	Interest Adjusted Cost Rank[3]
Aetna Life	$559.20	$167.27	$19.93	8	$191.63	$ (4.43)	9	8
Banker's Life of Iowa	510.60	140.79	8.81	4	172.08	(22.48)	5	1
Connecticut General	553.40	120.67	60.73	10	186.82	(5.42)	8	6
Continental Assurance	557.40	140.07	45.33	9	172.69	12.71	10	10
Equitable Life Assurance Soc.	468.20	89.47	(3.27)	1	128.48	(41.96)	1	2
John Hancock	507.60	128.62	8.15	3	166.62	(39.34)	3	4
Massachusetts Mutual	553.00	176.94	13.62	5	215.82	(25.26)	4	3
Metropolitan	500.00	87.98	14.02	6	114.58	(13.58)	7	9
New York Life	471.80	87.14	(1.34)	2	126.04	(40.24)	2	5
Prudential Life	488.00	88.94	17.06	7	125.74	(19.74)	6	7
Average	$516.90	$122.79			$160.05			
Dividends/Premium		23.8%			31.0%			

Source: *Best's Review, Life Edition*, December, 1974, pp. 45-50. Percentages calculated.

[1] Ordinary life insurance policy, male age 35.

[2] Net cost = 20 years Premiums − 20th year cash value − 20 years dividends.

[3] Rank among the 10 insurers presented in this table.

as the 20-year gross premium – cash value – dividends. There were only minor changes in the ranks among the 10 insurers on net cost. The Equitable Life Assurance Society of New York ranked lowest on net cost on both scales, while Connecticut General ranked tenth on the projected dividend scale, but eighth on the actual dividend paid.

A calculation such as that given in Table 6–1 may lead the buyer to believe that insurance has been provided at little or no net cost and that comparisons of cost are of little importance. This, of course, is an incorrect assumption. The insurer has no secret gold mine or oil well out of which to pay for insurance service. Insurance is provided by contributions of the insured group and by interest earnings on the funds that are pooled. The low or negative net cost figures given in Table 6–1 reflect the fact that the policyholder has foregone interest earnings which would have been received if the money had not been used to pay a higher premium. What has happened is that the insurance company has taken the policyholders' funds and earned interest on them, which has been almost sufficient to pay for the insurance service and death claims. The insurance buyer should be cautioned that dividend projections are only estimates and are not guaranteed. An insurer could easily show a superior estimated performance by exaggerating its future dividend scales. Small changes in interest earnings, expenses, or mortality costs could cause significant changes in these dividends, as demonstrated in Table 6–1.

Interest-Adjusted Method. A more scientific way to estimate the true costs of life insurance is the interest-adjusted method. This method considers the time value of money. Under it, the interest earnings lost by the insurance buyer on premiums devoted to life insurance are counted as part of the cost. The last two columns of Table 6–1 show how the ten large insurers ranked by using both the traditional net-cost and the interest-adjusted methods. Several rank changes are evident. For example, Banker's Life Insurance Company of Iowa was fifth on the net-cost method, but first on the interest-adjusted method, while New York Life was second on the net cost, but fifth on interest-adjusted cost.

One may appreciate the difference between the net cost and the interest-adjusted method of calculating life insurance costs by considering the following example of two insurers, *A* and *B*.

	Dividends Plus Cash Values	
	Insurer	
Years	*A*	*B*
1	$ 100	$ 0
5	500	300
10	1,000	600
15	1,500	1,400
20	2,000	2,000

Each policy pays the policyholder $2,000 by the end of the 20th year, but Insurer *B* offers much lower interim values. Insurer *A* would have a lower interest-adjusted cost than Insurer *B* because of the time value of money.

Shoppers' Guides. Consumer guides to insurance are available giving cost ranks and other information on various insurers. Used carefully, these guides can be of considerable assistance to the buyer, particularly in eliminating weaker and high-cost insurers. For example, the second edition of the *Shopper's Guide to Straight Life Insurance,* published by the Pennsylvania Insurance Department in 1973, gave interest-adjusted cost rankings of $10,000 and $25,000 straight life participating life insurance policies for the 35 largest insurers operating in Pennsylvania. It ranked the highest and lowest cost participating companies among all insurers in the state, and also gave rankings for nonparticipating insurance and term insurance. Three age levels were covered—ages 20, 35, and 50. The guide effectively demonstrates that the same gross premium does not necessarily mean the same cost, that different premiums do not necessarily mean different costs, and that the same cost and premium do not necessarily mean equal cash values or dividends. In using shoppers' guides, one should examine carefully the methods and assumptions made in the calculations. Affected insurers should be contacted to see that these methods and assumptions are justified in the light of the insurer's current practices.

In summary, although there are substantial differences in costs among insurers, there is no easy or quick way in which an average buyer can determine the lowest cost insurer in life insurance.[13] As an initial guide one can determine which insurer appears to have the lowest expense ratio and the highest average rate of interest return on investments. If possible, a further investigation of mortality experience would be valuable. Net-cost comparisons can be very misleading and should probably be either completely avoided or interpreted with extreme care because of the inherent difficulties of forecasting cost results. Finally, cost should not be considered in isolation, since the elements of financial strength must also be carefully weighed.

Financial Strength

In life insurance, probably the two most important elements of financial strength are: the safety of the investments, and the relative size of policyholders' surplus, which includes all types of reserves for contingencies and any contributed capital of the owners.

Safety of the Investments. Investment data for life insurers are reported by several rating agencies that gather information from the annual statements furnished by each insurer to the commissioner of insurance in each state in which the insurer operates. The information is public and any analyst can obtain it directly by inquiring at the state insurance commissioner's office.

[13] One relatively scientific method of determining the cost of existing life insurance to the policyowner has been outlined by Joseph M. Belth in "The Cost of Life Insurance to the Policy Owner—A Single Year Attained Age System," *Journal of Insurance* (December, 1961), pp. 23-31. This method, while as good as any the author has observed, involves more arithmetic than the average policyowner is likely to be willing or able to undertake. The method also involves making estimates of dividends and so is subject to error from this source.

The record of investment safety in the life insurance industry is one of the best of all industries in the United States. For example, during the depression period from 1929 to 1939, only 19 life insurance companies, representing about 5% of all companies then operating, retired with initial losses to policyholders of $1 million or more. The initial losses totalled $130 million, 50% of which was later recovered as other companies took over the retired insurers' business. In the same period, 12,000 banks were reported to have failed, with loss to depositors of $3 billion.[14] The final losses to policyholders of life insurers were approximately .2% of the average assets of the companies then operating. It seems fair to state that this record of safety has reduced the risk of loss to policyholders as close to zero as is feasible for any type of saving under modern conditions.

Relative Size of Policyholders' Surplus. The adequacy of reserves may be studied for life insurers in the same manner as for property-liability insurers. The ratio of policyholders' surplus to total assets may be compared with the average for the industry, and any existing trends determined. For example, in 1973 this ratio was about 2% for stocks and 11% for mutuals in the life insurance field.[15] Compared to property-liability insurers, life insurers operate with net worth which is much smaller in proportion to reserve liabilities. This is due to several factors, chief among which is the more stable and predictable loss experience in life insurance compared to property-liability insurance. Life insurers also have a much larger proportion of total assets invested in conservative securities such as bonds and mortgages than is true for property-liability insurers.

Ratings of Financial Services. The analyst of a life insurer's financial strength should also consult opinions of rating agencies such as Best or Dunne. These opinions encompass the quality of the investments, net cost of insurance to the buyer, significant operating ratios, and management efficiency. For the most favorably situated insurers, a "policyholders' recommendation" is given by Best, summarizing Best's opinion of the results and safety margins of the insurer. For example, the top Best rating states, "The results achieved by the company have been most favorable. In our opinion it has *most substantial* over-all margins for contingencies. Upon the foregoing analysis of the present position we recommend this company." For insurers of lesser stature, Best uses the adjectives "very substantial," and "considerable." If the rating is omitted entirely, the insurer is not considered to be sufficiently strong, its history may be too short (less than five years), or insufficient information was available for a rating. Best does not rate fraternals or assessment associations.

For insurers with the two lowest ratings (substantial and considerable) and for new, small insurers about which little information is available, the potential

[14] A. M. Best, "Rating in the Financial Structure of Insurance Companies," *Administrative Problems in Corporate Insurance Buying*, Insurance Series No. 96 (New York: American Management Association, 1952), p. 8.

[15] Calculated from data in *Life Insurance Fact Book 1974*, p. 66.

policyholder is advised to use caution before committing long-term insurance and financial planning programs to them. In all doubtful cases the policyholder should contact the insurance commissioner in this state for further information and opinion.

Service

The element of service in the selection of a life insurer has two aspects: the amount of service to be obtained from the agent, and the amount of service to be obtained from the home office of the insurer. The element of service in life insurance is fully as important as in property-liability insurance, although it is not often recognized as such.

Service from the Agent. The agent can act merely as an order taker, or can develop and maintain over the years a comprehensive plan of insurance design to meet the unique needs of the client. The agent can personally write letters on behalf of the customer, take care of details such as beneficiary changes, and handle premium collections as a convenience to the client, or the agent can ignore demands for aid or refer the client to the home office for answers. The agent can sell a policy that comes closest to meeting the real needs of the client or one that nets the greatest commission, regardless of whether the policy is appropriate.

No matter what quality of service is obtained, the premium is the same, so it behooves the insurance buyer to determine how much in the way of service can be expected of an agent. The variations in service can spell the difference between a satisfactory insurance arrangement and one that fails to accomplish for the insured many things which are possible, but which oftentimes the insured does not know of at all. In judging the degree and quality of service that may be received from an agent, one can get some indication by the methods employed in selling the coverage; evidence of professional accomplishments such as possession of the CLU designation:[16] length of time the agent has been in the business; and references from outside impartial sources.

Service from the Home Office. Service from the home office of the insurer is very important. The life insurance policy often is a long-term contract involving thirty or forty years of premium payments, and twenty or more additional years of annuity payments either to the insured or to beneficiaries. The dispatch with which these payments are handled is vital to the success of the insurance plan. Insurance companies often pride themselves on paying death claims of thousands of dollars within hours after the proof of loss has been submitted. Because agents come and go, the service of the insurer as a continuing influence over the years is of greater importance than it would be if the insured could deal with one agent indefinitely.

[16] CLU stands for Chartered Life Underwriter. This designation is given by the American College of Life Underwriters, Bryn Mawr, Pennsylvania, after the full-time life insurance agent has passed a series of ten comprehensive examinations in life insurance and related fields.

SUMMARY

1. Since not all companies writing insurance are alike in such matters as price of the product, financial strength, and quantity and quality of services offered, the prudent insurance buyer will make an analysis of the particular insurer before entrusting it with his financial security.
2. The first step in the intelligent selection of an insurer is to make sure that each insurer to be analyzed offers a comparable insurance contract. The factors of the cost of insurance, the financial strength and stability, and the quantity and quality of services offered are all interrelated. The final selection of the insurer should be withheld until all factors have been studied.
3. Some notion concerning the cost of the insurance service may be obtained by an examination of the ratio of losses and expenses to premiums earned for individual insurers and resulting underwriting gains or losses.
4. Examination of published underwriting experience of stock and mutual insurers reveals no consistent cost differences according to type of organization.
5. The financial strength of an insurer may be judged by the ratio of policyholders' surplus to liabilities, by Best's ratings, by the adequacy of reserves for contingencies, by the soundness of investments, and by the trends in loss and expense ratios. The tests should be compared for several continuous years.
6. Quantity and quality of service rendered, economy, and convenience in the administration of one's insurance program are important factors in the selection of an insurer or agent. Studies reveal considerable dissatisfaction with some agents, brokers, and insurance services. The individual needs of each buyer should be weighed in selecting agents or insurers.
7. The sound selection of a life insurer involves the same general pattern of analysis as is true in selecting a property liability insurer. Special care should be taken to see that the contracts being considered are identical, that misleading dividend comparisons are avoided, and that the interest earnings on the assets are considered. The personal service rendered by an agent differs widely in life insurance and is a significant factor in the selection of a particular insurer. Willingness of the home office to render aid in fitting life insurance to the individual needs of the buyer is also an important factor.

QUESTIONS FOR REVIEW AND DISCUSSION

1. A writer stated, "Insurance company insolvencies have caused a clamor for some method under which claimants against insolvent companies would be paid for their losses. The number of insurance companies that have failed in recent years has been small, but it is the number of policyholders affected that causes the clamor rather than the number of insolvencies."
   (a) Look up the statute in your state to determine the nature of the insurance company insolvency law, if any, and report on its provisions.
   (b) Do you believe insolvency statutes should apply to insurers only or should they relieve any creditors, such as creditors of a retail store, of loss from insolvency of the debtor? Discuss.
   (c) Should insolvency plans be financed by all insurance buyers,

through higher premiums, or by general tax revenues? Discuss.

2. Is there anything inherent in the legal organization of an insurer that would tend to make a given type of insurer superior over another type in: (a) management, (b) cost, (c) financial strength? Discuss.
3. Often the problem of selecting an insurer is solved by a diligent search to find a company that will accept the buyer's application. Explain why this might be true.
4. *A* argues that the insurer with a high loss ratio is actually more desirable than one with a low loss ratio because a high loss ratio is the best evidence that management is returning to the policyholder group a larger proportion of the premium dollar than the company with a low loss ratio. Criticize this argument.
5. Explain the terms:
   (a) Loss ratio.
   (b) Expense ratio.
   (c) Net underwriting profit.
6. Why is it true that the loss ratio of an insurer writing at a lower premium than another may be larger even though actual losses are identical? What significance does this have in the analysis of mutual company figures?
7. Consult a service such as *Best's Insurance Reports* to obtain a list of insurers that have discontinued business in the previous year. Develop a classification of the reasons for discontinuance. What light does this investigation throw on the problem of financial strength of insurance companies?
8. "The most significant single ratio that tests the financial strength of an insurer is the ratio of policyholders' surplus to total liabilities." Explain the logic behind such a ratio.
9. The text states, "Insurance is a service in which the cost must be estimated in advance by the insurer." Explain the significance of this statement with regard to the problem of selecting insurers on the basis of prices quoted for coverage.
10. Explain why a 1:1 ratio of policyholders' surplus to total liabilities means $2 of assets behind each $1 of liabilities.
11. Under what conditions should an analyst be satisfied with a ratio lower than 1:1 for a fire insurance company?
12. One insurance manager attempts to buy from insurers with substantial underwriting profits, while another manager believes that buying from insurers just breaking even on underwriting is best. With whose point of view do you sympathize? Explain.
13. Jack is seeking automobile insurance for a fleet of cars and his agent recommends the policies of the Maine Insurance Co., Portland, Me., whose financial data Jack immediately looks up in *Best's Key Rating Guide*. He discovers the following facts:

Total assets	$4,301,000
Policyholders' surplus	$1,723,000
Loss reserves	1,226,000
Unearned premium reserves	1,168,000
Net premiums written	4,289,000
Underwriting losses, last 5 years	(832,000)
Underwriting loss, latest year	(555,000)
Investment gains, last 5 years	362,000
Investment gains, latest year	138,000

(a) Calculate the ratio of net worth to debt. Explain the meaning of this ratio. How does it compare with industry averages?
(b) Calculate the ratio of premiums to net worth. Explain the meaning of this ratio.
(c) Assess the significance of the underwriting results of this insurer to Jack.
(d) On the basis of your analysis would you recommend that Jack

accept his agent's recommendation? Under what conditions? Discuss.

14. What advantages and disadvantages are inherent in the use of Best's ratings as a measure of the financial strength of insurers?

15. An insurer of property-liability lines reports the following financial information for the latest operating year: Premiums written, $10 million; losses and expenses, $11 million. Ratio of premiums written to policyholders' surplus, 10:1.
(a) What is the apparent surplus position of the insurer?
(b) If losses and expenses had been $9 million, what would the insurer's surplus position have been?
(c) How do your answers to (a) and (b) above illustrate the advantages and disadvantages of high financial leverage? Explain.
(d) How does this example explain the caution exhibited by many insurers in accepting new insurance business?

16. (a) In life insurance, what is the advantage of a nonparticipating rate?
(b) Of a participating rate?
(c) Which do you prefer? Why?

17. What are the three elements of cost in life insurance? For each element, indicate how possible future trends might affect the cost of life insurance.

18. What dangers exist in selecting a life insurer on the basis of net-cost illustrations?

19. In what ways does the analysis of the financial strength of a life insurer differ from that of a property insurer?

20. (a) Referring to Table 6–1, calculate the dollar difference in net cost for the purchaser of a $20,000 ordinary life insurance policy among the insurers ranked one and ten on net cost. Is the difference significant to an average buyer?
(b) Using Table C–2, page 670, calculate the net difference in value between two contracts, the first promising a dividend and cash value total of $1,000 in 10 years, and the second offering $1,000 total in 15 years if money is worth 6%? What is the relationship of this calculation to the interest-adjusted method of figuring the cost of life insurance? Explain.

21. Why has the life insurance industry achieved such a good record of financial strength over the years?

22. The Pennsylvania Insurance Department *Shopper's Guide* revealed that for a male age 20 for $10,000 of nonparticipating, straight life insurance The Travelers Insurance Company and the Surety Life Insurance Company each quoted an annual premium of $118. However, the 20-year interest-adjusted cost index for Travelers was $3.77 compared to $6.29 for Surety Life. Since neither policy pays dividends, account for the different rankings on interest-adjusted cost.

23. A pilot purchased a long-term, noncancellable, disability income policy from an insurer with a clause giving the right to obtain a refund of 80% of the premium if the policy is kept 10 years. This clause increased the regular premium by 30%. After seven years, the insured received a letter from the insurer offering a full refund of the 30% extra premium, stating that it had found the benefit "uneconomical" to keep in force. The insurer itself was in financial difficulties, but made no reference to this fact in the letter.
(a) What action should the pilot take?
(b) How might such a difficulty have been avoided?

Chapter *Seven*

FUNCTIONS AND ORGANIZATION OF INSURERS

One of the most difficult and challenging problems faced by business lies in the area of organization. The insurance industry is certainly no exception to this statement. Since World War II the insurance industry has been undergoing a basic change in its internal organization structure, a change which some say has raised more problems than it has solved. To understand the reason for these changes it is necessary to see what an insurance company does, why it does it, and what alternatives there are in the way functions may be performed.

FUNCTIONS OF INSURERS

The functions performed by any insurer necessarily depend on the type of business it writes, the degree to which it has shifted certain duties to others, the financial resources available, the size of the insurer, the type of organization used, and other factors. Nevertheless, it is possible to describe the usual functions that are carried out, and it should be remembered that the specific nature and extent of each function varies somewhat from insurer to insurer. These functions are normally the responsibility of definite departments or divisions within the firm. The chief activities that are carried on by insurers are:

1. Production (selling).
2. Underwriting (selection of risks).
3. Rate-making and statistical control.
4. Managing claims.
5. Investing and financing.
6. Accounting and other record keeping.
7. Providing certain miscellaneous services, such as legal aid, marketing research, engineering services, and personnel management.

Production

One of the most vital functions of an insurance firm is securing a sufficient number of applicants for insurance to enable the company to operate. This function, usually called *production* in an insurance company, corresponds to the sales function in an industrial firm. The term production is a proper one for insurance because the act of selling an insurance policy is production in its true sense. Insurance is an intangible item and does not exist until a policy is sold.

The production department of any insurer supervises the relationships with agents in the field. In firms, such as direct writers, where a high degree of control over field activities is maintained, the production department recruits, trains, and supervises the agents or salespersons. Its responsibility runs deeper than this, however. Many insurers support marketing research departments whose job is to assist the production department in the planning of marketing activities, such as determining market potentials, designing and supervising advertising, conducting surveys to ascertain consumer attitudes toward the company's services, and forecasting sales volume.[1]

In firms using independent agents as the primary channel of distribution, the extensive use of facilitating services in the production of business is not common. Special agents are used to explain company policies and to serve as the chief point of contact between the home office and the field forces. The chief job of selling is left to the independent agency force.

Underwriting

Underwriting insurance has to do with all the activities necessary to select risks offered to the insurer in such a manner that general company objectives are fulfilled. Underwriting is performed by home office personnel who scrutinize applications for coverage and make decisions as to whether they will be accepted, and by agents who produce the applications initially in the field. The location in the organizational structure of authority to make final underwriting decisions varies considerably between insurers and between lines of insurance. In some organizations (generally in the property-liability insurance area) agents can make binding decisions in the field, but these decisions may be subject to post underwriting at the home office because the contracts are cancellable upon due notice to the insured. In life insurance, agents seldom have authority to make binding underwriting decisions. In all fields of insurance, however, agency personnel usually do considerable screening of risks before they are submitted to home office underwriters. In some companies agents are often referred to as underwriters.

The Objective of Underwriting. The main objective of underwriting is to see that the applicants accepted will have a loss experience similar to that assumed when the rates were formulated. To this end, certain standards of selection relating to physical and moral hazards are set up when rates are calculated, and the underwriter must see that these standards are observed when a risk is accepted. For example, it may have been decided that a company will accept

[1] A study of these activities among insurers was made by the author and was reported in "Marketing Research As an Aid to Insurance Management," *Journal of Insurance* (December, 1957).

no fire exposures situated in agricultural areas or will take no one for life insurance who has had tuberculosis within a period of five years.

The underwriter, in reviewing an application for fire insurance where a building is located at the edge of an agricultural area or in reviewing an application for life insurance in which the individual had tuberculosis four and one-half years ago, asks the question: "Can I make an exception for these applications, or must I reject them because they do not come within the technical limitations of my instructions?" In answering these questions, the underwriter visualizes what would happen to the company's loss experience if a very large number of identical risks were to be accepted. If the aggregate experience would be very unfavorable, the underwriter will probably reject the applications.

In sound underwriting, it is recognized that while profitable business is an important object, it is a mistake to accept only business in which it is extremely certain that no losses will occur. To do so would no doubt make the job of the producer more difficult, if not impossible, and would mean too low a volume of business to support operations. As in many things, a happy medium must be sought between the extremes of very safe and very hazardous exposures on which to write insurance.

Services That Aid the Underwriter. In life insurance the underwriter is assisted by medical reports from the physician who made the examination of the applicant, by statements made by the applicant, by information from the agent, by an independent report (called an inspection report) on the applicant prepared by an outside agency created for that purpose, as well as by advice from the company's own medical advisor. In fire and liability insurance (as well as life insurance), the underwriter has the services of reinsurance facilities, mapping departments to report on the degree of concentration of exposures in any one area, and credit departments to report on the financial standing of applicants.

Company Procedures That Aid the Underwriter. The underwriter is also guided by fairly definite company procedures regarding the various physical and moral hazards that affect the probability of loss in given lines of business. In fire insurance, for example, a great deal of assistance is given by the rules that set up definite classes of building with definite characteristics, such as type of construction, type of occupancy, degree of protection by city services, and exposure to various physical hazards. Unless there is something unusual about the structure or its occupancy, there is very little problem of selection because most of the important underwriting decisions have already been made. In assessing the moral hazard, however, serious problems may arise for which few rules have been promulgated. One rule that is widely observed is that if a serious moral hazard is known to exist, the business is rejected outright and no attempt is made to accept it at higher than normal rates or to impose other restrictions. The difficulty lies in judging whether or not a moral hazard actually exists. Judgment of the underwriter is of paramount importance to the general success of any insurance company, and in the matter of assessing the moral hazard the quality of the underwriter's judgment is put to one of its severest tests.

Policy Writing. Part of the work of the underwriting department may be most concisely described as *policy writing*. In property and liability insurance, the agent frequently issues the policy to the customer, filling out forms provided by the company. For this reason, the agent is often termed an underwriter. A check upon the work of the agent to determine the accuracy of rates charged, whether or not a prohibited risk has been taken, and other matters is done by the *examining section* in the home office of the insurer. In life insurance, the policy is usually written in a special department, whose main task is to issue written contracts in accordance with instructions from the underwriting department and, since most policies are long-term in nature, to keep a register of them for future reference.

Conflict Between Production and Underwriting. Because the underwriting department has often turned down business that has been previously sold by an agent, an apparent conflict of interest has arisen between these two areas. The problem is similar to that which exists between credit and sales in other firms, with a good sale ruined because credit is not approved. The conflict is, of course, only apparent. Neither the agent nor the underwriter will profit long by too strict or too loose underwriting. Too strict underwriting will tend to choke off acceptable business and may create unnecessary expenses involved in cancelling business already bound by the agent. Too loose underwriting may involve losses of such substantial size that the company may be forced to withdraw entirely from a given line, to the detriment of the agent.

Rate-Making and Statistical Control

Closely allied to the function of underwriting is that of *rate-making*, a function which is extremely technical in most lines of insurance. (The details of rate-making will be discussed in Chapter 26.)

Rate-Making. In general, rate-making involves first the selection of classes of exposure units on which to collect statistics regarding the probability of loss. In life insurance this particular task is relatively uncomplicated since the major task is to estimate mortality rates according to age and sex, and, in some cases, by occupational groups. In other fields, such as fire and workers' compensation, very elaborate classifications are necessary. In the latter field, for example, several hundred classes of industries are distinguished and a rate is promulgated for each.

Once the appropriate classes have been set up, the problem becomes one of developing reliable data for each class over a sufficiently long period of time. Converting the data thus accumulated into a useful form for the purpose of developing a final premium becomes the next step. This involves incorporating estimates of the cost of doing business into the premium structure on an equitable basis. The rate-making function involves estimation of the cost of including certain policy benefits, or of changing policy provisions or underwriting rules, as well as the cost of writing business on which no data whatsoever have been accumulated.

Actuarial Services. The rate-maker must have considerable skill in solving the various mathematical problems that face the insurer, a class of problems described as *actuarial*. It is through actuarial services that estimates can be made of the real meaning of data collected by the company from inside and outside sources. For example, if losses begin to rise in a certain class of business, does this mean that the rates will have to be restudied and revised upward, and if so, by how much? Or are such losses evidence of a mere random experience for which no significant conclusions can be drawn? What are the necessary sizes of the various reserves that must be provided? What results can be expected in losses and premiums if a new underwriting policy is followed, if a different accounting method or loss table is used, if there is a change in the investment earnings of the company? Solutions to these and many other questions are usually sought from the actuary.

Statistical Control. By its very nature, statistical control is vital to the success of insurance management. Not only are valid statistics required by tax and regulatory authorities, but, as will be seen, these data are essential to various rate-making organizations. The compilation of industry-wide statistics is necessary, in order that actuarially sound rates can be made. Few industries rely on such statistics to the extent that the insurance industry does. The insurance industry was among the first to utilize advanced computers to perform the many tasks required of accounting and statistical departments.

Managing Claims

Settling losses under insurance contracts and adjusting any differences that arise between the company and the policyholder describe the function of *claims management*. Claims management is often accomplished in the field through independent adjusters who are employed to negotiate certain types of settlements on the spot. Such adjusters sometimes have considerable legal training. The claims department of an insurer will have the responsibility of ascertaining the validity of written proofs of loss, investigating the scene of the loss, estimating the amount of the loss, interpreting and applying the terms of the policy in loss situations, and finally approving payment of the claim. These functions are more extensive in property liability insurance than in life insurance because of the higher frequency of losses, the predominance of partial losses, and the uncertainty of the amount of loss in individual cases.

The felicitous management of claim settlements is of paramount importance to the success of an insurer. Reluctant claims settlement brings with it public ill will, which may take years to overcome.[2] Oftentimes, negotiations with the claims department is the only direct contact that the insurance buyer has with the insurer. A bad impression received on that occasion may result in loss of business, court action, regulatory censure, or even suspension of the right to

[2] As was stated by one authority: "There is nothing quite so private as public relations. The insurance profession must handle each loss with every person in a satisfactory way. Public relations is the stone stalagmite and personal experience is the drop of water that builds the stone."

carry on business in the jurisdiction involved. On the other hand, an overly liberal claims settlement policy may ultimately result in higher rate levels and loss of business through lower premiums charged by competitors.

Investing and Financing

When an insurance policy is written, the premium is generally paid in advance for periods varying from six months to five or more years. This advance payment of premiums gives rise to funds held for policyholders by the insurer, funds that must be invested in some manner. Every insurance company has such funds, as well as funds representing paid-in capital, accumulated surplus, and various types of reserves. Selecting and supervising the appropriate investment medium for these assets is the function of the *investment department*. Investment income is a vital factor to the success of any insurer. In life insurance, solvency of the insurer depends on earning a minimum guaranteed return on assets. In property and liability insurance, investment income has accounted for a very substantial portion of total profits and has served to offset frequent underwriting losses.

Since the manner in which insurance moneys are invested is the subject of somewhat intricate government regulation, the investment manager must be familiar with all the laws of the various states in which the company operates. Investments must also be selected with due regard to the financial policies of the insurer. Property insurers typically have a combined capital and surplus ranging between 30% and 50% of total assets, and funds equivalent to this may be invested in common and preferred stocks. The extent to which this is done depends upon the class of business written and upon the need for liquidity. Life insurers, on the other hand, have few of their assets invested in common and preferred stocks, primarily because the nature of the life insurance obligation dictates that guaranteed amounts be repaid to policyholders.[3] To accomplish this, bonds and mortagages are usually selected as the major investment medium. Large insurers have separate departments for major classes of investments, such as for real estate loans, policy loans, and city mortgages.

Financing refers to the planning and control of all activities that are related to the supplying of funds to the firm. Normally in insurance, few outside funds have to be raised since most of the normal financing requirements are met by reinvested profits. However, problems such as determination of dividend policies, meeting state solvency requirements, and handling the occasional negotiations for both long- and short-term capital sources fall within the province of the chief financial officer.

Accounting

The accounting function for insurance management has essentially the same purpose as accounting for the operating results of any firm, namely, to record,

[3] Life insurers as a group had only 10.3% of their total assets invested in common and preferred stocks as of 1973. State laws impose definite restrictions on the extent to which life insurers may invest in these stocks.

classify, and interpret financial data in such a way as to guide management in its various policies.

Miscellaneous Functions

Various functions such as legal advice, marketing research, engineering services, and personnel work are often performed for an insurer by individuals or firms outside the company or by a specialized department set up within the company.

Legal Advice. The function of the legal adviser is to assist others in the company in their tasks. Underwriters receive aid in the preparation of policy contracts and endorsements so that the company's intention will be phrased in correct legal terminology. In the administration of claims, particularly in disputed claims, legal aid is important and if court action is required, the legal staff must represent the company.

Legal aid is required in drawing up agency contracts, in investigating bond indentures and real estate titles, in preparing reports to the insurance commissioner, and in advising on insurance legislation. Hardly any phase of an insurer's many activities can be effectively performed without competent legal advice. Most large insurers have their own legal departments. Others use outside counsel only. All companies use outside counsel on occasion.

Marketing Research. Reference has already been made to the role of marketing research in assisting the production department. As yet, marketing research is not usually performed within the firm, except in the case of very large companies. When carried on, the marketing research typically involves only selected types of research, such as testing and developing effective advertising. Such research can be a vital factor in the long-run success of any insurer. The success that direct-writing insurers have had in winning markets away from those insurers using the indirect channel of distribution has increased the interest of the latter in marketing research.

The role of marketing research is to narrow the area within which executive judgment must operate; that is, to make for more scientific decision making than is possible by merely playing hunches. Marketing research can assist management in many ways, and its usefulness is not confined to production alone. For example, one firm conducted psychological surveys among a sample of policyholders to determine what basic motivations existed that affected their behavior toward the insurer. Results of this and other research led the company to establish a program of policyholder participation in company decision making.

Engineering Services. Engineering services are utilized, particularly in the field of property insurance, as valuable aids to rate-making and underwriting. It is the function of the engineer to advise with respect to the conditions—that is, hazards—which make losses more likely. The services of the engineer in loss-prevention and salvage operations are extremely important to the insurance mechanism.

Information concerning the physical characteristics of exposed property is necessary for intelligent underwriting. Rate-making classifications are usually developed on the basis of physical characteristics, and rate charges and credits are made on this basis. For example, the engineer provides information that will help answer the question, "How long will fireproof glass resist breaking when subjected to the heat of a burning building?" If a building has such glass, the underwriter is in a much better position to assess its importance than that underwriter would be without such information. Again, the engineer may provide answers to the following questions: "How much money will it cost to restore a burned building to its former condition? Is it economically feasible to raise this sunken ship? For safety, in the event of an explosion, how far should an oil tank be placed from a building? Do seat belts really prevent or reduce injury in automobile accidents?" The usefulness of such information to the insurer is readily apparent.

Personnel Management. Personnel management normally includes selection and discharge of employees, keeping employment records, supervision of training and educational programs, administration of recreational and fringe benefit programs, and other similar functions. Most large companies and many small ones have separate personnel departments. Regardless of the size of the firm, personnel management is an essential function. Insurance, particularly life insurance, has experienced a somewhat more rapid turnover of employees than other industries. The need for giving increased attention to the problem of turnover and discovering the causes of this condition has increased the scope and importance of personnel management among insurance companies.

INTERNAL ORGANIZATION OF INSURERS

The matter under present consideration is that of deciding the best methods of organizing the concern in order that these functions may be performed most efficiently. Two major types of organization—internal and external—will be discussed. *Internal organization* problems are those relating to how the insurer controls and organizes its internal activities by such methods as the use of product divisions, territorial divisions, organization by groups or fleets, and multiple-line or all-line systems.

Territorial Organization

The type of organization used by a given insurer and the types of departments created depend upon the particular problems it faces. The most common basis is a centralized management with departments organized on a functional basis, as illustrated in Figure 7–1. However, other bases, such as territorial, are commonly used, often concurrently with the functional type. The insurer in Figure 7–1, for example, recognizes territorial organization in its underwriting of fire and marine lines.

An insurer may create branch offices for certain major geographical regions. Many insurers organized in the eastern part of the United States have

ORGANIZATION CHART OF LARGE STOCK INSURANCE GROUP, HANDLING ALL LINES

Figure 7-1

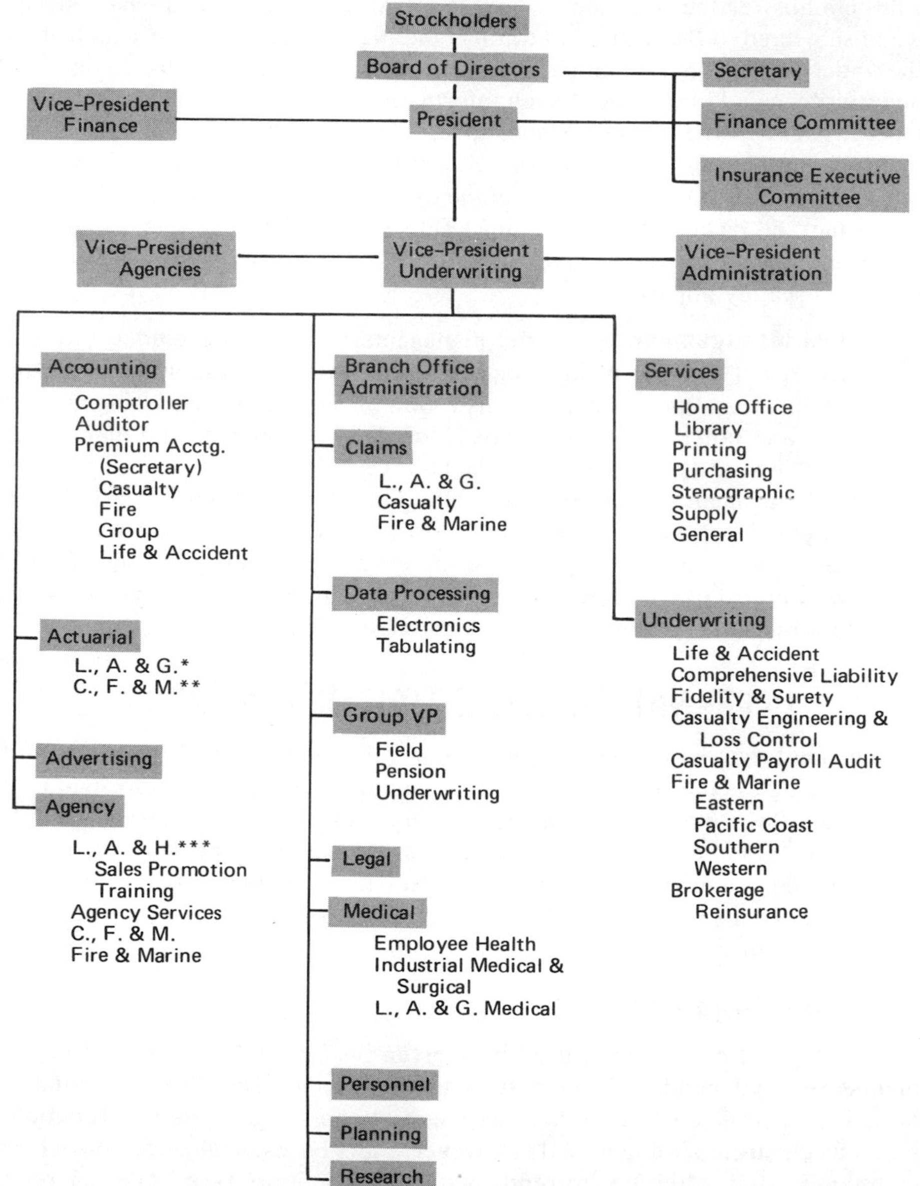

* Life, Accident, and Group.
** Casualty, Fire, and Marine.
*** Life, Accident, and Health.

established branch offices on the West Coast. Certain functions, such as investment and finance, legal, actuarial, and general accounting, are often carried out by a central office; while other functions, such as underwriting, claims, rate-making, and production are decentralized in each of the branches. Decentralization is a general practice when the size of distant markets increases to the point that it is more efficient to make certain decisions at a local level rather than to refer everything to a central office. An example of such a decision might be the underwriting of certain risks where frequent contact with the insured is necessary. Dealing from afar might be unwieldly, inefficient, and ultimately cause a loss of the business.

Product Organization

In some insurance operations, particularly among multiple-line insurers, the problems arising from differing classes of insurance are so technical and specialized that it is inefficient to have all types of business handled by the same staff. In these cases, the business may be organized according to product divisions. For example, as illustrated by Figure 7–1, the insurer may divide the underwriting function by line of business, in this case, life and accident, comprehensive liability, and fire and marine.

In a life insurance company, it is common to find separate divisions handling group life insurance, group disability insurance, industrial life insurance, and group pensions. Within each group, major functions such as underwriting, accounting, claims, production, and policyholder service may be performed, with other functions carried on by the home office.

In property and liability insurance, particularly in multiple-line companies, separate divisions are commonly created for the major types of insurance, such as fire, inland marine, bonding, liability, automobile, and workers' compensation. Again, each division will perform certain major operating functions and use the centralized facilities of the insurer for the service functions, such as actuarial, investment, legal, and general accounting. The degree of autonomy of product divisions varies with each firm, with some divisions being almost completely self-sufficient, and others being highly dependent on the centralized administration for service and for various aspects of decision making.

Group Organization

Insurance in the United States developed early along essentially specialized lines. It was felt by most organizers that the technical problems of underwriting insurance were such that they could be handled best by having each company concentrate on a given type of coverage. In this manner, each peril could be studied separately and more rapid progress in developing suitable methods of insuring could be developed than if the efforts of the company were spread out over all kinds of perils. Furthermore, it was believed that it would be easier for the states to determine more accurately the financial ability of the insurer to assume the risks that it intended to insure if its operations dealt with a single peril. Accordingly, most state laws were drawn up giving insurers authority to write only specific types of coverage, such as fire and allied lines, liability, bonds, and life insurance. Reserve requirements in each state generally differed, depending on what type of insurance was underwritten. Usually there were three types of companies—property, casualty, and life—whose underwriting authority was limited to specific kinds of insurance.

The Early Growth of Group Organization. In a system where a company is authorized to write only certain lines of insurance, several problems become apparent. A fire insurer might have built up an organization of agents that handled its business. The agents, however, might wish to sell all kinds of insurance. This necessitated the use of several different insurers. It was natural that the fire insurer would find it desirable to seek authority to broaden its offerings to include whatever its agents demanded. Since it could not offer all types of insurance itself, oftentimes it allied itself with a casualty insurer whose underwriting authority included the type of insurance needed. This alliance was usually accomplished by the formation of a "group" of companies with centralized management and common ownership. It was the motive of obtaining wider agency representation and of securing diversification of business that led to the initiation of group operations.

In 1947, the National Association of Insurance Commissioners, an association of insurance regulatory authorities, approved a recommendation to sponsor what became known as multiple-line legislation, which eliminated the statutory limitations that gave rise to group organization. Multiple-line laws, which have been adopted in every state, now permit insurers to write different classes of insurance within a single firm. Thus, it has been suggested that group-type management will cease to grow and many gradually be abandoned by the industry.

Importance of Group Organization Today. In spite of the advent of multiple-line and all-line powers, group organization in insurance management continues to be of great importance. There were approximately 135 stock company groups operating in 1974. The large fleets of insurers controlled a large majority of the total property and liability premium volume of all insurers. Furthermore, two thirds of the leading groups of insurers continue to handle a very large amount of life and health insurance business through controlled subsidiaries. It is estimated that half of all groups have one or more life companies.

Reasons for the Continuing Importance of Group Organization. There are several probable explanations for the continued importance of the group-type organization, even though the original reason for its formation no longer exists. First, there appear to be no compelling reasons to suggest that consolidation would necessarily be more efficient from a management viewpoint than the present system. In fact, the problems facing multiple-line operations are such that the evidence seems just the opposite. Except for certain functions, such as investment operations, general accounting, and top policy making, which can be performed more efficiently on a consolidated basis, it is likely that decentralized and separated managements are more satisfactory. Underwriting, for example, is still a relatively specialized task and often requires years of training before competency is achieved. In companies attempting to combine into one policy many types of coverage, underwriting problems have been difficult to solve because of the shortage of individuals competent to analyze more than one type of coverage. Certainly, to undertake an entirely new type or organization is expensive; and unless there is a strong likelihood of greater efficiency from it, reorganization would not be indicated.

Second, the present type of organization is particularly adaptable to experimentation with new underwriting techniques. In meeting the competition of direct-writing organizations, for example, many stock companies have formed subsidiary companies to try such innovations as continuous policy forms, direct billing, and new policy combinations. If successful, such experiments may be extended.

Third, present companies are decentralized geographically in many cases, and it would be difficult to consolidate effectively several companies organized in different states. Many such concerns have been advertised for years, and consolidation might mean the loss of this investment and the goodwill that it represents. Work force might be lost, and training capable replacements would be an expensive procedure.

Finally, there has been a trend for property insurance companies to enter the life insurance field. Multiple-line laws in most states, however, do not permit consolidated firms to sell life insurance along with other types. A separate organization is necessary. This requirement fits into the established pattern of group type organization.

Multiple-Line Organization

Companies commonly described as *multiple-line* are those firms that underwrite many types of property and liability insurance within the administrative framework of a single organization. Only rarely may such companies handle life insurance directly, but usually must do so through a separate company. The multiple-line type of organization is urged as a method of permitting the simplification of insurance contracts. It is felt by most insurance authorities, for example, that requiring a separate policy for every type of coverage is an inefficient technique and quite unnecessary. Why not combine, say, fire, windstorm, automobile, residence liability, residence burglary, and a personal property floater into one "package policy" designed for the homeowner, who would be able to have just one company, one policy, and one agent for most insurance needs? If this were possible, it is argued, the agent would have a much larger commission from personal lines and would be able to service each customer more satisfactorily than if having only a small portion of the customer's total business. Furthermore, the customer would be able to purchase many coverages that customer might not buy individually, thus enabling the insurer to obtain a wider spread of risks.

A disadvantage of the system of compartmentalization of insurance lines lies in the inflexibility that it introduces into the insurance business. An insurer can write only the lines in which it is specifically authorized. Thus, if a new type of insurance protection is needed, special authority must be sought in the state legislature before the coverage can be offered. As noted previously, all states have now passed multiple-line legislation.

As can be seen from the preceding discussion of group organization, the insurance industry has moved slowly in altering its basic organization form to accommodate the new multiple-line powers. It is not surprising that a type of organization that grew up over the last one hundred years, one to which the industry has adjusted, will not give way overnight to a new type. Multiple-line powers have created new problems for which solutions will be developed only gradually. Reference has already been made to the lack of trained personnel, particularly in underwriting. The lack of a body of statistical data on which to base rates for new policy combinations is another roadblock that will be overcome only as time permits the accumulation of data. New merchandising methods to accommodate the changed concept of insurance packages must be developed in such a way that existing agents can be used effectively and compensated fairly. Since a package policy involves new selling techniques and requires a substantial increase in the average premium charged per policy, devices such as premium financing and training tools for agency personnel must be developed by the industry. Finally, new methods of regulating multiple-line companies must be developed. Basic questions such as what should be the reserve requirements for the new package policies; how often should multiple-line companies be examined; how should rates that are fair, adequate, and not excessive be developed; and what new license requirements should be imposed for insurance agents—are examples of issues that must be resolved in the regulatory sphere.

In spite of the various problems, multiple-line legislation has opened up new fields to insurers. The new types of contracts which multiple-line laws have permitted have become known as multi-peril policies, policies under which several different types of perils, formerly written under separate contracts, are now combined into one, e.g., homeowners and commercial multiple-peril contracts. In 1964, these contracts accounted for about 11% of premiums collected by major property-liability insurers (see Table 5–2), but by 1974 this percentage had risen to 17.8%. During this same period premiums collected under fire and allied lines declined from 14% to 8.8% of total.[4]

The new contracts have not been without their underwriting problems. For example, over the period 1966–1970, stock company groups lost money on homeowners multiple-peril policies each year, but made underwriting gains in commercial multiple-peril policies each year.[5] It may be concluded that in spite of problems of adjusting to multiple-peril organization and in the uneven underwriting results in multiple-peril contracts, the substantial growth in the latter field is very likely to continue in the years ahead.

[4] Calculated from Table 5-2, page 105.

[5] Calculated from *Best's Aggregates and Averages, 1971,* pp. 18-21.

All-Line Organization

All-line organization refers to that type of arrangement by which an insurer may write literally all lines of insurance under one administrative charter. There are about thirteen states in which this is permitted by state law.[6] However, many insurers, through company fleets, write all lines and for all practical purposes seem to enjoy the same advantages as insurers who offer such coverages under one administrative framework. One of the great problems in effecting full all-line underwriting is the securing of agency personnel trained to handle literally every type of insurance. Insurance is considered by some to be too complex a subject for all types of agents to be competent in any area in which they choose to write business. Another problem is that of finances. It takes a considerable investment in time and money for an insurer and its agency plant to enter the life insurance business, whether this is done through merger or whether the life insurance business is started from scratch. Nevertheless, all-lines underwriting seems to be gaining favor among insurers. In many property and liability agencies at the local level, a life man or woman has been employed to handle the increasingly important source of agency business—life and health insurance premiums.

THE MERGER MOVEMENT

Additional evidence of the interest in multiple-line and all-line underwriting among insurance company managers is the "urge to merge." Mergers of insurance companies into consolidated units has been a major trend in insurance company organizational change in the post-World War II period. Of the approximately 300 stock insurers retiring from business during the period 1954–64, for example, about 40% represented mergers with other insurers.[7]

Mergers in the insurance business may be classified according to the type of firm initiating the merger: insurance, financial, or industrial companies.

Insurance Company Initiated

The first type of merger has already been described in the discussion of multiple-line and all-line companies which have formed groups and holding companies. The major impetus to these mergers was to take advantage of legislation permitting the combining of formerly separate insurance operations into various types of insurance packages for better and cheaper distribution of insurance service to the consumer. There is also the desire of insurance companies to enter financial fields such as mutual funds, computer leasing, banking, and real estate. These companies include such giants as CNA Financial, US Life Corporation, American General, Transamerica, and Republic Financial.

[6] Alabama, Alaska, Connecticut, Delaware, Georgia, Maine, Mississippi, North Dakota, Oregon, Rhode Island, South Carolina, Tennessee, and Wisconsin. See Hugh Harbison, "Legal Environment for All Lines Insurance," *All Lines Insurance,* edited by Dan McGill (Homewood, Illinois: Richard D. Irwin, Inc., 1960), p. 23.

[7] Derived from *Best's Insurance Reports, 1964,* pp. 966B-704B.

Financial Company Initiated

The second type of merger occurred with the acquisition of insurance companies by concerns such as banks and finance companies. The major impetus behind these mergers appears to be the desire of financial firms to broaden their line of financial services to include insurance. Examples of firms making such acquisitions include American Credit Corporation (whose holdings include six insurance companies, both life and property), Capital Bankshares, Family Finance Corporation, Financial General Corporation, Investors Diversified Services, and CIT Financial Corporation.

Industrial Company Initiated

The third type of merger occurred when noninsurance and nonfinancial corporations began to acquire existing insurance firms or form new ones to complement their other activities in manufacturing, retailing, or service. Examples of such mergers include International Telephone and Telegraph (which purchased Hartford Fire Insurance Co.), Leasco Data Processing (which purchased Reliance Insurance Co.), Sears Roebuck and Co. (which formed Allstate Insurance Co.), J.C. Penney Co. (which formed its own life and property-liability subsidiaries), Deere and Co. (which controls Rock River Life Insurance and Rock River Insurance Co.), and Ford Motor Company (which formed three insurers covering life and nonlife lines).

Advantages to Insurers

To illustrate some of the advantages of mergers to the insurance firm, consider the case of an insurance group formerly operating in property and liability insurance which decides to acquire a life company. The life company may have a large number of agents selling only life and health insurance. These agents have clients whose general insurance business may be solicited as well. A life agent who is not trained to handle general business or is not interested in doing so may turn over prospect lists to the insurer's local agents who specialize in this field. In return, the insurer's local agents may provide the life agent with many leads for additional sales of life and health insurance.

Acquiring a life insurer may be profitable. The life insurer may have a substantial income from investments which may bolster the earnings of the general lines insurer. Life insurance operations have had a better record of underwriting profit than general insurance and the combined operation may thus produce higher and more stable underwriting profits. It is well known that many property-liability insurers depend on investment profits to offset underwriting losses on their general lines. The life insurance operating lends considerable stability to an otherwise erratic profit performance among property-liability insurers.

Forming a holding company offers an insurer several financial advantages. For example, a holding company can raise capital through issuance of debt securities, a procedure not permitted an insurer. Holding companies can take credit in their balance sheets for nonadmitted assets (e.g., office furniture) not permitted for an insurer. An insurer may list only assets readily available for the payment of debts. Holding companies, which are not subject to investment restrictions of insurers, may compete with other financial institutions on a more equal footing. Holding companies also permit an insurer the benefit of affiliation with a noninsurance firm without threatening the ability of the insurer to fulfill its insurance obligations.

Finally, through mergers, insurers have obtained infusions of fresh management skills which helped operating efficiency. For example, some insurers have reported that new managers have improved methods of collecting premiums and have installed new financial techniques which have helped insurers reduce unnecessary cash balances.[8]

Advantages to Financial Firms

A financial complex may acquire one or more insurers for reasons similar to those which motivate insurers to enter financial and related lines of activity. Among the reasons are:

1. The customer may be offered a "department store" of financial and related services. For example, life insurance and equities such as mutual funds often go hand in hand as an appealing plan for achieving financial security. The department store concept is especially significant in selling packages of benefits through payroll deduction, which in the future may commonly include fire and automobile insurance as well as life insurance, mutual funds, or pension plans.
2. Trained personnel are in short supply, and the merger may better utilize existing agents to handle more than one line. Very often the existence of a trained sales force in a life insurer motivates a mutual fund organization to acquire the insurer in order to obtain a ready-made sales crew.
3. Earnings may be stabilized for the combined operation. When earnings in one type of insurance are low, they may be offset by profits elsewhere.
4. There may be income tax advantages in a holding company operation. For example, a life insurance company is subject to federal income tax on its reserve base. If the insurer desires to expand its reserve basis to enlarge its operations, higher taxes may result. The holding company form of organization permits an expansion through separate subsidiaries, thus minimizing the adverse income tax.
5. Profits may be increased by better utilization of each partner's resources. For example, a loan company generally borrows so that it may lend out at higher interest rates. An insurer, on the other hand, collects funds in advance and invests or lends these funds (usually at low rates) until they are needed to pay losses. A merger of the two types of firms may increase the profits of both by reducing borrowing costs of the loan company and increasing effective interest returns of the insurer.

Advantages to Industrial Firms

An industrial concern may acquire insurance firms for several reasons. Among these reasons are:

[8] "Diversification Haunts the Insurance Industry," *Business Week*, August 24, 1974, p. 52.

1. The firm may feel that it can utilize excess surplus in the insurer to better advantage than the insurer can. Several factors have caused insurance profits to fall considerably below those of comparable industries or companies. For example, Leasco Data Processing Company, with assets of about $75 million in 1968, acquired the assets of Reliance Insurance, whose assets were nearly $600 million. The financial leverage was used to acquire computers for leasing purposes. Insurers tend to have a large cash flow which is relatively stable over the business cycle; this cash flow often attracts an industrial concern in need of capital for expansion.
2. Many concerns such as retailing or service companies can sell insurance products effectively through existing distribution outlets. Thus, they may utilize their existing marketing position and store locations more profitably through broadened product lines. Allstate has been able to sell insurance through Sears Roebuck retail stores very effectively; similar operations have been implemented by the J. C. Penney Company. Again, automobile manufacturers can effectively sell their own insurer subsidiary policies through dealer outlets.

Disadvantages of Mergers

Merger activity has not always been advantageous to the parties involved. Insurers have sometimes entered new lines of business in which they were inexperienced and suffered unexpected losses. For example, Continental Corporation, a large insurance holding company, lost nearly $100 million between 1969 and 1972 in its Diners Club subsidiary before finally earning a small profit of $1.1 million in 1973 on this venture. CNA Financial paid $30 million for a group of mutual funds and $150 million for Larwin, a real estate concern. Nothing was earned on mutual funds, and $35 million was lost in the second quarter of 1974 by Larwin in the tight real estate market of 1974.[9] Such losses drain funds from insurance reserves which may be needed to finance underwriting activity.

Another problem associated with mergers has been to subject insurers to greater losses from fluctuations in security prices, particularly common stocks. For example, in one group of 480 large insurers, stock market losses in 1974 caused policyholders' surplus to decline by about 20%. This drain coincided with unusually large underwriting losses in 1974, amounting to about 10% of policyholders' surplus.[10] These losses can cause serious disruptions in operations by enlarging the ratio of premiums written to surplus, leadng to more restrictive underwriting.

Possible Effects of Mergers on Insurance

We may speculate about the likely future effects on insurance operations as a result of the organization changes described above, particularly the effects of the merger movement. Many of the effects described below already are in evidence and may be expected to develop further.

[9] *Ibid.*

[10] Insurance Information Institute, *Insurance Educators Letter*, Vol. IV, No. 4 (April 2, 1975).

Greater Market Concentration. If the trend toward holding companies and mergers continues as it has in the past, the obvious and immediate effect will be a tendency for a greater dominance by a few large national and international companies which control an increasing proportion of the insurance business. With greater concentration in the industry, there may be a tendency toward more federal regulation as a way of obtaining better levels of consumer protection than sometimes is achieved with state regulation. Perhaps specialized governmental agencies will have to be set up to deal with the problem of regulating the insurance functions of conglomerate enterprises.

Marketing Orientation. There may be a tendency for future generations of insurer management to be more consumer-oriented than they are product- or actuarially-oriented. The days may be numbered for those who are oriented toward handling a single line of financial service which they first ''invent'' and then try to sell. Greater emphasis will be on studying consumer needs first and then trying to meet needs with appropriate products. Competition for work force will be greater, particularly management personnel who have ''the broad picture.''

Sales Effort and Compensation. Insurance salespersons may continue the trend toward becoming professional family financial counselors. The day of the part-time door-to-door insurance agent, real estate salesperson, or tax consultant appears to be passing. The straight commission compensation system in life insurance may gradually give way to the salary-bonus system as has already occurred in group life insurance. Life insurance agents will increasingly be able to offer diverse insurance lines, particularly automobile and homeowners coverages. Property-liability personnel will continue to offer increased services in the fields of life and health insurance and pensions.

Product Lines. The tendency toward selling packages such as (a) insurance and mutual funds; (b) life insurance and variable annuities; (c) mortgage loans, life insurance, and property-liability insurance, will continue to grow. The opportunities for combinations of equity products, insurance, and financial products seem limitless. Furthermore, the insurance holding company or financial holding company will be expected to offer a considerably broader range of services to the consumer than it does at present. Adjusting and claims handling, engineering, credit reporting, computer services, real estate services, trust services, estate planning, accounting, tax services, and many others may be routinely offered.

Group Marketing. The new forms of business organization in insurance will have a reinforcing effect upon the increasing tendency toward group marketing, or so-called mass merchandising. Life insurers have long been established in selling through payroll deduction systems in life and health insurance. The same systems are now being applied to property-liability insurance, equity products, and other services.

EXTERNAL ORGANIZATION OF INSURERS

A great deal of the organization in insurance has to do with group cooperation. This cooperation is accomplished through associations of various kinds designed for very definite purposes. Many vital tasks in insurance could not be accomplished without such cooperation. Only a few of the many associations can be described here, for a complete listing of all of them would fill a volume.[11]

Rate-Making Organizations

Rate-making organizations are of high-ranking importance. Even though it might appear that such groups would be in violation of antimonopoly laws, most states specifically authorize rate-making groups. This type of cooperation is essential because many companies do not have a sufficiently large volume of business in certain lines to enable them to develop rates that are statistically sound. When the experience of many companies is pooled, however, as is done by a rate-making organization, there is a large enough body of data to permit a higher degree of scientific rate calculation. The rate-making organization is usually supported financially by member companies, but in some states the government owns and operates the agency. This is common in the field of workers' compensation insurance. State regulation has general jurisdiction over insurance rating practices to see that the rate-making association does not dispense excessive or discriminatory rates. Rate-making cooperation is common in fire, automobile, bonding, inland marine, and workers' compensation insurance. In life insurance, while there are no rate-making bodies as such, a similar result is achieved by the universal adoption of certain standard mortality tables.

The influence of rate-making cooperation goes beyond the mere setting of fairly uniform rates. If companies are to charge similar rates, it follows that most of them must also plan fairly similar amounts for losses and expenses. In order to achieve this result, policy provisions must be quite uniform, or the cooperating insurers would not experience loss ratios that were uniform. Thus, rate-making bodies have worked toward uniform policy provisions and standard policies in general. This has had a far-reaching influence on the insurance business and has enabled an orderly development of the coverage. As will be seen, the standardization of policies is widespread. Another influence in some lines of insurance has been the control exercised by rate-making bodies over allowances for agency commissions and other expenses. This has controlled, at least partially, competitive bidding for agents' services and has kept the production cost of insurance at a reasonable level in most lines of insurance.

A prominent example of a rate-making organization is the Insurance Services Office (ISO), which makes rates in 13 lines of property and liability insurance for its member companies. ISO conducts actuarial research, makes rates for some insurers, offers advice to others on rating problems, acts as a

[11] *The Insurance Almanac,* published annually, contains the names and descriptions of hundreds of types of insurance organizations.

statistical agent for the submission of experience data to regulatory authorities, develops standard policies, files forms to state insurance departments, and offers management advice to its member companies. This organization replaced several predecessor organizations, including the Insurance Rating Board, the Multi-line Insurance Rating Bureau, and the Insurance Data Processing Center.

Loss-Prevention Groups

Another important cooperative organization in insurance has been in the field of loss prevention. One of the best known of such organizations is the National Board of Fire Underwriters, an association of stock fire insurance companies dedicated to fire prevention. Underwriters Laboratories, originally formed through the cooperation of fire underwriters for the purpose of testing combustibility of various materials at the World's Fair in Chicago in 1893, has grown in influence and scope of activity until today its seal of approval is famous. This seal is looked for by most buyers of products such as electrical appliances, building materials, and fireproof containers, where the factor of fire safety is of importance. In liability insurance, the National Safety Council has had similar influence.

Reinsurance Organizations

Reinsurance is largely accomplished through cooperative activity among insurers and is one of the vital types of external organization that serve the essential needs of underwriters.

Reinsurance may be defined as the shifting by a primary insurer, called the *ceding company,* of a part of the risk it assumes to another company, called the *reinsurer*. That portion of the risk kept by the ceding company is known as the *line,* or *retention,* and varies with the financial position of the insurer and the nature of the exposure. A reinsurer may also pass on risks to another reinsurer, a process known as *retrocession*. Very often a ceding insurer is also a reinsurer at the same time, taking part in a *reinsurance treaty* under which each member insurer participates in sharing risk. Reinsurance arrangements are international in nature, with Lloyd's of London being an important factor in the world reinsurance market.[12] Very large exposures, such as the Golden Gate Bridge in San Francisco, are insured and reinsured around the world, so that in case of a catastrophe no one insurer is likely to suffer disastrous financial consequences.

Uses and Advantages of Reinsurance. One may wonder why an insurer that has gone to all the expense and difficulty of securing business would voluntarily transfer some of it to a third party. There are several reasons for this, the main one being that the primary insurer is often asked to assume liability for loss in

[12] Other important world reinsurers include Munich Reinsurance Co., Swiss Reinsurance Co., North American Reinsurance Co., General Reinsurance Co., and American Reinsurance Co.

excess of the amount that its financial capacity would permit. Instead of accepting only a portion of the risk and thus causing inconvenience and even the ill will of its customer, the company accepts all the risk, knowing that it can pass on to the reinsurer the part that it does not care to bear. The policyholder is thus spared the necessity of negotiating with many companies and can place insurance with little of the delay that such a procedure would involve. Using a single policy with a single premium also simplifies insurance management procedures. The policy coverage is not only more uniform and easier to comprehend, but the added guaranty of the reinsurer also makes it that much safer.

From the viewpoint of the insurer, reinsurance not only distributes the risk, but it also has other uses and advantages. Stabilized profits and loss ratios are an important advantage in the use of reinsurance. It is true that oftentimes good business must be shared with others, but in return some bad business is also shared. In the long run, it is usually considered more desirable to have a somewhat lower but stable level of profits and underwriting losses than it is to have a higher but unstable level. This is not to imply that reinsurance arrangements necessarily reduce average profit levels, but they do iron out fluctuations that would normally occur. Furthermore, reinsurance does not always mean the loss of premium volume, for one of the results of reinsurance is the procurement of new business. As a member of a group of ceding companies organized to share mutual risks, one ceding company must usually accept the business of other insurers. Some companies obtain a significant portion of their total premium volume in this manner, and others engage exclusively in the reinsurance business.

Reinsurance is also used to allow for a reduction in the level of unearned premium reserve requirements. For new small companies especially, one of the limiting factors in the rate of growth is the legal requirement that the company set aside premiums received as unearned premium reserves for policyholders. Since no allowance is made in these requirements for expenses incurred, the insurer must pay for producers' commissions and for other expenses out of surplus. As the premiums are earned over the life of the policy, these amounts are restored to surplus. In the meantime, however, the insurer may not be able to finance some of the business it is offered. Through reinsurance, the firm can accept all the business it can obtain from its agency force and then pass on to the reinsurer part of the liability for loss, and with it the loss and unearned premium reserve requirement.

Finally, reinsurance may be used to retire from business or to terminate the underwriting on a given type of insurance. If a firm wishes to liquidate its business, it could conceivably cancel all its policies that are subject to cancellation and return the unearned premiums to the policyholder. However, this would be quite unusual in actual practice because of the necessity of sacrificing the profit that would normally be earned on such business. It would probably be impossible to recover in full the amount of expense that had been incurred in putting the business on the books. Through reinsurance, however, the liabilities for existing insurance can be transferred and the policyholders' coverage remains undisturbed. If an insurer desires to retire its life insurance business and to cease underwriting this line, it may do so through reinsurance. Since the life insurance policy is noncancellable, the policyholder has the right to continue the protection. If it were not for reinsurance, the insurer would find it difficult, if not impossible, to achieve its objective of relieving itself from the obligation of seeing that the insured's coverage is continued.

Types of Reinsurance Agreements. Organization for reinsurance is found in many forms, from individual contractual arrangements with reinsurers to pools whereby a number of primary insurers agree to accept certain types of insurance on some prearranged basis.

Facultative Reinsurance. The simplest type of reinsurance may be described as an *informal facultative agreement*, or specific reinsurance on an optional basis. Under this arrangement a primary insurer, in considering the acceptance of a certain risk, shops around for reinsurance on it, attempting to negotiate coverage specifically on this particular contract. A life insurer, for example, may receive an application for $1 million of life insurance on a single life. Not wishing to reject this business, but still unwilling to accept the entire coverage, the primary insurer communicates full details on this application to another insurer with whom it has done business in the past. The other insurer may agree to assume, let us say, all loss above $100,000 on this contract for a certain percentage of the premium. The primary insurer then puts the contract in force. The reinsurance agreement does not affect the insured in any way. Informal facultative reinsurance is usually satisfactory when reinsurance is of an unusual nature or when it is negotiated only occasionally. Such an arrangement becomes cumbersome and unsatisfactory, however, if reinsurance agreements must be negotiated regularly.

Occasionally an insurer will have an agreement whereby the reinsurer is bound to take certain types of risks if offered by the ceding company, but the decision of whether or not to reinsure remains with the ceding company. Such an arrangement may be called a *formal facultative contract* or a facultative treaty, and is used where the ceding company is often bound on certain types of risks by its agents before it has an opportunity to examine the application. If the exposure is such that reinsurance is not needed or desired, the ceding company may retain the entire liability. In other cases it will submit the business to the reinsurer, who is bound to take it. Such reinsurance agreements are often unsatisfactory for the reinsurer because of the tendency for the ceding company to keep better business for itself and pass on the more questionable lines to the reinsurer.

Automatic, or Obligatory, Agreement. To protect all parties concerned from such a tendency as described above, to speed up the transaction, and to eliminate the expense and uncertainties of individual negotiation, reinsurance may be provided whereby the ceding company is required to cede certain amounts of business, and the reinsurer is required to accept them. Such an agreement is described as *automatic,* or *obligatory*. There are several types of such agreements, called *treaties,* because often each member to the agreement accepts reinsurance from the other. The amount that the ceding company keeps for its own account is known as its *net retention,* and the amount ceded to others is known as the *cession.*

Two basic types of treaties have been recognized: *pro rata treaties,* under which premiums and losses are shared in some proportion, and *excess of loss treaties,* under which losses are paid by the reinsurer in excess of some predetermined deductible or retention. In the latter, there is no directly proportional relationship between the original premium and the amount of loss assumed by the reinsurer.

There are many varieties of *pro rata treaties,* but perhaps the two most common are the surplus treaty and the quota share treaty. *Surplus treaties* cover only specific exposures—policies covering individuals or business firms—while *quota share treaties* cover a percentage of an insurer's business, either its entire business or some definite portion thereof. Illustrations of these agreements follow. Under an *excess line,* or *first surplus, treaty*, the ceding company decides what its net retention will be for each class of business. The reinsurer does not participate unless the policy amount exceeds this net retention. The larger its net retention, the more the other members of the treaty will be willing to accept. Thus, if the ceding company will retain $10,000 on each dwelling fire exposure, the agreement may call for cession of up to "five lines" or $50,000 for reinsurance. The primary insurer could then take a fire risk of $60,000. On the other hand, if the ceding company is willing to retain only $5,000 on a residential fire exposure, it may have only four lines acceptable for reinsurance, and could not take more than $25,000 of fire insurance on a single residence.

First surplus treaties call for the sharing of losses and premiums up to a stated limit in proportion to the liabilities assumed. Sometimes a second surplus, or even a third surplus, treaty is arranged to take over business that is beyond the limits set by the first surplus treaty. The surplus treaty is probably the most common type of reinsurance in use today.

Under quota share treaties, each insurer takes a proportionate share of all losses and premiums of a line of business. An illustration of the quota share treaty is the *reinsurance pool* or *exchange*. Pools are usually formed to provide reinsurance in given classes of business, such as cotton, lumber, or oil, where hazards are of a special nature and where the mutual use of engineering or inspection facilities provides an economy for participating members. Each member of the pool agrees to place all described business it obtains into the pool, but it shares some agreed proportion, such as 10% or 16.67%, of the total premiums and losses. Quota share treaties are especially suitable for new small firms whose underwriting capacity is limited, and who would be unable to get started without such an arrangement because of their inability to meet the drain on surplus imposed by unearned premium reserve requirements.

It is not uncommon for a primary insurer to find that, while it is willing to accept up to $10,000 on each exposure insured in a given class, it is unable to stand an accumulation of losses that exceeds $50,000. To impose a limit on such losses, a type of treaty known as the *excess of loss treaty* has been developed whereby the reinsurer agrees to be liable for all losses exceeding a certain amount on a given class of business during a specific period. Normally, such treaties are used when there is a danger of catastrophic losses. Such a contract is simple to administer because the reinsurers are liable only after the ceding company has actually suffered the agreed amount of loss. Since the probability of large losses is small, premiums for this reinsurance are likewise small.

A variation of the excess of loss type of reinsurance is the *spread of loss treaty* under which the primary insurer decides what loss ratio it is prepared to stand on a given kind of insurance, and agrees with a reinsurer to bear any losses that would raise the loss ratio above the agreed level over a period of, say, five years. Thus, the ceding company has spread its losses over a reasonable time period and, in effect, has guaranteed an underwriting margin through reinsurance. In this way an unusually high loss ratio in a poor underwriting year is averaged in with other years, and the reinsurer is obligated to pay only when the five-year loss ratio exceeds the stipulated amount.

There are many variations of reinsurance agreements under which the losses of the primary insurer are limited. The main advantages of such agreements are: (1) underwriting profits are more or less directly controlled; and (2) the agreements are simpler to administer than other types of reinsurance because it is not necessary to render continuing reports to the insurer (called *bordereau*) nor to keep books on each reinsurer's share of total risks assumed. The disadvantages include: (1) while underwriting profits are set at a minimum, the premium for reinsurance is set in such a way that profits of the ceding company are limited and any benefits from good underwriting experience must be shared heavily with the reinsurer; and (2) underwriting is said to become careless because the ceding company personnel know that losses are limited through reinsurance, and forget that ultimately the ceding company must pay for loose underwriting in the form of higher reinsurance premiums.

SUMMARY

1. The major functions of an insurer are: (a) production (selling), (b) underwriting, (c) rate-making and statistical control, (d) claims management, (e) investing and financing, (f) accounting, and (g) miscellaneous functions, such as legal aid, marketing research, engineering services, and personnel management. These functions are performed both by the home office and by the agency staff in the field.
2. Underwriting is the task of selecting subjects for insurance in such a way that the assumptions underlying the rate structure are realized in practice. It is the underwriting, claims-handling, and rate-making tasks which are most nearly exclusive functions of insurance. The other functions, while they are necessary to carry out these basic tasks, are not exclusively insurance functions, since they are common to most business enterprises.
3. There are two general types of organization in insurance: internal and external. Internal organization refers to the way in which an individual insurer or its subsidiaries, if any, carry out their tasks. External organization refers to the work

done through cooperative groups such as safety, rate-making, or engineering associations.

4. Distinguishable internal organizational concepts are product and territorial organization. In general, as an insurer grows, it is more likely to use some form of territorial decentralization and for very large insurers, this is accompanied by decentralized product divisions.
5. Two central plans for internal organization may be identified: (a) single-line organization and (b) multiple-line organization. The former plan describes the pattern of organization typically used by insurers that write only specific lines of insurance, such as fire or life. This plan has led to what is known as group operations, or company fleets, whereby insurers merge into units under centralized control for the purpose of offering a more complete and diversified insurance service than is possible for each company operating separately. Multiple-line organization, on the other hand, describes the plan of operation used by insurers authorized to write several lines of insurance within the framework of a single administrative entity. Multiple-line organization has become legally possible in the United States since World War II.
6. Because single-line organization and its related group type of operation have evolved over many years in the United States, it is doubtful that it will be suddenly replaced by the multiple-line organization, which has created many basic changes and problems for insurers. Rather, it is likely that the two systems will coexist for an indefinite period.
7. The insurance industry is characterized by a more extensive use of cooperative groups and associations than is true of almost any other industry. Most of these associations are formed because it has been found that it is more economical to pool resources for carrying out tasks which are mutually needed than to perform them individually. Indeed, some tasks, such as rate-making, loss prevention, and reinsurance, can be performed in no other way.
8. Reinsurance is an important example of one task that is accomplished by external organization. The uses of reinsurance include distribution of risk, stabilization of profits, reduction of legal reserve requirements, and facilitation of retirement from business. The major types of reinsurance agreements are facultative, pro rata, and excess of loss.

QUESTIONS FOR REVIEW AND DISCUSSION

1. (a) How has the merger movement in insurance affected insurance organizations and functions?
   (b) What advantages of mergers to the insurer seem to you to be the most important? Why? Do you see any possible disadvantages?
   (c) What effects are possible as a result of the merger movement?
2. A sales manager told a group of agents that the broadened product line of the company, which through merger included variable annuities, permitted an average agent to triple commission income by combining ordinary life insurance with individual variable annuities in the same package. This was true even though the average first-year commission of ordinary life was 50% compared to 10% for the variable annuity.
   (a) What might account for the phenomenon noted?
   (b) What problem inherent in broadened product lines does this example illustrate? Explain.
3. In a study by the New York Insurance Department of 350 insurers which had ceased business in that

state, the overwhelmingly major reason for financial difficulty lay in inadequate underwriting. Explain the connection between inadequate underwriting and the financial difficulty referred to.

4. (a) Explain what is meant by the "conflict between underwriting and production" in insurance.
(b) Do you agree that such a conflict is real, or is it only apparent?

5. It is stated in the text that there are two major classifications of organization in insurance. Name and describe each type.

6. (a) What basic legal problem gave rise to group organization?
(b) Now that this legal hurdle has been largely eliminated, will group organization disappear? Why or why not?

7. What major problems are inherent in a multiple-line organization?

8. What is retrocession, and how is this concept related to the internationalization of insurance?

9. Do not rate-making organizations carry on what amounts to price-fixing, and is this not in violation of the Sherman Antitrust Act? Discuss.

10. It has been stated that action through groups is often more effective than action by individuals. Recently a number of insurers reduced their production allowances in the rate calculation for certain types of insurance. The reduction, which resulted in a cut in commission rates to agents, was strongly opposed by agents, who took legal action through their association, the League of Independent Insurance Producers, to prevent this reduction. It was charged that the insurers acted in concert to restrain trade in violation of the Sherman Antitrust Act. Suggest possible reasons for the desirability of action at the group level rather than action by individual agents in such a problem.

11. (a) Which function has been more important to most insurers—investing or financing? Why?
(b) Are there any important differences in the functions of investing and financing among life insurers as opposed to property and liability insurers? Explain.

12. The policyholder is said to be injured if claims management is either too liberal or too strict. Explain.

13. Bring to class a report of an article illustrating the application of marketing research in insurance. Do you think this function is likely to increase or to decrease in importance in the future? Explain.

14. It is stated that the facultative reinsurance agreement is the simplest of all kinds of reinsurance. Explain, giving in your answer a definition of reinsurance.

15. A certain insurer is willing and able to assume all the risks on residential fire offered to it in a certain city. However, it fears a catastrophic-type loss in case of a forest fire, which could destroy the whole city. Suggest a type of reinsurance agreement that would solve this problem.

16. (a) Explain what is meant by a first surplus treaty and give an illustration of its application.
(b) How does the agreement differ from quota share reinsurance?

17. Insurer *I* has written a fire insurance policy on *A* in the amount of $2 million on *A's* factory. *I* has a net retention of $100,000 on any one fire loss, and it has a pro rata first surplus treaty of nine lines, a pro rata second surplus treaty of five lines, and it has facultative reinsurance of $500,000 on *A's* plant. It now seeks an excess of loss treaty that pays any loss in excess of $25,000 on any one risk.
(a) If *I* has a loss of $1 million on account of a fire at *A's* plant, how will the loss be distributed under the existing reinsurance treaties? Explain.
(b) If *I* is able to obtain the excess of loss treaty, how much would it be able to recover from the excess of loss reinsurance? Explain.

PART III *Fundamentals of Insurance Contracts*

Chapter *Eight*

LEGAL PRINCIPLES OF INSURANCE CONTRACTS

Insurance is effected by legal agreements known as contracts or policies. A contract, contrary to many impressions, cannot be complete in itself, but must be interpreted in light of the legal and social environment of the society in which it is made. This chapter is concerned with the specific legal doctrines which underlie the insurance contract.

PRINCIPLE OF INSURABLE INTEREST

A fundamental legal principle underlying all insurance contracts is *insurable interest*. Under this principle, an insured must demonstrate a personal loss or that insured will be unable to collect amounts due when the insured peril occurs. Insurable interest is always a legal requirement, because to hold otherwise would mean that an insured could collect without personal loss. This would establish a moral hazard and would be deemed contrary to public policy. The doctrine of insurable interest is also necessary to prevent insurance from becoming a gambling contract. In life insurance, an important reason for requiring insurable interest is to remove a possible incentive for murder.

Insurance follows the person and not the property. Thus, insurance is said to be *personal*. A policy can be written covering a certain piece of property and an individual may be named as the one who would suffer a financial loss if the peril were to occur and cause damage. However, if at the time of the loss the individual named no longer had an interest in the property, there would be no liability under the policy. For example, suppose that *A* owns and insures an automobile. Later *A* sells the car to *B* and shortly thereafter the auto is destroyed. *A*, who has no further financial interest in the car, cannot collect under the policy. *B* has no protection under the policy since *B* is not named as an insured or as having any interest in the auto at the time the policy was written.

What Constitutes Insurable Interest?

The legal owner of property having its value diminished by the occurrence of an insured peril, has an insurable interest and can collect if able to demonstrate that a financial loss has occurred. However, in many cases a loss occurs when an individual is not a legal owner. In other words, ownership is not the only evidence of insurable interest. For instance, *C* leases a building under a long-term lease whereby the lease may be cancelled if a fire destroys a certain percentage of the value of the building. *C* has an insurable interest in the building because of the lease.

There are other rights under contract which are sufficient to establish an insurable interest in property, the continued existence of which affects the contract and its value to the insured. Thus, the holder of a contract to receive oil royalties has an insurable interest in the oil property so that in the event of an insured peril, indemnity can be collected, the amount of the indemnity being measured by the reduction in royalty resulting from the insured peril.[1] Likewise, legal liability growing out of contracts establishes insurable interest in property. For example, garage operators have an insurable interest in the stored automobiles for which they have assumed liability.

Secured creditors, such as mortgagees, have an insurable interest in the property on which they have lent money. Building contractors have an insurable interest in property on which they have worked because they have a mechanic's lien. In each of the two cases, loss of the building would endanger the ability to collect amounts due. However, *general creditors*—ones without specific liens on the property—are not regarded as having a sufficiently great property right to give them an insurable interest. In most states, however, a general contractor who reduces a debt to a judgment then has an insurable interest in the debtor's property. A business person has an insurable interest in the profits expected from the use of property and in the expenses incurred in managing that property.

In life insurance, an insurable interest is always presumed to exist for persons who voluntarily insure their own lives. An individual may procure life insurance and may make anyone the beneficiary regardless of whether the beneficiary has an insurable interest. Of course, there are practical limits as to the amount of life insurance an individual may obtain.

Sometimes parties will attempt to avoid the insurable interest requirements in life insurance and try to use the contract as a wagering agreement. Courts will usually set aside such contracts, however. For example, two individuals met in a saloon and after a short acquaintance, one agreed to insure his life and then assign the policy to the other if reimbursed for the premium. The insured person died and the insurer refused to pay when the facts surrounding the application became known. The court upheld the insurer's refusal to pay on the grounds that the transaction was conceived to use the life insurance policy as a means of effecting a wager. The intention was to avoid the requirement of insurable interest by having the *cestui que vie* (person whose life is insured) take out the policy with the sole purpose of transferring it to another who had no insurable interest.

One who takes out life insurance on another's life, must have an insurable interest in that person's life. Thus, a corporation or other business firm may

[1] See *National Filtering Oil Co.* v. *Citizens Insurance Co.*, 106 N.W. 535 (1887).

insure the life of a key person because that person's death would cause financial loss to the firm. A wife may insure the life of her husband because his continued existence is valuable to her and she would suffer a financial loss upon death. The same statement may apply to almost anyone who is dependent on an individual. A father may insure the life of a minor child, but a brother may not ordinarily insure the life of his sister. In the latter case there would not usually be a financial loss to the brother upon the death of his sister, but in the former case the father would suffer financial loss upon the death of his child. A creditor has an insurable interest in the life of a debtor because the death of the debtor would subject the creditor to possible loss.

When the Insurable Interest Must Exist

In property and liability insurance it is possible to effect coverage on property in which the insured does not have an insurable interest at the time the policy is written, but in which such an interest is expected in the future. In marine insurance a shipper often obtains coverage on cargo it has not yet purchased in the anticipation of buying cargo for a return trip. As a result, the courts generally hold that in property insurance, insurable interest need exist only at the time of the loss and not at the inception of the policy.

On the other hand, in life insurance it is the general rule that insurable interest must be in existence at the inception of the policy, but is not necessary at the time of the loss. This follows because life insurance is not a contract of indemnity, while property liability insurance, with certain exceptions, is generally so considered. Also, the courts view life insurance as an investment contract. To illustrate, assume that a wife who owns a life insurance policy on her husband later obtains a divorce. If she continues to maintain the insurance by paying the premiums, she may collect upon the subsequent death of her former husband, even though she is remarried and suffers no particular financial loss upon his death. It is sufficient that she had an insurable interest when the policy was first issued. In a similar way, a corporation may retain in full force a life insurance policy on an employee who is no longer with the firm. A creditor may retain the policy on a life of a debtor who has repaid an obligation. In other words, in life insurance the general rule is that a continuing insurable interest is not necessary.[2]

PRINCIPLE OF INDEMNITY

The *principle of indemnity* states that a person may not collect more than the actual loss in the event of damage caused by an insured peril. Thus, while a person may have purchased coverage in excess of the value of the property, that person cannot make a profit by collecting more than the actual loss if the property is destroyed. Many insurance practices result from this important principle. In general, only contracts in property and liability insurance are subjected to this doctrine, although there are exceptions where statutes have

[2] In Texas the rule pertaining to a continuing insurable interest has neen modified by statute so that this statement is not strictly true in that state.

modified its application. Life and most health insurance policies are not contracts of indemnity.

The principle of indemnity is closely related to insurable interest. The problem in insurable interest is to determine whether any loss is suffered by a person insured, whereas in indemnity the problem is to obtain a measure of that loss. In the basic fire insurance contract, the measure of "actual cash loss" is the current replacement cost of destroyed property less an allowance for estimated depreciation. In liability insurance, the final measure of loss is determined by reference to a court action concerning the amount of legal liability of the insured for negligence. Very often the estimate of an insurance adjuster is accepted as the measure of loss without the necessity of formal court action. In any event, the purpose served by the principle of indemnity is to place the insured in the same position as before the loss.

One of the important results of the principle of indemnity is the typical inclusion of clauses in insurance contracts regarding other insurance. The purpose of such clauses is to prevent the insured from taking out duplicating policies with different insurers in the expectation of recovering more than the actual loss. Typically, such clauses provide that all policies covering the same risk will share pro rata in the loss. Thus, by operation of this type of clause, if Jones carries $4,000 fire insurance in Company *A* and $6,000 in Company *B*, the two insurers will divide a $1,000 fire loss, 40% and 60%, respectively.

As noted above, there are some exceptions to the application of the principle of indemnity in property insurance. In about half of the states, *valued policy laws* have been passed whereby the insurer must pay the entire face amount of the fire insurance policy in the event of total loss of the insured object.[3] Ocean marine and some inland marine contracts are valued, and it is assumed that the insured will take out insurance equal to the full value of the object. Finally, it is becoming increasingly common to permit the sale of replacement insurance, contracts under which there is no deduction for depreciation in the settlement of losses on depreciable property. Exceptions to the principle of indemnity will probably continue until it is felt that they begin to constitute a moral hazard, giving the insured an incentive to destroy the property in the hopes of making a gain.

PRINCIPLE OF SUBROGATION

The *principle of subrogation* grows out of the principle of indemnity. Under the principle of subrogation, one who has indemnified another's loss is entitled

[3] Since most losses are partial, valued policy laws have relatively little actual effect in insurance. They apply usually only to real estate. Rather than appraise every piece of real estate, most insurers probably find it less expensive to pay an occasional total loss that has been insured for an amount in excess of its actual value. Valued policy laws exist in Arkansas, California, Florida, Georgia, Kansas, Louisiana, Minnesota, Mississippi, Missouri, Montana, Nebraska, New Hampshire, North Dakota, Ohio, South Carolina, South Dakota, Tennessee, Texas, West Virginia, and Wisconsin. Several states have repealed these statutes on the grounds that the only insureds who are benefitted are those desiring to defraud insurers. Georgia's law, passed in 1971, provides that if the building burns within 30 days of the date of the policy coverage, the loss is subject to settlement on an actual cash value basis.

to recovery from liable third parties, if any, who are responsible. Thus, if *D* negligently causes damage to *E*'s property, *E*'s insurance company will indemnify *E* to the extent of its liability for *E*'s loss and then have the right to proceed against *D* for any amounts it has paid out under *E*'s policy. One of the important reasons for subrogation is to reinforce the principle of indemnity; that is, to prevent the insured from collecting more than the actual cash loss. If *E*'s insurer did not have the right of subrogation, it would be possible for *E* to recover from the policy and then recover again in a legal action against *D*. In this way *E* would collect twice. It would be possible for *E* to arrange an accident with *D*, collect twice, and split the profit with *D*. A moral hazard would exist and the contract would tend to become an instrument of fraud.

Another reason for subrogation is to hold rates below what they would otherwise be. In some lines of insurance, particularly liability, recoveries from negligent parties through subrogation are substantial. While no specific provision for subrogation recoveries is made in the rate structure other than through those provisions relating to salvage, the rates would have to be higher if such recoveries were not permitted. A final reason for subrogation is that the burden of loss is more nearly placed on the shoulders of those responsible. The negligent should not escape penalty because of the insurance mechanism.

Subrogation does not exist in lines where the principle of indemnity does not apply, such as life insurance and most types of health insurance. Also, subrogation does not give the insurance company the right to collect against the insured, even if the insured is negligent. Thus, a homeowner who negligently, but accidentally, burns down the house while thawing out a frozen water pipe with a blowtorch, can collect under his fire policy; but the insurer cannot proceed against the owner for compensation. Otherwise, there would be little value in having insurance.

It is not uncommon for an insurer to waive rights of subrogation under certain circumstances where, by so doing, there is no violation of the principle of indemnity. Suppose, for example, that a manufacturer has agreed to hold a railroad not liable for losses arising out of the maintenance of a spur track that the railroad has placed on the manufacturer's property. In effect, the manufacturer has assumed legal liability that would otherwise be the responsibility of the railroad. Now assume that a spark from one of the railroad's engines sets fire to the manufacturer's building and the railroad is found to be negligent, and hence legally liable for the ensuing damage. The insurer will pay the loss, but under its rights of subrogation will proceed against the railroad. However, the manufacturer has previously agreed to assume all losses arising out of the existence of the spur track. Therefore, any amount collected becomes the ultimate liability of the manufacturer because of the hold harmless agreement. If this were not the case, the manufacturer would have been in the position of collecting for the loss from the insurer but returning it to the railroad because of the hold harmless agreement. Therefore, the insurer will waive the subrogation clause in the first contract because to enforce it would mean that its insured would not be compensated at all.

An insured who acts in such a way as to destroy or reduce the value of the insurer's right of subrogation violates the provisions of most subrogation clauses and forfeits all rights under the policy. For instance, suppose *F* collides with *G* in an automobile accident. *F* writes *G* a letter of apology and implies that *F* is to blame. It is later determined that *G* is palpably negligent and had it not been for *F*'s statement, *F*'s insurer would have been able to subrogate against *G* for amounts paid to *F*. The insurer may deny liability to *F*.

Subrogation rights of the insurer cannot be avoided by a settlement between the primary parties after the insurer has paid under the policy. In such a case the insurer is entitled to reimbursement from the insured who has received any payment from the negligent party.

The insurer is entitled to subrogation only after the insured has been fully indemnified. If the insured has borne part of the loss through the application of deductibles, inadequate coverage, or because of legal costs involved in collection against third party claims, the insurer may claim recovery only after these costs have been repaid. For example, assume that *H*'s house, valued at $40,000 and insured for $28,000, is totally destroyed through the negligence of *I*. *H* sues *I*, but is able to collect only $20,000. *H* also collects $28,000 from his insurance company. The insurer enjoys subrogation only after *H* has been fully indemnified. Therefore, the insurer is entitled only to $8,000 and not the full $20,000 that was recovered from *I*.[4]

PRINCIPLE OF UTMOST GOOD FAITH

Insurance is said to be a contract of *uberrimae fidei,* or *utmost good faith*. In effect, this principle imposes a higher standard of honesty on parties to an insurance agreement than is imposed in ordinary commercial contracts. The principle of utmost good faith has greatly affected insurance practices and casts a greatly different light on the interpretation of insurance agreements than many persons often suppose, as will be seen. The application of this principle may best be explained in a discussion of representations, concealments, and warranties.

Representations

A *representation* is a statement made by an applicant for insurance before the contract is effected. Although the representation need not be in writing, it is usually embodied in a written application. An example of representation in life insurance would be "yes" or "no" to a question as to whether or not the applicant had ever been treated for any physical condition by a doctor within the previous five years. If a representation is relied upon by the insurer in

[4] There are occasional exceptions to this rule when the contract so provides. In credit insurance, for example, the insurer and the insured would share the amounts collected from negligent third parties in the proportion that each party's loss bore to the total loss. In automobile insurance deductible settlements, it is fairly common for an insured not to recover 100% of the deductible, even if full recovery is made from a third party.

entering into the contract, and if it proves to be false at the time it is made or becomes false before the contract is made, there exists legal grounds for the insurer to avoid the contract.

Avoiding the contract does not follow unless the misrepresentation is *material* to the risk. That is, if the true facts had been known, the contract either would not have been issued at all or would have been issued on different terms. If the misrepresentation is inconsequential, its falsity will not affect the contract. However, a misrepresentation of a material fact makes the contract *voidable* at the option of the insurer. The insurer may decide to affirm the contract or to avoid it. Failure to cancel a contract after first learning about the falsity of a material misrepresentation may operate to defeat the insurer's rights to cancel at a later time, under the doctrines of waiver or estoppel.

It is generally held that even an innocent misrepresentation of a material fact is no defense to the insured if the insurer elects to avoid the contract. The applicants for insurance speak at their own risk and if they make an innocent mistake about a fact they believe to be true, they are held for their carelessness. Thus, let us say that a person in applying for insurance on his automobile states that there is no driver under age 25 in his family. However, it turns out that his 16-year-old son has been driving the family car without his father's knowledge. Lack of this knowledge is no defense when the insurance company refuses to pay a subsequent claim on the grounds of material misrepresentation. It is not necessary for the insurer to demonstrate that a loss occurred arising out of the misrepresentation in order to exert its right to avoid the contract.[5] Thus, in the above case, let us assume that *A* has the accident himself and then it is learned for the first time he has a 16-year-old son driving. Since this situation is contrary to that which *A* had previously stated, the insurer may usually legally refuse payment. However, if the court holds that a statement given in the application was one of opinion, rather than fact, and it turns out that the opinion was wrong, it is necessary for the insurer to demonstrate bad faith or fraudulent intent on the part of the insured in order to avoid the contract.[6] For example, let us say that an applicant is asked, "Have you ever had cancer?" and the applicant says "No." Later it develops that the applicant actually had cancer. The court might well find that the insured was not told the true state of his health and thought that he had some other ailment. If the question had been phrased "Have you ever been told you had cancer?" a "yes" or "no" answer would be clearly one of fact, not opinion. An honest opinion should not be grounds for recision.

Concealments

A *concealment* has been defined as "silence when obligated to speak." A concealment has approximately the same legal effect as a misrepresentation of

[5] In some states, Missouri, for example, there are exceptions to this statement. In these states, the loss must find its present cause in the fact misrepresented before the insurer may deny liability.

[6] See E. W. Patterson, *Essentials of Insurance Law* (2d ed.; New York: McGraw-Hill Book Company, Inc., 1957), pp. 382-396, for an interesting discussion of this point.

a material fact. It is the failure of an applicant to reveal a fact that is material to the risk. Because insurance is a contract of utmost good faith, the applicant is required to exercise a higher standard of honesty than might prevail in an ordinary commercial transaction. It is not enough that the applicant answer truthfully all questions asked by the insurer before the contract is effected. The applicant must also volunteer material facts, even if disclosure of such facts might result in rejection of the application or the payment of a higher premium.

In insurance, the applicant is often in a position to know material facts about the risk that the insurer does not. To allow these facts to be concealed would be unfair to the insurer. After all, the insurer does not ask questions such as "Is your building now on fire?" or "Is your car now wrecked?" The most relentless opponent of an insurer's defense suit would not argue that an insured who obtained coverage under such circumstances would be exercising even elementary fairness.

The important, often crucial, question about concealments lies in whether or not the applicant knew the fact withheld to be material. The tests of a concealment are: (1) Did the insured know of a certain fact? (2) Was this fact material? and (3) Was the insurer ignorant of this fact? The test of materiality is especially difficult because often the applicant is not an insurance expert and is not expected to know the full significance of every fact that might be of vital concern to the insurer. The final determination of materiality is the same as it is in the law of representation; namely, would the contract be issued on the same terms if the concealed fact had been known? There are two rules determining the standard of care required of the applicant: one, the stricter, applies to ocean marine risks; the other applies to insurance on land risks.

Ocean Marine Risks. In marine insurance, as it developed in early England, ships were often insured after they had set sail. Thus, there was no way for the insurer to inspect the ship. Usually the shipper had a better knowledge of the actual conditions of the risk than did the underwriter. Furthermore, since insurance was necessary to the expanding overseas trade in England, there was a desire to do everything possible to nurture the growth of this significant activity. Accordingly, very strict rules governing disclosures were adopted. Lord Mansfield, sometimes called the father of English insurance law, writing in 1776,[7] held that even innocent concealments could void the contract:[8]

> Although the suppression should happen through mistake, without any fraudulent intention; yet still the underwriter is deceived, and the policy is void; because the risk run is really different from the risk understood and intended to be run, at the time of the agreement.

Following this philosophy is the British Marine Insurance Act of 1906, which holds that as a test of concealment in marine insurance, the assured is deemed to know every fact or circumstance which in the ordinary course of

[7] The student may recognize this year as that during which Adam Smith published his famous *Wealth of Nations*, in which the philosophy of individual responsibility was so ably propounded and applied to business generally.

[8] Patterson, *op. cit.*, p. 450, quoting *Carter* v. *Boehm*, 3 Burr. 1905, 1909 (1776).

business ought to be known, and failing to reveal it, is guilty of concealment. The philosophy is recognized by our courts.

Land Risks. In land risks, the United States courts have been unwilling to apply the same standards of *uberrimae fidei* as they have in ocean marine risks. English courts, however, generally apply the same standards to all risks. In land risks, insurance companies generally inspect the properties they insure or have an opportunity to do so. Thus, they do not rely so heavily on the accuracy of statements by the insured, who often does not have sufficient knowledge of the facts about the risk and their significance to the insurer. Decisions have been rendered in the United States whereby failure to disclose the fact of a recent fire of incendiary origin by an unknown party or of the use of kerosene lamps in the picking room of a cotton factory did not constitute concealments. In general, the nonmarine, or land, rule is that a policy cannot be avoided unless there is fraudulent intent to conceal material facts. Thus, in nonmarine risks, a fourth test of concealment is added to the three mentioned on page 175. This test is: Does the insured *know* that the insurer does *not* know of a material fact? Under this test, intentional withholding of material facts with intent to deceive constitutes fraud. Assume that *H* learns that his wife *W* is going to "end it all" in the family auto by driving over a cliff. *H* immediately obtains collision insurance on the vehicle without telling all he knows. As a result, *H* is guilty of a concealment and the insurer may avoid the contract. Here *H* knows about a material fact; the insurer does not know of it; and *H knows* the insurer is ignorant of it. Furthermore, *H* has no right to assume that the insurer should know of it.

In life insurance, cases of concealment are not common because of the reluctance of courts to enforce the doctrine strictly and because of the general use of a very long list of questions in the application concerning the applicant's background. An applicant's failure to disclose the fact that he had been threatened with murder and was carrying a gun for protection was held not to be a concealment.[9]

In determining which facts must be disclosed, if known, it has been held that facts of general knowledge or facts known by the insurer already need not be "disclosed." There is also the inference from past cases, though not a final determination, that the insurer cannot defend on the grounds of concealment those facts that are embarrassing or self-disgracing to the applicant.

Warranties

A *warranty* is a clause in an insurance contract holding that before the insurer is liable, a certain fact, condition, or circumstance affecting the risk must exist. For example, in marine insurance the contract may provide "warranted free of capture or seizure." This statement means that if the ship is involved in a war skirmish, the insurance is void. Or a bank may be insured on condition that a certain burglar alarm system be installed and maintained. Such a clause is condition precedent and acts as a warranty.

[9] *New York Life* v. *Bacalis*, 94 F. 2d 200 (C.A. Fla. 1938).

A warranty creates a condition of the contract, and any breach of warranty, *even if immaterial,* will void the contract. This is the central distinction between a warranty and a representation. A misrepresentation does not void the insurance unless it is material to the risk, while under common law any breach of warranty, even if held to be minor, voids the contract. The courts have been somewhat reluctant to enforce this rule, and in many jurisdictions the rule has been relaxed either by statute or by court decision.

Warranties may be express or implied. *Express warranties* are those stated in the contract, while *implied warranties* are not found in the contract, but are assumed by the parties to the contract. Implied warranties are found only in ocean marine insurance. For example, a shipper purchases insurance under the implied condition that the ship is seaworthy, that the voyage is legal, and that there shall be no deviation from the intended course. Unless these conditions have been waived by the insurer (legality cannot be waived), they are binding upon the shipper.

A warranty may be promissory or affirmative. A *promissory warranty* describes a condition, fact, or circumstance to which the insured agrees to be held during the life of the contract. An *affirmative warranty* is one that must exist only at the time the contract is first put into effect. For example, an insured may warrant that a certain ship left port under convoy—affirmative warranty—and the insured may warrant that the ship will continue to sail under convoy—promissory warranty.

DISTINGUISHING LEGAL CHARACTERISTICS OF INSURANCE CONTRACTS

There are several legal characteristics of insurance contracts and their issuing parties which distinguish them from other contracts and contracting parties. Reference has already been made to some of these characteristics, such as the fact that insurance is a contract of indemnity, is personal in nature, and is a contract of utmost good faith. Additional characteristics are analyzed below.

It is important to distinguish insurance policies from other commercial contracts for several reasons. First of all, for tax and regulatory purposes, the insurance business is viewed quite differently from other businesses. Special statutes have been passed to give insurance firms particular tax status, some of which are especially favorable to the insurer. Insurers are exempt from federal bankruptcy statutes and are liquidated by state insurance commissioners under special regulation.

Second, the type of agreements made by firms is of value in determining whether or not this firm should be classed as an insurance company and thus whether or not it is conforming to all of the regulations under which insurance companies must operate. Issuing insurance policies may be outside the authority of the corporate charter, thus subjecting the officers to liability for *ultra vires* acts. The Supreme Court of the United States has held that the variable annuity contract is sufficiently differentiated from insurance as to require regulation of issuing companies by the Securities and Exchange Commission as well as by insurance commissions in the various states in which they operate.[10]

Finally, whether or not an agreement is indeed an insurance contract affects the way in which it may be enforced in legal actions. A separate body of law and decisions affect the enforcement of contracts classified as insurance, as compared with contracts which are classed as ordinary commercial transactions. The question arises as to whether a given contract is in conformity with state insurance law.

For example, it has been held that certain commercial agreements which appear as though they might be insurance agreements are not insurance in a legal sense. These include: contracts entitling certificate holders to medical services at free or reduced rates, a guarantee to an employee of payment for services on goods damaged or destroyed by fire, an agreement to protect an employee against other striking employees, and an agreement by a bicycle association to keep members' bicycles in repair and to replace them if stolen.

On the other hand, the following contracts have been held to constitute insurance contracts: guarantee of payment of the principal and interest of mortgage loans, contracts guaranteeing rent, contracts guaranteeing value of corporate stock on a certain date, and comprehensive guarantee of automobile tires. It was held that a corporation which undertook for specific consideration to guarantee a revenue per acre of farming land to the owner was an insurance company.[11]

It may be seen that in determining whether or not a contract is insurance or whether the issuing party is an insurance company is not always obvious. Certainly, the following factors are not the controlling ones in making such a determination: whether or not the term "insurance" appears in the contract or company name, a statement that the contract is *not* to be considered insurance, and the term or mode of payment. Rather, the courts look to the true nature of the promise or acts to be performed and the circumstances under which they will be performed.

Among the legal tests which have been used to determine whether or not a given transaction constitutes legally enforceable insurance are the following:

1. There must exist an insurable interest by the party seeking insurance.
2. The agreement of insurance must conform to the legal requirements of a contract offer and acceptance, consideration, legal purpose, and capacity of parties. The agreement can include transactions which in substance are contracts although legally they may not be so. Thus in New York a conditional sale of merchandise involving the cancellation of the debt upon death has been held to constitute a contract of insurance.[12]
3. There must exist some risk, some chance of loss, some uncertainty as to loss from designated perils.

[10] *S.E.C.* v. *Variable Annuity Life Insurance Company,* 359 U.S. 65, 75-78 (1959).

[11] *American Jurisprudence* (Rochester: Lawyers Cooperative Publishing Co., 1960), 29, 440-445.

[12] Harold Van B. Cleveland, "The Status of Self-Insured Employee Benefit Plans," *The Journal of Insurance,* Vol. 27, No. 2 (June, 1960), pp. 7-8.

4. The assumption of loss must be a part of a general scheme to distribute losses among a large group of persons bearing similar risks. The requirement, attributed to W. R. Vance,[13] is also part of the statutory definition of insurance in several states.
5. The insurer must assume the risk of loss. Payment to the insured may be in money or in services.

Not all state insurance laws define insurance, and those which do may have definitions which do not conform to all of the above requirements. For this reason, no single statutory definition is totally satisfactory. For example, New York's statutory definition requires that benefits of monetary value be given to the insured as a result of a fortuitous event (requirement 3 above), but the laws of Massachusetts do not require a fortuitous event. The laws of Kentucky specify that the event be a "contingency" and the laws of California specify that it be a "contingent or unknown" event.[14]

More specifically, in analyzing insurance contracts, courts are concerned with several legal characteristics, only the most important of which will be discussed in the remaining sections of this chapter. Among these characteristics are those describing (1) the peculiar ways in which insurance must conform to the requirements of any valid contract; (2) the classification of an insurance contract as aleatory, conditional, and one of adhesion; and (3) the legal status of the insurance agent or broker in effecting valid contracts.

Insurance and the Requirements of a Contract

A *contract* is an agreement embodying a set of promises that are enforceable at law, or for breach of which the law provides a remedy. These promises must have been made under certain conditions before they can be enforced by law. In general, there are four such conditions, or requirements, which may be stated as follows:

1. The agreement must be for a legal purpose; it must not be against public policy or be otherwise illegal.
2. The parties must have legal capacity to contract.
3. There must be evidence of agreement of the parties to the promises. In general this is shown by an *offer* by one party and *acceptance* of that offer by the other.
4. The promises must be supported by some consideration, which may take the form of money, or by some action by the parties that would not have been required had it not been for the agreement.

Insurance contracts must meet these essential requirements. The peculiar problems involved in applying the requirements to insurance are discussed below.

[13] W. R. Vance, *Handbook of the Law of Insurance* (St. Paul: 1951), pp. 1-2, and H. S. Denenberg, "The Legal Definition of Insurance," *Journal of Insurance*, Vol. 30 (September, 1963), p. 339. It has been held, however, that a single isolated transaction is enough to constitute insurance in some states, including New York. See New York Insurance Law, Section 41 (3) (4), and Denenberg, *op, cit.*, p. 336.

[14] Denenberg, *op. cit.*, pp. 328-329

Legality. As indicated before, to be legal the insurance contract must not violate the requirement of insurable interest, nor may the contract protect and encourage illegal ventures. Obtaining insurance on life or property without an insurable interest would violate antiwagering statutes and could lead to arbitrary and intentional destruction of the subject matter. In early England, it was not uncommon to allow private individuals to take out insurance on the lives of public figures, such as the king. The premiums for such contracts would vary daily, depending on reports from the sickbed. Such a policy would be unthinkable today.

Capacity. Parties to the policy of insurance must have legal capacity to contract. There have been instances where a minor has exercised the legal right to rescind an agreement (before reaching the age of majority) and to recover the full cost of the premium without any adjustment for the value of insurance protection received.[15] This follows because a minor is a legal infant and does not have the power to make binding contracts except for necessary items of support actually furnished. The courts have not yet come to the point of interpreting insurance to be a necessary item in the support of an infant. Several states, however, have passed statutes granting a minor who has reached a certain age (14½ years in New York) the power to make binding contracts of insurance.

Other parties who have no legal capacity to contract are: (1) insane persons—those who do not have the ability to understand the nature of the agreement into which they enter; (2) intoxicated persons; and (3) corporations that act outside the scope of their authority as defined in their charters, bylaws, or articles of incorporation.

Offer and Acceptance. In insurance the agreement is effected by one party making an offer and by the other party accepting that offer. Until there has been both an offer *and* an acceptance, there is no contract. To be valid, an offer must be communicated effectively to the offeree. An offer can be withdrawn at any time before it is accepted. Therefore, it becomes important to determine, in many cases, what constitutes a legal offer. If *A* goes to an agent to purchase insurance and the agent fills out an application that *A* signs, has the agent made an offer which *A* accepts by signing the application? If so, the insurance is in force. If not, when is the contract in effect? The answers to these questions are vital in determining when coverage attaches and can often spell the difference between collecting and not collecting for a loss.

It is the general rule in insurance that it is the *applicant,* not the agent, who makes the offer. The agent merely solicits an offer. When the contract goes into effect depends upon the authority of the agent to act for the principal in a given case. In property and liability insurance, it is the custom to give the local agent authority to accept offers of many lines of insurance "on the spot." If the

[15] See *New Hampshire Mutual Fire Insurance Co.* v. *Noyes,* 32 N.H. 345. It should be added that a minor who does not rescind the contract upon reaching the age of majority is thereafter bound by it.

insurer wishes to escape from its agreement, it usually may cancel the policy upon prescribed notice. In life insurance, the agent generally does not have authority to accept the applicant's offer for insurance. The insurer reserves this right, and the policy is not bound until the insurer has passed on the application. If the insurer wishes to alter the terms of the proposed contract, it may do so, and this is construed as making a counteroffer to the applicant, who may accept or reject it.

A legal offer by an applicant for life insurance must be supported by a tender of the first premium. Usually, the agent gives the insured a *conditional receipt,* which provides that acceptance takes place when the insurability of the applicant has been determined. Thus, let us say that *B* applies for life insurance. tenders an annual premium with the application, passes the medical examination, and then is run over and killed by a truck, all before the insurer is even aware that an application has been made for insurance. *B*'s beneficiaries may collect under the policy if it is determined that *B* was actually insurable at the time of the application and had made no false statements in the application.

An applicant for life insurance who does not pay the first annual premium in advance has not made a valid offer. In this case, the insurer's agent transmits the application to the home office, where it is acted upon and questions of insurability are determined. The insurer sends the policy back to the agent for delivery, and the agent is instructed to deliver the policy only if the insured is still in good health. This constitutes, on the part of the insurer, an offer that may be accepted by paying the annual premium at the time of delivery.

In summary, the offer in insurance can be made in either of two ways: (1) by filling out an application and rendering other considerations required of the applicant, and (2) by offering a completed policy to the applicant. Normally, the offer is effected by means of the first method, but occasionally, and especially in life insurance, the second method is used, depending upon the power of the agent in the circumstances.

Consideration. All contracts that are legally enforceable must be supported by a consideration, and insurance is no exception. A *consideration* has been defined as a legal detriment, or more simply, as the act or promise that is bargained for. The insured's consideration is made up of monetary payment plus an agreement to abide by the conditions of the insurance contract. The insurer's consideration is its promise to pay indemnity upon the occurrence of certain perils, to defend the insured in legal actions, or to perform other matters, such as inspection or collection services, as the contract may specify.

Oral Contracts of Insurance

While most insurance contracts are written, oral agreements of insurance are very common and the courts will enforce them. Often an oral agreement for insurance is made and a written notation, called a *binder,* is issued as evidence of the oral contract until the full written policy is issued. If it were not for binders, it might be difficult to prove that an oral contract ever existed. Even if there were witnesses, it would be difficult to obtain an accurate statement of just what the agreement was. Also, in many cases the insurer's agent is found to lack authority to bind contracts orally. Some states have passed statutes requiring certain types of contracts, such as life or fire, to be in writing, and sometimes the provisions of the insurer's charter will not allow oral contracts. Therefore, oral contracts are to be discouraged wherever possible.

Parol Evidence Rule

Under the *parol evidence rule*, when an oral contract is reduced to writing, the written contract is to be construed as the entire agreement; and oral testimony to change it is inadmissible except under certain circumstances. Therefore, oral agreements that do not find themselves expressed accurately in the written contract are not enforceable, and it is dangerous for the insured to rely on them.

Effect of Mistakes

When an honest mistake is made in a written contract of insurance, it can be reformed if there is proof of a mutual mistake or a mistake on one side that is known to be a mistake by the other party where no mention was made of it at the time the agreement was made. A mistake in the sense used here does not mean an error in judgment by one party, but refers to a situation where it can be shown that the actual agreement made was not the one stated in the contract. If *A* believes to be the owner of certain property, and insures that property, *A* cannot later demand all of the premium back solely because he found out that, in fact, he was not the owner of the property. This was a mistake in judgment or an erroneous supposition, and the courts will not relieve this kind of mistake.

As an example of mistakes found in life insurance policies, an insured paid up his policy and through a mistake by the insurer, the endorsement stated that the value of the paid-up contract was $5,495.26, including interest. Actually the proper value was $1,994.65. The insured sued for the larger amount, and the court held that an honest mistake had been made by the company and that it was "inconceivable that a successful businessman would think that a policy which on his death paid $2,765 would at any time acquire a surrender value of $5,495.26!"[16] In another case the insurer issued a $1,000 life policy and by an error of one of its clerks included an option at the end of 20 years to receive an annuity of $1,051 rather than $10.51. The mistake was discovered 18 years later. When the insurer tried to correct the error, the insured refused payment of the smaller amount. In a legal decision, the court held that the mistake was a mutual one, the error of the insurer being in misplacing a decimal point, and the error of the insured being in either not noticing the error, or if he noticed it, in failing to say anything, an action amounting to fraud.[17] These decisions also illustrate the fact that insurance is a contract of *uberrimae fidei,* of utmost good faith on both sides.

[16] *Flax* v. *Prudential Life Ins. Co.*, 3 Life Cases (2) 105, Fed. Supp. (1956).
[17] *Metropolitan Life Ins. Co.* v. *Henriksen,* 126 N.E. (2d) 736 (Ill. App. Court—1955).

Aleatory and Conditional Contracts

Insurance is classed as an *aleatory* contract, of which the outcome depends on an uncertain event. Thus, the obligation of the insurer to perform is dependent upon chance and is *conditional* upon the occurrence of some insured peril and upon the occurrence of certain other conditions, such as the adherence to policy provisions or requirements by the insured. The insurer is bound to pay the insured a much larger sum of money, under some conditions, than the insured has paid the insurer in the form of premiums. Thus, the conditions are a part of the bargain. In contrast, an ordinary commercial transaction is one in which there is roughly an equal exchange of values between the parties and few, if any, conditions which must be observed to effect the bargain.

Contract of Adhesion

The insurance contract is said to be contract of *adhesion,* the result being that any ambiguities or uncertainties in the wording of the agreement will be construed against the drafter—the insurer. The insurer has the advantage in drawing up the terms of the contract to suit its particular purposes; and, in general, the insured has no opportunity to bargain over conditions, stipulations, exclusions, and the like. Therefore, the courts place the insurance company under a legal duty to be explicit and to make its meaning absolutely clear to all parties.

For example, in the fire insurance contract, courts construe policies with conflicting loss settlement provisions covering the same property in such a way as to favor the insured, so that the insured is not deprived of recovery. In automobile insurance, a court construed an accident involving a car which left the road after being struck by a flying piece of ice to be covered under comprehensive rather than collision, an interpretation which favored the insured because no deductible applied to the claim.[18] In life insurance, ambiguities involving the effective date of a policy have been construed in such a way as to favor the insured. For example, some life insurance policies are antedated, that is, dated before the coverage actually begins. A majority of courts held that the one-year suicide clause runs from the earlier date of the policy and not the date the policy became effective.[19] Such an interpretation favors the beneficiary, since if the insured's suicide occurs after the one-year period stated in the suicide clause, the beneficiary may collect the full amount of the policy whereas if suicide occurs within the one-year period, only a return of premiums is tendered.

In interpreting the agreement, the courts will generally consider the entire contract as a whole, rather than just one part of it. In the absence of doubt as to meaning, the courts will enforce the contract as it is written. It is no excuse that the insured does not understand or has not read the policy. The insured is bound by its terms, regardless.

[18] *Gruenther* v. *American Indemnity Co.,* 17 N.W. (2d) 590.
[19] E. W. Patterson, *op. cit.*, p. 99.

LEGAL POWERS OF INSURANCE AGENTS

Reference has been made frequently to the significance of the agent in insurance contracts. The powers of insurance agents to vary the terms of the contract, to put the insurance in force, to deal with the insured, to handle settlements, and to perform many other affairs are of vital importance to a sound knowledge of insurance. An insurance corporation, after all, is a legal entity only, and it must function through agents of various kinds.

An *agent* is a person given power to act for a principal, who is bound by the acts of authorized agents. The power of a given insurance agent cannot be determined easily by reference to whether the agent is called a general, a special, or a local agent. The reason for this is that there is little uniformity in insurance terminology, and a general agent in property insurance has far different powers and functions from the general agent in life insurance. Furthermore, the sense in which insurance practitioners use the terms for various types of agents may not be comparable to the sense in which attorneys view the terms.

For example, the law recognizes two major classes of agents: general and special. A *general agent* is a person authorized to conduct all of the principal's business of a given kind in a particular place. A general agent is the company itself, legally speaking, in that capacity. As such, the general agent can add or detract from a printed form, waive the terms of contracts, accept or reject risks, change rates, and do almost everything the company itself could do. In life insurance, the general agent has few or none of these powers, but in property insurance the general agent often has at least some of these powers.

In the legal sense, an agent does not necessarily have to be a person serving in the channel of distribution for insurance, but may be any representative of the insurance corporation, such as the treasurer or the chief underwriter, who is given certain authority. An agent may fall in the classification of a *special agent*, a person who has authority to perform only a specific act or function and has no general powers. If anything occurs that is outside the scope of this authority, the agent must obtain special power to handle it. An agent who handles matters outside the scope of this authority may or may not bind the principal, depending on certain circumstances.

Source of Authority

The basic source of authority for all insurance agents (using the word agent in its broad sense) comes from stockholders or policyholders and is formulated by the charter, bylaws, and custom. The agent in the channel of distribution for insurance is of greatest concern to us at this point, however, and the discussion will be confined to that agent. There are three distinct sources of authority for the agent: from the agency agreement, by ratification, and by estoppel.

Agency Agreement. The first source of authority, the agency agreement, is by far the most common. Agents generally obtain their authority to write insurance directly from the principal by an instrument known as an *agency agreement*. This agreement sets forth the specific duties, rights, and obligations of both parties. Unfortunately, the agreement is oftentimes inadequate as a complete instrument, and the agent may do something which the principal did not intend. This situation gives rise to other methods by which an agent is said to receive authority from the principal.

Ratification. An agent can also obtain authority by a process known as *ratification*. That is, an individual may perform some act concerning another person without authority at all, and this act may be assented to at a later time by the person involved. Thus *A* writes an insurance policy covering *B*'s house against loss by fire. *A* is not authorized to do this by an insurer. However, *A* later persuades insurer *C* to accept this risk, and thus becomes *C*'s agent by ratification.

Estoppel. A third way in which an agent can obtain authority is through a process known as agency by estoppel. *Estoppel* is a legal doctrine under which a person may be required to do something, or to refrain from doing something, that is inconsistent with previous behavior. Suppose in the example above, insurer *C* continues to allow *A* to sell insurance even though *A* does not have an agency agreement with *C*. Every time *A* sends in a policy, *C* accepts it. Gradually *A* becomes known as *C*'s local agent in the community and no attempt is made to inform the public differently. To the public, *A* has the power to bind *C* to fire insurance contracts as is the custom with other local agents. Now, *A* writes coverage on *D*'s house and before the policy is ratified by *C* the house burns. May *C* deny liability on the grounds that *A* had no authority to write the policy in the first place? It is very probable that the courts would say that because *C* had led the public to believe that *A* had authority to bind it, to allow *C* to escape payment would work a hardship on an innocent party, and the law would provide a remedy. *C* is *estopped* from denying liability, and *A* has become an agent by estoppel.

In summary, one can obtain the authority of an agent either expressly or by implication. One can have actual authority, or if not, one can have *apparent authority*, and may still bind the principal. Authority includes customary powers and all the powers necessary to carry out the job of an agent. Secret limitations on authority that are not customary will not be effective as to innocent third parties. Courts have often extended an agent's authority beyond the actual authority because of these principles. For example, a company denied its liability under a policy of life insurance on the grounds of false statements in the application. It was shown that the agent had taken the responsibility of answering the questions for the insured, and that the agent had answered incorrectly even though the correct information was received. The court held that knowledge of the agent is knowledge of the company and that to deny liability would be inequitable. The insurer had to pay.[20] Of course, if the insured knew of the wrong answers recorded by the agent, the insured would be guilty of fraud and could not collect. Most courts refuse to hold that an applicant signing the application warrants the truth of everything in the application.

[20] *Atlas Life Insurance Co.* v. *Eastman,* 320 Pac.2 397 (Okla. 1957).

Estoppel Versus Waiver

A *waiver* is the voluntary relinquishing of a known right. Estoppel prevents one from asserting a right because of prior conduct that is inconsistent with such an assertion. The two legal doctrines are vital in an understanding of the law of agency. Often they are not clearly distinguished, even in court actions, and sometimes they are used interchangeably. The two doctrines are of interest primarily in understanding how the acts of insurance agents may or may not be binding upon insurers. To illustrate, in a case involving an accidental death policy, a lower court dismissed the suit on the evidence that proofs of loss were not filed as required under the policy. A higher court found that the company's agent had told the insured that it would do no good to file a proof of loss because there was no liability for payment for accidental death. The court decided that such an action amounted to a *waiver* of the requirement to file a proof of loss.[21] Had it not been for the doctrine of waiver, the beneficiary would have had no chance of collecting on this policy.

Estoppel operates when there has been no voluntary relinquishing of a known right. Estoppel operates to defeat a "right" which a person, technically speaking, possesses. When the enforcement of this right would work an unfair hardship on an innocent party who has been led to rely on certain conduct or actions of another person, the courts will deny the right under the doctrine of estoppel. Waiver and estoppel situations oftentimes arise when the policy is first put into force. Let us say that an agent writes a fire insurance policy with the full knowledge that some condition in the policy is breached at the time it is issued. For example, the insured might be engaged in a type of business that the insurer has instructed its agents not to write and has excluded in the policy. The agent issues the policy anyway, and there is a loss before the insurer has had an opportunity to cancel the contract. Most courts would say that the action by the agent constituted a waiver of the breached condition, and the insurer would be estopped from denying liability.

Agents Versus Brokers

In most areas of insurance, middlemen, known as brokers, operate. A *broker* is the legal agent of the insured and does not have the same powers as a local agent although operating at the same level. A broker is employed by the individual seeking coverage to arrange insurance on the best possible terms. The broker has contacts with many insurers, but does not have an agency agreement with them. Thus, the broker is free to deal with any insurer that will accept the business. The broker cannot bind any insurer orally to a risk because the broker has no prior arrangements such as would be described in an agency agreement. Thus, in dealing with a broker, one should not assume coverage the moment the insurance is ordered. One is covered only when the broker contacts an insurer that agrees to take the risk.

[21] *Keel v. Independent L. & A. Insurance Co.*, 99 So.2 225 (Fla. 1957).

Legal Uncertainties

Although the legal principles discussed in this chapter are general rules which normally govern the settlement of disputes under insurance contracts, it should not be assumed that they apply invariably, or that settling insurance disputes is simple and routine. In many cases, courts have not upheld a given principle because of the particular facts of a given dispute, lawyers' courtroom tactics, legal errors, or the predilections of judges.

To illustrate, ambiguities in the insurance contract may not always be construed in favor of the insured (principle of adhesion) if the insured is a large corporation which has negotiated as an equal party with the insurer in designing a particular type of contract. Influence of a state insurance commissioner may cause some insurers to grant coverage or settle claims more favorably to the insured than would otherwise be indicated by the strict terms of the policy. Difficulties experienced by laypersons in understanding insurance contracts has caused some insurers to rewrite policies in simpler, nontechnical language, but this new language may introduce further uncertainties which can only be interpreted by the courts in future cases.

In spite of attempts to make the intention of the parties and the legal principles of insurance contracts clear to all, many legal uncertainties remain, necessitating recourse to the courts and to legal counsel by the insured in settling insurance disputes.

SUMMARY

1. An understanding of legal principles is vital to a proper understanding of the insurance contract itself. There are several differences in the application of these legal principles to life insurance as opposed to general insurance.
2. Insurable interest is necessary for any insurance contract to be valid. The principles of indemnity and subrogation are closely related to the principle of insurable interest. Both are necessary to reinforce the principle of insurable interest.
3. Because insurance is a contract of utmost good faith, breach of warranty or a material misrepresentation on the part of the insured can void the coverage. A concealment has the same legal effect as a material misrepresentation.
4. Insurance is effected by means of a legal contract and must meet the general requirements of contracts. Thus the insurance contract must not be against public policy, must be enacted by parties with legal capacity to contract, must be effected with a meeting of the minds, and must be supported by a consideration. Oral contracts of insurance may be valid, although they should usually be avoided whenever possible. Insurance is a contract of adhesion and any ambiguities are construed against the insurer. Insurance is an aleatory and conditional contract.
5. Insurance is effected through agents who have varying degrees of authority, depending upon the custom in different lines of insurance and upon the doctrines of waiver and estoppel. Brokers are agents of the insured, not the insurer, and cannot bind coverage orally

QUESTIONS FOR REVIEW AND DISCUSSION

1. E. W. Patterson, writing in *Essentials of Insurance Law,* states: Subrogation is a windfall to the insurer. It plays no part in rate schedules (or only a minor one).... Even as to tort-feasors, it is arguable that since the insurer is paid to take the risk of negligent losses, it should not shift the loss to another.
(a) Do you agree with this statement either in whole or in part? Explain.
(b) State the general arguments for including subrogation clauses in insurance contracts.
2. Suit was filed by an insured to change the wording of a paid-up life insurance policy (*Alldredge* v. *Security Life and Trust Co.,* 92 So.2 26, Alabama, 1957). The insured claimed that the company's general agent signed an agreement which would entitle the insured to a paid-up $7,000 policy on the payment of only four annual premiums of $322.28 each. Neither the policy nor the application therefor referred to this written instrument.
(a) Do you think the suit should be successful? Why or why not?
(b) Upon what legal doctrines does your decision rest?
3. In *National Indemnity* v. *Smith-Grandy, Inc.* (150 Wash. 109), Smith-Grandy, an auto dealer, telephoned a general agent in Seattle to place coverage on a truck that was then in transit from Detroit to Seattle. The dealer was told that coverage would commence immediately, which was at 3:15 p.m., on June 7, 1955, the day of the conversation. But the written policy which was subsequently issued stated that the coverage was from 12:01 a.m., June 7, 1955, to June 7, 1956. It was learned later that at 2:15 p.m., the truck had been in an accident that resulted in a claim against Smith-Grandy for $200,000. The insurer refused to pay the claim because the accident occurred before 3:15 p.m. In a suit against the insurer, Smith-Grandy argued that the time stated in the written policy governed the effective time of coverage, but the insurer defended on the basis of the agent's testimony that the coverage was not placed until 3:15 p.m.
(a) How should this case be decided?
(b) Explain the legal doctrines involved in this case.
4. *B*, the employee of a small manufacturer, applies for a fire insurance policy on the manufacturing plant because if the building burns, *B* knows he will lose his job. The agent refuses to write the policy. Upon what grounds is this refusal probably based? Explain.
5. A movie producer has spent $1 million making a movie satirizing the life of a popular public figure. The producer applies for a life insurance policy on this individual in the amount of $1 million. Will the life insurer issue the policy? If so, why? If not, why not?
6. *X* borrows $1,000 from *Y*, who demands that *X* allow him to take out a life insurance policy on *X*'s life as security for the debt in case *X* dies. Later the debt is repaid, but *Y* keeps the policy in force. Five years later, *X* dies. May *Y* collect? Why, or why not?
7. Under what conditions, if any, is it necessary to prove insurable interest on the part of a beneficiary in life insurance? Explain.
8. In *Liberty National Life Insurance Co.* v. *Weldon* (3 Life Cases 2 669, Alabama, 1957), the insurer issued a life insurance policy on a two-year-old girl. The applicant for the insurance was the child's aunt. The parents knew nothing about the insurance. Later the aunt poisoned the child, was found guilty, and was executed. In your opinion was the requirement of insurable interest met in this case? Why?

9. *A* is thinking of purchasing a car. *A* takes out an insurance policy on the car and orders the car delivered to another city where *A* intends to take possession and to close the deal. Before *A* becomes the legal owner, the car is destroyed. In the meantime, the former owner has dropped the insurance coverage on the car.
(a) Who suffers the loss?
(b) Is there any effective insurance covering this loss?
(c) Would your answer be different if the car had been destroyed after *A* had taken title, bearing in mind that the insurance was placed *before* title was taken?

10. Distinguish between the doctrine of insurable interest and the principle of indemnity.

11. *D* has a house valued at $15,000. *D* takes out insurance in two companies, each policy in the amount of $15,000. If the house is totally destroyed, can *D* collect in full from both companies? Why, or why not?

12. In an important case (*Securities Exchange Commission* v. *Variable Annuity Company*, 359 U.S. 65), the U.S. Supreme Court, in a split decision, held that the variable annuity was not "insurance" and was subject to SEC regulation. The variable annuity guarantees a lifetime payment of "units" to the annuitant. The units are expected to fluctuate in value over the period since they represent a cross section of traded common stocks. The court stated:
Insurance involves some investment risk-taking on the part of the company. The risk of mortality assumed here, giving these variable annuities an aspect of insurance. Yet it is apparent, not real; superficial, not substantial. In hard reality the issuer of a variable annuity that has no element of a fixed return assumes no risk in the insurance sense. It is no answer to say that the risk of declining returns in times of depression is the reciprocal of the fixed-dollar annuitant's risk of loss of purchasing power when prices are high and gain of purchasing power when they are low. We deal with a more conventional concept of risk bearing when we speak of "insurance." For in common understanding "insurance" involves a guarantee that at least some fraction of the benefits will be payable in fixed amounts. The companies that issue these annuities take the risk of failure. But they guarantee nothing to the annuitant except an interest in a portfolio of common stocks or other equities—an interest that has a ceiling but no floor.
(a) Do you believe that a variable annuity fits the definitional requisites of insurance presented in this chapter? Explain.
(b) Can you think of insurance contracts that might not meet the court's requirement that an insurance contract must have some element of a fixed return.
(c) Do you agree that the variable annuity has an interest that has "a ceiling but no floor"? Discuss.

13. *A* is killed in an auto accident in which *B* has been held to be negligent. *A*'s life insurer pays $50,000 under *A*'s life insurance policies. Does the insurer have the right to sue *B* for this amount? Why, or why not?

14. *T*'s house, valued at $10,000, is burned for a total loss through *U*'s negligence. *T* collects $6,000, the full face value of the fire insurance policy. *T*'s insurer sues *U* and collects $5,000. How is the $5,000 divided between T and the insurer? Explain.

15. In an application for life insurance, the applicant stated that he had no illness, that he went to a physician only twice a year for a checkup, and that he had no application for insurance pending with any other company. Shortly after the policy was issued, the insured died. The company denied liability when it was discovered that the insured

had seen a doctor six times within ten weeks preceding his application. Furthermore, the insured had applied to another insurance company for $50,000 of life insurance at the same time.
(a) May the insurer properly deny liability?
(b) What legal doctrine of insurance is involved in this case?
(c) What is the test of materiality in a representation?

16. Distinguish between a concealment and a misrepresentation.

17. (a) What two standards of care are imposed in determining whether or not a concealment will void a policy?
(b) Explain the reasons for these two standards of care.

18. An applicant for fire insurance failed to reveal various threats that, unless a certain sum of money was paid, the house would be burned. Do you think this would constitute a concealment?

19. Differentiate between (a) warranty and representation; between (b) promissory warranty and affirmative warranty.

20. There was a plot to burn a house for fire insurance. Ten gallons of gasoline were poured over the floors. One of the plotters went into the house to retrieve some bedspreads, but something went wrong and the gasoline ignited before he could escape. In a suit to recover on the arsonist's life insurance, the insurer denied liability on the grounds that the whole thing was an illegal venture. (*Taylor* v. *John Hancock Mutual Life Insurance Co.,* 132 N.E.2 579 (Ill. App. 1956). Do you think this defense is valid? Explain.

21. What is the connection between legality in an insurance contract and the requirement of insurable interest? Explain.

22. An applicant for life insurance in the amount of $6,500 did not submit his first premium with his application. The policy provided there would be no liability until a policy was issued and delivered during the lifetime and good health of the insured and upon payment of the full first premium. Two days after the application, the applicant passed his physical examination. However, the insurance company wrote its district manager that it would accept the policy only for a higher premium. In the meantime, the agent told the applicant that he had passed his physical, and collected the first annual premium. The company never issued the policy, for within 30 days after the original application, the applicant died of a heart attack. The estate of the insured sued on the grounds that the insurer's silence was implied acceptance of the risk, and it should be estopped from denying that a contract had been made. In your opinion, does the action of the agent and the silence of the insurer, pending an answer from the district manager, constitute sufficient evidence as to allow estoppel to be invoked? Discuss. (*Hayes* v. *Durham Life Insurance Co.,* 96 S.E.2 109 (Va. 1957).

23. What two elements constitute the consideration in an insurance contract?

24. Are all oral contracts of insurance binding? Discuss.

25. (a) Under what conditions can a mistake be corrected in an insurance policy?
(b) Do you think the insurer could have tried the case in Question 3 on the theory of correction of a mistake in the policy? Discuss.

26. Why is the principle of adhesion important in the interpretation of insurance contracts?

27. What is the doctrine of uberrimae fidei?

28. Distinguish between the powers of a general agent and those of a special agent.

29. By what three methods may one become an agent for another?

30. (a) Distinguish between the doctrines of waiver and estoppel.
(b) Give an illustration of each.

Chapter *Nine*

COMMON CHARACTERISTICS OF INSURANCE CONTRACTS

There are many similarities in insurance contracts which can best be studied and analyzed at one time. For example, most contracts contain certain exclusions, such as for loss due to war, loss to property of an extremely fragile character, and loss due to the deliberate action of the named insured. Most property insurance contracts require the insured to notify the insurer of loss as soon as practicable, and usually require that the insured prove the loss. An understanding of these common elements greatly facilitates the understanding of insurance contracts generally, even when a given policy applies a different name to a certain type of provision or condition. The following analysis supplies an outline of the more significant provisions common to most insurance contracts.

THE INSURING AGREEMENT

One of the first things in any contract is a statement of the essence of what is agreed upon between the parties. In insurance, this is found in the *insuring clause,* or *insuring agreement,* which normally states what the insurer agrees to do and the major conditions under which it agrees. The insuring agreement normally starts out, "In consideration for the premiums herein paid and the conditions agreed to, the ―――――― Insurance Company hereby insures the above named person. . . ." The exact nature of what is promised is then set forth. The insured promises only to pay the premium and to conform to the conditions of the policy. Conforming to the conditions is a part of the consideration, so technically the insured just agrees to pay a consideration. The most important, and in fact, the crucial part of the agreement is the statement of what the insurer promises.

NAMED PERIL VERSUS ALL-RISK

There are two general approaches used in framing insuring agreements. One, the traditional, is the named peril approach, and the other, which is being used more and more extensively, is the all-risk approach. The *named peril* agreement, as the name suggests, lists the perils that are proposed to be covered. Perils not named are, of course, not covered. The other type, *all-risk,* states that it is the insurer's intention to cover all risks of loss to the described property *except* those perils specifically excluded.

The insuring agreement of a typical automobile insurance policy is illustrative of the named peril approach. The agreement may state:

> The company agrees with the insured . . . in consideration of the payment of the premium and in reliance upon the statements in the declarations and subject to the . . . terms of this policy . . . to pay. . . .

The policy then lists and describes the various perils against which coverage may be purchased under a particular form. Such perils are usually loss to the insured arising out of the ownership, maintenance, and use of the automobile, and include such losses as may result from negligent operation causing damage to others, loss from collision, loss from fire and theft, and loss from injuries to the insured and passengers while riding in the car.

Typical of the all-risk approach is the insuring agreement of the personal property floater, which undertakes to insure "all risks of loss of, or damage to, property covered except as hereinafter provided." The policy then goes on to impose various limitations upon types of property covered (for example, automobiles, boats, and business property are excluded) and upon certain perils that are excluded (loss resulting from war, mechanical breakdown, and breakage of fragile articles).

DEFINING THE INSURED

All policies of insurance name at least one person who is to receive the benefit of the coverage provided. That person is referred to as the *named insured*. In life insurance he is often called the *policyholder*. In addition, many contracts cover other individuals' insurable interest in the described property or cover them against losses outlined in the policy. These individuals are often called *additional interests* or *additional insureds,* and they normally receive coverage somewhat less complete than that of the named insured.

For example, the family automobile policy covers not only the registered owner of the automobile, but in addition grants exactly the same coverage to the spouse if a resident of the same household. The policy also covers *any* other persons who are driving with the permission of either the named insured or the spouse, provided they are not driving the automobile in connection with any automobile business such as a service station, a garage, or a parking lot.

In a fire policy (New York Standard, 1943), likewise, the policy covers not only the named insured but also legal representatives of the named insured. Thus, if the named insured dies, the policy, by virtue of this provision, is effective in covering the estate until it is settled. In the comprehensive personal liability policy, the insured includes not only the named insured, but also the spouse and the relatives of either if they are living in the same household. In addition, the policy insures any employee of the insured who is operating certain farm equipment in the scope of employment, any person under age 21 in the care of the insured, and any person or organization legally responsible for losses growing out of the use of animals or watercraft owned by an insured. Thus, if the named insured lends a horse to a neighbor and while the neighbor is riding, the horse breaks away and injures someone, the neighbor is covered under the named insured's liability policy.

THIRD-PARTY COVERAGE

Many contracts of insurance may provide coverage on individuals who are not direct parties to the contract. Such persons are known as *third parties*. The rights of third parties are outlined in each contract and vary considerably.

In life insurance the beneficiary is a third party and has the right to receive the death proceeds of the policy, under conditions that are usually determined in advance by the named insured. The beneficiary can be changed at any time by the insured, unless this right has been formally given up—i.e., the insured has named the beneficiary irrevocably. The beneficiary's rights are thus contingent upon the death of the insured, unless the beneficiary has been named irrevocably. Similarly, a person such as a creditor, to whom a policy has been assigned, has certain rights as a third party to receive death proceeds and perhaps certain claims on the cash value of life insurance policies.

In the workers' compensation insurance contract, the agreement is between two parties, an employer and an insurance company. The insurance company agrees to make such payments to employees as are required under the laws of the state relating to compensation of workers who suffer job-connected injuries. The insurer's obligation is directly to the injured worker, who is a third party under the contract. Depending on state law, the worker may bring legal action against the insurer for benefits even though the worker was not a direct party to the agreement.

In medical payments insurance, coverage that is granted under automobile policies and under various liability policies is essentially a third-party coverage. Under it, individuals who are not contracting parties are covered for injuries they may suffer under certain conditions, such as while riding in the automobile of the named insured or while on the property of the named insured. The insurer is obligated directly to the third parties, just as in workers' compensation insurance.

In the field of property insurance, very often the third party is the one who has loaned money on property covered under the policy of the named insured. For example, in fire insurance, the lender is usually covered under what is known as the standard mortgagee clause; and in automobile insurance, under what is known as a loss payable clause. The lender is entitled to recover first if the property is damaged by a peril covered under the policy, with any excess going to the owner. The lender is entitled to advance notice in case the policy is about to be cancelled for any reason and is usually permitted to pay the premium if the insured fails to do so. The lender's rights are not lost merely because the insured violates some provision of the policy and thereby loses his or her rights under the contract. Thus, if the insured uses his vehicle as a public rental vehicle, thereby suspending coverage under the automobile policy, the lender is still entitled to the recovery of the interest in case the vehicle is destroyed. The insurer pays the lender and, through subrogation, enjoys all the rights that the lender had against the insured. In this way the insured cannot benefit from payment to a third party when the insured was not entitled to payment personally.

EXCLUDED PERILS

Practically all contracts of insurance exclude from coverage certain perils, those factors causing losses. Normally a separate section, with all the excluded perils listed and described, appears in the contract. It is vital that the exclusions be noted and understood. Providing for exclusions is the drafter's way of describing and delimiting the insuring agreement to make it definite and unambiguous.

One complicating factor in the analysis of insurance contracts is the fact that most policies define and delimit the peril in such a way that it is partially covered, but not completely so. Thus, in the basic fire policy, fire from specific causes may be excluded, such as fire caused by order of civil authority. In the extended coverage endorsement, explosion is covered, but no explosion which results from bursting of steam boilers, steam pipes, steam turbines, or other rotating parts of machinery owned or controlled by the insured. In life insurance, death from war may not be covered. In accident insurance, some policies restrict coverage to those accidents which stem from given sources such as travel accidents and nonoccupational accidents.

Perils may be excluded or limited in various ways for at least three different reasons:

1. Some perils are excluded because they are basically uninsurable.
2. Others are excluded because it is intended to cover them elsewhere, such as in another type of policy.
3. Still others are excluded because it is intended to charge extra for them under an endorsement which may be added to the policy at the option of the insured.

Perils That Are Basically Uninsurable

In all types of insurance it is very common to exclude loss arising out of war, warlike action, insurrection, and rebellion because losses from such sources cannot be predicted with any degree of reliability, and are often catastrophic in nature. Likewise, perils such as wear and tear, gradual deterioration, and moth and vermin are excluded because losses from this source are not accidental, and are in the nature of certainties and hence uninsurable (except at very high premium rates). For a similar reason, losses to property resulting from deliberate action by the insured are excluded, such as arson, faulty workmanship, or voluntary increase of the hazard. In life insurance, suicide within two years (one year, in some policies) of the application is an excluded peril for the same reason.

Perils To Be Covered Elsewhere

Some perils can be more easily covered in contracts that are specially designed for them. Thus, the personal automobile policy excludes losses arising out of business uses of the vehicle, and commercial automobile coverage excludes, under well-defined conditions, personal uses of the vehicle. The problems of insuring business and personal risks are entirely different and policies are designed for each purpose. The exclusion serves the purpose of eliminating duplicate coverage. A similar exclusion is found in fire insurance forms, liability contracts, and inland marine policies. Another example of this type of exclusion is in the exclusion of certain water damage and flood losses from fire forms. Such perils present special problems and must be insured separately.

Perils Covered Under Endorsement at Extra Premium

The third type of exclusion may be illustrated by the provision in the standard fire policy that the policy shall not cover riot or explosion unless fire ensues, and in that event for loss by fire only. In subsequent endorsements, the perils of riot and explosion are customarily added back into the policy at an extra premium. In this way those insureds who do not require additional coverage of certain perils may choose a more limited form of coverage.

EXCLUDED LOSSES

Most insurance contracts will contain provisions excluding certain types of losses even though the policy may cover the peril that causes these losses. For example, the fire policy covers direct loss by fire, but excludes *indirect* loss by fire. Thus, the policy will not cover loss of fixed charges or profits resulting from the fact that fire has caused an interruption in a business. Separate insurance is necessary for this protection. Neither does the policy cover losses caused by the application of any law (such as building codes) requiring that a more expensive type of construction be used in replacing a building destroyed by fire.

Similarly, in health insurance, if the policy is designed to cover hospitalization expense due to the peril of illness, it will often exclude the cost of doctor bills that result from this same peril. In automobile insurance, loss due to the peril of collision will not include losses to the property of others from this peril. Such losses must be covered under separate agreements.

EXCLUDED PROPERTY

A contract of insurance may be written to cover certain perils and losses resulting from those perils, but it will be limited to certain types of property.

For example, the fire policy excludes fire losses to money, deeds, bills, bullion, and manuscripts. Unless it is written to cover the contents, the fire policy on a building includes only integral parts of the building and excludes all contents. The automobile policy gives only very limited protection to personal property carried in the vehicle. The automobile policy also gives somewhat more limited protection to nonowned vehicles than it gives to owned vehicles of the insured. The liability policy usually excludes the property of others in the care, custody, or control of the insured.

Why are certain types of property excluded from insurance coverage? There may be a variety of reasons, many of which are interrelated. First, it may be the intent of the insurer to cover certain types of property under separate contracts. A good example is the general pattern of excluding property relating to a business from policies designed primarily to insure property for personal uses. Thus, automobiles used as taxis are excluded from coverage under the family automobile policy. Second, the property involved might be subjected to unusually severe physical or moral hazards or be especially susceptible to loss. The exclusion of bullion and manuscripts in the fire policy, for example, is made at least in part for this reason. Finally, property might be excluded because of difficulties in obtaining accurate estimates of its value at the time of loss. Special treatment of items such as works of art is often necessary, as is the insurance of intangible property, such as accounts receivable.

EXCLUDED LOCATIONS

The policy may restrict its coverage to certain geographical locations. Relatively few property insurance contracts give complete worldwide protection. Fire insurance is usually restricted to property in set locations, with only a small part of the coverage, say 10% of the face amount, applicable when some of the property is located elsewhere than on the chief premises of the insured. Automobile insurance is usually limited to cover the auto while it is in the United States, its possessions, or Canada. If the car is in Europe or Mexico, for example, coverage is suspended.

CLAUSES LIMITING AMOUNTS PAYABLE

In defining the coverage of an insurance contract, it is usually necessary for the insurer to limit the dollar amounts of recovery by including clauses such as deductibles, franchises, coinsurance arrangements, time limitations, dollar limits, and apportionment clauses. A policy may contain one or more of these clauses. The clauses serve many different purposes and it is not always possible to ascribe a single reason or even a group of reasons for the use of any one of them. In general, however, the clauses are used to reduce the costs of offering the insurance service; to prevent too many small, expensive-to-administer claims; to achieve a greater degree of fairness in the rate structure; and to place an upper limit on the insurer's obligation on any one policy. These purposes are aimed at converting the insuring agreement from a vague promise to indemnify into a definite, measureable contract which meets the requirements of insurable risks.

Deductibles

It is very common to stipulate that a definite dollar amount, say $50, will be borne by the insured before the insurer becomes liable for payment under the terms of the contract. For example, most people are familiar with the use of $50 and $100 deductibles in automobile collision insurance. More recently, $50 deductibles have been used in fire insurance contracts applying to all claims except those stemming from the occurrence of certain common perils, such as fire, lightning, explosion, and smoke. The purpose of these deductibles is to eliminate small claims. Small losses are expensive to pay, sometimes causing more administrative expense than the actual amount of the payment. It is to the insured's advantage that such deductibles be available, for oftentimes the insured is able to save considerable sums in the insurance cost by their use. For example, in automobile insurance the saving in the annual premium by the use of a $100 deductible for collision claims rather than a $50 deductible might amount to $35. This is the equivalent of saying that to reduce the deductible from $100 to $50 costs $35. The insured would be paying $35 a year for $50 of added coverage, an extremely high rate compared to that charged for the entire contract.

Franchises

A *franchise* is a deductible, expressed either as a percentage of value or as a dollar amount, under which there is no liability on the part of the insurer unless the loss exceeds the amount stated. Once the loss exceeds this amount, however, the insurer must pay the entire claim. Sometimes this franchise is termed "disappearing deductible," because the deductible has no effect once the loss reaches the specified amount. In ocean marine insurance it is common to use a franchise agreement expressed as a percentage. Thus, the policy might provide that there shall be no loss payable on wheat unless the loss equals or exceeds 3%, except for losses caused by fire, sinking, stranding, or collision. But once the loss reaches this level, the insurer is responsible for 100% of the claim.

There is more logic to the use of a franchise than a straight deductible if the sole purpose is to eliminate small claims. However, a straight deductible also eliminates many small claims which the insurer will never have to pay, and it eliminates a portion of large claims as well. In this way a straight deductible keeps down total loss payments. Likewise, the insured who must pay some part of each claim has additional incentive to minimize the frequency of loss.

Coinsurance

The term coinsurance has different meanings in insurance. In health insurance and credit insurance the coinsurance clause is simply a straight deductible, expressed as a percentage. Its purpose in health is to make the insured bear a given proportion, say 20%, of every loss, because it has been found through experience that without such a control, the charges for doctors and other medical services tend to be greatly enlarged, thus increasing the premium to a prohibitive level. The insured who must personally bear a substantial share of the loss is less inclined to be extravagant in this regard.

In fire insurance, the coinsurance clause is a device to make the insured bear a portion of every loss *only when underinsured*. Underinsurance is looked upon as undesirable for two reasons. First, insurance companies are in business to restore their policyholders to the same position they were in before the loss. They obviously cannot accomplish this objective unless the insured is willing to protect the whole value of the property.

Second, it costs relatively more to insure the business of individuals who are underinsured than it does to handle the business of individuals who purchase insurance equal to the full value of the object—that is, those who take out "full insurance to value." This follows because most losses are partial, and the probability of partial losses is higher than the probability of total losses. Rates depend on the probability of loss. Consequently, it follows that the *rate* charged for partial losses should be higher than the rate charged for total losses. No one knows whether a loss will be total or partial. Yet there is a tendency for the average person to assume that this loss will be partial and therefore underinsure in order to save premium cost.

The typical coinsurance clause prorates any partial losses between the insurer and the insured in the proportion that the actual insurance carried bears to the amount required under the clause. Usually 80% or 90% of the sound value is the amount required.[1] Thus, if there is a building with a $10,000 sound value written with a 90% coinsurance clause, $9,000 of insurance is required. The insured who carries at least this amount collects in full for any partial loss. But the insured who carries half of this amount, or $4,500, collects only half of any partial loss. The insured who carries $6,000 collects two thirds of any partial loss. The amount collected in any case may be determined by the formula:

$$\frac{\text{Amount of Insurance Carried}}{\text{Amount of Insurance Required}} \times \text{Loss} = \text{Recovery}$$

If the loss equals or exceeds the amount required under the clause (if the loss is nearly total), there is no particular penalty invoked by the coinsurance clause. Thus, if in the above case the loss were $9,000 at a time when the insured is carrying only $6,000 of insurance, substitution in the above formula yields the following:

$$\frac{\$6{,}000}{\$9{,}000} \times 9{,}000 = \$6{,}000$$

[1] Sound value means the actual cash value of the property; that is, the replacement cost less an allowance for depreciation.

The recovery is $6,000, the amount of insurance carried, and there is no particular penalty other than the fact that the insured did not carry sufficient insurance to cover the entire loss. In the above case, if the loss were $1,500, the recovery would be $1,000.

By use of the coinsurance clause, the burden is placed upon the insured to keep the amount of insurance equal to or above the amount required by the clause. Failing in this, the insured becomes a coinsurer and must bear part of any partial loss.

Dangers of Coinsurance. There are several factors which, by increasing the value of exposed property without corresponding adjustments in the amount of insurance coverage, might cause an insured to become a coinsurer unintentionally. If inflation increases the replacement cost of the insured's property, the insured is required to increase the amount of coverage or suffer coinsurance penalties. Other factors include unexpected or temporary increases in inventory, increases in supplier prices for replacement goods, and increased investment within the plant or store which modifies or improves the building or its equipment. In one case, a dealer in farm machinery had decided to take on a new line of vehicles and, on the morning of an explosion which destroyed the store, had received a large shipment of parts for the new line. The dealer suffered severe coinsurance penalties in the loss settlement. In another case, a manufacturer had spent $20,000 per machine to modify it to produce at closer tolerances than had been the case when the machines were purchased for $40,000 each. This increased investment subjected the owner to sharp reductions in the effective insurance coverage through coinsurance penalties.

Perhaps the only really satisfactory solution to these problems is to maintain an appraisal program under which periodic reviews by qualified appraisers are undertaken. Such personnel may be indispensable in proving the amount of the loss, representing the insured in negotiations with loss adjusters, and alerting the insured to needed changes in insurance program and coverage.

Coinsurance in Residence Policies. The coinsurance clause as described above has only limited application to insurance contracts covering residences. In general, the clauses are so written that the insured will not suffer coinsurance penalties in the same way as is true with commercial contracts. In residence policies, the coinsurance clause has an application with replacement cost insurance.

Coinsurance Credits. In return for accepting a coinsurance clause for the contract, the insured is offered certain credits in rate. For example, a typical reduction in the building rate for the 90% coinsurance clause is 25% for mercantile buildings and 5% for manufacturing establishments. For 100% coinsurance, the reduction is 30% and 10%, respectively. The reduction is somewhat less when applied to contents, being 20% for the contents of mercantile structures for the use of a 90% coinsurance clause. By accepting the coinsurance clause, obtaining the lower rate, and buying the minimum amounts of coverage required, the insured can obtain greater insurance coverage for the same total premium that would be paid for a smaller amount of coverage written without the coinsurance clause. In many jurisdictions the insured is not given the opportunity to purchase coverage without the coinsurance clause attached.

Coinsurance Rationale. The higher rates necessitated by underinsurance and the rationale of the coinsurance clause in fire policies may be illustrated in four simple hypothetical case examples.

Case 1—Full Coverage. An insurer is attempting to calculate a pure premium for 10,000 uniform buildings, each valued at $10,000. (The pure premium is that number of dollars which will pay for fire losses only and is not adjusted for the cost of doing business.) It is assumed that 99% of the buildings have no losses; and of the remaining 100 buildings, 50 suffer a 10% loss during the year, 40 suffer a 50% loss, and 10 suffer a total loss. It is also assumed that each building's owner covers the property 100% to value, or $10,000. The pure premium calculation is as follows:

	Insurance in Force	*Losses*	*Fire Losses Payable*
	$ 99,000,000	0	0
	500,000	10%	$ 50,000
	400,000	50%	200,000
	100,000	100%	100,000
Total	$100,000,000		$350,000

$$\text{Pure Premium} = \frac{\$350{,}000}{\$100{,}000{,}000} = .0035 = \$.35 \text{ per } \$100 \text{ of value, or } \$35 \text{ per building}$$

In this case the insurer must charge each building owner $35 to pay for the expected fire losses. The corresponding fire rate would be $.35 per $100 of insured value.

Case 2—50% Coverage. Assume all facts the same as in Case 1 except that each insured decides to insure only 50% to value:

	Exposed Value	*Insurance in Force (50%)*	*Losses*	*Fire Losses Payable*
	$ 99,000,000	$49,500,000	0	0
	500,000	250,000	10%	$ 50,000
	400,000	200,000	50%	200,000
	100,000	50,000	100%	50,000*
Total	$100,000,000	$50,000,000		$300,000

* Limited by the face amount of the policy to 50% coverage.

In this case the insurer must pay out $300,000 in losses. However, if the insurer has charged the $.35 rate as developed in Case 1, it will have collected only $175,000 from policyholders ($50,000,000 × .0035). It will therefore suffer a net deficit of $125,000 due to underinsurance.

Case 3—Charging Higher Rate. Assume all facts the same as Case 2 except that the insurer decides to charge a higher rate in order to prevent the deficit.

Since total losses payable in Case 2 are $300,000 and there is $50 million of insurance in force, the pure premium must equal .006 ($300,000/$50,000,000) or $.60 per $100. This contrasts with the situation in Case 1 where a rate of only $.35 per $100 was needed.

Rather than charge a higher rate for coverage, the insurer may utilize the coinsurance clause, which reduces loss payments to the individual insured.

Case 4—Use of Coinsurance Clause. Assume the same facts as Case 2, except that the insurer attaches a 100% coinsurance clause to each policy. The rate charged is $.35 per $100 of value, which produced a net deficit without the use of coinsurance.

	Insurance In Force	*Insurance Required (100%)*	*Percent Recovery*	*Fire Losses Incurred*	*Amount Payable by Insurer*
	$49,500,000	$ 99,000,000	50	0	0
	250,000	500,000	50	$ 50,000	$ 25,000
	200,000	400,000	50	200,000	100,000
	50,000	100,000	50	100,000	50,000
Total	$50,000,000	$100,000,000		$350,000	$175,000

Premiums collected (.0035 × $50,000,000)	$175,000
Deficit	0

In this case, the insurer eliminated what would have been a net deficit by reducing loss recoveries by means of the coinsurance clause. Policyholders have suffered $175,000 of losses through coinsurance penalties. Presumably it is immaterial to the insurer whether a $.60 rate is charged or the coinsurance clause is used to effect ''equity'' in the rate structure. The insurer might offer the insured a choice: the higher rate ($.60 in the above example) or allow attachment of a coinsurance clause and pay the lower rate ($.35). In practice, however, coinsurance credits are not as large as this example suggests.

Time Limitations

Time is of the essence in most insurance policies. There are specified limits of time set forth, for example, during which the loss must be suffered, the insurer to be notified in event of loss, the claims to be paid, and the proof of loss to be submitted. We are now interested primarily in the time limits that affect the dollar amount of coverage. To illustrate, in health insurance contracts, and for that matter in nearly all contracts guaranteeing the payment of an income or periodic indemnification for loss, there are often waiting periods before recovery begins. There are also time limitations that restrict the maximum period for which payments may be made. Thus, in a policy that pays an income to the insured who becomes permanently disabled, it is very common to provide that no income shall be payable during the first 7 or 30 days of disability. Such a provision has the same purpose as a straight dollar deductible, namely, to eliminate small claims and to reduce the cost of coverage. In addition, the policy may provide that the income shall continue for one year, two years, ten years, or life, as the case may be. The insurer always specifies what time limit shall be imposed. This is necessary in order to meet the requirement that an insurable risk must be definite and measurable.

Time limitations are found in many kinds of insurance contracts other than health insurance. In business interruption insurance, the insurer promises to pay for profits and necessary continuing expenses lost as the result of an interruption of normal business operations due to the occurrence of a named peril. The payment necessarily depends primarily on the length of time the business was shut down as a result of the named peril. In life insurance, the contract is often settled with the beneficiary by paying the proceeds in the form of an income, rather than in a lump sum. When this is done, the length of time the income is to continue is spelled out in the policy.

Dollar Limits

Most insurance contracts provide for maximum dollar limits on recovery for given types of losses. In addition to the limits imposed by the face amount of the policy, there are two general types: specific limits and aggregate limits.

Specific dollar limits restrict payments to a maximum amount on any one definite item of property or from a named peril, as provided in the policy. *Aggregate dollar limits* restrict payments to some maximum amount of any one group of items of property. Thus, in the fire insurance ''special'' form, applicable to a dwelling, the policy has a specific limit of $250 on liability to plants, shrubs, and trees from any one loss. In addition, there is an aggregate limit which provides that no more than 5% of the amount of insurance may apply to plants, trees, and shrubs in any one loss.

Another example of dollar limits is found in the manner in which insurers restrict their liability for losses resulting from bodily injury liability. Usually there is a specific limit of liability for damage to any one person, and there is an aggregate limit of liability applicable to loss in any one accident. Thus, if the limits of liability are expressed as ''$10,000/$20,000 BI,'' it means that the company will be liable for no more than $10,000 to any person in a given accident, and in no case for more than $20,000 per accident in the event that more than one person files a claim for which the insured is liable.

Apportionment Clauses

Practically all contracts of indemnity and many valued contracts contain *apportionment clauses* that limit the insurer's liability in case other insurance contracts also cover the loss.

For example, a contract may agree to pay the insured a certain income on a valued bais if the insured becomes permanently and totally disabled. It might stipulate, however, that in case the insured is collecting under other disability contracts as well, the indemnity will be reduced to the point that the insured will be prevented from collecting more than, say, three fourths of the income received prior to the disability. Sometimes the effect of the apportionment clauses is quite severe because one insurer may limit its liability to its proportion of all insurance covering the property regardless of whether the other insurance policies apply to a particular loss. As an example, suppose *A* has a building valued at $10,000. *A* has fire policies in two companies, *X* and *Y*, in the amount of $5,000 each. The policy in company *X* is written to cover windstorm losses through the use of the extended coverage endorsement, and the policy in company *Y* does not contain this endorsement. Company *X*'s policy contains an apportionment clause. In case of a windstorm loss of $1,000, company *X* pays only the proportion that its policy bears to all fire insurance on the property, or one half. Thus, the insured collects $500 from company *X* and nothing from company *Y* because company *Y*'s policy did not insure against windstorm. The only solution to this problem is to make sure that all policies insuring the property are identical in their coverage.

The purpose of apportionment clauses, sometimes known as pro rata liability, or distribution, clauses is to establish some procedure by which each insurer's liability may be determined when more than one policy covers the property. In the absence of such clauses, the insured might collect more than the actual cash loss, and a moral hazard could be created. In most property insurance lines, these clauses simply provide for an apportionment of coverage in the same proportion that the amount of each policy bears to the total insurance. In other lines, such as automobile, the clause provides that with regard to certain losses, such as accidents involving a nonowned car or those involving medical payments claims, the policy will be "excess over any other applicable coverage." That is, the contract is to apply to losses only after the limits of liability of all applicable insurance contracts have been exhausted. In ocean marine insurance, it is the general rule that the limits of liability of the first policy to be written on a given exposure must be exhausted before subsequently issued contracts will have any liability. Other policies, such as the personal property floater, do not permit other insurance to be written on the described property. If it is found that other insurance has been written, this will act as breach of warranty and may void the coverage.

COMMON POLICY CONDITIONS

All insurance contracts are written subject to certain conditions. Breach of these conditions is usually grounds for refusal to pay in the event of loss. Therefore, the conditions should be read with care, even though in some cases the insurer does not insist upon exact compliance. Most of the conditions have to do with such matters as loss settlements, actions required at the time of loss, valuation of property, cancellation of coverage, and suits against the insurer.

Fraud

Many contracts state that misrepresentation or fraud will void the contract. This condition may be inserted in the contract as much to serve as a warning to the insured as it is to state a condition that would be enforced by the courts even if the policy said nothing about it.

Notice of Loss

Most contracts of insurance require the insured to give immediate written notice of any loss, if practicable. If it is not practicable to do so, the loss must be reported within a reasonable time. For example, if a forest fire destroys *A*'s summer cabin that is situated in a remote area, *A* may not be able to reach outside communications for several days. If *A* made an attempt to notify the insurer as soon as reasonably possible, *A* would still be able to collect on the insurance policy. The purpose of this provision is to give the insurer a reasonable opportunity to inspect the loss before important evidence to support the claim and establish the actual amount of damage is dissipated. As another example, a person injured in an accident may be unable to give immediate notice of loss. However, failure to notify the insurer promptly would not violate the notice of loss provision in the health insurance policy.

Proof of Loss

The insured is given a certain period, usually 60 or 90 days, to render a formal proof of loss. It is not enough that the insurer be notified of the loss; it is necessary for the insured to prove the amount of the loss before being able to collect. Usually the company adjuster or agent aids the insured in preparing the proof, but the burden is on the insured to accomplish the task. In this connection, the insured must submit to examination under oath as to the accuracy of proof; must produce all books of account, bills, invoices, etc., that might help in establishing the loss; and must cooperate in any reasonable way to assist the insurer in verifying the proof.

In some cases, establishing the proof of loss is an extremely specialized and expensive task. In ocean marine insurance, for example, specialists known as *average adjusters* may spend years collecting all the proofs of loss resulting from a sunken ship and involving hundreds of cargo owners, in order that a final settlement can be made and the loss apportioned among the various insurers that are liable. In large fire losses, adjusters from all over the nation may spend months in the destroyed area reconciling all conflicts over claims for losses.

Appraisal

Most contracts of property insurance provide that if the two parties cannot agree on a loss settlement, each may select a competent and disinterested appraiser to determine the loss. An impartial umpire, selected and paid by each party, settles any remaining differences. Although this somewhat expensive procedure is not resorted to often, it must be complied with in many states before suit can be brought for recovery under the policy where the cause of the suit is failure to agree on the actual cash value of the loss.

Preservation of the Property

Most contracts of property insurance contain provisions requiring the insured to do everything possible to minimize losses to insured property when the insured peril occurs. In fire insurance, the insured must protect the property from further damage. This means, for example, that the insured must take all reasonable steps to cover up property that has been removed from the building to protect it from rain or exposure. If the insured fails to do this, the insurer may be relieved from any further liability for loss.

Ocean and inland marine policies contain a clause known as the *sue and labor clause,* which requires the insured to "sue, labor, and travel for, in and about the defense, safeguard, and recovery of the property insured hereunder." This may may be interpreted to mean that the insured is required to hire salvors to protect a stranded ship from further loss, to hire guards to watch over a wrecked truck and its cargo, and to bring suit against a party liable for loss. The insurer agrees to be responsible for these expenses, in addition to paying the full limits of liability under the policy for loss. Thus, if the insured pays a salvage company $5,000 to save a stranded ship, but the effort fails and the ship becomes a total loss, the insurer will indemnify the insured for full value of the ship plus the $5,000 fee for salvage.

Cancellation

All contracts of insurance specify the conditions under which the policy may or may not be terminated. In general, life insurance and certain health insurance contracts may be terminated by the insured but not by the insurer except for a limited period named in the "contestable" clause. Property and liability contracts may usually be cancelled by either party upon specified notice.

Property and liability insurance policies usually state that the insurer may elect to end its liability for losses after a five or ten days' notice. This gives the insured time to obtain coverage elsewhere and prevent any lapse of protection. In such cases the insurer is obligated to return any unearned premium on a pro rata basis. Thus, if the premium has been paid in advance for three years and the insurer cancels after one and one-half years have expired, it is obligated to return one half of the premium to the insured. However, if the insured cancels, the policy usually provides for a short-rate return of premium. In the above case the insured would get back only about 40% of the premium instead of one half. The reason for the difference in methods of refunding premiums lies in the fact that if the insured cancels before the end of the full term, the insurer should be entitled to some compensation for the extra cost involved in short-term policies. Furthermore, if there were no penalty involved in such cancellations, there might be a tendency for better risks to drop out, leaving the insurer with the poorer risks, i.e., adverse selection would result. If the insurer cancels, however, the insured should not be penalized for the short-term coverage.

Until recently, few if any restrictions were imposed by the insurer on the right to cancel a property or liability insurance contract. Due to the tendency of some insurers to cancel policies without adequate explanation, in 1969 the state of New York required insurers to specify the grounds for cancellation of certain nonbusiness contracts, furnish the facts on which the cancellation is based, and show that these facts revealed some fault on the part of the insured.[2] The automobile insurance policy contains a cancellation provision which imposes certain restrictions on the rights of the insurer to cancel. (See Chapter 16.) In most contracts, however, no reason need be given when either party elects to cancel such a contract as described.

In life insurance and in certain other types of contracts, such as noncancellable disability income policies and credit insurance, there is no cancellation privilege given the insurer. If the insurer could cancel at will, the insured might be deprived of coverage at the very moment it was needed most because in these lines certain events that indicate the imminence of loss usually become apparent; thus the insurer would be warned of impending liability.

Where a policy is not cancellable by the insurer but is subject to termination by the insured, there is no provision for return of premium as such to the insured. All premiums paid in are considered earned by the insurer. In life insurance, upon surrender of the policy, the insured is entitled to what are known as nonforfeiture values, which may have accumulated under the policy. These values originate from premium payments, but they are not identified as such in the policy; rather they form a pool of funds that in effect are excess premiums paid in and held for the insured as savings. (This feature is discussed in Chapter 21.)

Assignment

An *assignment* is the transfer of the rights of one person to another, usually by means of a written document. In insurance it is common to allow the insured to assign his rights under the contract to another person. Usually such permission must be specifically granted. The person granting the right is called the *assignor* and the party to whom the right is granted is called the *assignee*. In life insurance the policy provides that if another person is to be given any rights under the contract, such as the right to receive death proceeds to the extent of a debt that existed between the assignor and the assignee, the insurance company must be notified. In the event of the death of the insured, such as assignment must be honored before any named beneficiary receives payment. This is very common when a lender requires protection before granting a loan to a borrower.

Often when a property is sold, it is desired to transfer the existing fire insurance policy to the new owner. This transfer ends the necessity of cancelling the old policy, taking a short-rate return of premium, and placing a new policy in force. Permission of the insurer is required for such an assignment. In ocean marine insurance it is the usual practice to allow assignment of the coverage on cargo shipments without prior consent of the insurer. The assignment is accomplished by means of a document known as a *cargo certificate,* which may be endorsed somewhat in the same way as a negotiable instrument as the goods change hands in their journey from producer to final consumer.

[2] New York Insurance Code, Chapter 189, Section 167-b.

The reason for requiring permission of the insurer before policy rights may be assigned is that insurance is a personal contract and one of utmost good faith, and the underwriting of it requires investigation into the personal characteristics of the insured. To allow assignments without consent of the insurer could impose obligations and risks that were never contemplated in the original contract.

SUMMARY

1. There are two general approaches to insuring agreements—the named peril and the all-risk approaches. The tendency is to expand the use of all-risk contracts as time goes on.
2. It is common to cover many more than one individual as insureds under most insurance policies. These secondary interests normally do not receive as broad coverage as is given to the named insured. Policies also give certain privileges to third parties, who are not direct parties to the contract. In fact, many insurance agreements are chiefly for the benefit of third parties.
3. All contracts of insurance contain exclusions. There are excluded causes of loss or excluded perils such as war, wear and tear, and intentional damage. There are often excluded losses and excluded property so that even if an insured peril occurs, not all the loss it may cause is covered. Most policies exclude or limit losses caused in certain locations, such as while the goods are away from a named location or abroad.
4. The practice of limiting amounts payable is common to insurance contracts. Thus, there are various kinds of deductibles, franchises, coinsurance arrangements, time limitations, named dollar limits of liability, and apportionment clauses. These clauses serve purposes other than merely keeping down the insurer's loss payments. They may encourage the insured to take out complete insurance to value or they may discourage this course of action. They also serve to control the moral hazard and to define the insurer's obligation more precisely than would be possible without them, thus converting what might be an uninsurable risk into one that is insurable.
5. The major conditions of the insurance contract which follow fairly standard wording are fraud, notice and proof of loss, appraisal, preservation of the property at the time of loss, cancellation, and assignment. Each of these clauses is intended to make the risk acceptable to the insurer.

QUESTIONS FOR REVIEW AND DISCUSSION

1. The insuring agreement of the personal property floater reads: "Perils insured. All risks of loss of or damage to property covered except as hereinafter provided." Should one assume from this that one has all-risk coverage for the property described? Explain.
2. John lends his car to Jim, who drives it to a nearby town where he has an accident that damages the front end. Later Jim lends the car to his friend Jack, who forthwith runs into a pedestrian and is sued for $5,000. Assuming John has complete automobile insurance

coverage, which of the above accidents, if any, is covered? Why?

3. *A* has a comprehensive personal liability policy. His married son, *S*, lives next door. A gardener who was to work on *A*'s lawn made a mistake and started to work on *S*'s lawn instead. *S* had been digging a trench for a water pipe. The gardener stumbled over the half-covered trench and broke his leg. He sues *S*. Does *S* have coverage under *A*'s comprehensive liability policy? Why?
4. *T* is the beneficiary under *X*'s life insurance policy. *X* dies and it is discovered that *X* has named *Y* as a new beneficiary to replace *T*. *T* sues the insurer, holding that as a third party he had certain rights that were violated. Assess the position of *T*.
5. *D* is a worker employed at the plant of *Z*. *D* is injured and is awarded a lifetime income of $137 per month from *Z*'s workers' compensation policy. Later, *Z* goes out of business. Ten years later *D*'s payments suddenly stop. Does *D* have any rights to proceed against the insurance company, or must *D* sue *Z*? Explain.
6. Explain the major reasons for excluding certain perils from insurance contracts.
7. Differentiate between excluded perils and excluded losses, giving examples of each type.
8. An automobile policy excludes coverage of nonowned autos if they are furnished for the regular use of the named insured, but covers such cars if they are only occasionally used.
   (a) Explain the probable reason for this.
   (b) Is this exclusion sound from the standpoint of basic insurance principles? Why or why not?
9. The personal property floater excludes loss against breakage of eyeglasses or glassware unless occasioned by certain named perils such as fire, theft, and lightning.
   (a) Why is such property excluded?
   (b) If you were designing a new policy, under what conditions would you cover such property? Discuss.
10. *A* is offered the choice of a major medical policy with a $100 deductible or with a $500 deductible. There are five members in *A*'s family and the deductible applies on a calendar year basis to each individual in the family. The cost of the policy with a $100 deductible is $200 a year while the cost of the policy written with a $500 deductible is $70 a year. Which policy should *A* take? Why?
11. Explain the difference between a franchise clause and a straight deductible by use of an example.
12. A certain fire insurance policy is written with a 90% coinsurance clause in the amount of $45,000. The actual replacement cost of the structure, less depreciation, is found to be $100,000.
    (a) What amount may be collected under this policy in the event of the following losses? (1) $1,000, (2) $5,000, (3) $50,000, (4) $80,000, (5) $90,000. Explain your answer.
    (b) Does the clause reduce recovery below the amount insured in all of the above cases? Why?
13. Answer Question 12(a) if the amount of insurance carried had been $60,000 instead of $45,000.
14. (a) Explain the reasoning behind the use of the coinsurance clause in Question 12.
    (b) Is there any other way in which to accomplish the purpose other than through the use of coinsurance? Explain.
15. A certain residential fire insurance form allows up to 10% of the face amount of insurance to apply to losses described as "rental value," but in no case may the recovery exceed 1/12 of this amount in any one month.
    (a) If the policy is for $12,000 and the rental value of the property is $150 per month, how much can be collected if the insured is displaced for two months?

(b) What type of dollar limits are illustrated in this case?
(c) What purpose is served by such limits?

16. The double indemnity provision in a life insurance policy provides that twice the face amount of the insurance will be paid for certain types of accidental death, providing death occurs within 90 days of the accident.
(a) What purpose is served by this type of time limitation?
(b) Is the time limitation in accord with sound insurance principles? Explain.

17. A certain health insurance policy providing an income in the event of permanent and total disability stipulates payments for two years in case of illness, but lifetime payments are provided if the disability is caused by accident.
(a) Account for the difference in the time limits noted.
(b) Are these limitations in accordance with sound insurance principles? Explain.

18. The standard fire insurance policy provides that "this company shall not be liable for a greater proportion of any loss than the amount hereby insured shall bear to the whole insurance covering the property against the peril involved, whether collectible or not." Would the principle of indemnity be violated if this clause were not included? Give an illustration.

19. Why is it unnecessary for a policy to state that fraud will void the contract?

20. While *A* is vacationing in Florida, *A*'s tool shed in Ohio burns and a neighbor notifies *A* that the shed was a complete loss. *A*, returning to Ohio ten days later, notifies the insurance company of the fire and is surprised to find that the insurer denies liability. On what grounds does the insurance company's denial rest? Explain.

21. *Y*'s house and its contents become a total fire loss, but *Y* has only a vague idea of what property actually was destroyed because there was no inventory of the household goods.
(a) How might *Y* go about establishing the loss?
(b) Is it likely that *Y* will be able to collect full indemnity, assuming that *Y* was fully insured? Why, or why not? Discuss.

22. What machinery is usually provided in an insurance contract to handle settlements of loss when the insurer and the insured disagree as to the amount of the claim? Explain.

23. Why are life insurance policies not cancellable by the insurer while fire insurance policies are?

24. Under what conditions may an assignment to a third party of an insurance contract be preferable to cancellation and subsequent rewrite in the name of the third party?

25. It is customary to give substantial allowances in the rate for the use of coinsurance clauses in fire insurance. Assume that a certain base rate is 1% of value annually and that a reduction of 25% in this rate is made for the use of a 90% coinsurance clause.
(a) How much insurance must be carried on a $10,000 building to avoid coinsurance penalties, and what would be the cost of this insurance annually?
(b) If the insured does not have the coinsurance clause and therefore pays the full 1% rate, how much insurance could the insured carry for the same net premium?
(c) Explain the principle illustrated here about the use of coinsurance.

Chapter *Ten*

FIRE AND MULTIPLE-LINE INSURANCE

While fire is a most valuable servant of the human race, it has also proved to be a most destructive enemy. Each year in the United States, it is estimated that about 12,000 lives are lost in fires. In 1973, property valued at over $2.6 billion was destroyed. This chapter concerns the peril of fire and insurance techniques to reduce the risk of loss from this source and from other perils frequently associated with fire.

THE PERIL FIRE

Data collected by the National Fire Protection Association reveal that in 1973 in the United States there were approximately one million building fires and 1.6 million fires not involving buildings, such as in aircraft, motor vehicles, forests, and ships. Table 10–1 shows the incidence of fire losses by major classes of occupancy.

Residential fires are the most numerous type of building fire, accounting for about 36% of the total losses. Mercantile and other commercial building fires tend to be severe, for while they are fewer in number they cause over 50% of the total damage caused by all fires. It should then be noted that although the aggregate fire loss has been increasing steadily in the United States, total property exposed has increased tremendously and the rate of loss has actually declined to the point where best estimates place it at one third of the 1900 level.

The causes of fire, as estimated by the National Fire Protection Association, are summarized in Table 10–2. The largest single source of fire is electrical, followed closely by heating and cooking and smoking and matches.

Other perils, such as windstorms, tornadoes, and explosions, take their toll annually, both in lives and property. A relatively new source of catastrophic loss, disorders, began to make its appearance on the U.S. scene during the period 1965–1969. During this period, disorders caused over $202 million of payments for loss due to fire, riot, vandalism, and other perils which had their origin in civil and racial disorders, beginning with the riots in the Watts area of

LOSS BY FIRE, BY TYPE OF OCCUPANCY, 1973

Table 10-1

Occupancy	Percent of Total Dollar Loss
Residential	36.5
Mercantile and Office	12.2
Manufacturing	12.1
Storage	9.9
Public Assembly	5.1
Educational	3.3
Basic Industry, Utility, Defense	2.5
Miscellaneous Building	1.6
Institutional	.8
Subtotal	84.0
Non-Building Losses	16.0
Total	100.0

Source: National Fire Protection Association estimates reported in *Insurance Facts 1975* (New York: Insurance Information Institute, 1975), p. 36.

CAUSES OF BUILDING FIRES, 1973

Table 10-2

Causes	Percent of Total Fires
Electrical	18.2
Heating and Cooking Equipment	17.7
Smoking-Related	12.3
Incendiary and Suspicious	10.1
Children and Fire	7.6
Open Flames and Sparks	7.5
Flammable Liquids	7.2
Trash Burning	3.8
Exposure	2.7
Lightning	2.3
Spontaneous Ignition	1.6
Gas Fires and Explosions	1.0
Explosions from Fireworks, Explosives	.5
Miscellaneous and Unknown Causes	7.5
Total	100.0

Source: National Fire Protection Association estimates reported in *Insurance Facts 1975* (New York: Insurance Information Institute, 1975), p. 37.

Table 10-3

A RECORD OF CATASTROPHIES, 1970-1974 INSURED LOSSES EXCEEDING $30,000,000

Date	Place	Peril	Estimated Loss
May 11-12, 1970	Texas Panhandle	Tornado, Wind, Hail	$ 50,000,000
August 3, 1970	Southeastern Texas	Hurricane "Celia"	309,950,000
February 9, 1971	Los Angeles County, California	Earthquake, Fire	31,600,000
June 17-25, 1972	Florida, Georgia, South Carolina, North Carolina, Virginia, West Virginia, Ohio, Michigan, Pennsylvania, Maryland, Delaware, D.C., New Jersey, New York, Connecticut, Rhode Island, Massachusetts, Vermont, Maine	Hurricane "Agnes"	97,853,000
March 31, 1973	Georgia, South Carolina, Virginia	Wind, Hail, Tornadoes	33,352,000
April 19-26, 1973	North Dakota, South Dakota, Minnesota, New Mexico, Texas, Oklahoma, Arkansas, Alabama, Missouri, Illinois, Iowa, Louisiana, Mississippi, Florida, Georgia	Wind, Hail, Tornado	33,105,000
May 26-29, 1973	21 eastern, southern, midwestern states	Wind, Hail, Tornadoes	76,490,000
April 2-5, 1974	Alabama, Arkansas, Kentucky, Georgia, Illinois, Indiana, Mississippi, North Carolina, Ohio, Oklahoma, Tennessee, Texas, Virginia, Michigan, Missouri, South Carolina, West Virginia	Wind, Hail, Tornadoes	430,566,000
June 8-9, 1974	Oklahoma, Kansas	Wind, Hail, Tornadoes	47,512,400

Source: *Insurance Facts 1975* (New York: Insurance Information Institute, 1975), pp. 43-45.

Los Angeles in 1965. The largest single set of losses from this source followed the assassination of Dr. Martin Luther King in April, 1968. Table 10–3 illustrates the need for protection against the financial loss. The losses shown in the table are only the insured losses. Uninsured losses, which were probably large, are not reflected. For example, hurricane "Agnes" is estimated to have caused over $3 billion of flood losses. Most of the losses were uninsured although flood insurance had become available from a new federal program prior to the disaster.

THE STANDARD FIRE POLICY

It appears that no matter what measures are taken to prevent fires and other perils, a certain number of losses will occur. While theoretically all fire losses except a very small portion are preventable, modern industrial society has not yet organized itself in such a way that these losses are actually eliminated. Therefore, it becomes the primary function of the insurer to redistribute the burden over a large group in such a way that no one suffers a catastrophic loss from fire. Because most property insurance is written with fire insurance as a base, considerable attention is given here to the standard fire policy.

Before 1873, fire insurance contracts were not standardized, meaning that they often contained different wording or wording which was mutually incomsistent when more than one policy was written on the same property. Such a system often involved not only omissions in coverage, but also produced conflicts which were not in the best interests of policyholders. Each insurer devised its own agreement and there was no attempt to integrate coverage to provide uniform protection. For example, one insurer might include a provision in its policy that if another contract were written to cover the risk, the first policy would be void. The second contract covering the risk might contain the same provision and the insured might, under some interpretations, be without protection altogether when the loss occurred.

The uncertainties introduced by individualized contracts led the state of Massachusetts, in 1873, to establish a standard contract form. In 1880 this form became mandatory for all insurers doing business in the state. In 1887, New York followed suit, using a slightly different form. This latter form was then required in several other states and has become, with only slight modification, the standard of the industry. There was a revision in 1918 and again in 1943. The insuring agreement of the 1943 Standard Fire Policy is reproduced in Figure 10–1, and its major provisions are discussed below. Except for minor variations in some states, substantially identical wording is used in all states.[1]

The Insuring Agreement

The insuring agreement of the standard fire policy, reproduced in Figure 10–1, is of basic importance to a sound understanding of the contract and

[1] Texas, Minnesota, and Massachusetts have adopted a standard fire policy with differ ing provisions, which need not be discussed here.

THE INSURING AGREEMENT OF THE STANDARD FIRE POLICY

Figure 10-1

IN CONSIDERATION OF THE PROVISIONS AND STIPULATIONS HEREIN OR ADDED HERETO AND OF the premium above specified, this Company, for the term of *years specified above* from *inception date shown above* At Noon (Standard Time) to *expiration date shown above* At Noon (Standard Time) at location of property involved, to an amount not exceeding the amount(s) above specified, does insure *the insured named above* and legal representatives, to the extent of the actual cash value of the property at the time of loss, but not exceeding the amount which it would cost to repair or replace the property with material of like kind and quality within a reasonable time after such loss, without allowance for any increased cost of repair or reconstruction by reason of any ordinance or law regulating construction or repair, and without compensation for loss resulting from interruption of business or manufacture, nor in any event for more than the interest of the insured, against all **DIRECT LOSS BY FIRE, LIGHTNING AND BY REMOVAL FROM PREMISES ENDANGERED BY THE PERILS INSURED AGAINST IN THIS POLICY, EXCEPT AS HEREINAFTER PROVIDED,** to the property described herein while located or contained as described in this policy, or pro rata for five days at each proper place to which any of the property shall necessarily be removed for preservation from the perils insured against in this policy, but not elsewhere.

Assignment of this policy shall not be valid except with the written consent of this Company.

This policy is made and accepted subject to the foregoing provisions and stipulations and those hereinafter stated, which are hereby made a part of this policy, together with such other provisions, stipulations, and agreements as may be added hereto, as provided in this policy.

deserves some specific comment and explanatory statements. It will be observed that the consideration for the contract consists of *both* a specified premium and an agreement to the provisions and stipulations which follow. Failure to pay the premium or to abide by these provisions means a failure of the consideration, and hence may lead to a failure of the contract itself if the insurer gives notice of cancellation.

Policy Term. Reference is made to noon standard time as being the time of inception and termination of the contract. This is intended to avoid disagreements that might arise over other time measurements, such as daylight saving time or solar time. If the fire commences during the policy period, all the damage caused by the fire is covered, even if part of the damage is done after the expiration of the policy. Thus, if a fire begins at 11:55 a.m. on the day the policy expires and most of the loss is caused after 12:00 noon, the policy pays the whole claim.

Actual Cash Value. The insuring agreement states that only the actual cash value of the property at the time of loss will be reimbursed, not to exceed the amount that it would cost to repair or to replace the property with material of like kind and quality. Some insureds might interpret this to mean that the insurer will restore all the burned property with material of like kind and quality. However, the insurer sets the replacement cost as a maximum reimbursement. *Actual cash value* is interpreted to mean replacement cost at the time of loss less any depreciation. Thus, if it costs $1,500 to rebuild a 40-year old roof that is almost worn out, the insurer normally will not rebuild the roof, but will make a cash settlement of an amount far less than this to allow for depreciation. Fire insurance is a contract of indemnity, and it is intended to put the insured in the same financial position with respect to damaged property after a loss as before the loss. The insured may buy coverage that will eliminate the deduction for depreciation, but this involves another type of insurance with an additional premium.

In the case of buildings, factors such as obsolescence and a deteriorated neighborhood may be considered in arriving at the actual cash value. In a well-known case,[2] an old brewery was totally destroyed by fire. It had been insured for a substantial amount, but at the time of the fire was obsolete because the National Prohibition Act had made the brewing business illegal. The question was raised as to the amount of the recovery permitted under these circumstances, since the replacement cost less depreciation was substantially more than the building was worth as part of an illegal business. While no definite rule for measuring obsolescence was laid down, the decision established that obsolescence could be considered in reducing the recovery *below* the actual replacement cost less depreciation. In the case of personal property, replacement cost is the cost that would be incurred by the owner in obtaining comparable goods. This amount might be well above the original purchase price, if the trend were rising prices.

The actual-cash-value basis for settling losses may not be used if the state in which the loss occurs has a valued policy law. Valued policy laws apply generally only to real property which is totally destroyed, not to partial losses. However, courts have held that if a building is only partially destroyed but the insured actually suffers a total loss due to a building ordinance which prohibits rebuilding of the damaged property, the insured is entitled to recover the full face amount of the policy.[3]

Interest of Insured. Recovery is limited to the extent of the legal financial interest of the insured in the property. This interest need not be sole ownership of the property, as was required in the 1918 form, nor must the interest be explained in the policy; but it must be proved at the time of any loss. Say that *A* and *B* own a house jointly, *A* insures the house in his name, and *B* is not named as an insured. In the event of loss, only *A* will recover and then only to the extent of his ownership, presumably one half of the value of the house. Thus, all interests should be named in the policy, or they cannot be paid in the event of loss.

Direct Loss. The words "direct loss by fire, lightning and by removal from premises. . . ." are of great importance. By *direct loss* is meant loss, the

[2] *McAnarney* v. *Newark Fire Insurance Co.*, 159 N. E. 902.
[3] *Gambrell* v. *Campbellsport Mutual Insurance Co.*, 177 N. W. 2nd, 313 (1970).

proximate cause of which is one or more of the three sources listed in the insuring agreement. No indirect loss, such as loss resulting from interruption of business or manufacture, is covered. Separate coverage is provided for this type of loss.

There have been many controversies in insurance over the meaning of the words "direct loss by fire." In the 1918 Standard Fire Policy, the peril lightning was not automatically covered and had to be added by endorsement to the basic contract. Many fires were caused by lightning and it became necessary to differentiate that part of the loss caused by lightning from that caused by fire, because the policy covered only direct loss by *fire*. Thus, if a building were struck by lightning, split in two, and then caught fire and burned to the ground, the policy would restore the value of a building that had been split in half, and not a whole building.

To avoid such difficulties, the 1943 Standard Fire Policy added lightning to the basic coverage, but the same problem still exists with regard to other physical perils (such as windstorm) for which protection may be added by endorsement. Suppose a building burns and leaves one wall standing. A week later this wall falls down during a windstorm and damages the insured's building that is situated next door. Is this a fire loss or a windstorm loss? It can be argued that if it had not been for the fire, the windstorm would not have had an opportunity to blow down the wall; therefore the fire is the proximate cause of loss. On the other hand, it might be argued that the wall might have stood indefinitely had it not been for the windstorm; therefore the windstorm was the proximate cause of loss. The doctrine of proximate cause says that a peril may be said to cause a loss if there is an unbroken chain of events leading from the peril to the ultimate loss. Adjusters and sometimes ultimately the courts have the responsibility of interpreting each case in the light of this doctrine in order to ascertain the real meaning of "direct loss by fire."

Sometimes the question is raised as to what constitutes fire. A *fire* may be defined as combustion in which oxidation takes place so rapidly that a flame or a glow is produced. Rust is a form of oxidation, but of course is not a fire. Scorching or heat is not fire. Furthermore, the fire must be *hostile;* that is, it must be of such a character that it is outside its normal confines. Fires intentionally kindled in a stove are not covered in the policy, nor are articles accidentally thrown into the stove. Such fires are said to be *friendly*. However, once the fire escapes its confines, it becomes hostile and all loss resulting directly from it is covered. Direct loss by fire also includes such losses as damage from water or chemicals used to fight the fire, and broken windows or holes chopped in the roof by fire fighters since these are often an inevitable result of the fire itself.

Location. The insuring agreement makes it clear that the coverage applies only while the insured property is at a location specified in the declarations, unless a fire threatens and the goods are moved away to a safe place for the sake of preserving them from destruction. The danger of fire varies greatly depending on the location of the property, and the insurers wish to restrict their coverage to areas that they have had an opportunity to inspect and approve. However, permission is granted to remove the goods to another place for a limited time, set at five days, for safety. Extensions of this period to 30 days are typical in endorsements that modify the basic agreement.

The insuring agreement also provides that it may be amended by later endorsements. Without such permission, a question might be raised as to which provision holds, the basic agreement or later stipulations. It is clear that later amendments govern the coverage, even if they directly contradict earlier provisions, unless the basic agreement specifically prohibits such amendments.

Assignment. Because the insurer wishes to reserve the right to choose the one with whom it will deal, the contract provides that assignment of the policy rights will not be valid without the written consent of the insurer. The personal element in insurance is an important underwriting characteristic and without this provision, the original insured might assign the policy to someone who is a poor moral risk.

The usual reason for an assignment is to transfer an insurance policy to another individual who has purchased the covered property. The assignment avoids the necessity of cancelling the existing contract and taking a short-rate return of premium for the unexpired term of protection, only to replace the coverage with a new policy. Usually the insurer will give its permission to make such an assignment.

Conditions and Stipulations–165 Lines

The New York Standard Fire Policy (1943) contains 165 lines of provisions and stipulations that form the basis of the insurance coverage. Some of the provisions are amended by later endorsement, but by and large the 165 lines set the pattern for all later insurance protection and deserve careful attention. Reference should be made to Figure 10–2 for an identification of the lines discussed in the following comments pertaining to the conditions of the policy.

Excluded Property. Lines 7–10 refer to excluded property, which is divided into two classes—property which may not be covered at all under the Standard Fire Policy, and property which may be insured by specific endorsement. Separate coverage is provided for property such as money and securities, because the special underwriting problems that arise make it desirable to give that class of property special attention. Bullion and manuscripts need to be described carefully before insurance can be granted.

Excluded Perils. Lines 11–24 name the perils that are excluded from coverage. For example, if there is an invasion or a war that results in a fire and this fire destroys the insured property, it is the position of the insurer that the proximate cause of loss is war, not fire. War is a peril that is almost universally excluded in private insurance contracts. Likewise, if the insured deliberately fails to call the fire department until after the fire has a good start, coverage will probably be denied because the proximate cause of loss was the willful neglect of the insured to use all reasonable means to save the property.

CONDITIONS AND STIPULATIONS OF THE STANDARD FIRE POLICY

Figure 10-2

Concealment, fraud. This entire policy shall be void if, whether before or after a loss, the insured has willfully concealed or misrepresented any material fact or circumstance concerning this insurance or the subject thereof, or the interest of the insured therein, or in case of any fraud or false swearing by the insured relating thereto.

Uninsurable and excepted property. This policy shall not cover accounts, bills, currency, deeds, evidence of debt, money or securities; nor, unless specificially named hereon in writing, bullion or manuscripts.

Perils not included. This Company shall not be liable for loss by fire or other perils insured against in this policy caused, directly or indirectly, by: (a) enemy attack by armed forces, including action taken by military, naval or air forces in resisting an actual or an immediately impending enemy attack; (b) invasion; (c) insurrection; (d) rebellion; (e) revolution; (f) civil war; (g) usurped power; (h) order of any civil authority except acts of destruction at the time of and for the purpose of preventing the spread of fire, provided that such fire did not originate from any of the perils excluded by this policy; (i) neglect of the insured to use all reasonable means to save and preserve the property at and after a loss, or when the property is endangered by fire in neighboring premises; (j) nor shall this Company be liable for loss by theft.

Other Insurance. Other insurance may be prohibited or the amount of insurance may be limited by endorsement attached hereto.

Conditions suspending or restricting insurance. Unless otherwise provided in writing hereto this Company shall not be liable for loss occuring

(a) while the hazard is increased by any means within the control or knowledge of the insured; or

(b) while a described building, whether intended for occupancy by owner or tenant, is vacant or unoccupied beyond a period of sixty consecutive days; or

(c) as a result of explosion or riot, unless fire ensue, and in that event for loss by fire only.

Other perils or subjects. Any other peril to be insured against or subject of insurance to be covered in this policy shall be by endorsement in writing hereon or added hereto.

Pro rata liability. This Company shall not be liable for a greater proportion of any loss than the amount hereby insured shall bear to the whole insurance covering the property against the peril involved, whether collectible or not.

Requirements in case loss occurs. The insured shall give immediate written notice to this Company of any loss, protect the property from further damage, forthwith separate the damaged and undamaged personal property, put it in the best possible order, furnish a complete inventory of the destroyed, damaged and undamaged property, showing in detail quantities, costs, actual cash value and amount of loss claimed; **and within sixty days after the loss, unless such time is extended in writing by this Company, the insured shall render to this Company a proof of loss,** signed and sworn to by the insured, stating the knowledge and belief of the insured as to the following: the time and origin of the loss, the interest of the insured and of all others in the property, the actual cash value of each item thereof and the amount of loss thereto, all encumbrances thereon, all other contracts of insurance, whether valid or not, covering any of said property, any changes in the title, use, occupation, location, possession or exposures of said property since the issuing of this policy, by whom and for what purpose any building herein described and the several parts thereof were occupied at the time of loss and whether or not it then stood on leased ground, and shall furnish a copy of all the descriptions and schedules in all policies and, if required, verified plans and specifications of any building, fixtures or machinery destroyed or damaged. The insured, as often as may be reasonably required, shall exhibit to any person designated by this Company all that remains of any property herein described, and submit to examinations under oath by any person named by this Company, and subscribe the same; and, as often as may be reasonably required, shall produce for examination all books of account, bills, invoices and other vouchers, or certified copies thereof if originals be lost, at such reasonable time and place as may be designated by this Company or its representative, and shall permit extracts and copies therof to be made.

Appraisal. In case the insured and this Company shall fail to agree as to the actual cash value or the amount of loss, then, on the written demand of either, each shall select a competent and disinterested appraiser and notify

Added provisions. The extent of the application of insurance under this policy and of the contribution to be made by this Company in case of loss, and any other provision or agreement not inconsistent with the provisions of this policy, may be provided for in writing added hereto, but no provision may be waived except such as by the terms of this policy is subject to change.

Waiver provisions. No permission affecting this insurance shall exist, or waiver of any provision be valid, unless granted herein or expressed in writing added hereto. No provision, stipulation or forefeiture shall be held to be waived by any requirement or proceeding on the part of this Company relating to appraisal or to any examination provided for herein.

Cancellation of policy. This policy shall be canceled at any time at the request of the insured, in which case this Company shall, upon surrender of this policy, refund the excess of paid premium above the customary short rates for the expired time. This policy may be canceled at any time by this Company by giving to the insured a five days' written notice of cancellation with or without tender of the excess of paid premium above the pro rata premium for the expired time, which excess, if not tendered, shall be refunded. Notice of cancellation shall state that said excess premium (if not tendered) will be refunded on demand.

Mortgagee interests and obligations. If loss hereunder is made payable, in whole or in part, to a designated mortgagee not named herein as the insured, such interest in this policy may be canceled by giving to such mortgagee a ten days' written notice of cancellation.

If the insured fails to render proof of loss such mortgagee, upon notice, shall render proof of loss in the form herein specified within sixty (60) days thereafter and shall be subject to the provisions hereof relating to appraisal and time of payment and of bringing suit. If this Company shall claim that no liability existed as to the mortgagor or owner, it shall, to the extent of payment of loss to the mortgagee, be subrogated to all the mortgagee's rights of recovery, but without impairing mortgagee's right to sue; or it may pay off the mortgage debt and require an assignment thereof and of the mortgage. Other provisions relating to the interests and obligations of such mortgage may be added hereto by agreement in writing.

the other of the appraiser selected within twenty days of such demand. The appraisers shall first select a competent and disinterested umpire; and failing for fifteen days to agree upon such umpire, then, on request of the insured or this Company, such umpire shall be selected by a judge of a court of record in the state in which the property covered is located. The appraisers shall then appraise the loss, stating separately actual cash value and loss to each item; and, failing to agree, shall submit their differences, only, to the umpire. An award in writing, so itemized, of any two when filed with this Company shall determine the amount of actual cash value and loss. Each appraiser shall be paid by the party selecting him and the expenses of appraisal and umpire shall be paid by the parties equally.

Company's options. It shall be optional with this Company to take all, or any part, of the property at the agreed or appraised value, and also to repair, rebuild or replace the property destroyed or damaged with other of like kind and quality within a reasonable time, on giving notice of its intention so to do within thirty days after the receipt of the proof of loss herein required.

Abandonment. There can be no abandonment to this Company of any property.

When loss payable. The amount of loss for which this Company may be liable shall be payable sixty days after proof of loss, as herein provided, is received by this Company and ascertainment of the loss is made either by agreement between the insured and this Company expressed in writing or by the filing with this Company of an award as herein provided.

Suit. No suit or action on this policy for the recovery of any claim shall be sustainable in any court of law or equity unless all the requirements of this policy shall have been complied with, and unless commenced within twelve months next after inception of the loss.

Subrogation. This Company may require from the insured an assignment of all right of recovery against any part for loss to the extent that payment therefor is made by this Company.

In Witness Whereof, this Company has executed and attested these presents; but this policy shall not be valid unless countersigned by the duly authorized Agent of this Company at the agency herein-before mentioned.

Excluded Losses. Lines 28–37 exclude three types of losses: (1) those occurring while the hazard is increased by any means within the control or knowledge of the insured, (2) those occurring while the building is vacant for a period beyond 60 consecutive days (this period is often extended in some territories), or (3) those occurring as a result of explosion or riot, unless fire ensues and then for the fire loss only. The first type of loss involves situations in which the insured may change the basic character of the risk by some action, such as switching the use of the building from a garage to a manufacturing establishment. The insurer is entitled to be told of this situation, and if it is not, the coverage is suspended. Often this exclusion is waived for residential property.

Cancellation. The provisions within lines 56–67 specifically set forth the terms under which the policy may be cancelled by the insurer or by the insured. Termination is effective five days after the written notice of cancellation is communicated to the policyholder. The policy remains in force during the five days, which are counted from midnight on the day in which the notice is received to midnight five days later. The notice must either be accompanied by a return of the unearned premium or contain a statement that the pro rata unearned premium will be returned to the insured. Neither party to the contract is required to give a reason for cancellation. The purpose of the five-day notice is to give the insured an opportunity to place the coverage elsewhere.

Mortgage Clause. Lines 68–85 contain the provisions that govern relationships with any mortgagee named in the declaration of the policy. The form that extends the basic fire policy contains further elaboration of the provisions relating to the mortgagee in the so-called standard mortgagee clause. This clause has the effect of creating a separate agreement between the mortgagee and the insurer, almost as if the mortgagee had taken out a separate policy covering its interest in the property.

The mortgagee requires some kind of protection because if the property were destroyed, it is much less likely that the debt would ever be paid. A mortgagee has the possibility of protecting its interest in insured property in at least four ways:

1. Separate insurance for the mortgagee's interest.
2. Assignment by insured.
3. Loss payable clause.
4. Standard mortgagee clause.

Separate Insurance for the Mortgagee's Interest. The mortgagee can purchase separate insurance covering its interest. This plan has the disadvantage, however, that both the mortgagee and the mortgagor will be placing coverage on the same values, since the mortgagor has an interest equal to the entire value of the property, and not just its equity. For example, if there is a house valued at $20,000 with a $15,000 mortgage on it, the interest of the mortgagee is $15,000 and the interest of the owner is $20,000. If each purchased separate coverage, there would be a total of $35,000 of insurance on the house, far more than is necessary to protect the value exposed.

Assignment by Insured. The mortgagee could be protected by means of an assignment. The insured could simply take out a policy and then assign its benefits to the mortgagee, after obtaining the permission of the insurer. The difficulty with this method is that if owner defaults on the premium or otherwise violates a policy provision, the coverage may be cancelled and with it the protection of the mortgagee. In other words, the mortgagee receives no better protection under an assignment than is enjoyed by the person making the assignment.

Loss Payable Clause. The mortgagee could be protected by a loss payable clause. Such a clause simply states that the loss, if any, shall be payable to the person named. However, if the insured were to violate the policy, such as defaulting on the premium, no loss would be payable and the loss payee would receive no payment in most jurisdictions, which treat the loss payable clause as an assignment of any rights to payment belonging to the insured. If the insured has no rights to collect, neither does the loss payee in these jurisdictions.

Standard Mortgagee Clause. The mortgagee may be protected by the standard mortgagee clause, which was designed to overcome the limitations of the other methods and is now in almost universal use. Under the standard mortgagee clause, the mortgagee has certain rights and obligations. Among its rights are:

1. To receive any loss or damage payments as its interest may appear, regardless of any default of the property owner under the insurance contract, and regardless of any change of ownership or increase of the hazard.
2. To receive 10 days' notice of cancellation, instead of five days.
3. To sue under the policy in its own name.

Among the obligations of the mortgagee under the standard mortgagee clause are:

1. To notify the insurer of any change of ownership or occupancy or increase of the hazard that shall come to the knowledge of the mortgagee.
2. To pay the premium if the owner or mortgagor fails to pay it. (In most jurisdictions this has been interpreted to mean that the mortgagee must pay the premium only if it wishes to enjoy the protection under the policy. In some states, and in the forms used widely on the Pacific Coast, the mortgagee covenants to pay the premium on demand, even if it does not wish to maintain the insurance.)
3. To render proof of loss to the insurer in case the owner or mortgagor fails to do so.
4. To surrender to the insurer any claims it has against the mortgagor to the extent that it receives payment from the insurer. The insurer may under some conditions deny liability to the owner or mortgagor and therefore retain, through subrogation, all rights that the mortgagee may have had against the mortgagor. To illustrate, assume that the mortgagee, protected under the standard mortgagee clause, has a $10,000 mortgage on a $15,000 building, and there is a $5,000 fire loss caused deliberately by the insured. The insurer denies liability to the insured, but must pay the mortgagee $5,000. The mortgagee must now surrender to the insurer $5,000 of its claim against the mortgagor. Or the insurer has the right to pay the mortgagee the entire $10,000 debt, obtain an assignment of

the mortgage, and collect in full against the mortgagor. In this way, the mortgagor does not obtain any of the benefits of payment to the mortgagee through a reduction of debt. Instead of owing the mortgagee, the mortgagor owes the insurance company.

Pro Rata Liability. Lines 86–89 state that the insurer shall not be liable for a greater proportion of any loss than the amount insured bears to the whole insurance covering the property, whether or not this insurance is collectible. The pro rata liability clause is simply an apportionment clause. The clause is designed to enforce the principle of indemnity and to prevent the insured from collecting more than one policy covering the property. Thus, if there are three policies in the amount of $5,000, $3,000, and $2,000 covering a loss of $1,000, the insurers are obligated for one half, three tenths, and one fifth of the loss, respectively. If the $2,000 policy is not collectible because the insurer is insolvent, its share of the loss, $200, is not made up by the other policies.

It is worth noting that the pro rata liability clause applies only to policies that cover the same legal interest. If there is more than one interest involved, such as in the case of a lessee and an owner, and there are two policies on the property, each insurer must pay to the fullest extent of its liability and the payment will not be reduced by action of the pro rata liability clause. For example, suppose a lessee spends $10,000 improving a property and insures this value. Since the value of all permanent improvements to real estate revert to the landlord upon expiration of the lease, the landlord also has an interest in the improvements, and may insure them. Since there are two interests, there may be two policies of $10,000 each. In the event that a fire destroys the entire property, both insurers would have to pay to the fullest extent of the insurable interest of each insured.

Requirements When Loss Occurs and Appraisal. Lines 90–161 of the standard fire policy spell out the procedures that are to be followed when a loss occurs, in order that disagreements and expensive court litigation may be avoided. These procedures must be followed before suit can be filed under the policy.

In case loss occurs, there are several obligations that must be met by the insured. Violation of any of these obligations may jeopardize the protection. They include: (1) giving immediate written notice to the company or its agent, (2) protecting the property from further damage, (3) separating damaged from undamaged property and furnishing an inventory of all property, (4) filing detailed proof of loss within 60 days of the loss, and (5) submitting all evidence available to the insurer's adjuster to aid in determination of the amount of the loss as may be reasonably required.

If the adjusters and the insured cannot agree on the amount of the loss, the policy details the procedures that must be followed before any legal action can be taken. It provides that each party, upon the written demand of the other, must select an impartial appraiser, who will then select an umpire to arbitrate any disagreements that still exist after the appraisers have rendered their separate judgments as to the amount of the loss. The insurer reserves the right to take over the damaged property and to pay the insured its sound value, to repair or rebuild it, or to make a cash settlement for the amount of the loss. Normally the last method is used. These are company options, not those of the insured. The insured may not elect to abandon the company property that has been partially or totally destroyed and demand payment therefor. Once the proof of loss is agreed upon by all parties, payment is due within 60 days. This gives the insurer time to investigate further, if it wishes, or to raise the money for payment in the event the loss is so large as to require liquidation of securities or collection from reinsurers. Finally, the policy provides that any legal suit must be commenced within 12 months of the loss. This provision places a sort of statute of limitations on all disputes and prevents indefinite prolongation of uncertainty about them.

Subrogation. Lines 162–165 provide for subrogation rights of the insurer in case the insured has legal rights against liable third parties for any loss.

FIRE AND MULTIPLE-LINE INSURANCE FORMS

It may be observed that the basic fire policy is not complete in itself, since it does not describe in detail the property which is to be covered, nor does it go into sufficient detail as to the terms, conditions, limitations, and exclusions which will further define the precise nature of coverage. There is a definite need to tailor coverage to meet the specific and differing insurance needs of business firms and individuals. This is accomplished by adding to the policy amendments called *forms*.

At first, very simple forms were added to the basic fire policy, accomplishing little more than describing the general nature of the property to be insured. Gradually, more complex forms were developed extending coverage to many different perils and to additional property, such as outbuildings, landscaping, and property when it was away from the main premises.

With the development of multiple-line legislation forms became even more complex and complete. They extended the basic fire policy on a different basis than formerly to include liability, theft, and transportation perils all in one policy. It is generally conceded that the new multi-peril policies will become more and more common and will gradually replace the more traditional forms. In 1973, multi-peril policies accounted for 17.4% of total property-liability insurance premiums, compared to 11% in 1964.

In the following discussion, fire and multi-peril forms are classified according to the basic purposes they serve. There are at least four objectives accomplished with forms:

1. To describe accurately the property which is to be covered and to place various kinds of limitations on the coverage of this property.
2. To extend the basic policy to cover additional perils.
3. To allow automatic coverage on property which fluctuates in amount, such as stock in trade or which is situated at different locations and is moved from location to location throughout the term of the policy.
4. To cover losses, such as indirect losses, which are excluded in the basic policy.

The first three types of forms are discussed below, and the fourth is reserved for more detailed treatment in Chapter 11.

Figure 10–3 presents a schematic outline of two major ways in which property interests may be insured in the United States, namely, fire coverages and marine coverages. All fire coverages are built upon the standard fire policy and its 165-line set of terms and conditions. Marine coverages are designed primarily for the risks of transportation and certain types of fixed location property whose main purpose is in connection with transportation and communication (e.g., radio towers, bridges, piers, wharves).

Each of the fire forms shown in Figure 10–3 may be used in conjunction with other forms and endorsements which modify its terms. For example, a merchant may use a special form designed for its class of business under the special multi-peril (SMP) program, but may modify it to be either on an all-risk basis or upon a named peril basis, depending on his need. Certain endorsements may change the way in which the deductible operates, the way in which coverage is assigned to different locations, the way in which coinsurance applies, etc. It is not uncommon to find that fire forms and endorsements for a complex property occupy an entire file drawer and require considerable study to learn just what insurance applies in case of a given loss.

Describing the Property and Its Coverage

Those forms which describe the property and its coverage may be classified according to residential and business properties.

Residences. The typical residence may be insured under several forms, each of which differs primarily in the degree to which it extends the protection given by the basic fire policy. A typical form will define what is meant by dwelling coverage as opposed to contents coverage; the extent to which coverage is given to trees, shrubs, and plants; the amount of coverage given to property located away from the main premises; and the amount that can be ascribed to indirect losses, such as rental value or additional living expenses.

Dwelling Buildings and Contents—Broad Form. A widely used form to insure residence buildings is the *dwelling buildings and contents—broad form*. It is mainly for residences not qualifying for coverage under the homeowners form. For example, a homeowners form must be issued for a minimum amount of $8,000. The broad form defines insured property and interests to include the following: the dwelling itself; additions to the building occupied as a private residence; materials and supplies located on the premises intended for use in construction, alteration, or repair of the dwelling; garages or storage buildings on the premises which are not used for business purposes; and personal property of any type owned by the insured or by a resident employee engaged in the service of the insured while the property is on the insured premises.

The form extends coverage to personal property located away from the premises up to 10% of the amount of insurance, but not less than $1,000 of coverage. Thus, personal articles or clothing of a son or daughter in college

THE STRUCTURE OF PROPERTY INSURANCE COVERAGE

Figure 10-3

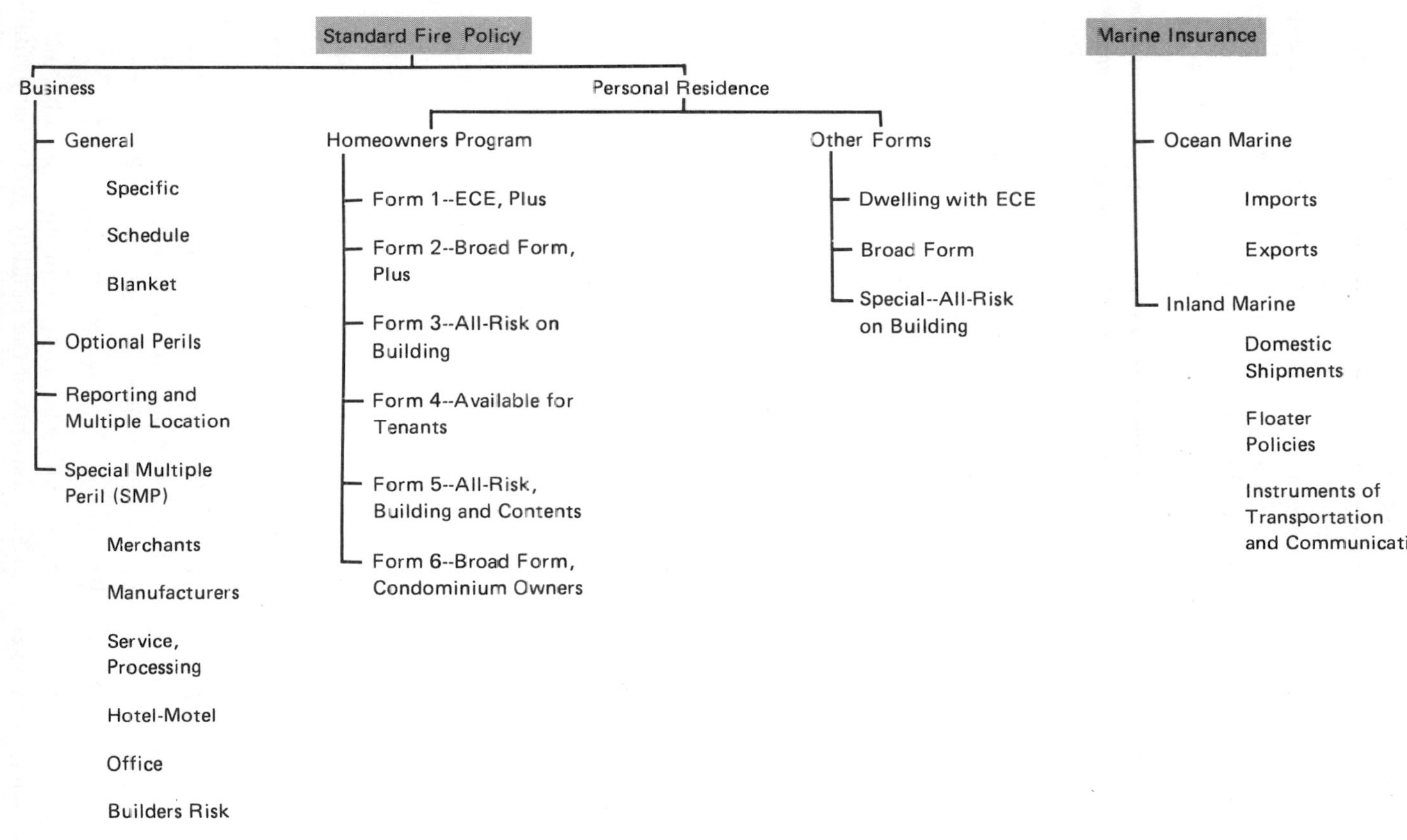

would be covered under the parents' dwelling policy, so long as the loss did not exceed 10% of the amount of insurance. Property such as animals, automobiles, motorcycles, aircraft, and certain business property are excluded under this form. The form extends coverage to loss of rental value of the building or to additional living expenses incurred if the dwelling should burn and cause the insured expenses above and beyond the normal living expenses. Rental value and additional living expense coverage are each limited to 10% of the amount of insurance as additional insurance.

The form covers damage to trees, shrubs, plants, and lawns from certain listed perils up to 5% of the face amount of insurance or $250 for each shrub or tree. There is also a $100 deductible clause in most jurisdictions.

In many territories, the insurer is required to give the insured 30 days' notice of cancellation instead of five days specified in the standard fire policy. Reasons for cancellation must also be given; these may include nonpayment of premium, new facts which would have made the property unacceptable from the start, substantial change in the property, or hazards which have been increased by neglect or omission of the insured.

If any goods are damaged as a result of being removed from the premises due to fire or lightning, they are covered for loss except from theft for a period of 30 days at places to which they are removed for safekeeping. Coverage for removal is limited to five days under the standard fire policy.

Finally, the form adds, with certain limitations, protection known as *replacement cost insurance*. Under this insurance, the company makes no deduction for depreciation if the insured has been carrying coverage equal to 80% of the full replacement cost of the building. An insured who has not been carrying coverage equal to 80% of the full replacement cost might not suffer a full deduction for depreciation. Under the terms of the replacement cost protection of the broad form, the insured may still make a claim for that portion of the full replacement cost of a loss which the amount of insurance carried bears to 80% of the full replacement cost of the building. For example, assume that a residence, replaceable at $10,000 and insured for $6,000 on the broad form, suffers a fire loss of $1,200. It is agreed that the depreciation applicable to the destroyed portion is $600. Eighty percent of the full replacement cost is $8,000. The insured may recover six eighths (75%) of $1,200, or $900. It is required that the insured actually replace the property if the loss is more than $1,000 or 5% of the face amount of insurance, whichever is greater. In this case, the insured would have to effect repairs or collect $600, the actual cash loss. The insured will never recover less than this amount, and may recover more through replacement cost coverage.

The Special Form. The *dwelling buildings special form* differs little from the broad form regarding the description of insured property. The central feature of the special form is that it offers building coverage on an all-risk basis, rather than on a named peril basis.

Business Property. Forms defining what is to be included as a business building, what must be classified as contents of the building, and what limitations of coverage are imposed are much more numerous than in the case of residential forms. The reason for this lies in the many varied types of businesses in operation with special hazards applicable to each. Special forms have been designed, for example, for schools, restaurants, service stations, lumber mills, and many other classes of occupancies. In many territories, a so-called *general form* is used, and space is left in it to insert the definition and description of the property to be insured.

General Form. Since the fire insurance rate applying to buildings is lower than that applying to contents, it is to the insured's advantage to broaden the description of the building as much as possible. A typical description of a building will include permanent attachments such as engines, boilers, pumps, tanks, signs, flagpoles, fences, awnings, and storm windows. Also, fire extinguishers, floor coverings, cooking and cooling equipment, window shades, and even janitors' supplies and employees' uniforms may be counted as a part of the building if they are related to the landlord's servicing of the structure.

The general form describes stock as all merchandise, raw materials, goods in process, packaging materials, labels, etc. It will describe separately all items to be known as furniture, fixtures, and machinery, to include such things as machine parts, manuscripts, electrical appliances, tools, and accounting records. The general form also provides for coverage on what are known as improvements and betterments. These items are usually investments made in the building by the lessee. Even though they will belong to the landlord at the termination of the lease, the tenant may insure their value until the lease has expired.

Under the general form, coverage may be one of three bases: specific, schedule, or blanket. Under *specific coverage,* separate items of stock, machinery, buildings, etc., are listed on the face of the policy with a definite amount of insurance after each item, which is insured separately. Under *schedule coverage,* which is a variation of specific coverage, property at two or more locations is listed and specifically insured. Under *blanket coverage,* property at several locations may be insured under a single item. For example, the policy could provide $87,500 of insurance on all contents at plants in five different cities. Or under blanket coverage, classes of property usually insured specifically might be lumped together and be insured as a single item, such as $10,000 on stock, furniture, fixtures, and machinery.

Typical Clauses in Business Property Forms. Business fire insurance forms often contain important clauses that affect the property to be covered. It is very usual, for example, to find clauses excluding from coverage the cost of excavations, brick or concrete foundations, and underground flues or pipes. The reason for these exclusions is to enable the insured to carry less coverage for purposes of meeting the requirements of the coinsurance clause, since these items are normally not destroyed in a fire. Very often the form will exclude damage to electrical machinery which is caused by electrical short circuits. The form may provide coverage for goods within 100 feet of a building, such as goods that are on platforms or in streets and alleys near the building. It will usually provide a limited amount of protection to cover the cost of removal of debris following a fire.

Extending the Coverage to Additional Perils

Another group of forms extends the basic policy to cover additional perils. Again, these forms may be classified as pertaining to residential or business properties.

Residences. The basic fire policy covers only fire, lightning, and loss while goods are removed from the premises for safety from threatened loss due to the perils insured against. Practically all residential property is protected against many additional perils through the use of one or more of several forms that offer varying combinations of protection.

Extended Coverage Endorsement. One of the first, and still the most widely used, endorsements to broaden the list of perils insured against is the *extended coverage endorsement* (ECE). This endorsement adds windstorm, hail, explosion, riot, riot attending strike, civil commotion, aircraft, vehicles, and smoke, as defined. The endorsement states that the above-named perils will be substituted for the word "fire" in the basic policy as the case requires. Special definitions of windstorm, hail, smoke, etc., are provided. For example, the term "smoke" means only smoke due to sudden faulty operation of a heating or cooking unit, and specifically does not mean smoke from fireplaces or industrial apparatus. "Explosion" as a peril does not include bursting of steam boilers, rupture or bursting of water pipes, or concussion, such as a sonic boom. Loss from vehicles belonging to the insured or loss caused by any vehicle to fences, driveways, walks, or lawns, is excluded. When extended coverage is added to the basic fire policy, it must be written for the entire amount of indemnity as provided against fire. If some policies are written on the property without the endorsement, an apportionment clause, discussed previously, reduces the recovery from an extended coverage loss to that proportion of the loss that the policies having extended coverage bear to the total insurance on the property.

Dwelling Buildings and Contents—Broad Form. The dwelling buildings and contents—broad form extends even further the coverage against ten added perils. In addition to the ECE perils named above, the form covers loss due to damage done by burglars; glass breakage; vandalism and malicious mischief; weight of ice, snow, or sleet; collapse of buildings; water damage to or freezing or leaking of plumbing, heating, and air conditioning systems (freezing and water damage are two separate perils); damage from falling objects (such as trees); electrical damage to appliances and wiring; and explosion of a hot water system.

The broad form also offers broader and more inclusive definitions of several perils insured than is true of the ECE. For example, the ECE defines "smoke" to include only smoke from a faulty heating or cooking unit which is connected to a chimney. Smoke from fireplaces is excluded. In the broad form, smoke only need be "sudden and accidental" and must arise from a source other than argicultural smudging or industrial operations. Thus accidental emission of smoke from a fireplace would be covered, as would smoke from a source outside the building. As another example, the broad form does not exclude sonic boom as an explosion, while the ECE excludes sonic boom. Finally, the broad form covers loss to the dwelling (not to fences, driveways, or walks) caused by vehicles driven by the insured, whereas such losses are excluded in the definition of vehicle damage in the ECE.

Permission is granted for the insured to leave the premises vacant or unoccupied without limit of time, to make alterations or repairs, and to conduct activities usual to the operation of a home. Thus, the normal "conditions suspending insurance," stated on lines 31–35, are removed.

The broad form excludes perils such as war, nuclear explosion, landslide, flood, earthquake, backing up of sewers and drains, and losses occurring outside of the United States or Canada.

Dwelling Buildings Special Form. An even more comprehensive attempt to broaden the coverage for residential property is found in the dwelling buildings special form. This form utilizes the all-risk approach and attempts to cover all risks of physical loss except those perils and losses specifically enumerated. In other words, if a property is covered by this form and is damaged in any way, the loss may be presumed to be covered unless there is a specific exclusion listed. This form cannot be used to cover contents, however; only buildings may be covered. Typical exclusions include damage due to wear and tear, termites, rust, dry rot, mechanical breakdown, earthquake, flood, radioactive contamination, and war or military action of any kind. In addition, certain types of loss to property are excluded, such as loss to retaining walls by landslide or water pressure, and loss to undrained plumbing or heating systems by freezing while the building is vacant. A $50 or $100 deductible applies to all losses with only a few exceptions.

Homeowners Program. The ultimate in comprehensive protection for residences, however, is found in what is known as the *homeowners program*. The homeowners program is an outgrowth of several attempts by the insurance industry to provide a package of protection for the average homeowner that would provide a more balanced and a more generally adequate program of insurance at a lower cost than would be true if the coverages were purchased separately. Such a policy was made possible by multiple-line legislation, and it is known as a *multi-peril policy*. The homeowners policy was developed in 1958 by the Multi-Peril Insurance Conference, an advisory and rating organization for insurance companies. There is a single standard skeleton policy with which is used one or more of six standard forms together with an assortment of endorsements to provide flexibility in coverage.

A basic objective of the homeowners program is to provide an opportunity for the homeowner to purchase in one policy almost any of the variations of fire insurance and extended peril coverages previously discussed, plus such coverages as personal liability insurance, medical payments insurance, and theft. The distinguishing feature of this type of policy is that *definite minimum amounts of coverage* in each of the above categories may be required and *one indivisible premium* is charged. Thus, the insured must buy a certain minimum package of benefits and cannot select specific coverages. Yet, there is sufficient flexibility in the amounts required so that the form can fit the needs of most residents. A brief outline of the six basic forms of the homeowners program follows:

Form 1. Standard form. Covers dwelling, contents, and private structures. Contains coverage for fire, lightning, extended coverage, vandalism and malicious mischief, theft, limited glass breakage, additional living expense, comprehensive personal liability, medical payments, and damage to property of others.

Form 2. Broad form. Same as Form 1 except that additional perils are covered. Thus, loss from falling objects, weight of ice, collapse of building, specific forms of water damage, glass breakage, and freezing are all covered.

Form 3. Special form. Applies all-risk protection to fixed property only. Similar in coverage to the dwelling special form, described previously.

Form 4. Residence contents broad form. Applies *broad named peril coverage* to contents and personal property. Designed especially for tenants who do not want building coverage or owner-occupants who are not eligible for all-risk coverage on their buildings, e.g., apartment houses. Form includes theft, personal liability, medical payments, physical damage to the property of others.

Form 5. Comprehensive form. Provides *all-risk coverage* on both building and contents and includes coverage for personal liability, theft, medical payments, and physical damage to property of others. Contents coverage is similar to that of the personal property floater.

Form 6. Homeowners condominium. Provides broad form coverage similar to Form 4 with some adjustments for the particular needs of owners of condominiums (e.g., coverage for assessments for losses on jointly-owned property).

Although Form 2, the broad form, is the most widely sold of the various forms of coverage, Form 5 is the only form giving all-risk protection on both real property and personal property. Homeowners Form 2 contains the following major coverages, with minimum applicable limits:

Coverage A	Dwelling building	$8,000
Coverage B	Appurtenant private structures	10% of Coverage A
Coverage C	Unscheduled personal property	50% of Coverage A
Coverage D	Additional living expense	20% of Coverage A
Coverage E	Comprehensive personal liability	$25,000
Coverage F	Medical payments	$500 a person $25,000 per accident
Coverage G	Physical damage to property of others, regardless of legal liability	$250 per occurrence

Coverages B, C, and D above, although determined by a percentage applied to Coverage A, operate as additional insurance. Thus, a homeowner would have a minimum of $8,000 coverage on a home, plus $4,000 on personal property. The insured has worldwide coverage for personal property off the premises, except that there is a limit of 10% of Coverage A (but not less than $1,000) for property in a secondary residence.

Coverage C excludes coverage on certain classes of personal property: animals, birds, fish, motorized vehicles (except unlicensed vehicles such as power mowers used in the maintenance of the premises), aircraft, property of nonrelated roomers, business property away from the premises, tape players and tapes used in autos, and separately described property specifically insured.

Limited coverage on money ($100), manuscripts or securities ($500), and on silverware or guns ($1,000) is provided but the limits may be increased by endorsement for extra premium. "Money" is defined broadly to include bullion, coin collections, and bank notes. The form limits coverage on watercraft, jewelry and furs, and trailers to $500 each. Trees, shrubs, plants, and lawns are limited to $250 on any one item, and to 5% of Coverage A in any one occurrence. Coverage under Form 2, as well as other forms, may be extended to apply to secondary residences, subject to a $5,000 minimum on Coverage A.

The perils and losses covered in Homeowners Form 2 are similar to those listed previously for the dwelling buildings broad form coverage, except that Form 2 includes certain additional perils such as theft and fire legal liability. The homeowners program was altered in 1976 in some states to permit a new, simplified writing, together with some minor coverage changes. If successful, the new program will be extended nationwide.

Two types of deductibles are used in homeowners policies, a disappearing deductible, and a flat deductible. Generally the deductibles apply across the board to all perils. A common type of disappearing deductible provides that no liability exists for payment unless the loss from each occurrence exceeds $50. If the loss falls between $50 and $500, the insurer pays 111% of the loss. For losses above $500, no deductible is charged. Thus, for a loss of $100, the insurer would pay 1.11($100 – $50), or $55.50; for a loss of $200, 1.11($200 – $50), or $166.50; and for a loss of $500, 1.11($500 – $50), or $500. If the insured accepts a flat deductible, a premium credit is given equal to 10% for a $100 deductible, 20% for a $250 deductible, and 25% for a $500 deductible, subject to a maximum credit of $45, $150, and $225, respectively, for deductibles of $100, $250, and $500.

The chief advantages claimed for insuring under the homeowners program are:

1. The homeowner is able to secure broad protection at much less cost than if all the coverages were purchased separately. The package contains most of the insurance that the average homeowner needs and should have. However, a homeowner who does not want all the protection listed may insure on one of the traditional forms.
2. The three-year premium paid under the program might amount to as much as $500 or more, and this is said to provide sufficient commission income to give the agent more incentive to service the needs of the average homeowner in a more comprehensive fashion than has been true in the past.
3. Finally, the underwriters secure a broader base of insurance and there is less adverse selection in these policies. It follows that the total loss ratio should be lower for the policy as a whole and hence more profitable. This makes possible more liberal underwriting with fewer exclusions.

In practice the homeowner has often been able to secure protection under one of the homeowners forms for a premium no higher than that for simple fire and extended coverage. Nevertheless, Homeowners Form 5, which offers superior coverage to any of the other forms, is considerably more expensive, and the rates increase more than proportionately as coverage increases.

Business Property. Extensions of the basic fire policy to various business exposures have not progressed as rapidly as has been truc of personal risks. In general, the subject of extending coverage to additional business property perils breaks down into extending coverage on buildings and extending coverage on contents and other items of personal property used by business.

Extending Coverage on Buildings. Coverage on buildings is not common on an all-risk basis, as it is in the case of personal residences. The business person may extend coverage in the standard fire policy through use of the extended coverage endorsement or by means of an *optional perils policy*. Under the optional perils policy, protection may be obtained against explosion, riot and civil commotion, vandalism and malicious mischief, and aircraft and vehicle damage. Separate protection against such perils as earthquakes may be purchased. In some territories, such as the Pacific Coast, the basic fire policy may be extended to cover this peril. Insurance against many other perils, commonly called "allied lines," may be purchased. Thus, damage due to faulty sprinkler systems, or the liability resulting therefrom, may be insured. Special coverages for certain types of property, such as boilers and machinery, have been devised.

Extending Coverage on Personal Property. Coverage on personal property belonging to a business enterprise may be purchased on the forms previously described in connection with buildings. In addition, such coverage is available on an all-risk basis. There are two basic groups of forms that cover the personal property of business on an all-risk basis: one group for establishments carrying stocks of goods held for sale (wholesalers and retailers), and one group for manufacturing establishments.

Under the personal property of wholesalers and retailers group, there are three main types of coverage; namely, inland marine forms, block forms designed specially for given types of risks, and forms known as the commercial property coverage program. The first two, inland marine forms and block forms, will be discussed in Chapter 13, which deals with inland marine insurance.

The commercial property coverage form, which is attached to the standard fire policy, is designed for a wide range of retail and wholesale merchants, and provides an all-risk coverage on stock in trade, furniture and fixtures, with improvements and betterments protection available optionally. The form is available for almost every type of merchant except those specifically named, such as jewelers and furriers, for whom special inland marine forms are provided;[4] and establishments such as restaurants, florists, pawnbrokers, and pet shops, which present special underwriting problems.

[4] These forms are the Jewelers' Block Policy and the Furriers' Block Policy.

The commercial property form has a $100 deductible that applies to all but certain listed perils.[5] It covers property wherever located in the United States, and while in transit in Canada. Among the excluded perils are freezing, flood, rising water, seepage, earthquake, landslide, war, inherent vice of the goods, radioactive sources, mysterious disappearance, and honesty of the insured or an employee. Most of these excluded perils do not apply to goods in transit. Certain types of property are specifically excluded as well, such as unattended property in a vehicle; damage to steam boilers; automobiles; neon signs; and furs, jewels, gold, and silver in excess of a limited amount. The commercial property coverage is written with 80% coinsurance, and various discounts are available for the use of such loss-prevention devices as guard service, burglar alarm systems, and iron protective screens. For additional premiums, the insured may extend the coverage to such items as money up to $250 in any one occurrence, personal effects, debris removal, and damage to the building done by burglars.

The *special property form* is designed for manufacturing, processing, or service establishments and offers all-risk coverage on personal property of the owner and the property of others in the care, custody, or control of the insured, subject to certain limits. The coverage is offered as an endorsement to the special multi-peril policy. In general, coverage is parallel to that offered under the commercial property coverage form.

The Special Multi-Peril Policy. Perhaps the most comprehensive development in multiple-line insurance is the special multi-peril policy (SMP) for given types of commercial and institutional organizations. Introduced in 1960 as a special form for motel risks, the special multi-peril policy was expanded gradually until by 1966 it was revised to be adapted to the needs of retail and wholesale establishments; apartment houses; offices; and institutional, service, manufacturing, and processing exposures. After 1966, the program was substantially revised so that a set of general rules apply to the various coverages issued under the SMP program. Endorsements to tailor the coverage to particular needs were revised and reissued, so that now under the SMP policy it is possible to provide most of the property and liability insurance needs of eligible risks. These include:

1. Forms for a wide range of merchants under the commercial property all-risk coverage form.
2. Forms for manufacturing, industrial processing, and service establishments on the all-risk basis.
3. Forms for offices, builders, public and institutional organizations, physicians and surgeons, hotels and motels, condominium owners, and others. In addition, endorsements for special types of property (also insured under inland marine forms) are available under the SMP policy: radium, fine arts, cameras, musical instruments, physicians' and surgeons' equipment, and neon signs. In some states a multi-coverage account plan is available giving special rate credits where premiums exceed $5,000 per account on large risks.

[5] For example, fire, extended and additional extended coverage perils, and theft.

Coverages which may be offered under the SMP policy include four major classes: general property, liability, crime, and boiler and machinery. Only general property insurance and liability insurance are mandatory, and they must, with certain exceptions, be written to cover both a building and its contents. Available as optional coverages are extra-expense insurance, valuable papers insurance, newly acquired property coverage, business interruption insurance, off-premises coverage of property, and personal effects coverage. About the only major types of coverage which cannot be written on the SMP policy are automobile insurance, surety bonds, and life or health insurance.

Flexibility in use of the SMP policy is made possible by the use of numerous endorsements. The insured can elect all-risk coverage on a building and its contents, or may use only named peril forms. Forms may be reporting or nonreporting. It is even possible for more than one insurer to share general property coverage, and still have other types of coverage underwritten by a single insurer. Such flexibility may be quite valuable for large risks.

The SMP policy automatically covers newly acquired buildings subject to a limit of 10% of the amount of insurance or $25,000. It covers personal property at newly acquired locations again subject to limits of 10% of the amount carried on other personal property, but not over $10,000. If the insured removes personal property for cleaning or repair, there is coverage up to 2% of the amount of insurance carried on other personal property, but not over $5,000. The policy also covers personal effects of others and valuable papers up to $500 each, trees and shrubs up to $1,000 (not more than $250 on any one tree or shrub), and extra expenses of $1,000.

The SMP policy may be written with the same types of deductible clauses employed in the homeowners program. Coinsurance of 80% is a general requirement, except that for losses both less than $10,000 and less than 5% of the amount of insurance the requirement of obtaining an inventory of undamaged property, as stated in the basic 165 lines of the standard fire policy appearing in the form, is waived. Valuation of property for the purpose of determining losses is on an actual cash value basis, with certain qualifications for books of account, manuscripts, film, tape, disc, or other storage media for electronic data processing equipment. The policy also contains the standard exclusions for perils such as war, building ordinance, flood, earth movement, wear and tear, and inventory shortages.

Rates charged for insurance under the SMP policy are at least 15% less than those charged for coverages purchased separately. As the insurance industry gains experience with multi-peril contracts, and as knowledge of the savings and of the superior protection available increases, it seems likely that their use will continue to grow.

Covering Changing Values in Varying Locations

An important purpose of this type of form is to adjust insurance protection to business firms that have many plants located in different geographical areas or that wish protection to be adjusted automatically to constantly changing values at these plants. It would be cumbersome, indeed, if a business enterprise carrying on a nationwide operation involving 10 manufacturing or processing plants and 20 warehouses and other distributing centers had to purchase a separate policy for each location. For example, there would undoubtedly be much duplication of coverage when goods were shipped from one location to another (being insured by both the sender and the receiver) and many instances of omission of insurance protection altogether (each party believing the others to have taken care of the insurance).

Reporting forms are designed to adjust insurable coverage on contents to changing property values at one location or in different locations. Reporting forms have several advantages: (1) the amount of insurance protection is automatically adjusted to changes in values of property at different locations; (2) new locations are automatically covered; (3) the insured does not have to pay premiums on limits of liability in the policy, but rather pays premiums according to the actual values at risk; and (4) the possibility of having gaps in coverage or duplication of insurance is virtually eliminated.

The industrial property policy program may be written on a reporting basis, as may be the commercial property policy program. In addition, there are in common use many other multiple-location forms, each designed to fit specific types of risks or to allow variations in the way in which values are reported and the premium determined.

A typical multiple-location reporting form is the one known as Multiple-Location Reporting Form 1. When the insured has two or more locations, he or she estimates the highest value of personal property at each location and pays a deposit premium (there is a minimum premium of $500) based on the average values for all locations. The rate applied is an average rate determined by applying at each territory the rate in that territory multiplied by the average value of the goods to be located there. Each month the insured is required to report to the company what the actual values were at each location on a specific date. If the insured understates the actual value and later suffers a loss, there is a penalty in the recovery and only that portion of the loss that the amount reported bears to the actual values at risk can be recovered. Thus, if the insured reported $50,000 of inventory at location C, and it was determined that the true value was $60,000, only five sixths of any subsequent partial loss could be recovered. Also, if the insured fails to make a report on the required date, recovery is limited to the values reported on the last date a report was made; thus, the insured is denied the feature that gives automatic protection when values rise between reporting dates. For example, if on January 1 the insured reports correctly $10,000 of values at location D and on January 15 there is a loss of $15,000 (made possible because incoming shipments of goods raised the values exposed), the entire loss is paid if it falls within the limitation of liability at location D. However, if the loss occurred on February 15 and no report had been made on February 1, when it was due, the limit of liability would be $10,000.

To avoid the necessity of making monthly reports and yet to secure the advantage of automatic coverage at newly acquired locations, the insured may elect another type of multiple-location form known as Form 5, in which a coinsurance clause of at least 90% is required. This form is suitable for risks with varying locations and which have little fluctuation in total values and where it is impossible or inconvenient to render monthly reports. If values fluctuate considerably, the insured would be subject to coinsurance penalties unless the amount of insurance was constantly adjusted. However, the insured has automatic coverage at any one location, and thus is fully protected as long as sufficient insurance is carried to avoid coinsurance penalties.

SUMMARY

1. The perils of fire, windstorm, explosion, etc., annually cause great loss of life and property in the United States. Fire loss alone amounts to nearly $2 billion annually. Insurance against these losses is among the best developed and widely accepted types of insurance in existence, with the standard fire policy being the basic contract on which most property insurance coverages are based.
2. The standard fire policy is divided into three parts—the insuring agreement, the conditions and stipulations, and the various types of forms. The insuring agreement and conditions form the basic part of the contract and have been standardized throughout the United States. They cover such matters as what basic perils and property are covered or excluded, how losses shall be adjusted, termination of the contract, interests of others including a mortgagee, and rights against negligent parties.
3. The form in fire insurance is necessary to complete any insuring agreement against property losses. It serves four major purposes, the first three of which are discussed in this chapter and the fourth in the next chapter: (a) to describe accurately the insured property and the various kinds of limitations and extensions applying to it; (b) to extend the basic contract to cover additional perils; (c) to give automatic coverage on property which fluctuates in value, such as stock in trade, or which is moved about from one location to another, i.e., reporting and multiple-location forms; (d) to cover losses which are indirectly a result of fire or other perils.
4. Forms may be analyzed under two main headings, those applying to residences and those applying to business property. The main dwelling forms are the special form, extended coverage endorsement, replacement cost endorsement, dwelling buildings and contents (broad form), and the homeowners program. The chief business forms include the general form, the optional perils policy, the commercial property coverage form, the special multi-peril policy, the multiple-location reporting forms, and reporting forms.

QUESTIONS FOR REVIEW AND DISCUSSION

1. Coverage C of homeowners forms defines personal property as that which is usual or incidental to the occupancy of the dwelling. The form excludes "business property while away from the described

premises." Which of the following losses do you think should be paid under the homeowners policy?

(a) $4,000 worth of business tools belonging to the insured stolen from his employer's truck parked in the insured's driveway.

(b) A valuable mold for forming fiberglass bodies for racing cars while it was away from the insured's premises. The insured made racing car bodies as a hobby.

(c) A small garden tractor used on the premises was destroyed.

(d) The insured loaned an electric range to a tenant of a building owned by the insured. The range was destroyed by fire.

2. Insurance companies support various organizations such as the National Board of Fire Underwriters and the National Fire Protection Association which aim at reducing the losses from fires that occur annually in the United States.

(a) A certain agent suggests that this activity, if completely successful, would put insurance companies out of business. Comment.

(b) Is it in the best interests of insurance companies to attempt to eliminate loss from fire or other perils? Discuss.

3. *Z* owns a 20-year-old house. When new, it had a life expectancy of 50 years and was valued at $10,000. What could be collected from a $10,000 fire insurance policy in the event of a total loss, under the assumption that it would take $15,000 to replace the house? Explain your answer.

4. Assume that coverage on *Z*'s house in Question 3 is written on the dwelling buildings special form, which provides for replacement cost insurance. The loss is partial, and it is estimated that $2,000 would replace the lost portion with new materials.

(a) What will the recovery be? Show your calculations.

(b) How would your answer be changed if it were shown that instead of $15,000 it would take $30,000 to replace the house today? Explain.

5. Jones's factory is destroyed by fire, and it is estimated that it will take three months to rebuild the factory and to resume operations. The cost of this delay is calculated at $20,000 because of loss of profits and fixed charges that continue regardless of the volume of operations. Is this amount recoverable under the standard fire policy? Explain.

6. *A* owns a residence and insures it for $15,000 on the standard fire policy with extended coverage. The contents, valued at $10,000, are insured for $5,000 on the same policy. Show the extent to which the following losses would be covered and give your reasons in each case:

(a) Smoke damage from a fireplace necessitates a $70 repainting job in the living room.

(b) A valuable antique wooden table worth $500 is accidentally damaged by heat when it is placed too near a hot air register.

(c) A grass fire threatens *A*'s house. For safety, *A* removes all contents and places them in three warehouses, as follows: Warehouse X, $4,000; Warehouse Y, $3,000; Warehouse Z, $3,000. Water damages the goods at Warehouse Z and causes a $2,000 loss two days after they have been stored there. Also $500 worth of goods is stolen from Warehouse Y.

(d) A neighbor's house burns. Fire fighters' trucks gouge deep holes in *A*'s yard.

(e) Three teenage boys "have it in" for *A* and cause $25 of damage to the lawn hoses by slashing them with knives.

7. In a recent case a windstorm damaged the roof of a building, allowing rain to enter. The water caused a short circuit in the electricity. Food in a freezer thawed when the electricity went off and was ordered destroyed by health authorities. The insured carried the

standard fire policy with extended coverage. The insurer denied liability under the contract for the loss of the spoiled food.
(a) Upon what probable grounds would the insurer reject the above claim?
(b) Do you agree with the insurer? Why or why not?

8. In a fire the following items were included on a proof of loss form. Discuss the extent to which these losses, if any, are insured under the standard fire policy:
(a) $50 of cash in a locked box.
(b) One share of A. T. and T. in the same box.
(c) A deed to a summer residence.
(d) Loss of a water heater valued at $150 when heat from the fire caused it to explode.
(e) $500 loss of an old oak tree damaged by fire.
(f) How would your answers in (a)-(d) above be changed if the coverage had been Homeowners Form 2 instead of the standard fire policy? Explain.

9. *D* claims that the exclusion in the standard fire policy for losses due to increase of the hazard by the insured might serve to exclude almost any loss where the insured was negligent, such as fire loss from a carelessly discarded cigarette. Comment.

10. *T* has a house insured for $20,000 with a $15,000 mortgage. The mortgagee is protected by a loss payable clause. A fire occurs, and it develops that the $2,000 loss is uninsured because *T* has forgotten to pay the premium and the policy lapsed.
(a) May the mortgagee collect? Why?
(b) What is the most satisfactory way for the mortgagee to protect its interest? Why?

11. What rights and obligations does the mortgagee have under the standard mortgagee clause?

12. Smith insures a retail building under three policies, as follows: Insurer A, $5,000; Insurer B, $10,000; Insurer C, $15,000. At the time of a $6,000 fire loss, it is discovered that Insurer A is insolvent and is not paying any claims. How much can Smith collect from each insurer? Why?

13. What is meant by "the form" in property insurance, and what four purposes are served by it? Explain.

14. Mayer insures his palatial mansion for $50,000 under the dwelling buildings special form. A few months after he spent $20,000 in oriental landscaping, the building was completely gutted by fire and $10,000 worth of landscaping was lost. What limits of liability for this loss exist under the policy?

15. Kammack insures a $30,000 private business college building for $12,000 under a policy containing an 80% coinsurance clause. The policy is written on a form that contains a clause excluding the value of foundations from the coverage. If it is determined that the building's foundation is valued at $10,000, what effect does this clause have on the recovery for the loss? Explain.

16. Name the perils covered under the extended coverage endorsement.

17. In California there have been a series of losses due to the slow movement of earth which becomes loosened when water used for lawns seeps down and causes the shale to slip. Underman's house is one of those affected. When a large crack in the foundation occurred, Underman submitted a claim. The insurer paid the loss and immediately cancelled the policy. A month later Underman's house fell into the bay when the entire cliff gave way. Underman made a claim for loss, but the insurer rejected the claim, arguing that the loss occurred after the policy was cancelled. Discuss the rights of the parties.

18. What advantages and disadvantages are there for the average homeowner under the homeowners program that covers multiple-peril risks?

19. An insured retailer was covered under an all-risk commercial property coverage, which excludes losses from "mysterious disappearance," including losses which are revealed by taking inventory periodically. A quarterly inventory showed that more than 1,000 tires, valued at $11,000, were missing. The insured obtained testimony from a party who had actually been convicted of the theft of seven of the missing tires, but the insurer denied recovery under the inventory exclusion. Should the insured be entitled to recover for presumption of theft? Discuss.

20. Why have reporting forms been developed? Discuss.

21. A certain hardware wholesaler is insured under the Multiple-Location Reporting Form 1. He has ten warehouses located throughout the United States. He has been unable to provide satisfactory monthly reports because his accounting system is not arranged to provide the necessary information conveniently. Suggest a different form that will give adequate protection automatically, but that will not require the monthly reports. What dangers may exist in the use of this form? Explain.

22. In a recent court case, *Lipschultz v. General Insurance Co.*, (9 C.C.H., Fire & Casualty, 1064), windstorm had broken the supply lines to a power substation a half mile from the insured premises. There was no wind damage at the premises. As a result, the operation of a supermarket suffered a loss from spoiled goods due to temperature increases in refrigerated containers. The supermarket owner had carried no consequential loss coverage and argued that the loss was a direct loss by windstorm, which was covered under his extended coverage endorsement to the fire policy on the market. Should the owner collect? Why or why not?

Chapter *Eleven*

CONSEQUENTIAL LOSS COVERAGE

The common contracts of fire insurance cover only *direct* loss from given perils. Direct losses are those where the damage has been caused by the fire either coming into contact with the subject matter or causing an unbroken chain of events leading to the destruction of the subject matter. Direct loss policies invariably exclude losses that result from the peril insured against but not caused *directly* by it. Such losses, which are described as *consequential,* may be added by endorsement to the standard fire policy. To cover consequential losses represents the fourth purpose of the endorsement.

BASIC CHARACTERISTICS OF CONSEQUENTIAL LOSSES

The nature of consequential losses can best be understood by use of an example. Suppose a small manufacturer suffers a serious fire that shuts down its plant for two months while repairs are being made. The manufacturer is fully insured against *direct* loss by fire but carries no consequential loss coverage. The fire policy pays for the replacement cost of lost raw materials, goods in process, and finished goods, as well as repairs to machinery and buildings. However, the manufacturer finds that it is necessary to keep certain key employees such as plant managers and salespersons on the payroll to help with the reorganization and to render service to customers. In addition, there are other expenses, such as taxes, insurance premiums, interest, heat, light, power, and depreciation, that are incurred regardless of the volume of operation. Finally, the manufacturer has not been able to earn any profit on the unsold finished goods nor upon the volume of goods that would normally have been produced during this period. The sum of such losses may be so severe that the manufacturer is unable to continue in business. Consequential damage contracts have been devised to indemnify for this type of loss.

The importance of consequential losses has long been recognized in personal insurance lines. Life insurance, for example, is intended to replace lost income due to the premature death of the breadwinner. Disability income insurance is designed to restore income lost as a result of total disability. In property insurance, however, consequential losses have not generally been recognized for the serious exposure that they really are. In a study of 21 losses of steel manufacturers, for example, it was found that in 15 cases the consequential loss exceeded the direct physical loss.[1] The physical loss was placed at about $381,000, while the consequential losses were estimated to be $2,654,000, or about seven times as great as the direct losses. The largest single direct loss was $86,800, while five of the consequential losses exceeded $400,000, the largest amounting to $675,973. While comprehensive data on the premium volume from consequential business are not available, there is little question that it accounts for a small portion of the total fire insurance written. The central reason for the failure to insure such an important exposure appears to lie in the somewhat complicated techniques employed to put the coverage into effect. Furthermore, agents have found consequential loss coverage difficult to understand completely and have thus not been able to educate their clients to the need. In addition, loss settlements have been somewhat involved because it has been difficult to determine precisely the true amount of dollar losses.

CLASSIFICATIONS OF CONSEQUENTIAL LOSS CONTRACTS

A consequential loss contract is usually written as an endorsement to the standard fire policy or is listed on the form. The perils insured against usually include fire and extended coverage. The perils of riot, civil commotion, vandalism, and malicious mischief may also be insured against. Thus, if the interruption of business or other consequential loss results from damage to property by any of the major perils in the contracts, the insured is indemnified. Consequential loss contracts may be divided into time and nontime element contracts.

TIME ELEMENT CONTRACTS

Time element contracts are those contracts which measure the indirect loss in terms of so many dollars per unit of time that passes until the subject matter can be restored.

Rental Value and Additional Living Expense Insurance

Perhaps the most commonly sold type of time element consequential loss insurance is rental value and additional living expense insurance, which is included automatically in most dwelling forms. The purpose of this insurance is to reimburse the tenant or the owner for the loss of use or loss of rent of property made uninhabitable because of the occurrence of one of the insured perils, such as fire. The coverage thus supplements the direct loss of property by making an indemnity for subsequent indirect loss—namely, the loss of rent, the amount depending on the time during which the building is untenantable.

[1] R. E. Lauterbach, "Business Interruption," Insurance Series No. 115 (New York: American Management Association), pp. 43-44.

Dwelling Coverage. Suppose a homeowner lives in a dwelling whose rental value including furnishings is $200 a month. A fire occurs and the building cannot be used again for three months. In addition to the house, the homeowner has lost $600, because to obtain comparable quarters, that sum would have to be paid for shelter. The homeowners form on which the owner had direct fire coverage would pay this sum in addition to the direct loss by fire, subject to certain limitations. Furthermore, if the insured must incur expenses in addition to the normal living costs because of the fire, these expenses are also insured. Thus, the insured who must live during part or all of the period in a hotel because cheaper quarters are not available, and incurs a total of $500 a month to maintain normal living standards, may recover the extra costs occasioned by hotel accommodations. A tenant who is required to maintain rent regardless of fire or other peril also needs this type of coverage.

Some dwelling forms (not homeowners forms) limit the amount of rental value indemnity to 1/12 of the amount of applicable coverage for each month of untenantability. In basic dwelling forms, the rental value and additional living expense insurance is limited to 10% of the basic amount of insurance on the building (not as additional insurance). In homeowners forms, the limit is 20% of the amount of insurance on the dwelling, and the coverage is applied to additional insurance. This means that if an insured takes out $30,000 of insurance under the homeowners form, there will be an additional $6,000 of coverage on rental value and additional living expense, and in the event of total loss of the building, the insurer could be liable for as much as $36,000 of indemnity. In basic dwelling forms the limit would be $30,000, with no more than $3,000 of this amount applicable to rental value and additional living expense.

There are several special features of rental value insurance:

1. The coverage is on an indemnity basis. Recoveries are limited to what the tenant or owner would have lost had the insured peril not occurred. If under the lease the tenant is excused from paying rent if the premises become uninhabitable because of fire, then the owner cannot recover for lost rental income.
2. Noncontinuing expenses must be deducted from rental value indemnities. If the fair rental value is $200 a month, but $20 is the value of maintenance and repairs, the true loss is $180, not $200.
3. Protection is extended to the time it takes not only to restore the building, but also the time it takes to refurnish the building (assuming the building is rented on a furnished basis).
4. The insured peril must occur during the policy term, but the rental indemnities may extend beyond the expiration date of the original policy.
5. The indemnity is based on the time it takes to restore the property with *due diligence and dispatch*. Unreasonable delays in rebuilding are not compensable. The form provides coverage up to two weeks for untenantability due to restrictions imposed by local building ordinances.
6. Special arrangements can be made when the property is rented on a seasonal basis. A beach house, for example, can be insured under the condition that indemnity is payable only if the period of untenantability falls during a specified time during the vacation season.

Business Risks. When rental insurance is written on business risks, a few additional complications may arise. The following aspects should be noted:

1. Any extra losses incurred because of building laws or ordinances are excluded.
2. Most forms do not apply on a "rented or not" basis. Thus the insured must prove that had the fire not occurred a certain amount of rental income could have been reasonably expected. Indemnity is on a loss-sustained basis. If the building were only half occupied, and there was no expectation that the rate of occupancy would normally have increased during the period of untenantability, the insured could recover only on the basis of 50% occupancy.
3. Business forms usually include a pro rata liability clause similar to the 1/12 per month limitation on basic dwelling forms. Thus the insured who has rentals totalling $12,000 per year but takes out only $6,000 of rental value insurance can recover only $500 per month during any period of untenantability (1/12 × $6,000).
4. If the insured's rental income is on a contingency basis (for example, geared to the tenant's sales), a special form is provided under which the premium is subject to audit at the end of the year and is adjusted to the actual rental income received. Settlement of losses is made on the basis of the expected future rental income, based on past experience. Thus if the rental income in the latest year was $12,000, but it is determined that the tenant's sales are up by 10% in the current year, the insured may receive indemnity based on an annual rental income of 110% of $12,000, or $13,200.

Business Interruption Insurance

Business interruption insurance undertakes to reimburse the insured for profits and fixed charges lost as a result of damage to the property from a named peril. It is generally a contract of indemnity;[2] thus, one of the important problems in this line of insurance is to acquire a firm understanding of methods to determine losses which, by their very nature, depend on future events. Because the future is an unknown quantity, this problem is sometimes complicated.

Basic Characteristics of Business Interruption Insurance. The business interruption contract has certain fundamental provisions that are frequently a source of much misunderstanding. The policy will indemnify the insured subject to the following conditions:

1. There must be physical damage to property by a fire or other insured peril.
2. There must be a shutdown of business and this shutdown must result from the physical damage caused by the named peril (and not from some other cause such as a strike or a shortage of supplies).
3. During the period of shutdown, it must be established that the business would have continued to operate had it not been for the occurrence of the insured peril.
4. The peril must occur during the policy term at the described location.
5. During the period of shutdown, the business would have continued to earn profits and to incur continuing expenses.

If the business had only been breaking even at the time of occurrence of the insured peril, there would be a question raised as to whether any profits would have been earned. If it were found that no profits would have been made even if the business had not been shut down, no real loss from this source would have been incurred, and hence no indemnity for lost profits would be paid. Of

[2] Occasionally valued policies are written in the London market.

course, if the business is earning its fixed charges, these would be reimbursed. Thus, even though a business is losing money, there is an insurable value to the extent that it is earning its fixed charges. As might be surmised, it might be a considerable source of conflict to resolve the question as to what profits might be in the future.

Business Interruption Value. The value of the possible loss may be measured by different methods, but the central idea is to examine the income statement of the firm and derive from this statement the various items of income and expense that are to be insured. An example of such a technique follows.

Total gross earnings from all sources derived from the use and occupancy of the described building		xxx
Less:		
Cost of materials consumed in the manufacturing process, or the cost of goods sold in a mercantile business	xx	
Cost of supplies	xx	
Sales taxes	xx	
Bad debts	xx	
Ordinary payroll*	xx	
Total		xxx
Remainder—Profits and all other expenses		xx

* May be insured for limited periods, if desired, under most forms.

In other words, the process of isolating the insurable value is to deduct from total gross earnings all expenses and costs that are variable—that is, those that may be discontinued if a fire or other peril were to cause a shutdown of the business. The amount so obtained is the *insurable value* and forms the basis of the loss settlement.

Coinsurance. The importance of determining business interruption value (sometimes referred to as use and occupancy value, because all value is supposed to result from the use and occupancy of the damaged building) becomes even more evident when it is realized that most business interruption forms contain a coinsurance clause. Coinsurance requirements vary from 50% upward, depending on the amount of coverage desired. If the business concern elects to take the 50% form, it is required to carry at least 50% of its annual insurable value. Failing to carry this amount, it becomes a coinsurer.

To illustrate, assume that the sum of the annual fixed charges and profits during the prior year is $96,000. When the policy was originally issued, the insurable value was $80,000; the firm now carries $40,000 of business interruption insurance. In the event of a shutdown for three months and assuming an even rate of operations and earnings, the firm will have lost 3/12 of its year's profits and fixed charges, or $24,000. Does the firm collect this amount? No, because it has not been carrying the amount of insurance required by the coinsurance clause. Since it carries $40,000 and is required to carry $48,000 (one half of its annual insurable value of $96,000), it collects only 40/48 of the loss, or $20,000. To avoid coinsurance penalties of this nature, the insured may follow one of four courses:

1. The insured may take care to see that the policy amount is always equal to or greater than the amount required by the coinsurance clause. This requires that careful forecasts be made of future operations and that coverage be tailored accordingly, or that continuous adjustments in the amount of coverage be made to correspond with actual profits.
2. The insured may be permitted under some jurisdictions to add an *agreed amount endorsement* to the policy. Under this endorsement the insured agrees to take out a stated amount of insurance and this amount is a substitute for a coinsurance clause. That is, if the insured pays premiums based on the agreed amount of gross earnings at the beginning, there will be no coinsurance penalty, even if later experience reveals that actual gross earnings exceed the estimates agreed upon by the insurer when the policy was first taken out.
3. The insured may take out insurance on the earnings form.
4. The insured may employ an endorsement known as the *premium adjustment endorsement*. Under this endorsement, the insured may purposely carry larger limits that he or she would normally be required; and after the policy period is over, the premium is reduced if actual business interruption value falls below the amount taken. If it turns out that the actual business interruption value exceeds the amount taken, however, coinsurance penalties apply. The insurer's liability is also limited to some proportion (according to the percentage of coinsurance) of the actual business interruption value. In the case above, suppose the insured had elected the 50% form of gross earnings in the amount of $100,000, even though the insurable value at the inception of the policy was $80,000. At the end of the year it is determined that the actual insurable value was $96,000. The insured would pay a premium based on 50% of $96,000, or $48,000, and would have had $48,000 of coverage had any loss occurred.

How Much Insurance Should Be Carried? The question frequently arises, "How much business interruption insurance should be carried?" The answer depends upon what the firm believes the maximum loss might be. Coinsurance forms are available that allow the insured to carry as little as one half of its annual insurable value. However, if the firm has reason to believe it might take as much as a year to restore the business to regular operations, it should, of course, carry insurance equal to its full insurable value. Generally, insurance on no more than one year's insurable value is available. It should be remembered that some firms may operate on a seasonal basis, and a few months' operations might account for an entire year's profits. If the peril occurs just before the operating season which lasts only three months, a whole year's profits might be lost and probably a good part of the year's expenditures for fixed charges would not be earned. Such a situation would, of course, justify carrying insurance on the profits and fixed charges of a whole year. The policy does not require that the lost profits or charges be incurred in any particular time period, so long as they do not exceed the time that it reasonably takes to restore the building and to resume operations.

On the other hand, the loss may be only partial; that is, if the business is only partially shut down, indemnity can be collected for the partial loss. If it takes an entire year to make repairs and to restore normal operations and the firm is forced to reduce operations by one fourth of its normal level, the indemnity would be one fourth of the annual insurable value, assuming the operations to be level throughout the year.

Incurring Expenses to Reduce Loss. Sometimes it is possible to expedite repairs by incurring costs that would not normally be necessary. For example, special parts might be flown in by air express, or overtime allowances may be paid to workers. If such costs succeed in reducing the time of interruption, they will be reimbursed by the insurer so long as the total amount does not exceed the amount that would have been payable had the expediting funds not been spent. Thus, if it would normally have taken three months to restore operations, but by spending $3,000 extra, the insured is able to reduce the period of interruption to two months, the insurer will pay the insured the $3,000 providing the monthly loss from earned profits and fixed charges would have otherwise equalled or exceeded $3,000.

Special Provisions. The basic business interruption policy limits payments to the length of time it reasonably takes to restore the property physically to normal operating conditions so that the same level of operation exists as existed before the loss. The insured is given up to 30 days' additional time to process damaged raw stock to the same stage of manufacture as existed at the time of the loss, but no such indemnity is available for finished stock. If a civil authority, such as a local government, prohibits access to the insured's premises because of other damage in the area arising out of the insured peril, the policy provides up to two weeks' indemnity for loss from this source. However, no indemnity is payable in the case a building ordinance, strike, or lease agreement results in a delay in rebuilding. Electrical power failure is excluded as a source of loss unless fire ensues and then coverage pertains only to the resulting fire. If a larger building replaces the destroyed structure, indemnity is adjusted for the length of time it would have taken to rebuild a comparable building of the same size as the one destroyed.

An endorsement is available to alter some of the basic requirements just noted. Under the terms of the *extended period of indemnity endorsement,* the period of loss is defined to mean that period necessary to return to normal business operations, and not just the period necessary to reopen business physically. For example, a small manufacturing company may suffer a fire which stops physical operations for three months. At the start of business, however, its chief customers have found new suppliers, and it may take several more months to obtain new customers and to achieve the same level of operation it enjoyed prior to the fire. The extended period endorsement is offered in units of 30 days, so that the above manufacturer could purchase three units of coverage, or as much as needed. If the manufacturer is able to resume normal operations in less than 90 days, it can recover only for the shorter period, since the contract is on an indemnity, or actual loss-sustained, basis.

Forms Available. The most common form in use in business interruption insurance is known as the *gross earnings form,* which requires the use of coinsurance. For certain types of mercantile and other nonmanufacturing risks, another form, known as the *earnings form,* is available without coinsurance.

Gross Earnings Form. Gross earnings forms are of two varieties—one for mercantile, or nonmanufacturing, risks and one for manufacturing risks. In the mercantile form, gross earnings are defined as the total sales and other earnings less the cost of goods sold, and materials and supplies or outside services, the cost of which may be discontinued in the event of interruption. This definition corresponds generally to a typical accounting concept of gross earnings for a retailer or wholesaler. For the manufacturer, gross earnings are defined in terms of sales value of production, plus the sales of finished merchandise and other earnings, less the cost of raw stock, supplies, merchandise sold, and services purchased from outsiders for resale. The sales value of production is simply the estimated gross sales (less discounts, returns, bad debts, and prepaid freight) less beginning inventory of finished stock plus ending inventory of finished stock. Gross earnings is a simple and easily understood concept. All that is needed to determine insurable value is to find gross earnings, as defined. The form requires a minimum coverage of 50% of gross earnings in order to avoid coinsurance penalties. If the insured wishes to cover ordinary payroll, 80% coinsurance is required.

Earnings Form. Designed especially for small business firms, the earnings form has no coinsurance clause and thus overcomes the disadvantages of coinsurance penalties, which may be substantial in some cases because of fluctuations in earnings which often characterize small business firms. The rate is higher under this form than for the gross earnings form, and recoveries are limited to 16⅔%, 25%, or 33⅓% of the total amount of coverage in any one month. "Earnings" are defined as the sum of the net profit, taxes, rents, payroll expense, and all other operating expenses earned by the business. To assure full recovery for any loss, the insured must carry sufficient limits so that the selected limit will cover the total earnings for any one month. Suppose, for example, that a retail store obtains one fourth of its year's earnings, as defined, in the month of December, not an uncommon occurrence. To recover in full for a shutdown during the month of December, the firm must carry policy limits equal to four times its December earnings. This limit is not cumulative, but applies monthly. There is no prorating of coverage for loss periods less than one month. Suppose the firm has $20,000 of coverage with a 25% monthly limitation, and is shut down for 40 days. It is established that the loss during the first 30 days is $6,000, and the loss for the remaining 10 days is $2,000. The recovery is limited to $5,000 for the first 30 days (one fourth of $20,000), plus $2,000 (and not one third of $5,000) for the remaining 10 days. Thus, if the firm believes that the maximum period of shutdown is three months and that the maximum loss in any one month is $5,000, it should take $15,000 of coverage with a 1/3 monthly limitation.

Coverage similar to that given by the earnings form is also available to users of the special multiple-peril (SMP) form; it is called the *loss of earnings endorsement*. The insured has a choice of 1/3, 1/4, or 1/6 of the total amount of coverage. This means that the insured who wishes may carry as little as three times, or as much as six times, the maximum monthly indemnity desired. Since the SMP policy has broad coverage, loss because of interruption is covered from such perils as looting at and during a riot or civil commotion, or explosion of a steam boiler, in addition to the normal perils such as fire and windstorm.

Business Interruption Rates. Rates for business interruption insurance are usually based on the 80% coinsurance fire rate applicable to the building. In New York, they are based on the contents rate. A typical charge would be 90% of the rate applicable to the building, if the business interruption policy has a 50% coinsurance clause, or 70% of the building rate if the business interruption policy has an 80% coinsurance clause.

For the earnings form, rates vary according to the monthly limitation percentage, and are somewhat higher than the regular gross earnings form. Rates in most territories vary from 85% to 110% of the 80% coinsurance building rate. Thus insureds must pay a rate which is 20% to 50% higher than the gross earnings form in order to escape the coinsurance clause. This price may be worth it, however, in view of the severe loss recovery penalties sometimes imposed under the gross earnings form.

Criticisms. Business interruption insurance has been criticized among other things for its complexity, uncertainty of loss adjustments, and for the operation of the coinsurance clause. The insured often cannot understand, for example, being required to purchase a minimum of 50% of annual gross earnings, even though it is extremely unlikely to be shut down 50% of a year. The effect of this requirement is to force the insured to pay for more insurance than could be collected in most circumstances.

Even the insured who carries, say, an amount equal to 50% of annual gross earnings is not assured of full recovery for losses during shutdowns of periods less than six months because of coinsurance. For example, if business had been 50% higher during a given year and the policy was not properly written, recovery for any one month would be reduced to two thirds of that month's actual loss. To illustrate, if the gross earnings were estimated at $120,000 annually but were actually running at the rate of $180,000 and the coinsurance requirement were 50%, the insured could collect only 6/9 of any partial loss. To avoid this result, the insured must either continuously adjust the amount of coverage, use an agreed amount endorsement, or make a very liberal estimate of earnings and attach the premium adjustment endorsement. Such action requires a high level of advice from a qualified agent or risk manager.

Contingent Business Interruption Insurance

It sometimes happens that a firm is forced to shut down, not because a peril occurred and damaged its plant, but because a peril forced the shutdown of the plant belonging to a supplier or an important customer on whom the firm depends. Thus, a manufacturer of air conditioners may find that its plant is shut down because the supplier of compressors has suffered a fire. The consequential loss is just as severe, perhaps, as if the fire had occurred at the firm's own plant because it may require several months to obtain another supplier. Similarly, a firm may find that its chief customer has cancelled orders because of a fire or other disaster at its plant.

To meet such situations, *contingent business interruption insurance* has been devised. The regular business interruption policy will not cover the losses described above because the insured peril did not cause any damage at the firm's own plant. Insurable value for contingent business interruption insurance is calculated in the same manner as it is for business interruption insurance. Since oftentimes the interruption of a supplier's plant will only reduce the operations of the firm's plant, insurable value may be correspondingly reduced. Of course, the form is designed to cover losses only when the reduction of business stems from the occurrence of an insured peril, and not from any other source. Thus, if a customer decides to buy from another source, such an event is not compensated under this policy. It is only where there is a direct connection between damaged property from an insured peril at another plant and the consequent reduction of business that indemnity is payable.

Extra Expense Insurance

Certain types of business firms do not find it possible or expedient to close down following the destruction of their physical plants. Such firms as laundries, newspapers, dairies, public utilities, banks, oil dealers, and ice companies will often continue their businesses using alternative facilities. The closing of these firms would deprive the public of a vital service or would involve a complete loss of goodwill or loss of business to competitors. If the firm is not shut down, even if using other facilities, the business interruption policy is not liable. However, the firm may have incurred great costs for such things as rental of new quarters for its staff, purchase of extra transportation facilities, rental of substitute equipment at high cost, and overtime allowances to employees. To cover such expenses when the firm's operations have not been interrupted, the *extra expense policy* has been devised. Some forms of extra expense insurance limit the allowances in such a way that no more than 40% of the policy amount can be paid in any one month and that the total amount must be distributed over at least three months.

Extra expense insurance may be written in conjunction with business interruption coverage. However, it should not be confused with the expense-to-reduce-loss coverage given in connection with a business interruption policy.

Extra expense coverage is designed primarily for indemnification of the extra costs of operations that are necessitated by a destruction of physical facilities. Expense-to-reduce-loss coverage repays the insured for extra costs and expenses involved in expediting, at higher than normal costs, the rebuilding of the destroyed facilities in order to reduce the period during which the business is interrupted. Expense-to-reduce-loss coverage is also written in connection with extra expense insurance, and payments are made to the extent that the expenses are incurred to reduce indemnity otherwise payable under the extra expense policy. This gives the insured some incentive to return to normal operations as soon as possible.

Leasehold Interest Insurance

A *leasehold* may be defined as an interest in real property that is created by an agreement (a lease) which gives the lessee (the tenant) the right of enjoyment and use of the property for a period of time. A leasehold may become very valuable to the lessee because changing business conditions, improvements in the property, and good management may increase the rental value of real estate considerably above the rental due under the lease. For example, the *Y* Department Store may negotiate a 20-year lease on its store building calling for a rental payment of $12,000 a year. Due to a growing business community, comparable property might rent for $15,000 within five years after the lease has been signed. This increase in value creates what is known as *leasehold interest,* or *leasehold value.*

Given the situation described above, what insurance problems are raised? If the lease is lost because of the occurrence of a fire or other physical damage to the building, the *Y* Department Store might be forced to sign a new lease calling for an increased rental of $3,000. It is very common in leases to provide that the agreement is void or voidable if the premises are destroyed by fire, or if a certain percentage of the sound value of the premises is destroyed by fire, or if the premises are so damaged that they cannot be restored within a given number of days. It is this source of loss that is insurable under a form of coverage known simply as *leasehold interest insurance.* In the preceding illustration, such a policy would provide indemnity for the loss of $3,000 a year for the unexpired term of the lease, which is 15 years. The policy, giving consideration to the interest factor, defines the loss as the present value of a sum of payments of $3,000 compounded annually at 4%. The form provides a table that enables the insured to see what the indemnity will be for each dollar of leasehold interest value. When the policy is written, the value of the lease at that time is estimated and this amount is named as the face amount of the policy. As time goes on, the amount for which the insurer may become liable is diminished because the remaining period of lease grows shorter each year. The premium, therefore, is computed on the average leasehold value over the life of the lease.

Leasehold value probably changes constantly just as the market opinions vary daily as to the value of common stocks listed on the stock exchange. While there is no daily market in real estate or in leases that tells precisely what these fluctuations are, they no doubt occur and should be estimated periodically so that the leasehold interest insurance form can be kept current. Such an estimate should be made by a qualified appraiser at least annually, as the policy is renewed.

Forms are provided for other types of interest in property that result from the loss of a leasehold. For example, an insured lessee might spend $10,000 remodeling the outside of the leased building. A fire occurs inside and as a result, the lease is cancelled. The lessee stands to lose $10,000 because the permanent improvements revert to the landlord at the expiration of the lease. This loss, it will be noted, does not stem from direct damage by fire, but from indirect loss by fire which caused cancellation of the lease. Hence, the indirect loss is not covered under the standard fire policy. Such a loss is insurable, however, under a leasehold interest insurance policy covering tenants, improvements, and betterments. A similar loss, also insurable under such a form, is the loss of prepaid rent that is not returnable if the lease is cancelled.

Most leases provide that the option to cancel in the event of destruction of the premises lies with the lessor (owner). If the lessor does not cancel the lease, of course there is no loss and, hence, no idemnity is payable under the policy to the lessee. The policy provides that if the lessee cancels, there is no payment due. Normally, if the rental value of the property has increased, it is very likely that the lessor will exercise the option to cancel the lease in the event of fire. If the lessor does cancel, the property may be rented to the same tenant on a month-to-month basis at a higher rent, in which case the policy pays the lessor the difference between the old rent and the new rent. If the lessor does not cancel, the lessee stands to lose the use of the premises until it is made tenantable again, in which case the leasehold interest policy indemnifies for the loss of use of the property until it is repaired.

Excess Rental Value Insurance

The question arises, "Suppose the rental value of the property has *fallen* since the lease was signed and it is the landlord, not the lessee, who loses by cancellation of the lease in the event of fire, or other insured peril?" In this case, a policy known as *excess rental value* may be written to cover the landlord's loss. Coverage under this policy parallels that given the lessee under the leasehold interest form.

NONTIME ELEMENT CONTRACTS

Nontime element contracts or coverages are used to insure those losses that result from fire, but where the loss cannot be measured by either direct damage by fire or in terms of elapsed time.

Profits Insurance

Profits insurance differs from business interruption insurance in that the latter covers profits that would have been earned in the future had the fire or other insured peril not damaged the firm's plant. *Profits insurance* covers the loss of the profit element in goods already manufactured but destroyed before they could be sold. Suppose that a plant is manufacturing refrigerators and is disabled by fire. Among the lost property, stored in a warehouse, are finished refrigerators with a sales value of $10,000. This figure includes an expected profit of $2,000. The standard fire policy indemnifies the insured only for the replacement cost, which would be $8,000. The business interruption policy would not cover the $2,000 loss of expected profit because the policy applies only to refrigerators which would have been produced during the period of interruption by fire, and not those already produced. To receive full indemnity for its $2,000 loss, the manufacturer would have to be covered by profits insurance.

Profits insurance serves a vital need. If a business person could replace the lost finished goods immediately at the same cost, the expected profit could be realized on the new goods. Oftentimes, however, the goods cannot be replaced in time for their expected market. Thus, goods ready for shipment to buyers who need them for a seasonal sale probably cannot be purchased elsewhere in time to realize the expected profit. The purchasers will buy elsewhere and the profit will be lost.

Profits insurance is written for manufacturers, not merchants. A merchant would receive the same protection through a business interruption insurance policy since the business of the merchant is selling finished inventory and the policy is designed to cover the lost profits and expenses from lost future sales.

In some jurisdictions a manufacturer may insure its goods for their selling price rather than for their replacement cost, or cost of production. In such a case, profits insurance is obviously not needed. Profits insurance covers only finished goods, not goods in process, which come under the loss settlement procedures of the business interruption policy.

Accounts Receivable Insurance

Accounts receivable insurance attempts to indemnify an insured for the loss brought about because of the inability to collect from open account (unsecured) debtors because a fire destroyed accounts receivable records. If a catastrophe such as fire makes it impossible to prove the existence of a debt because there are no records of the transaction, some debtors may refuse to honor their obligations. Most debtors are honest and will pay, but a loss from unscrupulous debtors may result as a consequential loss from fire or other peril.

Accounts receivable insurance is written as an all-risk cover, with the only exclusions being war and infidelity of the insured's main partners or officers. Insureds are required to make a deposit premium and to report the value of their outstanding receivables each month. An audit at the end of the year determines the actual premium. Nonaudited forms are also available. The coverage applies only while the accounts receivable records are on the premises, but for an additional premium the records may be covered while at another temporary location. It may be required that records be stored in a vault or a safe when the business is closed.

Indemnity under accounts receivable insurance is made for: (1) uncollectible accounts, the sole reason for which is the damage or loss of records, less an allowance for normal bad debts, less any debts that can be reestablished or proven by other methods or other records; (2) interest on loans made necessary by the loss; and (3) excess collection expense or the reasonable cost of reestablishing proof of an account. To establish the amount of the loss in the absence of accounts receivable records, projections from accounting data for prior years are made, with adjustments for seasonal or cyclical fluctuations. The rate for this coverage, as is true of most consequential loss contracts, is based on the fire rate in the territory served.

Temperature Damage Insurance

In many types of business firms, such as bakeries, cold-storage plants, dairies, and greenhouses, the maintenance of a certain temperature is vital to the prevention of loss. A fire may disrupt the power supply, and before it can be restored, a rise or fall in temperature may have caused a great loss even though there was no *direct* loss by fire. Such losses would not generally be covered under the standard fire policy. Yet it is vital that their insurance not be overlooked.

In most jurisdictions insurance against such consequential loss from fire is accomplished by means of an endorsement known as the *consequential loss assumption clause*. This clause broadens the definition of loss on the standard fire policy to include many types of damage due to changing temperature.

Rain Insurance

Rain as such seldom causes any direct damage to property. The accumulation of water due to extended rainfall, of course, does cause much loss to property in the form of flood or rising water, but such coverage is generally not available from private insurers. Rain, itself, however, may be a source of considerable *indirect* loss because its occurrence may greatly reduce the expected profits of promoters of an outdoor or public event. *Rain insurance* is designed to cover the loss of profits and fixed charges or extra expenses due to rain, hail, snow, or sleet of anyone having a financial interest in an event that is dependent on good weather for its success.

Rain insurance, forms for which were revised extensively in 1970, is written on two forms, the basic form and the optional form. The former is written on an indemnity basis, with losses restricted to those which actually occur; the latter form is written on a valued basis. Both forms require that a minimum amount of rain must fall, say 1/10 of an inch, before any losses are payable. The insurer may, at its option, restrict coverage under the valued form to equal not over 100% of the net expenses or 60% of the gross revenues on the last similar day not affected by rainfall. Under the valued form, the insurer is liable for the full amount of insurance scheduled for the event, if other conditions are met.

Rain insurance must be applied for at least seven days prior to the time the event is scheduled, and once issued, the insurance cannot be cancelled. This provision protects the insured from having coverage cancelled in case rain threatens, and protects the insurer from demands for premium refunds in case the insured sees that there is not going to be any rain after all and tries to cancel the coverage just before the event.

The advisability of purchasing rain insurance depends on the promoter's estimate of the actual effect of rainfall on anticipated attendance and the resulting profit. In some areas rain is so common that it does not discourage attendance substantially, while in other locations, even a light rainfall will ruin attendance. If an event is very popular and is sold out by advance ticket sales that are nonrefundable, the profit is assured in advance and there is no reason for rain insurance. Among the possible users of rain insurance are sponsors of auction sales, sporting events, boat excursions, carnivals, fairs, conventions, and dances.

SUMMARY

1. The major contracts of insurance covering indirect or consequential losses are classified under two headings: time element and nontime element coverages. Time element policies measure the loss in terms of given time periods, while nontime element coverages use some other basis in measuring loss.
2. Consequential losses are often greater than the loss of property destroyed directly by fire or other peril. Yet, they are often overlooked in an otherwise complete insurance program.
3. The most important single type of time element contract is called business interruption insurance, which is designed to indemnify the insured for loss of profits and fixed charges that are occasioned by stoppage of business due to some named peril.
4. Other time element contracts of insurance are: (a) contingent business interruption insurance, which indemnifies for losses due to interruption of the business of a major supplier or customer; (b) extra expense insurance, which indemnifies for the extra cost when a named peril occurs and, while not causing a business shutdown, necessitates a higher cost of operation than normal; (c) additional living expense insurance, which indemnifies for higher living costs necessitated by occurrence of a named peril that renders a home unusable; (d) rental value insurance, which indemnifies for loss of rents when fire renders a building untenantable; (e) leasehold interest insurance, which indemnifies the tenant for loss of a valuable lease cancelled before its usual termination due to occurrence of fire or other named peril; and (f) excess rental value insurance, which indemnifies a landlord who loses a favorable lease due to occurrence of fire or other named peril.
5. Examples of nontime element contracts of insurance are: (a) profits insurance, which indemnifies the insured for loss of profits expected from the sale of finished goods; (b) accounts receivable insurance, which indemnifies for failure to collect accounts rendered uncollectible because a fire or other named peril destroys the records that give evidence of the debts; (c) temperature damage insurance, which indemnifies for loss due to temperature changes brought about by the occurrence of some named peril; and (d) rain insurance, which indemnifies for the loss of profits and expenses incurred when rain or other types of precipitation decrease expected attendance at some public event.

QUESTIONS FOR REVIEW AND DISCUSSION

1. In *Palatine Insurance Company* v. *O'Brien* (68 Atl. 484), the insurer refused to pay rent indemnity during the time that the insured property was rendered untenantable because the city refused to issue a permit while it was considering a change in the zoning law.
   (a) Is such a restriction common in rent forms?
   (b) Why would such a restriction be imposed?
2. A circus owner purchased a rain insurance policy covering the period beginning two hours before the opening and continuing throughout the circus. Early in the morning of the day of the circus it rained heavily and turned cold, but the rain stopped entirely at noon. The grounds of the circus were soaked and the weather continued cold and threatening, but no rain fell during the two-hour period prior to

opening nor during the circus. Nevertheless, attendance at the circus was poor. Discuss the liability of the insurer for indemnity to the circus owner.

3. "In a sense, life insurance may be properly termed a consequential loss contract." Explain.
4. Gerdes takes out a business interruption insurance policy against the perils of fire, lightning, riot, and civil commotion. As a result of a riot connected with a labor disturbance, the employees fail to show up for work during the following three days and the plant is closed. Under what conditions may Gerdes apply for loss of profits and fixed charges under the policy? Discuss.
5. Distinguish between time element and nontime element coverages.
6. If business improves considerably during the year, the individual purchaser of business interruption insurance may fail to collect in full for a partial loss under the policy. Why is this possible? Explain.
7. How should a firm go about determining how much business interruption insurance to carry? Discuss.
8. *Z* operates a concession at a beach resort for only four months during the year. *Z*'s agent recommends a business interruption policy covering an entire year's profits and fixed charges. *Z* objects, saying that if the concession is interrupted for only four months, the policy indemnifies for that period only. Discuss.
9. A lumber mill is shut down when a fire destroys its main saw carriage. The daily loss of continuing expenses and profits amounts to $1,000. It is determined that repair parts can be flown in at an extra cost of $500 over rail transportation and if this is done, the mill can resume operations three days earlier than it could if the parts were shipped by rail.
(a) Under the typical business interruption policy, will the insurer reimburse the mill for the $500 difference? Why?
(b) In this case, what is the limit of indemnity payable? Explain.
10. A small manufacturing plant is destroyed by fire and it is determined that it will take four months to rebuild it. However, the owner wishes to build a larger plant and it is estimated that the rebuilding time will be five months because of the larger size. For how many months will the business interruption policy apply? Explain.
11. On January 1, 1952, *A* leased a building to *B* under a 20-year nonrenewable lease calling for an annual rent of $1,800. The lease contains a clause under which the lease is terminated in the event that fire destroys 25% or more of the value of the building. On January 1, 1962, *B*, realizing that if it became necessary to obtain other comparable quarters in case of a major fire the cost would be $250 a month, seeks an agent's advice. *B* informs the agent of the above facts and also reports spending $4,000 to lower the ceiling of the building and to refinish the exterior. What insurance policies, and in what amounts, should *B* consider? Explain.
12. The Myrtles Dairy asks its agent to look into a business interruption insurance policy, but the agent, upon inquiry, recommends that this type of insurance would not be suitable for the dairy. The agent recommends another policy. Why might business interruption insurance not be appropriate for the dairy and what other policy would the agent probably recommend?
13. Under what circumstances would a rent insurance policy duplicate the coverage granted under a business interruption insurance policy?
14. Hendershot purchases rent insurance under a dwelling form that limits the recovery to 1/12 of the applicable insurance. The applicable insurance is 10% of the face amount of the policy. The fair

rental value of the home is $180 a month. The policy is written in the amount of $12,000. It is estimated that $20 per month represents the average cost of maintenance and repairs. How much can Hendershot collect under the rent insurance if the home is:
(a) Completely untenantable because of fire for two months?
(b) Tenantable, but approximately one half of the area is unusable until it is repaired, and the repair period will last three months?

15. Answer Question 14 on the basis that Hendershot's policy had been for the face amount of $20,000.

16. The insurance manager of the *T* Manufacturing Company is concerned about the possibility that sales to the chief customer of the firm may be cancelled because of fire damage to the customer's plant. The manager is particularly concerned with the expected profit on a shipment of finished parts ready for sale, parts that would not have a market for any other buyer.
(a) Is such a risk insurable?
(b) Would profits insurance cover the risk?
(c) What methods of handling this risk, other than insurance, might be used?

17. Why is profits insurance, as a general rule, not sold to retailers or wholesalers? Explain.

18. The ABC Company sells raw materials on open account to a certain manufacturer. Due to fire in the manufacturer's plant, accounts in the amount of $20,000 prove to be uncollectible by the ABC Company. Is this loss payable under accounts receivable insurance?

19. The Dumbe Company takes out $100,000 of business interruption insurance on the gross earnings form with 50% coinsurance. It is estimated that gross earnings are $200,000. The Wize Company also estimates gross earnings at $200,000, but takes out $150,000 coverage on the gross earnings form with 50% coinsurance and with the premium adjustment endorsement. In each case actual gross earnings turn out to be $250,000.
(a) Contrast the coverage coinsurance effect and the premium due for each of these firms.
(b) If Wize's gross earnings had increased to $400,000, would it have been subject to coinsurance penalties or would a premium increase have been due? Why or why not?
(c) Could Wize have collected as much as $150,000 if gross earnings had been $250,000? Why or why not?

20. A manufacturer gives you the following estimates of operations for the coming year: net sales, $500,000; beginning inventory of finished goods, $100,000; ending inventory of finished goods, $150,000; rent from a leased building, $100,000; purchases of raw stock, $200,000; beginning inventory of raw stock, $50,000; ending inventory of raw stock, $100,000; supplies consumed in production, $100,000; services purchased from subcontractors in the production process, $50,000; ordinary payroll, $200,000. The manufacturer estimates that the maximum period during which operations might be interrupted is six months. However, the manufacturer does not wish to insure ordinary payroll.
(a) What is the business interruption value for this manufacturer? Show your work.
(b) Insurers require that if ordinary payroll is excluded, in whole or in part, a minimum of 80% coverage to value must be taken out by the insured. Discuss the possible logic behind this requirement.
(c) Calculate the minimum coverage required in this case if the manufacturer rejects coverage on ordinary payroll and contrast it with the business interruption value as determined in (a) above. Is the manufacturer carrying more insurance than is needed?

Chapter *Twelve*

TRANSPORTATION INSURANCE

Insurance on the risks of transportation of goods is one of the oldest and most vital forms of insurance. All types of trade depend heavily upon the availability of insurance for successful and expeditious handling. If it were not possible to trade with others, it would not be feasible to manufacture goods on a mass-production basis. Without mass production, life as we know it would be entirely different and probably not as comfortable and easy.

Insurance played a vital part in stimulating early commerce. In Roman times, and earlier, contracts known as *bottomry* and *respondentia* governed the terms under which money was borrowed to finance ocean commerce. Under these contracts, the lender of money took as security for a loan either the ship itself, in the case of bottomry bonds, or the cargo in the case of respondentia bonds. However, if the ship or cargo were lost as a result of ocean perils, the loan was cancelled. If the voyage were successful, the loan was repaid and substantial interest charged mainly because the interest included an allowance for the possibility of loss of the security; this extra charge was essentially an insurance premium.

Today, even as in ancient times, shippers of goods are seldom in a position to assume the risks of transportation perils. They have constantly sought means to transfer these risks to others. The perils of transportation are so many and so varied that the shipper is in no position to make subjective judgments of their importance and to make allowances in selling prices. In addition, much trade is accomplished with the use of borrowed money. Normally, the lender is unwilling to commit funds unless satisfactory arrangements have been made to meet the risks of transportation.

THE PERILS OF TRANSPORTATION

The perils that may cause a loss to goods being transported may be appreciated by realizing the inability to control adequately or completely the forces of nature, or to prevent human failure as it affects the safe movement of goods. For example, in spite of radar, sonar, the gyroscope, the compass, and all the other modern safety devices, frequent ocean tragedies occur. Ocean storms can capsize even the largest ocean vessels. Huge waves driven by hurricane winds often dump tons of sea water on a vessel and cause damage to cargo stowed inside. Engine failure may subject a ship to the mercy of a storm, driving the ship aground, where it quickly breaks up by the pressure of waves grinding it against rocks and sand. Poor visibility still causes collisions, and fires occur frequently. Goods are sometimes lost as a result of basic dishonesty, negligence, or incompetence of the crew handling them or through faults in the management of the vessel. Likewise, loss of goods shipped on land comes from sources such as overturn of the vehicle, collision, fire, theft, flood, rough or careless handling, and unusual delays that result in spoilage.

THE LIABILITY OF THE CARRIER

The question arises, "Is not the carrier of the goods responsible for their safe movement?" The answer is, "Yes, to some extent." The common-law liability of the carrier differs depending upon the country in which the transportation conveyances are chartered, the applicable statutes, custom, the type of shipping, and other factors.

The Carrier's Liability in Ocean Transportation

In the field of ocean shipping, the carrier, or shipowner, is responsible only for failure to exercise "due diligence." The responsibility of the carrier, which is spelled out by the Carriage of Goods by Sea Act, passed in the United States in 1936, is to make the ship seaworthy; to employ proper crew, and to equip and supply the ship; and to make all holds and other carrying compartments safe and fit for the goods stored there. In addition, the carrier must exercise due care in loading, handling, stowing cargoes, etc.

The Act lists specific causes for which the carrier is definitely *not* liable. For example, the carrier is not liable for loss resulting from:

1. Errors in navigation or management of the vessel.
2. Strikes or lockouts.
3. Acts of God.
4. Acts of war or public enemies.
5. Seizure of the goods under legal process.
6. Quarantine.
7. Inherent vice of the goods.
8. Failure of the shipper to exercise due care in the handling or packing of his goods.
9. Fire.
10. Perils of the seas.
11. Latent defects in the hull or machinery.
12. Other losses where the carrier is not at fault.

Even though the carrier must prove that it was not to blame, the shipper of the goods has little claim against the carrier for loss of goods by some force outside the control of the carrier, such as windstorm or other perils of the sea.

The Carrier's Liability in Land Transportation

The common-law liability of the land carrier is considerably greater than that of the ocean carrier, but it is still not absolute. In addition to being responsible for failure to exercise due diligence, the land carrier is responsible for *all loss* to the goods except for the following causes:

1. Acts of God.
2. Act of public enemy or public authority.
3. Acts or negligence of the shipper.
4. Inherent vice or quality of the goods.

Acts of God. *Acts of God* have been interpreted to mean perils such as earthquakes, storms, and floods, which could not have been reasonably guarded against. Fire is not an act of God and hence the carrier is liable for damage caused by these perils to goods in its custody. However, loss caused by the breaking of a rail due to sudden and intense cold[1] and loss caused when a train was held up because of a heavy snowstorm[2] were held to be perils falling within the scope of the definition "act of God" and the carrier was held not liable.

Acts of Public Enemy or Public Authority. The term *public enemy* has been interpreted to mean the action by forces at war with a domestic government, not acts of gangsters, mobs, or rioters. Thus, the carrier is liable for losses of goods by organized criminals as well as by a single thief. However, the carrier is not liable for loss when the goods are taken by legal process against the owner, such as the confiscation of contraband.

Acts or Negligence of the Shipper. Under the heading *acts or negligence of the shipper* come such causes of loss as improper loading or packing, or where the nature of the goods is concealed. Thus, if packages contain glassware but are not clearly marked "fragile," the carrier may be excused from loss due to breakage. Loss from poor packing that was visible to the carrier when the goods were accepted for shipment falls upon the carrier. But if it can be proved that the loss was caused by improper packing which was not readily apparent when the goods were accepted for shipment, the carrier is excused from any liability.

Inherent Vice or Quality of the Goods. A loss from the *inherent nature of the goods* may be illustrated by losses due to decay, heating, rusting, drying, or fermentation. In one case the shipper sent a car of Christmas trees from Vermont to Florida. When the trees arrived, it was found that they had sustained damage by mold and rot. Investigation revealed that the trees had been shipped with excessive moisture and were locked in a steel car. As the train proceeded south, temperatures rose and the heat ruined the shipment. The carrier was held not liable because the loss stemmed from the inherent nature of the goods.[3]

[1] *McPaddin* v. *New York Central Railway Co.*, 44 N.Y. 478 (1871).
[2] *Ward* v. *Chicago, St. Paul, M & O Railway Co.*, 137 N.W. 995 (Neb. 1912).
[3] *Austin* v. *Seaboard Air Line Railway Co.*, 188 Fed.2d 239 (1951).

Need for Transportation Insurance

The preceding discussion reveals that many types of transportation losses fall outside the responsibility of the common carrier. Furthermore, common carriers have been slow to settle losses for which they are legally liable. In land transportation it is common, moreover, for the shipper to send goods under what is known as a *released bill of lading*. The effect of shipping goods under a released bill of lading is to limit the dollar liability of the carrier for any loss to the goods. In return, the shipper obtains a lower freight rate. In effect, the difference in freight rates is intended to compensate the shipper for the added risk of loss which must be assumed. Thus, a shipper may use outside insurance in order to achieve a prudent level of security and safety.

It is possible, of course, to shift the risk of transportation losses to the consignee of the goods. For example, goods may be shipped under terms such as f.o.b. mill or f.o.b. factory. These terms mean that the selling price does not include the cost of freight or insurance and that the title to the goods is transferred to the buyer when the goods are laid down for shipment at the railway siding or at the pier. However, suppose the buyer does not pay and the goods are returned. The seller is now subjected to the risk of loss while the goods are being sent back. Again, the shipper may buy materials on the same terms as it ships. Thus, the shipper becomes liable for loss to incoming shipments. It should be clear that it is not feasible to avoid the risk of loss entirely by trying to shift it to the buyer. There is no satisfactory substitute for insurance as the major way of handling the transportation risk.

OCEAN TRANSPORTATION INSURANCE

Insurance has been developed and has attained a high degree of refinement in modern-day commerce. As world trade grew and values at risk became larger, the need for coverage became more apparent. Larger ships and more refined instruments of navigation made long voyages possible and with this development, insurance protection was looked upon almost as a necessity. The major source of underwriting capacity was in England, probably because England was among the first to develop a refined system of admiralty law, a very necessary adjunct to successful insurance underwriting.

Major Types of Coverage

The four chief interests to be insured in an ocean voyage are:

1. The vessel, or the hull.
2. The cargo.
3. The shipping revenue or freight received by the shipowners.
4. Legal liability for proved negligence.

If a peril of the sea causes the sinking of a ship in deep water, one or more of these losses can result. However, each of these potential losses can be covered under a corresponding insurance policy.

Hull Policies. Policies covering the vessel itself, or *hull insurance,* are written in several different ways. The policy may cover the ship only during a given period of time, usually not to exceed one year. The insurance is commonly subject to geographical limits. If the ship is laid up in port for an extended period of time, the contract may be written at a reduced premium under the condition that the ship remain in port. The contract may cover a builder's risk while the vessel is constructed.

Cargo Policies. Contracts insuring cargo against various types of loss may be written to cover only during a specified voyage, as in the case of a hull contract, or on an open basis. The latter is probably the most common type of contract. Under the *open contract,* there is no termination date, but either party may cancel upon given notice, usually 30 days. All shipments, both incoming and outgoing, are automatically covered. The shipper reports to the insurer at regular intervals as to the values shipped or received during the previous period. The shipper declares the classes of goods and the ports between which these goods move. There is usually a limit of values that may be insured on a single vessel and a limit on the goods stowed on deck.

Ocean cargo is often shipped under what is known as a *cargo certificate*, an instrument which entitles the holder to collect any losses that would have been paid under the basic cargo policy covering the goods. The certificate is used because it can be negotiated from one person to another, entitling each subsequent owner of the goods to collect on the insurance in case of loss. Each seller transfers the certificate of insurance to the buyer. In this way, ocean commerce and foreign trade are greatly facilitated because it is unnecessary for each transferee of goods to arrange for insurance; all who have a financial interest are automatically protected.

Freight Coverage. The money paid for the transportation of the goods, known as *freight,* is an insurable interest because in the event that freight charges are not paid, someone has lost income with which to reimburse expenses incurred in preparation for a voyage. Under the laws of the United States, the earning of freight by the hull owner is dependent on the delivery of cargo unless this is altered by contractual arrangements between the parties. If a ship sinks, the freight is lost and the vessel owner loses the expenses incurred plus the expected profit on the venture. The carrier's right to earn freight may be defeated by the occurrence of perils ordinarily insured against in an ocean marine insurance policy. The hull may be damaged so that it is uneconomical to complete the voyage, or the cargo may be destroyed, in which case, of course, it cannot be delivered.

The owner of cargo has an interest in freight arising from the obligation to pay transportation charges. There are two typical arrangements for handling the shipping charges. First, freight may be guaranteed to the carrier, payable in all events. This type of freight is a part of the invoice cost and is insured by the cargo owner as a part of the value of the goods. Since payment of the freight is guaranteed to the carrier, the carrier does not insure its payment. Second, freight may be contingent, payable only if the goods are delivered. The carrier insures this type of freight. However, the cargo owner is normally required to pay freight charges on goods arriving in damaged condition. Thus, the cargo owner may also insure contingent freight and there then exists a double insurable interest. Freight insurance is normally made a part of the regular hull or cargo coverage instead of being written as a separate contract.

Legal Liability for Proved Negligence. In the *running down clause (R.D.C.)* in ocean marine insurance policies covering the hull, the hull owner is protected against third-party liability claims that arise from collisions. Collision loss to the hull itself is included in the perils clause as one of the perils of the sea. The R.D.C. clause is intended to give protection in case the shipowner is held liable for negligent operation of the vessel which is the proximate cause of damage to certain property of others. The vessel owner or agent of that owner who fails to exercise the proper degree of care in the operation of the ship may be legally liable for damage to the other ship and for loss of freight revenues. The R.D.C. clause normally excludes liability for damage to cargo, harbors, wharves, piers, or for loss of lives or personal injuries.

To provide liability coverage for personal injuries, loss of life, or damage to property other than vessels, the *protection and indemnity* (*P. & I.*) *clause* is usually added to the hull policy. This clause is intended to provide liability insurance for all events not covered by the more limited R.D.C. clause, except liability assumed under contract. Similarly, the policy may be extended to insure the shipowner's liability under the Federal Longshoremen's and Harbor Workers' Compensation Act.

Perils Clause

In 1779, Lloyd's of London developed a more or less standard ocean marine policy containing an insuring clause, the wording of which has been retained almost in its original form in policies issued today. The wording, which has been the subject of repeated court decisions interpreting almost every phrase, is as follows:

> Touching the adventures and perils which we the assurers are contented to bear and to take upon us in this voyage; they are of the seas, men of war, fire, enemies, pirates, rovers, thieves, jettisons, letters of mart and countermart, surprises, takings at sea, arrests, restraints, and detainments of all kings, princes, and people, of what nation, condition, or quality soever, barratry of the master and the mariners, and of all other perils, losses, and misfortunes, that have or shall come to the hurt, detriment, or damage of the said goods and merchandise, and ship, etc., or any part thereof.

It will be noticed that this clause might be interpreted as an all-risk contract since it makes reference to certain named perils "and *all other* perils, losses, and misfortunes." However, the courts have interpreted the quoted phrase as "all other *like* perils." Hence, it cannot be said that the policy is an all-risk contract although it is very broad in its coverage. Essentially, the insuring clause covers perils *of* the sea and not all perils. Perils *on* the sea, those not finding their inherent cause arising out of the sea, are not insured unless they are specifically mentioned. Fire, for example, is a peril *on* the sea and is insured by specific mention. Examples of perils *of* the sea are action of wind and waves, stranding, and sinking. Gradual wear and tear caused by the ocean is not considered a covered peril.

The insuring clause is not interpreted as providing coverage against the perils of war, even though a broad implication is present that such is the intention. Losses from pirates, assailing thieves, or overt dishonest actions by the ship's master or crew (barratry) are similar to burglary and robbery protection on land and are not losses from war. Pilferage is not covered, but may be added by endorsement. The *free of capture and seizure* (*F.C.&S.*) *clause,* which is present in most modern policies, specifically excludes all loss arising out of war. War coverage is not available from private insurers today, although the United States government provided this protection during World War II by creation of a special body known as the War Shipping Administration.

Deductibles

Ocean marine insurance policies have two chief types of deductible clauses:

1. Memorandum clause.
2. Free of particular average (F.P.A.) clause.

Memorandum Clause. One of the most common of the deductible clauses is known as the *memorandum clause*. Attached to cargo policies, this clause lists various types of goods with varying percentages of deductibles that apply on a franchise basis. Thus, the memorandum clause may specify that there will be no loss payment for loss to tobacco under 20%, nor to sugar under 7%, nor to *any* partial loss to cheese or certain other perishables. This means that if there is a partial loss to a shipment of tobacco and the damage is less than 20%, each package considered separately, no loss will be payable; but if the loss exceeds 20%, the entire amount of the loss will be reimbursed to the owner.

Free of Particular Average Clause (F.P.A.). Some policies covering the cargo and the hull may obtain a type of deductible known as the *free of particular average clause*. In ocean marine insurance terminology, the word average, stemming from the French word *avarie,* means loss or damage to a ship or a cargo. *Particular average* means a partial loss to an interest which must be borne entirely by that interest. Particular average is contrasted to *general average,* which will be explained shortly. The free of particular average clause (F.P.A.) usually provides that no partial loss will be paid to a single cargo interest unless the loss is caused by certain perils such as stranding, sinking, burning, or collision. Often the F.P.A. clause is limited to those losses under a certain percentage, such as 3%.

In interpreting what is a partial loss, each package is insured separately. A total loss of one package in a shipment is not considered as particular average but as a total loss of a part. Let us say that the clause reads, "warranted free from particular average under 10% unless general." The shipment consists of 100 bags of coffee. If one bag of coffee is completely destroyed, the policy will cover the loss even though it constitutes only 1% of the value of the shipment. No indemnity would be paid, however, if there is a partial loss to each unit of an amount less than the stipulated percentage that constitutes the franchise deductible. The words "unless general" mean that if there is a partial loss falling in the category of a general average claim, the loss will be paid regardless of the percentage. The ocean marine insurance policy always provides full coverage for general average claims.

General Average Clause

The *general average clause* refers to losses which must be partly borne by someone other than the owner of the goods that were damaged or lost. General average losses may be total or partial, while particular average losses, by definition, are always partial. To illustrate, suppose that a certain cargo of lumber, wrapped in a large bundle, is stored on deck. To lighten the ship during a heavy storm that is threatening the safety of the whole voyage, the captain orders the lumber, worth $5,000, to be jettisoned. The action of the captain is successful in saving the ship and all the other interests. Such a sacrifice would be termed a general average and those interests that were saved would be required to share a pro rata part of the loss. Thus, if the ship and freight interests were valued at $100,000, and the other cargo interests at $95,000, the shipowner would have to pay one half (100/200) of the value of the lumber. The other cargo interests would share 95/200 of the loss and the owner of the lumber would bear 5/200 of the loss. All ocean marine policies provide coverage for general average claims which may be made against the insured.

General average claims must meet certain requirements before they can be properly described as "general average." The sacrifice must have been *voluntary*; it must have been reasonably *necessary*; it must have been *successful*. If in the above case the lumber had washed overboard just before the captain ordered it jettisoned, the loss would not be termed a general average because it was not a voluntary sacrifice. This is true even though the result of the loss saves the other interests. Likewise, if the ship sinks, even though the sacrifice was voluntary, there will be no general average contributions because the sacrifice was not successful in saving the other interests.

General average claims extend to many types of loss other than mere jettison. Suppose a fire breaks out and water used to put it out causes loss to otherwise untouched cargo. Since fire fighting is considered to be a voluntary effort and is necessary to save the other interests, such losses would be paid as general average claims, assuming the effort is successful. Again, assume that a ship is stranded and engine damage is sustained in an effort to get the ship free, or that certain expenses are incurred when a ship is voluntarily sent into a harbor during a storm. These examples may both qualify as general average claims, assuming always that there is absence of negligence on the part of any interest seeking indemnity in bringing about the peril which threatens the voyage. No general average claims will be paid as a result of sacrifices made because of perils which are not covered by the ocean marine contract.

Sue and Labor Clause

A clause of basic importance to the ocean marine insurance policy is known as the *sue and labor* clause. A typical clause reads:

> And in case of any loss or misfortune, it shall be lawful and *necessary* (to and for the Assured) . . . to sue, labor and travel for, in and about the defense, safeguard and recovery of said goods and merchandises, or any part thereof, without prejudice to this insurance; . . . and to the charges whereof, the said Assurers will contribute according to the rate and quantity of the sum hereby insured.

Under this clause, the insured is required to do everything possible to save and preserve the goods in case of loss. The insured who fails to do this, has violated a policy condition and loses the rights of recovery. This means that the insured must incur reasonable expenses such as salvage fees, attorney's fees, or storage, which may be reimbursed by the insurer, even if such expenses fail to recover the goods. It is possible to recover for a total loss plus sue and labor charges even if the face amount of the policy proceeds is exhausted.

Abandonment

In ocean marine insurance, two types of total losses are recognized, actual and constructive. *Actual total loss* occurs when the property is completely destroyed. *Constructive total loss* occurs when, even though the ship or other subject matter of insurance is not totally destroyed, it would cost more to restore it than it is worth. Under American law, before constructive total loss is said to have occurred, the damage must equal 50% or more of the ship's value in an undamaged condition, while under English law, damages must exceed 100% of the ship's sound value. In most hull policies, the English rule is stated as a policy provision. Such a provision says that if it costs more to repair the ship than its agreed-on value as stated in the policy, the ship may be abandoned to the insurer and the insured collects the full amount of the policy. The salvage then belongs to the insurer, who is usually in a better position to dispose of it than the insured, since the insurer deals with salvors all over the world and is experienced in such matters. Abandonment is not permitted in any line of insurance except marine.

Subrogation

The ocean marine insurance contract provides for subrogation rights against liable third parties for damage to insured property. (The principle of subrogation was discussed in Chapter 8.)

Warehouse-to-Warehouse Clause

Under the terms of the *warehouse-to-warehouse clause,* such protection as is afforded under the insuring agreement extends from the time the goods leave the warehouse of the shipper, even if it is located far inland, until they reach the warehouse of the consignee.

Other Insurance Clause

Unlike other forms of insurance, the ocean marine contract specifies that if there shall be more than one insurer covering a given interest, each policy shall contribute to the loss in the order of the date of its attachment. Where two or more policies attached on the same date, each would contribute in the proportion that the face amount of each policy bears to the total insurance. For example, suppose a hull valued at $100,000 is insured for $75,000 by Company A on January 1; for $15,000 by Company B on January 2; and for $10,000 by Company C on January 2. The hull suffers a $60,000 loss. Under the other insurance clause, Company A would have to pay the entire amount, since it had coverage attached before that of Companies B and C. If the loss had been $85,000, Company A would have paid $75,000 and Companies B and C would have divided the remaining $10,000 of loss in the proportions 3/5 for Company B and 2/5 for Company C.

Coinsurance

While there is no coinsurance clause as such in the ocean marine policy, losses are settled as though each contract contained a 100% coinsurance clause. Ocean marine contracts are usually valued. Total losses result in an enforceable claim for the entire limit of liability as stated in the policy, and partial losses are determined, insofar as possible, by sale of the damaged article or by independent appraisal.

In general, since it is usual for the insured and the insurer to agree on a full valuation in advance, there are no coinsurance penalties involved. Occasionally, however, the value of a cargo may rise or fall during the course of shipment. Assume that a certain shipment is valued at $1,000 at the time of shipment and at the time of arrival, it is found to be damaged. To determine the loss, the article is sold in damaged condition and brings $600. It is determined that if the article had been undamaged, it would have brought $1,500. Thus, the loss is $900. The ratio of $900 to $1,500, or 60%, is the percentage of sound value which is lost. This percentage is then applied to the amount of original valuation, $1,000, and the insured recovers $600, or two thirds of the loss. The insured has received a total of $1,200 on cargo worth $1,500. If there had been $1,500 of insurance, the insured would have received 60% of $1,500, or $900, from the insurer and $600 from the sale of the damaged goods, or a total of $1,500. Since there was a failure to carry the full value of the goods, even though this failure was inadvertent, the insured becomes a coinsurer.

Usually cargo policies contain wording which values cargo at invoice plus 10%. The additional 10% coverage provides a hedge against the possible rise in value of a shipment and the resulting coinsurance penalties. If the value of cargo falls, it is possible, of course, for the insured to collect more than the actual cash loss. Since the insured seldom has control over fluctuations in value or over conditions causing losses, little or no moral hazard exists.

Warranties in Ocean Marine Insurance

There are two types of warranties in marine insurance—express and implied. *Express* warranties are written into the contract and become a condition of the coverage relating to potential causes of an insured event. *Implied* warranties are important too; however, they are not written into the policy but become a part of it by custom. Breach of warranty in marine insurance voids the coverage, even if the breach is immaterial to the risk.

Express Warranties. Express warranties are often used to effect certain exclusions. Examples of express warranties are:

1. The F. C. & S. (free of capture and seizure) warranty.
2. The S. R. & C. C. (strike riot and civil commotion) warranty.
3. The delay warranty.
4. The trading warranty.

F. C. & S. Warranty. Under the *F. C. & S.* warranty, both parties agree that there shall be no coverage in case of loss from such perils as capture, seizure, confiscations, weapons of war, revolution, insurrection, civil war, or piracy.

S. R. & C. C. Warranty. Under the *S. R. & C. C.* warranty, it is agreed that the insurer will pay no loss due to strikes, lockouts, riots, or other labor disturbances.

Delay Warranty. Under the *delay* warranty, the insurer excludes loss traceable to delay of the voyage for any reason, unless such liability is assumed in writing.

Trading Warranty. A class of express warranties known as *trading warranties* is important in ocean marine insurance. Examples of trading warranties are warranties restricting the operation of the ship to a given area, such as a certain coastal route; warranties specifying that the insurance issued represents the true value of the ship or other interests; and warranties restricting the time during which the ship may operate, such as only during the open season on the Great Lakes.

Implied Warranties. There are three implied warranties in marine insurance. These relate to: seaworthiness, deviation, and legality.

Seaworthiness. If a ship leaves port without being in safe condition, the implied warranty as to seaworthiness has been breached and the entire coverage is immediately void. If the ship were seaworthy when it left port but became unseaworthy later on, the warranty is not breached. Seaworthiness involves such factors as having a sound hull, engines in good running order, qualified captain and crew, proper supplies for the voyage to be undertaken, and sufficient fuel.

Deviation. The warranty as to deviation is breached when a vessel, without good and sufficient reason, departs from the prescribed course of the voyage, but without the intention of abandoning the voyage originally contemplated. The liability of the insurer ceases the moment that the ship departs from its course; but mere intention to deviate, not accompanied by an actual change of course, does not relieve the insurer of liability. Undue delay may constitute a deviation. The deviation or delay does not have to increase the hazard of the voyage in order to release the insurer because any breach of warranty, regardless of whether or not the warranty was material to the risk, voids the contract. Even if the ship later resumes course and then suffers a loss, there is no coverage unless later negotiations with the insurer have restored the insurance.

There are certain causes which will excuse a deviation that has not been authorized by contract. These fall into two main groups: unavoidable necessity and aiding in saving human life. *Unavoidable necessity* may be proved when a ship is blown off course, puts into a port of distress, deviates to escape capture, is taken over by mutineers, or is carried off course by a warship. *Aiding in saving human life* is illustrated when a ship deviates to help a vessel in distress. It is to be noted, however, that deviation to save *property* only is not permitted.

Legality. The implied warranty of legality is one that is never waived. If the voyage is illegal under the laws of the country under whose dominion the ship operates, the insurance is void. Under the laws of the United States, insurance on a ship engaged in running rum would be void, but such a purpose might not be illegal under the laws of another country, and in that country the insurance contract would be enforceable. To provide insurance against illegal enterprise is obviously against public policy and this accounts for the fact that the illegality warranty cannot be waived.

LAND TRANSPORTATION INSURANCE

In the early period of industrial development, buyers of goods generally took delivery at an ocean port and conducted most of their business from that port. With the growth of inland centers of commerce, inland shipments of ocean cargo by way of railroad or canal became common, and pressure grew for an extension of the ocean marine contract to cover the perils of land transportation. The warehouse-to-warehouse clause was developed to meet this need. But the ocean marine contract was not suited to the needs of land transportation insurance, and so there developed a branch of insurance known as inland marine.

The Marine Definition

Inland marine insurance is defined in what is known as the *nationwide marine definition* of the National Association of Insurance Commissioners. This definition, first formulated in 1933 and completely revised in 1953, serves as a guide for regulatory authorities in governing rating procedures, underwriting methods, contract provisions, and other matters. The five subjects of insurance that are recognized include contracts covering: imports, exports, domestic shipments, instrumentalities of transportation and communication, and "floaters," which are policies on movable property.

One of the important reasons for adopting a uniform definition of what constitutes marine insurance arises from the fact that rate regulation applicable to fire insurers is generally much more rigid than that applicable to marine underwriters. Before the definition was adopted, there was a tendency for marine underwriters to insure subjects, such as property in fixed locations, which normally would have been insured by fire underwriters. The greater flexibility in rating and in coverage enjoyed by the marine underwriters had a tendency to undermine the rating formulas imposed upon fire underwriters, who were rapidly losing business. In general, the common requirement of all subjects of insurance in the marine definition is that there must be some element of transportation or communication involved in their handling. This means, for example, that real estate which has nothing to do with transportation or communication cannot be insured under a marine insurance policy. As for personal property, it is possible to insure such goods under either a marine policy or a multiple-peril policy, regardless of whether the goods are situated at a fixed location or are in transit. This has been made possible by the adoption of multiple-line laws that give an insurance company the right to design contracts which are all-inclusive in nature.

The nationwide marine definition does not distinguish between inland or ocean marine insurance. It permits insurance on certain classes of goods and contains a section of prohibited risks. In general, the basis for differentiating permitted from prohibited risks is mobility.

Imports and Exports. Imports and exports may be covered under marine contracts so long as the perils of transportation are included. When goods lose their identity as shipments, they are no longer eligible for coverage under a marine policy. Thus, an import loses its characteristics as an import when it is sold and delivered by the importer, removed from storage and placed on sale as part of the importer's stock in trade, or delivered for manufacture or processing.

Domestic Shipments. Domestic shipments may be insured under a marine contract so long as the policy covers the perils of transportation. Goods qualify for coverage while they are in a fixed location of a customer who has them on consignment, or in a warehouse of a carrier where storage is incident to their transportation. However, such goods may not be covered under a marine contract while they are at the factory or warehouse location of the owner.

Instrumentalities of Transportation and Communication. Bridges, tunnels, piers, wharves, docks, pipelines, power transmission and telephone lines, radio and television towers, outdoor cranes, and loading bridges are among the so-called instrumentalities of transportation and communication which may be insured under a marine insurance contract. However, there are some restrictions on the coverage of these objects. For example, bridges and tunnels are not eligible under the marine policy if the only perils to be insured are fire, lightning, windstorm, sprinkler leakage, hail, explosion, earthquake, riot, or civil commotion. In other words, the policy would have to insure such transportation perils as collapse or cave-in, in addition to those listed above, before the property would be eligible for marine insurance.

Floaters. The marine definition lists 25 types of floater policies which may be issued. Seven of these policies cover private individuals, and the remainder are designed for either business use or personal use. A *floater* policy may be used to insure goods of a movable nature wherever they may be located, whether in transit or in the permanent location. However, floaters are often much more restrictive than this, and cover goods only under certain conditions while away from their normal location. Floaters may be all-risk or specified peril, most being of the latter type. Examples of personal floaters are those that cover personal property, tourists' property, personal effects, and furs and jewelry. Examples of business floaters are those that cover patterns and dies, contractors' equipment, animals, property on exhibition, jewelers' stocks, merchandise held on a floor-plan financing basis, and signs.

Inland Transit Policy

A basic contract covering domestic shipments primarily by land transportation systems is known as the *inland transit policy*. Sometimes called the *annual transit floater,* this form of insurance is designed for manufacturers, retailers, wholesalers, and others who ship or receive a substantial volume of goods. The contract usually covers shipments by rail and railway express, public truckers, and may cover coastal shipments by ship between ports on the eastern coast of the United States and the Gulf of Mexico. It covers goods in the hands of other transportation agencies when in connection with rail, railway express, or steamer shipments. Shipments by mail or by aircraft are not usually covered unless specifically named in the policy.

Perils. There is no standard form for the inland transit policy, but all such contracts follow a similar pattern. The contracts are typically written on a named peril basis, covering the perils of transportation, which include collision, derailment, overturning of vehicle, rising water, tornado, fire, lightning, and windstorm. Sometimes the policy covers theft of an entire shipping package, but it seldom covers pilferage except when the goods are shipped by express. In general, the policies exclude loss due to strike, riot, civil commotion, war, delay of shipment, loss of market, illegal trade, inherent vice of the goods, leakage, or breakage unless caused by one of the basic perils insured against. Among the types of property excluded are accounts, bills, deeds, evidences of debt, money, notes, securities, and exports after arrival at seaboard. Variations in these provisions are frequently negotiated between the parties. For example, an all-risk form for the inland transit policy is available for certain types of shippers, with the insuring clause reading "This policy insures against all risks of loss or damage to the insured property from an external cause (including general average and/or salvage charges and expresses) except as herein excluded."

Loss Limits. The inland transit policy normally has several types of liability limits. For example, there will be a limit of loss of a given amount, often 5% of the annual estimated shipments, while the goods are in the custody of any one shipping agency. There will be a limit of 10% of the annual estimated shipments in any one casualty. For purposes of loss settlement, goods are valued at invoice cost plus any prepaid or advanced freight or other costs due on the goods.

Rates. If the common carrier assumes the liability for loss of goods at their full valuation, the rates are considerably higher than if the goods are shipped under a released bill of lading, whereby someone else assumes liability for losses above a certain amount. The express agency, for example, charges 10 cents per $100 for any declared valuation in excess of $50, whereas the insurance rate will probably be about half of this amount,[4] depending upon the individual circumstances of the shipper's business. Furthermore, the insurance coverage is broader than the protection given by the express company, which insures only for the amounts for which it is legally liable. This liability is less than complete or absolute. A deposit premium is required by the insurer, and the final premium is determined by audit.

Important Conditions. The inland transit policy, as is true of most inland marine insurance contracts, is characterized by somewhat different conditions and provisions than prevail in the ocean marine policy. For example, if other insurance is applied on the risk, the policy provides that it is excess only. It is important that two policies with identical provisions not to be placed in force, or each would be ''excess'' over the other. The inland transit policy contains a 100% coinsurance clause, which formalizes the unwritten similar condition in ocean marine contracts. It also has a cancellation clause which provides that either party may end the agreement, with five days' notice being a typical requirement if the insurer cancels. In contrast to the situation in ocean marine insurance, the inland transit policy may not be assigned or transferred without the written consent of the insurer. Unless otherwise provided, coverage under the inland transit policy is limited to the continental United States and Canada.

Trip Transit Insurance

For the individual or business firm that makes only an occasional shipment, the trip transit policy is especially applicable. Covering on a named peril basis, this policy is written for a specific shipment of goods between named locations. The type of conveyance may be either a common carrier or a private carrier of some type, such as a horse-drawn vehicle, a public trucker, or a trailer. It is common to insure household furniture, merchandise, machinery, or livestock under trip transit insurance contracts. The perils insured, conditions, and exclusions are similar to the inland transit and blanket motor cargo contracts. For example, leaking, marring, scratching, or breaking are excluded unless caused by certain named perils. This limitation is of special interest to shippers of household goods that are susceptible to damage by freight car movement.

As in other forms of transportation insurance, the trip transit policy is an inexpensive method of obtaining protection as compared to shipping under bills

[4] Rates differ but are usually within the following ranges for each $100 of value: railway express, $.04—$.07; rail freight, $.02—$.04; truck, $.07—$.10; coastal steamer, $.12½—$.18.

of lading that are not released. In a given situation, the freight charges under a released bill of lading were $1.00 per 100 pounds and charges for full value declared, $1.50. Thus, the carrier in effect charged $.50 per 100 pounds for "insurance" on the full value of the goods. Yet, a trip transit policy was available for only 10 cents per 100 pounds. Therefore, the insured could effect a saving of 40 cents per 100 pounds by using the trip transit policy. In many cases, however, the effect of minimum premiums is such that it may be cheaper not to use a trip transit policy but to rely on full common carrier liability for protection.

SUMMARY

1. Insurance on the risks of transportation, particularly ocean transportation, was one of the earliest forms of insurance to be employed. It has proved vital to an expanding industrial economy dependent on mass production and consequent need for wide distribution of goods.
2. Two of the factors increasing the demand for transportation insurance are the seriousness and frequency of losses from transportation perils and the fact that the legal liability of the common carrier for safe shipment of the goods is neither absolute nor complete.
3. The major types of policies in ocean marine insurance are contracts covering (a) the hull, (b) the cargo, (c) the freight, and (d) the legal liability of the carrier for proved negligence. The coverage is broad, but it is still on a named peril basis.
4. Ocean marine policies contain many types of deductible clauses. The two most common are the memorandum clause and the free of particular average (F.P.A.) clause. The former clause excludes losses to certain commodities on a franchise basis. Free of particular average conditions means that the policy will not pay for any partial loss to a single interest.
5. General average refers to a situation where all interests must contribute to a voluntary sacrifice, made for the good of all, which is successful in saving the ship from total loss.
6. Warranties in ocean marine insurance are of extreme importance and any breach, no matter how slight, voids the contract. Express warranties are typified by trading warranties of various kinds. The implied warranties are those of seaworthiness, deviation, and legality.
7. Insurance on the perils of land transportation grew out of contracts of ocean marine. The marine definition delineates five types of insurance to be allowed as marine insurance, with no distinction now being made between ocean and inland marine. The five groups are contracts covering (a) imports, (b) exports, (c) domestic shipments, (d) instrumentalities of communication and transportation, and (e) floater risks. The one element common to all these contracts is that the subject of insurance is essentially mobile, either actually or constructively.
8. The inland policy, the blanket motor cargo policy, and the trip transit policy are three basic contracts covering the perils of land transportation. In general, it is cheaper and better to use these policies than to rely on insurance covering the interest of the common carrier or upon the common-law liability of the common carrier for safe carriage of the goods.

QUESTIONS FOR REVIEW AND DISCUSSION

1. A television play recently featured a drama about the experiences of a captain who insisted upon keeping with him at all times an aide whose qualifications as a sailor were in doubt. It developed that the captain was partially blind and relied on the good vision of this aide to help him perform his duties. What insurance implications does this story have to the shipowner? Explain.
2. In a recent case (*Bolta Rubber Company* v. *Lowell Trucking Corporation*, 37 N.E.2d 873) a trucking company insured under a motor cargo policy to protect its legal liability as a common carrier. The policy contained a warranty that each insured truck would be equipped with a burglar alarm in good working order. A truck was held up. It was determined that the burglar alarm system had been turned off at the time of the holdup. The trucker was held liable for $1,000. The policy contained the Interstate Commerce Commission endorsement required for truckers in interstate commerce. Discuss the liability and rights of the insurer and the trucker.
3. List at least six causes of loss for which an ocean-going common carrier is not liable at common law.
4. A ship is lost by collision with an iceberg. The owners of cargo claim that the tragedy would not have occurred if the captain had steered a more southerly course. In your opinion, is the captain guilty of negligence, or is the loss caused by one of the acts of God over which no control is exercised and for which liability does not exist on the part of the common carrier?
5. In *Vernon* v. *American Railway Express Company,* S.W. 913 (Mo. 1920), the court held that extraordinarily hot weather was a cause for which the common carrier was not liable. Under what conditions might the court have held otherwise, i.e., that the carrier would be liable?
6. If the common carrier is responsible for the safe carriage of the goods, why is insurance necessary? Explain.
7. Explain the function of the released bill of lading in transportation insurance.
8. Why is an ocean cargo certificate considered such a valuable device in facilitating foreign commerce?
9. What basic interests are insured in ocean transportation insurance?
10. The antiquated wording in the 1779 Lloyd's ocean perils clause is retained in its essential outline in modern-day policies. Suggest reasons for this.
11. What coverage is added to the ocean marine contract by the R.D.C. clause? by the P.&I. clause? Contrast these two clauses.
12. A shipment of 1,000 bags of flour valued at $5 per bag is shipped by ocean transport from San Francisco to Rio de Janeiro. The shipment is insured under an ocean marine open cargo insurance policy containing the following clause: "*Free of particular average* under 3% unless caused by the vessel being stranded, sunk, burned, or in collision, each package separately insured." One hundred (100) bags of flour are damaged to the extent of $500, by a peril insured against.
    (a) Explain briefly the term "free of particular average" as it is used in ocean marine insurance.
    (b) What is the amount of the liability, if any, of the recovery by the shipowner for this damage by fire?
13. A shipowner insures his $100,000 hull under a typical ocean marine hull insurance policy for $75,000. A fire causes damage resulting in a repair cost of $10,000. What is the extent, if any, of the recovery by

the shipowner for this damage by fire?

14. The *S. S. Victory* lost all power after going under the Golden Gate Bridge of San Francisco. The captain immediately tossed out the anchor, but due to the heavy current produced by the tide, found that the vessel was drifting dangerously near the rock-ledged coast. Rather than risk drifting onto the rocks before any power could be developed, the captain called for two tugs to come out and pull the vessel clear. The *S. S. Victory* is valued at $2 million, the collect freight expected from pursuance of the voyage is stated at $75,000, and the total cargo carried is valued at $725,000. The cargo of the Smith Company is valued at $5,000.
(a) Would Smith Company incur any liability as a result of this action? If so, what would such liability be?
(b) Would the insurer pay such a loss?

15. The *S. S. Victory* runs aground as it enters the harbor at Honolulu. Due to various contingencies, it is impossible to refloat the vessel before a storm strikes. Considerable damage is done to the vessel and the cargo, especially to the Number 3 hold in which the Smith Company's merchandise (pens and pencils) is packed. The pens and pencils are so badly battered that in order to save the shipment from being a total loss, it is necessary that $2,000 be spent on reconditioning them. The Smith Company seeks recovery from the insurer for the entire $5,000 for which the shipment is insured on the grounds that there is actually a total loss. Do you agree? Why or why not?

16. (a) Explain in your own words the meaning of general average.
(b) Why should the various interests be required to pay such claims?

17. "A particular average is not a total loss of a part of a shipment." If this is so, just how would you describe particular average?

18. A ship ran aground and the captain hired salvage vessels to pull it off before an approaching storm broke it upon the rocks. The salvors worked all night, managing to save most of the crew, but the ship was a total loss. Is the recovery under the ocean marine policy limited to the full value of the ship? Explain why or why not.

19. Why is abandonment permitted in ocean marine insurance and not in most other lines of insurance?

20. A shipowner insures a ship with Company T on July 1 for $100,000. Later, on July 5, fearing insufficient coverage, the shipowner takes out another $50,000 policy with Company U.
(a) In the event of a $30,000 loss to the hull, how would the two companies divide the claim? Explain.
(b) What would the settlement be if the loss were $60,000? Explain.

21. Contrast the situation in Question 20 to a similar case in which the cargo is insured by the owner under the inland transit policy.

22. A shipper of grain to a foreign port by ocean transportation insured its goods for their full value, $25,000, under an ocean marine cargo policy. When the goods arrived, it was found that they had suffered a 50% damage. However, the price of grain had fallen so that the remaining grain brought only $10,000 on the open market.
(a) For what amount is the insurer liable? Explain.
(b) What would your answer have been if the price had risen instead and the remainder of the shipment had brought $15,000? Explain.

23. Does the fact that most ocean marine policies are "valued" introduce a moral hazard in their underwriting? Explain why or why not.

Chapter *Thirteen*

FLOATER CONTRACTS

The practice of insuring property at a fixed location or while it is being transported by a common carrier is well established. The need for coverage is universally recognized and owners of such goods rely on fairly standard contracts to protect them. A more difficult insurance problem is the risk of loss associated with property which is either not at a fixed location or is not being transported by a common carrier.

For example, Contractor Brown owns $50,000 worth of equipment that is used in building bridges and roads. This equipment includes such items as cranes, tractors, diggers, winches, hoists, small tools, cement mixers, and cable. The equipment is being moved constantly from job to job and is exposed to losses from many types of perils, such as landslide, theft, flood, fire, windstorm, collision, explosion, and vandalism. Since the equipment is seldom located at any one place very long, coverage under traditional fire insurance forms is not suitable. Because the equipment is not being moved by, nor is in the custody of, common carriers, the usual transportation insurance forms are not applicable. Clearly, there is a need for giving specialized attention to Brown's problem. The answer is found in a ''floater'' policy, more particularly in the contractors' equipment floater, which is discussed in this chapter.

Similarly, how may one be assured of reimbursement for loss to goods while they are temporarily in the care and custody of others? For restitution in case of loss, must one rely solely on the good faith and, perhaps, the generosity of the holders of goods on consignment, goods at the warehouse, or property being repaired? Discussion of these and other questions form the content of this chapter.

The term *floater policy* has never been satisfactorily defined, but it is generally understood to be a contract of property insurance which satisfies three requirements:

1. Under its terms the property may be moved at any time.
2. The property is subject to being moved; that is, the property is not at some location where it is expected to remain permanently.
3. The contract insures the goods while they are being moved from one location to another, that is, while they are in transit, as well as insuring them at a fixed location.

Contracts which qualify as floaters have been classified by the National Association of Insurance Commissioners in the nationwide marine definition under two headings: those designed for individuals, and those covering businesses or individuals.

INSURANCE ON FLOATING PROPERTY—PERSONAL

Personal articles not only represent a more sizable investment than many homeowners realize, but they are also subject to many more hazards, both physical and moral, than is true of real property. Theft of real property, for example, is next to impossible; but theft of movable property is not uncommon, as FBI reports document all too well. Water damage, freezing, and breakage are among the other perils especially destructive to personal property. A person who purchases a home on a long-term mortgage with a relatively low down payment will have only a small investment in the home. The purchaser will probably have several times that amount invested in furniture, clothing, garden equipment, jewelry, and other articles. In a typical home of a middle-class family of four, the contents probably cannot be replaced for less than $6,000 to $10,000. Accurate data on the average amount of physical peril insurance on personal property do not exist, but the experience of local agents generally places the average amount at far less than the true replacement cost of the property.

Gradually, however, more people have become aware of the facts of underinsurance and the growing cost of replacing personal property. A substantial demand exists for comprehensive insurance contracts that cover personal articles of all types. Several approaches have been used by underwriters in meeting this demand. One approach has been the use of endorsements that extend the scope of the basic fire policies on dwelling contents. Homeowners policies, now widely used, provide that 50% of the coverage on the dwelling shall be written on personal property, but only 10% or 20% of this amount shall apply while the property is away from the described premises. No particular provision is made under homeowners policies for articles of unusual value. Furthermore, except on Homeowners Form 5, coverage on personal property is not on an all-risk basis, and specific types of property, such as tape recorders designed for use in cars, motorized vehicles, and property of persons not related to the insured, are excluded.

Another approach has been to offer inland marine floater policies on specific types of property, such as jewelry, furs, equipment, cameras, stamp collections, musical instruments, and outboard motorboats. A third approach has been the sale of comprehensive all-risk floaters that cover personal property of almost any description, wherever located.

The Personal Property Floater

The *personal property floater* (PPF) is an all-risk policy covering personal property on a blanket basis. One of the oldest of the inland marine floaters, this contract has gained widespread acceptance, and because of its basic importance, it will be analyzed in detail.

The personal property floater may be written to cover not only specific items of property for stated amounts, but it may also cover *all* other nonbusiness personal property without scheduling each item separately. While there are different versions of the personal property floater, depending on which company issues the floater and which rating organization happens to sponsor it, the contract has become quite standardized.

Property Covered and Excluded. The personal property floater covers scheduled and unscheduled personal property of a nonbusiness nature belonging to or borrowed by the insured or members of the insured's household. Also included, at the insured's option, are the property of visitors while on the described main premises and the property of servants while located off the premises, if the servant is actually engaged in the insured's service and has custody of the property at the time of the loss. The policy also covers loss to the real property of the insured if it is damaged in the course of a theft or attempted theft.

Various items of personal property are excluded from coverage because other types of insurance are designed for them or because their use involves hazards too great for an all-risk policy. For example, automobiles, aircraft, and motorcycles are excluded because special forms of coverage are designed for them. Animals, business or professional equipment (except books and instruments in the insured's residence at the time of loss), and property at an exhibition are subject to unusual hazards and are covered under more limited policies.

Certain types of property are excluded from coverage unless the loss is caused by certain named perils. Thus, eyeglasses, glassware, statuary, marble, bric-a-brac, porcelains, and other fragile articles (watches, jewelry, and cameras excepted) are not covered unless the loss was occasioned by theft, vandalism or malicious mischief, fire, lightning, windstorm, earthquake, or other listed perils.

Limits of Liability. The personal property floater has many clauses that limit the liability of the insurer for losses. The most important ones are listed below.

1. There is an aggregate limitation of the face amount of the policy, applying to all losses of scheduled property.
2. There is a limitation of $250 applying to any one loss of *unscheduled* items of jewelry, watches, or furs, unless this amount has been increased in the scheduled portion of the policy. Under another endorsement, the coverage on jewelry, furs, and watches may be increased on an all-risk basis to $1,000, subject to a $250 limit per item. There is an aggregate limit on all *scheduled* property. The insurance liability for loss cannot exceed the stated value of each scheduled item.
3. Liability for loss cannot exceed 10% of the aggregate amount as regards property ordinarily kept at residences other than the principal residence. This limitation does not apply to property kept at another residence on a temporary basis. However, it is expected that if two permanent residences are maintained, separate policies will be purchased in order to avoid granting free insurance.

4. There is a limit of liability of $100 on any one loss of money or $500 on any one loss of notes, securities, stamps, transportation tickets, or other valuable documents. Note that throughout the policy year, the insured could collect on several losses of $100 in money, but not more than $100 each time. Coverage can be increased to $500 on money and $1,000 on securities.
5. The limitation on recovery for loss cannot exceed the actual cost to repair or to replace with materials of like kind and quality at the time of the loss. In the past there has been a tendency for some insurers not to make any deduction for depreciation, especially for items insured on a scheduled basis, but the policy definitely provides that it is to be considered a contract of indemnity.
6. On permanent improvements to dwellings not owned by the insured, there is a limitation of liability of 10% of the aggregate amount of insurance applying to damage caused by certain named perils.
7. Outboard motorboats may be endorsed to the property item, but not to exceed $500. Coverage on boats is on a named peril basis.

Perils Excluded. Like every all-risk policy, the personal property floater has a number of excluded perils. Among these are war, mechanical breakdown, extremes of temperature, deterioration, moths, vermin, inherent vice, nuclear fission, and damage caused by refinishing, renovating, or repairing. In addition, certain types of water damage to unscheduled property are excluded. Prior to 1959, there was no exclusion for flood, surface water, waves, backing up of sewers or drains, or seepage. Losses from this source were so serious that it was decided to eliminate this coverage, but only insofar as the loss is caused at the premises owned or controlled by the insured. Thus, property away from the residence is still covered for water damage. Furthermore, the water loss exclusion does not apply to certain scheduled property such as jewelry, furs, musical instruments, and art objects. A final exclusion is that of loss caused by animals kept by an insured or a resident employee.

Coinsurance and Deductibles. The personal property floater does not contain a coinsurance clause, but the rules provide that the policy may not be issued unless the insured purchases limits equal to or exceeding 80% of the exposed values. The purpose of this rule is to help overcome the problem of underinsurance. The values stated by the insured for each type of property are only estimates and are not a binding limit upon recovery; nor will a coinsurance penalty for breach of warranty be involved if these estimates are incorrect, or if the insured later acquires values beyond those stated. However, there are exceptions to this general statement in certain territories, such as in four metropolitan counties of New York where the amounts stated are converted into actual limits, and newly acquired property is covered only to the lesser of two amounts, 10% of the amount of the policy or $2,500.

The personal property floater permits the use of a $50 deductible against each loss, for which a rate credit of 40% is given. This deductible applies only to *unscheduled* property, and the rate credit is applied to the premium charges for that property. Furthermore, it is not a flat deductible that applies to all losses to unscheduled property because losses from certain named perils are not subjected to the deductible. These perils include theft, fire, lightning, windstorm, hail, smoke, explosion, riot, civil commotion, aircraft, vehicles, and rupture of a steam or hot water heating system. The deductible applies to theft from an unattended and unlocked automobile and to mysterious disappearance, and all losses except from the above-listed perils. Although the deductible is generally optional, it is mandatory in some jurisdictions, such as in the four metropolitan counties of New York referred to previously.

Rating. The personal property floater rate is computed by adding a "loading" to the basic contents fire rate. The *loading* is a charge based upon the amount of insurance and upon the territory in which the principal residence is located. In metropolitan areas, for the first $5,000 of coverage, the loading ranges from nearly .9% of the stated values to 3%. Rates for the next $5,000 of coverage are approximately one half of the rates for the first $5,000. For amounts over $20,000 the rates vary from .07% to .3%. Considering that the personal property floater provides the equivalent of fire, extended coverage, theft, and transportation insurance, plus the all-risk feature which takes care of unknown perils, the premium seems reasonable.

Bailed Property

A bailment exists when one has entrusted personal property to another, such as occurs in the case of laundries, repair establishments, and garages. Special forms of insurance are available to *bailees,* the owners of such establishments, to cover loss to bailed goods for which they might be liable. Homeowners forms also cover such losses subject to a coverage limitation of 10% to 20% of the amount of insurance.

INSURANCE ON FLOATING PROPERTY—BUSINESS

The nature of business property makes necessary more complex types of floaters, some examples of which are discussed in the following paragraphs.

Block Policies

The term *block* in insurance language, while having no precise meaning, connotes the general idea of a contract which is somewhat broader than the traditional forms of inland marine or fire insurance. A *block policy* covers *en bloc,* on an all-risk basis, the stock in trade or the equipment belonging to a business firm, no matter where the property happens to be located. In Chapter 10 the coverages known as the commercial property program (a development in multiple-line underwriting) were described. This program comes very close to providing for wholesalers and retailers generally what block forms provide for specific types of business firms. Since block policies on jewelers, furriers, camera and musical instrument dealers, and equipment dealers have been issued for many years by inland marine insurers, these and a few other types of firms are not eligible for the commercial property coverage program. Block policies will be discussed in some detail because of this fact and because these forms tend to set the pattern for the more general commercial property coverage program as it is extended to more types of commercial institutions.

Jewelers' Block Policy. One of the oldest and broadest of all block contracts, the *jewelers' block policy*, is written to insure all the stock in the trade of a typical jeweler on an all-risk basis. Thus, such property as jewels, watches, precious metals, glassware, and gift items are covered whether they belong to the jeweler or to a customer, or whether they belong to another firm and are in the store on consignment and the jeweler is legally liable for their safety or has a financial interest in them.

The jewelers' block policy covers not only property belonging to the jeweler as an owner, but also property of the customer bailor. Thus, the jewelers' block policy is another example of bailee liability insurance. Its coverage may be extended to insure property anywhere in the world, and while in transit to or from the jeweler's place of business, such as while the property is in the hands of messengers, salespersons, customers (on approval), common carriers, other jewelers, repairers, the post office, or the railway express agency.

The jewelers' block policy excludes several perils, such as war and dishonesty of employees, and it also excludes certain types of property, such as goods shipped by regular mail instead of registered mail. The jeweler is commonly required to provide loss-prevention systems, such as burglar alarms.

Camera and Musical Instrument Dealers' Policy. Another significant example of the block idea in inland marine insurance is the *camera and musical instrument dealers' form*. An all-risk policy, it covers all goods typically stocked by camera and musical instrument dealers while the goods are in transit or at any location in the United States or Canada. Like the jewelers' block policy, it covers both owned property and goods of others in the insured's custody for repair, delivery, or storage. For the dealer to be eligible for this policy, at least 75% of the dealer's business must be in cameras or musical instruments. Radios, televisions, and stereo sets are not considered musical instruments, but for insurance purposes they may be stocked by musical instrument dealers and insured under the policy so long as their sales do not exceed 25% of the dealer's total sales. Certain types of property, such as goods delivered to customers on conditional sales contracts, goods in the course of manufacture, accounts, bills, money, furniture, and fixtures, and tools and machinery, are excluded.

Equipment Dealers' Policy. A third example of an all-risk block form is the *equipment dealers' policy,* designed for retailers and wholesalers of heavy agricultural and construction equipment, such as road scrapers, bulldozers, pneumatic tools, compressors, harvesters, tractors, binders, reapers, plows, and harrows. The policy covers property belonging to others in the insured's control, but excludes automobiles, trucks, motorcycles, aircraft, or watercraft, which are insured under automobile forms. Covered territories include the United States and Canada, except for shipments via the Panama Canal. Other provisions are similar to the two block forms already discussed.

Scheduled Property Floater Risks

Many types of movable business property are insurable under a form known as the *scheduled property floater,* a general or skeleton form to which is attached an endorsement describing specific types of property and the conditions under which they are insured. The basic form contains fairly standard provisions such as subrogation, appraisal, loss adjustment, cancellation, and misrepresentation and fraud clauses. Losses are settled on an actual cash value basis. The policy provides that it is to be excess over any other collectible insurance on covered property. Some of the scheduled floaters are all-risk, but a majority are on a named peril basis.

Included among the various types of property insured under the scheduled property floater are: contractors' equipment, mobile agricultural equipment, office machinery, salespersons' samples, theatrical equipment, railroad rolling stock, oil-well drilling equipment, patterns and dies, goods on exhibition, neon and mechanical electric signs, radium, livestock, and instrumentalities of transportation and communication. Because inland marine floater forms covering these types of property are similar in nature, only two commonly used floaters—the contractors' equipment floater and the livestock floater—will be discussed here.

Contractors' Equipment Floater. One of the most important classes of property insured under the scheduled property floater form is contractors' equipment. The *contractors' equipment floater* is typical of most of the floaters on scheduled property that are listed above. Contractors have a special need for protection against the many perils that can cause loss to movable equipment. Very large sums are often invested in a single piece of equipment which is used under conditions that are basically dangerous. Fire, landslide, collision with other equipment, falling rock, and flood are not uncommon causes of total loss.

Contractors normally work under time deadlines, with severe penalties applying if the deadlines are not met. If important items of equipment are damaged or destroyed at a time when most of the owner's ready capital is already invested in the job, the need for immediate indemnity for the loss becomes apparent. Without insurance, the contractor may lose not only the funds invested in equipment, but also the profits on the job in which the funds were employed because of construction delays incurred while credit arrangements are made for equipment replacements.

Not all contractors' equipment floaters are the same, but, in general, the following perils are covered: fire, lightning, collision or overturning of a vehicle on which the equipment is being transported, explosion, collapse of bridges, windstorm, earthquake, landslide, flood, and theft. Sometimes deductibles are applied to certain types of perils, such as theft and collision. The form usually contains the following perils exclusions: wear and tear, war, riot, strike, civil commotion, infidelity of employees, overloading of lifting equipment, and damage of electrical apparatus unless caused by fire.

The contractors' equipment floater insures such items as tractors, steam shovels, cement mixers, scaffolding, pumps, engines, generators, hoists, drilling machinery, hand tools, cable, winches, and wagons. In fact, all items of equipment used by a contractor, except motor vehicles designed for highway use, such as trucks, trailers, and road tractors, are covered. The contractor may schedule all items, with a given amount for each, or may name a blanket amount of coverage, in which case an 80% (or higher) coinsurance clause is required. The floater covers property whether it is owned, leased, or borrowed. Insurance attaches no matter where the property is located. However, property permanently situated at a given location is not eligible for coverage under this floater. Property such as designs, plans, surveying equipment, and underground cable, is usually excluded.

While there is no standard rating system for the contractor's equipment floater, the fire rate in each territory usually serves as a basis. The rate is then modified on a judgment basis according to the particular perils and exclusions stated on the given contractors' equipment floater and according to the type of equipment mainly involved. The annual premium will typically range between 1% and 3% of the value of the equipment insured.

Livestock Floater. Illustrating the flexibility of coverage that is possible in inland marine floaters on scheduled property is the *livestock floater,* available to owners of cattle, horses, hogs, sheep, and mules, whether these animals are kept for farming purposes or otherwise. This floater, which is on a named peril basis, gives worldwide insurance to the owner against loss by death or destruction of the animal due to such perils as fire, lightning, windstorm, hail, explosion, riot and civil commotion, smoke, aircraft, collision with vehicles, theft, overturn of conveyances, earthquake, flood, and sinking or stranding of vessels while the animals are being transported.

Among the excluded perils are war, mysterious disappearance, escape, and infidelity of an employee or a person to whom the property is entrusted, except a carrier for hire. Certain types of losses are excluded, such as loss of use, extra expense occasioned by loss of the animal, and accidental shooting by the insured. Neither death due to sickness or disease nor veterinary expenses are covered under this form, unless the proximate cause of the loss is one or more of the perils insured against.

An optional perils rider, available at extra cost, may be endorsed on the livestock floater to cover death or destruction due to accidental shooting by someone other than the insured or employees of the insured, attack by dogs or wild animals, collapse of building, drowning, and artificially generated electricity.

Miscellaneous Business Floaters

There is a wide variety of miscellaneous business floaters, each designed to meet a specific need for insuring property in a given situation. While no attempt will be made to list them all, or even to classify them, two will be discussed as examples of the wide range of risk management problems which can be at least partially solved by the use of inland marine floaters.

The Conditional Sales Floater—Its Economic Rationale. Of all retail sales of consumer goods, it is estimated that approximately one third represent credit sales, and that of all credit sales, one third are installment sales. Thus, the value of unpaid-for property in the hands of credit buyers is tremendous. In December, 1975, there was about $162 billion of consumer credit outstanding.[1] The question arises, "Who loses if the goods are destroyed by some insurable peril before they are paid for?" Clearly, the seller has an interest in the goods to the extent of the unpaid balance, and the buyer has an interest to the extent of equity. Legally, the buyer is required to pay for the goods even if they are destroyed, because the buyer usually signs a note for the unpaid balance and is obligated to repay the note. In practice, however, it may turn out that the buyer has no funds and is more or less judgment proof. The loss then falls on the seller.

Aside from the fact that collection of debts for goods that have been destroyed may be difficult and expensive, many sellers hesitate to force collection because of the danger of losing the goodwill of a customer who may not consider that it is fair to make payment for goods that "still belonged to the finance company." These customers need replacements for the lost property and represent a source of continued business which normally will be profitable. An antagonistic debt collector may cause the loss of this business.

Finally, many sellers consider it illogical to insure stock "to the hilt" while it is in their possession, only to expose the goods to possible loss when they are in the home of a customer with little or no equity in them and with the attitude of indifference toward loss which often characterizes an individual in these circumstances. Furthermore, scheduled property forms and block policies usually exclude from coverage property sold to others. For example, the jewelers' block policy excludes property sold on the installment plan. A conditional sales floater is necessary for complete coverage for the jeweler who sells a substantial volume of goods on credit.

Because of these considerations, the conditional sales floater has assumed somewhat greater significance as a tool of risk management to manufacturers selling on installment contracts, to sales financing institutions, and to retail credit stores.

The conditional sales floater may be written to insure: (1) only the seller's interest in the goods, in which case the floater is known as a *single interest form;* (2) both the seller's and the buyer's interest under what is called *double interest form;* or (3) on a *contingent basis,* where indemnity is paid to the creditor only if the debtor cannot be made to pay.

If a loss occurs under a single interest form, the customer's debt is cancelled and the seller recovers the amount of the unpaid balance. There is no insurance on the customer's equity in the goods as is true in the double interest form.

In the double interest form, if goods are destroyed by an insured peril, both the equity of the buyer in the goods and the unpaid debt are covered. For

[1] *Federal Reserve Bulletin* (February, 1976), p. A45.

example, suppose Keeling has purchased a stereo set for $500 and still owes $300 on it at the time the set is destroyed by fire due to failure of a component. Fortunately, the creditor carries insurance on the double interest form of the installment sales floater. Keeling may recover the $200 already paid and the store recovers the $300 unpaid balance. The remaining debt of $300 is cancelled. The policy is considered excess over any other insurance which covers building contents, there is no collection from the installment sales floater. Once the full purchase price has been paid, the installment sales floater coverage is terminated.

Under the contingent form, the customer's debt is not cancelled, nor is the customer's equity in the goods covered. The seller is obligated to make full effort to collect the unpaid balance due. If the unpaid balance proves uncollectible, the insurer reimburses the seller for this loss. Contingent forms are written at a rate equal to approximately two thirds of the rate of the other forms because the insurer expects to pay only for losses where the seller's customer is financially insolvent or has disappeared.

Although conditional sales floaters are not standardized, they usually cover the perils of the extended coverage endorsement to dwelling policies, perils of fire and lightning, transportation perils, water damage, earthquake, collapse of building, breakage in transit, and theft. Some insurers write all-risk coverage on certain goods, such as household appliances. Typical perils excluded are stealing by the buyer, inherent vice of the goods (for example, scratching, bending, and breakage of fragile articles), faulty internal wiring of electrical appliances, war, and illegal trade. Sometimes a flat dollar deductible is used for goods such as musical instruments, which are especially subject to breakage.

Shipments by Mail. The United States Postal Service is not a common carrier and has no liability for the loss of goods entrusted to it unless they are insured by the post office. Therefore, anyone using the mails, and especially those sending a considerable volume of shipments annually by the mails, is in need of obtaining protection for the shipments. The insurance industry has designed forms to meet the needs of almost everyone, from the person sending only a relatively small volume of mail, to the shippers of very large values of securities and currency. The following list summarizes the major policies of this nature:

1. Parcel-post policy—covers merchandise shipments only.
2. First-class mail floater—three forms are available for different classes of customers sending securities, coupons, stamps, and other papers of value by first-class or certified mail.
3. Registered-mail floater—covers bonds, stocks, currency, bullion, precious metals, warehouse receipts, and other valuable shipments by registered mail or express.

Policies issued by private insurers generally offer the advantages of greater convenience, broader coverage, lower cost, and faster claims service than post office coverage. These advantages are more apparent to the large shipper than to the occasional shipper. For example, shipments under a registered-mail policy are covered from the moment they leave the premises of the sender until they arrive at the premises of the addressee, and not only during the time they are in the hands of the post office or the express company. Under the first-class mail floater, it is not necessary to wait in line at the post office to purchase insurance each time a shipment is mailed nor to trust a messenger to make proper arrangements each time. Each of these policies discussed below is all-risk, with the chief exclusion being for the peril of war.

Parcel-Post Policy. Covering shipments on an all-risk basis from the time they are in the custody of the post office until final delivery, the *parcel-post policy* is available for merchandise but not for money or securities. Perishable merchandise, packages not labeled "return postage guaranteed," packages bearing descriptive labels on the outside, and shipments not made in accordance with the General Parcel Post Act of 1912 are among the excluded items of property. There is a limit of liability of $100 on unregistered and $500 on registered mail.

First-Class Mail Floater. Users of the first-class mail floater enjoy all-risk coverage on incoming or outgoing shipments by first-class or certified mail. While the rates are somewhat higher than those charged for the registered-mail policy, considerable savings and added conveniences are effected for certain types of shipments by the use of first-class mail instead of registered mail. There are three forms of the first-class mail floater: Form A, Form B, and the Transfer Agents Mail Policy.

Form A allows coverage up to $250,000 per package and $1,100,000 per addressee, applying from the moment the package is placed in the hands of a messenger for mailing until it reaches the addressee. Government bonds and their coupons are not covered under this form. The insured is not required to insure every item of first-class mail sent, but only those items on which payment of premium to the insurer is recorded and rendered. No insurance is given to shipments not thus recorded.

The measure of loss is the market value of similar property purchased by the insured in the available market plus loss of interest, shipping, and insurance charges, not to exceed 125% of the amount of insurance. Thus, if a shipment of negotiable securities is lost, and by the time the loss is known it would cost 25% more to replace the securities than the stated value of the shipment for insurance purposes, the shipper can still recover for the increased value under Form A.

Form B of the first-class mail floater enables the insured to avoid the requirement of recording each shipment and of paying a premium based on the values thus recorded. Furthermore, Form B covers only shipments made by the insured, whereas Form A covers both incoming and outgoing shipments. Loss is limited to 100% of the amount of insurance.

A first-class mail floater designed for bond indenture trustees, transfer agents, and registrars who send by first-class mail issues of their own securities is the *Transfer Agents Mail Policy*. The limit of recovery for a single first-class package is $100,000 and for registered mail is $1 million. The policy gives the insured the right to have lost securities duplicated or reissued on behalf of the issuing company, and the insurer agrees in the contract to pay for this cost and to guarantee against any loss resulting from the negotiation of the lost securities in case they fall into unauthorized hands.

Registered-Mail Floater. The *registered-mail floater*, one of the oldest of inland marine floater policies, gives all-risk protection to a wide variety of shipments, including currency and precious metals, by either registered mail or express. Depending on the rate charged, coverage may be worldwide or restricted territorially. Except for currency, there are no stated limits of insurance; the coverage is equal to the values reported by the insured. If it is determined that the insured reported the full market value of securities at the time of mailing and the value of these securities had risen by the time of the loss, the amount payable to the insured may be higher than the original declared amount, subject to a maximum of 125% of full market value at the time of shipment.

SUMMARY

1. Of the various floater policies covering personal nonbusiness property belonging to an individual, the best known and most widely used is the personal property floater (PPF). This form, written on a blanket basis, insures on an all-risk, worldwide basis with relatively few exclusions of property or perils.
2. Bailments of property give rise to a demand for property insurance on bailed goods even though often no legal liability exists on the part of the bailee for damage to the goods of others which are in the bailee's custody. The bailee has a representative insurable interest in such goods if not legally liable for their destruction.
3. Coverage on bailed property may be provided by either or both the bailee and the bailor. Bailees' customers policies are designed to pay for the loss of bailed goods from specified perils regardless of the legal liability of the bailee. Typical among the many types of bailees' customers forms is the furriers' customers policy, an all-risk contract designed to cover the concentrations of values in furs left for storage or for repair at furriers.
4. Block policies, issued on an all-risk basis to specific types of retail and wholesale concerns by inland marine insurers, are significant because they have tended to set the pattern for all-risk insurance on floating business property, issued under the commercial property policy program. Common block policies are the jewelers' block, the camera and musical instrument dealers' block, and the equipment dealers' block.
5. In contrast to block forms, scheduled property floaters, generally issued on a named peril basis, cover an extremely wide variety of floating business property. Examples of the different needs met by these forms are the contractors' equipment floater and the livestock floater.
6. Because of the increasing importance of credit sales in the United States, the conditional sales floater, covering unpaid-for property in the hands of buyers, has assumed some significance as a tool of risk management in retail stores, in sales finance institutions, and for others who take installment sales risks. The conditional sales floater insures the goods against loss from named

perils and may cover the interest of the buyer and seller.

7. The parcel-post policy, the first-class mail floater, and the registered-mail floater, used by those who ship valuables by mail, may be arranged in an economical and convenient manner to meet the widely varying needs of these individuals.

QUESTIONS FOR REVIEW AND DISCUSSION

1. Indicate, with your reasons, which of the following losses are covered under a personal property floater written with a $50 deductible:
   (a) A dog belonging to the neighbors has chewed up the insured's patio lounge pad.
   (b) The insured's dog has chewed up the insured's lounge pad.
   (c) A squirrel has gnawed a hole in an expensive coat left on an outdoor table.
   (d) Thieves take $75 from an insured locker in an athletic club. Six months later another $80 is taken in the same manner.
   (e) Valuable carpeting, sent to the cleaners, was damaged by a mothproofing process.
   (f) Thieves stole some blank checks belonging to a church, filled in various amounts, and negotiated the checks.
   (g) A rug was damaged by discoloring when a servant used household ammonia and water to clean it. The insurer denies payment on the grounds that the loss was not accidential and that the insured could have prevented the loss by a quick application of acetic acid but failed to do so.
   (h) Wind caused a hole in a roof during a storm; water seeped in and caused an electrical short circuit; a freezer, filled with frozen food, warmed up and the meat spoiled. The insurer denies recovery because of the exclusion for "mechanical breakdown."
   (i) A toilet runs over and water seeps through ceiling joists and damages a valuable chair below.
   (j) The insured borrows some silverware from a neighbor for use at a party. Thieves ransack the house that night and the silverware is among that taken. They also take a fur coat belonging to one of the guests who is staying overnight.
   (k) A $500 watch disappears mysteriously. It was not scheduled on the insured's PPF.
2. Is there a duplication of coverage carried by a bailee under a bailee's customers policy and the insurance provided for a bailor under a personal property floater? Explain.
3. (a) Draw up a list of (1) excluded perils, (2) excluded property, (3) excluded territories, and (4) type of loss limitations found in common block type floaters that cover business property.
   (b) What similarities and dissimilarities among block policies can you observe? (Do not confine your inquiry necessarily to forms discussed in the text.)
4. (a) What is the chief difference in approach used by drafters of block policies and those of scheduled property floaters?
   (b) Suggest reasons for not using the block idea for users of scheduled property forms.
5. (a) Select three examples of scheduled property floaters not discussed in the text and compare them under the headings: (1) covered property, (2) covered perils, and (3) loss limitations and exclusions.
   (b) What other factors do these forms have in common? (You may use forms supplied you by a local agent or a home office in your area.)
6. The West Furniture Store has a conditional sales floater issued on

a contingent basis. George Homan has just taken advantage of the generous credit terms offered by this store and furnished his home with $2,000 worth of furniture, with a down payment of $200. Returning from a short vacation, George finds his house burned to the ground. Since he has not taken out fire insurance on the goods that he assumed to be owned by the West Furniture Store, he shrugs his shoulders over the $200 loss and goes on another shopping trip, only to be met by West's credit manager at the door demanding the next installment before any further credit is extended.

(a) If the credit arrangements by West are typical, is George required to pay his unpaid debt? Why?

(b) What type of conditional sales floater available to West would have made George's shopping trip more enjoyable? Why?

7. The firm of Overman, Meyer, and Mann, security dealers, does not wish to ship ordinary stock certificates to customers by registered mail because of the inconvenience and expense involved in this type of shipment. Yet, they do not wish to send these securities uninsured in the ordinary mail.

(a) Suggest a policy that will fit their needs.

(b) What form of this policy do you recommend? Why?

8. The Alamo Jewelry Company sells valuable diamonds and watches by mail.

(a) Why would the parcel-post policy not be an appropriate solution to Alamo's insurance needs?

(b) What policy would you recommend? Why?

Chapter *Fourteen*

THE LIABILITY RISK

One of the most serious financial risks covered by insurance is that of loss through legal liability for harm caused others. Losses from this source have been so frequent and serious in the United States that special legislation, no-fault laws, have been passed in the area of automobile liability. Negligence as a basis for determining liability for industrial accidents and illness has been eliminated by adoption of workers' compensation laws. Public attention has recently been focused on another area of negligence, that of medical malpractice suits, and legislative solutions to the handling of this risk have been proposed.

Illustrative of the sometimes catastrophic losses occurring because of negligence is the following case: An 11-year-old boy was hit on the right side of the head in a schoolyard fight. He was taken to the hospital, but no evidence of skull fracture was found when X-rays were taken; he was sent home although he was pale and groggy and perspiring heavily. When he did not improve, his father took him to the hospital that night and this time doctors decided to operate. They removed a large blood clot pressing on the brain. It was determined that had the doctors operated immediately the first time, the boy would have made a good recovery; because of the delay, however, permanent brain damage occurred. The boy was left mute and paralyzed from the neck down. The family sued the doctors, the hospital, and the school district for negligence and was awarded damages of $4,025,000, one of the largest settlements of this type on record.[1]

To protect themselves against such judgments, medical doctors have had to carry malpractice insurance on which premiums have been rising steadily. In one case, for example, it was reported that a neurosurgeon in New York State in 1970 paid $4,700 annually for this insurance; by 1975 the premium had risen to $14,000.[2] Of course, these costs must be passed on to patients, aggravating the problem of high medical costs. In other cases, doctors have ceased to practice in given areas because of high insurance costs or inability to secure

[1] *Time,* March 24, 1975, p. 60.
[2] *Ibid.*

insurance on any items, thus depriving the public of needed medical services. For these and other reasons, our system of settling disputes arising from legal negligence has produced great controversy.

BASIC LAW OF NEGLIGENCE

The basic law of negligence has many threads which are sometimes difficult for the layperson to disentangle. To see what this basic law is all about, one needs first to understand what conditions must be met before an act is considered such that it gives rise to actionable negligence. Next, one must appreciate what defenses are recognized by the courts for the protection of defendants. No matter how wrong a defendant may have been, if a suitable defense which satisfies the law can be raised, the defendant may be shielded from liability. Finally, it is necessary to appreciate how this interaction of negligence and defenses operates in the many different sets of relationships that make up our culture—that is, relationships such as the employer-employee relationship, the landlord-tenant relationship, the buyer-seller relationship, the principal-agent relationship, and the driver-pedestrian relationship. Additional standards of conduct are applied in each relationship. The law is extremely complex and is changing constantly; therefore, only a summary of highlights can be given in this text.

TORTS

A *tort* is a legal injury or wrong to another that arises out of actions other than breach of contract in which courts will provide a remedy by allowing recovery in an action for damages. A legal *injury* results when a person's rights are wrongfully invaded. Examples of such rights are the right of personal privacy, the right to enjoy one's property unmolested, and the right to be free from physical injury. Examples of torts are libel, slander, assault, and negligence. Conduct may give rise to criminal action, civil action, or both, against the offender. We are mainly concerned here with protection against the financial consequences of civil action arising out of only one of these torts, negligence, which arises from the omission or commission of an act. Insurance against intentional torts, such as false arrest, libel, slander, trespass, battery, and assault, is also available.

THE NEGLIGENT ACT

By *negligence* is meant failure to exercise the degree of care required by law. What is required by law is understood to be the conduct which a reasonably prudent individual would exercise to prevent harm.

A Negative Act

A negligent act may be the failure to do something as much as it is the positive doing of something. It arises from a breach of legal duty to another.

One may drive an automobile into the rear of another car. As such, this is a positive act. A negligent act may be a negative, as failing to signal a turn.

Negligence may be the failure to act when there is a duty to act. Thus, a gas company was held liable for a loss when it had agreed to inspect a customer's gas pipe, but failed to do so.[3]

A Voluntary Act

A negligent act is one which is done *voluntarily*. If an act is done involuntarily, the act is excusable. If such were the case, the plaintiff could not collect damages. For example, it is easy to see that if one person puts a gun into the hand of another, directs the second person's aim at a target, and helps pull the trigger, the second person is hardly a free agent; and if the shot injures a person, there is doubt that the second person is necessarily negligent.

A negligent act is not excused because there was no intention to cause harm. Unintentional injury to another may give rise to both criminal and civil action at law. Negligent acts are essentially those in which the defendant may try to be excused by saying "I didn't mean to."

The law does not expect perfection to be the standard by which conduct is judged. The care expected of a trained physician who is a specialist is higher than that expected from an intern or even a general practitioner. The degree of care expected from a child is different from that expected of an adult. The care expected of an automobile driver is not interpreted in the light of what might have been, had the driver been able to take full advantage of hindsight in avoiding an accident, but in the light of the decision that any reasonable person would have made in an emergency when there was no time to consider all the possible alternatives.

An Imputed Act

Liability for a negligent act may be *imputed* from another person. Thus, one is liable not only for one's own acts, but also for the negligent acts of servants or agents acting in the course of their employment or agency. Employers may be sued because of negligent acts of employees. Liability for the negligence of another can rest upon a contract to assume that liability. Thus, a baseball club may be held liable for accidents arising out of the use of a ball park owned by the city and leased from it, simply because the club had assumed such liability under the lease. Under so-called dramshop laws in many states, a tavern owner may be held liable for damages resulting from the operation of dispensing alcoholic beverages. Thus, if a customer becomes inebriated, and because of this state wanders into the path of a car on the way home from the tavern and becomes injured, the tavern operator may be held liable for the loss. In some states, parents may be held legally liable for the damage caused by their children who negligently drive the family automobile or who perform other torts, because the state law requires that the parents assume such liability.

[3] *Trimbo* v. *Minnesota Valley Natural Gas Company,* Minnesota Supreme Court, 110 N.W. 2d 168 (1961).

Proximate Cause of the Loss

A negligent act, to give rise to action for damages, must of course be the *proximate* cause of the loss. There must be an unbroken chain of events leading from the negligent act to the damage sustained. Suppose *A* negligently damages *B*'s car and as a result *B* is late for an important business engagement. *B* charges that, as a result, a sale was lost which would have netted $10,000. Can *B* add $10,000 to the claim for damages? Carrying the example further, suppose *B* claims that not only did he lose the sale, but as a result of losing it, he also lost his job. Further, because of the lost job his wife had to go to work, necessitating the expense of purchasing a second automobile and the hiring of a nurse for the children. May *B* also add these expenses to his claim? It is clear that the court must draw a line in determining proximate cause, or a host of sources for damage claims would open up.

DEFENSES

Even if a person is guilty of a negligent act, certain defenses can be used to bar liability for such negligence.

Contributory Negligence

At common law, if both parties are to blame in a given accident, neither party may collect from the other for damages arising out of negligence. One must come into court with "clean hands." The one who was partially to blame was guilty of contributory negligence and may not collect against another, even if the other was 90% to blame and the plaintiff was only 10% to blame.

Assumed Risk

Under certain circumstances, a defendant may raise the defense that the plaintiff has no cause of action because the plaintiff assumed the risk of harm from (1) the conduct of the defendant, (2) the condition of the premises, or (3) the defendant's product. Managements of baseball parks are sometimes sued when baseballs hit members of the viewing crowds. Assuming that reasonable care has been exercised in providing appropriate wire screens, courts usually hold that a person who views a ball game is assuming the risks normally attributed to viewers and must accept the consequences of any normal result of a baseball ga.ne.

Expanding Application of Liability

Courts tend increasingly to impose liability in new factual settings. For example, traditionally a manufacturer might be held liable for making a faulty product such as a gas tank which leaks, causing an accident. Recent decisions in California held a manufacturer and a dealer liable for loss from what was defined as an unsafe gas tank design. In another case, an owner of a chimpanzee which caused ten persons to get hepatitis was held liable. Before this case most suits involved situations in which an animal caused an injury, not an illness. In still another case, an airline was charged with undue delay in obtaining proper medical treatment for a passenger who suffered a heart attack.

Weakening of Defenses

The area of workers' compensation was the first major example of social insurance in the United States. All states have now passed this type of legislation, which represents an abandonment of the principles of negligence law in determining liability for occupational injury. Before these laws were passed (most such laws were enacted in the decade 1910-1920), the principles of negligence governed and an employee had to seek damages at law from the employer for occupational injuries. Because this system proved inefficient, time consuming, and generally unsatisfactory, especially for the employee, it was replaced by workers' compensation laws. The employee now receives a payment for on-the-job injuries according to a schedule set up for this purpose, regardless of who is to blame, if anyone, for the injury.

Similar principles have recently been applied in several states which have passed no-fault laws regarding bodily injuries in automobile accidents. In some of these laws, the rights of the plaintiff to bring legal action for negligence against other drivers have been restricted.

The defense of contributory negligence likewise has been weakened in various ways. In a few states, statutes have been enacted that replace this principle with one termed *comparative negligence*. Under this doctrine, the liability of the defendant is reduced by the extent to which the plaintiff was contributorially negligent. If the plaintiff was 20% negligent, the defendant is liable for only 80% of the plaintiff's damages. In some states, the plaintiff recovers nothing if more than 50% at fault.

Another way in which the defense of contributory negligence has been weakened is in the *last clear chance rule*. Under this rule, a plaintiff who was contributorially negligent may still have a cause of action against the defendant if it can be shown that the defendant had a last clear chance before the accident to avoid injuring the plaintiff, but failed to do so. Thus, it is possible that a jaywalker may collect if hit by a motorist who had a chance to swerve, but failed to do so.

Res Ipsa Loquitur

Another illustration of the trend toward absolute liability lies in the more frequent use of a rule known as *res ipsa loquitur*—"the thing speaks for itself." Under this rule, a plaintiff may sometimes collect without actually proving negligence on the part of the defendant. It should be noted that under common law, before an action can be sustained against a party, negligence must be shown; that is, it must be shown that there was some failure on the part of the defendant to use the degree of care required of a reasonably prudent person in the same circumstance. Testimony of witnesses and of the injured parties must usually be brought to bear upon the case.

Res ipsa loquitur may be applied to establish a case against the defendant when (1) the defendant is in a position to know the cause of the accident and the plaintiff is not, (2) the defendant had exclusive control of the instrumentality which caused the accident, and (3) the use of the instrumentality would not normally cause injuries without the existence of negligence in its operation. As may be guessed, this doctrine has been used frequently in premises and product liability cases.

Expansion of Imputed Liability

Still another evidence of the stricter view of negligence taken by society today is the passage of what are known as *vicarious liability laws*. The effect of vicarious liability laws is to place liability on the owner of a car for the negligence of the driver, thereby expanding the common-law rule applicable to employers and principals. About 39 states have such laws. Thus, in these states, under certain circumstances, the owner of a car may be held liable simply because in good faith he or she loaned the car to another, and such other person negligently caused harm.

Changing Concepts of Damage

Another factor worth noting in assessing the trend toward absolute liability is the more liberal interpretation of what type of damages may be allowed in negligence actions. Courts generally allow as damages claims for medical bills, loss of income, loss of life, property damage, and other losses for which the proximate cause was negligence. Thus, damages have usually been allowed for such things as pain and suffering, and loss of the conjugal relation by a husband. However, more recently, damages have been awarded for such intangible losses as mental anguish, presumably under the theory that pain and suffering need not be physical to establish damages.[4]

Increased Damage Awards

Not only have the courts tended to widen the types of cases for which damages are awarded, but they have also tended to increase greatly the amount of these damages.

Various reasons have been advanced for the tendency of courts to be more generous than they formerly were in assessing the awards given in negligence actions. The effect of inflation in reducing the purchasing power of the dollar has undoubtedly had a considerable effect. The existence of liability insurance, it is claimed in some quarters, has caused juries to be more generous than they would be if it were known that the plaintiff would have to pay damages personally. An organization of attorneys known as the National Association of Claimants' Compensation Attorneys (N.A.C.C.A.) has had some influence in obtaining larger judgments for claimants. This organization has been instrumental in

[4] Harold Chase, "Changing Concepts of Legal Liability and Their Effect on Liability Insurance," *Proceedings*, 82nd Annual Meeting, Fire Underwriters Association of the Pacific (March 5-6, 1958), p. 24.

advancing the use of ideas and methods known to be successful in obtaining larger awards than would otherwise be the case. The use of visual aids in a courtroom to illustrate vividly the scope of the damage done and the seriousness and reality of pain and suffering is an example of such methods.[5] The N.A.C.C.A., greatly criticized by some for its activities in attempting to increase court judgments, vigorously defends its methods as only a realistic approach to what it feels is the task of raising awards that were in the past, and still are, too low for adequate compensation of injured plaintiffs.[6]

Guest-Host Statutes

About the only significant exception to the general trend toward absolute liability in our society has been the passage of what are known as *guest-host statutes*. These laws relate to the standard of care owed by an automobile driver to a passenger. The general effect of the laws is to reduce the standard of care owed to a guest in a car in such a manner that the guest, in order to prove liability for the negligence of a driver, must prove that the driver was guilty of gross negligence, or willful injury, such as might be the case if the driver were intoxicated. Under the guest-host laws, ordinary negligence will not be sufficient to sustain a case against the driver. In a number of states, guest-host statutes have been declared unconstitutional.

CONTRACTUAL LIABILITY

Under the concept of contractual liability, one's liability may be imputed to another by contract. For example, a city may require that a street paving contractor hold the city harmless for all negligence arising out of the operations of the contractor. In this way, suits that might otherwise be directed against the city will be directed against the street contractor. Similarly, a railroad may make a contract with the manufacturer that if there is any negligence action arising out of the operation of the railroad's locomotives or trains which have entered the manufacturer's property on a spur track in order to pick up shipments, the manufacturer will assume the liability. The railroad's liability has thus been transferred by means of a contract. Other common contracts by which liability is transferred are leases and contracts to perform services to supply goods.

EMPLOYER LIABILITY

Employers are still subject to the law of negligence with respect to employment not covered by workers' compensation laws. Workers' compensation laws do not, however, cover many classes of employees. For example,

[5] An amusing treatment of the courtroom antics and graphic, if not too dignified, methods sometimes used by attorneys in injury cases is given by Alexander Rose, *Pay the Two Dollars* (New York: Simon and Schuster, Inc., 1957).

[6] For an able presentation of the view on this subject taken by a member of the N.A.C.C.A., see Leo S. Karlin, "Bodily Injury Awards—Where Are We Going," *Insurance Law Journal* (September, 1957), pp. 568-569.

often farm workers and workers of an employer who hires less than a specified number of people are excluded from coverage. Railroad employees and sea workers are also exempt from workers' compensation laws.

The duties owed by an employer to employees, breach of which may give rise to liability, are the following:[7]

1. The employer must provide a safe place to work.
2. The employer must employ individuals reasonably competent to carry out their tasks.
3. The employer must warn of danger.
4. The employer must furnish appropriate and safe tools.
5. The employer must set up and enforce proper rules of conduct of employees, as they relate to safe working procedures.

To illustrate the operation of these standards, if a garage provides a jack to raise automobiles, but does not take steps to see that it is in good working condition, and the employee using this jack is injured because the jack breaks due to no fault of the worker, the employer has probably breached a common-law duty to the employee. If an employer fails to warn a new employee of the existence of explosives in a storehouse or hires an untrained worker to handle explosives, with resulting injury to an innocent worker, grounds exist for damage suits. An employee who disregards danger signals or fails to use the tools provided and is injured as a result is guilty of at least contributory negligence and under common law cannot recover. This would not affect the worker's right to workers' compensation.

The employer may utilize the common-law defenses in suits by employees, providing these defenses have not been lost for one reason or another. For example, a worker brings an action against an employer for some breach of care and the employer argues that the worker was partly to blame (contributory negligence defense); or the worker should have known there were certain risks on the job and cannot complain because one of these risks materialized (assumption of risk).

LIABILITY OF LANDLORDS AND TENANTS

In situations that involve the operation of real property, the owner or tenant owes a certain degree of care to those who enter on the premises. In most states, the degree of care is governed by the status of the person who is involved. The common law recognizes three classes of individuals who enter premises: invitees, licensees, and trespassers. The degree of care owed to an invitee is highest, and to a trespasser, lowest.

An *invitee* is an individual who is invited on the premises for his or her own benefit as well as for that of the landlord or tenant. Typical invitees are customers in a retail store, and guests at a hotel or at a public meeting. *Licensees* are those who are on the premises for a legitimate purpose with the permission

[7] Thomas Gaskell Shearman and A.A. Redfield, *A Treatisc on the Law of Negligence*, I, 438; II, 441-442.

of the occupier. Typical licensees are police officers and fire fighters; others, who may be licensees or invitees, are milk delivery drivers, messengers, and meter readers. *Trespassers* include all those other than invitees and licensees who are on the premises.

No care is owed to a trespasser, but an owner cannot set a trap for or deliberately injure a trespasser. If the trespasser is injured by or through some hidden hazard, the landlord or tenant is not liable. In the next higher status is the licensee, to whom the landlord owes the duty to warn of danger and to refrain from causing deliberate harm, but no other duty. Ordinary care is owed an invitee. It is not sufficient only to warn an invitee of danger; in addition, positive steps must be taken to protect an invitee from a known danger, and to discover unknown dangers.

Illustrating the concepts above, consider the owner of a retail store who has just polished the floors to such a high degree of slickness that they constitute a definite hazard to safe walking. A burglar enters the store at night, slips, and breaks a leg. Clearly the owner is not required to pay any medical bills or otherwise compensate this trespasser. If a delivery driver had a similar accident, the courts would probably hold the owner innocent of negligence providing the owner had taken reasonable steps to warn people that the floors were slick. However, if a customer slipped and broke a leg on a slick floor, the courts would award damages if the storeowner could have taken reasonable steps to reduce the hazard.

There is a modern trend to abolish the classifications of trespasser, licensee, invitee, and to hold the occupier of the land liable for failure to exercise due care under the circumstances. Within this trend, that the plaintiff was a trespasser, a licensee, or an invitee is merely one of the circumstances but the classification is not controlling.

Assumption of Liability by Tenant

If a landlord leases a building, the question arises as to what extent the landlord is responsible for injuries to tenants. In general, when the landlord releases possession of the building, the tenant takes on whatever duty the landlord owes to members of the public. In some instances, the landlord is liable to a third person because the landlord has retained possession of the area where the third person was injured. For example, in the hallways of an apartment house occupied by several tenants, the owner has been held liable for negligence to tenants and to members of the public. In one case involving a tenant who tripped and fell over a crack in the cement slab leading to her apartment, a substantial judgment was rendered when the tenant's leg had to be amputated.[8] In another case the landlord was held liable when a tenant was injured by a loose front porch floorboard which had been poorly repaired.[9]

In most states it is common and it is legal to require, by terms of the lease, that the tenant assume whatever liability the landlord may have had (or to

[8] *Petrillo* v. *Maiuri,* 20 CCH Neg. 572.
[9] *Koleshinske* v. *David,* 20 CCH Neg. 264.

reimburse the owner for liability) for injuries to members of the public or to employees of the tenant. However, there are some types of liability of an owner that cannot be so shifted. Examples are liability for the violation of a safety ordinance; failure of a subcontractor to comply with such ordinances; or failure of the contractor to exercise reasonable care in excavations, blasting, or the use of fire.

Attractive Nuisance Doctrine

Under a doctrine which has become known as the *attractive nuisance doctrine,* the liability of the occupier of land to children may be changed so that a trespasser who happens to be a child is considered, in many jurisdictions, to be an invitee. Various legal fictions have been invented to accomplish this result, among which are that there is an implied invitation to children; and that there is an intention to harm because the landlord has placed an allurement of some kind known to attract children, who are incapable of recognizing or appreciating the danger involved. The courts, in utilizing the attractive nuisance doctrine, usually consider the age of the child in rendering judgments. The decisions in the field of attractive nuisance are contradictory among the various states. Judgments have been rendered in favor of children for injuries received when the child has ventured on a railroad track that was supposed to be fenced[10] and when a child was lighting matches over the gas tank of an abandoned vehicle in a vacant lot. In these cases it is clear an ordinary trespasser would have no claim, but because the trespasser happened to be a child, damages were awarded.

PRODUCT LIABILITY

A manufacturer, wholesaler, or retailer is required to exercise reasonable care and to maintain certain standards in the handling and selection of goods in which it deals. If injury to person or property results from the use of a faulty product, there may be grounds for legal action in the courts. Such actions are generally based on these grounds: breach of warranty, strict tort, or negligence.

Breach of Warranty

A warranty may be expressed or implied. Often a seller gives a written or an express warranty on goods or services sold, and it is the breach of this written contract that may give rise to a court action. However, under the Uniform Commercial Code the seller is held to have made certain unwritten or implied warranties concerning a product. These warranties are two: (1) the seller warrants that the goods are reasonably fit for the purpose for which they are intended, and (2) the seller warrants that when the goods are bought by description instead of by actual inspection, the goods are salable in the hands of the

[10] However, a court refused to charge a railroad with negligence when an 11-year-old boy was injured on an overhead wire as he climbed atop one of the railroad's freight cars. The court said it would be asking too much to require the railroad to make its property "child proof" along its 275 miles of track. *Dugan* v. *Pennsylvania Railroad,* 6 CCH Neg. 32d 443.

buyer. Breach of implied warranty is most often used as the basis of suits for faulty products.

There is an implied warranty that goods are fit for a buyer's particular purpose when the seller knows the buyer's purpose and the latter relies on the seller's judgment in making the purchase.

The following cases illustrate the liability of a manufacturer for faulty products. These cases may be brought by the injured consumer directly or by a retailer who has paid a judgment as a result of selling a faulty product, particularly in the case of foods, medicine, explosives, or weapons. For example, a manufacturer paid a judgment of $111,000 when a fire resulted from the heating of some roofing primer in order to thin it.[11] The manufacturer had provided no warning that the mixture would release explosive gases when heated.

Retailers have paid losses resulting from their handling of products. In one case, a dealer sold floor stain under his own private brand. Due to faulty manufacture, the mixture exploded, causing a loss to the user; but the court held that the dealer was liable because he must answer for a product he has accepted as his own. Breach of the implied warranty of fitness has formed the basis of most suits against restaurants that serve poisoned food, and against drugstores that sell faulty medicines or cosmetics.

Strict Tort

Under strict tort liability, the manufacturer or distributor of a defective product is liable to a person who is injured by the product regardless of whether the person injured is a purchaser, a consumer, or a third person such as a bystander or pedestrian. It must be shown that there was a defect in the product and that the defect caused harm. It is no defense that there was no negligence or that the defect was in a component purchased from another manufacturer.

Negligence

Another basis for liability is negligence. A person injured because of the use or condition of a product may be entitled to sue for damages sustained on the theory that the defendant was negligent in the preparation or manufacture of the product or failed to provide adequate instructions or warnings. A manufacturer is held to have the knowledge of an expert with respect to the product involved and must, therefore, take reasonable steps to guard against the dangers or inadequacies apparent to an expert. A court has said:

> [A] person who sells an article which he knows is dangerous to human life, limb, or health to another person, who has no knowledge of its true character, and fails to give notice thereof to the purchaser, is liable in damages to a third person who while in the exercise of due care is injured by use of it which should have been contemplated by the seller.[12]

In a famous early case it was held that a manufacturer or a vendor has no liability for negligence unless it had a contractual relationship with the injured

[11] *Panther Oil & Grease Mfg. Co.* v. *Segerstrom,* 224 Fed. 2d 216.
[12] *Farley* v. *Lower Co.,* (Mass.) No. 18431 (1930).

party.[13] Thus, an injured person could bring action only against a retailer with whom there was a contractual relationship, and not against the manufacturer. Later cases brought about a relaxation of this defense, known as lack of privity between the injured party and the manufacturer. A landmark case, *MacPherson* v. *Buick Motor Company,*[14] which concerned the breaking of a defective wheel, established the precedent that in the court's language, "If the nature of a thing is such that it is reasonably certain to place life and limb in peril when negligently made, it is then a thing of danger." It should be emphasized, however, that a manufacturer or a seller does not guarantee the safe use of the product. For example, a court refused to indemnify damage incurred when a sparkler set fire to a child's dress. The court reasoned that there would have been little danger if the article had been used properly.[15]

PROFESSIONAL LIABILITY

Closely related to negligence product liability is the area of negligence law known as professional liability. Just as a manufacturer is required to make a product reasonably fit for its intended purpose, so is the seller of services required to use reasonable care not to injure others in the performance of these services. There are two variations of this type of liability: (1) the liability of individuals such as physicians, accountants, insurance agents, lawyers, pharmacists, and others who render a professional service, and (2) the liability of contractors who perform work which, when completed, results in injury to someone. Insurance against the former has been identified as *malpractice* or *errors and omissions insurance,* while contracts covering the latter are known as *completed operations insurance.*

Malpractice Liability

The standard of care required of physicians, accountants, attorneys, or other professional persons is broadly interpreted to mean that these individuals must possess the degree of skill, judgment, and knowledge appropriate to their calling and conduct themselves accordingly to recognized professional standards. These standards naturally vary from profession to profession and are changing constantly as each particular field develops. Failure to take X-rays of a patient's hip cost one physician a judgment of $38,000. The injury was diagnosed as a bruise instead of a fracture, and resulted in severe complications.[16] The same failure prior to when it was considered standard procedure to take X-rays following accidents would not have constituted negligence.

In the field of medical malpractice, damage claims appear to be especially numerous and serious in recent years. In one jurisdiction it was estimated that about 1 in every 35 medical doctors is sued annually for malpractice. Although

[13] *Winterbottom* v. *Wright,* 10 M.&W. 109, Eng. Rep. 402 (ex. 1842).

[14] 217 N.Y. 382

[15] Suel O. Arnold, "Products Liability Insurance," *Insurance Law Journal* (Oct., 1957), p. 618, citing *Beznor* v. *Howell,* 203 Wis. 1, 233 N.W. 788.

[16] *Agnew* v. *Larson,* 5 CCH Neg. 2d 23.

only in about one out of seven or eight cases examined by a special study group was there any substantial evidence of negligence by the practitioner, yet in about one fourth of the suits the doctor-defendant lost.[17] Malpractice verdicts have often been large,[18] and the physician may often be at a procedural disadvantage. For example, in a California case, the physician, a specialist in vascular surgery, employed a standard diagnostic procedure to determine the specific nature of the patient's difficulty. This procedure involved the injection of certain drugs, which for unknown reasons caused the permanent paralysis of the patient from the waist down. The physician had previously performed 50 such injections, with no adverse effects. The doctrine of *res ipsa loquitur* was employed, thus permitting the jury to find for the plaintiff unless the doctor could prove no negligence. A verdict of $250,000 was handed down, but it was later reduced to $215,000. Use of the doctrine of *res ipsa loquitur* in medical malpractice cases appears to have had the effect of turning the doctor into an insurer, and may result in unwillingness of the doctor to try new procedures and treatment for fear of financial bankruptcy if the treatment fails.[19]

Insurance agents under general principles of agency law have been frequently held to be liable for negligence. For example, if an agent agrees to obtain insurance for a client and then, through neglect, fails to do so, the agent may be held liable for losses which the client incurs because of lack of appropriate coverage.[20] If the policy was obtained but it turns out to be worthless because the insurer was insolvent, the agent can be held liable.[21] Agents have also been held liable in cases where their clients fail to comply with a warranty or condition in the policy and the insurer is thereby relieved from liability.[22] In one case, a client told his regular agent that he was about to lease a building in another state. The agent did not request to see a copy of the lease or make any other inquiry. Later the client was held liable for a $41,000 fire loss to the building, because the terms of the lease made the lessee liable. The agent was held liable for the loss for not advising the client of the potential liability in the lease, nor recommending appropriate insurance.[23]

An insurance agent is also subject to damage suits by the insurers represented for failing in a common-law duty, such as loyalty or obedience which

[17] R. Crawford Morris, "Medical Malpractice—A Changing Picture," *Insurance Law Journal* (May, 1956), p. 319. See also G. H. Graser and P. D. Chadsey, "Informed Consent in Malpractice Cases," *Williamette Law Journal*, Vol. 6 (June, 1970), pp. 183-191, and W. A. Aitken, "Medical Malpractice: The Alleged Crisis in Perspective," *Insurance Law Journal*, (Feb., 1976), pp. 90-97.

[18] Morris, *op. cit.* Morris cites cases occurring over a two-year period involving verdicts of courts as follows: San Francisco, $250,000; San Diego, $210,000; Tennessee, $200,000; Texas, $100,000; Wisconsin, $97,000; federal jury, $123,000.

[19] *Ibid.*, Morris gives an excellent bibliography of legal cases on medical malpractice including 61 cases in which it was held that the doctrine of *res ipsa loquitur* is applicable to doctors.

[20] *Adkins and Ainley* v. *Busada,* 270 A. 2d 135 (DC App. 1970).

[21] *Annot.*, 29 ALR2d 171, 174 (1953).

[22] *Ibid.*

[23] *Hardt* v. *Brink,* 192 F. Supp. 879, 881 (D Wash. 1961). See also Joseph R. O'Connor, "Liability of Insurance Agents and Brokers" (Madison, Wisconsin: Defense Research Institute, 1970).

an agent owes to the principal. For example, the insurer may prohibit the agent to bind coverage on a certain class of property. The agent, in disobedience to these instructions, writes the insurance and a loss occurs before the insurer has a chance to cancel the policy. Because the agent was the authorized representative of the insurer and had the power to bind it and because members of the public are not bound by private instructions of a principal to an agent, the insured has a legal right to collect. The insurer may then come against the disobedient agent for indemnification.

Even attorneys have not escaped malpractice suits for negligence in the conduct of their professions. In one case an attorney was successfully sued for $100,000 when it was determined that he failed to perform adequate research in a divorce case. The attorney had neglected to claim the husband's military pension as community property in the property settlement, and as a result the wife was unable to share in more than $322,000 estimated pension income.

Completed Operations Liability

A contractor who carelessly installs a water boiler or an electrical appliance that later explodes or causes a fire and resulting damage to the property or person of another may be held liable for negligence arising out of the faulty installation. This is known as completed operations liability, under which the damage must occur after the contractor has completed the work and it has been accepted by the owner or abandoned by the contractor. Examples of completed operations liability include the following cases: A contractor was held liable for extensive property damage when a rubber hose connection broke in an air-conditioning system several months after the installation and admitted many gallons of water to the attic.[24] In another case, a contractor was involved in litigation 17 years after he repaired an iron railing; it was alleged that faulty repair work caused injury to a person leaning on the railing.[25] An electrical contractor paid $12,000 for the death of a three-year-old child electrocuted by an improperly installed outlet on which the work had been completed 15 months prior to the accident.[26]

It should be noted that if the conduct of a contractor causes injury while the contractor is still in control of the operation, the liability is similar to that of an owner or a tenant of real property. Insurance contracts differentiate, however, between these two types of liability.

LIABILITY FOR ACTS OF AGENTS

Under the doctrine of *respondeat superior*, a master is liable for the acts of servants if the servants or agents are acting within the scope of their employment.[27] An employee thus imposes liability on the employer for negligent

[24] *Saunders* v. *Walker*, 86 Sou. 2d 89.
[25] *Hanna* v. *Fletcher*, 8 CCH Neg. 2d 1017.
[26] *Kurdziel* v. *Van Es*, 6 CCH Neg. 2d 1080.
[27] *Singer Mfg. Co.* v. *Rahn*, 132 U.S. 158.

harm to a third party even if the employee is acting contrary to instructions, so long as he or she is doing the job. If an employee is told to solicit orders for a product, and in so doing carelessly runs into the customer, the employer will probably be required to answer for the agent's act. If the employee is instructed not to call on *X*, but calls on *X* and injures him, the employer cannot plead in defense that the agent acted contrary to instructions.

There is a distinction between acting as an agent or a servant and acting as an independent contractor. In the former, the employer not only controls what is to be done, but also directs the manner in which it shall be done. In the latter, the employer pays the contractor for completing a certain job, but does not exercise any control over how it is done. It is logical that the employer is not held liable for the carelessness of an independent contractor to the degree as for the carelessness of an agent or a servant. There are, however, exceptions to this rule.

LIABILITY OF AUTOMOBILE OWNERS AND OPERATORS

Under common law an automobile owner or operator is required to exercise reasonable care in the handling of automobiles. Three situations may be distinguished in this important area of negligence:

1. Liability of the operator.
2. Liability of owner for negligence of others operating the car.
3. Liability of employers for negligence of their servants or agents using automobiles in their employer's business.

Liability of the Operator

The typical damage suit in the field of automobile liability is one which charges the operator with carelessness, which is the proximate cause of either bodily injury or property damage to an injured third party. As in the other areas of liability, it is impossible to lay down a comprehensive statement of what constitutes negligence in the operation of an automobile. In some states, departures are made from the common law by adoption of the rule of comparative negligence and the last clear chance doctrine.[28] In certain cases, guest-host statutes operated to lessen the liability of operators to passengers.

Liability of the Owner Who Is Not the Operator

The question arises, under what conditions can an automobile owner be held liable for damages when not personally to blame for the alleged negligence? If one gives a loaded gun to a child and tells the child to entertain himself or herself and the child accidently injures or kills someone, the owner of the gun might well be held guilty of negligence. Does the same situation hold if one lends one's car to a person without investigating this person's qualifications to

[28] See page 293 for a discussion of these concepts.

handle the car and there is a subsequent injury to another through the operator's negligence? The courts have generally agreed that the automobile is not a "dangerous instrumentality" in itself and that one is justified in assuming that the borrower of an automobile is competent to handle it unless there is obvious evidence of incapacity or known recklessness. Illustrating this is the case of an employer who successfully defended an action charging negligence in failing to examine a bus driver who, having recently returned to work from an illness, suffered a fatal heart attack and crashed the bus, causing injuries to the plaintiffs.[29]

There are, however, several exceptions to the general rule that an owner is not liable for acts of operators of automobiles. In 25 states[30] so-called vicarious liability laws have the effect of making the parent of a minor child liable for damage done by negligent operation of the car by a minor. Usually the owner-parent has signed the minor's application for a driver's license, and in so doing, is bound to be responsible for the minor's negligence. In six states,[31] any person furnishing a car to a minor is liable for the minor's negligence. In 13 jurisdictions,[32] the owner is liable for personal injuries or property damage done by the negligence of *any* driver.

In addition, there is a tendency for courts to rely more and more on the doctrine of *respondeat superior* in deciding the liability of the owner for negligence of an operator driving with the owner's permission. There is no question about the right of an injured third party to recover from the employer of an employee negligent in the course of employment, but some have questioned the propriety of making an owner liable for the acts of a gratuitous borrower of a car. Yet, there is a tendency for the courts to decide that the permissive user is really the agent of the owner and hence the owner must answer for the agent's carelessness.[33] The inconsistency in this viewpoint was stated as follows:

> If I agree to take friends in my automobile to visit their relatives or am otherwise on a mission for their convenience and benefit, it is hard to see that an agency relation exists, much less that of master and servant. Any benefit accruing to me or any "business" that I may have is the purely social end of accommodating not myself but my friends. Under these facts, then how can I suddenly become the master by relinquishing the operation of the automobile to the friend? Yet decisions so finding are almost universal, including the appellation of "gratuitous servant or agent."[34]

[29] *General Electric Company* v. *Rees,* 5 CCH Auto Case 2d 330.

[30] Arizona, Arkansas, California, Colorado, Connecticut, Delaware, Florida, Hawaii, Idaho, Indiana, Kentucky, Louisiana, Maryland, Mississippi, Montana, Nevada, New Mexico, North Dakota, Ohio, Oklahoma, Rhode Island, Tennessee, Texas, Utah, and Wisconsin.

[31] Delaware, Idaho, Kansas, Maine, Pennsylvania (under 16), and Utah. Arizona and Virginia provide that liability exists only if the minor is not licensed.

[32] California, Connecticut, District of Columbia, Florida, Idaho, Iowa, Massachusetts, Michigan, Minnesota, New York, North Carolina, Rhode Island, and Tennessee.

[33] R. Parke and M. Orona, "Automobile Owner's Liability: Anomaly or Enigma?" *Insurance Law Journal* (March, 1957), p. 155.

[34] *Ibid.*, citing *Mazur* v. *Klewans*, 34 CCH Auto Cases 180; *Droppelman* v. *Willingham,* 17 CCH Auto Cases 421; *Flynn* v. *Kurn,* 1 CCH Auto Cases 387.

Another application of the agency relationship in establishing liability of an owner for negligence of an operator is the so-called *family-purpose doctrine* recognized in approximately half the states. Under this doctrine, an automobile is looked upon as an instrument to carry out the common purposes of a family. Therefore, the owner ought to be responsible for its use when any member of the family uses it because this member is actually the agent of the family head and is carrying out a family function. Yet the courts have not seen fit to extend this doctrine to any instrument or possession, such as a bicycle or a boat, in common use by a family. It would appear that the family-purpose doctrine is a legal fiction to establish the liability of the person most likely to be able to respond financially for damages incurred in the use of the automobile. In an Illinois case, a car owner was even held liable to a third party for the negligent driving of a thief who took a car in which the owner had left ignition keys, in violation of an ordinance to the contrary.[35]

Liability of Nonowners

Even those who do not own automobiles may be liable for damages through their negligent operation if by some legal construction the nonowner can be shown to be responsible. The legal construction normally employed is *respondeat superior*. The employer is liable for the negligent actions of employees whether their acts were in or out of an automobile. The ownership of the automobile is immaterial in such cases. In a famous early case, a life insurance company was held liable for a $10,000 judgment arising from the negligence of one of its salesmen driving in his own car on the way to a convention.[36] The defendant's argument that the salesman was really an independent contractor whose actions are not binding on the insurer was dismissed. In general, the courts are not sympathetic to the independent contractor argument.

MISCELLANEOUS LIABILITY

The preceding examples illustrate the major areas of negligence liability. In a similar way, legal decisions form the framework of the common law of negligence of many other types of relationships in modern society. For example, there is a body of decisions (and some statutory enactments) surrounding the area of liability of a parent for the negligent acts of children, of the liability of a trustee to beneficiaries for mishandling of trusts, and of the liability of owners of animals for destruction or injuries caused by these animals. Detailed inquiry into the liability law for these and other areas is beyond the scope of this text.

UNIVERSAL NO-FAULT

Because of the complexity, delays, cost, and other weaknesses in our basic system of negligence law in compensating victims of accidents, much

[35] *Ney* v. *Yellow Cab Company,* 3 CCH Auto Cases 2d 888.
[36] *Dillon* v. *Prudential Insurance Co.*, 242 Pac. 736 (1926).

discussion has taken place of the idea of extending the no-fault principle in workers' compensation and automobile insurance to accidents in general. As indicated above, courts are already tending to make negligence more and more absolute. Professor Jeffrey O'Connell has proposed a system of universal no-fault in which manufacturers, professional persons, and others would be given exemption from negligence suits.[37] Damages for pain and suffering would not be allowed except perhaps for serious injuries. In return for such exemptions, these persons would, on a voluntary or elective basis, carry insurance guaranteeing that injured persons would receive indemnity for out-of-pocket losses, regardless of whether the product or service was defective. Such insurance would be expensive, because more persons would receive benefits than do presently. Most injuries now go uncompensated because it is not feasible to bring court actions for negligence unless losses are relatively large. Even if suits are brought they are often slow, uncertain, and expensive.

Although universal no-fault is probably a long way from adoption in the United States, it is possible that the principle may be employed on a piecemeal basis over the years ahead, as the disadvantages of the negligence system become more apparent in given areas. For example, Indiana passed a law in 1975 limiting medical malpractice claims to $500,000, and limiting any one insurer's liability under this insurance to $100,000. A patients' compensation fund was established to pay claims above the $100,000 limit up to $500,000. This fund is supported by a surcharge on premiums. Attorneys' fees are limited to 15% of the award. Similar bills have been introduced in other states.

SUMMARY

1. Negligence is the failure to exercise the degree of care required of a reasonably prudent individual in the same circumstances. Negligence which is the proximate cause of injury to the property of another may, in the absence of effective defenses, give rise to substantial court judgments against the responsible party.
2. Common-law defenses bar liability for a negligent act: contributory negligence and assumed risk. There are also statutory and contractual defenses available.
3. There is an unmistakable tendency for courts to impose liability. That is, there is a trend toward "absolute" liability. Evidence of this trend includes a weakening of the common-law defenses and the recognition of new theories of liability.
4. An employer owes employees certain duties, the breach of which may give rise to damage suits against the employer. In most cases, an employer's liability to employees is governed by workers' compensation statutes.
5. The degree of care owed by a landlord or a tenant to members of the public and others who are on private property depends, at common law, on whether the person is said to be an invitee, a licensee, or a trespasser. The highest degree of care is owed to an invitee; the lowest degree of care is owed to a trespasser.

[37] Jeffrey O'Connell, *Ending Insult to Injury* (Urbana, Illinois: University of Illinois Press, 1975).

6. Liability of a manufacturer or a vendor for damage caused by faulty products is well established. Product liability actions are based on either some failure on the part of the manufacturer to exercise reasonable care in the manufacture of a product, or on the part of the vendor for breach of express or implied warranty concerning the appropriateness of a product for its intended use, or on strict tort liability.
7. Professional liability exists for individuals holding themselves out as qualified to render a professional service but who fail to meet the standards of care or practice looked upon as normal by other members of their profession.
8. Under *respondeat superior,* a master is liable for the negligent acts of servants or agents performed while the employee is acting within the scope of the employment. This holds true even if the employee is acting contrary to instructions. It is under this doctrine that an employer is usually held liable for the negligence of an employee who is driving an automobile while performing the employer's business.
9. An automobile operator is liable for negligence in the operation of his or her car; and in many cases the owner of the car, if someone other than the operator, may be held liable as well. The family-purpose, last clear chance, and *respondeat superior* doctrines and vicarious liability laws have operated to extend and to tighten the liability law applicable to owners, nonowners, and operators of automobiles.

QUESTIONS FOR REVIEW AND DISCUSSION

1. A writer stated, "At first the courts were extremely suspicious of the liability insurance contract. Some courts held that it would be against public policy to permit a person to insure himself against the results of his negligence, on the theory that such insurance would have the effect of encouraging recklessness."
   (a) What attitude seems best to characterize the courts in modern society on this subject?
   (b) How does this attitude compare with that expressed in the quotation? Discuss.
2. Many states have guest-host statutes, which have the effect of converting a rider in an automobile from the status of an invitee (guest) to the status of a licensee. Does the existence of such laws represent an additional evidence of the "trend toward absolute liability"? Why or why not?
3. In connection with guest-host statutes, referred to in Question 2, a court held that an owner is not a guest in his own car even though the trip is purely social.
   (a) If the owner is not a guest, what status does the owner presumably occupy with respect to a friend who is driving?
   (b) What is the significance of the fact with regard to the possibility of an owner suing for damages if a friend is driving the car and is involved in an accident in which negligence is proved?
   (c) How would the situation differ if the owner were driving and the friend were suing for damages?
   (d) Discuss the implications of this case with respect to the "trend toward absolute liability."
4. Some courts have held that if the state workers' compensation board issues a safety order to regulate the conduct of employees on the job, and if a member of the public is injured as a result of the violation of this order by an employee, the employer is liable unless it can be proved that the conduct was excusable. Is this an

example of the "trend toward absolute liability," or is it a normal consequence of the common-law duty of an employer to protect members of the public from harm? Discuss.

5. Look up the employer's liability statute, if any, in your state or in a nearby state. To what extent does the statute eliminate or change the common-law of the employer?
6. In a famous English case in 1837 (*Priestly* v. *Fowler,* 3 M and W 1; 150 Eng. Rep. 1030), a worker was injured when the employer's wagon in which he was riding broke and collapsed. He sued his employer for damages and won in a lower court, only to have the decision reversed in the higher court, in which the judge ruled: (1) that to allow damages would result in a host of cases in which an employer could be held liable for almost any negligence or omission on the part of any of his employees, (2) that it would mean that the employer had to take better care of his servant than he did himself, and, furthermore, (3) that the employee was not bound to accept service with the employer and if he wished to avoid danger to himself he could refuse to take such service.
(a) Which of the common-law defenses does this case illustrate?
(b) Did this decision put the employee in a better or a worse position than a member of the public?
(c) It had been suggested that this decision grew out of the *laissez-faire* economic philosophy which was at its height at the time this decision was rendered. Explain why this might be true.
7. In a recent study by Dr. Hans Zeisel, 500 trial judges were asked to keep a record of personal injury cases, noting how the jury decided the case and how the judge would have decided it without a jury. The findings were: (1) In 79% of the cases both judge and jury agreed—for the plaintiff in 50% of the cases, and for the defendant in 29% of the cases. (2) In 21% of the cases they disagreed, the judge finding for the plaintiff in 10% of the cases while the jury found for the defendant, and vice versa in the remaining 11%. In case of disagreement it was found that if the defendant was a corporation, the jury tended to favor the plaintiff by a substantial margin; and if the defendant was a governmental body, the jury favored the plaintiff by an even greater margin.
(a) If you were a plaintiff in a personal injury trial, do you think it would generally be to your advantage to seek a jury trial, according to the above findings? Why or why not?
(b) Do you believe that the study above supports the often-heard statement that juries have a "soak-the-rich" attitude? Why or why not?
(c) What relevance, if any, does this study have to liability insurance and its influence on the outcome of jury trials? Discuss.
8. In the case of *Union Carbide* v. *Stapleton* (6 CCH Neg. 2d 337), the employer gave an employee a physical examination upon his leaving the employment of the employer due to illness. The worker was found to have been suffering from tuberculosis, but he was not informed of this fact. In your opinion, was this a breach of one of the common-law duties required of employers? Discuss.
9. A worker was hired to mow a lawn with a power mower and was injured when his foot slipped under the skirt at the rear of the mower. The worker sued the employer and the vendor of the machine, claiming that the mower lacked certain specific safety features, such as guards, which would have prevented the accident.
(a) In your opinion should the worker win the case?

(b) If so, what implications would this have for the manufacturers of goods intended for buyers of relatively inexpensive merchandise?

10. The owners of a swimming beach were sued by the parents of a boy who drowned when he swam into deep water and the lifeguard failed to reach him in time to save him. The plaintiffs argued that the defendant beach owners should have had more lifeguards. The defendants tried to prove that they had enough guards for normal needs and that the boy was guilty of contributory negligence in swimming out into deep water which, rather than the absence of a sufficient number of lifeguards, was the cause of his death (*Spiegel* v. *Silver Beach Enterprises* [6 CCH Neg. 2d 874]).
(a) Decide who should win this case. Why?
(b) How does this case illustrate the basic requirements of a negligent act?

11. In the case of *Jamieson* v. *Woodward & Lothrop* (6 CCH Neg. 2d 1172) a manufacturer of rubber ropes with loops at each end, designed as an exerciser, was sued by a user of its product. The plaintiff's eye was injured when the end of the rubber rope slipped from her foot as she was performing an exercise illustrated in the instruction booklet. The plaintiff alleged that the manufacturer did not warn of the possibility of such danger in his instructions. Who should win this case? Give reasons based on your knowledge of product liability.

12. Tweed, age 59, a casketmaker from California, visited his doctor, a general practitioner, complaining about a pain in his right shoulder. The doctor diagnosed it as arthritis, ignoring a suggestion by a consulting radiologist that "a tumor must also be considered." The pain got worse in spite of 41 costly shots of a steroid drug over a three-month period. Tweed went to an orthopedic surgeon who X-rayed the shoulder and misdiagnosed the problem. Eight months later an associate of the orthopedic surgeon happened to see the X-rays and identified the illness as bone cancer. If the malignancy had been spotted in its early stages, Tweed might have been saved; instead the illness was classified as terminal. Tweed sued both the original doctor and the surgeon; Tweed's lawyer settled out of court for $300,000. Do you think that the elements of negligence existed in the above case? Is a doctor liable for failure to cure a patient? Compare this case with one in which a mechanic fails to discover a leaking brake fluid line, which later causes an accident.

13. A prominent attorney was interviewed as to his views on why medical malpractice suits are becoming more common. His answer was that "because medical malpractice is becoming more common and is increasingly being recognized by the average patient." Do you agree? Suggest other possible reasons.

14. The American Medical Association and the American Hospital Association have suggested a plan to settle malpractice suits; each injury would be settled for a specified amount of money as under workers' compensation. A spokesperson stated, "many injuries result not because of negligence, but because medicine is an inexact science and often things happen at the hand of God."
(a) Under the negligence system is a doctor liable for things which happen "at the hand of God"?
(b) Will the workers' compensation system satisfy most patients in their claims for malpractice? Discuss.

15. In 1958 an accounting firm in Illinois was ordered by the supreme court to pay $24,265 to a firm for which it had undertaken annual audits for several years. During this time a bookkeeper had managed to embezzle a large sum of money, undetected by the auditors. Was this decision instrumental in turning the C.P.A. firm into an insurance company as to its client? Discuss.

16. In *Ward* v. *Arnold* (8 CCH Neg. 2d 790), a woman hired an attorney to draw up a will for her husband, making her the beneficiary of his estate. The attorney drew up the will and mailed it to the husband with instructions to sign it in the presence of three witnesses. The husband signed it, but no witnesses were present. When the husband died, his will was ruled invalid and the property was distributed as though the husband had died intestate. As a result, the husband's brother inherited $15,262, half the estate, which would have otherwise gone to the wife. The wife sued the attorney for malpractice. Do you think her suit should succeed? Why?

17. The doctrine of comparative negligence has replaced the contributory negligence rule in some jurisdictions and has long been used as an informal method of settlement. Consider the equity of this doctrine in the following case: A wealthy defendant causes $100 of damage to the automobile of a poor plaintiff, who has been adjudged 10% to blame for the accident. There is $4,000 of damage to the car of the defendant who was 90% to blame.
(a) What amount would the plaintiff recover at common law?
(b) What amount would the plaintiff recover under comparative negligence?

18. A plaintiff alleged that while walking across a street, he was struck by a car which had first been hit by the defendant's car, propelling the struck car into the crosswalk. The plaintiff received a concussion, a sprained foot, and bruises. Doctor bills were $118. The defendant's car had been stolen and the plaintiff charged negligence and violation of a city ordinance because the defendant had left the keys in the ignition, making it easy for a thief to steal the car. Decide the case.

19. Locate a few cases in each of the areas listed below (consult a source such as the *Insurance Law Journal*) and write a summary of these cases together with your evaluation of what constitutes a reasonable standard of care.
(a) Trustee liability.
(b) Parents' liability.
(c) Liability for damage done by animals, either domestic or wild.

20. A woman purchased a refrigerator and three years later received a severe electric shock when she grasped the door handle. The manufacturer proved that after purchase, the door handle had been serviced because it didn't close properly and that, therefore, the manufacturer did not have exclusive control over the machine and, hence, could not have been directly liable for the damage (*Ryan* v. *Zweck Wollenberg Co.* [3 CCH Neg. 2d 724]). Decide the case, stating the principles of product liability governing your answer.

21. *A*'s automobile was struck by an approaching vehicle belonging to *B,* who had swung out of his lane to avoid striking another vehicle whose driver, *C,* was negligently backing out of his driveway without looking. *A* sued *B* for damages, but *B* defended on grounds of no negligence. *A* contended that it was *B*'s car that actually did the damage. Who should win this case? Why?

22. Can it be established that violation of a traffic ordinance, in itself, should constitute proof of negligence? Discuss the pros and cons.

23. Is there any "justice" in holding one parent liable for a child's careless driving, and absolving another parent, whose child's carelessness in the riding of a horse causes injury of another person? Discuss.

24. In the case of *Gothberg* v. *Nemerowski* (108 N.E. 2d 12, Ill. App. [1965]) a minor telephoned a broker of insurance and arranged to get coverage on his auto. The broker's office wrote to the applicant that insurance had been ordered as of the date of the meeting. Later the applicant called the broker to ask if the coverage was effective then, and obtaining an affirmative reply, asked the person who had answered the telephone (the broker was out of the office) to repeat this to the applicant's mother, who would not let him drive the car until she knew he was insured. Prior to the date the applicant sent in the balance of his premium, he had an accident and a judgment of $20,000 was rendered against him. The applicant sued the broker for this sum but the broker denied liability on the grounds that he was under no legal duty to procure insurance until the balance of the premium had been sent in. Decide this case: explain your reasoning, based upon your understanding of the liability of insurance agents and brokers.

25. The purchaser of a used Volkswagen was injured when a gust of wind blew the car from the icy road into a tree. The purchaser sued the manufacturer on the grounds of lack of controllability of the car. It was brought out in the trial that the plaintiff had experienced wind deflections on prior occasions.
(a) Do you think the suit will succeed? Discuss.
(b) How, if at all, would the prior wind deflections affect the case?

26. In a 1974 Georgia case, an insurance agent had undertaken to review annually a client's business interruption insurance to avoid coinsurance penalties. The policy required that coverage equal to 70% of the potential loss. When a loss occurred, the coverage was found to be inadequate. When the client sued the insurer the lower court held for the insurer, stating that no recovery can be had if the policy does not provide the coverage contracted for and the insured has been furnished with a copy of the policy. The case was appealed to the Georgia Supreme Court. How should this case be decided? Why?

Chapter *Fifteen*

LIABILITY INSURANCE CONTRACTS

Liability insurance is an outgrowth of, and is in fact an inevitable result of, those legal relationships in society which permit the bringing of successful lawsuits against individuals for negligence. This is a key factor in understanding the scope of and the reasons for the liability contracts to be discussed in this chapter. As it became recognized that negligence formed the basis for a damage suit, a demand arose for protection against the financial consequences of such suits.

At first the courts frowned upon liability insurance in the belief that contracts of this nature would tend to encourage reckless conduct and thus result in more injuries to persons and property. Later it was recognized that there was a true need for financial protection and that existence of insurance did not cause an unwarranted degree of irresponsible conduct. Today the law takes the attitude that *failure* to obtain liability insurance against the consequences of negligence does in itself constitute irresponsible financial behavior. For example, all states have enacted legislation imposing penalties for failure to provide some sort of financial protection against negligence in the operation of automobiles.

MAJOR CLASSES OF LIABILITY INSURANCE CONTRACTS

Liability insurance contracts have developed to parallel the major classes of legal liability. As may be expected, the insurance industry has formulated hundreds of policies, but it would be superfluous to consider them all. The classification below gives typical examples of each major class of contract. Only a few of these policies have been selected for analysis here, with the emphasis being placed on elements that are common to all.

The major types of liability insurance contracts are:

1. Business liability
   a. Employers' liability and workers' compensation
   b. Owners', landlords', and tenants' liability

   c. Manufacturers' and contractors' liability
   d. Products and completed operations liability
   e. Contractual liability
   f. Contingent liability
   g. Comprehensive general liability
2. Professional liability (malpractice)
   a. Physicians', surgeons', and dentists' malpractice
   b. Lawyers' professional liability
   c. Insurance agents' and brokers' errors and omissions liability
3. Personal liability
   a. Comprehensive personal liability
   b. Special liability contracts
4. Automobile insurance

In the classification above, automobile insurance has been singled out for special attention in Chapter 16 because of its economic importance and the particular hazards and problems surrounding this line of insurance. Actually, of course, the automobile risk is a type which is common to each of the three other classes—business, professional, and personal liability. In addition, types of coverage other than liability, for example, physical damage and medical payments, are discussed as they apply to automobile insurance.

SOME ELEMENTS COMMON TO ALL LIABILITY INSURANCE CONTRACTS

No matter what type of liability a policy applies to, there are certain features which appear in all liability insurance contracts.

Insuring Agreements

Practically all liability insurance contracts include three insuring agreements: the insuring clause; the defense, settlement, and supplementary payments; and the definition of the insured.

The Insuring Clause. Some insuring agreements contain separate clauses for bodily injury and property damage, and sometimes the two are combined into one insuring clause such as the following:

> To pay, on behalf of the insured, all sums which the insured shall become legally obligated to pay as damages because of bodily injury, sickness or disease, including death at any time resulting therefrom, or because of injury to or destruction of property, including loss of use thereof, sustained by any person and caused by accident.

The following points apply to the interpretation of this typical agreement.

1. The policy of liability insurance almost invariably states that the insurer is bound to pay only the sums which the insured is legally obligated to pay. Unless specifically insured, voluntary payments are not covered, even if made in good faith because of what is felt to be a moral obligation to the injured party. This, of course, does not mean that every case must be brought into court to determine legal obligation—it is estimated that over 95% of all cases are settled out of

court—but it means that there must be some breach of care giving rise to actionable negligence.

2. There is no limitation or restriction of coverage concerning to *whom* it is that the legal obligation may be owed. In other words, if the insured injures a person, rich or poor, important or unimportant, native or foreigner, sane or insane, and it is determined there is a breach of care giving rise to actionable negligence, the policy covers.
3. The act causing the injury must be accidental. However, the insured can be covered for torts other than negligence, such as libel, slander, assault and battery, which are not accidental. It will be recalled that a basic requirement of an insurable peril is that it be fortuitous in nature. In spite of this, most liability policies now appear without the "caused by accident" clause. Instead, wording is substituted under which the insurer is liable for any "occurrence" giving rise to legal liability. Even though these policies declare that injuries caused intentionally by the insured are excluded, there is the probability that use of the "occurrence" wording does give more coverage than the "caused by accident" wording. The word "accident" suggests a sudden, unexpected, and abnormal event, while the word "occurrence," when modified to exclude intentional acts, connotes unexpected and abnormal events, but not necessarily sudden events. For example, suppose a contractor is blasting for an excavation for a new building and, while there is no immediate damage observable to a neighboring property, over a period of days the earth is so shaken that the foundations of the nearby buildings are damaged. Under "caused by accident" wording, there may be some doubt that this injury is covered since the contractor should know the probable consequences of his actions and there is no sudden damage due to the blasting. Under the "occurrence" wording, unless it is demonstrated that the contractor deliberately continued actions known to be destructive, the liability for the damage would be recovered.

Defense, Settlement, and Supplementary Payments. With respect to such insurance as is afforded by this policy for bodily injury liability and for property damage liability, the company shall:

1. Defend any suit against the insured alleging such injury, sickness, disease, or destruction and seeking damages on account thereof, even if such suit is groundless, false, or fraudulent; but the company may make such investigation, negotiation, and settlement of any claim or suit as it deems expedient.
2. Pay all premiums on bonds to release attachments for an amount not in excess of the applicable limit of liability of this policy, all premiums on appeal bonds required in any such defended suit, but without obligation to apply for or furnish such bonds.
3. Pay all expenses incurred by the company, all costs taxed against the insured in any such suit and all interest accruing after entry of judgment until the company has paid or tendered or deposited in court such part of such judgment as does not exceed the limit of the company's liability thereon.
4. Pay expenses incurred by the insured for such immediate medical and surgical relief to others as shall be imperative at the time of the accident.
5. Reimburse the insured for all reasonable expenses, including loss of earnings up to some limit such as $25 a day, incurred at the company's request; and the amounts so incurred, except settlements of claims and suits, are payable by the company in addition to the applicable limit of liability of this policy.

In words substantially similar to those above, all contracts of liability insurance provide in the insuring agreements to pay for the legal defense of the insured and other related costs. The importance of this agreement is indicated by the fact that liability insurance has sometimes been termed defense insurance because in a majority of cases liability suits are settled out of court by negotiation between attorneys, and the insured knows that the worry and care of negotiations are assumed by the insurer. The following points concerning the defense clause are worth noting:

1. The fact that the insurer agrees to defend any suit, even if it is groundless, false, or fraudulent, relieves the insured of the worry and expense of nuisance cases, where the plaintiff is relying on the fact that in many cases a reputable business house will settle a small but groundless claim rather than go to the expense of defending itself in court. The insurer already has a legal staff, the cost of which is distributed over many similar claims in a given year and can thus handle each case economically. Without insurance, a defendant might wish to retain counsel even if the amount involved were small. It should be noted that the word *any* does not mean that the insurer will defend a court action falling outside the scope of a negligence action.
2. Sometimes courts require that the alleged wrong-doer post a bond to guarantee that, pending the outcome of a negligence action, he will not dispose of property subject to confiscation if the case goes against him. In cases where a decision has been lost in the lower court and is appealed to a higher court, a bond must be posted to guarantee that if the defendant loses in the higher court, the judgment will be paid. The insurer agrees to pay the premium on these bonds, plus any accrued interest after the date of the judgment.
3. Under the other terms of the liability policy, the insurer has the right to require the insured to appear in court personally in legal actions arising under the policy.
4. The insurer agrees to pay for such immediate medical relief to others as shall be necessary at the time of the accident.
5. The insurer does not deduct the cost of defense from the applicable limit of liability for damages, but instead pays for these costs over and above all limits of liability for damages. It may turn out that the defense costs exceed the judgment finally handed down.

Definition of the Insured. All contracts of liability insurance specifically set forth who is to be considered the insured. The concept of the insured individual in liability policies is generally very broad, and the wording differs for each type of policy. In the case of a business firm, the intent is to include all partners, officers, directors, or proprietors in their capacity as representatives of the particular business. In personal liability insurance, the policies include as insureds all members of the family who are permanent residents of a single household. It is not uncommon to write liability contracts naming other parties as additional insureds, for payment of an extra premium.

Exclusions

Among the various liability insurance contracts, certain exclusions appear almost universally. Among these are:

1. In the case of business policies, all nonbusiness activities giving rise to damage suits are excluded. In personal contracts, all business pursuits giving rise to damage suits are excluded.

2. There is an attempt in each policy to exclude all sources of liability intended to be covered in other contracts, or intended to be covered by a special provision for an extra premium. Thus, the comprehensive general liability policy covers products or contractual liability only if specific payment is made for this coverage and it excludes professional liability since this is insured under separate contracts.
3. Nearly all liability contracts exclude damage to property belonging to or rented to the insured, or property in the care, custody, or control of the insured, under the general theory that a person cannot be liable to himself for his own negligence. The insured is expected to obtain physical damage insurance, such as fire or lightning insurance, to cover the accidental loss of property which he owns or for which he is legally liable for loss.

The question sometimes arises as to the conditions under which property is in the care, custody, or control of the insured. For example, if a mechanic is working on the fan belt of an engine in a customer's car, and the fan blade accidentally breaks off and puts a hole in the radiator, is the damage covered under the garage liability policy or is it excluded under the construction that the car is in the care and custody of the insured and hence damage to any part of the car is excluded? A liberal policy interpretation would hold that the damage is covered and that only damage to property actually being worked on is excluded. Thus, in one case a contractor installed a heat exchange unit. While it was being tested, but before the job was abandoned, damage resulted. The court held that the damage was covered.[1] In another case, however, the court held that damage to a concrete retaining wall by a bulldozer was excluded because the wall was ''in the care, custody, and control'' of the contractor at the time of the damage.[2] There seems to be no general rule applicable to such cases, except the general rule that always applies—ambiguities in contractual language will be construed against the insurer.

Some insurers offer broadened policies under which the ''care, custody, and control'' exclusion is considerably liberalized. Of special interest to contractors, the *broad form property damage liability program,* as it is called, spells out in considerable detail just what property is covered and under what terms.

Limits of Liability

Under all policies of liability insurance, there are limits of liability of various sorts. For example, in the comprehensive general liability contract, the limits might be $100,000 for bodily injury liability for any one person, and $300,000 for each accident. For property damage liability, there might be a limitation of $50,000 for each accident. This means that if three or more of the insured's customers are injured in a single accident, there is an aggregate limitation of $300,000, with no coverage for each individual claim to be in excess of $100,000. If there is more than one insured named in the policy, the question arises, ''Are these limits of liability applicable to each insured, thus doubling or tripling the stated limits?'' The answer is ''No.''

[1] *Boswell* v. *Travelers Indemnity Company,* 8 CCH Fire and Casualty Cases 936.

[2] *Jarrell Construction Company* v. *Columbia Casualty Company,* 8 CCH Fire and Casualty Cases 642.

The question also arises as to whether a given accident can be interpreted as a series of accidents so as to apply the limit of liability per person or per accident to each separate "accident," thus greatly increasing the insurer's liability. In a famous case a truck negligently ran into a train derailing 16 freight cars.[3] In its action against the insured truck owner, the railroad argued that since the cars were owned by 14 separate owners, in reality there were at least 14 separate accidents and the insured's limit of liability applied to each one of them. This contention was rejected and the court held that there was only one accident within the normal meaning of the word. The principle is also applied to the field of products liability insurance, where the liability limits apply to all claims arising out of any one batch or lot of goods or products. Let us say that a manufacturer with a $50,000 limit of coverage for products liability sells a bad lot of a certain medicine and 1,000 injured customers make claims of $1,000 each over its use during the ensuing six months. The maximum amount the insurer will pay for damages arising out of these 1,000 claims is $50,000, not $1 million. One accident is defined in such a way that it applies to one lot of goods. Since there might be many claims arising out of the use of one lot of goods and since the limits of liability apply to the sum of these claims, the need for much higher limits in products liability than are commonly purchased is apparent. The manufacturer might be severely underinsured in the mistaken belief that the liability limits apply to every claim.

Subrogation

Practically all contracts of liability insurance are subject to the right of subrogation by the insurer against any liable third party. This right is very important. It may turn out, for example, that while the insured is held legally liable for some act of negligence, someone else had agreed to assume this liability by contract or is held liable because the insured is the agent or servant of a third party. If the insurer pays the claim, it has a right to any such claims that the insured may have had against others.

Notice

Like all insurance policies, liability contracts require immediate notice of accident and notice of claim or suit. It is especially important that this condition be complied with since otherwise available witnesses may be dispersed and evidence dissipated so as to make it difficult or impossible to determine later what actually happened. Such information is vital to the successful defense of the insured and without prompt notice, the insurer is greatly handicapped.

BUSINESS LIABILITY INSURANCE

Among the business liability contracts listed on page 312, we shall give somewhat detailed consideration only to the comprehensive general liability policy because this contract includes all the perils covered by the others except

[3] *St. Paul-Mercury Indemnity Company* v. *Rutland Railroad,* 5 CCH Auto.2d 894.

the employers' liability and workers' compensation policy, which will be discussed in a later chapter.

Comprehensive General Liability

The *comprehensive general liability* (CGL) policy is a scheduled form that permits the insured to combine many types of liability coverage in one contract. It is issued on an all-risk basis so that if legal liability arises out of some event not listed, but also not specifically excluded, coverage is provided. The policy is issued to a wide variety of business enterprises.

The following classes of liability may be insured under the CGL:

1. Liability arising out of the use of premises.
2. Liability arising out of manufacturing, contracting, or other business activities of the insured.
3. Medical payments.
4. Contingent liability (independent contractors).
5. Products and completed operations liability.
6. Contractual liability.

In addition, it is usually possible to insure all automobile liability under a form which is a combination of the CGL and the comprehensive automobile liability policy. Insurance on the exposures listed above may also be purchased separately under separate contracts. For example, the first type of liability listed is essentially the coverage provided in the owners', landlords', and tenants' liability policy which insures liability arising out of the ownership, maintenance, and use of a premises. The second listed coverage is that provided by the manfacturers' and contractors' liability policy which insures liability arising out of manufacturing or contracting operations. The phrasing of the coverage in the CGL is such that claims arising out of any operation in any way connected with or required by the insured's business are covered. Thus, a claim arising out of a roadside sign is covered because the sign would be interpreted as "incidental or necessary" to the business operation. Elevator liability is automatically covered.

It is significant that for each of the perils named, the CGL provides automatic coverage on newly acquired premises, elevators, or other hazards arising during the policy term. Thus, if a new building is purchased or leased, a new elevator installed, or a new type of business purchased or begun, the insurance adjusts automatically to provide coverage. Naturally, when the policy is audited at the close of the year, an additional premium is charged for any such new exposures. The automatic coverage applies only to exposures falling within the class of those already insured. For example, if the insured had elected not to take products liability insurance, there would be no automatic coverage for claims arising from this source.

Insuring Clause—Occurrence Basis

In the CGL, the act causing the injury must be accidental in the sense that an occurrence produces results which are accidental and unintended by the insured. The occurrence itself need not be accidental. The latest revision of the CGL (1973) defines an occurrence as "an accident, including continuous or repeated exposure to conditions, which results in bodily injury or property damage neither expected nor intended from the standpoint of the insured." Thus, the insured could perform some *deliberate* act, but if the results of this act caused a loss, as defined, which was neither expected nor intended by the insured, the policy would cover. There is no requirement that the loss result from some *sudden* act by the insured because an exposure to conditions over a period of time is covered.

The following losses have been held by courts to be compensable by insurers as accidents: loss due to radium exposure over a period of seven months in which the employer had furnished defective protective equipment,[4] loss due to beryllium poisoning over an eight-year period,[5] and loss to windows by hydrofluoric acid due to improper cleaning precautions.[6]

Medical Payments

A typical agreement covering medical payments under the CGL reads as follows:

> To pay all reasonable expenses incurred within one year from the date of accident for necessary medical, surgical, and dental services, including prosthetic devices, and necessary ambulance, hospital, professional nursing and funeral services, to or for each person who sustains bodily injury, sickness, or disease, caused by accident and arising out of the ownership, maintenance, or use of the premises, or operations necessary or incidental thereto.

Medical payments coverage applies only to expenses incurred within one year of the accident, and payments are made only to individuals *other than the insured*, regardless of the legal liability of the insured for the accident. The purpose of medical payments coverage is to compensate the insured for costs that would normally be incurred when members of the public are injured on the insured's property, regardless of legal liability. Of course, the injured person may feel that he or she has a legal claim for further damages, in which case there is nothing to prevent that person from bringing an action, even after receiving medical care under the medical payments section of the policy. Medical payments claims do not affect the liability sections of the CGL.

The medical payments coverage as commonly attached to the CGL has some important limits and exclusions. There is a dollar limit per person, usually $250 or $500, and a dollar limit per accident, commonly $25,000 or $50,000. Medical payments claims arising from use of faulty products are usually excluded because these claims would be covered by products liability coverage. There is no coverage applicable to tenants who do not reside on the premises, and no coverage to tenants living off the premises for accidents incurred on those parts of the premises rented to them. All medical claims arising from the

[4] *Canadian Radium & Uranium Corp.* v. *Indemnity Insurance Co. of North America,* 108 N.E.2d 515.

[5] *Beryllium Corp.* v. *American Mutual Liability Insurance Co.,* 223 Fed. (Ind.) 71.

[6] *Cross* v. *Zurich General Accident and Liability Insurance Co.,* 184 Fed. (Ind.) 609.

use of automobiles are excluded, inasmuch as separate coverage for automobiles is available. Automobile medical payments coverage, incidentally, is generally much more comprehensive than other medical payments insurance.

Contingent Liability

Contingent, or *protective, liability* is the liability imposed on the insured by law for actions of independent contractors. Not all liability can be passed on by an owner to the contractor, even if the contractor is willing to assume it by agreement. The building owner, for example, may still be liable to members of the public if an independent contractor engages in hazardous activities such as blasting. Contingent liability insurance covers this risk.

Products Liability

As written in the CGL, *products liability* includes the liability of the manufacturer or the vendor arising out of the handling of faulty products or their containers, as well as completed operations. This coverage is vital to most insureds and a careful study of it is warranted.

Products liability is distinguished from general liability in that the injury or damage must occur *away* from the premises of the insured and after the insured has relinquished possession and control of the product which caused the loss.[7] In one case, for example, a plaintiff tapped a glass jar lightly and the jar exploded, cutting her seriously. The court found the manufacturer liable because the explosion was caused by a faulty annealing process in the manufacture of the glass.[8] If an accident similar to this had occurred *on the premises* of the vendor, the general premises liability portion of the CGL would have covered the loss. Since it is common to purchase different limits of coverage on different types of liability exposures, it makes a difference as to which liability coverage is applicable to a given loss. A firm may have $100,000 limits for general premises coverage but only $25,000 on products liability.

Similar reasoning holds for services performed by the insured on the premises of others. If a loss occurs while the worker is on the job, the general liability section of the CGL would cover. Once the worker has left the job, the products liability (completed or abandoned operations) section covers the loss. However, losses arising from pickup or delivery operations, existence of tools left on the job, and uninstalled equipment or leftover materials, are covered under the general liability portion, by contractual provision.

The fact that the insured intends to perform additional work in the future does not necessarily mean that the job is unfinished and that, therefore, the general liability portion of the policy covers. If, for example, a flooring contractor installs a new floor in the living room, intending to do the dining room at a later time, but leaves the job for a temporary period, it will be considered that

[7] There is an exception to this general rule for restaurants, where coverage attaches for losses occurring while food is being consumed on the premises.

[8] *Trani* v. *Anchor Hocking Glass Corp.*, Conn. Sup. Ct. of Errors (July 12, 1955) 5 CCH Neg.2d 34.

the living room has been completed, and any losses arising from defective workmanship are covered under the completed operations liability.

In one case a salesperson applied some wax on a customer's floor but did not remove it. Later on someone slipped on the floor and a claim for injuries resulted. The salesperson's employer carried general liability coverage but did not carry completed operations liability. The court found that the installation was one of completed operations and that no liability under the general liability policy existed.[9] Because of the fine distinction that exists between the general liability coverage and the products liability coverage, it is advisable that a company carry both types of insurance so as to prevent possible disagreements over the question as to who, if anyone, is to pay the loss.

The products liability section of the CGL contains a business risk exclusion, intended to eliminate the responsibility of the insurer for losses due to liability of the insured for loss of use of tangible property of a customer due to some failure in the insured's products or services to meet performance standards. If an insured fails to construct a building on time or installs an inadequate heating system, causing a loss in rental income to the customer, there is no coverage under products liability. However, if the heating system is repaired poorly and later explodes causing a shutdown of the building, a loss of use, liability coverage is effective. Likewise, if a manufacturer's insecticide is faulty and the customer loses farm crops due to insect infestation, any liability for the resulting loss would be paid.

If a manufacturer discovers a bad batch of products and incurs expense in withdrawing them from the market, the CGL does not cover such expense. Separate insurance, known as *recall insurance*, is available in nonstandard markets for this exposure. However, there are detailed provisions in the contract requiring the insured to take all reasonable steps to prevent further loss once a bad batch of products is identified and to repair faulty work. Under the sistership exclusion, products liability coverage excludes loss claimed for damage when goods are recalled, such as expenses to restock a grocer's shelves.

Products liability insurance applies equally to damages caused by the container of the goods as well as by the goods themselves. Thus, if a bottle of liquid explodes and the glass causes injuries to the holder, the policy covers the resulting damages.

Products liability insurance applies to all accidents that give rise to losses suffered during the policy term regardless of when the article or service causing the accident was sold or rendered. It is not unusual for products liability claims to arise several years after the goods are sold. The insurance applies not only to the goods that were sold but also to any free samples or premium merchandise given away with the goods at the time they were sold.

Major CGL Exclusions. The CGL excludes automobile exposure unless it is combined with automobile coverage, which is usually written as a separate contract. (However, liability loss due to the operation of mobile equipment or

[9] *United States Sanitary Specialties Corporation* v. *Globe Indemnity Company*, 7 CCH Fire and Casualty Cases 1193.

from parking nonowned automobiles on the premises of the insured is covered.) Aircraft liability is excluded, as well as liability from the operation of watercraft away from the premises. There are the usual exclusions due to war, workers' compensation claims, and to property in the care, custody, and control of the insured.

Liability in connection with vending machines is not covered unless this type of protection is specifically included at an extra premium. All liability assumed under contract, except for warranties of goods or products, is excluded from the products liability section of the CGL; such liability is covered under contractual liability. Finally, liability arising from the responsibility imposed by a liquor law is excluded. Known as the *dramshop exclusion*, this provision appears in most liability contracts because in some states the dramshop laws make the seller or distributor of alcoholic beverages liable for losses which can be traced to the use of alcohol sold or distributed by him or her. Thus, an intoxicated person may leave an establishment dispensing liquor and injure someone or destroy property. Under the state's dramshop law, the liability might be traced back to the insured establishment. This liability is excluded under the policy but may be covered by payment of an additional premium.

Vendors' Endorsement. Because of the importance of the products liability hazard, many retailers refuse to handle the goods of a manufacturer or a wholesaler unless they are provided with evidence that the distributor has protected them with products liability insurance. This is usually accomplished by naming the retailer as an additional insured on the wholesaler's or the manufacturer's products liability policy. This endorsement covers not only claims based on breach of the manufacturer's warranty, but also those claims based on the retailer's negligence, or upon the retailer's own warranty of the goods. An extra premium is, of course, charged for this endorsement. Since the retailer often carries products liability insurance as well, the effect of the vendors' endorsement is to provide higher limits of liability for products hazard claims.

Contractual Liability

A source of liability that is often overlooked by business firms stems from agreements they have signed with others assuming liability that might otherwise be attributed to someone else. Typical examples are railroad spur track agreements, leases, easements, contracts with suppliers of goods or services, contracts with municipalities for the performance of certain services (say, snow removal) or for construction, elevator maintenance agreements, and purchase order agreements. Under these agreements, the liability assumed is not necessarily restricted to negligence liability but may be for any accidental occurrence, such as fire.

Railroad Spur Track Agreements. One of the oldest and best known sources of contractual liability arises out of agreements with railroads to "hold harmless" the railroad for certain losses growing out of the installation, maintenance, or use of a spur track run into the insured's property for convenience in loading and unloading materials and supplies. These contracts are not standardized but usually provide that if one of the railroad's locomotives causes fire damage to the property of some third party or if accidental injury results from the use of the spur track, the property owner will be responsible for the resulting expenses and losses.

Even if both the railroad and the property owner have general liability insurance, the property owner has no coverage against these claims unless he or she has contractual liability coverage insuring such contracts. Let us assume that due to the negligence of the employees of both the railroad and the property owner, someone is killed by one of the railroad's engines. A judgment is obtained against both the railroad and the property owner and is paid by each party's liability insurer. The railroad's insurer now sues the property owner for recovery of the amounts paid on behalf of the railroad, arguing that the railroad's liability was assumed by the property owner under the hold harmless agreement. The property owner must pay this amount and may not look to the insurer for legal defense unless contractual liability insurance was purchased, either separately or under the CGL. Note that both parties were protected by general liability insurance, but that because of the hold harmless agreement, the property owner suffers an additional loss.[10]

Leases. Under the typical lease, the lessee agrees to assume any liability that would otherwise be attributable to the lessor for any damage caused by the lessee or by any person due to poor building maintenance or due to the neglect of any person, including tenants or occupants of the building. It is significant to note that the agreement provides that if anyone causes a loss for which the lessor is held liable, the lessee must pay. Thus, even if a landlord is held directly liable at law for negligence, the lessee or the insurer of the lessee must reimburse the landlord. The same principle applies to most contractual liability agreements. In a leading case, for example, an electrical contractor had assumed liability in a construction contract with the city of New York. Through negligence of one of the city's employees, the city was held liable for a judgment of $85,000, which it was able to collect from the electrical contractor under the hold harmless clause of its construction contract.[11]

The CGL normally lists and insures without extra charge five types of contractual liability agreements called "incidental contracts": lease of premises, sidetrack agreements, elevator and escalator maintenance agreements, easement agreements in connection with a railroad grade crossing, and agreements required by municipal ordinance in connection with work for the municipality. The policy automatically covers all *written* agreements of these types during its policy term. Any other agreements, such as those arising out of the use of leased equipment, must be covered by separate endorsement and a premium paid therefor. Insurers are generally not willing to issue a blanket endorsement covering all types of agreements which might be signed during the policy term.

[10] A case very similar to this actually occurred and is described in *St. Louis Police Relief Association* v. *Aetna Life Insurance Co.*, 154 S.W.2d 782.

[11] *Thiebault* v. *City of New York,* reported in 135 New York Law Journal, 108.

PROFESSIONAL LIABILITY (MALPRACTICE) INSURANCE

Because general liability policies usually contain exclusions for all claims arising out of error or mistake of a professional person in the performance of the duties of the profession, separate policies covering this important form of legal liability have been developed. These contracts are sometimes referred to as *malpractice* and sometimes as *errors and omissions policies,* depending upon the type of professional person utilizing them. Essentially the two contracts are quite similar, however, and have many provisions in common. Examples of three of these policies follow, with the peculiar characteristics of each analyzed.

Professional Versus Other Liability Contracts

Important differences between professional liability and other liability insurance contracts exist:

1. In professional liability insurance, the insurer often needs the permission of the insured to settle claims out of court by tendering sums in return for releases of liability by the plaintiff. The practice of out-of-court settlement is very common in other liability claims, but it is easy to see that to allow this in the case of professional liability would tend to damage the reputation of, say, a doctor who might become known as a person who admits malpractice by settling claims in this manner. Therefore, even though it might be less expensive for the insurer to pay a claim regardless of its validity, the professional person has the right to insist that the insurer defend him or her in the courts.
2. The professional liability policy is usually written with only one major insuring clause, with no distinction made between bodily injury or property damage liability, and with no limit *per accident*. Usually there is a limit of liability *per claim* stated. Thus, if the policy has a $25,000 limit of liability per claim and a $100,000 aggregate limit, and two damage suits arise out of a single error, say one by the patient and another by the patient's spouse, the limits of liability would be $50,000 ($25,000 per claim). Other liability policies, on the other hand, invariably state the limits of liability in terms of so much per accident or per occurrence.
3. The professional liability policy does not restrict its coverage to those events that are "caused by accident" because usually the act which gives rise to a claim is deliberate. The event has an unintended result but may not always be described as accidental. For example, a druggist may sell a patent medicine for the relief of itching. If this medicine causes a severe allergic reaction in the customer, certainly the result is unintended, but the act of selling the drug was deliberate. Medical malpractice insurance would cover such a loss. However, the policy always excludes illegal or criminal acts from its coverage.
4. The professional liability policy usually does not exclude damage to property in the care, custody, or control of the insured, as do general liability contracts. Normally this type of loss will be at a minimum since, for the most part, the contracts cover personal injuries.
5. Unlike other liability policies and products liability in particular, professional liability contracts protect the insured against all claims which had their basis in the service or the acts performed during the policy term. It is not necessary for the claim itself to be made during the policy term, but the professional error must have been committed during the policy period.

6. The products liability policy insures claims arising out of a breach of warranty of the vendor regarding the goods. If a retailer says a product is good for a certain purpose and it turns out to be definitely wrong for this purpose, "an action lies" for which the policy must respond. In the professional liability policy, however, there is generally an exclusion for any agreement guaranteeing the result of any treatment. A suit by a patient, irritated because the treatment failed when the doctor promised it would succeed, is thus not covered. The policy responds to suits based on a physician's error, mistake, or malpractice in rendering the service, but not to any warranty for successful results, which cannot be guaranteed. Similar clauses are found in other types of professional liability contracts.

Medical Malpractice Insurance

One of the major professional liability contracts is the physicians', surgeons', and dentists' liability policy. In it the insurer agrees to pay:

> All sums which the insured shall become legally obligated to pay as damages because of injury arising out of malpractice, error, or mistake in rendering or failing to render professional services in the practice of the insured's profession described in the declarations, committed during the policy period by the insured or by any person for whose acts or omissions the insured is legally responsible.

The insuring clause refers to "injury" and not to bodily injury. Thus, the clause covers a broad range of claims, such as mental anguish, false imprisonment, slander, and libel, based on professional acts. The insuring agreement refers to acts arising in the "practice of the insured's profession." If a patient slips on a wet doormat while entering the premises, however, this is not part of a professional service and the malpractice policy would not cover any damages. The professional person thus needs premises liability insurance as well as professional liability coverage. Very often professional liability insurance is provided by a rider on the general liability policy, and thus in practice there is normally little difficulty arising from problems of this sort.

The insuring agreement covers the insured's liability for the act of a nurse, assistant, technician, etc., but does not cover the personal liability which might attach to such a person. The nurse, assistant, or technician is expected to provide professional coverage separately. Often the insurer permits this coverage to be endorsed on the employer's policy.

Because of the increasing frequency and severity of medical malpractice claims, some contracts now limit the time during which coverage exists under a policy or its renewal after its termination to some period, such as three years. Thus, coverage would have to be renewed periodically for a retired physician wishing coverage for acts performed during the time of active practice. Under traditional contracts, coverage exists even if the claim is presented years after the alleged malpractice. Thus, a person age 21 might sue for a malpractice committed during childbirth.

Lawyers' Professional Liability

Another example of malpractice insurance is found in a more or less standardized contract that covers the professional liability of lawyers and attorneys.

This contract is now offered by most liability insurers on a form developed by the National Bureau of Casualty Underwriters. The contract is similar in wording to other professional liability contracts, with adaptations to fit the particular needs of lawyers. The insuring agreement is very broad, covering liability "because of any act or omission of the insured, or of any other person for whose acts or omissions the insured is legally responsible, and arising out of the performance of professional services for others in the insured's capacity as a lawyer." Like other professional liability contracts, it makes no reference to "accidents," and the insurer may not settle a claim without the permission of the insured.

The contract covers claims arising out of any act or failure to perform if the act or failure occurred during the policy term, with no time limit as to when the claim must be presented. Thus, if lawyer Brown fails to carry out properly a divorce proceeding for client Smith and ten years later it develops that Smith, having been illegally remarried, is charged with being a bigamist, the insurer will defend the suit and pay any judgment that arises even if the insurer is no longer carrying the policy on Brown. On the other hand, if Brown had never carried professional liability insurance before, and during the policy term Brown is sued by Smith for damages, the present liability insurer will still pay the claim providing it can be shown that when the policy went into force, Brown did not know nor could reasonably have foreseen that the earlier omission would have caused the suit by Smith. However, if Brown drops the policy after one year and Smith's suit is brought after the policy has expired, there is no coverage, as there would have been had the original error occurred during the policy period. If at the time Smith's suit is brought, Brown has a policy with another insurer, the first insurer must respond (providing the professional mistake occurred during the period the first policy was in force) and the second insurer's coverage is considered excess in case the limits of liability of the first insurer are insufficient.

Insurance Agents' and Brokers' Errors and Omissions Liability

The agents' and brokers' errors and omissions policy insures the agent against all loss which the agent must pay because of negligent acts, errors, or omissions of employees to clientele. While these contracts are not standardized, most insurers give the agent the option of protection against similar claims from the insurance companies represented. Usually the contract is written with a substantial deductible amount, say $500 or $1,000. The policy pays only if legal liability on the part of the agent can be proved, and does not respond to payments made to customers voluntarily in order to preserve goodwill. Like other professional liability contracts, errors and omissions insurance covers only *professional* mistakes.

The agent, to collect, need only show that the claim was brought during the policy term, regardless of when the professional mistake occurred. However, for the protection of the agent, the contract requires that if the insurer refuses to renew, the coverage is extended for one year against claims arising from mistakes occurring during the policy term. It might happen, for example, that an agent realizes on December 28 that an error was committed for which the agent is liable, there having occurred a loss which, because of the agent's mistake, was left uninsured. The professional liability insurer, learning of this, might refuse to renew the errors and omissions policy in the knowledge that a claim would not be submitted before the expiration of the policy on December 31. The provision granting coverage on such claims thus protects the agent from being unjustly denied recovery on the errors and omissions contract.

Important features in errors and omissions policies which should be examined include:

1. The extent of the coverage of agents' acts prior to the effective date of the policy.
2. The coverage of acts by outside agencies, such as appraisal companies.
3. The existence of territorial limitations, especially regarding coverage for international clients.
4. Limitations on the period stated for discovery of the loss.
5. The insurer's ability to settle a claim without the agent's consent and the agent's ability to admit liability.
6. The effect of illegal or unwarranted acts of the agent's employees or subagents.
7. Whether liability to the insurer is covered.

Not all policies will contain provisions concerning these points which will be satisfactory to the insured.

PERSONAL LIABILITY INSURANCE

Most insurance coverage on one's *personal* (nonbusiness) liability for negligence, other than automobile, is written on the *comprehensive personal liability policy* (abbreviated CPL), first introduced in 1944, and now incorporated in homeowners forms. Individual contracts on particular types of personal liability, such as golfer's liability, sportsman's liability, and dog liability, are occasionally written. The comprehensive personal liability policy is an all-risk contract and has few exclusions. It is intended for legal liability risks arising from the maintenance of a home, but also covers the insured's nonbusiness liability away from the residence.

Insuring Agreements

The insuring agreements of the comprehensive personal liability policy parallel those of the CGL in most respects, but differ in that:

1. The insuring agreement makes no reference to acts "caused by accident." Therefore, the coverage is on an occurrence basis.
2. Property damage and bodily injury liability are covered in one insuring clause and a single limit applies to both types. This procedure is becoming more common in liability policies, although at one time only the CPL was written in this manner.

3. Medical payments coverage is not optional as it is on the CGL, and it amounts to $250 or $500 per accident, unless the policy is endorsed for higher limits. The following medical payments claims, which must be based on an accident, are covered: (a) losses to persons on the premises with permission of the insured; (b) losses away from the premises if they were caused by activities of the insured, or by children, servants, or animals of the insured; (c) losses on premises where the insured is temporarily living (providing the insured does not own the premises) or on vacant land belonging to the insured. Medical payments on the CPL do not cover the cost of accidents to the insured himself or to anyone else residing with the insured. This restriction does not apply to medical payments as it is written on automobile liability contracts.
4. In defining the insured, the CPL includes not only the named insured but also the spouse and the relatives of either who are residents; together with any person under 21 living at the residence; and, with respect to the use of certain farm and garden implements, employees.
5. Liability to employees for injuries incurred are covered unless a workers' compensation policy is in force or is required under the laws of the state.

Exclusions

The major exclusions of the CPL are:

1. Business activities and professional activities, are specifically excluded, as on the CGL personal liability is excluded. However, the CPL covers business activities ordinarily incident to nonbusiness pursuits. Thus, if the insured walks downtown on personal business but goes to the office on an errand and bumps into another person when rounding a corner, the CPL covers any resulting claim.
2. Liability arising out of the use of aircraft or automobiles away from the premises. However, if a vehicle does not have to be licensed (e.g., riding lawn mowers, snowmobiles, golf carts) it is covered while on the premises.
3. Liability arising out of the use of large boats. The policy generally covers the average small pleasure boat, so long as it does not exceed certain dimensions (sailboats under 26 feet or power boats with less than 25-horsepower engines). Liability arising out of the use of larger craft must be handled by a separate contract or by a special endorsement to the CPL.
4. Destruction of property in the care, custody, or control of the insured.
5. Contractual liability except those contracts of liability relating to the premises, as might be the case under a typical lease.
6. Liability arising out of intentional acts of the insured. The question has arisen as to whether intentional acts of children giving rise to parental liability are covered. It has been held that since the parent did not perform the intentional act, the CPL applies to such cases as far as the *parent's* liability is concerned.[12] Suits against the *child* would not be defended where the child intentionally causes some loss, even if the child cannot know the full consequences of the act because of age. In one case, an insurer had to pay for the insured's liability for an unintentional injury to a storekeeper whose store he robbed. The insured fired his gun as a scare tactic to avoid being recognized as he fled the scene of the robbery, but accidentally injured the storeowner instead.[13]
7. Liability arising from secondary residences, such as beach houses or mountain cabins if owned by the insured. The insured is expected to purchase a separate policy for such property. Since in most areas the rates for the CPL are less than $15 a year for basic limits, this requirement does not impose an undue cost.

[12] *Arenson* v. *National Automobile & Casualty Insurance Co.*, 286 Pac.2d 816.
[13] *Vanguard Insurance Co.* v. *Cantrell* v. *Allstate Insurance Co.*, 1973 C.C.H. (Auto) 7684.

SUMMARY

1. The major classes of liability contracts are business, professional, personal, and automobile. The latter class has applications in each of the first three classes but, because of its special importance, is singled out for separate discussion in Chapter 16.
2. All liability contracts have certain elements in common. For example, the insuring agreements are fairly well standardized. The major differences lie in whether the event giving rise to a legal claim is interpreted to be an "occurrence" or an "accident." The occurrence basis, being broader than the accident basis, is a preferred wording from the viewpoint of the insured. Liability contracts vary in the definition of who is insured. All liability contracts guarantee that the insurer will bear the cost of defense in addition to paying any judgments up to the limits of liability.
3. Common exclusions peculiar to liability contracts include (a) nonbusiness activities in the case of business liability policies, and business activities in the case of nonbusiness liability contracts, and (b) damage to property in the care, custody, and control of the insured. Because of its inherent ambiguity, the latter exclusion has resulted in much litigation.
4. The comprehensive general liability contract (CGL) is one of the major policies of business liability insurance. A scheduled form written on an all-risk basis, the CGL may insure premises liability; liability arising out of manufacturing, contracting, or other business activities of the insured; contingent liability; medical payments; products and completed operations liability; and contractual liability. Any of the coverages are available on separate contracts.
5. Products liability insurance, which may be written with the CGL, is distinguished from general liability insurance in several ways, chief among which is that the accident giving rise to the claim must occur away from the main premises of the business and must arise out of a faulty product sold or a service rendered by the insured after the insured has completed work. Products liability insurance covers the loss no matter when the deficient product was sold or the faulty service was performed. It never covers loss to the product itself but only damage caused by its faulty manufacture.
6. Contractual liability insurance is necessitated by the existence of agreements whereby one party assumes the liability of another party by contractual agreement, often termed a "hold harmless agreement." Such an obligation is not covered under the concept of legal liability that applies to the general provisions of liability contracts and, therefore, special coverage is required.
7. Professional liability (malpractice) insurance covering liability for claims arising from professional errors or mistakes is distinguished from other liability contracts in a number of ways. Generally, professional liability contracts do not permit out-of-court settlements without the permission of the insured, are issued on a per-claim basis instead of a per-accident basis, and do not restrict their coverage to accidental occurrences. Professional liability policies will not cover dishonest or criminal acts nor will they insure any claim arising out of any guarantee that professional services rendered will accomplish a specified result.
8. Most personal liability insurance is written on the comprehensive personal liability policy (CPL). This contract, similar in wording to the CGL, is designed to meet the needs of the typical householder for premises liability as well as for

other liability arising from ordinary nonbusiness pursuits, such as sports, hobbies, and ownership of animals. Most coverage is in force under homeowners policies.

QUESTIONS FOR REVIEW AND DISCUSSION

1. In *Employers Insurance Company of Alabama Inc.* v. *Rives* (8 CCH Fire and Casualty Cases 676 [1955], a contractor installed some gasoline pumps and, due to his failure to tighten connections, gasoline leaked out underground and contaminated the well of a nearby property owner.
(a) Would the contractor's products liability policy cover this loss?
(b) If you were the attorney for the insurer, on what grounds might you attempt to deny liability under the policy? Explain.
2. In *Great American Indemnity Company of New York* v. *Saltzman* (8 CCH Fire and Casualty Cases 388), an insured had a general liability policy. Without permission, he entered an airplane belonging to another person to inspect it and started the engine. Because of his unfamiliarity with the controls, the insured could not stop the plane, which crashed into a hangar and caused substantial damage. The insurer refused to defend the insured in the resulting suit for damages.
(a) On what grounds is it likely that the insurer relied? Explain, with reference to appropriate policy provisions of the typical business liability policy.
(b) Do you think that the defense in (a) should be found to be good? Discuss.
3. The druggists' liability policy is a combination of professional liability and products liability, with the professional liability portion covering errors in compounding, delivery, or other handling of prescriptions or drugs. This policy gives the insurance company the sole right to settle claims. Is this provision typical of most professional liability contracts? If so, what dangers lie in it? If not, suggest a reason why the insurer might so provide.
4. *A*, a local agent, places *Y*'s general liability insurance in the Shifting Sands Insurance Company. *Y* has an accident in which she is held to be legally liable for $5,000 damages. When she submits her claim, it is discovered that the Shifting Sands Insurance Company is bankrupt. So *Y* sues *A* for $5,000, claiming that *A* negligently placed her insurance with an unsound insurer and is therefore guilty of breach of professional duty.
(a) In your opinion is *A* negligent? Why or why not?
(b) Assuming *A* is negligent, would her errors and omissions policy respond to this claim?
(c) Assuming *A* is not legally negligent but tenders *Y* $5,000 anyway because of what she feels is a moral obligation, will the errors and omissions policy cover the payment?
5. On the way to a meeting with a client, an attorney injures a third party in an automobile accident.
(a) Does such an occurrence arise out of the attorney's professional practice? If so, would the professional liability respond in damages? Why?
(b) Would your answer be different if the accident occurred because the attorney and his client were discussing a legal question while driving along and as a result of not paying attention to driving, the attorney caused the accident? Discuss.
6. In one case, a patient, *P*, alleged that his physician agreed to remove a growth by a method known as fulguration for a fee not to

exceed $150. The physician promised that the plaintiff would be cured in a few days and could resume his work, because the procedure would not involve any cutting into the abdominal wall. The procedure failed and as a result *P* was required to have an operation and spend a large sum of money. In addition, *P* was hospitalized for one month and could not return to work for a considerable period of time. *P* based his complaint on breach of contract—*Robins* v. *Finestone*, (5 CCH Negligence Cases 2d 16).

(a) Would the physicians' professional liability policy cover this loss?

(b) Would your answer have been the same if the suit were based on the fact that the physician had performed the operation in an unskillful manner? Explain.

7. What are the differences between professional liability contracts and other liability contracts? Discuss each kind.

8. In *Meiser* v. *Aetna Casualty & Surety Co.*, 98 N.W. (2nd) 919, the insured, a plastering subcontractor, spilled plaster on some expensive windows; in attempting to remove the plaster at the request of the owner, the windows were damaged. The plasterer was sued by the owner of the windows and the liability insurer under the CGL denied liability on grounds that the windows were "in his care, custody, and control," and therefore were excluded from coverage. Decide this case, stating your reasons.

9. In *Providence Washington Indemnity Co.* v. *Varella*, (8 CCH Fire and Casualty Cases 117), the insured had a CPL policy covering her residence and a hairdressing shop at another location. Later she moved her business to her home and after this relocation of the business, a patron was injured in a stairway accident. The insurer denied liability, under the CPL. The insured claimed that the CPL applies to all activities incidental to nonbusiness pursuits. Hence, her hairdressing activities were really incidental to running a home and should be covered. Is the insurer on sound grounds in denying liability? Why?

10. *C*, on a business trip, rents an outboard motorboat for some pleasure fishing. Due to careless handling, the boat runs into a swimmer, causing severe injuries. Will the CPL pay the claim? Why or why not?

11. A department store has a CGL policy with products liability covered. A woman came into the store to look at an automatic washer. After she purchased the washer, she asked to see once again how the bleach dispenser operated. During the demonstration of the machine, a metal strap snapped out and bruised her hand. Medical attention was necessary and a claim for damages resulted.

(a) Under which portion, if any, of the CGL policy would this claim be paid, if negligence is found?

(b) How, if at all, would your answer have changed if the accident had occurred after the washer had been delivered at the home of the buyer?

(c) What difference does it make as to which portion of the policy pays the loss? Explain.

12. The city of *Y* hires a contractor, *C*, to perform some work, and specifies that *C* name *Y* as an additional insured under his CGL. *Y* also requires *C* to sign a hold harmless agreement to the effect that *C* will assume any liability that *Y* might have arising out of the work which *C* is performing. *C* points out that such an agreement is unnecessary and, in fact, dangerous because the city would in effect be holding itself harmless for any liability arising out of the work.

(a) Do you agree? Why?

(b) In your opinion should the city not only require a hold harmless agreement but also be named as an additional insured? Discuss.

13. In *Maurice Pinoffs Co.* v. *St. Paul Fire & Marine* (315 Fed. Supp. 694), the insured imported canary seed which was sold in its original containers to eight feed and grain dealers. The seed was contaminated with chemical insecticide and caused the death of many birds. The insured had a CGL with products liability limits of $50,000 per occurrence, and also an excess cover, an umbrella liability policy. The first insurer paid its aggregate limit of $50,000, arguing that there was only one accident or occurrence. The excess insurer argued there were multiple occurrences and it was not obligated to pay anything until the limits of liability of the first insurer ($50,000 per occurrence) were paid first. The excess insurer argued that it was the sale of birdseed that was an occurrence and gave rise to liability, and each of the eight dealers sold the seed, creating a new "occurrence." Decide this case, stating your reasons.

14. A writer stated, "If both buyers and sellers, contractors and owners, and landlords and tenants will simply agree each to assume full responsibility for his own obligations according to law and each to rely on his own insurance for protection, the necessity for any sort of hold harmless clause in purchase orders, contracts, and leases will instantly cease." Do you agree? If so, why? If not, why not?

15. Which of the following claims, if any, would be defended under the CPL: (Give your reasons in each case.)

(a) A child riding a bicycle struck and injured a pedestrian. The child's parents were sued, but the supreme court found the child and not the parents liable.

(b) A child struck another child and threw him down an embankment, breaking his leg. The court found the parents liable because of their knowledge of the vicious propensities of the child.

(c) Two hunters, firing at the same time at a quail, injured a third hunter, who obtained a $10,000 judgment from each.

(d) The insured was sued when a guest tripped on steep stairs leading to the beach from an oceanside cabin which the insured maintained as a second residence.

(e) The insured's dog bit a "trespasser" who turned out to be the meter reader.

(f) The insured's dog, a police dog, killed another smaller dog in a somewhat uneven fight.

16. A customer of a department store purchased an electric heater which overheated and set fire to her home due to a failure in the electrical circuit. The customer brought action against the store for damages to her home plus the cost of a new heater. To what extent will the products liability policy of the store respond to this claim? Why?

17. A customer of the store in Question 16 hires one of the store's workers to apply some ceramic tile to the bathroom wall. Three weeks after the job is completed, one section of the tile comes loose and falls into the bathtub. Will the store's products liability policy respond to this claim? Why or why not?

18. The XYZ Manufacturing Company has purchased a CGL but has not bought contractual liability coverage with it. One day, the landlord informs XYZ that a nearby concern has brought an action against him arising out of XYZ's maintenance of the premises. It appears that XYZ's failure to control smoke emission has ruined certain raw materials through smoke deposits. The landlord observes that XYZ has agreed in the lease to hold him harmless for any claim arising out of the maintenance of the premises. Does XYZ have any protection against this claim under its CGL? Why or why not?

Chapter *Sixteen*

AUTOMOBILE INSURANCE

Automobiles, not an unmixed blessing in twentieth century America, were introduced in the United States at a time when mass-production methods were just becoming technically feasible. As a result, large numbers of automobiles were produced and sold before roads could be built or before other facilities were available to cope with the traffic problem. The industry has been able to accelerate the pace of manufacture of vehicles with a degree of speed and power that has tended to outpace the skill of drivers and the capacity of the highways. These two conditions, coupled with the fact that automobiles were cheap enough for nearly everyone to own, created an ideal climate for the growth of losses from liability claims, from collision, and from bodily injuries and deaths due to accidents. Insurance premiums have grown from an insignificant amount to a level where they are among the largest costs of owning and operating a car. Measured by premium volume, automobile insurance is by far the largest single segment of all property and liability insurance business, being almost as large as all other lines combined.[1]

THE HIGH COST OF AUTOMOBILE ACCIDENTS

The Insurance Information Institute[2] estimates that the economic losses from automobile accidents has increased from about $10.2 billion in 1960 to $30.4 billion in 1973, about $248 for each of the 122 million drivers that year. These costs include property damage; legal, medical, hospital, and funeral bills; loss of income; and the administrative costs of insurance. Deaths from motor vehicles, after rising sharply during the period 1961–1965, began to level off in the range of 53,000–56,000 annually after 1965. Automobiles deaths account for nearly half of all accidental deaths in the United States.

It is significant that in 1973, 23% of all drivers were involved in accidents. About 2.4% of these drivers were involved in fatal accidents. However, a disproportionate percentage of the total were young drivers. For example, drivers under 20 made up about 10% of all drivers, but accounted for 21% of all

[1] See Table 5-2, page 105.
[2] *Insurance Facts 1974,* p. 49.

accidents. Drivers between 20–29 made up about 21% of all drivers, but accounted for 30% of all accidents. Accident rates decline with age.

Death rates per 100,000 of population have remained fairly constant since 1925, ranging between 20 and 30 per 100,000 persons. Death rates per 10,000 registered vehicles, however, have declined steadily ever since automobiles came into widespread use.

According to data compiled by the actuaries of the New York State Insurance Department, the probability of a typical driver's having an accident over various periods of time is shown below:[3]

Years of Exposure	*Probability of Being Involved in at Least One Motor Vehicle Accident*
1	.24
3	.56
5	.75
10	.94
20	.99

Insurance Claims

Insurers have been faced with rising claims for all types of automobile insurance protection. Some statistics will illustrate the level to which claims have risen.

The average paid bodily injury claim increased from $1,129 to $2,044 over the 10-year period 1964–1973, a rise of 81%. Average property damage claims rose from $189 to $369 over the same period, an increase of 95%. In an effort to produce loss data to help auto manufacturers design safer and better cars, the Insurance Institute for Highway Safety conducts crash tests on different models. In tests of 1974 vehicles, for example, it was found that on balance, 1974 cars were no less susceptible to damage than 1973 models, and in some cases the damage was worse. For example, 1974 cars performed more poorly than 1973 models in front-end crash tests, but performed better in rear-end crash tests. Subcompact cars appeared to have higher loss frequency from collision than most other cars, but the cost of repair was a little less.[4] Through such findings it is hoped that eventually repair costs can be reduced and with them, insurance costs.

The federal government has begun to adopt minimum vehicle safety and antipollution standards aimed at improving the environment in which automobiles operate. For example, Motor Vehicle Safety Standard 215—Exterior Protection states that effective September 1, 1973, all new cars must resist a five-mile-per-hour impact, both front and rear, to meet specified damage criteria.[5]

[3] "Automobile Insurance . . . for Whose Benefit," *111th Annual Report of the New York State Insurance Department* (New York: Superintendent of Insurance, 1970), p. 157.

[4] *Insurance Facts 1974*, pp. 50-52.

[5] *Federal Motor Vehicle Standards and Regulations, Supplement 15* (Washington: U.S. Government Printing Office, March 15, 1972).

Causes of Automobile Accidents

There is no generally accepted or proved basic reason for accidents of any type, including, of course, automobile accidents. Explanations that automobile accidents are a result of psychological insecurity which is manifested by irrational behavior behind the wheel are interesting but unproved. About all that can be said is that certain factors can be identified which correlate with accident frequency and severity.

Statistical data reveal the conditions under which accidents occur, the types of drivers involved in the most accidents, etc. In Table 16-1, for example, data on major factors associated with fatal automobile accidents suggest that driving too fast and failing to observe the right of way of others are cited in about half of the cases. Driving errors are the predominant surface causes of loss in about three fourths of all fatal accidents. Other studies show that use of alcohol is undoubtedly one of the major causes of driving errors such as driving too fast.[6] Although safety belts are available in most cars, studies show that they are being used only 40% of the time. If safety belts were used all the time, between 8,000 and 10,000 lives annually would be saved in the United States. It is estimated that between 2,800 and 3,500 lives annually are being saved at present in cases where drivers have used them.[7]

CAUSAL FACTORS IN FATAL AUTO ACCIDENTS

Table 16-1

Factor	Percent of Accidents in Which Factor Was Cited
Driving too fast	25.2
Right of way violation	13.8
Driving left of center	12.0
Other driving errors	16.1
No improper driving stated	32.9
Total	100.0

Source: *Accident Facts, 1974 Edition* (National Safety Council, 1974), p. 48.

Other factors associated with automobile accidents from data gathered by the National Safety Council suggest the following conclusions regarding the nature of causal factors of accidents:

1. The probability of a pedestrian being killed by an auto is about one in five. Deaths caused by nighttime accidents are slightly more frequent than daytime accidents, but deaths caused by rural accidents are more than twice as frequent as those caused by urban accidents.
2. Superhighways are much safer than other roads, accounting for a third as many deaths as is true elsewhere.

[6] "Alcohol—A Factor in Half the Fatal Cases," *Accident Facts, 1972 Edition* (National Safety Council, 1972), p. 52.

[7] *Ibid.*, p. 53.

3. Highway deaths from riding bicycles are increasing twice as fast as other types of accidental deaths from automobiles.
4. Accidents occur slightly more often in areas without traffic-control markings or signals than where these signs are present.
5. Well over half of all accidents occur on weekends. Accidents occur less frequently in winter than in summer. Accidents rise during the year, peaking out in October.
6. Women drivers tend to have a lower accident rate than men. The rate of women drivers involved in fatal accidents per billion miles driven is 30, compared to 71 for men. However, this difference is not so great when all accidents, not just fatal accidents, are considered.
7. The death rate from motorcycles is about four times as great as that from overall motor vehicle death rates.
8. Defective tires and brakes account for about 68% of the defects found in vehicles involved in fatal accidents.
9. Nearly 80% of all accidents involve local residents. Apparently, unfamiliarity with local driving conditions is not a major factor in accidents.
10. Nearly 70% of all accidents occur on dry roads.
11. Death rates per 100 million miles are highest in the South and the Mountain States, and lowest in the West and in New England areas.
12. Among 20 countries surveyed, only Australia and Austria had a higher automobile death rate per 100,000 population than the United States. On a population basis, death rates less than half of that of the United States occurred in Mexico, Norway, and Spain. Comparisons on the basis of miles driven or number of vehicles registered are not available.

One should be cautious in drawing conclusions about the causes of automobile accidents from the above facts. For example, exposure to automobile accidents is far less in some countries than others, so it would be wrong to state categorically that Mexico is safer than the United States as a place to drive, based on the superior frequency record there. Nevertheless, it seems safe to conclude that good highways, uncrowded driving conditions, vehicles with protective features, and daylight all help reduce automobile accidents. Being under 25 is associated with factors that tend to result in more accidents, and being female is associated with factors that tend to result in fewer accidents than being over 25 or male, respectively.

Another conclusion seems to be that automobile accidents tend to accompany industrial development, rising incomes, and increased crowding of highways. Even though little can be done about the factors that produce accidents, perhaps more can be done to reduce the loss once it occurs. Examples of needed measures include the following: increased attention to safer and stronger cars, education to encourage more driver use of safety features, increased use of traveling first-aid vehicles to render more prompt and effective first aid to accident victims, and more emphasis on rehabilitation of injured persons. These are all areas which have been given relatively little attention, although similar measures have been applied very effectively in other areas.

Finally, it seems obvious that if highway safety is to be increased, the citizenry must seriously support stricter enforcement of traffic laws, particularly those relating to speeding and the observance of traffic signals.

THE NEED FOR INSURANCE

In the face of mounting costs of automobile accidents and the substantial probability of being involved in one, what should the average driver do to protect against the financial consequences of risk? For nearly everyone the answer has been insurance, in spite of its increasing cost. Insurance is almost a legal requirement in most states and is also far superior to running the economic risks without any protection (assumption of risk). Since most individuals own two automobiles at most, there is an insufficient exposure to allow self-insurance. Because of the personal catastrophic loss hazard involved in the liability risk, insurance is the only feasible solution.

THE FAMILY AUTOMOBILE POLICY (FAP)

Most automobile insurance contracts are written on three major forms—the *family automobile policy* (FAP), the *special package automobile policy*, and the *1955 standard automobile policy*. The FAP was introduced in 1956 and revised in 1958 and in 1963 as the basic coverage for noncommercial vehicles. Revisions in the FAP necessitated by no-fault laws are not reflected in the following discussion. No-fault laws are analyzed later in this chapter. The 1955 standard automobile policy, which formerly served the needs of both private and commercial automobile owners, is now employed primarily for commercial vehicles only. The special package auto policy, first introduced in 1959 and revised in 1963, is somewhat more limited than the FAP and generally costs less. The provisions of the three contracts are similar in most respects. An analysis of the FAP is given here because of its wide general use. Individual insurers often use slightly different forms to meet particular needs, to make their forms more salable, or to simplify them. Broadly speaking, however, an understanding of the FAP will enable the reader to analyze nearly any automobile contract. The five basic parts of the policy form are:

Section 1—Liability
Section 2—Medical payments
Section 3—Uninsured motorist protection
Section 4—Physical damage
Conditions

Section 1–Liability

Considerable similarity exists between the insuring agreements in Section 1 of the FAP and the insuring agreements in the liability contracts discussed in Chapter 15. Coverage is on an occurrence basis and the agreement to defend each suit arising out of the ownership, maintenance, or use of the owned, or of any nonowned, automobile is made part and parcel of the general insuring agreement to pay all bodily injury or property damage claims against the insured. The purpose here is to forestall the possibility that the insurer will be called upon to defend a suit against the insured even though the limits of liability under the contract have been exhausted or the suit did not even involve an automobile. Some courts have held that in liability policies the agreement to defend the insured is separate from the agreement to pay damages which the insured is legally obligated to pay. As a result of a decision of this type,[8] the FAP has combined its insuring agreement to reflect what has always been the actual intention of the insurer.

Illustrating these points, suppose that Carl carries liability limits of $10,000/$20,000 bodily injury ($10,000 each person, and $20,000 each occurrence) and $5,000 property damage. He is found to be negligent in an automobile accident and is required to pay a judgment of $4,000 to Jim, $3,000 to Sam, $11,000 to Harry for bodily injuries, plus $5,000 for the loss of Sam's building which was burned when Carl crashed into it. The FAP will respond in the amount of $17,000 for bodily injury liability, covering all of Jim's and Sam's claims, but only $10,000 of Harry's claim. Sam's property damage claim of $5,000 will be paid, plus all court costs and attorney's fees involved, if any. Later on, suppose Sam sues for an additional $3,000 under property damage liability when it is found that the fire also burned his new automobile. The FAP's limits have been exhausted for that accident and the insurer is not required to defend the second suit.

Persons Insured.[9] The FAP defines an insured in a very broad manner. Not only are all members of the named insured's household covered automatically, but so is anyone who is driving the owned auto with permission of the named insured or spouse.[10]

The policy further qualifies permissive use of the vehicle to include only those situations in which the user either had express permission or had good reason to believe that he had permission by implication, and that the use was within the scope of this permission. Note that a permissive user does not have the right to give someone else permission to drive,[11] nor the right to use the car for a purpose not contemplated by the owner when permission was given.

Not only does the FAP cover the named insured and permissive users, but, in addition, it provides certain coverage to those who are legally responsible for the use of the vehicle, providing the named insured or any additional insured using the auto at the time of the accident is first held to be liable. Thus, if an insured drives his or her personal car on an errand for an employer, and the insured is held liable for loss, and the resulting damage suit names the employer too, the employer is protected under the FAP.

With respect to nonowned automobiles (defined as cars not owned by or furnished for the regular use of the insured), the coverage is not quite so broad as it is with owned automobiles. The named insured and spouse have coverage

[8] *American Employers Insurance Company* v. *Goble Aircraft Specialities, Inc.*, 8 CCH Fire and Casualty Cases 437.

[9] Coverage of individuals other than the named insured is sometimes referred to as the *omnibus clause.*

[10] The definition of "named insured" includes spouse if a resident of the same household. No one else is empowered to give such permission.

[11] *Haines* v. *Linder*, 323 S.W.2d 505.

while driving *any* nonowned private passenger vehicles for business or nonbusiness use, if the car is not furnished for regular use. They also are covered for use of other types of nonowned vehicles, say commercial vehicles, if the use is not in connection with the insured's business. The insured is covered while driving any nonowned car. In addition, relatives who are residents of the named insured's household are also covered while driving a nonowned car providing this car is not regularly furnished for their use or being used for business purposes or used in the automobile business. To illustrate, assume that the named insured's son borrows a neighbor's car to run an errand and has an accident. The neighbor's car would be a nonowned car and hence the son is insured. However, if the neighbor's car were being used for business purposes or were a truck, the situation is different. The truck is not a private passenger automobile and coverage is not provided. Neither is coverage provided if the son is using the car to make a delivery in a business. However, the son would be insured under the neighbor's policy as a person driving with permission.

It may be observed that because of the way in which the FAP defines persons insured under the policy, it is impossible for two cars to be insured for the price of one. Suppose *A* and *B* decide to try to save on insurance costs and agree that *A* will take out insurance on his car, but use *B*'s car, which is to remain uninsured, to drive to work regularly. *B* will then drive *A*'s car and will be insured as a permissive user under *A*'s policy. Because of the definitions, *A* is not covered while driving *B*'s car because nonowned vehicles *furnished for regular use* are not covered under *A*'s policy. Since there is no insurance on *B*'s car, *A* is not insured as a permissive user of *B*'s car. The only person to have coverage under this arrangement is *B* while he is driving *A*'s car.

Because of the very broad definition of insured, in some cases an insurer may be required to pay liability claims which one insured may have against another insured. For example, the named insured lends her car to a neighbor who in negligently backing out of the garage strikes and injures the named insured. The named insured may now bring an action against the neighbor who is also an insured under the policy. The insurance company is required to defend the neighbor and pay any judgments which may be handed down in favor of the named insured. In other cases, the named insured and spouse may own two cars and have a collision. One spouse may bring an action against the other in such cases; the insurer must of course defend the suit.

What Is an Automobile? The FAP contains definitions of different types of automobiles, but does not define an automobile itself. Under existing rules, however, the FAP insures the following: private passenger cars, station wagons, jeeps, pickup trucks or farm trucks with a load capacity of 1,500 pounds or less, trailers designed for use with private passenger automobiles, and farm wagons or implements (for liability and medical payment only). Motorcycles, motor scooters, and other vehicles of fewer than four wheels must be insured under the 1955 standard automobile policy. Newly acquired cars are covered automatically, with premiums due from the date of acquisition. The insured is required to notify the insurer within 30 days after the date of acquisition if the new car is in addition to other cars covered under the policy and no other insurance on this new car exists. The FAP excludes coverage on newly-acquired cars which are insured elsewhere.

Exclusions of the FAP. In general, the exclusions in the FAP serve the purpose of eliminating wasteful duplication of insurance. For example, using a private car as a taxi or a public livery is excluded because this represents a business risk for which special coverage is designed. (But note that if the insured is held legally liable for an accident while riding as a passenger in a taxi, his FAP covers him.)

Liability for damage to property in the insured's care, custody, or control is excluded because physical loss of movable property is usually covered under fire insurance forms (for example, loss from vehicles in the extended coverage endorsement). Workers' compensation claims are excluded as are accidents for which an automobile business liability policy (for example, garage liability) would normally respond. Thus, if a service station employee is driving an insured's car while testing it and has an accident, there is no coverage under the FAP, since it is assumed that the station's garage liability policy will cover this type of claim. However, use by the insured of his or her private passenger car in an occupation or profession is not excluded, nor is the insured's similar use of a nonowned private passenger car.

Cancellation. The liability coverage under the FAP may be cancelled upon ten days' notice by the insurer, with pro rata refund of premiums. The 1963 revision of the FAP provided that the cancellation privilege is not available to the insurer, however, except for certain reasons. Nearly all states have statutes relating to midterm insurance cancellation provisions. Under these statutes, the policy may be cancelled by the insurer only for such reasons as follows: (a) the insured automobile is so defective as to endanger public safety, or is being used as a taxi or in such other specified ways as to increase the risk materially; (b) the insured has failed to pay premiums, has concealed material information, or has made material misrepresentations in the application; (c) the insured has moved to a territory where the insurer does not operate; (d) the insured has been convicted of criminal negligence or certain other traffic violations; (e) the insured has certain physical disabilities such as epilepsy, heart attack, or mental conditions. The list of exceptions is often so broad as to be virtually unrestrictive of the insurer's right to cancel. However, it should be noted that the insurer may not generally cancel the policy in midterm solely for the reason that the insured has had a large loss.

State laws also restrict nonrenewal practices of automobile insurers, such as requiring 10 to 30 days' notice of intent not to renew coverage.

Financial Responsibility Laws. The FAP provides that in states with financial responsibility laws it will "comply with the provisions of such law to the extent of the coverage and limits of liability required by such law." It is possible, for example, that the insured might have violated certain conditions in the policy, thus negating coverage, but under the laws of the state the insurer is required to make payment to an injured party regardless of its right to deny liability on the insured's behalf because of the violated conditions.[12] In such a case the insurer will make the required payment to an injured third party but may bring an action against the insured for reimbursement. The purpose of this provision in the policy is to make the FAP conform to those laws of the state that regulate financial responsibility of motorists within that state.

Other Insurance. The other insurance clause, which is very important, provides that if more than one policy applies to a given loss involving an owned car, the FAP will contribute on a pro rata basis with such other contracts. However, with respect to nonowned cars or temporary substitute automobiles, the FAP is to be considered excess. Thus, if Maude borrows Sybil's car and negligently injures someone, both owners being covered by the FAP, Sybil's policy is responsible to the extent of the limits of liability carried, and if damages exceed these limits, Maude's policy then contributes.

Section 2–Medical Payments

Medical payments insurance is automobile insurance designed to pay for medical claims of occupants arising from automobile accidents without regard to fault. Payment is made for *reasonable* expenses incurred within one year from the date of accident for necessary medical, surgical, X-ray, and dental services, including funeral expenses. Medical payments insurance covers all persons, including the named insured and residents of named insured's household, who are injured while occupying an owned or nonowned automobile (meaning entering, leaving, or while in or upon the vehicle) regardless of the question of negligence. Medical payments also cover the named insured and any resident relative who is struck by an automobile.

There are at least three important reasons for medical payments coverage. First, there is the fact that guests in an automobile might feel hesitant in bringing legal action against their host for negligent driving in order to recover for their medical bills. Yet, such action is technically required under the legal liability portion of the contract. Also, guest-host statutes in many states prevent successful negligence actions against drivers of automobiles unless *gross* negligence can be proved. Thus, without medical payments coverage, many medical bills simply would not be covered. Second, a negligent host would normally feel a moral obligation to provide for at least the medical bills of guests, even if it is determined that the host is not to blame for the accident. But in the absence of negligence, the insurer has no obligation to pay for such costs under the liability portion of the automobile contract. Third, experience indicates that if prompt settlement of all medical costs is made, there is much less likelihood that injured guests will bring negligence action, with its resulting defense costs and possibility of large judgments for such factors as loss of income and mental anguish. Medical payments coverage thus tends to minimize liability losses under the policy, with a resulting lower premium for the insured.

[12] *United States Casualty Co.* v. *Timmerman,* 180 Atl. 629 (1935), was one of the first cases upholding this provision.

Limits of Liability. Medical payments insurance is written with limits of liability between $500 and $5,000 per person. If there are six passengers in a vehicle and the owner has elected to purchase limits of say $2,000, there would be a total limit of $12,000 for all necessary medical costs arising from a single accident. It is possible that a passenger could collect under medical payments and also bring a negligence action against the driver and recover again for the same costs.[13] Medical payments insurance is actually a health insurance contract, which is not a contract of indemnity. The insurer reserves no right of subrogation in claims arising under the medical payments section, and if a passenger brings a successful action against the host, say for gross negligence, the insurer has no right to any collections made by the injured passenger.

Persons Insured. The contract of medical payments is in two sections, Division 1 for the named insured and members of named insured's household, and Division 2 for other persons.

Division 1 provides broad coverage, and compensable accidents are not confined to situations where the insured is a passenger in a car, but occur when the insured is occupying or is struck by an automobile or trailer of any type. Thus, the insured's family is covered for almost any automobile accident while a passenger or a pedestrian.

Division 2, covering medical costs of other passengers, gives complete coverage for injuries arising in the insured's owned automobile so long as the car is being operated by an authorized person (that is, the insured or persons driving with permission of the insured). As for nonowned cars, passengers are covered only if the insured, servants, or relatives are driving the nonowned car.

Exclusions. There are certain limitations on the application of medical payments insurance as outlined in the exclusions. For example, since use of the vehicle as a taxi or a public livery is excluded, medical payments insurance does not apply in such cases. The intent of the policy is to deny medical payments coverage to the named insured while operating a commercial vehicle (such as a truck) for business purposes, but not if it is used on personal business. If the insured is operating a nonowned passenger car on personal business, medical payments coverage is provided.

Other Insurance. The medical payments section provides that if medical payments insurance applies to a loss suffered when the insured is driving a nonowned automobile or a temporary substitute automobile, the other owner's coverage, if any, applies first and the insured's medical payments coverage is excess. Thus, if Lester, who has his FAP written with $500 medical payments, borrows Jim's car which is covered for $1,000 medical payments and has an accident which necessitates the expenditure of $1,250 in medical bills, Jim's policy will pay $1,000 and Lester's FAP will pay the remaining $250.

[13] This principle was upheld in *Severson* v. *Milwaukee Automobile Insurance Co.*, 3 CCH Auto 2d 1011.

Section 3–Uninsured Motorist Protection

Uninsured motorist protection is aimed at protecting the insured from loss by uninsured or hit-and-run drivers. Essentially the provision says, "If you should be struck and injured by a negligent motorist who happens to carry no liability insurance, you may bring legal action against your own insurer just as though your insurer covered the other party as well as yourself."

In most states, coverage is limited to bodily injury liability claims, and insureds are expected to carry physical damage coverage for losses to their own property. In a few states, however, the insured motorist protection applies to property damage (as excess coverage over physical damage protection) as well as bodily injury. In these states, a substantial deductible applies. Thus, a $250 deductible applies to such claims in Georgia and New Mexico; $200 in South Carolina and Virginia; $300 in West Virginia; and $100 in New Jersey and North Carolina. Uninsured motorist protection is compulsory in some states.[14] In New York the coverage applies to all residents, whether or not they are owners of automobiles, for accidents occuring in New York. A person residing in New York may purchase uninsured motorist protection for accidents which may occur outside the state.

Protection is extended to the named insured and any relative, passengers in the insured automobile, and other persons who would have a legal right to collect for bodily injuries suffered through the negligence of the uninsured motorist. Thus, the father of a minor child who was injured as a passenger would be protected. The uninsured automobile is defined to include hit-and-run automobiles, and other cars which are being operated without any applicable insurance protection. What constitutes an uninsured auto is carefully spelled out. For example, cars owned by the named insured, cars owned by political subdivisions or governmental agencies, trailer houses being used as a residence, or farm-type tractors or equipment except while operating on public roads, are not "uninsured autos" within the meaning of the coverage.

Uninsured motorist protection contains certain limitations. For example, if the insured were entitled to recover under a workers' compensation law for the bodily injuries suffered at the hands of the uninsured motorist, any liability under the policy is reduced by the amount of such compensation. Coverage under the uninsured motorist protection is excess over any other coverage available to the insured as an operator of a nonowned car. If the negligent uninsured motorist has other assets which are later attached by the insured, the insurer can recover the amounts paid to the extent of recoveries made by the insured against the guilty party.

Coverage under the uninsured motorist protection is usually limited to the basic limits of liability under the applicable financial responsibility law of the state. These limits are normally $10,000/$20,000 for bodily injury and $5,000 for

[14] As of 1971 the coverage was compulsory in Connecticut, Illinois, Maine, Massachusetts, Minnesota, New Hampshire, New York, Oregon, Pennsylvania, South Carolina, Vermont, Virginia, and West Virginia.

property damage. The uninsured or hit-and-run driver must be found negligent before the insurer must respond. In the event of disagreement over the question of negligence or the amount of loss, the parties are required to submit to an arbitration procedure to settle the differences.

Section 4–Physical Damage

The FAP combines liability and medical payments coverage with indemnification of the insured in case the insured's automobile is damaged by almost any type of peril, regardless of the insured's fault. It is obvious that the insured will not always be able to recover from a third party for damage to the vehicle. For example, the insured could be contributorially negligent, or the loss could be caused by perils other than collision (say theft). Thus, the FAP is really a schedule policy on which the insured may purchase insurance against loss due to legal liability, fire and related perils, medical costs, and theft. In other words, the FAP insures automobile owners against almost every type of loss to their automobiles or to themselves that arises out of the use of automobiles.

Physical damage coverage includes several types of indemnity, as follows:

Comprehensive loss
Collision loss
Fire, lightning, and transportation loss
Theft
Combined additional coverage
Towing and labor costs
Supplementary payments

Comprehensive Loss. *Comprehensive coverage,* as it applies in the FAP, covers all loss to the insured vehicle other than collision (subject to certain exclusions). To clarify what is meant by comprehensive, the contract specifies certain sources of loss which are to be construed as comprehensive and not as collision. Thus, breakage of glass or loss caused by missiles, falling objects, fire, theft or larceny, explosion, earthquake, windstorm, hail, water, flood, vandalism or malicious mischief, riot, and civil commotion are to be construed as comprehensive. In a case where the vehicle went off the road into the river and was damaged by water, the court held the damage to be done by collision and comprehensive insurance did not cover it.[15] Because of a lack of consistency in such cases and the resulting difficulty in predicting what a jury will decide, it would appear that an insured who desires complete physical damage protection against loss should take collision and comprehensive insurance.

Collision Loss. Collision with another object or upset of the automobile is normally subject to a flat dollar deductible amount of $50 or $100. Larger deductibles are permitted and corresponding reductions in the premium are granted. Collision coverage applies to a utility trailer, subject to an upper limit of $500. For large and valuable trailers, such as mobile homes, separate collision coverage must be purchased. Coverage against collision loss extends to

[15] *Ringo* v. *Automobile Insurance Co.,* 22 Pac.2d 887.

nonowned cars that the insured or any relative is driving, but such coverage is excess over any other valid and collectible collision insurance.

Collision is defined in the policy to include running into another object or upset. Interpretations have made it clear that the insured car need not be in motion itself nor does the collision have to be with another vehicle. For example, if a car strikes a cement barrier in the middle of the road and 20 miles later it is discovered that the engine is ruined because of a hole in the oil pan, the loss may be collected under collision insurance. Parked cars hit by another vehicle suffer collision damage.

Fire, Lightning, and Transportation Loss. One who does not wish to purchase a full, comprehensive coverage may secure a more limited coverage against the perils of fire, lightning, smoke, or smudge due to faulty operation of heating equipment in the premises in which the automobile is located, and by the stranding, sinking, burning, collision, or derailment of a conveyance in which the car is being transported.

The FAP provides a very limited coverage on personal effects damaged while they are in or upon the automobile. Loss is covered only if caused by fire or lightning while the effects are in or upon an *owned* car and is subject to a limit of $100. Thus, property burned while temporarily out of the automobile, or belonging to guests, or belonging to the insured while driving a nonowned car would not be covered. No extra charge is made for this insurance since it is a part of the comprehensive coverage.

Towing and Labor Costs. Under the FAP the car owner may elect to insure against towing and labor costs that result from a breakdown of the car. Coverage is limited to $25 in most states. Labor must be performed at the place of disablement.

Supplementary Payments. The FAP provides for compensation to the insured for loss of use of a stolen car at the rate of not over $10 per day, subject to an aggregate limitation of $300. The payment begins after a 48-hour waiting period and ceases when the car is returned to use or when the insurer settles with the insured for the lost vehicle.

The FAP agrees to reimburse the insured for liability for general average or salvage claims arising out of the transportation of the automobile. Such claims may arise, for example, when the vehicle is being transported on a ferry and there is a voluntary but necessary sacrifice of goods to save the ship during a storm. Each owner of cargo is required to contribute pro rata to the owner of the jettisoned property. The insurer of the car owner with such a liability must meet this demand.

Physical Damage Exclusions. Among the excluded perils of Section 3 of the FAP are war, use as a public livery, wear and tear, freezing, and mechanical or electrical breakdown. Damage to tires is excluded under the comprehensive coverage unless this damage is caused by certain described perils, namely, fire, vandalism, theft, or unless it is coincident with some other loss covered by the policy. For example, if the car is stolen and as a result the motor freezes up, or the tires are ruined through speeding over a rough road, the damage would be covered. The same damage caused by the insured's carelessness would be excluded.

Conditions

The major conditions of the FAP are similar to those of other insurance policies. The following comments concern those conditions which apply only to automobile insurance.

Premium. The FAP gives automatic coverage, without the requirement of notice to the insurer, on all newly acquired autos which replace the insured autos. Any premium adjustment needed is made as of the date of acquisition of the new vehicle. For new additions to a fleet, however, there is no automatic coverage unless the insured has all fleet cars covered with the same insurer and notifies this insurer either during the policy period or within 30 days of the acquisition that coverage is desired on the additional auto.

Two or More Automobiles. The FAP requires that if there is more than one automobile covered, the limits of liability apply separately to each vehicle unless a car and a trailer are involved in the same accident. In that event the liability limits apply as though there were just one vehicle involved, but the physical damage limits apply as if there were two vehicles involved. The effect of this is that any deductibles for physical damage insurance would apply separately to the car and to the trailer, but existence of a car and a trailer would not serve to double the liability limits.

Assistance and Cooperation. The assistance and cooperation condition is quite typical in all insurance contracts. In automobile insurance, it is particularly important because of a sentence stating:

> The insured shall not, except at his own cost, voluntarily make any payment, *assume any obligation,* or incur any expense other than for such immediate medical and surgical relief to others as shall be imperative at the time of accident.

It is common for individuals involved in accidents to say something like this to the other driver, "I'm very sorry. It was all my fault. My insurer will see that everything is taken care of." Oftentimes it is discovered that it was not the insured's fault at all but that because of a statement admitting guilt (which unhappily may be witnessed), the court finds the insured liable. In such cases the insurer appears to be justified in denying liability.

Subrogation. The FAP reserves the right of subrogation against liable third parties for physical damage and liability insurance, but not in the case of medical payments. If the insured does anything to prejudice such rights, a warranty has been violated and the insurer may deny liability under the policy.

Business Versus Nonbusiness Forms

The FAP, as the name suggests, is available only for nonbusiness consumers. Business consumers either take coverage under the 1955 standard automobile policy, or under an increasingly popular form known as the comprehensive automobile liability policy. In general, the provisions of the FAP and these two policies are similar, the chief differences arising from the fact that business vehicles tend to be more varied than is common for nonbusiness vehicles. The comprehensive automobile liability policy, for example, grants automobile insurance on power cranes, welding trucks or machinery, and air compressor trucks or spray rigs while such vehicles are being towed or driven to and from a job. However, such equipment as crawler-type tractors, concrete mixers, and graders, designed for use off public roads, are not considered to be automobiles unless they are being towed or carried to and from a job. Liability for such equipment is intended to be covered under the comprehensive general liability policy.

Nonownership Liability Insurance

Individuals may be liable for the use of automobiles even if they do not personally own vehicles of any sort. A person may be responsible as a result of directing the driving of a car, or because someone else is driving a car on his or her behalf.

There is automatic protection for nonownership liability under the FAP for the insured and spouse with the exception of cars furnished for their regular use, cars being driven without permission of the owner, or commercial-type vehicles used in business. By payment of additional premiums, a policy endorsement called *extended nonowned automobile coverage* may be added to the FAP granting coverage for cars regularly furnished to the insured and for business use of commercial vehicles. The same endorsement may be written to cover relatives in the same household. A similar endorsement may be added to the 1955 standard automobile policy. Also, nonownership liability coverage may be obtained for officers of corporations, partners of the insured, and co-owners of automobiles by endorsement to the basic contract covering operation of the vehicle.

An individual who does not own a vehicle may secure coverage for nonownership liability by use of the named nonowner endorsement on a standard contract which assumes that no automobile is owned. This coverage, like all nonownership liability insurance, is excess over other applicable insurance.

AUTOMOBILE INSURANCE AND THE LAW

In every state and in all the provinces of Canada, legislatures have passed some form of automobile insurance law designed to solve the problem of the uncompensated victim of financially irresponsible automobile drivers. In other words, the law has stepped in because without some system of financial guarantees, motorists are forced to use the method of assumption of risk whether they are financially able to or not. Most often they are not. Accordingly, legislatures have attempted various methods to cope with the problem. Laws have taken the following forms:

1. Financial responsibility laws.
2. Compulsory liability insurance laws.
3. Unsatisfied judgment fund.
4. Uninsured motorist endorsement.
5. No-fault and compensation laws.
6. Government auto insurance.

Financial Responsibility Laws

Financial responsibility laws represent by far the most common approach to the general problem of the uncompensated victim of the financially irresponsible motorist. There are two basic requirements of most such laws:

1. Motorists without liability insurance who are involved in an automobile accident must obtain and maintain liability insurance or other proof of financial responsibility (say, a surety bond) of a specified character for a given period, usually three years, as a condition of continued licensing of the operator and registration of the vehicle.
2. Motorists without liability insurance who are involved in an automobile accident must pay for the damages they have caused, or give evidence that they were not to blame, as a condition for the continued operation of their vehicle.

In their early development, financial responsibility laws often contained only the first requirement; but gradually the second requirement, called *security provisions,* was added. Financial responsibility laws have no penalty other than the suspension of driving privileges, and hence are not guarantees that the uncompensated victim will actually be paid. The effectiveness of the laws in this regard rests upon the hope that most drivers will be led to purchase insurance rather than face possible loss of their driving privileges.

Financial responsibility laws have the following points in common:

1. A great majority specify that insurance policies must have limits of $10,000/$20,000 bodily injury and $5,000 property damage liability, although a few states have limits of $5,000/$10,000 bodily injury liability. A few states have higher limits such as $15,000/$30,000 bodily injury and $10,000 property damage, or $20,000/$40,000 and $10,000.
2. A majority of laws do not apply to accidents where less than $100 (or $50) of property damage is caused and there is no bodily injury caused by the accident.
3. Most laws apply to both the owner and the driver.
4. A majority of laws specify that both the driver's license and the vehicle registration be suspended for violation of the law.
5. Over 90% of all laws provide that the insurer may not deny liability to the accident victim even if it is not liable to the insured because of some breach of policy condition. The insurer must pay the claim but may, of course, attempt to recover from the insured for payments made under these conditions.
6. In most states insurers participate in an assigned risk plan whereby drivers who have been refused coverage from one insurer may obtain coverage, sometimes at a higher rate, from another insurer. Each insurer agrees to take a certain number of so-called bad risks.
7. About 80% of the laws require that proof of future responsibility be maintained regardless of the negligence of the operator. Thus, an owner who does not carry liability insurance and who is involved in an accident causing bodily injury to

others through no fault of his own is still required to maintain proof or responsibility for the specified future period.

8. Driving privileges are restored to a driver once he has paid the amount of liability specified by the maximum legal limits, even though the actual judgment is much larger and is still unsatisfied. For example, if a $50,000 property damage judgment is obtained against Doe, Doe can get back his driver's license once the $5,000 which is usually specified as the maximum property damage liability limit has been paid.
9. Three fourths of the laws have reciprocity provisions whereby suspension of privileges in another state applies in the home state as well. Thus, if Doe is involved in an accident while on vacation in another state and a judgment is rendered against Doe in this state for damages, the home state treats this as though the violation had occurred there and will also remove Doe's driving privileges until the judgment is satisfied.
10. It is common to allow certain exceptions under the law, such as when the vehicle is legally parked at the time of an accident, or if the vehicle is legally owned by some governmental agency, or if it is being driven by a person using it without permission. Under such conditions the owner is not subject to the provisions of the financial responsibility law.

Weaknesses of Financial Responsibility Laws. Although financial responsibility laws are better than nothing, they have serious drawbacks as solutions to the problem of compensating victims of uninsured or financially irresponsible motorists. Major weaknesses include:

1. There is no assurance that all drivers will have liability insurance. The laws aim only at assuring financial responsibility for the irresponsible motorist's second and subsequent victims, not the first victim.
2. The penalty for not complying with the law is weak; the motorist is subject only to the loss of driving privileges.
3. There is no protection against hit-and-run, stolen car, or illegally driving motorists; enforcement procedures against these drivers is difficult and relatively unsuccessful. It is estimated that at least 15% or 20% of registered vehicles in the United States lack liability insurance.[16] Injury victims recover an average of only about half of their total loss from tort claims against negligent drivers.[17]
4. Because of lack of uniformity among states, such as differences in liability limits, settlements involving out-of-state drivers are often uncertain.
5. Drivers unable to obtain regular insurance to satisfy the financial responsibility provisions may also be unable to obtain satisfactory rates or complete coverage under assigned risk plans.
6. There is no recovery without provable negligence. Proof often involves difficult, expensive, and time-consuming procedures.

Those in favor of financial responsibility statutes are usually opposed to any further strengthening which probably would lead either to compulsory insurance or a compensation system similar to workers' compensation laws. The proponents point out that these laws, where they have been enforced effectively and are doing a good job of meeting the problem, have generally resulted in a very high percentage of insured drivers.

[16] U.S. Department of Transportation, *Motor Vehicle Crash Losses and their Compensation in the United States* (Washington: U.S. Government Printing Office, 1971), p. 28.
[17] *Ibid.*, p. 36.

Conclusion. General dissatisfaction with financial responsibility laws has resulted in a national movement to strengthen and extend them. Compulsory liability statutes and no-fault laws are being rapidly adopted in many states to solve the problem of compensating the victims of uninsured motorists.

Compulsory Liability Insurance Laws

Three states—Massachusetts, New York, and North Carolina—have gone one step further than the passage of financial responsibility laws and have adopted compulsory liability insurance statutes. In these states every resident must have purchased a specified type of liability insurance *before* being given a registration certificate or driving privileges. Connecticut, Maryland, and Rhode Island have laws that make the purchase of insurance compulsory for minors, with certain exceptions, while Illinois requires all trucks registered in the state to be covered by liability insurance, with certain exceptions.

Compulsory liability insurance has been in force in Massachusetts since 1927. New York's law, effective in 1957, and North Carolina's, effective in 1958, attempted to remedy some of the defects inherent under the Massachusetts system.

In Massachusetts every application for registration of a vehicle must be accompanied by evidence of bodily injury liability insurance with limits of $5,000/$10,000. In 1971 the law was amended to provide $2,000 of no-fault benefits, and property damage liability of $5,000 was made compulsory for the first time. The limits of compulsory liability coverage in New York are $10,000/$20,000 and $5,000, and in North Carolina, $15,000/$30,000 and $5,000. Between 1971 and 1975, some 23 states including New York passed no-fault laws, all but one of which (Kentucky) make liability insurance compulsory, indicating in varying degrees the dissatisfaction with the voluntary aspects of financial responsibility laws and with unlimited negligence liability as a basis for compensating victims for losses suffered from automobile accidents.

Unsatisfied Judgment Fund

The *unsatisfied judgment fund (UJF)* is a fund set up by a state to pay automobile accident settlements which cannot be collected by any other means.[18] If the negligent motorist is insolvent, does not carry liability insurance, or has voided insurance through violation of a policy provision, or if the insurer is insolvent, the innocent victim may collect from the unsatisfied judgement fund after every other means of collections is exhausted. The UJF is actually broader than compulsory insurance, since it covers cases in which insurance was carried but the damage is still uncollectible. However, the UJF is based on the principle of negligence; if there is no legal liability there can be no payment from the fund. Furthermore, the UJF has the right of subrogation; that is, it must be paid back by the negligent motorist if he obtains

[10] Unsatisfied judgment funds exist in New Jersey, Maryland, Michigan, North Dakota, New York, Manitoba, Alberta, British Columbia, Newfoundland, Nova Scotia, Ontario, and Prince Edward Island.

property on which liens may be obtained. In any case, the negligent motorist loses his driving privileges until the fund is repaid.

Uninsured Motorist Endorsement

The solution to the problem of the uncompensated victim of the uninsured motorist has been proposed and supported by private insurance companies in the form of an endorsement to the automobile policy known as the *uninsured motorists protection,* also known as the *uninsured motorist endorsement (UME).* Under the terms of this endorsement, which usually applies only to bodily injury claims,[19] if it is determined that an insured driver is injured by another driver who is uninsured, the insured driver's company will act as the insurer of the negligent motorist and pay any legal liability that the negligent uninsured motorist would be obligated to pay. The insurer naturally has the right to collect from the negligent uninsured motorist for any damages paid to the insured motorist.

The UME does not go so far as the UJF or compulsory liability insurance in solving the problem of compensating innocent victims of uninsured motorists, but it does overcome an important weakness in the typical financial responsibility law. For a small charge, an individual may be protected against bodily injury damage caused by uninsured motorists at least for minimum limits. While the individual does not always receive similar protection for property damage, physical damage insurance can always be purchaed for protection against property loss.

No-Fault and Compensation Laws

In recent years, there is a growing body of opinion that the economic importance of automobile accidents is such that we can no longer trust the legal liability system with the task of solving the problem of compensating the victims. It is argued that it is impossible to determine the precise degree of negligence in a given accident, even if any existed, and that too often the automobile accident victim is without any means to meet the cost involved. It is said that it is the person with the best lawyer and the most cooperative witness who is compensated, and the scientific method is conspicuous by its absence. The concept of fault in a society on whcels is not workable. In recognition of this argument a number of states have passed no-fault laws under which injured victims in automobile accidents must recover loss (up to a stated amount) under their own automobile policies rather than under tort liability policies of other parties.

Background of No-Fault. The problem of uncompensated victims of uninsured motorists has been studied intensively. Perhaps the best known work was written by Robert E. Keeton and Jeffrey O'Connell, whose book was a major

[19] The uninsured motorist protection applies to property damage, subject to deductibles ranging from $100 to $300, in Georgia, New Mexico, North Carolina, South Carolina, Virginia and West Virginia.

influence in initiating a national movement toward no-fault laws.[20] This movement was further motivated by the U.S. Department of Transportation in an extensive study of the automobile accident problem. The so-called DOT study was published in 28 volumes in 1970–1971. In 1971, the National Association of Insurance Commissioners, an advisory committee to the U.S. Department of Transportation, recommended that individual state legislatures pass no-fault laws. As of this writing, 23 states have passed such laws which, although not uniform in their provisions, are all aimed at overcoming some of the weaknesses in the tort liability system. In some ways the laws are similar in concept to workers' compensation statutes, which provide reimbursement for occupational injuries without regard to fault.

Weaknesses of Tort Liability. The major weaknesses of the tort-liability system in making compensation to victims of automobile accidents include:

1. The system, depending mainly on voluntary purchase of liability insurance to provide the funds for compensation, leaves many victims uncompensated because of absence of provable negligence or lack of insurance.
2. Victims suffering small losses are overcompensated, and victims suffering large losses are undercompensated.
3. Victims often suffer long delays in recovery due to the slow operation of the court system.
4. The costs of attorneys, insurance companies, and courts absorb too large a proportion of total loss claims.
5. There is insufficient use of and incentive for rehabilitation.
6. The system leads to dishonesty in claims and defense of suits.

The DOT study[21] revealed that over 91% of those with serious injuries received some form of compensation from one or more sources for their economic loss. Nearly half received medical benefits from their family medical insurance, and 35% benefited from auto medical expense insurance. Another 46% received medical settlements under tort liability. The following proportions of families with serious injuries or fatalities received compensation from the sources indicated: medical insurance, 48.2%; life insurance, 7.2%; auto medical, 35%; collision insurance, 29.1%; net tort liability claims, 45.9%; sick leave benefits, 8.1%; workers' compensation, 6.9%; social security benefits, 2%.[22] It was obvious that considerable duplication of benefits existed.

[20] Robert E. Keeton and Jeffrey O'Connell, *Basic Protection for the Traffic Victim* (Boston: Little, Brown and Co., 1966).

[21] U.S. Department of Transportation, *Economic Consequences of Automobile Accident Injuries*, Vol. 1 (Washington: U.S. Government Printing Office, 1970), pp. 26-28. This study was based on a representative national sample of persons drawn from records of reported accidents. Wage losses were based on actual pay rates of injured persons at the time of the accident, unadjusted for income taxes. Lost future earnings were based on average earnings for major occupational groups, as compiled by the Bureau of Census, discounted for interest, and adjusted for differences between male and female earnings, and for the maintenance cost of the disabled person. Lost future earnings of unemployed persons such as homemakers were estimated at $4,000 per year.

[22] *Ibid.*, p. 37.

Partly because of this duplication, it was discovered that those suffering relatively small economic losses recovered benefits which exceeded several times their total losses, while those with large claims recovered only a fraction of their total losses. Recoveries under tort liability equaled 60% of total recoveries. As shown in Table 16–2, the discrimination was much greater between people getting tort-liability settlements and those where such protection was unavailable. Thus, those with losses under $500 recovered 4.5 times their actual loss in reparations, while those with losses of $25,000 and over recovered an average of 30% of their losses.

Other important findings were:

1. Slightly less than half of all claimants were able to recover under tort liability.
2. The average time lapse between the accident and the final settlement was 16 months.[23]
3. Among all classes of injured persons, pedestrians were most successful and cyclists least successful in making recoveries under tort liability.[24]
4. Only 7% of those with serious injuries took physical or psychological therapy; .6% had vocational therapy.[25]
5. System expenses average $1.07 to deliver $1 in benefits to the injured automobile accident victims.[26] These expenses include claimants' expenses (mainly attorneys' fees), insurer litigation expenses, insurer sales and administrative expenses, court costs, and public costs of regulating liability insurers.
6. Many drivers do not purchase auto liability insurance. The DOT study estimated the liability insurance coverage for private passenger cars as follows:[27]

90% and over	3 states
85%-89%	8 states
80%-84%	9 states
75%-79%	9 states
70%-74%	7 states
65%-69%	3 states
Under 65%	5 states

Thus the automobile driver runs a substantial chance that the person with whom he or she is involved in an accident will not have insurance. Although the driver can often claim under the uninsured motorists endorsement, this coverage is usually limited to bodily losses and only where negligence of the other driver can be established.

DOT Recommendations. The DOT study made the following recommendations regarding the method of solving the problems which were discovered:

[23] *Ibid.*, p. 52.

[24] *Ibid.*, p. 55.

[25] *Ibid.*, p. 58.

[26] U.S. Department of Transportation, *Motor Vehicle Crash Losses and their Compensation in the United States* (Washington: U.S. Government Printing Office, 1971), pp. 49-51.

[27] U.S. Department of Transportation, *Driver Behavior and Accident Involvement: Implications for Tort Liability* (Washington: U.S. Government Printing Office, 1970), p. 205. Estimates for six states were not available.

Table 16-2

RATIO OF RECOVERIES TO LOSSES IN AUTOMOBILE ACCIDENTS

Economic Loss	Number of Persons with Some Recovery	Percent with Tort Recovery	Ratio of Net Recovery to Loss		Percent Tort to Total Recovery
			With	Without	
$1-$499	19,500	54.3	4.5	.8	92
$500-$999	42,700	62.6	2.6	.5	72
$1,000-$1,499	54,000	49.3	2.4	.7	79
$1,500-$2,499	95,600	46.9	2.0	1.0	63
$2,500-$4,999	109,300	43.6	1.6	.6	64
$5,000-$9,999	57,000	44.2	1.1	.6	63
$10,000-$24,999	28,200	52.3	.7	.4	72
$25,000 and over	42,600	41.8	.3	.3	42
Total	448,900	47.7	.6	.4	60

Source: U.S. Department of Transportation, *Economic Consequences of Automobile Accident Injuries*, Vol. 1 (Washington: U.S. Government Printing Office, 1970), p. 47.

1. After some experimentation and testing, state legislatures should move toward a compulsory first-party insurance covering all economic losses above certain voluntarily accepted deductibles of reasonable amounts.
2. The compulsory first-party insurance would be supplemented by voluntary additional liability coverage above the limits of the first-party insurance.
3. Victims should retain their present right to sue in tort for specified intangible losses, such as pain and suffering, but the right should be restricted to truly serious cases.
4. The private insurance industry, not public agencies, should administer the laws.
5. Benefits for the accident victim would be provided in such a way that automobile coverage would be primary insurance, and other sources of restoration (e.g., Blue Cross) would be secondary, thus avoiding duplication of coverage.
6. Emphasis on rehabilitation of the victim would be stressed.
7. Benefits provided under the first party coverage would be approximately of the following magnitude: medical costs, 100%, subject to a small deductible amount; income loss, up to $1,000 per month, for three years subject to reasonable waiting periods at the discretion of the insured; death benefits, $1,000 per person, with higher amounts optional with the insured; loss of services of nonemployed persons (e.g., housewives) up to $75 a week; property damage to the insured vehicle, in full or subject to optional deductibles up to say $1,000 or a third of the value of the car; nonvehicular damage to property of others, $10,000 per accident.

Expected Advantages. There are several advantages claimed for the DOT recommendations, including:

1. The cost of insurance would be reduced under the no-fault system because of elimination of overpayments of small claims, duplication of benefits, attorneys' fees, and court costs; voluntary acceptance of deductibles which would simplify settlements; and establishment of more scientific rating systems which would reflect protective features of vehicles and their susceptibility to damage. The major factor tending to increase insurance costs would be the compensation of victims now undercompensated. It is expected, however, that the net effect would be to lower insurance costs.
2. The system is aimed at protecting auto accident victims rather than serving the needs of tort feasors. These victims would know in advance what their benefits are and would escape the uncertainties of having to go to court or prove negligence. Delays in settlement would be reduced.
3. Loss prevention through the production of safer cars and highways would be encouraged.
4. Insurance should become more readily available because of decreased underwriting risk. Underwriting risk is less because it is easier to predict loss on a first-party basis than on a tort-liability basis which is subject to uncertainties in the jury trial system and abuse through exaggeration of losses.
5. Competition in insurance would be encouraged because of less underwriting risk.[28]

Arguments Against No-Fault. Those opposing no-fault, or who favor retention of the present system of tort liability, are in the minority, according to a public

[28] U.S. Department of Transportation, *Motor Vehicle Crash Losses and their Compensation in the United States* (Washington: U.S. Government Printing Office, 1971). pp. 133-146.

attitude survey sponsored by the DOT. In this survey respondents who had suffered injuries in auto accidents were divided into two groups, according to whether they had or had not recovered under tort liability. About 10% of the victims recovering from tort were opposed to the no-fault idea, compared to 12% of those not so recovering. In all about 22% of the nearly 460,000 victims surveyed were opposed.[29]

Major arguments of those injury victims opposed to no-fault included the feeling that the person at fault should pay (33%), expectation of higher insurance costs (36%), "it wouldn't be fair," (6%), and "would lead to careless driving" (9%). It was found that the general public tended to be better satisfied with its insurance experience than were those who had been seriously injured.

Perhaps the most powerful group to oppose the no-fault idea are attorneys who specialize in damage suits arising out of the tort liability system. Attorneys oppose the no-fault concept for two main reasons. First, it is assumed by many that there would be a reduction in the number of court cases filed and a consequent reduction in attorneys' fees. Second, many attorneys feel that if the right to sue for automobile injuries were restricted, similar restrictions would be later imposed in other areas. Personal rights to collect damages from negligent parties is a fundamental element in our legal system which upholds individual freedom and independence. In other words, no-fault auto insurance systems might set a dangerous legal precedent. A critical analysis of each of these arguments undermines each. First, most proposals for no-fault laws do not eliminate the right to sue when the damages are serious. It is therefore doubtful that attorneys' fee income would be greatly curtailed since most significant fees stem from serious cases anyway. Second, the precedent for no-fault principle already has been set in the passage of workers' compensation laws, which eliminate fault as a basis for settling occupational injury cases.

No-Fault Laws The first to experiment with the no-fault principle was the Canadian province of Saskatchewan, whose plan provided a schedule of indemnities in a manner similar to workers' compensation statutes. Thus, the injured victim's remedy for a broken arm or leg would be specified in the law. However the right to bring a negligence action for more serious losses was preserved. The law also established a state-controlled monopoly insurer to issue all liability insurance in connection with the plan. Another innovation in Canada is the optional extension on regular auto policies to all motorists driving outside the country of a limited no-fault coverage. For a premium of about $8 the motorist may add up to $5,000 of coverage for death, dismemberment, and loss of sight, or disability payments up to $35 a week for accidents outside of Canada. No jurisdiction in the United States passed a no-fault law until 1968, when Puerto Rico established a law. Massachusetts was second, its law becoming effective in 1971, and Florida, third, in 1972. Other states to pass no-fault laws were: effective in 1973, Connecticut, Michigan, and New Jersey; effective

[29] U. S. Department of Transportation, *Public Attitudes Supplement to the Economic Consequences of Automobile Accident Injuries* (Washington: U. S. Government Printing Office, 1970), p. 41.

in 1974, Colorado, Hawaii, Kansas, Nevada, New York, and Utah; effective in 1975, Georgia, Kentucky, Minnesota and Pennsylvania. Except for Kentucky (Kentucky's law is optional with the insured), each of the 16 laws mentioned above limit the right to sue for damages arising out of automobile accidents to serious accidents. These laws have been termed "modified no-fault."

Seven other states have passed laws which in reality provide only for expanded medical payments and disability income coverage on the traditional automobile insurance policy. The laws do not contain any limitations on the right for the injured victim to sue for damages. These laws have been none-too-accurately called "add-on no-fault laws." These have been passed in Arkansas (1974), Delaware (1972), Maryland (1973), Oregon (1972), South Carolina (1974), South Dakota (1972), Texas (1973), and Virginia (1972).

An example of an add-on statute is that in Texas, where the insured may recover $2,500 in medical hospital, funeral expenses, and 80% of lost income. The insured may obtain higher medical disability limits up to $10,000. The insured may also sue any negligent person for damages, but the insurer may reduce payment of any judgment by the amount it has already paid in no-fault benefits. The insurer may not proceed against liable third parties under subrogation rights for no-fault benefits paid to the insured. Injury sustained while committing a felony or fleeing lawful arrest is excluded. Presumably, there is less likelihood that the insured will bring negligence action against liable third parties than if this coverage did not exist, particularly for relatively minor losses. Thus, to some extent the negligence system involving third-party claims gives way to first-party claims.

An example of the provisions of modified no-fault laws are those of Massachusetts, Florida, and Georgia. The law in Massachusetts, known as the Personal Injury Protection (PIP) plan contains the following major provisions:

1. The insured must collect from his own insurance company for claims up to $2,000. These claims include medical and funeral expenses and up to 75% of lost wages.
2. Recoveries under tort liability are permitted for claims exceeding $2,000. However, tort recovery is permitted for pain and suffering if medical and funeral expenses exceed $500. Furthermore, tort liability is available for pain and suffering regardless of medical cost, if the injury causes death, consists of a loss of a body member, loss of sight or hearing, or a serious and permanent disfigurement or fracture.
3. Collision damage coverage subject to $100 deductible in one of two forms is a mandatory offering, as is comprehensive and loss-of-use coverage. The insured may elect to reject these coverages, however. Tort recovery for property damage claims is virtually eliminated.

The Personal Injury Protection plan amends the compulsory liability statute in Massachusetts, and excludes claims arising out of industrial injuries to prevent double recovery under workers' compensation statutes. Insurers may deny payment if the driver was operating the automobile under the influence of alcohol or drugs, committing a felony, or deliberately causing damage. Immunity from tort-liability claims up to $2,000 does not apply to accidents outside Massachusetts. An amendment to the law forbids cancellation of coverage of insureds who have clean driving records, are not drug or alcohol users, and can meet licensing requirements. Nonresidents involved in accidents in Massachusetts recover under tort liability in the usual way; however, nonresidents who are passengers in a car protected under the law may be entitled to benefits. In determining benefits, an allowance is made for the expenses of obtaining a replacement of the services performed by unemployed members of the household who are prevented from performing tasks for which they would not normally be paid. The insured may purchase coverage with a deductible amount ranging from $250 to $2,000, but is not permitted tort-liability recoveries for the amount of any loss suffered because of the deductible. Payments under the no-fault provisions are deducted from recoveries which may ultimately be paid under a tort-liability claim. Insurers in Massachusetts must make available to all drivers excess liability limits of $15,000/$40,000 for bodily injury and $5,000 for property damage.

Florida's no-fault law, which is compulsory, allows the auto crash victim to receive up to $5,000 in medical expenses and lost wages from his or her own insurer.[30] Tort liability suits above this amount are permitted if medical bills exceed $1,000 or if disability, loss of income, and medical expenses exceed $5,000. Some suits for pain and suffering are permitted.

Georgia's no-fault law provides $5,000 of no-fault coverage which includes $2,500 in medical expense payments, 85% loss of income up to $200 a week, essential services up to $20 a day, and $1,500 funeral expense. Loss of income benefits may be paid to survivors, who are also entitled to the $20-per-day loss-of-services benefit. The insured must be offered up to $50,000 of aggregate no-fault coverage but may elect not to accept this additional coverage. The law bars a tort liability suit unless medical expenses exceed $500; temporary disability exceeds 10 consecutive days; or the injury results in death, disfigurement, permanent disability, dismemberment, or bone fracture. In Georgia, no-fault benefits are not reduced by any benefits the victim may be entitled to under workers' compensation. Medical payments and uninsured motorist benefits, however, are excess over no-fault coverage.

Effects of No-Fault Laws. Perhaps one of the most important effects of compulsory no-fault coverage is the influence it should have on the proportion of drivers who are insured. Georgia, for example, was listed in the DOT study as having less than 65% of its drivers with liability coverage.[31] Thus, there should be a significant reduction in the number of traffic victims in Georgia who must bear their losses individually, rather than be able to recover from insurers. Another effect is the anticipated reduction in the number of court cases filed and in the subsequent reduction in bodily injury liability insurance costs (most laws do not apply to property damage liability). Preliminary results in Massachusetts suggest significant reductions in insurance costs.

[30] The Florida motorist may comply with the law in any of the following methods: no-fault insurance; by proving a net worth of $40,000; by posting collateral of $25,000; or by posting a surety bond.

[31] U.S. Department of Transportation, *Driver Behavior and Accident Involvement: Implications for Tort Liability* (Washington: U.S. Government Printing Office, 1970), p. 205.

According to studies by Brainard and Fitzgerald,[32] total auto insurance costs in Massachusetts in 1971 were reduced about 51% below the 1970 level under the old tort liability system. Liability insurance savings of $68.9 million were reduced by $18.5 million in the additional costs of the add-on costs of medical and disability coverage. However, early indications of loss experience with no-fault in Florida are that the savings are not as great as in Massachusetts. In Florida the law caused a smaller-than-expected savings in tort liability claims, which were reduced 24%, from the previous level, compared to a 69% reduction in Massachusetts.

Another effect, perhaps an unfortunate one, is the confusion in claims settlement likely to be brought about by the diversity of no-fault laws from state to state. For example, nonresident drivers in Massachusetts must recover under the tort liability system unless they are passengers in a resident vehicle. However, if Massachusetts drivers are driving out-of-state they receive no-fault benefits from their insurer and also may be able to bring tort action if the law in the state where the accident occurs so provides. In Florida, nonresidents may obtain no-fault coverage if their insurers provide no-fault coverage when the vehicle is in a no-fault state; otherwise, nonresidents must recover under tort liability. In any case, nonresidents in Florida must obtain Florida's no-fault coverage after they have been in the state 90 days.

Important contrasts occur in the laws passed so far. Differences exist in the amount of first-party coverage, the right to sue for pain and suffering, the right to bring tort-liability actions for amounts subject to be collected under the first-party coverage, and the treatment of property damage claims. The DOT study committee recommended that states experiment with different approaches until a satisfactory result is evolved. However, it seems that a considerable period of relative uncertainty and confusion might exist for an accident victim until there is reasonable homogeneity among the various statutes. Nevertheless, there seems little doubt that more no-fault laws will gradually be adopted and bring about substantial modification of the law of negligence method of compensating traffic victims. However, in many respects the laws passed so far fail to meet the goals recommended by the DOT committee.

Government Auto Insurance

In 1973 the first instance occurred in which a state government became the sponsor of a publicly-owned insurance company to offer automobile coverage in the United States. The insurer, known as the Maryland Automobile Insurance Fund (MAIF) was created to take over a restricted segment of the private automobile insurance market in Maryland. At the same time the legislature caused MAIF to take over the state's unsatisfied judgment fund and eliminated the assigned risk plan for insureds not meeting regular underwriting

[32] Calvin Brainard, "Massachusetts Loss Experience Under No-Fault in 1971: Analysis and Implication," *Journal of Risk and Insurance,* Vol. 40, No. 1 (March, 1973), p. 95; and Calvin H. Brainard and John F. Fitzgerald," "First Year Cost Results Under No-Fault Automobile Insurance: A Comparison of the Florida and Massachusetts Experience," *Journal of Risk and Insurance,* Vol. 41, No. 1 (March, 1974), p. 29.

requirements of private insurers. Liability coverage and $2,500 of medical and disability insurance became compulsory. Under the plan, the MAIF may insure only drivers who have been turned down by private insurers or whose policies have been cancelled for reasons other than nonpayment of premiums. Other drivers must continue to use private insurers. Among the reasons for a state government entering a heretofore exclusively private insurance domain were the following: (a) An inordinate number of drivers in Maryland had been placed in the assigned-risk pool at higher-than-average rates even though many of these drivers had clean driving records. (b) Private insurer rating systems produced rates judged too high and too complex in their application. (c) Claims settlements were often slow under private insurers, particularly for those in the assigned risk pool. Establishment of the MAIF demonstrates the willingness of government to compete with private insurers in areas where it is believed private insurer performance is lacking. It is too early to evaluate the success of the MAIF. However, similar laws have been introduced but not enacted in South Carolina and Louisiana, indicating considerable interest in the idea elsewhere.

Conclusions

Among the various attempted solutions to the problems of giving traffic victims fair, adequate, prompt, and efficient settlements for their losses, no one technique has prevailed. All make use of the insurance mechanism, however modified. So far no federal law has been passed to bring about great uniformity in no-fault laws being passed in the various states, although such measures have been introduced. It would appear that state regulation of automobile insurance will increase, particularly laws and regulations of a no-fault type. There is also the distinct possibility that more states will begin to offer their own versions of automobile insurance, as has been tried in Maryland.

SUMMARY

1. The cost of automobile accidents, in both absolute and relative terms, has been rising steadily in the United States for many years, posing a serious problem as to the most efficient and equitable manner in which the economic burden can be borne.

   If the real causes of accidents were known, steps might be taken to handle the risk by placing greater emphasis on reduction of hazard. Less emphasis would have to be laid on the reduction of risk to the individual through private insurance, a state fund of some sort, or assumption of risk by a person unable to bear it. One example of the significance of this point is the relationship of age to the probability of having an automobile accident. At present insurers seem to assign higher rates to certain classes of youthful drivers without any real knowledge as to what causal factors result in higher accident rates in youthful drivers.
2. Because a single automobile accident may be catastrophically expensive to the victims and because of the relatively high probability of loss, insurance is the only feasible method to protect against the risk involved.

3. The provisions of the family automobile policy (FAP) are representative of those found in most contracts covering the use of automobiles. The FAP is one of the most comprehensive contracts, insuring against losses due to legal liability for negligence, medical payments, and physical damage to the vehicle. Under the terms of the FAP, the words "insured" and "automobile" are defined broadly enough to protect the average car owner and to give nearly the same protection to anyone else driving the automobile with the owner's permission.
4. Liability coverage under the FAP covers against loss due to legal liability for damage to the person or property of others arising out of the ownership, maintenance, and use of the automobile. Medical payments coverage insures the loss due to accidental bodily injuries of occupants of a vehicle regardless of negligence of the insured driver. Physical damage Insurance reimburses the owner for physical loss of a vehicle from almost any peril, whether or not the insured caused the accident.
5. Because the definitions, exclusions, and conditions are as important as they are basic to an understanding of the FAP, they must be studied carefully to ascertain the scope of coverage. In general, coverage granted when the insured is driving nonowned cars is less comprehensive than when the insured is driving his or her own car.
6. Extensive studies of the problem of compensating victims for bodily injury and property damage suffered on the nation's highways have been made in recent years by the U. S. Department of Transportation. These studies have revealed a need for reform of the tort-liability system of compensating victims of highway accidents. This system has many serious weaknesses, such as paying some victims too much and others too little, being expensive to administer, failing to compensate many victims, and paying others only after extensive delays.
7. Among the approaches which have been tried to improve the effectiveness of the tort-liability system are financial responsibility laws, compulsory liability insurance, unsatisfied judgment funds, and no-fault insurance laws. The latter are the most recent measures and exist in only a few states. No-fault laws represent a basic reform in that, subject to certain limits, the negligence principle is abandoned and benefits are paid to victims by their own insurer on a first-party basis. No-fault laws are still experimental, but they offer considerable promise in improving the system. No-fault laws do not eliminate the need for liability insurance, which is still necessary to protect the motorist against loss due to liability for accident costs which exceed the exemptions specified in no-fault laws.

QUESTIONS FOR REVIEW AND DISCUSSION

1. "About one of four drivers are expected to have an accident in a typical driving year, but some have much higher probability of loss than others." Explain.
2. Suggest possible reasons why auto manufacturers do not make cars safer than they do, thus reducing insurance costs of operating them.
3. Which of the following factors are associated with higher accident rates on highways, according to available statistics? Which ones are not so related? (a) being a pedestrian at night, (b) driving on a country road as opposed to a superhighway, (c) riding a bicycle, (d) driving on weekdays, as

opposed to weekends, (e) being a woman driver, (f) being a nonresident driver, (g) driving in Mexico.

4. The medical-payments portion of the FAP limits liability for each person to that stated in the declarations, and states that this limit is "the limit of the company's liability for all expenses incurred by or on behalf of each person who sustains bodily injury as a result of any one accident." In the conditions of the policy, however, the policy states "when two or more automobiles are insured hereunder, the terms of this policy shall apply separately to each." In one case the insured covered two autos under one contract with medical-payments coverage of $3,000 on each. The insured's wife was injured while driving one of the autos and suffered medical expenses exceeding $6,000. Should the coverage be limited to $3,000, or $6,000? Why or why not?
5. Among the exclusions of the liability portion of the FAP are injuries to or destruction of property in the charge of the insured "other than a residence or private garage." Reasoning from general insurance principles, would you argue that this quotation implies that the policy intends to cover an insured's damage to his own garage in backing out and ruining the garage door? Explain your reasoning.
6. Since *Y*'s car is broken down, *Y* borrows his son's car to run an errand. The son, who lives with *Y* in the same household, does not have his car insured. If *Y* had an accident, would his FAP cover him? Explain why or why not.
7. *G*'s son gives permission for a neighbor to borrow his father's car, thinking it will be all right because the neighbor is a good friend of his family. Under the terms of the FAP, will the neighbor be covered while driving *G*'s car? Why?
8. Discuss the basic reason for the exclusion in the FAP of injury to employees of the insured.
9. Pauline has a collision loss of $2,300 under her FAP. After paying the loss her insurer sends a 20-day cancellation notice to Pauline by registered mail. What are Pauline's rights under the FAP?
10. Why does a driver need uninsured motorist coverage even in a state which has compulsory no-fault insurance?
11. *S* pulls a large house trailer behind his vehicle each year on a winter vacation which lasts four months. (a) Assuming limits of $5,000 property damage, what coverage is granted to *S* under the FAP if the trailer sideswipes another car, causing a $1,000 loss to the trailer and a $2,000 loss to the other car? (b) Would your answer be different if the trailer had been a small two-wheel camping trailer with sleeping accommodations for two? Why?
12. An insured's mentally deranged son, after becoming intoxicated, broke into the insured's locked vehicle, and while driving it at high speed, wrecked the vehicle. If the insured had comprehensive insurance but not collision insurance, what line of reasoning might lead to the conclusion that the damage was covered under the FAP? Discuss.
13. A thief steals the insured's car and wrecks it. Is this a collision loss or a theft loss? Discuss.
14. In *Harris* v. *Allstate Insurance Company* (309 N.Y. 72), the insured had driven rapidly over a portion of highway inundated by water. He lost control and the car went over an embankment. There was no collision insurance, but the insured had comprehensive insurance. Should the insurer pay the claim?
15. Many cases have concerned claims originating when an animal jumps on top of an automobile. In your opinion, is this a falling object or a collision? What difference does it make? Discuss.
16. An insured heard a large bang under his car, but continued to

drive. After he had gone a mile or so, the motor stopped. The insured did not examine the car, but had it pushed to the nearest garage, where it was determined that all the oil had leaked out of a hole in the oil pan and the engine was burned out. Is the insurer liable? If not, why not? If so, under what type of auto coverage? Why?

17. Josephine has $50 deductible collision insurance on her car, while Ellen carries $100 deductible. If Josephine borrows Ellen's car and has a collision in which $200 damage is done, which policy must respond and in what amounts? Why?

18. In the case of *Farm Bureau Mutual Automobile Insurance Company* v. *Boecher* (48 N.E.2d 895) the insured was involved in an accident while driving a car made available to employees by his employer, an auto dealer. The insured, who had never driven this particular vehicle before, applied for coverage under his private automobile policy and was denied protection on the grounds that the policy excluded coverage on nonowned cars. With reference to the provisions of the FAP, discuss the correctness or incorrectness of the position taken by the insurer.

19. A trade publication reported the following story:
A new approach to automobile insurance is being tried by one group of insurers. In their contracts, the individual operator is covered, regardless of what vehicle is being driven, in contrast to the usual practice of "insuring the automobile" regardless of who is driving it. The proponents of this plan argue that the present wave of granting rate credits "to an automobile" (under various "safe driver" plans), regardless of who is driving it, is unsound. The new contract covers only the named insured and does not extend to anyone else unless the other person is driving and the insured is a passenger.
(a) Is it true that it is the usual practice to issue insurance "on the automobile?" What is the fallacy involved here?
(b) What is meant by the argument that rate credits granted under merit rating plans now being tried are unsound?
(c) Would you feel that the new contract approach described here meets the needs of the average family? Why, or why not? Would it meet the needs of the average business? Discuss the pros and cons.

20. A method proposed to reduce the cost of automobile liability insurance is to issue all policies with a deductible clause of, say, $50 or $100. It is argued that drivers would be more careful if they had to pay the first $50 or $100 themselves in any liability claim for property damage, and a deductible would reduce the cost to insurance companies of paying small claims.
(a) Do you agree that these are sound arguments? Explain.
(b) What would be the probable attitude of accident victims under this arrangement?

21. A study of the effect of alcoholism on highway accidents reported that 80% of convictions for drunken driving involved social drinkers, not confirmed alcoholics. The study recommended a treatment program of education of the socially drinking public to the dangers of drinking and driving, coupled with severe penalties for those who overdrink socially and then drive. Based on these findings, in 1970 the city of Chicago conducted a campaign of public information and strict enforcement during the Christmas holidays, aimed at deterring the social-drinking driver. It was announced that persons convicted of drunk driving would be placed in jail for a minimum of seven days and would have their driving privileges suspended for one year. Assess the likelihood of success of this program, both on a temporary and a long-lasting basis.

22. An insurance representative stated that marketing automobile insurance on a group basis through employer, credit union, and labor union organizations may help solve many problems in automobile insurance. Suggest some of the problems which group automobile insurance may help solve. Show how these problems may be met through group underwriting.

23. What are the major weaknesses of the tort-liability system as a way to compensate injured victims for automobile accidents? What major group do you believe would resist vehemently the idea that the tort-liability system should be done away with? Discuss.

24. Analyze the law governing automobile financial responsibility in your state. Compare its provisions with the recommendations made by the DOT committee as goals for reform of auto compensation or no-fault statutes.

25. Analyze the arguments against no-fault laws. For example, do you believe these laws will result in drivers becoming less careful in their driving? What about the other arguments? Discuss.

26. In Oregon a no-fault plan was passed in 1971 with the following provisions: the plan would require all auto policies to provide benefits to the insured, any guest passengers, and pedestrians struck by an insured. There would be $3,000 of coverage for medical expenses, income loss coverage equal to the lesser of 70% of the loss of income or $500 per month for 52 weeks, and if the injured person is not employed, up to $12 a day for 52 weeks. All income benefits are subject to a 14-day waiting period; the insured may elect a $250 deductible on medical expenses. There are no tort exemptions, and the right to sue for pain and suffering is not changed. The plan does not cover property damage. In the fall of 1971 it was reported that insurance rates in Oregon were expected to rise between 8% and 15% as a result of the new law.
(a) Is this plan in harmony with the recommendations of the DOT study committee? Why, or why not?
(b) Why would rates be expected to go up under this plan, instead of down, as has been expected for other no-fault plans?

Chapter ***Seventeen***

CRIME INSURANCE AND BONDING

Crime against property in the United States is one of the most serious and most underinsured perils. It is estimated that less than 10% of loss to property from ordinary crime is insured. In addition, although statistics on losses are not available, facts suggest that loss from organized crime is tremendous. The crime loss problem has become so serious in recent years that the federal government has entered the field of burglary and robbery insurance.

LOSS DUE TO STEALING

Loss due to stealing has been rising steadily in the United States both absolutely and relative to population. Statistics gathered by the Federal Bureau of Investigation from police departments throughout the country on the rate of crimes against property during the period 1960–1973 are given in Table 17–1.

PROPERTY LOSS FROM CRIME, 1973 **Table 17-1**

Crime	Rate Per 100,000 Population	Percent Change From	
		1972	1960
Robbery	182.4	2.1	256.3
Burglary	1,210.8	8.0	140.3
Larceny-Theft	2,051.2	4.7	134.3
Auto-Theft	440.1	4.7	183.0

Source: Federal Bureau of Investigation, *Crime in the United States 1973*, Uniform Crime Reports (Washington: U.S. Government Printing Office, 1974), p. 1.

The total crime index (based on amount of crime per 100,000 population) has increased 120%.[1] Over period 1968–1973, crime against property increased 28%, compared to a 5% increase in population. Crime rates against property are about five times as high in cities over 250,000 as in rural areas. Property

[1] Federal Bureau of Investigation, *Crime in the United States 1973*, Uniform Crime Reports (Washington: U.S. Government Printing Office, 1974), p. 59.

crimes are highest in Western states and lowest in Southern states (5,340 vs. 3,225 per 100,000 inhabitants).[2] Over two thirds of all arrests for larceny were of persons under age 21. Females comprised 32% of all arrests for larceny.

Not a large percentage of property crimes are solved. The following percentages of property crimes were cleared in 1973: robbery, 27%; burglary, 18%; larceny, 19%; and auto theft, 16%.[3] In spite of the relatively low solution rate, 127 police officers were killed in 1973 and 30,280 were assaulted in the course of their work.

The Small Business Administration (SBA) made a study of the incidence and type of crime losses from a sample of 5,200 business firms representing the United States business population of 8 million firms in 1967–1968. The results represent the first available information of this type. Total crime losses were estimated to be over $3 billion in 1967–1968, of which burglary represented 31% and vandalism, 27%. Other types of crime, in order of relative size, were shoplifting, employee theft, bad checks, and robbery.

Burglary and theft loss goes relatively uninsured. According to the SBA study, approximately $1 billion of losses occurred from burglary and robbery in 1967–68. Total losses paid by insurance companies under policies covering these perils in 1968 approximated $60 million, or only 6% of the total.[4]

Crime tends to strike small business firms more frequently and cause the most severe loss. Firms with receipts under $100,000 had 36 times as many crime losses, relative to their gross income, as larger firms. These small firms were struck hardest for all types of crime except bad checks, which hit firms in the intermediate-size class more heavily, presumably because the very small firms know their customers better or are more careful in identification of customers before cashing checks. Crime loss tends to be greatest in the ghetto and least in rural areas for all types except bad checks, which tended to characterize all areas about equally. Small firms with under $100,000 of receipts constituted nearly 86% of all firms, had 9% of total receipts, but suffered 28% of losses. For these firms the losses amounted to .71% of their receipts, the highest relative loss of any size group. The largest firms lost only .02% of their receipts.[5] Because of such facts, insurance costs for small firms tend to be higher than for large companies.

Embezzlement

According to the SBA study, employee theft losses were estimated to have caused $381 million of losses in 1967–1968, or about 13% of total crime loss. It is very likely, however, that the total losses from employee stealing are much greater than this figure suggests, as swindled employers are reluctant to admit that they have been cheated by their own employees, and some losses remain undiscovered.

[2] *Ibid.*, p. 2.
[3] *Ibid.*, p. 29.
[4] *1969 Loss and Expense Ratios* (New York Insurance Department, 1970), p. 170.
[5] Small Business Administration, *Crime Against Small Business*, Senate Document 91-14 (Washington: U.S. Government Printing Office, 1969), p. 25.

Relatively little of the fidelity loss in the United States appears to be recovered through insurance. In 1968, for example, insurers paid out about $65 million in losses under fidelity bonds.[6] This represents 17% of the amount of loss reported in the SBA study, or 3.6% of the loss estimated by the FBI. Apparently, employers are as reluctant to insure the fidelity risk as they are to recognize that it exists.

Forgery

Forgery losses involving the passing of bad checks are among the most common types of dishonesty engaged in and yet are among the easiest to prevent. Most of such losses are caused by amateurs; it is estimated that only one third of the total check losses are caused by professionals. Forgery most commonly involves the issuance of entirely fictitious checks, although alteration of and false signatures upon legitimate checks are frequent. Most false checks are cashed in supermarkets, department stores, service stations, and taverns where large volumes of small transactions take place and where it is fairly uncommon to require a careful identification of the passer. Installation of devices to photograph every person cashing a check and the check to be cashed has reduced false check cashing in stores where this method has been adopted. However, some business firms, especially small ones, seem unwilling to take the necessary steps to prevent these losses. In addition to the objection that control measures are expensive, some store owners feel that to require identification of the customer might incur public ill will.

RISK MANAGEMENT OF THE CRIME PERIL

Management may attempt to handle the crime risk through several methods, including assumption, loss prevention, and insurance. Each of these methods is deficient in some respect. The method of assumption may invite ruin. Loss-prevention efforts tend to be haphazard and are often ineffective. Insurance methods suffer from adverse selection, high costs, and gaps in protection because of narrow definitions of perils.

Assumption

Evidence suggests that the method of assumption of risk has had serious negative consequences for many business firms. The SBA study reported that in three cities characterized by high crime rates, Boston, Chicago, and Washington, D.C., 20% of the businesses surveyed in 1966 were out of business by 1968, and 5% had moved to a new location. Survival rates were significantly higher in the areas with the lowest crime rates. Retailers were least likely to survive.[7] While these data do not prove that crime was the major cause of the

[6] *1969 Loss and Expense Ratios* (New York Insurance Department, 1970), p. 155.

[7] Howard Aldrich and Albert J. Reiss, Jr., "A 1968 Followup Study of Crime and Insurance Problems of Businesses Surveyed in 1966 in Three Cities," Appendix B to Small Business Administration, *Crime Against Small Business*, Senate Document 91-14 (Washington: U.S. Government Printing Office, 1969), p. 146.

business mortality noted, the association between these two factors seems apparent. Even though crime loss is still a relatively small .23% of total receipts, the losses can be catastrophic for some firms. Yet assumption remains perhaps the most generally used method of handling the crime peril.

Loss Prevention

Efforts to prevent crime loss appear to be the best solution to the problem, but total effectiveness even in the long run seems doubtful. Loss prevention can be considered in two perspectives—those efforts seeking reform of society to eliminate basic causes of crime, and those efforts attacking the symptoms of crime.

Sociological, economic, political, and legal reforms appear to be crucial in obtaining any permanent success in preventing the most serious losses from crime. As examples, these measures would include efforts to eliminate poverty, to reform prisons and the judicial system, to speed justice, and to help the criminal to adjust to society; medical research to cure mental and emotional disorders; improved community planning to eliminate crowding; and programs to improve education.

Efforts to control the crime problem by relieving its symptoms are also important. Among these efforts are police protection, private guards, burglar alarms, locks and shields, surveillance mechanisms, and sensing devices, which play a role in detecting and deterring crime once the criminal has initiated the act or has determined to do so. However, the three-city survey referred to previously reported little evidence that the presence of protective devices in areas previously without them had the effect of reducing the rate of burglaries in the two-year period.[8] The conclusion is suggested that protection and loss-prevention measures attacking symptoms alone have their limitations as a way to meet the crime risk. Also potentially valuable are such measures as community programs to show citizens how to cope with crime and to report observed crime, reducing the exposure to loss (for example, making more frequent bank deposits of cash receipts), installation of protective materials such as specialized glass to lengthen the time it takes to enter the premises, and use of devices to alert police.

Insurance

Even with rapid detection of crime, effective systems of court action, and rehabilitation efforts applied to the criminal, it appears that crime is a problem which will always characterize society. Insurance remains as a potentially effective device to spread the inevitable crime losses among insureds.

Unfortunately, insurance as a way to handle the crime risk suffers from serious weaknesses. Crime insurance is used sparingly and probably covers less than 10% of the total crime loss in the United States. Adverse selection is present, due to the tendency of those applicants who are most likely to suffer

[8] *Ibid.*

loss (such as pawn shops and jewelry and liquor stores) to apply for the most coverage. A moral hazard exists in the temptation of those who are insured to take advantage of opportunities to arrange a robbery or burglary with an accomplice in order to collect illegally from the insurance company. It is often difficult to establish the amount of the loss when it occurs because of inadequate inventory control methods or lack of adequate records. For example, a burglary to a retailer might occur, evidence of which is obvious, but the insured may try to include in the loss claim shortages of inventory which are in reality due to shoplifting or employee theft. It may be difficult for the claims adjuster to prove otherwise.

For reasons of high cost, lack of supply, or failure to appreciate the need, many businesses do not carry crime insurance. As shown in Table 5–2, burglary, theft, surety, and fidelity coverages accounted for only 2.2% of total property-liability insurance sold in the United States in 1974. Furthermore, this type of insurance has grown in premium volume only 75% over the period 1964–1974, compared to a 153% growth for property-liability insurance as a whole.

Losses from crimes against property[9] were estimated by the FBI in 1972 as follows: robbery, $91 million; burglary, $722 million; larceny of goods, $475 million; embezzlement loss, $2–$3 billion. Yet the total premiums of burglary and theft insurance in 1972 were only $130 million, and fidelity bond premiums were estimated at $200 million. Loss payments, of course, were probably only about 60% of premiums written. Thus, only about 6% of burglary and robbery losses and, conservatively, only about 5% of fidelity losses were covered.

Among the solutions which have been proposed for the problems which characterize crime insurance are the following:

1. Offer crime insurance through the federal government. This method is now being tried. (See below.)
2. Reduce what have been termed excessive agency commissions, which reduce the profitability to insurers and discourage them from making crime coverage more readily available.
3. Permit group crime coverage to be made available through trade associations.
4. Use deductibles and package policies to obtain greater spread of risk and hence less risk to the insurer.
5. Require more attention to loss prevention as a prerequisite to offering insurance.
6. Alter the premium structure by making the rate-making base the standard metropolitan area rather than the county. This would tend to produce lower rates for suburban businesses and would make firms in the urban areas share more fairly in the cost of crime.[10]

Even though insurance is not a total solution to the problem of managing the crime risk, it is one of the most immediately practical methods by which the

[9] *Insurance Facts 1973* (New York: Insurance Information Institute, 1973), p. 60. Percentages calculated.

[10] Herbert S. Denenberg, "Insurance Study," Appendix F to Small Business Administration, *Crime Against Small Business*, Senate Document 91-14 (Washington: U.S. Government Printing Office, 1969).

business firm may obtain financial protection against crime. If understood thoroughly, insurance and bonds can play an effective role in the war against crime.

CRIME INSURANCE AND BONDS

There are two basic types of financial protection against the catastrophic losses which can be caused by crime: surety and fidelity bonds; and burglary, robbery, and theft insurance. *Surety and fidelity bonds* provide guarantees against loss through the dishonesty or incapacity of individuals who are trusted with money or other property and who violate this trust. *Theft insurance*, on the other hand, provides coverage against loss through stealing by individuals who are not in a position of trust.

Insurance Versus Bonding

A *bond* is a legal instrument whereby one party (the *surety*) agrees to reimburse another party (the *obligee*) should this person suffer loss because of some failure by the person bonded (the *principal* or *obligor*). Thus, if a contractor furnishes a bond to the owner of a building, the surety will reimburse the owner if the contractor fails to perform as agreed upon and thereby causes a loss to the owner.

A bond may sound like a contract of insurance, but there are some important differences to be considered:

1. The bonding contract involves three primary parties, while the insurance contract normally involves only two.
2. In bonding, if the principal defaults and the surety makes good to the obligee, the surety enjoys the legal right to attempt to collect for its loss from the principal. In insurance, the insurer does not have the right to recover losses from the insured, for this would defeat the purpose of the contract.
3. In bonding, the surety sees as its basic function the lending of its credit, for a premium. It expects no losses, and reserves the legal right to collect from the defaulting principal. The insurance contract is set up with the presumption that there will be losses, and is viewed by its managers as a device to spread these losses among the insured group.
4. The nature of the risk is different. Usually a bond guarantees the honesty of an individual, as well as the capacity and ability of that individual to perform. These are matters within the control of the individual. The insurance contract, ideally, covers losses outside the control of the individual.
5. Finally, in insurance, the contract is usually cancellable by either party, and nonpayment of premium or breach of warranty by the insured is usually a good defense of the insurer in avoiding its liability. In a bond the surety is often liable on the bond to the beneficiary regardless of breach of warranty or fraud on the part of the principal. In addition, the bond often cannot be cancelled until it has been determined that all the obligations of the principal have been fulfilled.

Fidelity and Surety Bonds

Strictly speaking, all bonds are surety bonds, but it is convenient to classify them as fidelity bonds and surety bonds.

Fidelity bonds indemnify an employer for any loss suffered at the hands of dishonest employees. As such, the bonds are hardly distinguishable from insurance as far as the employer is concerned. While technically there are three parties to a fidelity bond—the employer (obligee), the employee (obligor), and the insurer (surety)—in practice the main parties are only two, the employer and the surety. The employees are often not even referred to by name, since they are covered on a blanket basis. The bond may be cancelled by either the surety or the employer, the surety has the right of subrogation against defaulting employees, and in other details fidelity bonding follows insurance practice.

Surety bonds, sometimes known as *financial guaranty bonds,* are contracts between three parties—the principal (obligor), the person protected (obligee), and the insurer (surety). Under the contract the surety agrees to make good any default on the part of the principal in the principal's duties toward the obligee. For example the principal might be a contractor who has agreed with the obligee for a given consideration to construct a building meeting certain specifications. The owner-obligee requires the contractor to post a bond to the effect that this contract will be faithfully performed. If the contractor fails in some way, the surety must "make good" to the owner and then has the right to recover any losses from the contractor.

Fidelity bonds are purchased by an employer for its own benefit, but surety bonds are purchased by the obligor for the benefit of some other party, the obligee. Fidelity bonds are concerned only with the honesty of the employee and not with the ability of the employee to perform certain work. In surety bonds, the obligee is concerned not only with the obligor's honesty but also with the *capacity* of the obligor to perform. Hence, the risk to the underwriter is greater on the surety bond than it is on the fidelity bond. The surety expects no losses in the case of the surety bond, since it is assumed that if the surety must make good the default of the principal, the principal will reimburse the surety. If it were otherwise, the surety would be a sort of business partner to the principal, a partner with great financial resources, to absorb any and all losses for the principal but without the chance of sharing in the principal's profits. In fidelity bonding, the surety's only hope of reimbursement is to recover from the defaulting employee; hence, losses are expected and planned for in the premium charged.

Requirement of Collateral

As an outgrowth of the fundamental nature of a surety bond, the surety often requires collateral before it will issue the bond. The surety bond is an instrument for lending the superior credit of the surety to the obligor in return for a premium payment. The surety may decide that the credit position of the obligor is strong enough so that definite collateral in the form of cash, securities, or property is unneeded; but in many cases such collateral is required as a matter of routine to protect the surety against losses, particularly in risky ventures. It may be inquired as to why an obligee requires a bond at all. If the obligee wants security, why does it not accept the collateral of the obligor directly? The answer lies basically in the fact that the obligee is usually in no position to assess the value of the many varieties of collateral that might be offered nor to attend to the details involved in obtaining legal security. The bonding company can perform the function much more economically and more efficiently than the typical obligee. Furthermore, many surety bonds are required by statute, and collateral may not be acceptable under the statute.

Types of Fidelity Bonds

Fidelity bonds may be classified in two groups: (1) those bonds in which an individual is specifically bonded, either by name or by position held in the firm, and (2) those bonds which cover all employees of a given class, called *blanket bonds*. Blanket bonds may also cover perils other than infidelity.

Bonds in Which an Individual Is Specifically Bonded. Bonds in which an individual is specifically bonded may be further classified as individual bonds or schedule bonds.

Individual bonds. *Individual bonds* name a certain person for coverage. If the employer suffers any loss through any dishonest or criminal act of the employee, either alone or in collusion with others, while the employee holds a position with the employer, the surety will be good for the loss up to the limit of liability, called the *penalty* of the bond.

Schedule bonds. *Schedule bonds* may list many employees by name and bond them for specified amounts, in which case the bonds are known as *name schedule bonds*. Additional names may be added or old names deleted upon written notice to the surety.

Position schedule bonds are those which list positions to be bonded and any employee in these positions is automatically covered. The employee is not identified by name in the bond, only by position. This form is especially suitable for the employer who has a rapid turn-over of employees. The employer may add coverage for positions that are created from time to time.

Some schedule bonds grant automatic coverage for a limited period on new names or new positions which may be introduced in order to grant a more complete protection to the employer using these bonds. The term of years for which coverage is provided varies from company to company.

Blanket Bonds. *Blanket bonds* have the following advantages over individual or schedule bonds which cause the use of blanket bonds to be heavily favored among most business firms:

1. Automatic coverage of a uniform amount on all employees is given, thus eliminating the possibility that the employer may select the wrong employee for bonding. An employer might believe, for example, that a common laborer is in no position to steal and thus fail to list the laborer under the bond or bond him or her for a very low amount. Yet it may turn out that this person is the one who admits thieves to the premises or cooperates with other employees in a plan to steal inventory.
2. New employees are automatically covered without need of notifying the surety. Thus, there is no need for setting up special records to handle premium adjustments when employees come and go or when seasonal help is hired. The only

requirement is that each new employee fill out an application form in order that the bonding company may investigate him or her.

3. If a loss occurs, it is not necessary to identify the employees who are involved in the conspiracy in order to collect, as is required on the individual or schedule bonds. It need only be shown that the loss was due to employee infidelity.
4. Because blanket bonds are subject to rate credits for large accounts, the cost may be no more than that of schedule bonds.

There are two major types of blanket bonds: the blanket position bond and the commercial blanket bond. These two bonds, whose terms are standardized by the Surety Association of America, differ primarily in the manner in which the penalty of the bond is stated. The *blanket position bond* has a penalty, ranging in amounts from $2,500 to $100,000, that applies to each employee. The *commercial blanket bond* has a penalty, ranging upward from $10,000, that applies to any one loss.

To illustrate this difference, consider the case of an employer who discovers a $20,000 loss involving three employees, each equally liable. Under a blanket position bond written for a $5,000 penalty, the maximum recovery would be $15,000. If only one employee had been involved, the recovery would be $5,000. The total limit and recovery for any one loss depends on the number of employees responsible for it, assuming all employees are equally to blame. Under the commercial blanket bond, the penalty of the bond is the limit of liability. The $20,000 loss would be covered fully if the penalty of the bond were $20,000 or more, regardless of the number of employees involved.

In deciding which type of bond is more appropriate, it should be noted that in case an employee or employees cannot be identified, the blanket position bond limit per employee is all that can be collected, even though it is unknown whether more than one employee is involved. This factor necessitates a higher penalty per employee than might otherwise be carried, and may result in a somewhat larger total premium on the blanket position bond than on the commercial blanket bond. The total premium on the blanket position bond is also slightly greater because of the higher maximum potential penalty that could be paid under this bond. This follows from the fact that there is no limit on the number of employees covered, and hence no limit on the aggregate loss that could be paid in any given time period.

Important Provisions of Fidelity Bonds. All fidelity bonds are characterized by certain standard provisions.

Continuity of Coverage. Most fidelity bonds are continuous until cancelled by either party. They have no expiration date, only an anniversary date. The premium may be paid annually, or a three-year premium may be purchased at the cost of two and one-half times the annual premium. In the latter case, the premium is due either in a lump sum at the beginning or it may be spread out over the period of the bond, 50% of the premium payable the first year, 30% the second year, and 20% the third year. The bond itself does not expire automatically on the anniversary date as do most insurance contracts. However, coverage on any one employee is automatically cancelled once an employer learns of any dishonest or fraudulent act committed by the employee either before or after the employee was hired. Thus, if an employer learns of a theft committed by an employee five years before being hired but decides to forgive the employee and give him or her a second chance, the employer does so at its own risk for any later stealing.

Noncumulative Penalty. The penalty of the bond is the maximum amount payable for any one loss or for any one employee. The employee may steal $5,000 each year over a long period of time under a bond where the penalty is say $5,000, but the total amount payable for losses traceable to the employee remains at $5,000.

Losses Covered. Fidelity bonds generally cover losses occurring while the bond is in force and discovered during this time or within a certain period, known as the *discovery period*, usually of two years' length, after the bond has been discontinued. If the loss occurs *before* the bond is effective, the loss is not covered under the typical fidelity bond. Some bonding companies write what are known as *discovery bonds*, whereby the loss is covered if it is discovered either during the period of the bond or within any discovery period following its cancellation, regardless of when the loss occurred. Discovery bonds are recommended for employers who have not previously bonded their employees, since there is no way of knowing how long an employee has been stealing.

Sometimes a bond may be cancelled in one company and replaced by another bond in another company. In such instances, the *superseded suretyship clause* provides that if a loss is discovered during the term of the second bond (but after the discovery period has elapsed under the first bond) and if the loss would have been paid under a prior bond had this bond been continued in force, the second surety will pay the loss. In this way an employer who wishes to change sureties may do so without fear of losing continuity of coverage. In effect, the superseded suretyship clause converts the second bond into a type of discovery bond.

Perils Covered. Most fidelity bonds cover any dishonest act or any criminal act of covered employees, but some bonds are restricted to certain crimes such as larceny and embezzlement. The difficulty with specifying such crimes is that there are different legal definitions for these crimes in varying jurisdictions. Thus, an employer can never be certain that coverage exists for all dishonest acts. Therefore, such restrictive wording should be avoided wherever possible. All blanket bonds use the broad wording in the insuring agreement.

Salvage. Recoveries of stolen property from employees, after the surety has fully indemnified the employer, are, of course, returned to the surety. If the surety has not fully indemnified the employer, say because the loss exceeded the penalty of the bond, some bonds require, under a *full salvage clause*, that any recoveries go to the employer until fully restored for the loss. This clause is similar to the rule in subrogation recoveries in insurance. Other bonds contain a *pro rata salvage clause*, which provides that such salvage will be divided between the surety and the employer in the proportion that each has suffered loss.

Suppose Jack takes $10,000 from the cash drawer one morning, goes on a wild spree in Florida, and when the surety's detectives arrive a month later, he has only $6,000 left. In the meantime Jack's employer has been paid $5,000, the penalty under the bond. If the bond has been written with a pro rata salvage clause, the $6,000 would be split evenly between the surety and the employer because up to that time each has suffered a $5,000 loss. Under the pro rata salvage clause, the surety and the employer each would have lost $2,000. Under a full salvage clause, $5,000 would be returned to the employer and $1,000 would go to the surety. In this way, the employer would be fully restored and the surety would have lost the $4,000 that Jack squandered, It obviously makes a difference to the employer which type of salvage clause is used.

Property Covered. Bonds covering employee dishonesty do not restrict the type of property for which indemnification is payable. Stealing of cash, inventory, equipment, securities, or any other property is covered. The property does not have to be owned by the insured, but may be merely held in trust for others to whom the insured may or may not be legally responsible. Sometimes there are territorial limits as to where the stealing may be insured. Usually, full coverage applies in the United States or its possessions or while the employee is temporarily in another country. Coverage for employees permanently located outside the United States should be arranged for by separate negotiations with the surety.

Restoration. When a loss is incurred, the question arises as to what happens to the amount of bond penalty available for other losses. In blanket bonds there is an automatic reinstatement of bond limits (or restoration clause) immediately after the payment of any loss. For example, under the commercial blanket bond written with a $50,000 limit, payment of $30,000 for one loss from one employee does not reduce the $50,000 penalty applicable to thefts by other employees. As to the employee who stole $30,000, however, only $20,000 remains as coverage for other stealing, no matter when it is discovered. Of course, all coverage in the future for this employee is cancelled. Since the blanket position bond limits apply separately to each employee, there is no need for a restoration clause.

Excess Insurance. Under bonds written with limits that apply to individual employees, it may sometimes be desirable to place larger limits on certain employees on an *excess* basis. Such coverage can be arranged without disturbing the primary bond and without, therefore, increasing the limits of the primary bond for all employees. Use of excess insurance on certain employees, while it may be more economical than increasing the limits of the primary bond, means that the employer must single out certain employees for higher coverage, an uncertain process at best since it cannot be predicted in advance which employee will steal.

Inventory Shortages. One of the most common types of loss from employee dishonesty is that of stealing various items of inventory. Yet, the existence of an inventory shortage does not necessarily mean that an employee is to blame;

shoplifting, sneak thievery, or natural evaporation or spoilage may account for the loss. In individual and schedule bonds there is no recovery under the bond for any loss unless the defaulting employee can be identified postively, including, of course, cases where the accounting system reveals an inventory shortage. In blanket bonds, where identification of the individual employee causing the loss is not a requirement, a question arises as to whether the bond will pay for a loss where an abnormal inventory shortage exists and where no explanation other than employee dishonesty could account for it. The bond provisions state that there must be conclusive proof that employees have been responsible for the shortage.

Types of Surety Bonds

Surety bonds may be classified in three categories: construction bonds, courts bonds, and miscellaneous surety bonds. A brief description of each type follows.

Construction Bonds. A commonly used surety bond is the construction bond. Construction bonds are classified as contract, bid, completion, and owners' protective bonds.

Contract Construction Bond. From the standpoint of premium volume, probably the most important type of surety bond is the *contract construction bond* (sometimes called a *final,* or *performance, bond*). The contract construction bond guarantees that those principals (contractors) involved in construction activities will complete their work in accordance with the terms of construction contracts and will deliver the work to the owner free of any liens or other debts or encumbrances. To the owner, particularly in the case of corporate or municipal owners who let contracts for large projects to the lowest bidder, the construction bond is an indispensable financial security mechanism. Only through use of a third-party guarantee, namely the guarantee of the surety company, can the owner realistically give a contract to the lowest bidder. Without the bond, the owner could not be sure that the lowest bidder would be able to perform the contract at the price stated. There is the possibility that the bidder has bid low just to get the work, and will be unable to finish the job at the bid price. With a bond the owner knows that if the contractor fails to perform, the surety will make good any loss involved. The cost of the bond is returned many times by the fact that owners are in a position to take advantage of the savings involved in competitive bidding. From the viewpoint of the contractor, the bond is highly desirable because the bond places each contractor on an equal footing in its bid, which can be calculated in the knowledge that a bid will not necessarily be looked upon with suspicion because it is low.

Bid Bond. A *bid bond,* in contrast to a contract construction bond, guarantees that if the bidder is awarded the contract at the bid price and under the terms outlined, the bidder will sign the contract and post a construction bond. The bid bond thus involves the same risk as the contract construction bond.

Completion Bond. Bid and contract construction bonds are required for the protection of the owner. The *completion bond,* on the other hand, is required by the lender or the mortgagee, who also may have an interest in the property because of financing arrangements. The completion bond guarantees that the person who borrows the money for the project (this may be either the contractor or the owner) will use the money only for the project and will ultimately turn over to the lender the completed building or project, free of any liens, as security for the loan. The completion bond, which is required only in case of private work, is a guarantee of the honesty and ability of both the borrower and the contractor, if they are different parties. A single job may involve all three types of construction bonds—the contract, the bid, and the completion bond.

Owners' Protective Bond. A form of the contract construction bond known as the *owners' protective bond* is issued for private construction only. The owners' protective bond provides that if the principal defaults, the surety has a direct obligation to take over and to complete the contract or to pay the loss to the owner in cash. This bond differs from the usual form of contract bond, in which the owner has to take over and complete the work in order to determine the loss. If the surety elects a cash settlement, the amount payable is the reasonable cost of completion, less the unpaid balance of the contract price, as determined by taking bids from at least three responsible contractors. The owners' protective bond differs also from other contract bonds in that unpaid laborers or material suppliers may take direct action against the surety instead of filing a lien and foreclosing, as is often the case under other contract bonds. The owners' protective bond further requires that the work be performed under the supervision of an architect.

Court and Miscellaneous Bonds. There are a large number of types of surety bonds used in connection with court proceedings. Examples are *fiduciary bonds*, insuring that a person appointed by the court to manage the property of others will carry out their trust; *litigation bonds*, insuring certain conduct by both defendants and plaintiffs; *license and permit bonds*, which are often used to guarantee the payment of taxes and fees; *lost instrument bonds*, which are required when individuals seek replacement of lost securities or other valuable papers; and *public official bonds*, which offer guarantees that public officials will perform their duties according to the law.

BURGLARY, ROBBERY, AND THEFT INSURANCE

As used in insurance contracts, the meaning of the terms burglary, robbery, and theft are important in the understanding of the extent of coverage. These terms always refer to crimes by persons other than the insured, officers or directors of the insured, or employees of the insured, coverage on which is provided by fidelity bonds.

Burglary is defined somewhat narrowly to mean the unlawful taking of property from within premises, closed for business, entry to which has been obtained by force. There must be visible marks evidencing the forcible entry. Thus, if a customer hides in a store until after closing hours, or enters by an unlocked door, steals some goods, and leaves without having to force a door or a window, the definition of burglary is not met under a burglary policy.

Robbery, on the other hand, is defined to mean the unlawful taking of property from another person by force, by threat of force, or by violence. Personal contact is the key to understanding the basic characteristic of the robbery peril. However, if a burglar enters a premises and steals the wallet of a sleeping night guard, this crime is not one of robbery because there was no violence or threat thereof. The person robbed must be cognizant of this fact. On the other hand, if the thief knocks out or kills the guard and then robs the guard or the owner, the crime would be classed as a robbery. Robbery thus means the forcible taking of property from a messenger or a custodian. Many contracts further define robbery according to whether it occurs outside the premises or inside, a higher rate being charged for outside robbery.

Theft is a broad term which is generally undefined in the insurance contract. Theft includes all crimes of stealing, robbery or burglary. Theft is a catchall term and is usually not distinguished from larceny. Thus, any stealing crime not meeting the definition of burglary or robbery is theft. Confidence games or other form of swindles are thefts, not robberies or burglaries.

Business Coverages

There are a variety of coverages covering the stealing crime peril for businesses. The following paragraphs describe a few examples, ranging from the least comprehensive to the most comprehensive coverage.

Safe Burglary Policy. The *safe burglary policy,* one of the oldest business crime policies, restricts its coverage to loss of property taken by forcible entry from a safe or a vault described in the declarations as the insured safe. Visible marks, such as those made by tools, explosives, electricity, or chemicals, must evidence the entry. If the safe combination is used or the lock is manipulated, there is no coverage. If the property owner is forced to give the combination, there is no coverage; such a loss is covered under a robbery policy. However, the safe burglary contract covers the loss when the entire safe is taken from the premises, even if the evidence is never found. The loss must be capable of being determined through books and accounts kept by the insured. Loss of these books in the safe is excluded; separate contracts (for example, valuable papers and accounts receivable) are available for this type of loss.

Damage to the safe or vault, to the building or its furniture, fixtures, equipment, or other property in the premises but outside the safe or vault is covered under the safe burglary policy, providing of course there has been evidence of an actual safe burglary. Any type of property (except books and records) stolen in a safe burglary is covered, not just money or securities; but if the burglar takes other property outside the safe, there is no coverage. Rates for this coverage depend on the fire and burglar-resistive properties of the safe, and upon the degree of hazard attached to the particular type of business involved.

Discounts are granted for policies covering more than one safe; where certain types of property, such as securities, constitute a given percentage of the total values exposed; or when certain protective devices are used.

Mercantile Open Stock Burglary Policy (MOS). Demand for crime insurance against the loss of stock on merchants' shelves as well as property contained in a safe gave rise to the *mercantile open stock burglary policy (MOS)*. The MOS covers loss by burglary (as usually defined) or by robbery of a night guard, while the premises are not open for business, of merchandise, furniture, fixtures, and equipment within the premises or within a showcase or show window. (The showcase may be outside the main premises, but must be within the building line of the premises.) Money and securities are not insured, nor are books, records, manuscripts, or furs taken from a showcase that was broken into from the outside. There is a limitation of $50 on any article of jewelry and $100 on any loss from a showcase that does not open directly into the building from the interior. The policy covers all loss incurred through damage to the premises and to other property during the covered burglary or robbery. However, vandalism and malicious mischief, war, loss occurring during a fire or when the hazard is increased, and loss to plate glass or its lettering are among the sources of loss excluded by the policy.

The MOS is written with a coinsurance arrangement requiring the insured to purchase coverage equal to the lesser of the following: (1) a certain percentage, ranging from 40% to 80%, of the value of the exposed property or (2) a dollar amount, called the *coinsurance limit*, which varies with the type of merchandise and its location. Failing to carry this amount, the insured may collect only that proportion of the loss as the amount of insurance carried bears to the amount required. This provision, which is designed to prevent underinsurance, may be illustrated as follows: A hardware store owner with $20,000 of stock may decide that thieves could never carry away more than $5,000 worth of merchandise at one time, and so this is the limit of coverage purchased. However, the MOS contract has a coinsurance percentage of 40% and a $10,000 coinsurance limit. Since 40% of the value of the stock is $8,000, and this is less than $10,000, the merchant would collect from the insurer only $5,000/$8,000, or ⅝ of any loss. To avoid coinsurance penalties, the merchant must carry at least $8,000 insurance in this case. The merchant may obtain rate reductions by accepting higher coinsurance percentages or limits.

For an additional premium of approximately 75%, the retail merchant may by endorsement broaden the coverage under the MOS to include any kind of theft, not just burglary or robbery of a night guard. The theft coverage is subject to a $50 deductible, and the coverage is written to exclude normal inventory shortages. The insured is expected to keep records so as to give reasonable evidence of abnormal stock losses. The additional charge for theft coverage amounts to 40% of the burglary premium for wholesale merchants or manufacturers. The size of these premiums gives a rough idea of the estimate that actuaries place on the additional perils introduced by broadening the coverage from burglary to theft.

Storekeepers' Burglary and Robbery Policy. The *storekeepers' burglary and robbery policy* is a package policy designed especially to fit the typical requirements of the small retail establishment. It covers seven perils in one policy: (1) safe burglary, (2) mercantile open stock burglary, (3) damage to money, securities, merchandise, furniture, fixtures, and equipment caused by burglary or robbery, (4) theft of money or securities from a residence or night depository of a bank, (5) kidnapping, meaning compelling a messenger or custodian to give the thief access to the premises for purpose of taking money, securities, merchandise, or equipment, (6) robbery, outside the premises, of the insured or a messenger of the insured, and (7) robbery inside the premises.

For each of the perils above, the policy contains a limit ranging from $250 or multiples thereof up to $1,000. There is a loss limit of $50 applicable to burglary of money or securities outside a safe, such as from a cash drawer or cash register. There is also a provision which limits the number of insured messengers at any one time to two for each location covered. Thus, if a retailer has this contract written for limits of $1,000, and two messengers each take $1,000 to a bank for deposit, the retailer is fully insured against robbery if both should be robbed. Premiums for the storekeepers' burglary and robbery contract vary with the class of risk, the territory, and the limits purchased. The premiums may range from a minimum annual premium of $12.50 to $82.50 for the first $250 of coverage. The charge for $1,000 of coverage is approximately two and one-half times the premium for $250 of coverage.

Money and Securities Broad Form Policy. The storekeepers' burglary and robbery policy gives limited protection against one of the chief crime perils facing a business enterprise—theft of money or securities. The *money and securities broad form policy* is designed to meet the needs of any business enterprise for money and security protection in any limits desired. Furthermore, the peril under this form is broader than just theft, and includes loss of money or securities due to destruction of any kind, including fire, and almost any type of disappearance or wrongful abstraction. Thus, if paper money blows out a window while it is being counted, if fire or flood ruins securities and paper money, or if money mysteriously disappears, the policy will cover. If money is taken from a cash drawer or a safe by manipulating the lock, the safe burglary policy does not apply since this is not a burglary under the definitions; but the money and securities broad form policy would cover the loss. In addition, coverage is given for damage to the premises or to furniture or equipment caused by burglary or robbery, and for loss of merchandise due to interior robbery. Notice that loss of merchandise due to *burglary* is not insured, and therefore there is still the need for the MOS burglary policy which insures this loss.

The main perils excluded under the money and securities broad form policy are war, forgery (may be insured separately), fire (this exclusion does not apply to money and securities), and employee dishonesty. Property such as manuscripts and records, plate glass and its lettering, money in a vending machine (unless the machine has a continuous recording and counting device) is excluded. Losses due to purchase or exchange of property or due to arithmetical errors or omissions are also excluded. Thus, if a clerk accidentally gives the wrong change, or if money is given as the purchase price for property whose value has been fraudulently misrepresented, these are not losses under the policy. However, if a thief poses as a bank messenger and thereby steals a sum of money intended for deposit, the loss is covered even though the owner voluntarily surrendered the cash to the thief.

The money and securities broad form policy is divided into two parts—loss inside the premises and loss outside the premises. Coverage outside the premises is limited to actual destruction, disappearance, or wrongful abstraction of money or securities from a messenger, armored car company, or from the home of a messenger. Loss of other property by robbery is covered only if it occurs in conjunction with the robbery of money or securities, or as the result of a theft in the home of a messenger. Coverage on the premises for property other than money and securities is limited to damage resulting from actual or attempted safe burglary or holdup, or by interior holdup.

If a loss occurs under the money and securities broad form policy, there is no reduction in the amount of insurance for subsequent loss. Furthermore, there is a one-year discovery period after expiration of the policy within which losses that occurred during the policy term may be discovered and paid.

Dishonesty, Destruction, and Disappearance Policy (3D). The dishonesty, destruction, and disappearance policy, abbreviated 3D, is a package contract with five parts: employee dishonesty coverage; money and securities broad form, inside the premises; money and securities broad form, outside the premises; money orders and counterfeit paper currency coverage; and depositors' forgery coverage.

The first three parts of this comprehensive contract are forms already analyzed in this chapter. The fourth coverage indemnifies the insured for loss in case counterfeit money or illegal or counterfeit money orders are accepted.

The fifth coverage, *depositors' forgery*, also known as *outgoing forgery*, covers the insured for losses suffered when checks are endorsed, when a check is issued to a person posing as a legitimate payee and the legitimate payee's signature is forged on the instrument, or when a check legally issued by the insured to a legitimate payee is endorsed and cashed by someone else without the authority of the legitimate payee. Court and legal costs involved in any suit over an allegedly forged instrument are also covered under the policy.

For an additional premium, an endorsement may be added to the 3D policy giving the insured protection in case of *incoming* check forgery. For example, losses incurred when the insured accepts a forged check in payment of merchandise or services may be insured. Incoming forgery coverage is somewhat hazardous in that it might encourage careless procedures in cashing any and all checks presented to the insured. For this reason checks cashed purely as an accommodation are excluded. Recovery on checks given for merchandise is limited to 75% of the insured's pecuniary interest in the check. Thus, if a customer gives a $100 check in payment for $80 of merchandise and receives

$20 in change, the insured's pecuniary interest is $100 and the recovery is limited to $75. This limitation on recovery helps to encourage careful check-cashing procedures.

In addition to incoming check forgery, mercantile open stock burglary, mercantile open stock theft, and certain other crime coverages may be endorsed on the 3D policy. Thus, the insured is provided a means of covering practically all crime exposures in one contract.

Personal Coverage

The *broad form personal theft policy* is the major form of theft insurance written for the typical homeowner. The broad form personal theft policy, defining theft as "any act of stealing," covers against loss by either theft or mysterious disappearance of any property from a private home, or from another depository such as another private dwelling, a public warehouse, a bank, or a trust company. The policy provides for limits of liability under the categories: loss on the premises or loss off the premises. Theft and crime coverage on personal residences is usually written as a division of the homeowners program.

Federal Crime Insurance

Because of difficulties in securing private insurance, particularly in some large city areas, the federal government of the United States began to offer crime insurance to the public in 1971 in certain states on a subsidized basis. Coverages are noncancellable and include burglary, robbery, and theft. Premiums are quoted so that the cost of crime coverage appears affordable to the average buyer. Although private insurers and their agents administer and market the coverage, the federal government, through the Federal Insurance Administration, is the bearer of the risk under the policies issued. As of 1975, about 5,000 businesses and 15,000 residences had been insured under this program in 15 states.[11]

In developing affordable rates the FIA employed statistics gathered by the Federal Bureau of Investigation (FBI). These data were compiled according to Standard Metropolitan Statistical Areas, as defined by the U.S. Bureau of Census. Each rating area is classed in accordance with the degree of crime existing in that area, according to FBI statistics. There are three ratings: low, average, or high. For example, a private residence on which $5,000 of crime coverage is written might receive a six-month rate of $40 in a low-risk territory, $45 in an average-risk territory, and $50 in a high-risk territory. An affordable rate is defined as one which a reasonably prudent person should be willing to pay given the costs and benefits for the territory.

To be eligible for federal crime insurance, the insured must (1) live in a state deemed eligible for the crime coverage; (2) meet certain protective device standards; (3) agree to permit inspections of the premises at reasonable times;

[11] Connecticut, Delaware, Florida, Georgia, Illinois, Kansas, Maryland, Massachusetts, Missouri, New Jersey, Ohio, Pennsylvania, Rhode Island, and Tennessee.

(4) agree to report to the insurer all crime losses, whether or not a claim is filed; and (5) accept the form of coverage prescribed by the FIA.

Residence Policy. The residential crime policy covers burglary, robbery, observed theft, or attempted theft of insured property, including damage caused by attempted theft. The coverage includes vandalism and malicious mischief on owned property. It may be written on one-, two-, three-, or four-family residences. The policy may be written in multiples of coverage from $1,000 to $10,000. It carries a deductible of $50 or 5% of the gross amount of loss, whichever is greater. The deductible is applied against the total loss, and not the policy limit. Thus if an insured had a $3,000 loss, but only $2,000 of coverage, the deductible of 5% ($150) would apply against $3,000 and the insured's recovery would be the full $2,000, the policy limit. The policy applies as excess coverage if the insured has other insurance. Thirty days' notice of cancellation is required. Other conditions are similar to those existing in commercial coverage of this nature. Annual premiums in the most hazardous area might be $60 for $5,000 of coverage.

Commercial Policy. Coverage under the commercial crime insurance policy is issued in amounts ranging from $1,000 to $15,000. There is a deductible between $50 and $200 per loss or 5% of the loss, whichever is greater. Businesses are assigned one of three ratings according to the degree of hazard for that line of business. Premiums vary according to class of business, territory of operation, sales volume, and amount of insurance.

The rating structure of commercial policies assumes that larger firms are more hazardous to insure than smaller firms; only a modest quantity discount for larger policy amounts is justified; and a different concept of an affordable rate exists in businesses as distinguished from residential policies. For example, while the owner of a residence with $5,000 of contents may pay $60 annually for coverage, a business firm with a $5,000 coverage and $100,000 of annual sales would pay over ten times that amount, presumably because of greater ability to pay and greater exposure to loss. The business policy, for example, covers the following perils: theft inside or outside the premises, kidnapping, safe burglary, theft from a night depository, and burglary or robbery from a night guard. Excluded from the business policy are the perils of embezzlement, war, revolution or rebellion, fire, nuclear reaction, and loss of manuscripts, records, or accounts.

SUMMARY

1. Crime statistics show that the perils of dishonesty and human failure cause more total losses than other major perils. Yet the crime peril is greatly underinsured. Prominent among the reasons for this underinsurance are the tendency for business firms to refuse to recognize that trusted employees can and do steal, and the lack of publicity that attends these crimes.
2. The two major types of crime protection are (a) bonds, and (b) burglary, robbery, and theft insurance. Bonds give protection

against losses due to defalcations of persons in a position of trust, while theft insurance gives protection against crimes of so-called outsiders.

3. There are some important differences between bonds and insurance, and an understanding of these differences is vital to an understanding of how crime protection contracts operate. Basic is the fact that bonds provide the surety's financial guarantee of the principal's honesty and ability, with the understanding that the surety can attempt to recover from the principal.
4. Fidelity bonds, which are similar to an insurance contract in their operation, appear in many forms which may be adapted to the needs of the particular business firm. They cover against loss due to dishonesty of employees, while surety bonds provide financial guarantees of both the honesty and the ability of the principal to perform according to a given agreement.
5. Fidelity bonds are continuous in term until cancelled, but their penalties are not cumulative from year to year. They generally cover only those losses that occur during the currency of the bond and which are discovered within a two-year period after its cancellation. The method of distributing any salvage under fidelity bonds may make a substantial difference to the employer in compensation for loss. The employer should give careful consideration to the method to be used to prove that losses have occurred. Proving losses under a fidelity bond is usually much more difficult than in other types of insurance.
6. The major classes of surety bonds are construction, court, and miscellaneous. Contract construction bonds have an important economic influence in all contract construction and in its financing in two ways: they facilitate competitive bidding and free competition in this important industry; and they enable the transfer of construction risk to parties better able to handle it, thus facilitating the growth of this industry and reducing the cost of construction. Surety bonds thus exert a much deeper economic influence than merely protection against crime.
7. Three major types of crime loss from outsiders are burglary, robbery, and theft. These perils are usually defined carefully in insurance contracts and their meanings differ from the meanings commonly ascribed to them by the layperson, who may make no differentiation among them. Crime policies have certain major underwriting characteristics that help to explain the insurance practices involving their use. Chief among these characteristics are the existence of underinsurance, a high degree of moral hazard, and a tendency toward adverse selection.
8. Contracts of insurance against each of the three major crime perils are available, both for personal and business use. In addition, all-risk coverage against loss of money and securities is available. The best known comprehensive crime policy for business is the 3D—dishonesty, destruction, and disappearance contract—which covers in one scheduled form fidelity insurance, broad form money and securities destruction insurance, and forgery and counterfeit money insurance. The broad form personal theft policy is probably the best known and most widely used form of theft insurance for individuals.
9. Since 1971 federal crime insurance on the perils burglary, robbery, and theft has been available to the United States public in 15 states at subsidized rates. This coverage is designed for crime areas where private insurance is often not available except at prohibitive cost.

QUESTIONS FOR REVIEW AND DISCUSSION

1. An employer discovered that an employee "borrowed" a small amount of cash from the company without prior permission. The employee repaid the sum and the employer kept the employee on the payroll. Two months later the employer applied for and received a bond covering all employees, but did not state anything about the incident. Later, the same employee was caught in another theft, but the bonding company denied recovery. On what grounds did the surety do this? Explain.
2. An employer has a blanket position bond with a $10,000 penalty. Three employees are caught in a scheme whereby fictitious employees are kept on the payroll and their names are forged on paychecks by the group. The total amount of theft is $36,000, of which $12,000 is finally recovered by the surety.
   (a) What is the amount payable to the employer under the bond? Explain your answer.
   (b) How would the salvage be divided under a bond with (1) a full salvage clause? (2) a pro rata salvage clause? Explain all calculations involved.
3. (a) Assuming no salvage in the case in Question 2, would the employer have been financially better to have secured a commercial blanket bond written for a penalty of $25,000? Why, or why not?
   (b) Discuss the merits of blanket position bond and commercial blanket bond.
4. The restoration clause has no applicability to the blanket position bond, as it has with the commercial blanket bond. Why?
5. Suggest reasons for the relative lack of acceptance of insurance against crime, in spite of the constant reminder of the danger of crime loss in the public media.
6. Data show that small business firms suffer higher relative losses from crime than large businesses. Suggest possible reasons for this.
7. Summarize the differences between: (a) surety bonds and fidelity bonds and (b) the bond and the insurance contract.
8. A certain dairy bonded all its financial personnel as well as its driver-collectors on a position schedule bond. A laborer in the yard made arrangements to purchase empty wooden butter cartons at five cents each for his "hobby." It turned out some months later that the laborer had systematically stolen several thousand dollars' worth of butter in the "empty" boxes as he passed through the check gate. How could the dairy automatically have protected itself against such a loss?
9. Writing on the subject of the tendency of management to ignore danger signals from dishonesty losses, an author stated: "Besides overlooking obvious danger signals, management often places undue confidence in its alarm systems. The principal alarms for embezzlement are the accounting system and the auditor. Both, for this purpose, are overrated. Most large embezzlements are hidden in accounting systems, remaining hidden through one audit after another. The internal accounting systems are not primarily established to detect fraud, and auditors can't audit what they can't find. More embezzlements are discovered by good luck than by good accounting." Comment. Does this imply that audits are completely useless? If not, what value might they have?
10. Judge Louis D. Brandeis was reported to have called fidelity insurance "an abomination," stating that it is ridiculous "to think of insuring management against the consequences of its own failure to know and supervise its trusted employees!"

(a) Discuss arguments for and against this position.
(b) Do the facts support Brandeis' opinion?
(c) What relationship does this argument have to the increasing dominance of professional managers in business as opposed to the former eminence of individual entrepreneur-owners?

11. Professor John D. Long writes: "Unless most persons in society are honest in most little matters and unless virtually everyone is scrupulously and compulsively honest in big matters, insurance will not function . . . (yet) some types of insurance, particularly dishonesty insurance, require instances of nonconformity to the law." Reconcile this apparent contradiction.

12. "Federal crime insurance is not aimed at 'taking over' crime insurance from private insurers. In this field total premiums were only $1.1 million in 1972 compared to $130 million by private companies."
(a) What is the aim of federal crime insurance?
(b) Why is federal crime insurance expected to grow slowly, in spite of subsidized rates?

13. The text states: "The cost of the (contract construction) bond is returned many times by the fact that owners are in a position to take advantage of the savings of competitive bidding."
(a) Explain what is meant by this statement.
(b) In constructing a building, what risks are taken by an owner who accepts a low bid only after investigating the successful contractor very carefully?

14. Harold Fried, a general contractor, submits a bid plus a bid bond for a certain job in the amount of $100,000. He is awarded the contract, but goes into bankruptcy after $75,000 of the work has been put into place. It is estimated that $35,000 will be required to complete the work.
(a) What is the liability, if any, of the surety under the bid bond?
(b) What is required under a bid bond?

15. (a) Assuming in Question 14 that the proper bonds have been issued, what action is required of the surety?
(b) What liability, if any, would exist if the estimate for completion of the work after Jones' bankruptcy were $15,000 instead of $35,000?

16. In an address to local agents, a bond underwriter stressed the following: "In looking over an application for a bond, the underwriter's first question is, 'Who is going to pay if the principal does not?' " Does this statement imply that the surety is not going to meet its obligations under the bond if a loss develops? If not, explain what steps the surety takes to insure that a loss to it will not occur.

17. (a) What particular advantages over other types of contract bonds are there in the owners' protective bond to (1) the owner and (2) the labor or material supplier?
(b) Suggest reasons for the requirement under this form that construction be handled under the supervision of an architect.

18. In the automobile insurance policy, the insurer has a clause stating that if it is required to make any payment under a financial responsibility act, which it would not have had to make except for this provision, the insured will reimburse the insurer for the amount so paid.
(a) Under what conditions might the payment referred to arise? (See Chapter 16.)
(b) What similarities are there in this provision to a surety bond?

19. Guido Rivas cannot find a policy covering his house against the peril of fire.
(a) Inform Guido as to the desirability of securing a replacement policy.

(b) Would a lost instrument bond be required before the insurer will replace the policy? Why or why not?

(c) Would your answer be the same if Guido had lost a stock certificate showing him to be the owner of 100 shares of General Motors? Why?

20. A burglar enters a jewelry store at night by forcing a window. Just as he begins his work of forcing open the safe, he is surprised by a night guard. There is a struggle, the guard is knocked unconscious, and the burglar escapes with his haul of gems taken from the safe. Is this crime compensable under the usual burglary policy? Why or why not?

21. An employer gave a messenger an envelope containing $1,000 for delivery at a certain location. When the messenger arrived, the envelope was missing. Under what policy, if any, would this loss be covered?

22. Indicate some of the possible weaknesses or limitations in the storekeepers' burglary and robbery policy from the viewpoint of the insured.

23. The manager of a clothing store maintains an average inventory of $15,000. The manager purchases an MOS policy of $6,000 with a coinsurance percentage of 60% and a coinsurance limit of $10,000.

(a) How much may the manager collect in the event of a $1,000 loss caused by robbery? Why? For a $2,100 loss caused by burglary? Why?

(b) How could the manager have made sure that it would be possible to collect in full for these losses? Explain.

24. (a) Distinguish, with an example, between incoming forgery and outgoing forgery.

(b) Which is the more hazardous from an underwriting standpoint? Why?

25. A loss of $3,600,000 was caused by the embezzlement of a trusted bank employee. The losses were suffered, but undiscovered, over a period of 13 years while the employee sought to recoup her losses in the stock and grain markets. The loss was undiscovered even though the bank had gone through three mergers during the period.

(a) What type of bonding problem is likely in such a situation?

(b) What solution to this problem is available?

Chapter *Eighteen*

INSURANCE AND SERVICE GUARANTEES

Insurance companies are frequently in a position to render certain services to an insured other than strict indemnification for loss due to insurable perils. In some cases certain contracts of insurance are purchased as much or more for these corollary services than for the indemnity payable in the event of loss. The nature of these services is not always apparent from reading the insurance contracts. The contracts discussed below illustrate a few examples of these services and point up the fact, stressed frequently in this text, that a full understanding of insurance involves more than a knowledge of the contract. The contract must be interpreted in the light of the economic and social environment within which it is operative.

This chapter analyzes four types of insurance which do not readily fit into the usual categories of insurance policies. These insurance contracts are: credit insurance, title insurance, boiler and machinery insurance, and plate glass insurance. In these contracts the insurer offers more than indemnification for loss. In each type there are somewhat different underwriting problems involved, and the element of service of the insurer assumes special importance.

CREDIT INSURANCE

Use of credit in modern economic societies is universally recognized as a key factor in facilitating growth.[1] Without credit it is very doubtful that the modern industrial economy could have developed at all. However, the use of credit has created many complex problems, not the least of which is the risk that debts will not be paid because of the occurrence of some peril that is often outside the control of the debtor. Among these perils are:

1. Death or physical disability of the debtor.
2. Destruction of accounting records which prevent the creditor from proving the right to collect from a debtor.

[1] One of the earliest works on credit insurance was published in 1848 by Robert Watt, and was entitled *Principles of Insurance Applied to Mercantile Debt.*

3. Failure of a financial institution in which funds have been deposited.
4. Failure of an insolvent business firm to repay a bank loan.
5. Failure of a homeowner or other property owner to repay a building loan because of insolvency.
6. Political action which prevents the debtor from repaying debts to creditors in a foreign country.
7. Insolvency of a business firm to which merchandise credit has been extended.

We shall be concerned primarily with the last type of credit risk, namely, the risk that commercial debtors will be unable to meet their obligations due to business failure of one type or another.

Kinds of Credit Insurance

Insurance exists in some form for all of the credit risks previously listed. Some of the specific kinds are described in the following paragraphs.

Credit Life Insurance and Credit Accident and Sickness Insurance. Insurance against failure to pay a debt because of death of the borrower is known as *credit life insurance*. This contract is not basically different from any contract of life insurance except for the manner in which it is arranged and marketed. Suffice it to say that credit life insurance should not be confused with other forms of credit insurance. A similar comment applies to *credit accident and sickness insurance*, which is arranged to liquidate payments on an installment debt during the time the debtor is disabled because of accident or sickness.

Accounts Receivable Insurance. Insurance protecting the creditor against failure or inability to collect a bad debt because accounting records have been destroyed by certain listed perils is known as *accounts receivable insurance* and was analyzed in Chapter 11.

Deposit Insurance. Insurance against the loss of deposits due to the failure of a bank or a savings and loan association is known as *deposit insurance* and is written only by agencies of the United States Government. The Federal Deposit Insurance Corporation insures bank deposits in all federally-chartered banks and in most state-chartered banks up to a maximum of $40,000. About 97% of all banks are insured. A depositor may obtain up to $40,000 coverage in each of any number of accounts maintained. Similar coverage is given to deposits in savings and loan associations by the Federal Savings and Loan Insurance Corporation. Deposit insurance proved its worth following the depression of the 1930's. After large numbers of people lost their life savings in banks which failed during the depression, the government created these insurance corporations in order to restore confidence in the banking system.

From the time its operations began in 1934 through 1972, the FDIC has handled 496 bank failures, in which losses to depositors amounted to only .4% of insured deposits. In 1972 the agency insured over 60% of the total deposits in insured banks.[2]

[2] *Annual Report of the Federal Deposit Insurance Corporation*, 1972.

Cash Loan Credit Insurance. The United States Government, through such agencies as the Federal Reserve System, the Veterans Administration, and the Small Business Administration, has sponsored various programs to insure cash loans made by banks to certain business enterprises that are unable to secure credit in any other way. While these guarantees are not strictly insurance (being more in the nature of a bond), they serve the same purpose; namely, to facilitate credit.

Loan Credit Insurance. Another significant credit insurance program is that of the United States Federal Housing Administration and the United States Veterans Administration in insuring long-term loans to property owners. The FHA, established in 1934, had about 5.2 million insured homes in 1973.[3] In the same year the Veterans Administration insured about 3.7 million homes for veterans.[4] The influence of credit insurance in home lending is greater than these figures would suggest, however, because about half of the new homes built under the FHA program are ultimately financed by private lending agencies. It is doubtful that long-term amortized mortgages would have been nearly so prevalent in the United States had it not been for the availability of insurance which guarantees the lender that someone would ultimately repay these loans. As it has turned out, the homeowner has been proven to be a good risk. Foreclosures accounted for only 2.8% of FHA home mortgage terminations in 1973.[5]

Insurance of Bonds. A development related to loan insurance is the practice of issuing insurance against the default of credit instruments such as municipal bonds in order to improve their investment quality and reduce interest costs. The American Municipal Bond Assurance Corporation (AMBAC), which issues such policies, estimates that a municipality may realize savings in bond interest ranging from $20,000 to $118,000 over the life of a $1,000,000 bond issue, depending on the quality of the bond and the length of the period of amortization. The insurance premium absorbs from 28% to 39% of the interest cost savings.[6] The insurance guarantee may reduce the risk enough to enable the sale of bonds by small municipalities which might not otherwise be able to issue their bonds at reasonable cost. AMBAC specializes in small and medium-sized issues which receive medium-grade ratings by agencies such as Standard and Poors.

International Business Guarantees. The insurance device has proved to be useful in government programs to stimulate international business. Through

[3] *1973 HUD Statistical Yearbook,* p. 344.

[4] *Ibid.*, p. 185.

[5] *Ibid.*, p. 185.

[6] American Municipal Bond Assurance Corporation, *Questions and Answers* (New York, 1971), p. 8. This company is a subsidiary of the Mortgage Guarantee Insurance Corporation, a private firm which issues loan insurance on some conventional mortgages issued by banks and savings and loan associations on home loans which are not subject to insurance by the Federal Housing Administration.

export credit insurance and foreign investment guarantees, the federal government has attempted to remove obstacles to the conduct of international business by reducing such risks as expropriation, inconvertibility of currency, war, cancellation of export licenses, and other international events outside the control of the individual business person. Export credit insurance, as well as domestic credit insurance, is in use in most industrial countries.[7] Such programs often involve services to collect accounts from foreign sources through extensive networks of banking and insurance facilities.

Domestic Merchandise Credit Insurance. In the United States, Canada, Mexico, and most European countries, sellers may obtain insurance against the insolvency of domestic debtors on credits arising out of the sale of merchandise on an unsecured basis. Such coverage has been sold in the United States since 1890. Insurance against failure to repay a cash loan is generally not available in the United States, except as it is applied for through a governmental agency in special programs such as those mentioned above. The volume of merchandise credit insurance is generally quite small, when compared with other major lines of insurance. Because it is so specialized in nature, relatively few insurers in each country compete for the business; and those who write it make it their chief line. In most countries credit insurers give only limited coverage, in that only certain business consumers, such as manufacturers and wholesalers, are eligible. Not all types of transactions are insured, not all perils are covered, and losses are not indemnified 100%. In the United States, for example, there are two main private insurers, the American Credit Indemnity Company and the London Guarantee Company. In 1974 their total premium volume, including amounts reinsured, was about $21 million, which was a small fraction of other types of insurance premium volumes. (For example, stock insurers wrote $36 million of premiums in glass insurance alone in 1973.) It is estimated that credit insurance policies covered about $25 billion of shipments in 1974. Thus, the coverage is not an insignificant economic factor in the business life of firms using it. The major insurer, the American Credit Indemnity Company, writes three fourths of all the merchandise credit insurance in the United States; and its contracts, which are very similar to those of the London Guarantee Company, are analyzed below.

Types of Credit Insurance

Credit insurance contracts as written in the United States may be classified in two categories: (1) back coverage and forward coverage, and (2) general coverage and restricted coverage.

Back Coverage Contract. Credit insurance contracts termed *back coverage* apply only to losses incurred during the policy term (one year). Under these

[7] F. T. Scafuro, *World's Principal Export Credit Insurance System* (Bank of America, 1968). This summary outlines the details of credit insurance systems in 34 countries. See also Mark R. Greene, "Export Credit Insurance—Its Role in Expanding World Trade," *Journal of Risk and Insurance* (June, 1965), pp. 177-193.

policies, claims can arise from sales made during the year prior to the commencement date of the policy. Back coverage contracts account for a majority of credit insurance in force.[8]

Forward Coverage Contract. Under the terms of *forward coverage* contracts, the policy indemnifies the insured for losses stemming only from accounts which were created by sales made during the policy term. Accounts already on the books when the policy is purchased are, accordingly, not insured. However, if on the last day of the policy term a credit sale is made which ultimately becomes a bad debt, the contract is applicable even if it is not renewed. There is always a time limit within which the account must be filed with the insurer as a claim in order to establish some termination of the insurer's liability.

General Coverage Form. Under *general coverage* policies, insurance covers all debtors falling into given classes of credit ratings on a blanket basis. Thus, the policy may specify that $100,000 of coverage applies to the bad debts of any debtor that has a 3A1 Dun and Bradstreet credit rating. However, the insurer often is willing to name specific customers of the insured for coverage in excess of the blanket limit. The blanket coverage is scaled down for firms with lower credit ratings. Automatic coverage on unrated accounts can also be provided, but the aggregate coverage on this group will not exceed the deductible. All back coverage policies are of the general coverage type.

Restricted Coverage Form. Under restricted coverage only debtors named specifically are insured. The amount of coverage is not based on credit agency ratings, and remains fixed for the full term of the policy unless cancelled by the insurer or the insured.

Establishing a Loss

To establish a loss the insured must first show what credit rating the debtor had at the time the goods were shipped. It is this rating which determines the limit of coverage under the credit insurance policy, unless the particular debtor has been specifically named for additional coverage beforehand. The policyholder must show that a legal obligation exists and that the debt arose because of bona fide sales of merchandise or services normally dealt in by the seller. Under the terms of the contract, a loss is said to have occurred under two general situations: (1) a debtor simply does not pay the account by the due date but is not insolvent, and (2) a debtor becomes legally insolvent as determined by specific events listed in the contract.

If the debtor is not insolvent but refuses to pay a legal obligation as defined in the contract within 3 months from the due date, the insured may file the account with the insurer as a claim. In other words, if a seller grants 60-day credit terms, the account is past due after 60 days. If the account is not paid within three months after the expiration of the regular 60 days of credit (a total

[8] In the American Credit Indemnity Company, back coverage policies account for over 95% of the company's total business.

of five months in this case), the insured may file this account with the insurer who will attempt to collect it. Failing to do so, the insurer will indemnify the insured for the loss, subject to the other terms of the policy. Because some insureds fear they will offend their debtor by such an action, they hesitate to file the account for collection with the insurer. If the account is not filed within the specified period (forward coverage policies require that this be done), the insured must then wait until the occurrence of one of 18 events listed in the policy defining the insolvency of the debtor. These 18 conditions include such events as the death or insanity of a sole debtor, sale of the debtor's assets by a court order, appointment of a receiver or filing of a petition in bankruptcy, calling of a meeting of unsecured creditors, or absconding of the debtor.

Deductibles

Loss settlements under the credit insurance contract can be subject to one or both of two kinds of deductibles: a stated dollar amount, and a percentage, 10% or 20% of the individual loss. The *dollar deductible*, called the *primary loss*, is intended to represent the normal credit losses of the firm. Since these losses are expected and are in the nature of a certainty, they are excluded from coverage. The amount of normal loss varies with the industry and is adjusted according to the experience of the individual insured. It is applied to the total of the insured's losses in a given policy term.

The *percentage deductible*, called *coinsurance*, is a flat deductible that applies to each individual loss. It is intended to control the moral hazard, the tendency that would otherwise exist for the insured to be careless in granting credit in the knowledge that if the debtor did not pay, the insurer would. The reasoning is that if the insured knows that at best only 90% of a given account can be collected from the credit insurer, the insured will be less tempted to sell to marginal credit risks, since collection of only 90% of an account from the insurer will usually not leave any profit. The coinsurance for poorly rated or nonrated accounts is increased to 20%.

As an example of these deductibles, assume that a firm has five bad debts in a given year, totalling $75,000. Assume that because of limits of liability governing the policy, effective coverage is $70,000. (This might be due, for example, to the fact that a customer has been extended $5,000 of credit beyond the applicable limits for this customer's credit rating.) Assume further that coinsurance is 20%, the primary loss is $4,000, and that all accounts are filed within 12 months of the date of shipment for collection. The settlement would be as follows:

Bad debts	$75,000
Uncovered losses	5,000
Losses allowed	$70,000
Less:	
Coinsurance, 20%	14,000
	$56,000
Primary loss	4,000
Loss payment	$52,000

Collection Service

Studies of credit insurance have documented the conclusion that many insureds look upon the collection services of the credit insurer as a very important part of the benefits secured under the contract.[9] Part of the efficiency of the efforts of insurers in this regard is due to the fact that failure to collect accounts placed with them by policyholders will normally result in a loss under the policy. Hence, the credit insurer has a greater stake in a given account than a typical collection agency, and will make strong efforts not only to collect the account but also to preserve the customer's goodwill in the knowledge that if the goodwill is sacrificed in the process of collection, the insured *and* the insurer may lose a good customer.

The services rendered by the credit insurer may be employed to bring about collections from distant buyers in an economical manner, a service of special importance to the small localized firm. Credit insurance does not permit a firm to disband its collection department or to dismiss its credit manager, since the insurer relies on credit screening as a basis for issuing the contract.

Advantages and Limitations of Credit Insurance

In view of the apparent usefulness of credit insurance, both to the firm which wants to protect itself against catastrophic credit losses brought on by the insolvency of some large accounts and to the firm which seeks to make use of the extensive collection facilities of the credit insurer, one may wonder why credit insurance has not been used more widely. The following arguments in favor of the use of merchandise credit insurance have been put forth:

1. It is illogical for a firm to insure its inventory against loss arising from various perils only to ignore the substantial possibility of loss when the inventory is sold and is represented on the books by accounts receivable. Records of bad debt losses show that the peril is substantial.
2. The use of credit insurance has important psychological benefits in reducing the fear of bad debt losses, thus removing a hindrance to expanded sales. A run of credit losses will thus not cause the credit manager to tighten up on all applications for credit, regardless of merit.
3. Use of credit insurance may in some cases enable the firm to accept applications for credit which would otherwise have been refused, because investigation of the account by the credit insurer reveals conditions which justify credit.
4. The use of credit insurance enables a firm to stabilize its operations by placing definite limits on the size of bad debt losses. The efficacy of the insurer's collection service is important to many users.

On the other hand, it appears that the following factors have been instrumental in limiting the growth of merchandise credit insurance in spite of the advantages claimed for it:

[9] See James G. Sheehan, "Credit Insurance from the Policyholder's Point of View" (Doctoral dissertation, The Ohio State University, 1955); John A. Churella, *An Evaluation of Credit Insurance and Its Effects on Business Management* (Baltimore: American Credit Indemnity Company, 1958); and Mark R. Greene, "An Analysis of Credit Insurance" (Doctoral dissertation, The Ohio State University, 1955). See also Clyde W. Phelps, *Commercial Credit Insurance as a Management Tool* (Baltimore: Commercial Credit Company, 1961), Chapter III.

1. The sale of credit insurance is limited to certain types of business firms—wholesalers, manufacturers, and certain firms providing services such as advertising agencies. Retailers are excluded because they sell to the final consumer whose credit is not normally believed to be insurable.
2. Many business firms feel they are better able to self-insure the credit risk because of the basic diversification of their accounts. The credit insurance contract best fits the firm that sells large quantities of goods on credit to relatively few customers, the failure of any one of which would jeopardize the firm's own solvency.
3. The operation of the deductibles in the credit insurance contract tends to limit recoveries in a typical year so that the insured usually pays most of the loss. This, of course, is the result of the way in which the insuring arrangement is planned because it is intended to cover only abnormal, excess, and unusually large losses, not the average normal credit loss. Nevertheless, many insureds have not understood this basic point and reject the insurance because the price is too high.
4. Credit insurance has not been promoted vigorously and the advantages claimed for it are relatively unknown by the overwhelming majority of business firms. Because it is a specialized and complex line of insurance, few general or local agents handling other lines of insurance are in a position to sell it to their customers. This situation is reinforced by the fact that the line is considered too hazardous to give the field agent authority to bind coverage without home office approval. The credit insurance contract is noncancellable, once issued, and must be tailored carefully to meet the individual needs of its user.
5. Conservative underwriting, brought on partly by lack of sufficient loss data to establish rates in which great confidence may be taken and partly by the element of adverse selection against the underwriter, has limited the growth of credit insurance. Competition of other insurers in the field is virtually nonexistent because of the specialized nature of credit insurance. On the other hand, factors, particularly in the textile trades, have combined the financing and the insurance functions in the outright purchase of a seller's accounts, thus eliminating the credit risk for many types of potential credit insurance users.

TITLE INSURANCE

Title insurance is a device by which the purchaser of real estate may be protected against losses in case it develops that the title obtained is not legitimate or can be made legitimate only after certain payments are made. Defects in titles may stem from sources such as forgery of public records, forgery of titles, invalid or undiscovered wills, defective probate procedures, and faulty real estate transfers. Thus, a person may occupy real property for years only to find that the one who conveyed title to this person was not the rightful owner. True ownership may lie in the possession of another, say a former spouse who had been wrongfully deprived of property rights.

Usually all rights in real property, such as encumbrances, liens, and easements, must be duly recorded in the courthouse of the county or the parish in which the real estate lies. Before title insurance became common, the real property buyer usually retained an attorney to search these records and render an opinion on the validity of the title. The attorney based this opinion in large part on an *abstract*, which is a brief history of title to the land. The abstract, which is usually developed by either the attorney or an abstract company, contains a record of the conveyances, liens, charges, county resolutions, court decrees, and other legal matters affecting the title to the land. The purpose of the abstract is to reveal the nature of any legal obstacle which may cloud the title or leave a way open for someone else to make a legal claim against the land. After examining the abstract and perhaps other matters which may not appear as a matter of public record, the attorney renders an opinion. The attorney, however, could be held liable only for negligence in the title search; and if it turned out that there was some unusual defect in title not discoverable by a reasonable and diligent search, there was no remedy for the unfortunate owner of the land. Thus, the need for a formal guarantee of the completeness and accuracy of the title search arose. Title insurance is essentially this guarantee. It should be observed, however, that if a title turns out to be defective, the remedy to the insured is a dollar indemnity and not possession of the property. The title insurance policy attempts to guarantee the merchantability of the title, subject to exceptions clearly set forth in the policy.

Special Characteristics of Title Insurance

Some of the differences between title insurance and other contracts of property and liability insurance may be summarized as follows:

1. The premium for title insurance is almost entirely intended to cover the necessary services in investigating possible sources of loss of title marketability, and not an expected loss. The title insurance company, in fact, expects no losses, feeling that if an adequate job of investigation is performed before the policy is issued, there will be no loss to pay on the policy. Some title insurance firms maintain extensive ''plants'' of real estate records in their area, and retain a staff of expert title attorneys, so as to render more rapid service to the purchaser.
2. Title insurance covers title defects which have occurred *before* the effective date of the policy but which are discovered *after* the effective date of the policy. Most other types of insurance cover only losses which occur after the effective date of the policy, and not before, under the general theory that to do otherwise would be to cause insurance to be taken out to cover a known loss. In the case of title insurance, the defect which causes a loss is not known at the time of the issuance of the policy. If the defect is known it is excluded as one of the sources of loss.
3. Title insurance contracts are not cancellable by either party, and the premium is fully earned once it is paid; that is, there is no refund of premium under any conditions.
4. Title insurance has no expiration date; the coverage is effective indefinitely. In other words, if a purchaser finds that the title is clouded 20 years after the effective date of the policy, and the defect causing this cloud occurred before this date, the policy covers any loss incurred. The policy contains no limitation as to when a claim can be made following a loss.

The Title Insurance Contract

There is no standard title insurance contract, but the general form of the insuring clause is fairly uniform. The insurer agrees to indemnify the owner against any loss suffered ''by reason of unmarketability of the title of the insured to or in said premises, or . . . from all loss and damage by reason of liens or encumbrances, defects, objections, estates, and interests, except those listed in Schedule B.''

Schedule B is a separate endorsement on which is listed all title defects or rights in the property found during the title search. The most usual of these defects are easements, mortgages, assessments, and tax liens. Often Schedule B will exclude from coverage those losses arising from "easements, liens or encumbrances, including material or labor liens, which are *not* shown by the public records, rights or claims of persons in possession or claiming to be in possession not shown of record, water rights, mining claims, taxes not yet payable, zoning laws, and any state of facts which an accurate survey and inspection of said land would show." The intent of these exclusions is to remove from coverage certain sources of defect in the title which exist at the time of title transfer, even if the title search did not reveal them.

The title insurance contract is certainly not an all-risk agreement, even with respect to the unknown defects. To illustrate, assume that Smith buys some land with the intent of constructing an apartment house. Unknown either to Smith or to the insurer, just before title is transferred, a zoning ordinance is passed prohibiting this type of construction on the land. Even though a loss accrues to Smith and it was unknown at the time of transfer, there is no liability.

Defense. Under the typical policy the insurer agrees to defend the insured in any legal proceedings brought against the insured concerning the title, assuming that the action involves a source of loss not excluded under the contract. The insured is required to notify the insurer of any such proceedings and to cooperate in any legal action by the insurer.

Premium. The premium in title insurance is paid only once, and it keeps the policy in force for the named insured for an indefinite period. If the property is transferred, a new premium must be paid for the protection of the new purchaser. The old policy is not assignable to the new buyer. Usually there is no reduction in premium, even if the property is transferred a short time after the prior purchase. Thus, if a residence is built in one year and is resold five times in the next five years, a title insurance premium might be charged five times. Since the premium presumably is charged chiefly for making the search, and since there is obviously less work to do on each succeeding title search (because less time has elapsed during which defects could have arisen), it would appear inequitable to charge the same premium for each policy. Premiums charged for a $20,000 policy might cost approximately $130. Premiums are based on the face amount of the policy, the territory, and on whether the insured is an owner or a mortgagee.

BOILER AND MACHINERY INSURANCE

Explosions caused by steam boilers, compressors, engines, electrical equipment, flywheels, air tanks, and furnaces constitute a serious source of loss which the layperson often does not recognize. Since the causes of boiler and machinery explosions are technical in nature, the danger is usually minimized by the would-be insured.

Special Characteristics of Boiler and Machinery Insurance

Boiler and machinery insurance has been developed along somewhat different lines from the usual insurance contract. First, recognizing that prevention of losses is even more important than indemnification of loss, insurers have taken on the service of inspection and servicing of boiler operations and technical machinery. Approximately one fourth of the total premium collected is used for the service function. The insurer typically sends an inspector to the insured plant two or more times each year, depending on the size of the firm. In many states these inspections substitute for an inspection required by law. Technical specialists examine boilers and pressure vessels both internally and externally, using special equipment to detect minute cracks, crystallization, deterioration of insulation, vibration, and general wear. Failure of a vessel to pass an inspection may mean imminent danger of continued operation. As a result, the insurer reserves the right to suspend coverage immediately if recommended repairs or replacements are not made.

Second, because of the technical nature and diversity of boilers, tanks, furnaces, and electrical equipment in use, the boiler and machinery policy specifies by endorsement the exact definition of "accident" applicable to each insurable object. The insurer requires a series of separate endorsements describing in detail the nature of the insured object and what will constitute an accident. An insured may have ten types of objects with a different definition of accident for each one. There is no blanketing of coverage for all machines and pressure vessels on one form. For example, one endorsement might list on a schedule of reciprocating pumps and compressors a "two-cylinder York ammonia belted compressor" with the definition:

> "Object" shall mean the complete unit which is designated and described in this schedule, including the shaft of said unit; but shall not include any electrical machine, nor any piping leading to or from the unit, nor any structure or foundation supporting the unit, nor any mechanism, appliance, or shaft connected to the unit.
>
> "Accident" shall mean:
>
> 1. A sudden and accidental breaking of the Object, or any part thereof, into two or more separate parts, but not the breaking of any gasket, gland packing, shaft seal, or diaphragm, nor the loosening of any assembled parts; or
> 2. A sudden and accidental burning out of the Object, or any part thereof, but not the burning out of any gasket, gland packing, or shaft seal; or
> 3. A sudden and accidental deforming of any shaft or rod of the Object, not caused by the cracking of such shaft or rod.
>
> An Accident arising out of a strike, riot, civil commotion or acts of sabotage, vandalism, or malicious mischief shall be considered "accidental" within the terms of this definition.

It may be appreciated that without such a careful definition, it might be possible for an insured to require compensation from the insurer for expensive machinery that actually did not break down but merely wore out.

Third, because the damage caused by an exploding boiler may result in legal liability for damage to the property or persons of others, direct loss to the property of the insured, and substantial indirect loss due to a shutdown of the plant, the single boiler and machinery contract provides coverage at once against different types of losses. Thus, the following types of insurance may be found in a single boiler and machinery policy:

1. Loss of the boiler or machinery itself due to accident, as defined.
2. Expediting expenses.
3. Property damage liability.
4. Bodily injury liability.
5. Defense, settlement, and supplementary payments.
6. Automatic coverage of newly-installed machinery for a period of 90 days.
7. Business interruption insurance.
8. Outage insurance.
9. Power interruption insurance.
10. Consequential loss due to spoilage of goods, from the accident, such as when a refrigeration system fails and meats spoil as a consequence.
11. Furnace explosion.

Because of the comprehensive nature of boiler and machinery insurance, there may be some overlapping of coverage with other property and liability insurance contracts. To avoid this as much as possible, the boiler and machinery contract contains provisions to the effect that for certain losses, such as bodily injury liability, the boiler policy is to be considered excess over any other applicable insurance. The policy also contains a unique feature in that an aggregate limit of loss is stated for the first four coverages listed above and loss payments are to be satisfied out of this aggregate limit in numerical order. Thus, if a policy has a $50,000 limit and $40,000 is paid out under the first coverage, $10,000 remains for the second. If no liability exists for this, the $10,000 is available to satisfy any liability for the third coverage, and so on, until the $50,000 is used up, after which the limits are exhausted for that particular accident. Separate limits of liability are commonly stated for all coverages from the sixth on. The insurer pays all defense, settlement, and supplementary payments over and above the aggregate limit. The net effect of these provisions is to maximize the benefits of the contract for the use of the insured in allowing the application of the policy limits where they are needed, and to avoid paying for duplicating coverage. All loss from the peril of war is excluded.

Insuring Agreements

The following comments describe the coverages commonly found in boiler and machinery policies, with emphasis on unusual features.

Loss of Property of Insured. Perhaps the chief reason for the purchase of boiler and machinery insurance is to replace, in the event of sudden or accidental loss, damaged machinery belonging to the insured, or to prevent the occurrence of such a loss. The insuring clause excludes loss when the proximate cause is fire, since fire losses are paid under the standard fire policy. Indirect losses are excluded but may be insured separately by endorsement. The insurer reserves the right to replace or to repair the property or to indemnify for its actual cash value.

Expediting Expenses. Under this clause the insurer agrees to pay for the reasonable extra cost of temporary repair or the extra costs of expediting the repair of the machinery, including overtime costs and the extra costs of express or other rapid means of transportation. Payments under this section may not exceed $1,000, or the amount payable under the first section, whichever is less.

Property Damage and Bodily Injury Liability. This coverage is identical to the typical agreement contained in the comprehensive general liability policy. The property damage liability contributes pro rata with any other applicable coverage, but the bodily injury liability is considered as excess. Bodily injury liability coverage may be eliminated by endorsement, and a premium reduction may be granted in return.

Defense, Settlement, and Supplementary Payments. This coverage, too, is identical to the typical agreement in general liability insurance coverages. The insurer assumes all legal defense of liability suits caused by the occurrence of an accident, as defined in the policy. This cost is paid above any amounts payable under other agreements.

Automatic Coverage. Under this endorsement the insurer agrees to cover accidents from all machinery of the same type as those specifically listed in the endorsement. (The coverage does not extend to just any additional equipment purchased.) The insured is required to apply for coverage on any additional equipment thus acquired within 90 days and to pay an additional premium thereon.

Business Interruption Insurance. One of the important types of loss stemming from the failure of a steam boiler or from other vital machinery is the shutdown of an entire plant. Thus, business interruption insurance, usually called *use and occupancy* in this line of insurance, is commonly added by endorsement to the boiler and machinery contract. The contract is similar to business interruption insurance as written in connection with fire insurance. It is available on the valued form or on an actual loss sustained basis. On the valued form a daily indemnity is stated, say $1,000 a day, with an aggregate limit, say $50,000. This amount is paid without proof of loss in case the plant is totally shut down. Proportionate parts of this amount are paid for partial shutdowns, which are measured by the reduction of sales or production due to the accident. Only shutdowns caused by described accidents are covered. The cost of this endorsement may be reduced by acceptance of waiting periods until indemnity begins.

Outage Insurance. *Outage* refers to insurance against loss incurred during the time that a piece of machinery has been put out of commission by the described accident. It is similar to extra expense insurance in that it is intended to cover the extra expenses of operation after an accident when the business is not wholly or partially shut down. For example, a heating plant boiler may fail, forcing the business to install temporary alternative methods of heating at considerable expense. A power plant failure may force the firm to purchase standby power from another source at extra cost. Outage insurance may be endorsed on the boiler and machinery policy to pay a set amount for each hour the object is "out" to pay for these extra expenses. Outage insurance is especially appropriate for office or apartment buildings, schools, and stores, where failure of an insured object would not usually stop operations but would cause considerable extra cost in keeping everything running.

Power Interruption Insurance. The *power interruption endorsement* is available on a boiler and machinery contract to provide coverage for two types of losses stemming from interruption of electricity, gas, heat, or other energy from public utilities: loss from interruption of operations, and loss from damage through spoilage to property of the insured. The first type of loss is paid on a valued basis, and it is not necessary to prove any losses. All that must be shown is that the outside power source failed for a period longer than five minutes. Indemnity is paid according to the length of time of the interruption. This type of loss is actually a combination of power plant business interruption and outage losses, but the contract makes no distinction between the two; and there is no necessity of proving that an actual loss was sustained.

The second type of power interruption loss is on an actual loss sustained basis and if the power or energy source is cut off for longer than a five-minute period, the insured may claim any amount of indemnity up to the policy limits, assuming it can be proved that spoilage of goods actually occurred. In other words, the actual loss sustained, rather than time, is the element that decides the amount of a valid claim. Thus, if a high wind destroys the power company's distribution facilities and electricity is cut off for ten hours, the insured may lose an entire cold-storage warehouse of perishable foodstuffs and might collect the entire amount of the policy.

Consequential Damage. Coverage similar to the second type of power interruption loss described above, but due to failure of an insured object within the insured's own premises, is provided on the *consequential damage endorsement*. In the case where an insured has a cold-storage warehouse filled with perishable foodstuffs and the refrigeration system is inoperative due to failure of the compressor system within the insured's plant, indemnity would be payable under a consequential damage endorsement but not under a power interruption endorsement. Firms such as cold-storage warehouses, breweries, creameries, florists, ice plants, and hothouses are among the more likely candidates for consequential damage and power interruption coverage.

Furnace Explosion. Coverage for losses resulting from the explosion of furnaces, as opposed to explosion of the boilers which they may service, is generally provided in one of the fire insurance forms or liability contracts covering the property. Alternatively, this coverage is available as an endorsement to the boiler and machinery contract. No general rule can be laid down as to which method is preferable, other than that care should be taken to see that this peril is recognized and that insurance against it, but not duplicating coverage, is provided.

PLATE GLASS INSURANCE

Plate glass has assumed great significance in modern architecture, not only as physical protection against the elements but also because of its advertising value. Use of plate glass in show windows is of great importance in successful merchandising. There are many uses of glass and types of glass objects, other than for plate glass windows, in which large investments are made and for which insurance is sought. Examples include glass signs, motion picture screens, halftone screens and lenses, stained glass windows, glass bricks, glass doors, neon signs, showcases, counter tops, and insulated glass panels.

Sources of Loss

Glass is susceptible to loss from many sources other than the usual perils of fire, windstorm, riot and civil commotion, and vehicles. Breakage from such sources as improper setting, excessive heat or cold, flying rock, and sonic boom illustrate the somewhat unusual nature of the perils which destroy glass. Of basic importance to the insured is the prompt repair of broken plate glass.

The Insuring Agreement

Since loss settlement procedures, common under insurance contracts of fire and related lines, are often somewhat delayed, a special contract known as the *comprehensive glass policy* has been developed under the rules of the National Bureau of Casualty Underwriters and the Mutual Insurance Rating Bureau. Under this policy the insured may purchase all-risk insurance against breakage[10] of glass from any source except fire or nuclear reaction. As is true in fire insurance, the insurer reserves the right to settle losses either in cash or by repairing or replacing the glass. Unlike fire insurance loss settlement procedures, however, it is the practice of insurers to replace the glass insured under the policy, and do so immediately after the loss. Insurance on the replacement glass continues as before without extra premium.

The comprehensive glass policy provides a place in the declarations for a detailed description of each plate of glass, the value of lettering and ornamentation, its position in the building, and its size. The insuring clause indicates that the insurer agrees:

1. To pay for damage to the glass and its lettering or ornamentation by breakage of the glass or by chemicals accidentally or maliciously applied.
2. To pay for the repair or replacement of frames when necessary.
3. To pay for the installation of temporary plates or boarding up of windows, when necessary.
4. To pay for the removal or replacement of any obstructions made necessary in replacing the glass.

Each of the last three agreements is subject to a loss limitation of $75 per occurrence. There is no dollar amount of liability stated.

[10] Scratching or defacing is not the same as breakage, and is not insured.

SUMMARY

1. Credit, title, boiler and machinery, and plate glass insurance have the common element that the insurer renders certain collateral services in addition to the indemnification and risk-reduction function.
2. There are at least seven kinds of credit insurance in existence. Merchandise credit insurance, issued to cover bad debts arising from unsecured open accounts with debtors who have become insolvent, is perhaps the oldest and best known type. While this coverage has existed for over 70 years in the United States, it has not become widely adopted.
3. Credit insurance seems useful when a firm has a few large accounts, the failure of any one of which would cause a severe and crippling loss, or when it is desired to use the credit and collection services of the insurer. A careful analysis must be made of the firm's exposure to loss and the policy must be tailored to fit these specific needs.
4. Some of the reasons that account for the relatively small volume of credit insurance business stem from the complicated nature of the contract, the use of deductibles that tend to place the average policyholder in the position of bearing most of the loss, conservative underwriting, absence of strong promotive efforts, and the tendency for most business firms to self-insure the credit risk or to handle it by loss-prevention methods.
5. Title insurance is purchased largely for the title investigation that accompanies it, although, of course, the protection it gives against losses caused by discovery of defects that impair the marketability of the insured title is also important.
6. Title insurance is distinguished from other insurance contracts in that it applies only to certain losses that existed before, but which are undiscovered at the time the policy is issued. Title insurance has no expiration date and the premium is paid only once. Far from all-risk in nature, title insurance excludes all known sources of loss as well as many unknown sources.
7. Boiler and machinery insurance exists because of the severe and crippling losses that can stem from an exploding boiler or broken machinery. Not only direct losses but also many types of indirect losses are so caused. Inspection of boilers and other insured machinery is an important feature of the boiler contract and accounts for a substantial element of cost in the premium.
8. The comprehensive glass insurance contract is a type of coverage that seems to find its justification more in the convenience it provides in the replacement of broken glass and in the comprehensive nature of its coverage than in the risk-reduction function, since it generally duplicates at least to some extent glass coverage granted on other contracts.

QUESTIONS FOR REVIEW AND DISCUSSION

1. The percentage of total loans insured by the Federal Housing Administration has declined over the years.
   (a) Does this imply that credit insurance on home loans is "on its way out"? Why?
   (b) What factors may account for the trend noted?
2. Why are political risks considered insurable by governments in international business guarantees, although they are considered uninsurable by private concerns?

3. E. M. Shenkman, in describing the policies of the first credit insurance company in Great Britain (formed in 1820), the British Commercial Insurance Company, stated that "The company understood to make good losses incurred by any debtor who became bankrupt, or sought relief under any Act of Parliament. But the insured must prove that the credit was given to the debtor when the latter's financial position was unimpeachable." How does the practice described in the statement above contrast with present-day methods of proving loss?
4. A credit manager of a steel supplier reported that credit insurance had helped increase the company's sales by 60% within 2 years. This was accomplished mainly by securing additional credit insurance coverage on accounts which were unrated but nevertheless worth additional credit. (If an account is unrated by a credit agency, usually only a small amount of insurance is granted on this account by the insurer.) It was found that sales increased in direct proportion to the firm's willingness to extend credit. In turn, the firm's ability to increase credit lines was made possible by a close working relationship with the firm's credit insurance underwriter, who agreed to increase credit insurance limits by degrees for one account from $10,000 to $100,000 within one year. If the credit insurance company was willing to increase its credit limits so extensively, for what reason did the credit rating agency apparently fail to give this customer a higher credit rating?
5. A writer stated, "The main cause of uncertainty in economic life is time. The function of insurance in an organized society consists in overcoming the disadvantage of time in the same way in which the means of transportation overcome the disadvantage of space."
(a) In what way is credit insurance an instrument to overcome the disadvantages of time? Explain.
(b) Can you say that this statement is true for other kinds of insurance? Why?
6. To what extent, if any, are bad debt loss reserves a substitute for credit insurance? Explain.
7. A writer stated, "Credit risk cannot . . . be transferred entirely to an external agency. . . . Some residual risk must always rest upon the shoulders of the independent businessman as a necessary consequence of engaging in business." Explain why this is true or untrue.
8. A user of credit insurance reported, "Some credit executives . . . indicate that the cost of credit insurance is extreme. Considering the terms of the policy, initial premium, monthly charges, coinsurance factor, and collection costs, the policy for our company is expensive. But it is expensive only if one takes the limited view of protecting accounts receivable . . . I operate with one assistant and would probably need two assistants for the sales volume involved . . . our salesmen may tap virgin territories and new accounts without fear that they will continually have static from the credit department. On the reverse of the coin, when the policy is purchased simply and solely to insure the accounts receivable and one lives within the limits of the policy without requesting increased coverages where needed, several things happen—the sales department is frustrated because the sales effort must be geared to the terms of the policy; the credit department tends to go along with the applicable credit agency ratings, not with credit reports; and good accounts that are not well rated remain undiscovered. To be effective the insurance program must be used aggressively and

persistently as a sales tool. As a sales tool, the cost is nominal; as an insurance expense, the price may be too high." Evaluate this statement. What are the limitations of this argument? Discuss.

9. In what way has insurance improved and facilitated credit for small communities? Discuss.

10. Identify at least seven varieties of credit insurance and indicate briefly their major differences.

11. (a) To what extent, in your opinion, should a bank be more willing to lend money to a firm whose open account credit is insured?
(b) Is there evidence that banks pay attention to this matter?

12. In view of the outstanding record of repayment of long-term home loans by homeowners, why is credit insurance necessary?

13. Why are retail firms not eligible for merchandise credit insurance?

14. The Jones Furniture Manufacturing Company, operated by A. M. Jones, has a credit insurance policy of the back coverage general form. The company's terms of sale call for a payment within 90 days after shipment. A sale is made to the Smith Retail Company, whose credit rating at the time of sale in Dun and Bradstreet is a rating to which $10,000 of credit insurance liability applies under the terms of Jones's policy. The sale was for $20,000. Payment is not made within the 90 days and Jones decides to wait a while. Thirty days later, payment still has not been received.
(a) What are Jones's rights under his credit insurance contract?
(b) If the Smith Company does not pay within 6 months after the date of shipment, what rights does Jones's have under his credit insurance policy if he has not filed a claim by then?
(c) For what reason might Jones have hesitated to file the account as a claim with the insurer? Are these reasons valid? Why?
(d) What payment will be made by the insurer if this is the only claim of Jones during the year and if the contract is subject to a $3,000 primary loss and 10% coinsurance? (Assume no recoveries of any sort.) Does use of these deductibles follow sound insurance practice? Why?
(e) Could Jones have obtained full coverage on this account?

15. How does the "factor" enter in as a competitor to credit insurance companies? (Consult an elementary credits and collection or finance text for reference to the operations of factors.)

16. Summarize the advantages and limitations of credit insurance as it is now written. As a project, consult a business firm or a local agency in your area that uses this type of insurance and obtain their evaluation and reaction to the arguments used in the text.

17. Ms. Adams objects to certain wording that she sees in her title insurance contract which states that she may recover for no losses that are discovered after issuance of the policy. Ms. Adams claims that there has been a mistake and what the insurer really intended was to eliminate all losses occurring before the contract is issued. Is Ms. Adams correct? If not, why not?

18. Of what benefit is title insurance if the insurer excludes all title defects occurring after the policy is issued and in addition all defects known to exist before the policy is issued? Explain.

19. (a) It is claimed that the premium for title insurance is unfairly high when the property is transferred frequently. Do you agree?
(b) What justification could the title insurer have for not reducing the premium where the property is transferred frequently?

20. A dishonest bookkeeper concealed the presence of tax arrears on a certain property in order to prevent discovery of an embezzlement.

Under what is known as *in rem* legislation, the property is sold for taxes and cannot be recovered by its former owner. In the transfer an agreement between the former owner and adjacent property owners regarding access rights to their rear driveway and garage is cancelled. The adjacent property owners find themselves without the legal right to cross the property and to enter their garages. This loss may be traced directly to tax liens existing on *neighboring* property. Assuming that one of these adjacent property owners purchased his property at the time these liens were in existence, and assuming the title insurance contract does not contain exclusions for tax liens of this nature, would the loss be normally recoverable under title insurance? Why or why not?

21. Under the Torrens title system, a property owner deciding to register property so notifies the court and submits all evidence of the title. A hearing is held for all interested parties, a tentative title is issued, and this title becomes final after a given period of time. All subsequent changes in title are registered with the court, and ownership is a public record. What advantages might this system have over the use of title insurance?

22. What three special characteristics of boiler and machinery insurance exist that distinguish this type of insurance from other lines? Explain each characteristic.

23. Distinguish between outage insurance, power interruption insurance, and power plant business interruption insurance.

24. (a) Why is power plant consequential damage insurance vital in many types of business firms?
(b) Which types of firms would you specify as candidates for this type of coverage?

25. A writer reported the following:
A department store in a small city had, within a fairly short period, three explosions of fuel oil vapor in the furnace of its boiler. In one of these accidents $25,000 of damage was caused, including the loss of plate glass windows. Many people, frightened by these explosions, stopped trading at the store and even crossed to the opposite side of the street to avoid passing near the store.
What moral do you see in this incident for the insurance manager of the department store?

Chapter *Nineteen*

LIFE AND HEALTH VALUES

So far we have considered mainly those problems caused by the destruction of property values, and the contributions of insurance to the solution of these problems. We shall now discuss some of the problems caused by the destruction of human values. Human values, aside from being more important to us from a personal standpoint, are far greater and more significant than all the different property values combined. The true wealth of a nation lies not in its natural resources or its accumulated property, but in the inherent capabilities of its population and the way in which this population is employed. The preservation of human life is of basic interest to all of us. A careful study of the specific types of economic loss caused by the destruction of life or health is vital to an understanding of the insurance methods available to offset these losses.

LIFE VALUES

A human life has value for many reasons. Many of these reasons are philosophical in nature, and would lead us into the realm of religion, esthetics, sociology, psychology, and other behavioral sciences. Of greatest interest here are economic values, although, of course, it is difficult to separate the discussion in such a way that an economic analysis would have no implications or overtones for other viewpoints.

A human life has economic value to all who depend upon the earning capacity of that life, particularly to two central economic groups—the family and the employer. To the family, the economic value of a human life is probably most easily measured by the value of the earning capacity of each of its members. To the employer, the economic value of a human life is measured by the contributions of an employee to the success of the business firm. If one argues that in a free competitive society a worker is paid according to worth and is not exploited, the worker's contribution again is best measured by earning capacity. It develops that earning capacity is probably the only feasible method of giving measurable economic value to human life.

There are four main perils that can destroy, wholly or partially, the economic value of a human life. These are:

1. Premature death.
2. Loss of health.
3. Old age.
4. Unemployment.

We shall discuss in this chapter only those problems arising from the first three of these perils. The peril of unemployment is analyzed in Chapter 24.

PREMATURE DEATH

The main economic problem arising when someone in the family dies, particularly the chief breadwinner, is the loss of earnings of this person.[1] The present value of these earnings is then the measure of loss. A method of determining this value is to find a sum of money which, when paid out in installments representing both principal and interest over the remaining working life of the worker, will produce, after taxes and allowances for the support of the worker, the same net income as the worker earned before. This amount, once calculated, represents the amount of life insurance that would be necessary to insure the full economic value of the person and to replace the net income which was formerly produced.

To illustrate, suppose a breadwinner age 35 is expected to earn an annual fixed amount, say $10,000, over the remaining working years. Assuming that retirement age is 65, the remaining working years number 30, and the worker would normally be expected to earn a gross amount of $300,000. From this sum the following deductions would be made: (1) an allowance for taxes, business expenses, etc., and (2) an allowance for the worker's own maintenance.

Assume that these items total $4,000 annually. The question is, "What sum of money now on hand would produce a payment of $6,000 a year and would last exactly 30 years?" If one assumes 6.0% interest, reference to an annuity table (see Table C–4, page 672) indicates that it would take exactly $82,588 to produce this income. This sum, when compared to the average life insurance per family in 1974 of $26,500, indicates to some degree the extent of underinsurance of the human life value.[2]

Several underlying factors in the preceding calculation should be observed. First, the peril of premature death always produces a *total* loss of human life value. Second, the human life value tends to decline with age, since each year that goes by means that the worker has one less year of income to earn. Third, the calculation of the human life value must assume a given value for the interest, the size of the worker's contribution to the family, future income tax rates, and a given level of total earnings. Changes in these and other

[1] Loss to a family caused by the death of dependents is, generally speaking, not susceptible to measurement by loss of earnings. There are definite measurable losses, nevertheless, such as the loss or investment in education, loss of unpaid-for services, and the cost of a funeral.

[2] See *Life Insurance Fact Book*, published annually by the Institute of Life Insurance, for current information about this amount and for other life insurance statistics.

factors could produce substantially different results in the final figure for human life value. For this reason, the calculation produces only a rough estimate of human life value, which is a very personal matter. Life insurance designed to offset the loss of human life value must take into consideration these and many other factors and should always be tailored to fit individual needs.

Needs Approach

Another method of measuring the loss to the family in the case of death of a person lies in what has been termed the *needs approach*. From this viewpoint, value lost is estimated in terms of the various uses to which the earnings would have been put had the individual lived to produce them. Thus, the value lost is measured by adding together sums necessary to meet certain family needs for income during various periods of life. For example, to pay last expenses such as funeral, debts, and taxes, $3,000 may be required. The sum necessary to provide a monthly income of $400 to the family during a 15-year child-raising period at 6% interest is about $46,600. The sum necessary to continue a monthly income of $250 to the widow for the remainder of her life, beginning after the 15-year family-raising period, would come to about $62,500 under the life income option of a typical life insurer if the widow were 50 years of age when the income payments began. To provide a college education for two children, an additional sum of say $20,000 (depending upon the school selected and the spending habits of the children) might be needed. These needs total $132,-100, a minimum figure as an estimate of the value lost when a breadwinner dies.

The following are examples of needs for income and cash which the life insurance estate may fill:

Income Needs	*Cash Sum Needs*
Readjustment income to ease the family adjustment to a lower income level.	Death expenses (funeral, doctor bills, debts, cemetery lot, taxes, etc.).
Family income during child-raising period.	Mortgage redemption.
Income to remaining spouse for life.	College education fund.
Retirement income for insured.	Gift fund.
	Fund for emergencies.

An advantage of the needs approach to an estimation of human life value is that it may focus attention on specific objectives in the purchase of life insurance. Life insurance purchased for a certain need can be arranged in the most appropriate way to provide funds for that need. Insurance bought to provide an income for children's education can be set up so that the insurer holds the funds until a given date and then pays out the income during the college period. Insurance is often purchased to offset high estate and inheritance taxes levied on the person's property after death. Without ready cash to pay these taxes, the asset might have to be sold at forced sale, thus causing unnecessary losses to dependents. Life insurance bought for this purpose can be paid in a lump sum to the estate of the deceased, and thus be made available for taxes and other costs. Life insurance purchased to pay off a mortgage can be set up so that no matter when the property owner may die, there is a sufficient amount of life insurance to liquidate the outstanding balance of the mortgage. The needs approach thus motivates the purchase of insurance for a given objective. Since these needs arise at different times throughout life, the needs approach also provides a guide as to which need should have priority and which type of insurance should be purchased.

Naturally this technique produces a different figure from the capitalization of income approach because of the different assumptions underlying it. The needs approach seems to be a more realistic approach to the problem of deciding upon types of life insurance to buy and when to buy them. The capitalization of income approach may be more useful in determining the total value of a human life for such purposes as justifying what loss occurred when one person was killed as a result of the negligence of another. Both methods reveal clearly that a human life is much more valuable economically than many realize, and that this value exceeds the amount for which life is commonly insured.

Loss to Business

A business firm has a somewhat more difficult task in determining the life value of a key employee, or of a partner, or of an important stockholder in a closely held corporation. If a key person dies, the firm may lose valuable customers whose loyalty depends on this individual. Plans on which the individual was working and in which the firm had invested much money may have to be abandoned. The extra cost of training or hiring a replacement may be substantial. Key employees may quit because of the death of a partner or an officer with whom they were closely associated. Each firm must make the best estimates it can of the loss exposure and insure accordingly.

Another source of loss to a business when a partner or a stockholder dies stems from the fact that this person's ownership in the business may pass to persons unfriendly to the firm, or may even result in liquidation of the firm in order to pay estate obligations. Competitors may obtain controlling ownership of the firm by purchasing shares from families of deceased stockholders. Those who have inherited the deceased stockholder's shares may enter the business but, because of inexperience, may cause losses or even bankruptcy. Life insurance arranged to offset or to prevent these losses is appropriately called *business continuation insurance*.

In a business continuation plan funded by life insurance, usually the owners of a business agree in advance as to what is to be done with the ownership shares in the event of death. For example, two partners own equally a business valued at $100,000. The chief asset of the business is a factory building. Neither partner has any family member capable of stepping into managment in case of death. Yet it is realized that the premature death of a partner will force the sale of the building to obtain money to retire that share of the business and to make money available for the use of the family. If the building were sold at forced sale, it is doubtful that $50,000 would be realized. To prevent this loss the partners enter into a *buy and sell agreement,* in which each agrees to buy the interest of the other if either dies. To fund the agreement and to insure that money for this purpose will be available, each buys life insurance of $50,000 on the life of the other. The buy and sell agreement binds each partner's estate to accept a certain valuation for this share and to sell it according to the terms of the contract.

The Probability of Loss

What is the probability that a person will die prematurely? Recall that for determining the economic loss of human life value we are not interested in *whether* a person will die, but *when* this death will occur. Even life insurance company examiners, who examine a person's application for insurance with utmost care, continually accept insureds who die within a year after taking out a policy in spite of their appearance of good health. For large numbers of people, however, actuaries have developed *mortality tables* on which scientific life insurance rates may be based. These tables, which are revised periodically, state the probability of death both in terms of deaths per 1,000 and in terms of expectation of life.[3] Table 19–1 illustrates the mortality experience in current use.

Table 19–1 shows that a person age 20 has an expectation of living for 50 years. At this age only 179 persons in every 100,000 are expected to die before they become 21. The probability of death at age 20 is thus .179%. At age 96 the death rate is slightly over 40%, since 400.56 per 1,000 are expected to die during that year. At age 100 it is assumed that death is a certainty. The probability of death expressed in a mortality table is based on *insured* lives and not the whole population. Death rates as stated in the 1958 CSO mortality table are greater at every age than death rates for the general population, even though it might appear that death rates for the general population would be larger. Aggregate death statistics include people of all ages and in any state of health, whereas insured persons presumably have been subjected to medical screening before acceptance. However, insurance mortality tables are purposely "loaded" to take care of certain contingencies (such as unusual fluctuations in death rates in a given year) and to make sure that all insurers, large and small, may use the table with safety. Nevertheless, for most purposes, the mortality table is a fairly accurate representation of the death rate.

The probability that a person will live is one minus the probability of death. There is a much greater *likelihood* of a breadwinner living to retirement age than dying before that time. Current mortality tables show that out of every 1,000 persons age 20, 687 males or 833 females will live to age 65. Table 19–2 gives estimates of the expectation of life at birth for selected years since 1900.

[3] The table in current use is the Commissioners Standard Ordinary Table (CSO), 1958, which is based on death rates recorded by insurance companies during the years 1950-1954. The CSO 1958 table replaced the CSO 1941 table, which was based on experience of the period 1930-1940. The 1941 table replaced the American Experience Mortality Table, which was based on data collected between 1843 and 1858. Different tables are used for different purposes, such as for annuities.

COMMISSIONERS STANDARD ORDINARY MORTALITY TABLE (1958)

Table 19-1

Age	Deaths Per 1,000	Expectation of Life-Years	Deaths Per 1,000	Expectation of Life-Years	Age
0	7.08	68.30	9.11	22.82	51
1	1.76	67.78	9.96	22.03	52
2	1.52	66.90	10.89	21.25	53
3	1.46	66.00	11.90	20.47	54
4	1.40	65.10	13.00	19.71	55
5	1.35	64.19	14.21	18.97	56
6	1.30	63.27	15.54	18.23	57
7	1.26	62.35	17.00	17.51	58
8	1.23	61.43	18.59	16.81	59
9	1.21	60.51	20.34	16.12	60
10	1.21	59.58	22.24	15.44	61
11	1.23	58.65	24.31	14.78	62
12	1.26	57.72	26.57	14.14	63
13	1.32	56.80	29.04	13.51	64
14	1.39	55.87	31.75	12.90	65
15	1.46	54.95	34.74	12.31	66
16	1.54	54.03	38.04	11.73	67
17	1.62	53.11	41.68	11.17	68
18	1.69	52.19	45.61	10.64	69
19	1.74	51.28	49.79	10.12	70
20	1.79	50.37	54.15	9.63	71
21	1.83	49.46	58.65	9.15	72
22	1.86	48.55	63.26	8.69	73
23	1.89	47.64	68.12	8.24	74
24	1.91	46.73	73.37	7.81	75
25	1.93	45.82	79.18	7.39	76
26	1.96	44.90	85.70	6.98	77
27	1.99	43.99	93.06	6.59	78
28	2.03	43.08	101.19	6.21	79
29	2.08	42.16	109.98	5.85	80
30	2.13	41.25	119.35	5.51	81
31	2.19	40.34	129.17	5.19	82
32	2.25	39.43	139.38	4.89	83
33	2.32	38.51	150.01	4.60	84
34	2.40	37.60	161.14	4.32	85
35	2.51	36.69	172.82	4.06	86
36	2.64	35.78	185.13	3.80	87
37	2.80	34.88	198.25	3.55	88
38	3.01	33.97	212.46	3.31	89
39	3.25	33.07	228.14	3.06	90
40	3.53	32.18	245.77	2.82	91
41	3.84	31.29	265.93	2.58	92
42	4.17	30.41	289.30	2.33	93
43	4.53	29.54	316.66	2.07	94
44	4.92	28.67	351.24	1.80	95
45	5.35	27.81	400.56	1.51	96
46	5.83	26.95	488.42	1.18	97
47	6.36	26.11	668.15	.83	98
48	6.95	25.27	1,000.00	.50	99
49	7.60	24.45			
50	8.32	23.63			

EXPECTATION OF LIFE AT BIRTH IN THE UNITED STATES

Table 19-2

Year	White		Nonwhite	
	Male	Female	Male	Female
1900	46.6	48.7	32.5	33.5
1920	54.4	55.6	45.5	45.2
1930	59.7	63.5	47.3	49.2
1940	62.1	66.6	51.5	54.9
1950	66.5	72.2	59.1	62.9
1960	67.4	74.1	61.1	66.1
1972	68.3	76.0	61.3	69.9

Source: National Office of Vital Statistics, United States Department of Health, Education, and Welfare.

This table reveals the great improvements that have been made in lowering the expected mortality rates over the years. It will be observed that since 1900 the expectation of life for white males has increased about 47%, compared to a 56% increase for white females. Life expectancy for nonwhite persons has increased at a much higher rate, approaching 89% for males and 109% for females. At the present time a white female can be expected to outlive a white male by about 7.7 years. These data have important effects in life insurance and annuity rate-making. For example, life insurance rates for women should be lower than for men. Furthermore, a woman age 20 can expect to outlive her husband about seven years if they are the same age. However, since it is common for a man's age to exceed that of his wife by a few years, it appears that a considerable period of widowhood is in store for the average wife. Thus, husbands should observe that, unless some provision is made, the probabilities are that the average wife will be a dependent widow for several years. The need for life insurance becomes immediately apparent and, because women live longer than men, the amount of insurance necessary to provide a given income is greater than if the beneficiary were a man.

Improvement in longevity has taken place at a much more rapid rate at lower ages than at higher ages. For example, the American Experience Mortality Table, based on data collected in the period 1843–1858, reveals that a child of two had an average life expectancy of 50 years, while the Commissioners Standard Ordinary (CSO) 1958 table shows a 2-year-old child with a life expectancy of nearly 67 years, a 34% increase. At age 50, however, under the American Experience Mortality Table, a person had an expectancy of living about 21 more years, while under current conditions the person may expect to live 23.6 years, an increase of only 12.4% over 100 years ago. Much of the explanation for this phenomenon lies in the fact that medical science has made its greatest strides in controlling diseases which do not primarily affect older age groups.

As shown in Table 19–3, diseases affecting primarily aged persons killed about as many persons in 1974 as was true in 1950. For example, cardiovascular-renal diseases and cancer accounted for 74% of all insured deaths in 1950, compared to 71% in 1974. Although these diseases are not confined to older persons, they occur much more frequently in this group than in the young. It seems likely that until important progress is made in the control of diseases affecting primarily the aged, life expectancy in the aged will experience only a slow lengthening.

DEATHS FROM SELECTED CAUSES AMONG INSURED INDIVIDUALS 1950 AND 1974

Table 19-3

Cause of Death	Deaths as a Percent of Total	
	1950	1974
Cardiovascular-renal diseases	57.0	50.4
Cancer	17.3	20.7
Pneumonia and influenza	1.9	2.7
Tuberculosis	1.3	.1
Diabetes	1.3	1.1
External causes:		
Motor vehicle accidents	3.1	3.0
Other accidents	3.6	3.4
Suicide	2.2	1.7
Homicide	.3	.8
All other causes	12.0	17.9

Source: *Life Insurance Fact Book 1975* (New York: Institute of Life Insurance, 1975), p. 88.

The probability of death arises rapidly with age. Figure 19–1 is a sketch of CSO 1958 death rates, on a semilogarithmic scale, with age levels represented on the horizontal axis and death rates on the vertical axis. Death rates during the first few years of life are higher than they are following ages 9 or 10. The death rate at age 1 is approximately the same as at age 19, with lower death rates falling in between these ages. After age 25, death rates increase at an increasing rate until age 40, but are still relatively low. At age 60, the death rate is over twice the rate at age 50, and by age 70 the death rate is nearly 2.5 times the rate at age 60. Thus, it is seen that after age 60 the death rates climb geometrically, until at age 99, the rate is assumed to be 100%.

Premium rates for life insurance tend to follow the same pattern as the curve represented in Figure 19–1. They rise steeply after age 40 until they tend to become prohibitive for new policyholders entering the insured group at advanced ages. For this reason very few people can afford to take out life insurance at an advanced age and most underwriters refuse to accept applications for term insurance from persons past age 65 because of the tendency for adverse selection beyond that age. Thus, if a person seeks life insurance at a time when it is needed, it is not available. It must be purchased at a time when

THE MORTALITY RATE, CSO 1958 MORTALITY TABLE

Figure 19-1

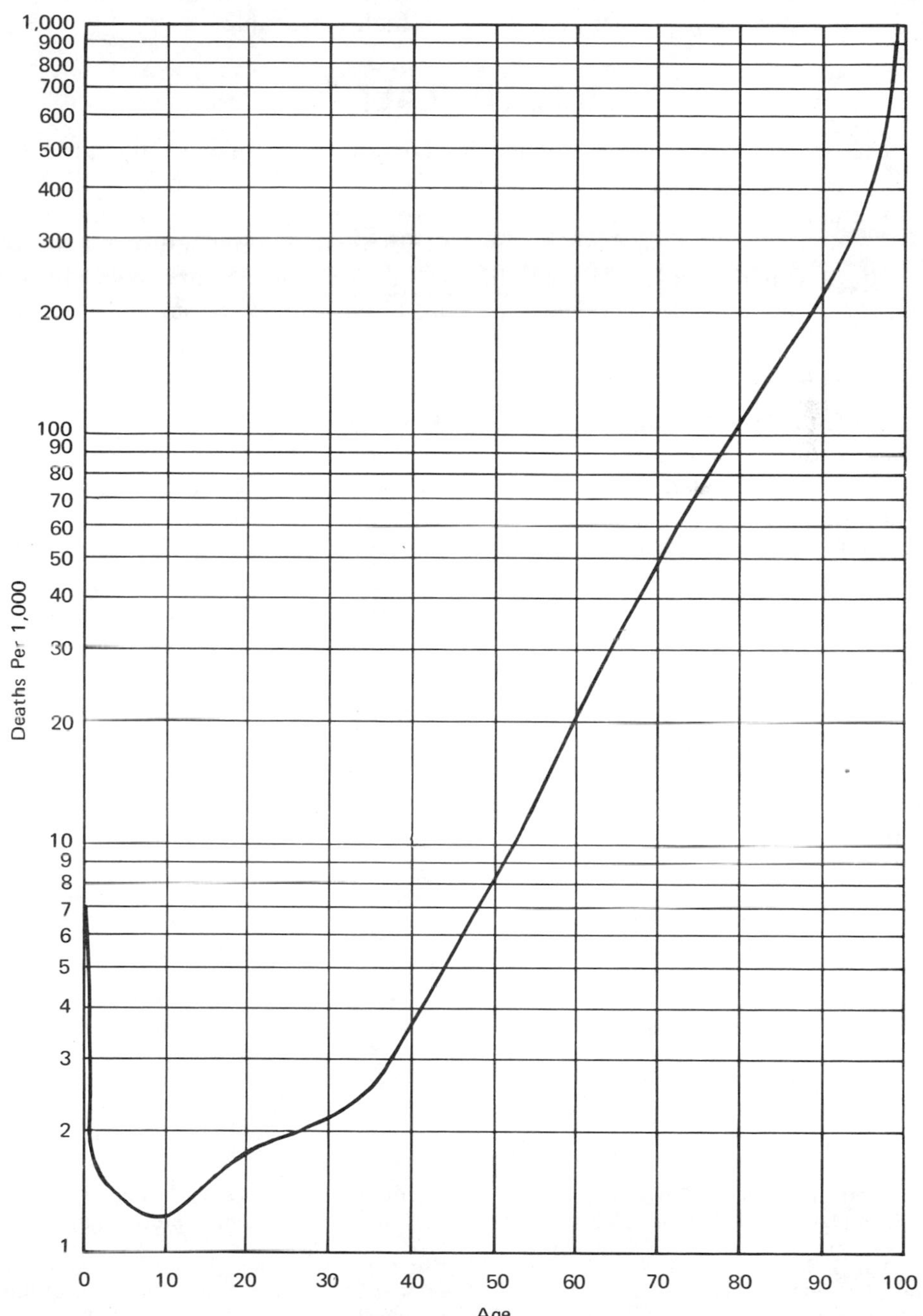

the probability of death is quite low. This same truth was observed in other lines (for example, fire insurance is not available after the house catches fire), namely, that insurance is a commodity the purchase of which must be arranged before the loss occurs or before it becomes highly probable.

LOSS OF HEALTH

The second major way in which human life value may be impaired or destroyed is loss of health. Loss of health is in many ways more serious than the premature loss of life because if a person is incapacitated from accident or sickness, that person's earning power is cut off completely or reduced greatly, and it becomes necessary to pay medical and hospital bills and to care for the individual. This imposes a considerable financial burden.

Income Loss

Losses from destruction of health may be measured in two ways: loss of earnings due to disability and expenditures for medical care. Income losses may be further divided into two groups: short-term and long-term. Short-term disabilities may be subdivided into those resulting from occupational causes and those from nonoccupational causes.

The Social Security Administration makes annual estimates of short-term, nonoccupational losses.[4] From these estimates can be derived estimates of losses in other categories, since among all nonoccupational losses, approximately 20% are short-term and 30% are long-term. The remainder are partial disability cases which may impair earning power but usually permit the person to work. Occupational injuries are estimated to cause a loss equal to about 1% of national income.[5] On this basis we may estimate total income loss in 1972 (in billions of dollars) from illness or accident in the U.S. to be over 6% of national income:

Short-term loss	
Nonoccupational	\$19.4
Occupational (.01 × \$947)	9.5
Long-term loss	
(\$19.4/.20) .30	29.1
Total	\$58.0
Percentage of national income lost through disability (58.0/\$947)	6.1

[4] Daniel N. Price, "Cash Benefits for Short-Term Sickness, 1948-72," *Social Security Bulletin* (January, 1974), pp. 19-30. Of estimated \$6.6 billion of benefits provided in 1972, 58% was in the form of paid sick leave.

[5] J. G. Turnbull, C. A. Williams, and E. F. Cheit, *Economic and Social Security* (New York: The Ronald Press Company, 1957), p. 298, citing Commission on Health Needs of the Nation, *Building America's Health, IV* (Washington: U.S. Government Printing Office, 1957), p. 303.

Such estimates, of course, do not take into consideration the vast amount of indirect losses from disability, such as lowered production efficiency and other additional expenses borne by employers and by families of disabled workers, nor do they count the loss of services of unpaid individuals such as housewives.

Medical Costs

Estimates place the expenditures for medical care in the United States at \$104 billion in 1974, or nearly \$500 per person. This compares with \$12 billion in 1950 or \$78 per person. Average per capita expenditures for medical care rose nearly sevenfold over this period. Similarly, the percent of gross national product devoted to medical care increased from 4.6% to 7.7% over the period 1950–1974. Tables 19–4 and 19–5 summarize some of the statistics relating to medical cost expenditures.

PER CAPITA EXPENDITURES IN THE U.S. FOR MEDICAL CARE, 1969 and 1974

Table 19-4

Type of Payment	1969	1974	Percent Increase
Hospital care	\$108.87	\$190.44	76
Physicians' services	57.67	88.47	53
Dental care	19.09	28.87	53
Other professional care	6.32	9.27	47
Drugs and sundries	31.57	45.14	43
Eyeglasses	8.49	11.02	30
Nursing home care	14.89	34.69	133
Administrative costs of insuring organization	10.06	19.67	97
Government public health	5.82	9.90	70
Miscellaneous health services	11.53	16.04	39
Medical research	8.72	12.50	43
Construction, medical facilities	12.18	20.36	67
Total	\$295.21	\$486.37	64

Source: Nancy L. Worthington, "National Health Expenditures, 1929-74," *Social Security Bulletin* (February, 1975), p. 13. Percentages calculated.

Data on health care costs support the following conclusions:

1. Per capita health care costs in the United States rose 64% over the period 1969–1974, an average of 13% annually. In 1974, 7.7% of the gross national product went for medical expenditures. The health care dollar is divided roughly as follows: hospital care, \$.39; physicians' services, \$.18; drugs, \$.09; all other, \$.34.
2. Payments for nursing home care have risen twice as fast as the average for all items of health care. The cost of doctors' and dentists' care has risen the least over the period 1969–1974.

DISTRIBUTION OF PERSONAL HEALTH COSTS IN THE U.S., 1960-1974

Table 19-5

Source of Payment	Percent of Costs Paid	
	1960	1974
Government		
Federal	9.3	25.5
State and local	12.4	12.1
Total public	21.7	37.6
Private agencies		
Individuals	55.3	35.4
Private insurance	20.7	25.6
Other	2.3	1.4
Total private	78.3	62.4

Source: Nancy L. Worthington, "National Health Expenditures, 1929-1974" *Social Security Bulletin* (February, 1975), p. 16.

3. The price of medical care is rising faster than any major item of the BLS consumer price index (CPI). From 1950–1973, for example, the total CPI rose 85% compared to 156% for the medical care component.
4. The costs paid by the federal government in providing increased health care services have risen dramatically in recent years. Major consideration of a formal system of national health insurance is under current discussion in Congress; it appears that through national health insurance the role of government will expand even further in the years ahead.
5. The cost of medical care borne by individuals directly has been declining steadily (see Table 19–5). In 1974 individuals paid out only about 35.4% of their total medical costs directly (compared to 55.3% in 1960), and the remainder is paid through private insurance or through the government. The proportion paid through private insurance has varied between 20.7% and 25.6% over the period 1960–1974.

The Probability of Loss

The preceding data show the tremendous aggregate cost of the loss of income through illness and accident and medical care expenditures. What is the probability that a person will be among the unfortunate individuals who are struck down annually? Again, there is no complete answer to the question, since data on illnesses and accidents are not nearly so well classified as mortality data.

Some notion of the probability of health loss can be obtained by examination of the statistics of hospital admissions. In 1973, for example, about one out of seven persons was admitted to the hospital. On the average about 3.3% of the total population is in the hospital at any given time.[6] In 1974 wage earners

[6] *Source Book of Health Insurance Data 1975-76* (New York: Health Insurance Institute, 1975), pp. 60, 61, 63.

lost an average of 3.4 days work as a result of some acute condition. As a proportion of average total days worked in a given year (approximately 250), time loss amounted to about 1.4%. However, the average American had 17.2 days of restricted activity during the year. It should perhaps be concluded that the probable amount of time loss due to bad health is closer to 7% than it is to 1%.

Although the probability of health loss is substantial, some individuals pay a larger share of total health costs than others. For example, persons over 65 constitute about 10% of the population but pay 27% of the total costs of health care. Similarly, persons under 19 constitute 16% of the population but pay 36% of the total costs of health care.[7] Health care data also show that illness is more severe among nonwhites than whites, among low-income groups than high-income groups, and among unemployed persons than employed persons. Females tend to have more illnesses than males, but are disabled for shorter periods of time. Single persons have more illnesses than married persons.

The uneven distribution of health care costs represents a problem which is ideally suited to solution through insurance. The average medical bill may not be excessive, but the variation is great and an unfortunate minority will suffer an unsupportable loss each year.

Causes of Illness

An indication of the causes of serious illness may be seen in Table 19–3, which shows the chief causes of death. The same factors also cause illness, of course, but the whole story is not told. Data shown in Table 19–6, for example, reveal that cancer causes only 10.5% of serious disabilities; yet cancer causes 20% of all deaths. Tuberculosis is a neglible cause of death, but it causes 3.5% of serious disabilities. Mental disease is a major cause of disability, but it is not even listed as a major cause of death in Table 19–3. The data in Table 19–6 reflect disabilities under which those afflicted are receiving income benefits from the Social Security Administration. In order to qualify for benefits, recipients must be disabled 5 months or longer and must be unable to perform any substantially gainful work due to a medical condition. The impairment must be expected to last for at least 12 months.

Analysis of illness data reveal certain differences by age, race, occupation, and sex. For example, heart disease is the major cause of disability for both men and women; the second most important cause of disability is emphysema for men, but arthritis for women. Tuberculosis and hypertensive heart disease are more heavily represented as causes of disability among black people than among white. Cancer strikes much more frequently at ages above

[7] Barbara S. Cooper and Mary F. McGee, "Medical Care Outlays for Three Age Groups: Young, Intermediate, and Aged," *Social Security Bulletin* (May, 1971), p. 5. Several extensive studies of national health have been made: by the Committee on the Costs of Medical Care, covering 8,758 families over the period 1928-1931; the National Health Survey, covering 703,092 households in 18 states in 1935-1936; and by the United States Public Health Service, the Social Security Administration, and the Office of Vocational Rehabilitation, covering 25,000 households in 1950, and periodically since then.

MAJOR CAUSES OF DISABILITY IN THE U.S. **Table 19-6**

Cause	Percent of Total Disabilities
Accidents	6.4
Illness	
Diseases of circulatory system	26.2
Bones and joints, including arthritis	13.3
Diseases of nervous system	12.4
Mental disorder	11.5
Cancer	10.5
Respiratory diseases	7.9
Tuberculosis and other parasitic diseases	3.5
Diabetes and other metabolic diseases	3.5
Digestive tract disorders	2.5
Genitourinary disorders	.8
Skin diseases	.4
All other	1.1

Source: U.S. Department of Health, Education, and Welfare, *Social Security Disability Applicant Statistics* (Washington: U.S. Government Printing Office, 1967), pp. 22-27. Data are based on 310,947 disabilities compensible under OASDHI in 1967.

45. For example, 10 times as many persons are disabled by cancer at age 60 or over than between the ages of 40–44. Skilled workers have more disability than unskilled workers.

OLD AGE

Old age is a condition that often destroys earning capacity just as does premature death or loss of health. It is certain that a young person will either die before reaching old age or the person will reach old age. However, a male age 20 has a considerably greater probability of reaching, say, age 65 than he does of not reaching age 65—he has roughly a 67% chance of getting "old."

For various reasons, relatively few individuals are able to earn much of their livelihood after reaching old age. Life insurance is directed against the peril of old-age dependency by providing a vehicle through which one can accumulate a savings fund which can be liquidated on a scientific basis by an annuity. In this way, one can create an income stream which will last as long as one lives.

Extent of Old-Age Dependency

Although people know that some day they will probably get old and will be dependent unless they make provision for themselves in some manner, statistics show that all too often the arrival of the date of retirement finds the individual with little guaranteed income and very little money or property. This situation has become of major economic interest because of the growth in the proportion of aged persons to the total population, the declining number of employment opportunities for these persons, and the increasing length of life which extends the average period during which they will be dependent on others. In 1900 only 4.1% of the population was age 65 or over. By 1970 this percentage had grown to 9.8, and actuarial projections place it at 10.6 by 1980.[8] In 1974 there were nearly 22 million people age 65 and over in the United States. The average life expectancy at age 65 in 1971 was 13 years for males and 16.8 years for females. Due to the increasing adoption of compulsory retirement rules, it is becoming more difficult for physically able aged persons to continue working.

Income Status

The 1968 Survey of the Aged indicated that about $60 billion was received by all persons age 65 and over in the United States. Of this sum, earnings represented 30%; retirement benefits, 37%; veterans and public assistance, 6%; income from assets, 25%; and miscellaneous, 2%. Only 4% were receiving private annuities such as from individual life insurance policies. Unmarried persons without benefits tend to rely on public assistance. About 20% of the aged couples who were drawing OASDHI were also receiving a private group pension. However, for about 60% of the aged couples, OASDHI constituted their only source of regular pension income.

The plight of the unmarried person with no retirement benefit was clearly shown. Nearly half of these individuals received less than $1,000, and the median income was only $1,020.

From these data we may draw certain conclusions about the probable economic outlook for persons in the U.S. reaching age 65 or over: (1) Seventy percent will be unable to hold their former jobs and will be unemployed; (2) about 96% will have no income from individually-purchased insurance or annuities; (3) nearly everyone will be able to draw social security, but only 40% will have other sources of income such as employer pensions to supplement this benefit; (4) many will be in poverty, especially single and black persons; (5) because of the trend toward earlier retirement and increasing life expectancy, economically deprived persons will have to endure their privation for a longer period than they did in the past.

Causes of Old-Age Dependency

The data cited above show beyond any reasonable doubt that, on the whole, people have not succeeded in preventing old-age dependency. There have been a number of explanations for this, some of which are given below.

1. The American economy is based on a high consumption pattern and people are urged through constant advertising to spend freely. In the effort to "keep up with the Joneses," saving for old age is ignored.
2. A long-term decline in interest rates (ending in the U.S. about 1950) prevented people from saving enough for their old age.

[8] Census Bureau, *Current Population Reports, Population Estimates,* Series P-25, No. 98, 114, 170, and 187.

3. A long-term inflation has reduced the ability to save because prices and acceptable standards of living rise faster than wages.
4. Children no longer feel obligated to care for their parents nor are they able.
5. The depression of the 1930's and personal misfortunes caused a loss of the life savings of many.
6. People do not earn enough to save sufficient amounts for old age.
7. Unions are responsible for declining employment opportunities of aged people.
8. Adoption of pension plans by business firms has caused the forced retirement of people able to work.

These explanations are, at least in some respects, more in the way of excuses than they are valid explanations of a cause which is outside the control of the individual concerned. Perhaps they might best be summarized under the heading, "refusal of most people to plan ahead," or the "tendency to live for today only," or the attitude "we'll get by somehow." Regardless of the merit, or even the truth, of the above explanations, the fact remains that while most people fail to save for a rainy day, a few succeed. The few who succeed generally have plans for succeeding, and as often as not, the insurance mechanism is an integral part of these plans.

SUMMARY

1. Human life values, often overlooked in the task of obtaining adequate insurance protection against financial losses, are undoubtedly more important and far greater than all property values. Four perils cause destruction of human life values—premature death, loss of health, old age, and unemployment.
2. Premature death causes great loss to families and to employers, a loss which may be objectively measured and insured. The probability of premature death is substantial in spite of striking improvements in longevity since 1900. According to current mortality tables, approximately 33 of every 100 people aged 20 will die before they retire at age 65. Data on the causes of illness suggest that major reductions in the mortality rate in the future will come when medical science conquers such afflictions as heart disease and cancer.
3. Increase in longevity has brought with it a rise in the rate of observable loss of health, since many who formerly would have died from illness are now kept alive, but in a state of semihealth. Loss of health causes more economic loss than the loss of life.
4. Ill health brings two major types of losses—loss of income during the period of disability and medical costs. Both types of costs have increased rapidly in the United States. While precise estimates of these costs are not available because of the many types of unmeasurable losses, it seems clear that losses of over 6% of the national income are being registered in the United States annually.
5. Long-term disability and partial disability can account for 80% of the loss of income from sickness and accident, while hospital and physicians' services account for about 55% of all expenditures for medical care.
6. Less than 40% of medical expenditures are being met directly and an increasing proportion of them are being met by the federal government. The proportion of

health loss paid through insurance has risen from 20.7% to 25.6% over the period 1960–1974.

7. Several studies have verified the finding that while medical costs and income losses on the average do not cause an intolerable financial burden, a disproportionate amount of the burden falls on relatively few individuals. This fact has undoubtedly stimulated the use of insurance as a method of spreading the loss more evenly.

8. The probability of living to old age is nearly twice as great as the probability of premature death. The extent of old-age dependency suggests that not only are people failing to save sufficient amounts for their declining years, but they have also tended to rely primarily on social insurance as a method of handling the risk of outliving their income. Relatively few old persons have annuities or life insurance proceeds on which to retire.

QUESTIONS FOR REVIEW AND DISCUSSION

1. It has been said that an average business person would not think of leaving a factory building uninsured, but the business person neglects to insure the lives of important key executives who may be more valuable than the building. Do you agree? In what way might a key executive be more valuable than the building?
2. How can the economic loss of a family breadwinner be measured?
3. It is estimated that over 33% of all women and over 20% of married women are employed outside the home.
   (a) In your opinion, does the earning capacity of a working wife give rise to economic value for which she should be insured?
   (b) Should the life of a wife and mother not employed outside the home be insured? Why or why not?
4. Juan is about to purchase a clothing business priced at $50,000, of which $10,000 represents inventory and fixtures. The remainder of the purchase price is attributable to goodwill. The business is expected to net $5,000 each year, after all expenses including the manager's salary have been paid.
   (a) If an appropriate capitalization rate for funds employed in similar enterprises is 15%, is the price of this business reasonable? If not, what is a fair price?
   (b) Would you expect to find a person whose earning capacity is $5,000 a year insured for a similar amount?
5. (a) In what way does the death of a partner or of a stockholder in a closely held corporation cause a loss to the business firm?
   (b) How can life insurance be employed to offset this loss?
6. Referring to Table 19–1, state the probability that (a) a person age 18 will live to age 19, and (b) a person age 97 will live to age 99.
7. (a) What explanations can you offer for the fact that the longevity for nonwhite people has increased at a faster rate since 1900 than for white people?
   (b) What significance does this have for life insurance?
8. Do observable data support or weaken the statement made in the text that "a considerable period of widowhood is in store for the average wife"?
9. The following statements were made by an investment analyst concerning a large industrial concern and the investment merit of its securities: " . . . the company shifted to a decentralized type of organization about six years ago. This move, however, did not yield the desired improvement in efficiency. . . . The deficiencies arising from too few centralized controls are now being corrected. A little

more than a year ago a new president took office. Since then the company has come a long way in tightening up its organization. . . . The company is fortunate in having a well-qualified chief executive to direct its improvement program . . . he combines a broad education in business with solid practical experience . . . he developed a central staff of experts to provide the specialized control and knowledge that formerly were lacking. . . ." What are the implications of this analysis with respect to a dependence on human life values?

10. With the tremendous strides in medical science, longevity has increased very significantly, especially at younger age levels. What is the chief reason for this and what implications does it have regarding life insurance?

11. Why is it difficult for a person past age 60 to purchase life insurance? (Refer to Figure 19–1.)

12. It is said that the decrease in death rates brings about an increase in disability rates.
(a) How is this true?
(b) What other factors have brought about an increase in disability rates?

13. Suggest possible reasons for the increase in the proportion of disposable income spent for medical care in the United States.

14. A survey by the Metropolitan Life Insurance Company revealed the following data on new long-term disability rates per 1,000 male employees: age 25–44, 1.5; age 45–54, 4.5; age 55–59, 15.5; and age 60–64, 51.0.
(a) Compare these disability rates with the death rates shown in Table 19–1. (Use the median age in each category.)
(b) What inferences can you draw from these comparisons as to the likelihood of disability versus the likelihood of death?

15. In the Metropolitan Life survey referred to above, a study was made of the status, after five years, of 401 men and 203 women employees who had been disabled for one year or longer. It was found that of the men, 61% were still disabled, 22% were dead, and 17% had recovered. Among women, these percentages were 56, 12, and 32, respectively. Judging from these data, which would you say is most important to have, if one had to choose between them—life insurance or long-term disability insurance? Why?

16. "A skewed distribution of medical costs lends itself to a solution via the insurance device in an admirable way." Explain why.

17. A recent study revealed that 80% of the aged who are not in the labor force left because of their health or because their employer asked them to leave. Over 77% of those aged individuals who are not in the labor force do not feel well enough to work. Finally, most aged persons discover that their occupational skills are obsolete.
(a) What implications does this study have to the problem of old-age dependency?
(b) Are these implications supported by any other findings?

18. Summarize the major factors in our economy that create an economic problem of old-age dependency.

19. Much has been heard of a population explosion throughout the world. What implications does this have for the problem of old-age dependency?

20. An employer is requested to adopt the policy of dropping the age 65 compulsory retirement rule in her company in order to permit many able-bodied older workers to continue working. The employer refuses, stating that the morale problem at younger age levels would be too severe if she did so.
(a) Why might a morale problem exist if this were done?
(b) What arguments would you use to counter the employer's position?

Chapter *Twenty*

LIFE INSURANCE

Few industries have equalled the consistent record of the long-term growth of life insurance. Yet, when measured against the potential market for life insurance, the sales have fallen far short of that market. No small reason for this is the failure of the consuming public to understand what life insurance really is, what it will do, why it is needed, and how it may be arranged. Part of the difficulty lies in the traditional methods of distribution which have been justified on the grounds that "life insurance is not brought; it is sold."

WHAT IS LIFE INSURANCE?

As a social and economic device, *life insurance* is a method by which a group of people may cooperate to ameliorate the loss resulting from the premature death of members of the group. The insuring organization collects contributions from each member, invests these contributions and guarantees both their safety and a minimum interest return, and distributes benefits to the estates of those members who die.

Viewed from an individual standpoint, life insurance is a method of creating an estate. It is a method of seeing to it that plans for accumulating property for the benefit of others, chiefly the family, are realized, regardless of whether the breadwinner dies prematurely or lives to "a ripe old age." The word "estate," unfortunately, carries a suggestion of death since the word is often employed to describe the aggregate property belonging to a deceased person. The meaning of *estate* is much broader, however, and will be used here to mean an aggregate of property, including income-producing property, whether it is to be used before or after the death of a person. In the last analysis, property is accumulated for the benefit of the living, not the dead, and the various plans for building an estate should recognize this fundamental precept.

It has been stated that most workers have two types of estates—the present or actual estate and the future or potential estate. The *present* or *actual estate* is the property that one has accumulated for dependents or oneself for the time when earning capacity will be cut off by premature death or old age. The *future* or *potential estate* refers to the property that one will normally accumulate to provide financial security for dependents if one lives long enough. Premature death means that the potential estate is never realized. Life insurance is a way of creating an actual estate for the benefit of dependents if the worker does not live to realize the potential estate, and it is a way of saving money for the actual estate to be used as a source of income in old age.

Protection Versus Savings Needs

Because a clear understanding of the purposes of life insurance is of such fundamental importance in appreciating what various contracts of life insurance will accomplish, these purposes are deserving of special emphasis. Life insurance can accomplish two objectives: to guarantee the existence of an estate out of which one's dependents may meet debts and receive an income if the breadwinner dies; and to save money as a part of one's own living estate, which is created for future needs for income. The first objective may be termed the *protection need* and the latter, the *savings need.*

Life insurance policies may be purchased to reflect each of these needs in varying proportions. *Term insurance* in its various forms is wholly dedicated to the protection need. Generally, there are no cash values whatever in term insurance and hence no possibility of the savings need being met.[1] Term insurance, thus, is designed entirely for death protection and to create an estate only in the event of premature death. On the other hand, *whole life insurance* is available in different forms to meet both the savings and the protection needs. These contracts may be arranged so that the savings need can receive as much emphasis as is desired, within certain limits. All whole life contracts have an element of protection which extends for the whole of the insured's life. *Endowment policies* emphasize the savings need, with only a small element of protection. Endowments and *retirement income contracts* are primarily savings contracts for a definite span of years with the added guarantee that if the insured does not live during this period to complete the savings plan, the insurer will complete it. These relationships are shown in Figure 20–1, which illustrates that different life insurance contracts contain varying proportions of savings and protection.

Ideally, a program of estate building should provide both savings and protection—savings if the estate builder lives, and protection when death occurs. Some individuals prefer to use term insurance for protection and to emphasize other types of investments, such as stocks, bonds, savings accounts, or real estate, for the savings need. Others prefer a contract such as whole life insurance in which modest protection and savings needs can be met in one contract. Still others may be interested primarily in a savings-type insurance policy such as the endowment in which the protection element is small. These individuals may use separate term policies to enlarge the protection element in their estate-building plans. There is no limit, of course, to the many different combinations of insurance contracts and investment plans which can be made.

[1] Certain long-period term insurance contracts have a small cash value, as will be explained later.

PROTECTION VERSUS SAVINGS IN LIFE INSURANCE **Figure 20-1**

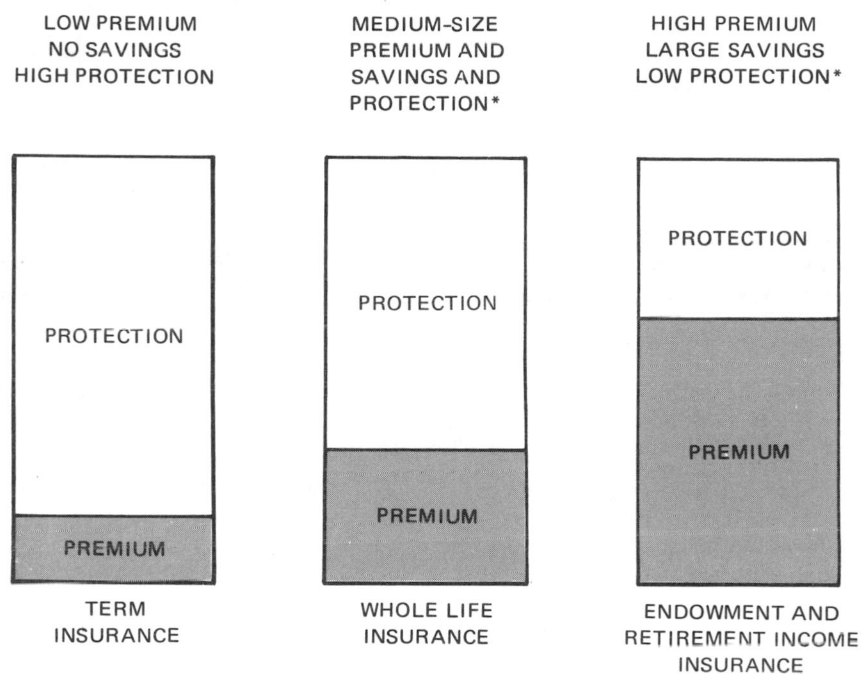

* (See page 432 for estimates of the dollar savings in different contracts.)

Permanent Versus Temporary Needs

Another way of thinking about the uses of various contracts of insurance is to consider whether the need is temporary or permanent. Of course, what would be a temporary need to one is a permanent need to another. Generally, whole life and retirement income contracts are considered to serve permanent needs, and term and endowment contracts are considered to serve temporary needs; hence these contracts have become known as *permanent* and *temporary* insurance, respectively.

To illustrate, examples of temporary needs would include the following: (1) Jane Roman wishes to borrow $5,000 for a period of four years for the purpose of attending medical school. Her uncle is willing to lend the money if Jane will take out a life insurance policy in favor of the uncle should Jane die before she graduates and is able to repay the loan. Jane will probably find that a five-year term policy will be the most economical form of insurance for her purpose. (2) Erik Stone, age 35, is raising a family and his youngest child is now age five. He wishes to guarantee his family a minimum of $400 a month for 15 years in the event of his death. A term policy may be arranged to fill this need. On the other hand, if Erik wishes to guarantee his wife a minimum income of $200 a month for the rest of her life in the event of his death, a term policy will not work satisfactorily since this need is continuous until Erik's death. As we have seen, Erik has a much greater probability of living to age 65 than of not living until that age. Hence, he would have to purchase a whole life contract, which may be kept in force indefinitely.

The Level Premium Contract

Life insurance is usually issued on a *level premium basis,* which means that the same premium is charged throughout the term of the contract. This was once a startling innovation, since it was reasoned that due to the rising probability of death with age, it would be impossible to charge a flat premium which would compensate for the rising mortality costs. The first insurance policies were issued for one year only and were renewable at the end of this year at a higher rate, providing the insured was still in good health. These contracts are still issued and are known as *yearly renewable term policies.*[2] The level premium idea is considered one of the most basic advances ever made in the development of life insurance. With this concept it became possible to issue policies for longer and longer periods until finally whole life contracts were made a regular part of the business. Actuaries, using refined mortality statistics, could calculate exactly how much had to be charged in the early years of the contract in order to make up for the rising mortality costs of the later years. This idea is illustrated in Figure 20–2.

Figure 20–2 gives a comparison of the annual rates charged for a level premium contract, term to 65, and the five-year renewable term policy per $1,000 of face amount. The insured, age 20, has the choice of purchasing the former contract at an annual premium of $8.54 for 45 years, or of paying successively higher rates which began at $3.73 and graduate to $29.90 at age 60. This ever-increasing rate follows the upward curve of mortality plotted on Figure 19–1, page 415. At age 40 the *break-even point* of these two contracts is reached. Above this age, the rate for a five-year renewable term policy rises above the rate for the level term. The overpayments in the early years of the term to 65 policy, together with interest, represented by the shaded area to the left of the break-even point in Figure 20–2, balance the excess underpayments area shown by the shaded area to the right of the break-even point.

The overpayment in the early years of a level premium life insurance policy is not really an overpayment in the sense that the insured is paying more than should be paid for protection. The insurer acts as a trustee of the premium funds, which belong to the policyholders as a group, and reduces the premium to reflect the interest earnings. The accumulation thus made is known as the *cash surrender value* or the *reserve.* If the insured desires, it is possible to borrow this value or recapture it completely upon lapsing the policy. In term policies which span many years, the size of the cash surrender value is relatively small; and for bookkeeping reasons, the insurer does not return any of

[2] However, modern contracts are practically always guaranteed renewable for specified periods without evidence of continued good health.

COMPARISONS OF ANNUAL NONPARTICIPATING PREMIUMS ON THE FIVE-YEAR RENEWABLE TERM CONTRACT AND THE LEVEL PREMIUM, TERM TO 65, CONTRACT

Figure 20-2

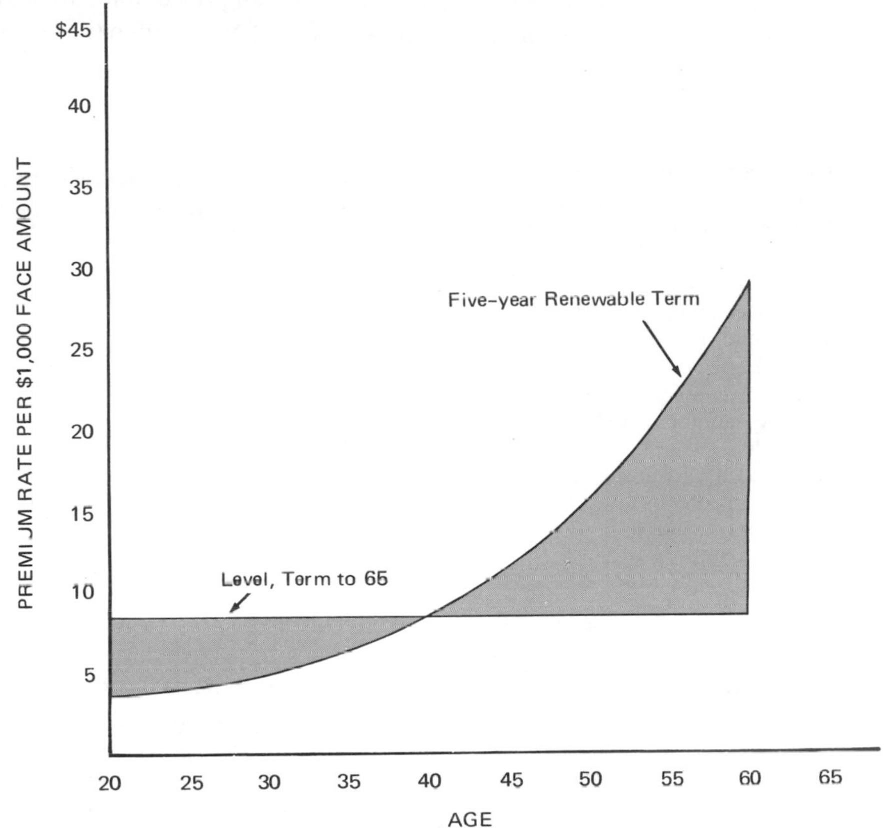

these amounts to the insured, although the premium is reduced below what it would be without the interest earnings that are made. On permanent contracts the size of the cash surrender value is substantial and constitutes the savings element referred to before.

The reason for having a savings element in life insurance, thus, is to smooth out premium payments over a long period of years. The insurer does not accumulate reserves merely to have funds with which to engage in the investment business or to set itself up as a savings bank. The reserve has its main purpose in meeting the very substantial burden of high mortality costs in the later years of the contract. Without the reserve, it would be impossible to offer continued protection beyond a certain age, roughly age 65. There are many needs for life insurance which extend beyond this age, such as a death expense fund, a fund to provide income for a dependent, and for tax purposes.

MAJOR TYPES OF CONTRACTS

The major contracts of life insurance are of three types—term, whole life, and endowment. There are also package contracts which represent combinations of these three basic types. Countless names are applied by individual insurers for specific policies issued, but all policies are simply combinations of the three basic types. Some of the more important of these combinations are listed below.

Term Insurance
- Level-term contract
- Decreasing-term contract

Whole Life Insurance
- Ordinary life contract
- Limited-payment life contract

Endowment Insurance
- Limited-term (e.g. 20 years) contract
- Retirement income contract

Package Contracts
- Family income policy
- Family maintenance policy
- Specials
- Modified life insurance policy
- Multiple protection insurance policy
- Juvenile insurance
- Family group policy
- Variable life contract

Another way to think of the structure of life insurance is according to the type of buyer (see Table 20–1). *Ordinary* insurance, a classification of contracts which includes all of the types listed above, is purchased mainly by persons acting individually. About 62% of all life insurance purchased in 1974 was ordinary. In addition, about 36% of all life insurance in force is purchased on a *group* basis, mainly through employers. Finally, about 2% of all life insurance is called *industrial*, consisting of policies of small face amounts (less than $1,000) whose chief buyers are low-income persons purchasing these contracts essentially to provide a burial fund.

Viewed still another way, life insurance may be seen in terms of the total face value of protection in force. Data are available under four major classes: ordinary, group, industrial, and credit. In 1975 a total of $2,140 billion of life insurance was in force, made up as follows: ordinary, 51%; group, 42%; industrial, 2%; and credit, 5%. Group, industrial, and credit insurance are discussed in Chapter 21.

Table 20–1 indicates the relative importance of the major types of life insurance purchased in the United States and the direction of the changes which are taking place in life insurance buying preferences. Americans have increased their purchases by an average of 6% annually in the 1970–1974 period. Group insurance is growing the most rapidly of the three major classes of insurance. This is due in part to the fact that group insurance can be marketed more efficiently than individual insurance and has an income tax

MAJOR TYPES OF LIFE INSURANCE PURCHASED IN THE U.S., 1964-1974

Table 20-1

Major Class of Insurance	Face Amount (Billions of Dollars) 1964	1974	Percent Increase 1964-1974
Ordinary	$ 79	$199	152
Group	25	114	356
Industrial	7	7	—
Total	$111	$320	188

Type of Ordinary Insurance	Insurance in Force on Individual Plans (Billions of Dollars) 1970	1974	Percent Increase 1970-1974
Term	$209	$ 312	49
Whole life	473	636	34
Endowment and retirement income	53	61	15
Total	$735	$1,009	37

Source: *Life Insurance Fact Book 1975* (New York: Institute of Life Insurance, 1975), pp. 16, 24. Percentages calculated.

advantage. The premiums for group insurance are usually deductible business expenses to the employer and generally need not be reported as taxable income to the employee. Group insurance growth has also been stimulated by the periodic increases in group coverage given to service personnel and federal employees who are covered under government-sponsored group plans.

Table 20–1 reveals that individual buyers have tended to favor term insurance over other type contracts. Over the period 1970–1974 insurance in force on term plans grew 49% compared to 34% for whole life contracts. Investment-type contracts and modified life policies increased only 15%. Bearing in mind that most group insurance is also on a term basis, it is clear that consumers increasingly tend to favor those contracts offering pure protection, i.e., the term contract. This is not surprising in view of the increasing need for protection occasioned by rising incomes and living standards. Surveys show that nearly half of all individual life insurance is purchased by persons earning between $10,000 and $25,000 annually. The average face amount of the individual ordinary life insurance policy has risen steadily over the years until by 1974 it had reached $7,690. In 1974 the average amount of life insurance in force per family in the United States was $26,500, double the level of $13,200 which was in force in 1964.[3]

Premium and Cost Differences

The prospective insurance buyer is usually presented with information such as the premium rates at different ages together with statements of the savings

[3] *Life Insurance Fact Book 1975* (New York: Institute of Life Insurance, 1975), p. 26.

element in each type of contract. The prospective buyer must then decide which type best fits the individual need. However, this selection may be difficult to make without further knowledge. Typical nonparticipating premium rates for common policies of insurance, issued at age 30, together with their cash values after 10 and 20 years, are shown in the table below.

Type of Insurance	Premium Per $1,000	Cash Value		10-Year* Cost	20-Year** Cost
		10 Years	20 Years		
10-year term	$ 5.45	$ 0	$ 0	$54.50	$147.00
Ordinary life	20.05	113	281	87.50	120.00
20-payment life	31.81	219	549	99.10	87.20
30-year endowment	46.96	397	1,000	72.60	(60.80)

* "Cost" = Sum of premiums minus cash value.
** 20-year cost of term is sum of 10 years of premiums for a policy issued at age 30 plus 10 years of premiums for a policy issued at age 40.

Thus, the 10-year term policy is seen to involve the lowest premium outlay; but since there is no accumulation of cash value, the total cost at the end of 20 years is larger than any of the other policies. This ignores the interest which one might have earned on the difference between the term premium and the higher cost policies. The premium on ordinary life is about three times the premium on 10-year term, but after 20 years its net cost appears lower than term if one ignores the interest element.

If one considers the interest element in this comparison, a very different result is obtained. Comparing the term contract to the ordinary life contract, the difference in premium is $14.60 annually per $1,000 ($20.05 − $5.45 = $14.60). If one saves this difference of $14.60 annually for 10 years at 5% in an insured bank account, the "cash value" would be $183.63, with comparable safety during the interim. (Refer to Table C–3 on page 671 for cash values under different interest assumptions.) At the end of the 10-year period the term policyholder has a savings account balance of $183.63, compared to only $113—the cash value of the ordinary life policy, a difference of about $50. Furthermore, if the term policyholder dies during the 10-year period, the beneficiary receives $1,000 plus whatever is in the savings account, whereas the beneficiary of the ordinary life insurance policyholder would receive only $1,000, the face amount. Increasing recognition of the time value of money has undoubtedly been at least partially responsible for the rising popularity of term insurance, as opposed to cash-value-type contracts.

Of course, "buying term and investing the difference" as the above procedure has been called, has some disadvantages relative to the ordinary life plan. First, one may not in practice faithfully "save the difference" in the separate account whereas one is more likely to maintain the ordinary life policy premiums. Second, the ordinary life policy offers certain income tax exemption on the accumulating interest element in the policy, whereas most interest in savings accounts is fully taxable. Third, the policyholder enjoys exemption from the claims of creditors for the cash value of the policyholder's ordinary life policy, a condition usually not applicable to savings accounts. Fourth, the owner of ordinary life has the option of continuing this protection as long as the owner wishes, whereas most term policies may not be renewed past age 65. Fifth, the ordinary life policyholder has the option of using certain settlement options which are not available to the savings accounts holder. For these and other reasons, those who wish to save through life insurance may consider this means a desirable one, even though they might accumulate more by separating their savings from their life insurance.

Term Insurance

As indicated before, *term insurance* contracts are issued for a specified number of years and usually do not contain any savings element. In this regard they are similar to other types of insurance in property and liability lines. Term contracts therefore provide a greater amount of pure protection per premium dollar than any other type of insurance. For example, a $100 annual premium would purchase approximately $18,300 of coverage on a person age 30, on a 10-year level-term contract. The same premium spent on whole life insurance would purchase about $5,000 of coverage, slightly over a fourth as much as that provided under the term contract. For this reason term insurance is used most often when:

1. The maximum coverage is desired and the amount available for premiums is limited.
2. The period during which the protection is needed does not extend past age 65.

Level-Term Contract. A *level-term contract* is issued for a constant amount during its term. Examples are 5-year renewable term, 10-year renewable term, 20-year renewable term, and term to 65. Level-term contracts are practically always renewable without evidence of insurability; thus, an objection is removed that was formerly attributable to this type of contract in that an insured's policy could expire and leave this person without protection and uninsurable. *Uninsurability* in life insurance generally means that a person's physical condition is such that it causes the failure to meet the minimum medical and other selection standards on which mortality tables are based. Other factors, such as occupation and credit standing, also enter into the meaning of insurability. About 3% of all applications for life insurance are rejected because of uninsurability. About 4% of all applications are accepted at an extra premium for unusual risk.[4] The probability of uninsurability is high enough that the right of renewal without medical examination is an important feature. In the case of most insurers, however, this right expires at age 60 or 65.

Decreasing-Term Contract. When the amount of pure death protection gradually declines each year on a term contract, the policy is described as one of *decreasing term*. The premium payable may be constant over the term, but the

[4] *Life Insurance Fact Book 1975* (New York: Institute of Life Insurance, 1975), p. 91.

insurance protection decreases. A good example of the use of decreasing-term insurance is in credit life insurance and in mortgage protection insurance. As an insured repays an obligation, such as a mortgage debt, the amount of coverage decreases steadily, corresponding to the declining balance of the debt. In this way the coverage is tailored to meet the need for which the insurance was designed. Since the face amount of decreasing-term insurance is, on the average, considerably less than the face amount involved in a level-term contract, the premium is correspondingly lower. Another manner in which decreasing-term insurance is employed is in the family income policy.

Convertibility. Most term insurance policies are *convertible* into a permanent form of coverage at or before the date of their expiration, without evidence of insurability. In this way persons may take out term insurance with the idea of maximizing their coverage during a period when their protection needs are at a maximum, and then convert their insurance to a permanent form of insurance for use in later years.[5]

Whole Life Insurance

As the name suggests, *whole life insurance* may be kept in force for as long as is desired or until the contract expires, which is never past age 100. There are many different ways of arranging premium payments for whole life insurance, ranging from continuous installments over a person's entire life (ordinary or straight life plan) to a single installment (single-premium whole life). In other words, an insured, at age 35, may pay a single sum, say $5,000 for a $10,000 policy, and never pay another premium. At the time of death the insurer pays the insured's beneficiary $10,000. If the insured does not have $5,000 with which to pay the single premium (and few are those who are able to do so), it may be paid by installments over whatever length of time is desired.

An *ordinary*, or *straight life, contract* is one so arranged that the premiums are payable as long as the insured lives. The contract is not paid up until one reaches age 100 or dies, whichever event comes sooner. (Sometimes additional cash payments or the use of dividends to pay up the contract will effectively convert the true ordinary life policy into a paid-up policy sooner than this.) A *limited-payment life policy,* on the other hand, is one which is so arranged that the insured pays a higher premium than would be required on the ordinary life plan so that a definite termination date can be established beyond which no further payments are due. The most common limited installment plans are 20-payment life, 30-payment life, and life paid up at age 65.

Figure 20–3 illustrates the various plans of whole life insurance. On the vertical axis may be read the face amount of the policy. This amount is made up of two parts, the amount at risk and the amount in the reserve fund. For example, line SP shows that if one pays for a whole life policy in one lump sum, one has a reserve fund of approximately $500 immediately after purchase. If the

[5] Some term policies require conversion before the protection period expires. Thus, the conversion and protection periods do not necessarily coincide.

HOW PREMIUM PAYMENT ARRANGEMENTS AFFECT RESERVE VALUES IN COMMON LIFE INSURANCE CONTRACTS

Figure 20-3

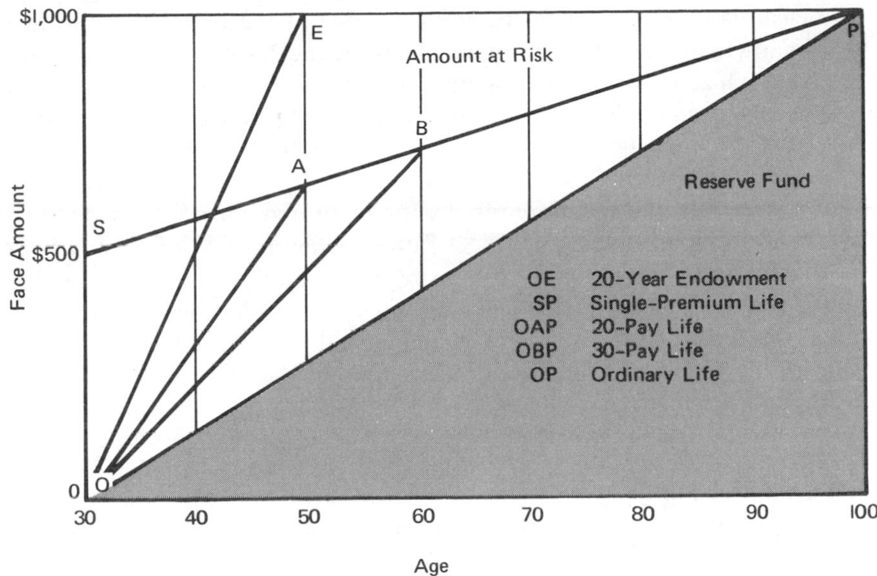

Note: The shaded portion represents the reserve fund in the ordinary life policy at different ages. The reserve fund in other policies is represented by the total area beneath each line, OE, SP, OAP, and OBP.

insured should die the next day, the insurer would pay the beneficiary the face amount of the policy, $1,000. It may be seen then that the *amount at risk* to the insurer was really only $500. On the other hand, for the ordinary life policy, represented by line OP, if the insured pays one premium, there would be no reserve fund available at that time; but if the insured should die the next day, the insurer would pay the beneficiary $1,000. Thus, the amount at risk is almost the full face of the contract. As time goes on, the reserve fund grows, since the premium paid in the early years exceeds the amount needed for mortality expenses. If the insured lives to age 100, the reserve fund reaches the full face of the policy and the insurer will consider the contract to have matured and will pay the insured $1,000.

There is a difference between a policy that is *paid up* and one that is *matured*. When conditions occur to obligate the insurer to pay the *face amount* of the policy, the contract is said to have matured and, hence, terminated. This occurs in the event of death or when the cash values equal the face amount of the contract. Line OE in Figure 20–3 represents the reserve line of the 20-year endowment contract. This line rises steeply so that 20 years after issuance of the contract, the cash values equal the face amount and the contract is terminated by maturity. Line OAP, on the other hand, representing the 20-pay life contract, rises to a certain point (point A) after which the policy is paid up. This means that the cash values, together with the interest which may be earned on this amount, will be sufficient to enable the insurer to meet its obligations to all policyholders, to contribute a share of the mortality expenses each year, and to build up the principal so that at age 100 the cash values will equal the face of the policy, $1,000. After age 50 (point A) the insured need pay no more premiums, but the cash value is not equal to the face value of the policy, as it is in the 20-year endowment policy. For a typical insurer, the 20-pay life contract with a face of $1,000 has a cash value of about $600 after it is fully paid. A whole life contract is really endowment at age 100 and is sometimes referred to in this way, because the face amount of the policy is equal to its cash value at age 100.

Figure 20–3 illustrates that the shorter the premium payment period, the higher the premium and the more rapidly the buildup of cash values. Thus, line OAP rises faster than line OBP since if one wishes to pay all premiums in a 20-year span, one must naturally pay more than would be necessary (and savings accumulate faster) if one had elected to pay the premiums over a period of 30 years. Of course, the faster the premium is paid up and the faster the reserve is built up, the less is the amount at risk. In any of the plans illustrated, at the time of death the insurer must pay $1,000 to the insured's beneficiary. However, the insurer loses less with the high-premium policy than it does with the low-premium policy. That is to say, the $1,000 paid to the beneficiary is made up of two parts—the reserve element and the protection element. The beneficiary collects the insured's own savings and in addition receives a contribution from other insureds. Insureds who live to age 100, receive back their own money. Consideration of this point shows why it is that the reserve is not entirely used up to compensate for the high mortality rate experienced by the insurer in the later years of the contract. The mortality rate at age 80 is 5½ times as great as the rate at age 60. At age 80 the mortality cost per $1,000 might be approximately $220 or higher. Thus, the reserve would be gone in a year or two if the full $1,000 were at risk. Actually, the amount at risk declines sharply as the reserve rises, and so the mortality costs are kept within bounds. Finally, at age 100 the mortality element is extinguished entirely. This is as it should be, for at age 100 actuaries consider death a certainty. As we have learned, it is not feasible to insure against certainties. The older one becomes, the more probable death becomes each year, and the amount at risk in the contract thus declines steadily in permanent whole life contracts.

Endowment Insurance

Endowment contracts are primarily savings contracts with an element of pure protection incorporated into the policy so that if the insured dies before the savings plan is completed, the insurer completes it.

To see how an endowment contract works, assume that Adam Mosby, age 35, sets for himself the goal of saving $1,000 in 20 years. If Adam could receive 4% interest in a savings institution, he would have to make annual deposits of $36.13 for 20 years for a total of $722.60 in order to reach his goal. Now assume that he wishes to have a guarantee that in the event of his death before the 20 years have passed, his wife will still receive $1,000. If he purchases renewable term insurance each year for the difference between $1,000 and the amount currently on hand, the total cost of the insurance would be about $163. The total outlay to him would be $885.60. If Adam purchased a 20-year endowment policy, he accomplishes this same goal for an annual premium of $46.50, or $930 for 20 years.[6] While the endowment contract may cost him somewhat more, there are certain features in this contract which partially offset the added cost.

Limited-Term Contract. *Limited-term endowment contracts* are those for a given period of years, usually 5, 10, 15, 20, or 30 years. A very common period is 20 years. Endowments are commonly used as savings for some specified purpose, such as for educational purposes, retirement, or travel funds. In this way, if the saver dies before the period has expired, the purpose for which the savings plan was set up can often be accomplished by the insured's dependents.

Retirement Income Policy. *Retirement income policies* are similar to endowments except that the former are arranged so that their cash values amount to a sum sufficient to provide $10 a month life income at retirement age, usually 65, for each $1,000 of face amount. Endowment policies are purchased for varying periods, such as a 10-year endowment, 20-year endowment, 30-year endowment, and endowment at age 65. They mature for their face value at the end of this term. At maturity, retirement income policies may have a cash value equal to about $1,400 for each $1,000 of face amount (some policies have different face amounts). The reason for this is that it requires about $1,400 to purchase a life annuity of $10 a month for a male at age 65. The face amount of the retirement income policy is still $1,000 and if death occurs before retirement, the insurer will pay $1,000 or the cash value, if it is greater. Since cash values mount rapidly under the retirement income policy, the insurance element in the contract is relatively small. (See Chapter 22.)

Package Contracts

Package contracts combine or modify the basic types of life insurance to meet specialized needs. The more common packages are described in the following paragraphs.

Family Income Policy. A *family income policy* is a combination of decreasing-term insurance and ordinary life insurance. It is nearly always issued on a level-premium basis. As its name suggests, the family income policy is designed to provide a large amount of pure protection during a time when children are young and at the same time to provide some permanent insurance. The *base* of the contract is usually ordinary life insurance, to which is added a decreasing-term *rider*. The insurance under the rider is commonly expressed as so many units of income at $10 a unit. Thus, a family income policy may be composed of $10,000 ordinary life insurance plus 10 units of decreasing-term insurance, $15,000 of ordinary life insurance with 15 units of decreasing-term insurance, etc. The policy is usually arranged so that the beneficiary receives $100 (or $150) a month for a specified period, and then $10,000 (or $15,000) at the end of

[6] The rates quoted assume 3% interest on reserves, CSO 1941, nonparticipating.

this period. The $10,000 ($15,000) is held by the insurer, and interest on this sum helps make the income payments.

The term rider is decreasing because the period during which the income would be payable in the event of death decreases as time goes on. For example, let us say that Amos takes out a $10,000 family income policy with a 20-year decreasing-term rider when he is age 25 and his youngest child is age one. The income is payable to his family from a period dating from his death until the time he would have been 45, or until the youngest child is 21. If Amos dies 10 years after the policy is issued, the payments are made for 10 years. If he dies 15 years after the policy is issued, the payments are made for five years, after which the $10,000 payable under the ordinary life insurance portion is settled. At the end of 20 years, if Amos has survived the period, the term rider expires and this portion of the policy is terminated. The premium is usually reduced accordingly and Amos may continue the ordinary life insurance portion as long as he wishes.

The family income policy is one of the most popular contracts of life insurance sold because it constitutes a small program of insurance in itself. It represents a balanced solution to the twin needs of both temporary and permanent life insurance. The term rider is generally available for varying periods—5, 10, 15, or 20 years—so that income may be provided until the children reach a certain designated age. Some insurers offer the term rider by itself without the necessity of the insured purchasing any permanent insurance along with it. Many insurers will also issue a term rider that may be attached to any permanent policy already issued on the life of the insured.

Family Maintenance Policy. The *family maintenance policy* is a combination of ordinary life insurance and level-term insurance and should not be confused with the family income policy. In both the family income and the family maintenance policy there is a base of protection in the ordinary life portion, but in the family maintenance policy the term protection does not decrease during the period of its existence. Suppose, in the example above, Amos has a family maintenance policy instead of a family income policy. The policy has a 20-year term rider attached. If Amos dies anytime within 20 years after taking out the policy, his widow receives an income for a *full 20 years*, and at the end, the face amount of the policy. If Amos survives the 20 years, the rider expires, as it did in the case of the family income policy, and Amos may continue the base policy indefinitely.

Specials. Many insurers issue *specials*—life insurance contracts with a specified minimum face amount at reduced prices. The economy rates involved in specials may stem from a number of sources. For example, it costs less to issue one policy for $5,000, or $10,000, than it does to issue 5 to 10 policies of $1,000 each. Reductions in cost may also be made because the contracts are issued only to *preferred risks,* individuals who pass very rigid underwriting standards. Savings may also stem from a reduction of the agent's commissions on the sale of the contracts. Each of these sources of economy appears to be a legitimate method of reducing the cost of distributing life insurance. Some insurers, however, make savings in what appear to be less legitimate ways. For example, specials may contain reduced schedules of cash values, fewer settlement options, less generous settlement options, or reduction of other services. It is not easy for the typical buyer to evaluate the differences, with the result that misleading comparisons may be made with regular contracts. Even though abuses of this kind may occur in the offering of specials, it appears desirable that insurers tailor their offerings to fit as closely as possible the varying needs of the public, particularly when reductions in distribution costs become possible.

Modified Life Insurance Contracts. *Modified life insurance contracts* are those in which the premiums are arranged so that they are smaller than average for the first 5 or 10 years of the policy and slightly larger than average for the remaining years of the contract This is done by combining term insurance with some form of permanent insurance so that the insured pays more than the term policy would cost, but less than the cost of the permanent insurance. Modified life contracts thus enable the insured to obtain a permanent insurance policy at a cost which is usually one half of what would normally be paid for the first five or ten years. The contract fits the needs of the young married person with a limited income who wants to develop a permanent insurance program but cannot afford to do so until his or her income rises. The solution could also be found in the purchase of straight convertible term insurance, but many persons would fail to convert term insurance into a permanent form because the premium increase is quite substantial. The modified life contract has the advantage that the insured need not take any positive action to convert the contract to a permanent form.

Multiple Protection Insurance Contracts. The *multiple protection insurance contract* employs term insurance to grant double, triple, or some multiple of the face amount of a permanent insurance policy for a set period, from 5 to 20 years, after which the protection is reduced to the face amount of the permanent policy. Thus, instead of using the term principle to reduce the cost of a set amount of coverage, as is true of modified life insurance, the multiple protection contract grants added coverage in a way very similar to the family maintenance policy.

Juvenile Insurance. Life insurance issued on children is called *juvenile insurance*. For very young children, say between the ages of 1 and 4, it is common to provide graded death benefits, so as to limit the life insurance coverage to modest amounts, often less than $500. As the child gets older, the coverage increases automatically until it reaches some limit, say $1,000, or a multiple thereof. Normally, coverage is issued on some permanent insurance form.

Jumping Juvenile Insurance. A package contract, sometimes called *jumping juvenile*, is issued in units of say $1,000 at some early age. The amount automatically increases to say $5,000 at age 21, without increasing the premium and without evidence of insurability. Often this insurance is sold as a savings program for college education.

Advantages of jumping juvenile insurance include the provision of permanent life insurance protection even if the child should become uninsurable later; the establishment of the savings habit at an early date; and the establishment of an insurance program at a low premium age. The disadvantage is that this plan takes away insurance dollars that might be better spent on the breadwinner. In view of the great underinsurance which exists on human life generally, it is doubtful if much expenditure for juvenile coverage can be justified.

Payor Clause. Insurers offer what is known as a payor clause on a juvenile policy which states that if the owner (usually the father) dies before the policy matures, all future premiums are waived until the child reaches age 21. This clause really amounts to additional insurance on the life of the father.

Family Group Policy. One of the most successful life insurance packages introduced in recent years is the *family group policy,* in which each member of the family is insured for different amounts. The head of the family normally obtains the most coverage and insurance on the spouse and children is limited to smaller amounts. Not uncommonly, if the owner of the policy is covered for $5,000, the spouse and the children will have $1,000 each. The $5,000 portion of the contract may be term or permanent insurance, but coverage on the spouse and the children is usually convertible term insurance. One premium is charged for the entire package which solves a common need, that of a limited amount of protection for the breadwinner's dependents, combined with insurance on the family head.

Variable Life Contract. Life insurance designed to help the amount to protection meet the loss in purchasing power caused by inflation has recently been introduced in the United States although its use is not yet widespread. The policy has been available in The Netherlands for several years. The reserves of the variable life contract are invested in common stocks and other equity type investments which fluctuate in value according to price changes in the stock market. Increases in the value of these investments are reflected in increased policy face amounts according to a formula stated in the contract. If the stock market declines, the face amount also declines; but some contracts contain a minimum death benefit equal to the original face amount. This policy will be discussed in Chapter 22.

SUMMARY

1. Life insurance is a method of creating an estate of income-producing property. It is the only method of creating an immediate estate in case of premature death; it serves as a hedge against the possibility that the insured may not live to carry out property accumulation plans.

2. The chief purpose of life insurance in estate planning is to provide for dependents in case of death of the breadwinner. A secondary purpose of life insurance is to save money for one's retirement or for other purposes. Policies are available which meet these twin purposes with many degrees of emphasis.

3. Life insurance is commonly issued on a level premium basis. Because death rates rise substantially over a long period of years, more money must be collected in the early years to offset the higher mortality costs of the later years. For this reason all policies except pure term insurance accumulate a cash value known as the reserve.
4. The reserve in life insurance not only serves to keep the premium level throughout the premium-paying period, but it also serves many other purposes. The insured may view the reserve as a savings fund to draw on in emergencies, as a buffer against the possible lapse of the policy, as collateral for a bank loan, or as a retirement fund. The reserve makes possible the continuance of life insurance beyond age 65, a period during which there are still many needs for protection.
5. The major types of life insurance—term, whole life, and endowment—may be purchased separately or in many different combinations to meet the specific needs of insureds. Of the three types, term insurance has grown most rapidly in recent years.

QUESTIONS FOR REVIEW AND DISCUSSION

1. (a) What is meant by the future estate? the present estate?
   (b) How does life insurance protect these estates?
2. It has been stated that life insurance is property. What general characteristics of property are possessed by life insurance?
3. It has been stated that the trouble with life insurance is that one has to die in order to collect. Is this an accurate statement? If so, why? If not, restate it more correctly.
4. "What is temporary for one person may be permanent for another." Explain, giving examples of what you consider to be permanent as opposed to temporary needs for life insurance.
5. All permanent life insurance contracts have cash values, but not all contracts with cash values are permanent. Do you agree? Why?
6. Why do life insurers issue contracts with an overcharge in the premium, while property and liability insurers do not? Explain.
7. A critic of life insurance stated, "Whereas that actuarial table of 1941 states that 4.59 out of every 1,000 men starting their 35th year would die in that year, as a matter of fact the experience of several large companies suggests that on the average only 2.9 out of every 1,000 men actually did die. Thus, you come upon the first of a series of life insurance overcharges. The major companies were tucking away $1.69 per annum per $1,000 in a perfectly obvious overcharge." Is this statement true or false? Would you draw the same conclusion from it as has been apparently drawn by the author of the remarks? Why?
8. Obtain the latest *Life Insurance Fact Book* and compare recent trends in the growth of each major type of life insurance—term, whole life, and endowment—for the last 20 years.
   (a) What do you observe?
   (b) How do you account for the trends noted?
9. "The idea of paying up a policy in 20 years rather than paying all my life is appealing, but it has certain drawbacks which often make this course of action of doubtful merit." Mention some of the drawbacks to which reference is made.
10. For what major purposes should term insurance be used? whole life insurance? endowment insurance? Defend your answers.

11. Philip Ramos, age 30, has a family of five, with children aged three, five, and ten. He earns $7,000 per year and figures that he can devote $500 a year to life insurance. He is covered by social security, and has a group life insurance certificate for $7,000 in connection with his employment.
(a) For what types of life insurance would you recommend that Philip spend his insurance budget? Defend your choices.
(b) How much death protection will your selections provide if Philip should die tomorrow?

12. Would your answer be any different in Question 11 if Philip Ramos, now age 49, earned $15,000 and his three children were aged 22, 24, and 29?

13. Payments cease 20 years after a 20-pay life or a 20-year endowment contract is issued, but at that time one is matured, while the other is paid up. What is the difference between a policy that is paid up and one that is matured?

14. A critic of life insurance asked, "Why is it that whole life policies endow at age 100 when most men are dead?" How would you answer the critic?

15. If one were to draw the appropriate line of a term-to-65 policy on Figure 20–3, where would the line be drawn? Why?

16. *Z* bought a $1,000 ordinary life policy at age 30 for an annual premium of $21.53. In five years its cash value was $86.66; in 10 years, $178.43; in 15 years, $273.82; and in 20 years, $370.83. A $1,000 term policy could have been purchased for a cost of $6.46 per year the first five years; $7.31 per year for the second five years; $9.87 per year for the third five years; and $13.02 per year for the last five years.
(a) What is the net cost of *Z*'s protection under each plan after (1) 5 years, (2) 10 years, (3) 15 years, and (4) 20 years? (Net cost = Premiums − Cash Value)
(b) How do you account for the differences noted?
(c) If *Z* had decided to "buy term and invest the difference," and had purchased the term contracts of $1,000 face amount, what would have been the cash value of the separate savings plan after 20 years assuming *Z* is able to earn 5% interest continuously over the period? (See Table C-3.) Do you think *Z* should have pursued this course, or should *Z* have purchased the ordinary life plan? Discuss the advantages and disadvantages.

17. *R* requests information concerning the family income policy. *R* wants to know (a) why the company does not pay the proceeds of the base policy immediately upon death of the insured, instead of at the end of the time period, and (b) why the income does not continue for a full 20 years from date of death, instead of stopping after the lapse of a 20-year period dating from the issuance of the contract. Suggest reasons for these conditions.

18. A certain insurer offers a family income policy with the following conditions: No base policy is required and the policy can be arranged so that the income may continue for any number of years desired, but not to exceed the period which would require payments after the insured reaches age 65.
(a) What type of basic life insurance is being used in this plan?
(b) What are the advantages over the usual family income policy?

19. One of the advantages claimed for permanent insurance is that it provides an automatic protection against lapse. How might this be done?

20. A certain insurer offers an ordinary life policy at age 25 at the rate of $18.56 per year per $1,000, and offers an "economy size" policy with a minimum face amount of $3,000, at the rate of $16.20 per year per $1,000. Explain the possible sources from which these savings might stem.

Chapter *Twenty-One*

CONTRACT RIGHTS IN LIFE INSURANCE

The contractual provisions of the life insurance policy are of special significance to the insured because it is through a wise use of certain of these contract rights that some of the most valuable benefits of the protection can be obtained. Furthermore, there are few contracts of insurance which contain more provisions directly bearing on the welfare of the insured. Life insurance is usually a long-term contract effective long after the death of the insured, and a clear understanding of at least the more important provisions is vital if the services of the insurer and the agent are to be employed effectively in carrying out the intentions of the insured regarding the estate.

NONFORFEITURE OPTIONS

The *nonforfeiture options* in life insurance guarantee that the savings element in the policy will not be forfeited to the insurer under any circumstances, but will always accrue to the benefit of the insured. There are three ways in which the insured may receive the cash value element: a lump sum paid in cash, extended term insurance, and paid-up insurance of a reduced amount.[1]

Cash and Loan Value Option

The *cash and loan value option* enables the insured to remove savings from the contract with or without terminating the contract. If emergency cash is needed but it is not desired to terminate the policy, the cash value may be borrowed from the insurer and interest paid on this loan. Since the insurer has calculated the original premium under the assumption that interest would be earned on reserves, interest is charged to anyone, including the insured, who

[1] Before the advent of nonforfeiture options (which are required by law in all states), there were cases where aged persons agreed to sell their policies to speculators when they could no longer continue the premium payments. The speculator's offer depended on the physical condition of the aged person, and a public sale often took place with the aged person present so he or she could be examined. Needless to say, the insured seldom fared well in these transactions. Elizur Wright, an early insurance commissioner in Massachusetts, was instrumental in outlawing these practices.

borrows these reserves. At the time the insured is using the reserve and paying interest on it, the insurer is crediting the insured's account with interest that it is earning on its assets. Thus, the insured may be paying 5% interest on an insurance loan and receiving 4% interest in the form of credits to the reserve account. The loan thus costs the insured only 1% interest. This cost is necessary because policy loans are offered as an accommodation to the insured and are relatively expensive to administer. The above arguments destroy the oft-expressed fallacy that it is inequitable for an insurer to charge an insured for the loan of the insured's own money. It is not actually the insured's money but that of the policyholders as a group. If the insured dies with an outstanding loan on a policy, the amount of the loan is subtracted from the policy proceeds. Otherwise, there is never any obligation to repay the loan. If the entire cash value has been borrowed, it is necessary, of course, for the insured to pay the annual interest in cash in order to avoid lapse.

Extended Term Option

If the insured has not selected an option, most insurers automatically use the *extended term option*. The cash value of the contract at the time of lapse is used to purchase a term policy for as many months or years as are allowed by the rates in effect at the insured's age when the lapse occurred. A table in the contract states just how long this period is at various ages. Thus, for one insurer an ordinary life policy issued at age 35 in force for 20 years has a guaranteed cash value of $370.83 per $1,000. If the insured wishes to terminate a contract, the options are to take the money in cash or to receive term insurance of $1,000 for 16 years and 325 days.

Paid-Up Insurance Option

The insured in the example above might select the *paid-up insurance option* and thus receive a paid-up ordinary life policy of $561. This means that no further premium payments would be necessary and that the insurer would pay $561 upon the insured's death no matter when it occurs. This is almost the same as if insured had purchased a single-premium ordinary life policy of $561 face amount for a lump sum premium of $370.83.[2]

The nonforfeiture options are very important to the insured. The insured cannot lose savings because of the inability to continue premium payments, and in addition the insured has the right to continue insurance protection in two different ways if so desired. This exposes a fallacy often heard in reference to ordinary life insurance, namely, that the trouble with it is that you have to pay premiums all your life. Actually, one may stop paying premiums at any time and elect one of the nonforfeiture options. The extended term option has benefitted many a widow who discovered that a policy which she thought had lapsed because of nonpayment of premiums was actually still in force under the

[2] However, the insured pays no acquisition expenses for insurance purchased under dividend options or nonfeiture options, and so it might be said that this is a very economical way to acquire insurance.

extended term option. The paid-up insurance option is especially valuable when old age reduces the ability to continue payment of premiums and yet continued protection is needed for a dependent spouse.

SETTLEMENT OPTIONS

Settlement refers to the way in which the insurer pays the proceeds of the contract. The *settlement options* describe the different ways in which the insured may elect to receive the proceeds of a policy. The insured may choose to receive the proceeds personally or to have the proceeds paid to the beneficiaries, whether the proceeds be death proceeds or a liquidation of the cash values of the contract. There are many settlement options and combinations thereof, but the most common are: lump sum option, fixed period option, fixed amount option, interest option, and life income option.

Lump Sum Option

Under the *lump sum option*, proceeds of the life insurance are paid in a lump sum, and the insurer's obligations are ended. The insurer exercises no further control over the money and the various services offered in connection with other options are lost. For this reason lump sum settlements are employed most often when the insured or the beneficiary needs the money for a purpose which may be best served by a cash amount, such as for liquidation of a mortgage, for payment of last expenses, or for paying taxes. A vast majority of all life insurance policies are settled under this option.

Fixed Period Option

Rather than being paid in a lump sum, the insured may select the *fixed period option* under which the insurer is directed to pay the policy proceeds in installments over a set time period. Under this option the insurer issues a supplementary contract (the old policy having been terminated) in which it agrees to pay the proceeds as directed. No extra charge is made for this service, although if a separate trust were set up to accomplish the same thing, a substantial cost would be involved.

As an example of a situation in which the fixed period option would be used, consider the following case. An insured, having provided for his family during the period when the children are young, wishes to set up an income for his wife, now age 36, to begin after their 7-year-old child is 18 and to continue until the wife is aged 60. Social security income ceases during this period and the insured observes that, without at least a minimum income, the wife may be unable to meet current expenses even if she works, since help from the children is generally not likely to be substantial. The problem then is to provide an income to begin after a set number of years have passed and to continue for a given number of years. Using the fixed period option, the insured instructs the insurance company that if he should die, the proceeds of the policy are to be held at interest until the wife is age 47 and then paid out to her over a 13-year period. At the end of this period the wife will be 60 and social security retirement income payments will commence. The amount of insurance proceeds necessary to accomplish this purpose may be calculated from special programming tables designed for this purpose. Thus, at 5% interest, it can be calculated that it would require $6,590 of proceeds to provide $1,200 a year for 13 years, the first payment being due at the beginning of the eleventh year, and the fund being exhausted at the end of the thirteenth year of payments.[3]

Fixed Amount Option

The *fixed amount option* is similar in purpose to the fixed period option except that under the former option, payment of the proceeds is arranged to provide a set income, with the *length of time* varying with the interest assumptions and the total funds available. An insured may wish to provide a certain minimum income to the family and will instruct the insurer to pay this income for as long as the proceeds may last. Excess interest lengthens the period, but does not vary the amount.

Interest Option

Under the *interest option*, the insurer holds the proceeds of the policy and pays an income consisting of interest only. The recipient may have the right to withdraw the principal. This option is often used in the following cases:

1. The proceeds of the policy may be intended to pay for last expenses, but it is not known just when these expenses will be payable. The proceeds are thus held at interest until needed and then withdrawn whenever the beneficiary wishes.
2. The proceeds of the policy are intended for use as an emergency fund for the spouse. The policy is settled under the interest option with the right of withdrawal of principal as needed.
3. Interest is needed to supplement family income, but the principal is intended to go to a child upon becoming age 21. The proceeds are left under the interest option with interest payable to the spouse, but without the right of withdrawal except by the named child upon becoming age 21.
4. It is desired to use the principal to meet income needs at a later time, but to pay out interest currently to supplement family income. The proceeds are left under the interest option until a certain time has elapsed, and then settled under the fixed period option, the fixed amount option, or the life income option.

Table 21–1 illustrates the amount of income from life insurance proceeds available under the settlement options discussed above. When insurance is viewed in terms of the income it will provide, the need for adequate protection becomes more evident to the average person.

Life Income Option

Under the *life income option*, the proceeds may be left in an annuity to guarantee the beneficiary a life income with or without any minimum number of guaranteed installments.

[3] Not all insurers will accumulate interest on death proceeds of insurance.

ALTERNATE INCOME USES OF LIFE INSURANCE PROCEEDS

Table 21-1

Fixed Period Option

Monthly Income Provided For Each $10,000 of Proceeds *	Time Period
$183.24	5 years
$100.58	10 years
60.03	20 years
49.40	life **

Fixed Amount Option

Insurance Proceeds	Time Over Which $100 a Month Will Be Paid
$ 5,000	4 years, 6 months
10,000	10 years
20,000	26 years, 11 months

Interest Option

Amount of Monthly Income Provided by $10,000 Proceeds	Interest Percentage
$25.00	3
33.33	4
41.66	5
50.00	6

* Assuming 4% interest.
** Female beneficiary age 60, lifetime payments with 10 years certain.

Significance of Settlement Options

In 1974 only 7% of the funds most likely to be used for income purposes (death benefits, matured endowments, and cash surrender values) were set aside for future payments under income settlement options. The remaining 93% was paid in lump sums.[4] It seems from these data that either life insurance is being used primarily for lump-sum needs or that policyholders as a group are somewhat unaware of the advantages of using income settlement options, or that alternative uses of insurance proceeds offer advantages, or that some combination of these conditions is present.

By the use of settlement options, insurance can be arranged to guarantee the income security of which it is capable. It has been stated previously that the

[4] *Life Insurance Fact Book 1975* (New York: Institute of Life Insurance, 1975), p. 47.

central purpose of life insurance is to replace income lost because of the premature death of the insured. If this is true, it is through income settlement options that the lost income can be replaced most economically and efficiently for the average person. Emphasis on settlement options furnishes a rationale for the purchase of life insurance and a guide for determining how much life insurance to purchase. In other words, the answer to the question of "How much life insurance should I buy?" may be answered "It depends mainly on how much income you wish to provide for yourself or your dependents." The principal sum necessary to furnish a given income level for different periods is then readily ascertainable.

Use of insurer services in managing the proceeds of the insurance costs the insured nothing extra. The proceeds are preserved from mismanagement by inexperienced beneficiaries, or from depletion by relatives or swindlers. The insured can rest in complete knowledge that fluctuations of the stock or bond market, a business depression, or other investment hazards will not interrupt the flow of income that is anticipated for beneficiaries.

Before using settlement options, however, the policyholder should compare carefully the proceeds promised by the insurer with proceeds available through alternative financial institutions. In recent years interest returns available in the open market far exceed the minimum interest guarantees, or even the interest guaranteed plus dividends, available from life insurers. To illustrate, as shown in Table 21–1, the policy may offer a female beneficiary age 60 lifetime monthly payments of only $49.40, with 10 years certain for each $10,000 of life insurance proceeds. This amounts to only $592.80 per year. A widow could take the $10,000 in a lump sum, deposit it in an insured savings and loan association or purchase a government bond, and obtain under today's conditions, at least a 6% return, or $600 a year, without using any principal and without risk. Under the life income option the payments are made up of both principal and interest and after ten years upon her death there would be no funds in her estate available for her beneficiaries.

CLAUSES PROTECTING THE INSURED AND THE BENEFICIARY

In addition to the inherent protective features involved in nonforfeiture and settlement options, there are other important clauses in the life insurance contract. Some of these clauses, which have as their purpose a guarantee that the life insurance contract will accomplish the purposes for which it is intended, are required by law.

Incontestable Clause

The *incontestable clause* states that if the policy has been in force for a given period, usually two years, and if the insured has not died during that time, the insurer may not afterward refuse to pay the proceeds nor may it cancel or contest the contract, even because of fraud. Thus, if an insured is found to have lied about his or her physical condition at the time application was made for life insurance, but this misrepresentation is not discovered until after the expiration of the incontestable clause, the insurer may not cancel the policy nor refuse to pay the face amount if the insured has died from a cause not excluded under the basic terms of the policy.[5] Thus, the incontestable clause serves as a time limit within which the insurer must discover any fraud or misrepresentation in the application or be barred thereafter from asserting what would otherwise be its legal right—namely, the right to cancel the agreement. Such a statute of limitations is not typical of most insurance contracts. The legal justification for this clause in life insurance is protection of beneficiaries from doubtful claims by an insurer that the deceased had made misrepresentations, after it becomes impossible for the deceased to defend against or to deny the allegation.

Suicide Clause

The *suicide clause* partially protects the beneficiary from the financial consequences of suicide. The clause states that if the insured does not commit suicide for at least a stated period, usually two years, after issuance of the contract, the insurer may not deny liability under the policy for subsequent suicide. If suicide occurs within two years of the issuance of the policy, the insurer's only obligation is to return without interest the premiums that have been paid. A one- or two-year period is justified on the grounds that if the applicant's plans to commit suicide have motivated the purchase of life insurance, it is likely that these plans will abate after as long as one or two years.

Reinstatement and Grace Period Clauses

Under the *reinstatement clause*, contracts may be reinstated within a certain period after lapse, usually three or five years, upon evidence of insurability. The policy lapses for nonpayment of premium, but the *grace period clause* always gives the insured an extra 30 days in which to pay any premium which is due before lapse takes place. Once the policy has actually lapsed, special application must be made under the reinstatement clause to restore coverage. Sometimes a new medical examination must be taken, but usually the insured is only required to make a statement of personal good health at the time of reinstatement. All premiums in arrears plus interest must be paid. Reinstatement reopens the incontestable clause for another two years, but generally the suicide clause is held not to be reopened. It is sometimes desirable to reinstate the old policy rather than to take out a new one because the old policy may have certain provisions, such as more favorable settlement options, immediate eligibility for dividends, or higher interest assumptions, which are not available

[5] Sometimes the policy excludes death from war or from certain aviation accidents. Refusal to pay claims resulting from these excluded perils would not be in violation of the incontestable clause no matter when the death occurred. It has also been held that in some cases of gross fraud there was never a valid contract in the first place, and that hence the incontestable clause was never in effect—e.g., in cases where the insured has another person take a medical examination there would not be a meeting of minds, and the contract would fail for want of a valid offer and acceptance.

in the new policy. Furthermore, no new acquisition costs have to be paid on the reinstated policy as they would on a new form. Since acquisition costs are substantial, amounting to about one year's annual premium on ordinary life policies, this is a great saving.

Automatic Premium Loan Clause

The nonpayment of a premium involves a lapse after expiration of the grace period. If the policy has a surrender value at the time of lapse, it may be surrendered for cash, changed into a different contract under extended term insurance, or become paid-up insurance of a reduced amount. To prevent a lapse, most insurers encourage the use of an *automatic premium loan provision*, which automatically authorizes the insurer to use cash values to pay the premium and thereby to establish a loan against the policy just as though the insured had borrowed this amount for another purpose. In this way the old policy continues as before without interruption, the only change being that there is now a loan against the policy.

Misstatement of Age Clause

Misrepresenting one's age in life insurance is material to accepting the risk and normally would become a defense against payment of the proceeds if it were not for the incontestable clause. Without some control over this hazard, it would become possible for people to understate their age for the purpose of obtaining a lower premium for life insurance and to overstate their age for the purpose of receiving a larger retirement income. Proof of age is therefore required before proceeds are paid. Under the *misstatement of age clause*, if it is determined that the person's age has been misrepresented, the insurer adjusts the amount of proceeds payable rather than cancelling the agreement altogether. The actual amount payable is the amount of insurance which would have been purchased for the premium paid had the true age been stated. For example, if the premium at the true age is $30 and the premium at the stated age is $25, the insurer will pay only 5/6 of the death proceeds otherwise payable.

Entire Contract Clause

The policy of life insurance generally contains an *entire contract clause*, which provides that the policy together with the application constitutes the entire contract between the parties. This clause is desirable for the protection of the insured and the beneficiary because without the clause it might be possible to affect the rights of the respective parties through changes in the bylaws or in the charter of the insurer. With fraternal insurers, the insured's rights can be changed if the fraternal organization's charter is duly changed.

Spendthrift Trust Clause

One of the legal rights granted to the life insurance owner in most states is the exemption of death proceeds and cash values from the claims of creditors.

Creditors of the insured cannot attach the cash value of life insurance for the payment of the insured's debts unless the insured has wrongfully bought or paid up a life insurance policy with money rightfully subject to creditor's claims. Neither may the insured's creditors attach the death proceeds of life insurance. This is an important right since the beneficiary is thus protected from the claims of the *insured's* creditors, and the indiscretions of the insured are not allowed to wreck the income security of the beneficiaries.

The question arises, however, "What about the *beneficiary's* creditors?" May the beneficiary incur large debts using as security the right to receive income from life insurance proceeds? This is technically possible unless the state law has a provision to the contrary, or unless the law has permitted the attachment of what is called the *spendthrift trust clause*. If the spendthrift trust clause is attached to a life insurance policy, the beneficiary's rights to the promised income cannot be attached by creditors in any court in the state of residence. Such a clause is a valuable security measure, for without it there might be a temptation for an unscrupulous creditor to persuade a beneficiary to purchase goods beyond the ability to pay, secure in the knowledge that the life insurance trust could be attached. Thus, society grants to life insurance special status not given to other types of investments. Endorsement of the spendthrift trust clause is legal in most states. To qualify for this clause, the proceeds must usually be settled under an income option. Once the income has been paid to the beneficiary, the protection is lost when and if the money loses its identity as life insurance proceeds.

MISCELLANEOUS CONTRACTUAL PROVISIONS

Several other types of contractual provisions are common to most life insurance policies. The following paragraphs describe the most common ones.

Dividend Options

Participating policies are those under which dividends are payable to the owner of the contract. The dividend is actually a partial return of the premium payment and reflects the experience of the insurer with regard to mortality and overhead costs and net investment income. All participating life insurance contracts provide certain options in the use of dividends. In general, the insured may: take the dividends in cash; leave them with the insurer at interest; use them to buy paid-up additions; use them to reduce premium payments; or use them to help pay up a permanent contract sooner than it would otherwise be paid.[6]

Dividends may be substantial in size and so the proper choice of a dividend option is important. For example, as shown in Table 6–1, page 134, dividends

[6] In 1970, dividends in life insurance were used for these purposes in the following proportion: taken in cash, 21%; left at interest, 28%; used to buy additional amounts of insurance, 27%; used to pay premiums, 24%; *Life Insurance Fact Book 1972* (New York: Institute of Life Insurance, 1972), p. 50.

among ten large life insurers over the period 1954–1974 averaged about 24% or the total premiums paid by policyholders over the 20-year period. Thus, the insured could have reduced premiums or could have purchased substantial amounts of additional life insurance with the dividends available. The use of dividends helps to pay up an ordinary life contract and in some cases may enable the insured to increase the reserve of a policy so that no more payments are necessary after age 65. (Contracts paying no dividends cost less initially and are called nonparticipating insurance.)

The use of dividends to purchase paid-up additions has four important advantages:

1. Since no acquisition charges are made in such cases, it is an economical way to buy additional life insurance.
2. Since no medical examination or other evidence of insurability is required, use of this option may enable the purchase of insurance when it is impossible to obtain coverage in any other way. Such use of dividend options is of obvious importance to persons in a doubtful state of health. Sometimes the insurer will require evidence of insurability if this option is selected after the policy is first taken out.
3. The paid-up additions themselves have a cash value which may be borrowed. Thus, the insured has available a large portion of the dividends if it becomes necessary to borrow the cash value of the paid-up additions. In the event of the insured's death, the beneficiary receives the additional life insurance (less the amount borrowed) even though the insured had the use of most of the dividend payments while living.
4. For individuals in the higher income-tax brackets, paid-up additions have a further advantage in that the interest earned on the dividends so employed has a tax-free status, whereas if they were left to accumulate at interest, the interest would be taxable. Dividends themselves, being considered a return of premium, are not taxable.

Extensions of Coverage

For an additional premium, most insurers will permit riders, which are actually in the nature of health insurance, to be attached to the life insurance policy.

Waiver of Premium Rider. The *waiver of premium rider*, which costs about 50 cents per $1,000 per year at age 30 for ordinary life policies, excuses the insured from paying any further premiums under the policy in the event of the insured's total and permanent physical disability from any cause before a certain age, usually age 60.[7] The policy will have the same cash values, death benefits, and dividends as it would have had if all premiums had been paid. Normally there is a waiting period of six months before the insurer starts to waive the premiums. The use of such a rider is recommended as a way of assuring that the life insurance estate will remain intact regardless of the insured's health.

[7] What constitutes total and permanent disability varies according to the interpretation by an individual insurer. A common definition is that the insured shall be considered unable to engage in a regular occupation for profit or remuneration. Total loss of eyesight, or loss of use of both hands or both feet, or one hand and one foot commonly constitutes evidence of total disability.

Disability Income Rider. Carrying the waiver-of-premium idea a step further, most insurers will endorse the life insurance policy to provide a monthly income of $5 or $10 for each $1,000 of face amount in the event that the insured is totally and permanently disabled. Known as the *disability income rider*, this endorsement becomes effective after a four- or six-months' waiting period, and terminates if disability has not occurred before the insured has reached age 55 or 60, or at the maturity date of the policy if this comes sooner. The income continues as long as the insured remains totally and permanently disabled, for life if necessary, but normally not beyond the maturity date of the policy or age 65, whichever comes sooner.

If disability continues to age 65, the policy generally becomes paid up. Often the insurer imposes certain restrictions concerning injuries that are intentionally self-inflicted or that are suffered as a result of war, while a passenger in a private aircraft, or while involved in a riot or civil commotion. The cost of disability income protection is relatively low, averaging about $3 annually for each $10 of monthly income for a person age 25. Because disability income protection is often available in separate policies on a more flexible basis than under life insurance policies, the importance of the disability income rider is diminishing.

Double Indemnity Rider. The *double indemnity rider* is an additional extension of coverage under which the insured's beneficiary may receive twice (and sometimes triple) the face amount of the policy if death is accidental. However, there are numerous restrictions on this benefit. For example, death from suicide, death which occurs after 120 days following an accident, death from all illnesses, death with no visible evidence of wounds or contusions, and accidental deaths due to war or aviation are excluded. While the charge for the double indemnity clause is not high, usually amounting to about $1.25 per $1,000 of face amount, coverage under the clause has the unfortunate tendency of leading the unsophisticated insured into believing that death protection has been doubled for a very small extra charge. Such could not be further from the truth. As we have seen, accidents are not the leading cause of death, and accidents that satisfy the definitions of the double indemnity clause are an even rarer cause of death.

Assignments

Rather than cash in a life insurance policy or borrow from the insurer, the insured may wish to *assign* the benefits to another, say a lender of money. This might be done because the bank may refuse to lend money to the borrower without insurance, or the borrower may have insufficient collateral to cover the loan, or the borrower is uninsurable for new coverage to protect a loan. Permission of the insurer is not necessary for the insured to assign a life insurance policy. However, the insurer must be properly notified in writing of an assignment, or the insurer is not bound by it. In the event of the insured's death, the usual procedure is for the insurer to pay to the holder of the assignment that part of the proceeds equal to the debt and the remainder to the named beneficiaries. The assignee need not have an insurable interest in the life of the insured. The insured may make a gift to someone through an assignment, for example.

Premium Payment

Most life insurers give the policyholder the right to pay premiums annually, semiannually, or quarterly. Many give the right to pay monthly. There is an extra charge, however, for paying other than annually. For example, if the annual premium is $100, the insurer may quote a semiannual premium of say $51. This is equivalent to charging $2 extra per year for the use of $49 for six months.[8] Reduced to simple interest terms, the cost is 4.08% for six months, or 8.16% annually. However, it may be worthwhile to the insured to pay at this rate because of the advantages of making installment payments as part of a budgeting program.

Excluded Perils

It is not common for life insurers to exclude many perils from coverage. Occasionally excluded are deaths caused by airplane accidents except for regularly scheduled flights on established airlines. Most insurers exclude only aviation deaths while on military activities. In wartime many insurers exclude deaths caused as a result of war. There is little uniformity in the excluded perils clauses, and the practices of each insurer should be studied carefully to ascertain the coverage. If a peril is excluded in a life insurance policy, the fact that there is an incontestable clause does not prevent the insurer from denying liability since it is held that the incontestable clause applies only to deaths from perils not excluded by the policy. Technically, the policy is not being "contested," because the insurer has simply elected not to cover certain causes of death. Fortunately, the average life insurance policy contains very few such exclusions. It is virtually a true all-risk agreement.

Beneficiary Designation

The insured may name anyone as beneficiary of a policy. The beneficiary does not have to have an insurable interest in the life of the insured. One of the great advantages of using life insurance as a method of estate creation is that the contract simultaneously provides for both the accumulation *and the distribution* of the property. The proceeds are payable directly to the beneficiary and do not pass through a probate court; hence the proceeds are not subject to the costs and delays that probate procedures sometimes involve. However, attention should be given to the way in which the beneficiary designation is made.

[8] If the insured now has $51 to make the premium payment and is required to pay the rest of the $100 premium in six months, we may accurately state that if the insured were willing to pay an additional $49 now, no credit would be needed.Thus, the amount of the credit needed to take advantage of the semiannual premium payment plan is $49.

Change of Beneficiary. The insured has the right to change beneficiaries without notice to those affected providing the insured has not named any beneficiary irrevocably. A *revocable beneficiary* has no control over the policy and has only contingent rights. Naming a beneficiary *irrevocably,* however, might amount to transferring all ownership rights in the contract to the person so named. It is done usually after a divorce or separation to give additional security to the beneficiary.

Secondary Beneficiaries. It is common to name *secondary*, or *contingent, beneficiaries*, so that if the primary beneficiary is not alive at the time of the insured's death, the proceeds will go to them. Since secondary beneficiaries are often children, care should be taken to name a guardian to receive the funds.[9] Otherwise, the court may appoint someone who would not have been satisfactory to the insured. Also, if both the insured and spouse, who is the primary beneficiary, were to die in the same accident and it is not determined who died first, the general rule is that the funds shall go to the secondary beneficiary.[10] However, if the spouse survives the insured, even for a little while, and then dies, the insurance proceeds go to the spouse's estate and would be inherited by the spouse's family. If the insured wishes to avoid this, it is possible to use what has been termed the *common disaster clause*, which specifies that the insurance proceeds will be under the interest option for a specified time, say two months, and if the primary beneficiary is alive then, the proceeds will be distributed to this person; otherwise they will go to secondary beneficiaries or to the insured's estate.

PROVISIONS OF INDUSTRIAL, GROUP, AND CREDIT LIFE INSURANCE

Although similar to other life policies in their benefits, the operation and methods of marketing industrial and group life insurance merit individual study.

Industrial Insurance

In 1974, 2% of all life insurance in force by private insurers in the United States was industrial insurance. *Industrial insurance,* sometimes called *weekly premium insurance,* is that form of life insurance in which the policies are typically less than $1,000 in amount and for which the premiums are quoted on a weekly basis, such as 5 cents or 10 cents a week, instead of so much per $1,000 of face amount as is true in ordinary life insurance. The premiums are typically collected directly by a salesperson who goes from house to house on a route known as a *debit*. Industrial insurance was originally designed as a burial policy for a wage worker who would otherwise buy no insurance because of difficulties in budgeting the premium payments involved. Today, however, it

9 This is usually done in a will.
10 This result is governed by the Uniform Simultaneous Death Act, which has been passed in most states.

cannot be said that only industrial workers have this type of coverage, for almost all classes of workers purchase industrial insurance. The rate of growth in this field of insurance has leveled off and the amount in force declined slightly for the first time in 1958. There are several reasons for this decline. Perhaps the most important lies in the growth of group life insurance, which has filled the need formerly supplied by industrial insurance. Another reason lies in the fact that large insurers who specialize in this business[11] have reclassified their business, formerly called industrial, to ordinary—or have eliminated new industrial sales altogether. It is possible to obtain ordinary life insurance for face amounts of less than $1,000. Furthermore, the economic status of most individuals in the industrial market has improved to the point where the chief selling feature of industrial insurance—its convenient premium—is no longer so important as it once was.

Group Life Insurance

Not to be confused with industrial insurance, *group life insurance* is commonly sold to employers of groups of workers ranging in size from ten to millions.[12] Unlike industrial insurance, group life insurance has shown a tremendous increase in the United States and at the end of 1974 constituted 42% of the total life insurance in force. In 1950, group insurance constituted 21% of the total, and in 1940, only 13% of the total.

Group life insurance is almost always issued on the term plan. The employer receives a master contract which outlines the provisions of coverage, and the employee receives a certificate that evidences participation in the plan. The amount of insurance usually depends on the employee's salary or job classification and may range from $1,000 to $100,000 or more. However, the typical amount per employee ordinarily ranges from $5,000 to $15,000 and averaged $11,645 in 1973.

In 1973, about 89% of all groups were employer-employee groups. Union, professional society, employee association, fraternal society, and savings or investment groups constitute the remaining associations which have arranged for group life insurance. Although 48% of all groups insured have fewer than 25 members, these groups have only 2.9% of all the group insurance in force. On the other hand, those groups with 500 or more members constitute only about 9% of the total number of groups, but account for about 82% of all group insurance in force. Many of the larger groups extended coverage to members in retirement, usually at reduced amounts.[13]

There are several underwriting and legal requirements of group insurance. Most of these are designed to prevent adverse selection:

[11] The developers and by far the largest insurers of industrial insurance are Metropolitan Life, Prudential Life, and John Hancock Life, in that order.

[12] The largest single group is composed of the three million federal civil service employees.

[13] *Life Insurance Fact Book 1974* (New York: Institute of Life Insurance, 1974), p. 32.

1. The group must not be formed exclusively for the purpose of obtaining the insurance.
2. A minimum proportion of the members of the group must be covered. If the employer pays all of the cost of coverage, all of the employees in eligible classes must be insured. If the employee contributes to the cost, 75% or more must be covered.
3. The coverage given to employees must be arranged so that the amount of protection received cannot be chosen by the employee. Rather, coverage is set according to income, employee class, or some other criterion.
4. In many states, the amount of coverage which can be written is limited by law. A common limitation is $20,000 per life, or 150% of a person's salary, whichever is larger, but in no case more than $40,000. Under federal law, if an employee receives term insurance protection exceeding $50,000 paid for by the employer, the employee must pay income tax on the value of the excess over $50,000.
5. If a member leaves the group, the policy may be converted to an individual policy within 30 days without a medical examination.

Group insurance generally costs the employee much less than an individual policy and has other advantages for several reasons:

1. The insurance is written without medical examination. The ability to work deems an employee well enough to receive coverage. If the employee resigns, insurance for that employee under the plan ceases; but the policy may be converted to an individual policy without evidence of insurability.
2. Other acquisition costs, such as sales commissions and policy issuance expenses, are greatly reduced.
3. The employer often contributes to the cost, either directly by paying a part of the premium, or indirectly by bearing part of the administrative costs. Increasingly the employer may pay the entire premium. Very commonly the employer pays all of the premium in excess of $.60 per month per $1,000 of face amount.
4. Mortality costs are lower because working groups are usually composed of active, healthy persons. Furthermore, a purpose for their organization exists other than to secure insurance.

Group life insurance can usually be arranged under one of the settlement options offered by the insurer under ordinary policies, although the master contract itself often provides fewer settlement options to choose from than are available on individual contracts. A recent development in group life insurance is to express coverage in terms of continuing monthly payments to surviving spouses in an amount related to the income of the employee. The period of payment is often a function of the employee's length of service with the employer at the time of the employee's death. Payments can also be made to extend for life, or to the age at which social security begins, or to cease at the remarriage of the spouse.

In the event of total and permanent disability on the part of the worker before a certain age, the usual group contract provides what amounts to a waiver of premium benefit. Other provisions such as waiver of premiums and grace period provisions apply to group insurance in a manner similar to individual coverage.

Some of the reasons for the growth of group life insurance are:

1. Group life insurance is a nonsalary inducement to productivity in business.
2. Taking up a collection when an employee dies is not necessary.
3. The value of up to $50,000 in benefits is federally nontaxable for the employee, yet the premiums are deductible for the employer.
4. Unions have successfully promoted group life insurance as a fringe benefit. Group life coverage is among the most popular of all fringe benefits.

Credit Life Insurance

Credit life insurance is that type of policy purchased to repay a debt if the borrower should die before the debt is discharged. Issued on a decreasing-term basis, the policy typically expires at or near the end of the repayment period. Coverage is issued on a group basis through lenders such as finance companies, banks, credit unions, and retail establishments. Data on credit life insurance are separated according to whether or not the term is ten years or less. (Life insurance purchased to protect mortgages of more than ten years is reported as part of ordinary life insurance.) Credit insurance first was used extensively only after World War II, when only about a billion dollars of face amount existed, compared to over $109 billion in 1974. Credit life insurance surpassed industrial life insurance first in 1963 and is now over 2.5 times as great. As of 1974 credit life insurance constituted 5% of all life insurance in force.

SUMMARY

1. The nonforfeiture options in the life insurance contract refer to those provisions that grant three methods of benefitting from life insurance with an accumulated reserve when one no longer desires to continue the original contract or is unable financially to do so. Cash value may be: (a) taken in a lump sum, (b) used to purchase extended term insurance, or (c) used to convert the existing policy into a paid-up policy of a reduced amount. Realization of this fact ends the common fallacy that one has to "pay all my life" on a whole life policy.
2. Settlement options refer to the contractual provisions under which the insured or the beneficiary may elect to receive the death proceeds or the cash values of life insurance. The insurer will agree to act, at no extra fee, as trustee of the proceeds for the benefit of the insured's family, holding the funds at interest, or distributing them as a guaranteed life income over a fixed period or as a fixed amount for as long as the proceeds last. Thus, the insured may economically plan the distribution of the estate that has been created in such a way as to guarantee that it will serve the purpose intended and will not be lost through mismanagement, theft, or other investment hazards.
3. In the typical life insurance contract, there are many clauses designed primarily for the protection of the insured and the beneficiary and which give the life insurance contract a preferred legal status over other types of property. Among these clauses are the incontestable clause, suicide clause, reinstatement privilege, grace period, automatic premium

loan clause, misstatement of age clause, entire contract clause, and spendthrift trust clause. These agreements reflect the basic social purpose of life insurance to provide for dependents who often would otherwise become a burden on the state.

4. Proper use of certain options can multiply the benefits to be received from the life insurance contract. The size of the insurance estate may be increased substantially through appropriate use of dividend options. The waiver of premium rider guarantees that the estate accumulation plans of the insured will not be interrupted because of permanent and total disability. The disability income rider replaces income lost because of permanent and total disability. The double indemnity rider is available to multiply death protection in the event of death through accidental means.
5. Since life insurance is usually purchased for the benefit of someone else, careful attention should be paid to the naming of beneficiaries and in planning for various contingencies so that the insurance estate will be distributed according to the wishes of the insured.
6. Industrial life insurance, which describes that type of insurance sold in amounts smaller than $1,000 and at a premium quotation of so much per week, appears to have neared the limit of its natural growth. It was designed for low-income individuals who could not purchase life insurance in any other way, and now constitutes only 2% of all private life insurance in force.
7. In contrast to industrial insurance, group life insurance has been expanding rapidly and now constitutes 42% of all life insurance in force. This type of coverage appears to be filling the place formerly occupied by industrial insurance in supplying life insurance to the working class at low costs. However, group life insurance, which is practically always issued on the term plan, is not by any means confined to the working class, but is used generally to insure all employees of a firm.

QUESTIONS FOR REVIEW AND DISCUSSION

1. (a) Differentiate between nonforfeiture options and settlement options.
   (b) What are the most important advantages of using income settlement options?
2. A certain insurer advertises that under its policies extended term insurance can be cashed in at any time, and that it will also participate in dividends.
   (a) What is extended term insurance, and why are these features an advantage to the insured?
   (b) Check the wording on a life insurance policy available to you to see if you can ascertain how the insurer handles these questions.
3. In a survey of insurers it was determined that about one fourth will consent to adding a spendthrift trust clause to their policies only upon request of the insured, while the remaining insurers include such a clause automatically.
   (a) What is the purpose of a spendthrift trust clause, and why is it a good idea to include this clause?
   (b) When can the clause be used?
4. A valuable use of the interest option is to leave the proceeds of the insurance at interest until the end of a specified period or until any minor beneficiary has reached majority, at which time the amount accumulated is distributed under another option, such as life income or fixed period. Yet, a survey of 100 insurers indicates

that less than half of them will allow such use.
(a) For what reasons is this use of the interest option valuable?
(b) Check a life insurance policy available to you to see if the insurer will allow this use of the interest option.

5. In order to join an insurance plan, the insured misstated his age to be 50 when he was actually 51. The oldest age permissible for entering the plan was age 50. After the lapse of the incontestable period, the insured died. When proofs of age were submitted, the insurance association denied liability and offered to return all premiums. The estate of the insured brought suit, complaining that both the misstatement of age clause and the incontestable clause prevented the insurer from denying liability. Apply your knowledge of these two clauses to decide this case. State the reasons for your decision.

6. Dividends in life insurance stem largely from mortality savings and excess interest earnings. If this is true, which types of policies may be expected to produce the greatest dividends in periods of general shortage of investment funds? in periods of oversupply of investment funds? Why?

7. Using the interest tables at the back of this book, calculate how much insurance proceeds at 5% interest would be required to provide $1,200 a year for ten years, payment to begin after a lapse of seven years during which interest is earned. Show your work.

8. Reyes requests your advice as to whether his life insurance dividends, which amounted to $1,000 last year, are taxable under the federal income tax law. Reyes was credited with $1,000 in dividends on his policies and under the option he has selected these dividends are held at interest and have earned $50 interest. Reyes is in poor health and does not wish to surrender any of his life insurance. Reyes received no cash.
(a) Advise Reyes about the taxability of these sums.
(b) Is Reyes making the best use of his dividends? Why?

9. Jane learns that she may pay her premium quarterly instead of semiannually, as she has been doing. Her annual premium is $40.42 per $1,000, $20.61 semiannually, and $10.51 quarterly. Calculate the simple interest cost involved for the privilege of paying quarterly instead of semiannually; semiannually instead of annually.

10. The insured had a policy with a double indemnity rider that provides twice the payment of the face amount if the insured were to come to death by drowning, directly, independently, and exclusive of all other causes, or of an external, violent, and accidental means. The insured was found dead, immersed in the bathtub. The insured was apparently in good health, and there was no evidence as to whether death resulted from an accident exclusive of all other causes.
(a) Would the question of whether or not the incontestable period had elapsed bear on this case? Why?
(b) Should the insured's beneficiary be able to collect this claim? Why or why not?

11. An insured failed to pay a quarterly premium due on February 12. The automatic premium loan provision kept the policy in force until May 12, at which time the cash value was $4.74, insufficient to pay an additional quarterly premium. Accordingly, the policy lapsed and the insurer purchased extended term insurance with the $4.74, thus extending the insured's coverage for 92 days. The insured died September 2. The insured's beneficiary claimed that the 92 days ran from the date of the expiration of the grace period, which would have meant that the insurance was still in force at the date of death. The insurer claimed that the 92 days ran from May 12. How should this case be decided? Why?

12. A writer argued that there are many advantages to borrowing on life insurance policies as compared with borrowing from a bank or another lender, such as ease and speed of the process, cheapness of interest, and lack of any pressure to repay. On the other hand, can you think of any disadvantages?

13. A policy lapsed October 25 and the insured sent a note to the insurer on November 6 saying, "I wish to drop my policy under the above number." The insurer wrote back and said, "As you requested, your policy was permitted to lapse on October 25." On November 14 the insured was accidentally killed. Should this claim be paid? Why or why not?

14. An insured was divorced and upon his remarriage he changed the beneficiary designation of his life insurance from his first to his second wife. The second marriage lasted five months, and in the divorce decree the second wife gave up all rights she might have had to any life insurance belonging to the husband. When the insured later died, it was found that he had not changed the beneficiary designation from the second wife and there was a court contest between the first wife and the second wife for the proceeds. Who should receive the proceeds? Why?

15. A court ordered an insured to use the cash surrender value of his life insurance if necessary to pay arrearages, amounting to $1,058, for his wife's support. The cash surrender value of the insurance was $14,725. The policies were in possession of the insured's son. The insured appealed this decision to a higher court. Do you think the court order should stand? Why?

16. An absolute assignment is one in which all rights in the property assigned are transferred to another person. In one case life insurance with a face amount of $110,000 was assigned as collateral to secure an $85,000 loan. The insured died and the insurance company paid $110,000 to the assignee. The insured's beneficiaries brought suit for the difference between the loan and the face amount of the insurance, claiming it was unjust for the assignee to keep all of it. How should the case be decided? Why?

17. The insured had elected to use the dividends to pay the premiums on a $5,000 life insurance policy. However, the insured failed to pay a premium of $16.05 due May 24. By June 24 the premium had still not been paid, so under the nonforfeiture option selected, the company applied the cash value to purchase paid-up insurance. On July 5 the insured sought reinstatement of the policy, but died the day before the application for reinstatement was approved. The insurer tendered to the beneficiary $639.25, which was the amount of the paid-up insurance plus accumulated dividends of $31.25. The check was refused and the beneficiary claimed the full $5,000. State with reasons how you think this case should be decided.

18. An insurer filed suit to rescind and to cancel a life insurance policy on the grounds that the insured gave false answers to some questions about a heart and blood condition. The insured died within a year of issuance of the policy, which had been "rated up" because of physical conditions revealed to the insurer by the examining physician.
(a) What right, if any, does the insurer have to cancel?
(b) Do you think there might be some valid defenses on the part of the beneficiary which might force payment of this policy?

19. An insured died of sunstroke two hours after being exposed to a temperature of 109 degrees. The

court upheld the insurer's refusal to pay double indemnity under the typical double indemnity clause in the life insurance policy. (a) For what probable reason did the insurer refuse to pay?
(b) Under what conditions is it possible that a death could have been caused by sunstroke and still obligate the insurer to pay double indemnity? Explain.

20. Do the same conditions exist today which gave rise to the sale of industrial insurance? If not, do you expect the gradual disappearance of this kind of coverage? Why?

21. In what ways are industrial insurance and group insurance different? How are they similar?

22. In group life insurance it is a basic rule that there must be some reason for the existence of the group other than the purchase of life insurance. Explain why this rule is insisted upon.

23. E. C. Mullendore, III, a wealthy Texas rancher, age 32, took out three life insurance policies for $5 million each. Most of the total premiums of about $250,000 had been financed by deferring payment to the sales agent for commissions. Just before the expiration of the grace period and after the second annual premium came due, Mullendore was fatally shot and the killer was never apprehended. It was then discovered that two physicians had filled out the medical forms on the insured without actually giving an examination. It was also discovered that Mullendore was in deep financial difficulty and lacked the money to pay the second year's premium. The insurer, which had retained only $40,000 of the risk and had reinsured the rest, refused to pay on the grounds of fraud. Do you think the insurer should have been required to pay? Discuss.

24. For each of the following policies, indicate which of the premiums listed below should apply at an issue age of 20: ordinary life, 20-pay life, 20-year endowment, life paid up at 65, endowment at age 65, and 5-year renewable term. (a) $16.19, (b) $17.27, (c) $19.35, (d) $26.45, (e) $46.14, and (f) $51.01.

25. For the policies (a), (b), and (c) in Question 24, suggest reasons for the relatively similar premium applicable to each.

26. A salesperson presented two plans of life insurance to an insured. In each case the premium was the same—$351.40 for a person aged 40. Plan I provided $10,000 protection under the 20-pay life plan and Plan II provided $15,180 protection under the ordinary life plan. In 20 years the paid-up insurance under Plan I was $10,000 and under Plan II, $8,956. Which plan is the better? What advantages do you claim for your choice? Explain.

27. In a comparison of the interest adjusted cost of nonparticipating term insurance over a 10-year period, it was determined that the lowest cost insurer charged $3.77 per $1,000, compared to $5.13 for the highest cost insurer. An agent argues that the differences reflect mainly differences in the quality of the product sold. Do you agree? What differences in the policy or the insurer might be reflected in the comparison?

28. Following a family argument, a wife told her husband that if she had a gun she would shoot him. The husband produced a gun, handed it to her, and told her to go ahead and shoot. The wife obliged and was later convicted of manslaughter. The insurer refused to pay accidental death indemnity on the insured's life insurance policy because it claimed the death could not be called accidental. Do you think the insured's death was (a) a suicide, (b) accidental? Should the insurer pay? Discuss.

Chapter *Twenty-Two*

ANNUITIES, LIFE INSURANCE, AND ESTATE PLANNING

Life insurance contracts issued on a permanent basis have cash values which may be used for many purposes, including that of providing retirement income. Separate contracts called annuities may also be purchased for retirement purposes. These contracts have no pure protection element and many authorities do not refer to them as life insurance. The important fact is, however, that one may combine life insurance protection with a savings plan for retirement, or one may save by methods which contain no element of death protection. Life insurance companies offer both types of plans as well as combinations of each. The suitability of various methods of saving for retirement is an important consideration in an analysis of how well the problem of old-age dependency may be solved.

THE ANNUITY

An *annuity* may be defined mathematically as a series of equal payments made at equal intervals of time. This is indeed a broad definition since it includes regular payments (called *rent* of the annuity) of almost any type and for any length of time and with no restriction on the length of the time interval. In the field of life insurance, we are primarily concerned with annuities of equal payments by an insurer to an insured (called the *annuitant*) on an annual basis (although the annual payments are usually expressed in terms of monthly installments) with the payment, composed of interest and principal, due at the end of the year (or month).

Often the word annuity also conveys the idea of lifetime payments, although mathematically the term of the annuity may be any length of time. In the following discussion, the expression *life annuity* means an ordinary annuity payable for life, that is, where the payment period, or *term*, is for the life of the annuitant. Income paid by an insurer for a specified length of time is usually referred to by one of the settlement options, such as fixed period or interest option. Broadly speaking, however, such payments constitute an annuity for a temporary period and are also called *short-term annuities*.

The *present value* of an annuity, or the cash equivalent of an annuity, is the amount of money that the insurer must have now in order to be able to pay the promised amounts over the term of the annuity. Due to the interest factor, the present value is, of course, smaller than the sum of all the promised payments. Thus, the present value of an annuity whose rent is $100 a year for 35 years at 6% interest is $1,449.82—less than half of the sum of all the payments, which total $3,500.[1] If the insurer has the sum of $1,449.82, it will be able to make payments to the annuitant of $100 a year, due at the end of the year, for 35 years, exhausting the principal at the end of this time.

In the long run, the interest assumed in the annuity agreement makes a substantial difference in the present value of the annuity. For example, the present value of an annuity of $100 a year for 35 years at 2.5% interest is $2,314.51, whereas at 3%, the present value is $2,148.72, some 7.5% lower. Thus, the rate of interest earnings is vital in choosing an insurance or annuity contract.

A life annuity, guaranteeing that an annuitant cannot outlive the income, is the reverse of the life insurance contract where the risk is not how long a person will live to receive an income, but whether death will occur before the expiration of a given term of the policy. Thus, it has been facetiously said that life insurance is insurance against "dying too soon," while annuities are insurance against "living too long." A mortality table is the basis of both life insurance and annuity contracts, although in the case of annuities, the tables employed reflect the greater longevity of annuitants. Since the cash values of the life insurance contract are often turned into annuity contracts at retirement age, or the death proceeds of the life insurance contract are settled on a *life income settlement option* (actually nothing more than a life annuity), there is an intimate relationship between life insurance and annuities.

TYPES AND USES OF ANNUITIES

Life annuities may be classified according to the following criteria:

1. The period during which a minimum number of payments is guaranteed.
2. When the rent begins.
3. The method of paying premiums.
4. The number of lives insured.
5. Whether the rent is fixed or variable.

[1] Table C-4, page 672, shows the present value of an annuity of $1 a year for varying periods. The formula for this value is:

$$a_{\overline{n}|}i = \frac{1 - (1 + i)^{-n}}{i}$$

which is read, "*a* sub *n* at rate *i* equals. . . ." In this expression *n* is the number of payment periods in the term of the annuity, and *i* is the rate of interest assumed. If one wishes to find the present value of an annuity of any amount for a given period, one simply multiplies the amount desired by $a_{\overline{n}|}i$ for $1.

Guaranteed Payments

The four major types of annuities classified according to the guarantee of payments are:

1. Straight-life annuity.
2. Period-certain life income annuity.
3. Installment refund and cash refund annuities.
4. Temporary life annuity.

Straight-Life Annuity. A *straight-life annuity* is one in which the rent of the annuity is paid only during the lifetime of the annuity, with no minimum number of guaranteed installments. If the insured dies the day after purchasing the annuity, there is no obligation for the insurer to return any of the purchase price. The sum paid in is held for the benefit of other annuitants. In the straight-life annuity, the annuity principle operates in its purest form. However, many individuals hesitate to use this form, particularly if they have heirs or dependents who would naturally like to participate in the estate upon the death of the insured. Under the straight-life annuity, the rent is higher than under the period-certain life income annuity or the installment and cash refund annuities, where some minimum number of payments must be made.

The price of annuities in recent years has been generally reduced because of rising interest rates. For example, a typical 1971 price of an immediate straight-life annuity (no refund at death) was $12,500 for each $100 monthly life income for a male age 65. This is equivalent to approximately a 10% return on the cost (using both principal and interest). A price of $15,000 was not uncommon a few years before that. Yet the price will still appear too high for many individuals who since 1969 may be able to earn up to 10% interest on funds invested in bonds with reasonably good safety ratings. If one purchases a well-rated bond, there is little chance of reduction of principal. In case of death of the bond owner, the beneficiary may sell the bond for its current market value or hold it until maturity. In the case of the straight-life annuity there would be no return to the beneficiary upon the death of the annuitant. The bondholder may run slightly more risk than the annuitant, but the principal can be preserved for the bondholder's heirs.

Period-Certain Life Income Annuity. When it is desired to obtain some minimum number of guaranteed payments, several different arrangements can be made. Under the *period-certain life income annuity*, the insurer agrees to guarantee 10, 15, or 20 years of payments to someone, and if the annuitant outlives this period, for the annuitant's lifetime.

Installment and Cash Refund Annuities. Other arrangements to guarantee a minimum number of payments under an annuity are the *installment refund* and the *cash refund annuities*. Under the refund annuity, the insurer subtracts from the value of the annuity at its starting date (that is, the present value) the total of all rents paid to the annuitant at the time of death. Any difference is paid to a beneficiary in cash or in installments, as the case may be. Slightly larger annuities are given for the installment refund type because the insurer will retain the funds for a longer period of time. If the insured spends $10,000 for a cash refund annuity at age 65 and draws $57 a month for 10 years, $6,840 would have been received in all. The beneficiary would obtain a cash refund of $3,160.

Temporary Life Annuity. Assume that it is desired to guarantee an income for the life of the annuitant, but to cease payment in any case after a certain period. Thus, the annuitant receives the rent for a stated number of years, but the income stops earlier if death occurs before the period is up. This situation might arise if the annuitant has a given income at some future period, say from a trust which matures in 15 years, or from social security benefits. If the annuitant survives the 15 years, there would be no need for rent from the annuity. If the annuitant dies before this time, the annuity will cease at that time. Such an arrangement is known as a *temporary life annuity* and is mentioned at this point only to illustrate the many arrangements for guaranteed payments which can be worked out to fit different needs for income.

Period When the Rent Begins

The rent of an annuity can begin as soon as the annuity is purchased, in which case the transaction is called an *immediate annuity*. Alternatively, the rent can begin at some future time, in which case the annuity is called a *deferred annuity*. Often the rent begins at retirement.

Method of Paying Premiums

An annuity can be wholly paid up in a lump-sum payment, or can be purchased in installments over a period of years. If the annuity is paid up at once, it is called a *single-premium annuity*. If it is paid for in installments, it is known as an *annual-premium annuity*. It is possible to view a permanent life insurance policy as a deferred annual-premium life annuity since the life income option permits the insured or the beneficiary to accept the proceeds as a life annuity as one of the settlement options. A similar observation applies to the retirement income policy. Single-premium deferred annuities are common methods of funding group pension plans. The pension of the employee is made up of the rents from a series of single-premium deferred annuities bought over the working years of the employee.

Number of Lives Insured

Two major types of annuities under which more than one life is covered are the joint and last survivorship annuity and the group annuity.

Joint and Last Survivorship Annuity. An annuity may be issued on more than one life. For example, the agreement might be to pay a given rent during the lifetime of two individuals, as long as either shall live. This, a very common arrangement, is known as a *joint and last survivorship annuity,* because the rent is payable until the last survivor dies. The rent may be constant during the entire period or may be arranged to be reduced by, say, onc third upon the death of the first annuitant. Thus, a husband and a wife both age 65 may elect to receive the proceeds of a pension plan on a joint and last survivorship basis, with an income guaranteed as long as either shall live.

To illustrate a comparison of rents, one insurer offers the following monthly rents at age 65 per $1,000 of proceeds:

1. Annuity 20 years certain and life	$6.11
2. Installment refund and life	6.91
3. Annuity 10 years certain and life	7.21
4. Joint and 2/3 to survivor for life	6.87
5. Straight life, no refund	7.76

If the wife is considerably younger than the husband, the rent on a joint and last survivorship annuity is quite low because of the obligation of the insurer to continue payments until the wife dies. Nevertheless, the joint and last survivorship annuity removes the risk of one person dying and leaving the other without a means of support.

Group Annuity. A group annuity is similar to an individual annuity except that it is issued to an employer or some other collective entity and covers all or selected members of the group as a unit. The group annuity is the oldest and best known method of funding a private pension plan. For various reasons the cost of issuing group annuities is less than that of issuing individual annuities. These reasons include savings in administration, savings in federal income taxes, and reduction of adverse selection.

Fixed or Variable Rent

Annuities may provide an income to the annuitant on a fixed or variable basis. *Fixed annuities* are paid in dollars, the number of which does not change during the time of the annuity. In *variable annuities* the rent can change periodically. The funds are invested by the life insurer in common stocks and other equity type investments which change in value daily. The monthly rent is paid in units, the number of which are specified when the annuity begins. The value of the units, and hence the income, fluctuates according to variations in the value of the underlying securities.

LIFE INSURANCE AND ESTATE PLANNING

Annuities and life insurance contracts with cash values are instruments through which one may develop plans for the accumulation and distribution of property, a process often referred to as *estate planning*. Estate planning usually makes use of life insurance and the annuity concept, but it involves much more. Among the problems which estate planning attempts to solve are long-term saving, investments, the development of wills and trusts, and tax planning.

Problems of Long-Term Savings

Success in long-term savings is usually more difficult to achieve than in short-term savings because of the existence of many problems whose solutions are often beyond the capability of an average individual without special guidance. These problems include:

1. Providing a certain amount, even though it is small, for regular savings.
2. Investing these savings in such a manner as to achieve *reasonable safety*. In judging safety, the fact that we are dealing with long periods of time should be considered, and hence investments that appear safe today may not be so in five years. Thus, there is a need for constant review and careful investment management.
3. Investing savings so as to achieve *reasonable liquidity*. Again, since long time periods are involved, it is not necessary that all accumulated savings be made in investments that may be turned into cash at a moment's notice. Such a high degree of liquidity is usually associated with a relatively low interest rate. Of course, a certain portion of savings should be in a highly liquid form so as to provide emergency funds when needed.
4. Making investments so as to achieve as *large a return as is consistent with safety and liquidity*. It is usually agreed that safety and liquidity should not be sacrificed to any great extent for the sake of a high promised return. This is not to disregard return as the least important of the three elements. A small difference in the interest return makes a substantial difference in retirement income over a long period of years.
5. Developing sound plans *for use* of the savings so as to achieve the desired objectives, such as making provision for dependents and for one's old age. Problems in this area include the development of wills and trusts and plans to minimize taxes, to insulate the estate from common investment perils, to minimize estate settlement costs, and to provide sufficient flexibility in the administration of an estate so that if conditions change after the estate planner is deceased, the plan may be altered according to the needs of the beneficiaries.
6. Securing *protection against inflation*. Steady deterioration of the money over long periods characterizes all industrialized economies, some more so than others. Before World War II, for example, it was thought that $300 a month in the United States for life would provide a comfortable retirement. Over the period 1940–1975 the value of the dollar declined approximately 75%, so that $300 would provide only about a fourth of the purchasing power anticipated at retirement. (See Table 22–1.) Long-term savings programs should be protected against this deterioration insofar as possible. Unfortunately there is no universally-accepted way to achieve this protection, and even those methods thought to be the best (e.g., purchasing common stocks on a regular basis) have not always worked satisfactorily.

Life Insurance as an Investment

Among the advantages and disadvantages of permanent life insurance as a vehicle for long-term savings, the following are cited:

1. The purchase of life insurance lends itself to a regular, consistent savings plan since it may be purchased in any denomination to fit the savings budget of individuals with varying incomes. The plan fits the psychological needs of most savers for a regular savings plan with a semicompulsory flavor.
2. The safety record of the life insurance investment has been above reproach. The probability of loss to policyholders from life insurance company failures is so close to zero as to enable an evaluation of the risk as negligible.
3. The liquidity of the life insurance investment is guaranteed by contract; the only qualification is that the policy contains a *delay clause* which gives the insurer a

period of six months or less, if necessary, in which to make a cash loan for a purpose other than payment of the premium. While this clause is seldom invoked by the insurer, it is there as a precautionary measure in case of repetition of a run during a financial panic similar to that which occurred during the depression of the 1930's.

4. The interest return on the life insurance investment is conservative. The policy generally guarantees a minimum rate, such as 3%, but the policyholder will usually receive a greater return through dividends. Still, studies reveal that unless the life insurance policy is held for relatively long periods, such as 20 years or longer, the return is usually beneath what can be obtained on other investments of comparable safety. For example, one study of 164 policies issued by 104 insurers revealed 20-year average rates of return as follows:

Rate of Return	*Number of Policies*	*Percent of Policies*
5.00-5.49%	7	4
4.50-4.99	26	16
4.00-4.49	53	32
3.50-3.99	35	21
3.00-3.49	21	13
2.50-2.99	18	11
Less than 2.50	4	3
	164	100

Thus, a saver through life insurance has a significant probability of obtaining 4% to 5% or more on the savings element, if careful shopping for the policy was done initially. However, when the policy is held only five or ten years, the return is much lower.[2]

5. Life insurance facilitates the development of sound plans to distribute an estate to beneficiaries. For example, settlement options give the insured flexibility in arranging income flows to those needing regular income for varying periods. Lump sum needs, such as funds for estate taxes and debit retirement, can be economically provided for. Protection of the estate from creditors' claims is possible through life insurance. This subject is amplified below.

6. Unfortunately, life insurance generally provides no inflation protection since under standard contracts all obligations and benefits are expressed in a fixed amount of dollars, and these dollars tend to decline in purchasing power over time. Recently, however, life insurers have introduced variable annuities and many are preparing variable life insurance contracts designed to help offset inflation. These contracts are discussed below.

Advantages of Estate Planning

Life insurance has long enjoyed a favored legal position which gives it advantages over other investments in arrangements which can be made for the eventual use of the savings. There is an unfortunate tendency for savers to ignore the problems involved in planning the wisest use of the fruits of their thrift. A lifetime savings program may be greatly diminished or its purpose deflected entirely by careless planning for the eventual settlement of the proceeds. For example, poorly drawn wills may cause the estate to be distributed to parties never contemplated by the saver. Imprudent tax planning may cause

[2] Joseph M. Belth, Editor, *The Insurance Forum,* Vol. 2 No. 9, (September, 1975).

the forced liquidation of assets at a fraction of their true value. Creditors' claims, attorneys' fees, court costs, and other claims may deplete the estate more than would be the case if careful attention had been given to estate planning.

Life insurance contracts provide a semiautomatic way of planning the disposition of an estate to overcome many of the hazards that confront unplanned estates. The life insurance estate is liquid so that it is not necessary to convert the assets into any other form in order to provide an income to the dependents. The estate is usually immune from creditors' claims. Interest credited on cash values is exempt from federal income taxes during the accumulation period. During the settlement period the annuity receives favorable tax treatment under current tax regulations.[3] Since life insurance proceeds are paid directly to the beneficiary, there are no probate or court costs or attorney's fees connected with this part of the insured's estate. Because the contract provides settlement options, no trustee's fees are assessed for the administration of the estate; the insurer performs these functions at no added cost. Estate and inheritance taxes can also be reduced through proper use of life insurance. Most states exempt from inheritance taxes life insurance proceeds made payable to named beneficiaries. Federal estate tax regulations do not exempt life insurance from this important tax, but it is possible to transfer a life insurance policy to a beneficiary while the insured is still living and thus remove assets from the insured's estate so as to avoid the estate tax.[4] Such a transfer may result in a gift tax, but gift tax rates are less than estate tax rates and exemptions are more generous.

One problem of life insurance in estate planning is the matter of inflexibility in the administration of the estate proceeds after the death of the insured. Life insurers may not always permit arrangements other than the stated settlement

[3] Tax regulations change constantly, but at the time of this writing, a life insurance investment, after being exempt from income taxes on interest accumulations, may often be distributed either to the insured or to beneficiaries with a low taxation burden. The present rules provide that the total cost of the contract shall be determined by adding all the premiums paid in. If the policy is cashed in, the gain, if any, is arrived at by subtracting the total cost from this cash value. Since the cost includes the amounts paid for pure protection, in effect, a tax deduction is given for the pure insurance element. However, there will seldom be an excess of cash values over total cost and, thus, little if any tax will commonly be due.

If the proceeds of a life insurance or an annuity contract are taken in installments, tax regulations are much more complicated. However, the basic principle currently used is relatively simple. Suppose the insured elects a life annuity with no refund. Assume the cash values are $17,000. The insured will receive a life annuity of about $100 per month at age 65. Tax authorities recognize that the $100 is part interest and partly a return of capital, and they, of course, tax only the interest. To determine the amounts representing capital, the $17,000 is divided by the approximate life expectancy (using tax tables) of the taxpayer. At 65 this period is 15 years. Thus, $1,133 is considered return of capital and the balance is therefore interest, which is fully taxable as ordinary income. Even if the insured outlives life expectancy, the tax is on only $67 a year. Because of these rules, taxes on life insurance are postponed to a time when other income of the annuitant is probably low, and the exemptions would be such that probably no taxes would have to be paid, assuming there is no other taxable income. Note that if the saver had put the $17,000 in the bank at 5% interest, the taxable income would be $850 annually.

[4] This may be done even though the insured continues to pay the premiums.

options, and once determined, these options cannot always be changed at will by the beneficiary. To avoid these difficulties it is not uncommon to have part of the insurance proceeds made payable to a trustee who may be instructed to use individual judgment in the administration of the money.

AN ILLUSTRATION OF ESTATE PLANNING

Although estate planning is a complicated topic, the essential elements may be expressed in the following steps:

1. Assemble the pertinent facts relating to the family, its income, assets, insurance and other resources applicable to its financial security.
2. Develop a statement of cash and income needs to be filled in the event of the premature death of the breadwinner.
3. Compare the needs and resources determined in the first two steps; determine what deficiencies exist and how they will be met.
4. Choose methods to dispose of the property in the estate, including the use of life insurance settlement options or trusts. A will is normally considered indispensable for effective estate planning.

It should be observed that estate planning is concerned mainly with financial needs in the event of the premature death of the breadwinner. Other risks, such as the risk of loss of property or loss of earning power through ill health, should not be forgotten. These topics are dealt with elsewhere in the text. Furthermore, it should be recognized that estate plans must be revised periodically. When the plan is first drawn up it is assumed that it will become effective immediately in case of the death of the breadwinner that night. Later the needs and resources change. For example, after a mortgage is paid off there is no continuing need for life insurance originally purchased to meet that obligation. The revised estate plan would reflect this fact. To illustrate the above steps, consider the following simplified case.

Step 1

Santos is age 40 and has a steady annual salary of $20,000. He has a wife age 35 and two children, Bill and Mary, ages 15 and 10, respectively. His present assets, insurance, and retirement program are:

	Value
House	$ 40,000
Personal effects, including cars	10,000
Bank savings	5,000
Mutual fund account	5,000
Life insurance:	
Individual, ordinary life (non-participating) plan, cash value $2,700	20,000
Group term plan, paid for by employer	20,000
Estate value	$100,000

OASDHI family benefit if Santos dies	$ 400	monthly until Bill is 18; $300 monthly until Mary is 18.[5]
Retirement income:		
Estimated OASDHI pension for wife and self	$ 300	monthly for life
Widow's benefit if Santos dies	$ 175	
Estimated employer-paid pension, joint and last survivorship basis, 2/3 to survivor for life (no death benefit before age 65)	$ 400	

Santos has a take-home salary of $15,000 annually. He is making regular savings of $300 a year in the mutual fund and is paying $300 a year for the ordinary life insurance policy, which was taken out when he was 30. Santos decides that if necessary he could spend an additional $1,000 a year in order to provide for his estate needs.

Step 2

Santos calculates his estate and retirement needs as follows (see Figure 22–1):

1. Educational funds for the two children	$20,000
2. Clean-up fund. Funds to pay last debts, funeral, taxes, and for readjustment period for the family. Santos' estate is not large enough to cause any estate tax problem at the present time.	5,000
3. Income to the wife	
As long as both children are under 18	700
As long as one child is under 18	600
After both children are in college until wife reaches age 62	400
After wife reaches age 62	400
4. To pay off the mortgage debt	20,000
5. Retirement income for wife and self, if living at age 65. Two thirds of this income is expected to be enough for the survivor.	10,000 annually 833 monthly

Step 3

Given the basic facts of assets, income, and financial requirements in case of Santos's premature death or in the event he lives to retirement, the next step is to compare needs with resources. If Santos dies, his major needs may be classed as for cash and for income. Cash needs are as follows:

[5] Under certain conditions, OASDHI benefits to dependent children may continue through age 22 if they are enrolled in college.

Figure 22-1

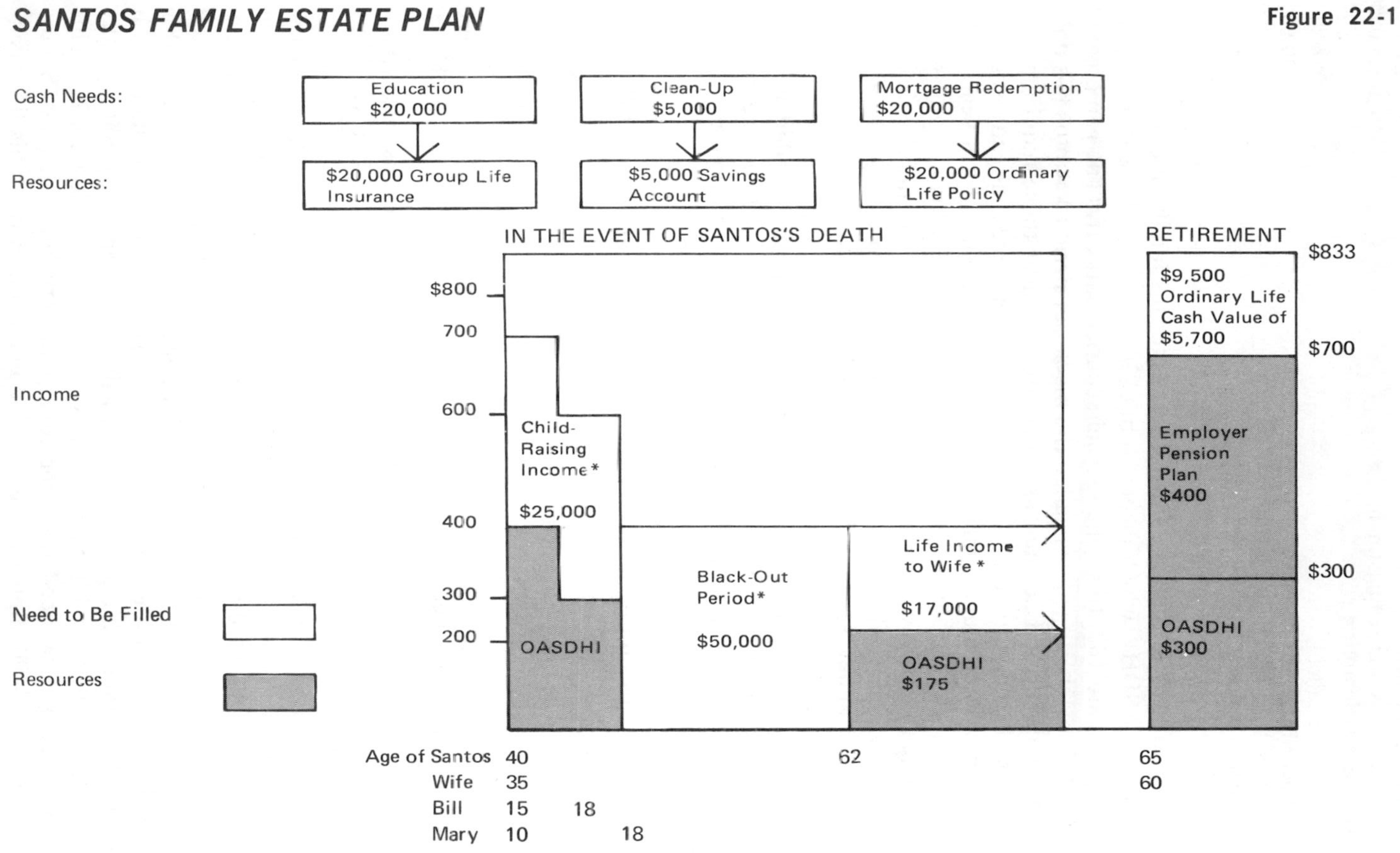

* Present value of sums needed, to be funded by life insurance.

Educational fund	$20,000
Last expenses and readjustment	5,000
Mortgage redemption	20,000
Resources available	$45,000
Proceeds, group term policy	20,000
Proceeds, ordinary life policy	20,000
Savings account	5,000
	$45,000

An important part of Santos's income needs for his family in case of death can be met by OASDHI, which meets all but $300 a month of the income goal until the children are 18, after which social security cuts off. (The gap created until the widow reaches age 62 is called the black-out period.) Santos has only $5,000 in his mutual fund account as a resource to meet these requirements. (He has planned to use his other resources for other needs, already shown.) Santos must provide enough capital to yield $300 per month for 8 years until Mary is 18, or about $25,000 (assuming 3.5% interest). Santos also must provide $400 a month to his wife starting in 8 years and lasting until his wife is age 62 (19 years), which would require a sum of $65,800 whose present value, at 3.5% interest, is about $50,000. Finally, Santos wants to provide a lifetime income of $225 monthly to his wife starting at age 62 to supplement the estimated $175 his widow would receive from OASDHI. The sum needed at age 62 for a lifetime income of $225 to his wife would be about $43,000. The present value of such a sum, assuming 27 years of interest accumulation at 3.5%, is about $17,000. (See Appendix C for sample interest tables.)

In summary, Santos's additional requirements for life insurance to meet income needs for his family in the event of immediate death are as follows:

Child-raising period	$25,000
Income to wife until retirement	50,000
Wife's retirement income	17,000
Total	$92,000
Less: $5,000 now in mutual fund	5,000
New insurance required	$87,000

Before Santos can decide what type of life insurance to buy for his estate plan, he should consider what additional cash requirement he needs, if any, for his retirement plan.

Santos has stated that his retirement income should be $10,000 annually, which is about two thirds of his current take-home pay. Since his employer pension and OASDHI together will meet $8,400 of this retirement ($700 × 12 = $8,400), he must make provision elsewhere for $1,600 annually. It is estimated that at the current rate of contributions to the mutual fund, the value of this account will be $17,000 if the fund earns an average return of 6% compound. If converted to an annuity at age 65, this sum will provide about $1,200 annually on a joint and last survivorship basis, with two thirds to his widow for life. This leaves a balance of $400 needed for the remaining retirement income. Santos may meet this last $400 annual retirement income need through his life insurance. The cash value of his $20,000 ordinary life policy, which is now $2,700, will be nearly $12,000 by the time he is age 65. Santos may convert about $9,500 of his policy, with cash value of $5,700, into an annuity which will provide the $400 of additional retirement income. The remaining $10,500 of the original policy, with about $6,300 in cash value, may be converted to a paid-up policy of approximately $9,000. The paid-up policy may be retained to meet continuing estate settlement needs and readjustment income for the wife in the event Santos dies first.

Since Santos's retirement income may be met with present resources, there is no need for buying cash value life insurance to supplement his retirement fund. If Santos wishes to save money for other purposes, of course, he may still decide that cash value life insurance is desirable.

If Santos has no further need for additonal savings, he may meet the additional $87,000 insurance requirement for the child-raising period and for his wife's life income through a term insurance plan. One method is to purchase a $25,000 10-year term insurance policy for the child-raising period, allowing this policy to lapse if Santos survives to age 48. The remainder of the program could be put on the term to age 65 plan in the amount of $62,000. Level protection is needed to age 65 because Santos's employer's pension carries no death benefit and almost the full amount will be needed until Santos retires and puts his retirement plan on the joint and last survivorship option, thus protecting his wife's retirement income. If Santos had selected decreasing-term insurance for this need and died just prior to retirement, his life insurance face amount would have been practically exhausted, since the protection under decreasing-term insurance reduces to zero at the end of the term period. In this event, his wife would have had no capital fund to bring her retirement income up to $400 since she would not yet be eligible for her widow's benefit under the husband's pension plan.

The cost of $25,000 of 10-year term insurance would be approximately $100 annually. The cost of $62,000 of nonparticipating term to 65 would be approximately $13.60 per $1,000 or $843. Thus, Santos's plan will cost $943 for the first 8 years, and $843 annually thereafter until age 65. This cost is well within Santos's limit of $1,000 annually to provide for his estate needs. Figure 22–1 illustrates the plan outlined in Step 3.

If Santos purchases the additional life insurance, his estate value will rise from its present level of $100,000 to $200,000. In this event, Santos's executor will be faced with federal estate tax liability. Depending on how Santos arranges his estate, this liability could run as high as $31,500 or as low as $2,000.[6] Santos's need for additional life insurance to cover the tax liability and other estate settlement costs will depend on what arrangements he makes. Professional assistance from attorneys, life insurance agents, tax consultants, and perhaps trust officers is needed to work out the best solution for the estate settlement plan and for the drawing of his will. Such a solution may involve

[6] For a good analysis of the tax effects of varying arrangements, see Robert I. Mehr, *Life Insurance Theory and Practice* (4th ed.; Austin: Business Publications, Inc., 1970), pp. 601-605. Estate taxes were reduced in 1976 by the Congress, a fact which alters the tax figures shown in this illustration.

setting up of one or more testamentary trusts to receive all or most of the estate property instead of utilizing settlement options under life insurance policies.

The strengths of the above estate plan are several. Santos has been able to meet his estate plan needs with a modest total outlay of $1,543 annually ($943 plus his current savings of $600) or a little less than 10% of his take-home pay. He should enjoy a modest protection against inflation through his mutual fund. Additional purchases of life insurance may be made with a definite objective in mind, and are not made solely because Santos may believe that "insurance is a good thing." He has the security that through his will, a trust, or settlement options of life insurance, his plan will actually be carried out after his death with minimum cost, and that other assets will not be depleted unnecessarily by being subjected to forced sale at sacrifice prices to pay estate settlement costs.

Among the weaknesses of this plan is limited protection against inflation. From the facts given it is not known whether Santos's employer's retirement plan offers any such protection. Santos should investigate to find whether he can choose to accept part of his pension as a variable annuity. Another alternative would be to convert the mutual fund into a variable annuity at retirement and, if permitted, to convert the cash value of his ordinary life insurance policy into a variable annuity to supplement his retirement income or his widow's retirement income, should Santos die first.

The program described is simplified for emphasis on the essential problems and approaches to estate planning. The average individual usually requires professional assistance in working out a plan.

Step 4

The final step in estate planning is to decide how life insurance and other property will be disposed of at Santos's death. A will is indispensable to a satisfactory plan. Otherwise, the property will be distributed according to the laws of the state, and the distribution according to law may not suit Santos's needs. Settlement options and beneficiary designations of life insurance must be chosen. In the above case, for example, the additional term insurance may be settled on a fixed-period option to coincide with the income periods Santos has planned for his family. The ordinary life and group insurance would be settled in a lump sum.

LIFE INSURANCE, ANNUITIES, AND INFLATION

We have examined the investment advantages and disadvantages of life insurance and annuity contracts as long-term savings methods from every viewpoint except how well they serve in an economy which in the past has been characterized by long-term inflation. This is obviously an important consideration, and it has caused much concern among life insurance and other fixed-dollar savers.

Inflation protection refers to the ability of an investment to withstand the long-term decline in purchasing power of the currency. Life insurance and annuity contracts give no inflation protection in the usual sense of the word. The savings in these contracts, being invested largely in bonds, are protected against deflation, but not against inflation. If the insured dies, the estate is often enhanced by a very large multiple of the amount of premiums that have been paid in. This constitutes a speculative element in the contract which has been equated to inflation protection by some, but this simile does not seem proper.

The Inflation Peril

How serious is the peril of inflation in robbing the fixed-dollar investment of its purchasing power? A measure of this threat may be observed by noting the rise of price indexes as seen in Table 22–1, which presents the figures of the Bureau of Labor Statistics Consumer Price Index in selected years since 1940. A long-term investment of $10,000 made in 1940 with interest compounded at 3% would have amounted to $28,139 in 1975 (35 years). However, the price index rose from 42.0 to 157.2. In terms of 1940 dollars, $28,139 would have declined by about 73% (100−42.0/157.2), or to about $7,600 in 1940 purchasing power. This is less than the actual number of dollars saved ($10,000), and so we might say that inflation has more than consumed the 3% interest earned during the period.

Some of the limitations of this measure of inflation should be considered. First, the index may not measure prices of the type of commodities in which the saver is interested. The index is based on the so-called market basket of a city wage-earner or a clerical worker and does not reflect differences in the amounts of goods people buy, or geographical differences in prices. A retired person may find that the prices of the things purchased have not risen so drastically.

Second, goods which may be heavily weighted in 1940 might not be important in 1975, nor may the quality of those goods be reflected in the price index.

CONSUMER PRICE INDEX, 1940-1975 (1967 = 100) — **Table 22-1**

Year	Index
1940	42.0
1945	53.9
1949	71.4
1955	80.2
1960	88.7
1965	94.5
1966	97.2
1967	100.0
1968	104.2
1969	109.8
1970	116.3
1971	119.8
1975*	157.2

Source: U.S. Department of Labor, Bureau of Labor Statistics.
* February, 1975.

For example, the housing and house furnishings in 1940 did not include many of the conveniences that are taken for granted today. The price of today's housing, while higher, may not reflect inflation so much as it reflects a higher standard of living. As someone has said, "it's not the high cost of living, but the cost of high living" which counts.

Third, in assessing the future seriousness of inflation, it should be recalled that the period under review, 1940–1975, was one of almost continual price increases. This may not be an entirely typical period, since it encompassed a period of three major wars (World War II, 1941–1945; the Korean War, 1950–1953; and the Vietnam War, 1965–1975). If one examines price changes since 1850, one observes large swings in price trends, which include long periods of decline. For example, commodity prices generally fell during the period following the Civil War until 1900, a span of over 30 years. Commodity prices also declined following World War I until 1933. If one had retired at the beginning of a long period of declining prices after having saved money during a period of rising prices, one would fare very well indeed with a program of fixed-dollar savings. In other words, there is no guarantee that inflation will be a continous phenomenon, uninterrupted by periods of deflation.

On the other hand, many believe that there is a built-in inflationary bias in the United States economy that results from certain factors which were not present during past periods when prices declined for substantial periods of time. For example, under the Full Employment Act of 1946, the federal government is committed to a policy of using federal powers to ensure full employment. This implies public works, taxation, and money management policies which aim at preventing price declines and accompanying depression. Strong labor unions reinforce the inflationary pressures by exerting an upward influence on wage rates. Continuance of defense expenditures necessitated by a cold war which gives no signs of letting up tends to encourage federal budget deficits. This causes constant new injections of credit for defense expenditures, which generate demand for scarce consumer goods and service. Thus, more money and credit in circulation compete for existing commodities and drive prices upward. The management of a huge war-induced public debt tends to favor policies which will keep interest rates lower than they might otherwise become, thus encouraging "easy money," a policy which promotes inflation.

It may be concluded that, although the inflation peril may not be inevitable, the long-run rise in prices is too much in evidence to ignore in plans for retirement. Ideally, one should hedge both ways. The long-term saver needs protection against both inflation and deflation.

Inflation and Retirement Plans

There are several methods currently in use in the United States to help the long-run saver offset inflation. First, federal social security provides for automatic adjustments in old-age retirement benefits for changes in the cost of living. Second, many employer-sponsored retirement plans have benefit formulas geared to wage changes. To the extent that wages keep pace with inflation, the corresponding retirement annuities will also be increased. Third, both life and nonlife insurers have developed new policies and methods to help meet the inflation peril.

Employer-Sponsored Annuities

In 1974 about 50 million persons in the United States were covered by group annuities of different types, both public and private. This was slightly over half of the labor force that year and the number has been rising steadily. In 1940 fewer than a fifth of all employees in private industry had pension plans. These plans together with individual plans and social coverages form an important part of the base of most persons' retirement coverage. For example, in 1973 about 6.1 million retirees received benefits from employer-sponsored plans, compared to about 17.7 million workers who received OASDIII retirement benefits.[7]

Inflation protection under employer-sponsored pension and annuity plans is achieved in two major ways. First, many plans have benefit formulas based on covered wages and length of service. A common method, for example, is to provide a pension equal to years of service times 1.5%, times the average wage in the five highest years in the ten years preceding retirement. Since wages tend to rise with inflation, a person's income is likely to be based on some realistic level at the time of retirement. Thus, if a person has worked 20 years under the above arrangement, the amount received will be 30% (20 × 1.5) of the final salary from the employer-sponsored plan. Second, many employers adjust the retirement income of employees during retirement in order to offset the effects of inflation. This protection is important since life expectancy for retirees has been lengthening and early retirement (before age 65) is increasingly common. If a male retires at age 60, for example, he may expect to live over 16 years, and females may expect to live about 20 years. If inflation averages 5% annually, the purchasing power of $100 will be reduced to about $37 within 20 years.

Life Insurance Methods

The insurance industry has developed some plans which are aimed primarily at offsetting the effects which inflation has had in reducing the value of life insurance protection and the value of retirement benefits from the cash values of life insurance contracts and annuities. These are (a) variable life insurance, (b) variable annuities, (c) a combination of mutual fund purchases and term life insurance, and (d) an insured mutual fund purchase plan.

Variable Life Policy

Proposals to offer life insurance protection which varies according to inflation are relatively new. These proposals appear to be taking two general forms: policies which specify that protection levels change according to some cost of living index, and policies which specify that protection levels vary according to changes in some designated stock market index. (The latter policies have been offered in the United States by a few insurers only since 1972.)

[7] *Life Insurance Fact Book 1975* (New York: Institute of Life Insurance, 1975), pp. 35-37.

Policies using the first method, the cost of living index, may be further subdivided into two categories, according to who bears the inflation risk. In the first category are arrangements in which the inflation risk is assumed by the policyholder and paid under one of several methods. For example, the insurer may offer the policyholder the right to purchase additional one-year term insurance as the cost of living index rises. The additional coverage is usually offered without medical examination and without heavy first-year acquisition costs. The rider permitting the additional coverage usually expires after 15 years or age 64, whichever comes earlier. The premiums to be charged and the maximum amounts of coverage which may be purchased are specified in the contract.

Policies in the second category are issued under contracts in which the insurer, not the insured, assumes the inflation risk. An example of these policies is that issued by the Life Insurance Company of Georgia, which has been offering such contracts since 1968 in 11 states.[8] The policy has a level premium, but contains benefits which escalate according to a cost of living index specified in the policy. Cash values are set relatively high and the premium is also relatively high when compared to fixed-dollar policies. For example, at age 25 the gross annual premium on the whole life plan is about 50% higher than the regular (nonescalating) basis.

Variable life policies using the stock market index may also be classified under two headings: those with a premium changing periodically according to the stock market index, and those with a fixed premium. The first plan has been in operation in The Netherlands for a number of years and is known as the Dutch design. A well-known example of the second plan was first outlined in 1969 and is known as the New York Life design.[9]

The Dutch design operates as follows. The whole reserve of the policy is held in a separate account whose assets are invested primarily in equities. The face amount varies according to the changes in the value of these equities. Some interest rate is assumed for the calculation of net premiums and reserves. If the value of the account in which the insured's funds are invested doubles, the face amount and the premium double. Premiums and benefits are expressed in terms of units instead of dollars. The insured pays a premium of so many units, the number of which are fixed during the life of the policy; but the value of the unit changes in a manner similar to the way in which the unit value of a mutual fund varies. The same actuarial principles which govern the calculation of reserves of regular fixed-dollar benefit life insurance policies apply to the variable life policy of the Dutch design.[10]

[8] John M. Bragg, F.S.A., "Life Insurance With Guaranteed Purchasing Power," in D. G. Olson and H. E. Winklevoss, *Variable Life Insurance* (University of Pennsylvania, 1971), pp. 47-60.

[9] Charles M. Sternhell, "The New York Life Benefit Design and its Practical Implementation," in Olson and Winklevoss, *op. cit.*, pp. 70-81. The plan was first outlined in a paper by John C. Fraser, Walter N. Miller, and Charles M. Sternhell before the Society of Actuaries.

[10] Mark R. Greene and Jacobus T. Severiens, "Variable Life Insurance in The Netherlands—A Case Study," *The Journal of Risk and Insurance*, Vol. XLI, No. 3 (September, 1974), pp. 511-521.

In the New York Life design, the reserve of the policy is held in a separate account in the same manner as that of the Dutch design. The assets are invested in equities, and the face amount of the life insurance protection varies with the value of these equities, but not in direct proportion. Furthermore, it is expected that there will be a minimum death benefit guarantee of an amount not less than the initial face amount of the policy. The cash and nonforfeiture values fluctuate in accordance with the changes in the equity account, but the premiums in dollars remain fixed. In the New York Life design the reserves per $1,000 of face amount are identical to the reserves per $1,000 face amount of a fixed-dollar benefit life insurance policy.

Unfortunately, variable life insurance based on stock market values offers no guarantee that the face value or the savings element will actually offset inflation, since the stock market and the consumer price index do not correspond one-to-one by any means, particularly in the short run. However, variable life insurance is an imaginative approach to the problem for which new solutions are badly needed.

The Variable Annuity

An ingenious scheme giving inflation protection for the retiree and one which is in actual use among many United States life insurers is the *variable annuity*.[11] The objectives of the variable annuity are to offer a method by which the long-term saver may accumulate retirement funds in *equities*—securities whose value tends to follow the fluctuations in the general price level. The basic idea is that if the general price level rises over the accumulation period, the value of savings will also rise, thus maintaining their purchasing power at a fairly constant level. If the general price level falls, the value of the savings will also fall; but their purchasing power will still remain fairly constant. In other words, the variable annuity attempts to provide funds for a retirement income which would have a varying dollar value but reasonably constant purchasing power. The regular annuities provide an income with a fixed-dollar value but a varying purchasing power. It is presumed that it is more desirable for the retired person to have an income with a value which in real terms is fairly

[11] The variable annuity was originated by the College Retirement Equities Fund. The Fund is a subsidiary organization of the Teachers Insurance and Annuity Association, a life insurance company selling life insurance only to faculty members of institutions of higher education. It has offered variable annuities to faculty members since about 1950. Until recently, difficulty in securing legal permission to offer variable annuities has prevented most other life insurers from entering this field. The Prudential Life Insurance Company of New Jersey has led a nationwide campaign to secure legislative approval for variable annuities, and in 1959 secured clearance from the New Jersey legislature to offer them.

The Securities and Exchange Commission regulates all variable annuity contracts, which are also subject to state regulation. By 1970, most states provided for the sale of these contracts. The Securities and Exchange Commission has exempted from registration group variable annuities under conditions described in the Investment Company Act of 1940 (Rule 3 (c) (3)), but individual variable annuity contracts must be sold with a full prospectus provided to each customer, as is true with new stock offerings and with mutual funds. The right of the SEC to regulate variable annuities was established after a lengthy court battle launched by insurance companies, in *SEC* v. *VALIC*, 359 U.S. 65 (1959), and *Prudential* v. *SEC*, 326 F2 383 (1964), 377 U.S. 953.

constant than to have an income with a fixed amount but a fluctuating real value.

Although the purchaser of a variable annuity accepts the risk that personal savings and income may decline if the stock market falls, the insurer accepts the mortality risk. The insurer guarantees some minimum rate at which the annuity will be paid, and the annuitant cannot outlive this income. Thus the variable annuitant is assured a lifetime income which should be high enough to offset inflation and to maintain a standard of living at the level of the time of retirement.

By 1975, about 1,600,000 persons in the United States were covered by variable annuities, an increase of over 27% over 1974. This may be compared to 2,900,000 persons covered under conventional annuities.[12]

How the Variable Annuity Works. In practice, the details of the variable annuity are somewhat involved, but the general way in which they operate may be described by an example. Suppose that *A* has purchased a variable annuity contract in 1950 when 45 years old and that annual premium payments of $1,000 were made until *A* was age 65. Each year the premiums are invested by the insurer in common stocks. Specific stocks are not bought for *A*'s account but for the account of the insurer, and *A* owns a small fraction of every security owned by the insurer. Thus, *A* owns a cross-section of a broadly diversified common stock portfolio, similar to the shares in a mutual fund.

During the 20 years that *A* pays premiums a total of $20,000 would have been deposited. If the annual premium of $1,000 had been saved at 5% compound interest, the value of the fund when *A* becomes 65 would be approximately $34,720. However, let us assume that due to inflation the value of the stocks is $56,600. This would represent nearly perfect adjustment to the rise in the Consumer Price Index since the value of *A*'s stocks, after depreciation for the declining value of the dollar, would be about $35,000 in terms of 1950 purchasing power.[13]

Under the variable annuity plan, *A* has 63% more funds than would have been available at a fixed interest rate, providing the stock market kept pace exactly with the cost of living. (The Standard and Poor's composite index of stock prices increased from 18.4 to 75.72 as of July, 1970, an increase of 311%.) If *A* had used a traditional annuity for a savings plan and had earned 5% on the funds a monthly life income (straight life annuity basis) of about $240 could be expected from the $35,000 fund.

Under the variable annuity, the insurer would express the $56,600 in terms of an annuity of so many units per month for life. The initial value of these units can be any arbitrary amount, say $1. Then *A* would have 56,000 units credit. Assuming the identical annuity rate as that which applied to the fixed-dollar annuity in the above example, *A* would be entitled to about 452.8 units per month for life, with an initial monthly value of $452.80. Assume that the stock market rises 3% in the second year of *A*'s retirement. Each unit is now

[12] *Life Insurance Fact Book 1976* (New York: Institute of Life Insurance, 1976), p. 43.
[13] Between 1959 and 1970 the dollar lost about 63% of its purchasing power.

worth $1.03 instead of $1.00 and *A*'s monthly retirement income in the second year would rise 3% to $466.38. If in the third year the stock market falls 10%, so does *A*'s annuity.[14] This is true regardless of what has happened to consumer prices or to living standards. The variable annuity concept assumes that in the long run, however, the stock market is a reasonable reflection of inflation and changes in living standards.

Interest in both fixed and variable annuities has been stimulated by two federal laws granting deferral of federal income taxes on funds used by individuals to purchase them. Under the Self-Employed Individuals Retirement Act of 1962 (Keogh Act), self-employed persons may save annually up to 15% of their income in approved plans, subject to a maximum of $7,500. Under the Employees Retirement Income Security Act of 1974 (ERISA), any employee whose employer does not contribute to a pension plan on behalf of the employee may save up to $1,500 annually on a tax-deferred basis. The growth of individual plans for retirement purposes seems assured and annuity plans will undoubtedly play a significant role in the efforts of individuals to augment their retirement security.

The question arises, "How has the variable annuity worked out?" Unfortunately, the variable annuity concept is too new to have built up a lengthy financial history over several business cycles, a history which can form the basis of any conclusive assessment of its value in stabilizing and building the purchasing power of a retirement income. Nevertheless, there is some convincing evidence that demonstrates the potential value of the variable annuity in assisting the long-term saver, without undue risk, in building a retirement income above that which would normally be attained using more conventional methods. Examples of such evidence are described in the following paragraphs.

College Retirement Equities Fund. A well-known variable annuity plan in effect for a substantial period of years is that offered by the College Retirement Equities Fund (CREF), a subsidiary of the Teachers Insurance and Annuity Association, a life insurance company chartered in New York and distributing insurance and annuities primarily to college personnel. Started in 1950 by special act of the New York legislature, CREF placed an initial value of $10 on its variable annuity accumulation unit.

The unit value reached $53.25 in 1972. Over the period 1953–1972 the average annual rate of return in CREF was 9.52%, but due to the stock market decline in 1972–1974, this return was reduced to 3.72% for the whole period 1953–1974.[15] The CREF unit dropped from $53.25 to $28.35, a loss of 53% in just two years, the largest two-year drop in CREF's history, demonstrating the

[14] The actual mechanics are more complicated. For example, during the period the annuity is being purchased the unit is called an *accumulation* unit. At retirement all of the accumulation units are converted into *annuity* units. The number of annuity units received depends upon the age at retirement, the number of payments guaranteed, and other factors. The stated value of the annuity may be changed periodically and remains stable for the given period. If the stock market goes down during one period, the annuitant's rent is not changed until the next period, when it is reduced enough to offset the higher rent the annuitant has been paid during the period of decline.

[15] *TIAA-CREF Annual Report,* 1974, p. 11.

dramatic declines in retirement benefits which are possible in variable annuities. However, the stock market recovered sharply in 1975, restoring a substantial part of the previous two-year loss. It may be concluded that on the average, the long-run saver may expect somewhere between 6% to 9% return in a variable annuity, subject to considerable fluctuations from year to year. This return corresponds roughly to long-term stock market returns.[16]

It has been urged that a retiree should aim at achieving an income which will not only offset inflation, but will also permit the retiree to maintain a standard of living corresponding to increases in productivity in the economy. It may be observed that if inflation averages 5% and productivity rises 4%, a retiree would need an average increase of retirement income of about 9%. Based on the 1953–1972 experience of CREF, the retiree would have achieved this objective, but due to stock market declines of 1972–1974, the retiree would have fallen considerably short. It seems clear that the long-term saver should not rely solely upon the variable annuity, but rather should hedge investments by placing at least a portion of annual retirement savings into fixed obligations such as bonds, mortgages, or traditional annuities.

Commercial Life Insurers. Approximately 75 life insurers have entered the variable annuity field in recent years. One of the first was the Variable Annuity Life Insurance Company (VALIC), now a subsidiary of American General Insurance Company of Texas. VALIC began writing variable annuities in 1956 and has had approximately the same investment results as CREF. Most other insurers began writing variable annuities in 1968.

Other Variable Annuity Plans. A number of governmental agencies have established optional variable annuity plans for their retirees. Wisconsin (1957), the Tennessee Valley Authority (1959), New Jersey (1963), New York City (1968), Minnesota (1969), and Oregon (1970) are examples. These plans have enjoyed modest success so far, but they have not been in operation long enough for full evaluation.[17]

Costs of Variable Annuities. Variable annuity contracts are more than simply investment vehicles, since they involve annuity rent guarantees, sales commissions, administrative expense limits, and sometimes a life insurance element (mortality charge) that guarantees the return of all of a saver's principal in the event of death before the rent of the annuity begins. Insurers make two types of charges: a percentage of each deposit for sales commissions, administration, and mortality expenses; and a percentage of accumulating assets designed to cover investment advisory services, mortality guarantees, and annuity rent guarantees. In some states premium taxes of up to 2.5% are also collected. A common deposit charge is 6% and a common asset charge is 1.3% or 1.4%

[16] Several studies on stock market returns have been made. One of the best known was completed by Lawrence Fischer and James H. Lorie, "Rates of Return on Investments in Common Stocks," (Chicago: The Center for Research in Security Prices, 1963), which revealed a 35-year average annual return of slightly over 8%.

[17] John P. Mackin, *Protecting Purchasing Power in Retirement* (New York: Fleet Academic Editions, Inc., 1971), pp. 208-223.

annually. In the discussion below, all of these expenses are for simplicity called administrative costs.

An analysis of these costs among 40 life insurers in 1974 revealed a wide variation in the administrative cost ratio (ACR) of the variable annuity.[18] The ACR is defined as the ratio $(S - A)/A$ where S equals the value of a savings account at some assumed risk-free interest rate, and A is the value of the same savings amount invested in the variable annuity after the deduction of all charges, the balance being accumulated at the same interest rate assumed for the separate savings account. The difference between S and A represents the interest-adjusted administrative costs on the assumed account balance after varying numbers of years.

The ACR is small at first, but rises steadily because of the effect of applying a constant percentage to the accumulating assets in the variable annuity account. Among the 40 contracts studied, using a 6% interest assumption, administrative cost ratios after 10 years ranged from 7.5% to 28.1%; after 20 years the ACR ranged from 9.6% to 45.7%. The median cost among 40 insurers after 20 years was 26% of the account balance. In other words, if it were not for all expenses and annuity benefits charged for by insurers, a long-term saver would have approximately 26% more money in the savings account. Of course, with a savings account, the saver would not have enjoyed the advantages of the various services and guarantees offered under the variable annuity. It is up to the saver to determine the value of the costs. The analysis demonstrates that it is worthwhile to shop for variable annuities carefully.

The Risk. It is clear that there is a significant risk to the buyer of variable annuities. As the 1974 stock market experience indicates, the value of the variable annuity unit can go down more rapidly than it goes up. Furthermore, for the saver to come out ahead of a regular savings plan with a fixed rate of interest, it is necessary to have superior investment performance to offset the administrative costs.

One of the ways in which the risk of the variable annuity is reduced is through *dollar cost averaging*. Dollar cost averaging refers to a plan under which a regular and fixed amount is invested in securities at differing prices over a period of time. Using this method the saver automatically acquires more shares when prices are low than when prices are high. Under this method the *average cost* of the purchases is always less than the average price at which purchases are made.

To illustrate dollar cost averaging, take a simple example of a person saving $1,000 regularly each year for three years in a given stock. Assume the price of the security to be $100 the first year, $50 the second year, and $100 the third year. The saver would acquire 10 shares the first year, 20 shares the second, and 10 shares the third year. At the end of the period the investor has saved $3,000 and now has 40 shares each worth $100, for a total value of $4,000, at an average cost of $75 ($3,000/40). The average price paid was $83.33

[18] Mark R. Greene and Paul Copeland, "Factors in Selecting Tax-Deferred Annuities," *CLU Journal* (October, 1975), p. 44.

$\left(\frac{\$100 + \$50 + \$100}{3}\right)$. Dollar cost average does not guarantee the success of an investment plan, of course, since if the average price continues to decline, the investor will lose part of the savings. However, if prices fluctuate and end up the period approximately the same as at the beginning, the investor will gain. As the above example shows, the saver was $1,000 ahead at the end of the three years, even though the price of the shares was $100 at both the beginning and the end. The variable annuity plan thus enables the investor to utilize the dollar cost averaging principle to compound the value of the investment. It also encourages regularity in the investment program, a principle which must be strictly observed if the benefits of dollar cost averaging are to be achieved.

Market Acceptance of Variable Annuities. Variable annuity options in CREF have been chosen by 95% of faculty members given the opportunity to adopt this plan. Acceptance ratios are less than 50% for several other public employee plans. The degree of acceptance seems to vary directly with income level, financial sophistication of employees, and the amount of the educational and promotional effort which accompanies the plan.[19]

Arguments for the Variable Annuity. We may summarize the chief arguments for the variable annuity as follows:

1. It enables the saver to obtain protection against the long-run decline in the purchasing power of the dollar both during the saving years and during retirement years.
2. It permits the saver to share in the economic growth of the nation in a way not possible with fixed-dollar investments. In this way the saver obtains participation in higher living standards as well as protection against lower living standards due to inflation.

Arguments Against the Variable Annuity. Opponents of the variable annuity stress the following arguments:

1. Issuance of these contracts by life insurance companies which have always been associated with secure, guaranteed investments may result in an adverse public reaction against established life insurance programs, especially among individuals who were sold a variable annuity as a result of the overzealous promises of a salesperson anxious to make a sale.
2. Due to an unfamiliarity with the basic assumptions of a variable annuity, many savers might be misled into believing that the value of the investment will always rise. If the stock market declines, they might become discouraged and drop the plan, thus losing any possible advantages from dollar cost averaging.
3. Since it is generally recognized that the stock market is an imperfect instrument in measuring changes in purchasing power, there will be some periods when the value of the annuity may bear no resemblance to actual changes in prices. An annuitant who had relied exclusively on this method as a way of retiring would face a serious dilemma if, for example, prices rose while the stock market fell, as has happened several times in the past.
4. If the annuitant retires at the time of a severe stock market slump, not enough may be realized to retire on and thus the annuitant would suffer loss of substantial principal.

[19] John P. Mackin, *op. cit.*, pp. 222-223.

5. The administrative costs of the variable annuity are substantial over a period of time.
6. There is no guarantee that all insurers who offer variable annuities will be able to achieve satisfactory investment results even in times when the general stock market index moves upward. Judging from the spotty record of the managements of mutual funds, who face the task of continuous investment of shareholders' funds, largely in common stocks, some variable annuity plans would not achieve results as good as those achieved by stock market averages.

In assessing these arguments it should be observed that if one is persuaded that investing all funds in the variable annuity is too risky, one may hedge by allocating a portion of savings to fixed-dollar benefit annuities or fixed-dollar savings during the accumulation period or the distribution period, or both. Most life insurers offer both types of savings plans and permit the saver to change allocations periodically.

Mutual Funds and Term Insurance Combination

There has been considerable interest in recent years in a plan designed by some life insurance companies and mutual fund managements to combine regular investment in mutual fund plans with term life insurance. The saver purchases shares in a mutual fund and at the same time buys term life insurance to meet death protection needs. This plan amounts to substituting equity-type investment for the fixed-dollar investment portion of the ordinary life insurance policy. The saver accepts the risk associated with common stock investment in the expectation that over the longer period the net gain in this combination plan will exceed that of the ordinary life plan.

A similar objective has also been achieved by savings plans under which the insured borrows the cash value of a life insurance policy and invests it in individual common stocks, or in a mutual fund on some regular basis. Under some conditions the interest on the life insurance loan is deductible for federal income tax purposes, thus reducing the net cost of borrowing by the amount of the tax deduction.

The success of combination plans rests upon the assumption that in the long run stock prices will rise sufficiently to reflect both inflation and the increases in national productivity, thus protecting the long-term saver against the possibility of suffering relative losses by devoting savings exclusively to fixed-dollar investments.

The Insured Mutual Fund

Plans are available under which the long-term saver may invest in a mutual fund, with the guarantees that if the total value of the investment after a 10- or 15-year period is less than the total outlay (original investment plus all loading charges), the insurer will make up the differences. In 1975 several mutual funds[20] were insured by the Harleysville Mutual Insurance Company, a

[20] Among the funds using such insurance in 1975 were Colonial Management Associates, National Securities and Research Corporation, Vanguard, Delaware Group, Alpha Fund, Provident Fund, and Fairfield Fund.

property-liability insurer which charged an insurance premium of 6% of the insured amount plus a 2% annual administrative fee. If the mutual fund rises in price, the investor may cancel the insurance policy and purchase a new ten-year policy on the increased value of the plan, thus locking in gains. At the same time, the investor enjoys protection against any decline below the original purchase price, plus fees.

In a study by Lipper Analytical Services of 2,696 different 10-year periods, it was found that among mutual funds which had been in business for at least ten years, 191 losses occurred; i.e., instances in which the ending value of the mutual fund was less than the initial value. This amounts to a loss frequency of about 7%, a measure of the probability of loss.[21] Thus the investor in mutual funds runs some risk of loss, which the insurance plan helps overcome.

The cost of risk transfer through insurance, when compared to other methods of obtaining investment security, may appear relatively high unless the expected gains in the mutual fund are above average. If one invests in a relatively conservative mutual fund whose expected gains are about average, say 7% annually, the cost of insurance may absorb a substantial portion of the expected gain. For example, if Perez puts $10,000 in such a fund and pays a normal sales load of 8%, the initial investment value is $9,200. The 10-year insurance premium, plus the administrative fee would amount to $800. If the fund earns 7% compound for 10 years, the ending investment value would be $18,097, a gain of $8,097. The ratio of the insurance costs to the gain is about 10%. By comparison, if Perez puts $10,000 into a 7% insured savings account for 10 years, there is no sales charge and the final investment value would be $19,671, a gain of $9,671. In this case Perez has had no insurance fee to pay and still has enjoyed complete safety of his investment. However, with the savings account there is no chance of gains beyond 7%, whereas in the insured mutual fund there is such a chance, depending on the fund selected. If the investor selects a volatile fund and the fund rises in value, the cost of the insurance may seem relatively small as a percentage of the gain. If the fund declines below its initial value or stays the same, the cost of insurance may loom large in the eyes of the investor when compared to what one could have earned in a regular savings account at no risk. However, if the fund falls below its initial offering price, the investor enjoys protection against the resulting capital loss. Presumably this plan will appeal to the risk-averse investor who still seeks the possibility of investment gains sufficient to offset inflation.

Conclusion

A basic conclusion which emerges from this discussion is that in all likelihood there will be continued periods of prosperity and depression, inflation and deflation. The variable annuity, which has much to recommend it, has enough weaknesses so that it ought not be relied on as the sole vehicle for retirement.

[21] Armon Glenn, "Guarantee Against Loss," *Barron's,* June 30, 1975, p. 22. See also, "Here's Another Way to Play the Market; An Insured Fund," *Wall Street Journal*, June 24, 1975, p. 13.

Fixed-dollar investments continue to have an important place in the long-range savings program, and regular annuities are among those investments.

An analysis of the manner in which people in the United States have invested their money reveals some interesting facts. As revealed in Table 3–2 (page 59) which shows the relative importance of various sources of savings in the United States, individuals have not lost their interest in fixed-dollar savings, in spite of inflation. Thrift institutions other than life insurers actually increased their market share of the total demand for long-term capital over the period 1970–1975. Life insurers are continuing their steady decline in the share of total capital furnished so that in 1975 they provided 11.4% of the total, compared to 12.5% in 1970. Life insurers furnished about 18% of long-term capital in 1960. On another comparison it was shown that in 1953, 36% of all new savings dollars went into insurance or pension accounts. By 1953 this percentage had declined to 23%.[22]

These adverse trends have accounted for at least part of the effort by life insurers to offer products to the public which will be more popular as long-term investment methods in periods of continuing inflation. In spite of their relative loss of market share of the consumer savings dollar, life insurers still account for a substantial segment of the total. Furthermore, life insurers have diversified into equity-type operations as a way of meeting the lessening consumer interest in the life insurance method of savings and their increased interest in equity products. For example, not only have insurers entered the variable annuity field, but they have also organized or purchased mutual funds to the extent that in 1974, of 275 funds analyzed by Arthur Weisenberger, 85, or 31%, were controlled by life and nonlife insurance companies.

SUMMARY

1. The annuity principle, the reverse of the life insurance principle, provides for an orderly liquidation of an estate in such a way that an annuitant cannot outlive retirement income. An annuity generally provides about twice the retirement income that can be provided by interest alone since the annuity contemplates the gradual depletion of principal.
2. The funds for the purchase of an annuity may be accumulated through permanent life insurance contracts, by separate annuity contracts, or through savings plans other than those sponsored by life insurance companies.
3. Saving for retirement through life insurance or an annuity contract has many advantages over traditional methods of saving; but, in common with investment media such as savings accounts, savings bonds, and other fixed-dollar methods, it contains no protection against gradual inflation.
4. While the inflation peril is probably not the absolute certainty that many believe, its threat warrants careful attention to methods designed to counter it. In an attempt to beat inflation, the saver should not lose sight of the other important desiderata in an investment program for retirement.

[22] *Economic Report of the President, 1975*, p. 273. Percentages calculated.

5. There are six major objectives to consider in a long-term savings program: (a) safety of the principal, (b) liquidity of the investment, (c) reasonable interest return, (d) choice of a plan most likely to lead to consistent savings, (e) formulation of sound plans for the eventual distribution of the estate, and (f) protection against inflation.
6. Traditional life insurance and annuity contracts lend themselves extremely well to meeting the first five objectives above, but make no attempt at meeting inflation. The variable life policy, mutual fund and term insurance combinations, the insured mutual fund, and the variable annuity have been proposed to remedy this defect, with most interest being centered in the variable annuity.
7. The variable annuity, a significant departure from traditional life insurance practice, is not a cure-all, but it holds sufficient promise to warrant careful investigation and experimentation as a way to permit the small saver to share in the long-term economic growth of the country and to obtain protection from inflation. Variable annuities should not be viewed as a substitute for, but rather as a complement to, traditional types of fixed-dollar investments.

QUESTIONS FOR REVIEW AND DISCUSSION

1. (a) A life insurance agent presented a client with the following figures concerning the purchase of ordinary life insurance versus term insurance:
   Annual premium for $20,000 ordinary life, age 35, $373. Annual premium for $20,000 term to age 65, $226. Difference available for outside investment, $147. Amount to which $147 per year will compound in 30 years at 5% interest, $10,213. Cash value of ordinary life policy in 30 years, $10,560. Conclusion, the client would need to earn 5% after taxes and investment expenses to equal the cash value of the ordinary life policy after 30 years.
   Criticize the agent's presentation and conclusion. If the agent's presentation were amended, what conclusions might you make about the wisdom of buying term and investing the difference?
   (b) The agent continued the presentation by stating that ordinary life insurance is a superior plan for retirement provision. The agent indicated that the $10,560 cash value of the ordinary life policy would provide $67.73 a month, while the separate savings fund would require a capital amount of $16,255 to equal this monthly income at an interest rate of 5%. Explain why the ordinary life plan is able to accomplish this feat.
2. Total purchases of life insurance measured by face amount of protection in the United States rose almost every year since 1945 (1973 experienced a drop in group life sales which caused total sales to decline about 3% that year). The average annual growth is about 8% to 9%, larger than the average annual rate of inflation. Account for this phenomenon in view of the fact that life insurance savings is not an inflation hedge, and the share of total savings in the economy accounted for by life insurance has been declining.
3. An economist, writing on the future of the dollar, observed that when the public begins to lose faith in the currency, wasteful consumption and misdirected investments suddenly become rational actions compared with the foolishness of saving money that is becoming worthless. Do you agree? Why or why not? What type of investment becomes "rational" in this situation? Why?

4. A writer stated "Suppose the head of your company called you in and said, 'We have been thinking about your retirement. We're going to offer you a choice, an income for life of $294.37 per month or 10 shares per month for life of American Telephone and Telegraph stock. You are to sell this stock every month and live on the proceeds.' " In what way does this plan (a) resemble, and (b) differ from, the variable annuity.
5. Develop a life insurance program for yourself, making any assumptions as to your estimated future income, family situation, employer pension program, OASDHI benefit, etc. which you feel are realistic and appropriate. Follow the steps outlined in the text and evaluate your program when you have finished.
6. One argument which has been used against the variable annuity is the fear that life insurance companies might gain voting control over companies in whose stocks they have invested. This, it is argued, would place insurance companies in fields in which they have no experience, to the detriment of the policyholder. What points might be raised for and against the argument?
7. One of the arguments for the variable annuity is that it should enable the long-term saver to share in the economic growth of the nation. If you were an opponent of the variable annuity, how might you answer this?
8. A sales agent of a mutual fund points out that there is little in a variable annuity not already available from a mutual fund, and that the company will agree to pay the proceeds of a savings program in as many installments and in whatever amounts are desired over a retirement period. What factor is the sales agent overlooking?
9. A financial writer stated, "Insurance has always been a contract in dollars. When it is no longer that, it becomes a mixture of investment trust and an insurance contract—neither fish, fowl, nor good red herring." The danger, it seems to this writer, is that people purchasing the variable annuity may do so under the impression that it provides the safety of an ordinary insurance policy. This can only be true if the days of deflationary and heavy declines in stock prices are entirely of the past." Do you agree?
10. Roger Babson, whose prediction of the 1929 stock market crash helped bring him fame in the field of finance, wrote in the *Commercial and Financial Chronicle* on January 7, 1960, "I don't see how buying Dow-Jones common stocks now can be a hedge against inflation. This is not to say they may not go higher, but these stocks are already too inflated to be bought as inflation hedges by intelligent people." Does this statement also pertain to the purchase of variable annuities at the time of that writing? Explain.
11. *T* argues that through dollar cost averaging she can always be assured that the average cost of the securities she purchases will be less than the average price of these securities, whether the market rises or falls.
(a) Explain how this can be true, using a numerical example.
(b) Does this mean that *T* cannot lose on her investment? Why?
12. A life insurance actuary stated, "If we are willing to face the truth for ourselves, we must admit privately that life insurance and pension funds as now issued are something of a gamble insofar as the proceeds have any definite foreseeable purchasing power." Formulate a reply to this argument from the viewpoint of one strongly committed to fixed-dollar savings as an exclusive method of saving for retirement.
13. In Germany, following runaway inflation in 1923, German life

insurers discovered that the expenses of maintaining existing life insurance policies in force exceeded the net revenues generated by them. To solve this problem many insurers ceased sending premium notices, attempting to convert all policies to a paid-up basis, and offered policyholders a special bonus for terminating their contracts.
(a) Why were such measures probably taken, instead of wholesale cancellations?
(b) What methods would you propose for life insurers to avoid problems such as this in the future?

14. A writer presented the following problem: An insured, age 50, owns $200,000 of life insurance; he is in the 30% estate tax bracket. Currently the life insurance carries a premium of $4,300 a year, has $53,000 of cash value and $85,000 of paid-up value. The insured is advised that he could reduce estate taxes by giving his life insurance to his wife and letting her pay the premiums with funds that he would give to her. However the insured rejects this solution because he would thereby lose access to the cash value of the policy and would be unable to borrow upon it. Suggest a solution to the insured's problem which would reduce his estate taxes, and at the same time, would retain for his use the cash value now locked up in his life insurance.

15. Explain why the present value of an annuity becomes less as the rate of interest assumed becomes greater.

16. "A life annuity is the reverse of a life insurance contract." Explain.

17. One use of a regular annuity is to enable a father to distribute part of his estate to his heirs while he is still living and yet enjoy the same retirement income from the remainder of his estate as he would have received from the entire estate invested conservatively.
(a) How can this be true?
(b) What advantages or disadvantages might there be for the heirs?

18. One insurer quotes the following annuity rents on a female, age 30: 10 years certain and life, $3.22 per $1,000 of proceeds; 15 years certain and life, $3.20; 20 years certain and life, $3.18; installment fund, $3.12. No quotation is available for a straight-life annuity at this age. Explain (a) why there is such a small difference in rents between these various annuity plans and (b) why the insurer does not publish quotations for the straight-life annuity at this age.

19. Differentiate between the 15-year temporary life annuity settlement and the fixed-period option for 15 years.

20. Would you logically expect to receive a higher or a lower life annuity from $10,000 of cash value in an ordinary life insurance policy or $10,000 of outside savings invested in an annuity when the annuitant reaches retirement age? Why?

21. Why would one logically expect to receive a higher income from a group annuity than from an individual annuity (assuming the same cash values available)? Explain.

22. Account for the substantial growth of group annuities in recent years as compared with the growth of individual annuities.

23. If you were to choose between a variable life insurance policy with the Dutch design and one with the New York Life design, which would you prefer? Why?

CHAPTER *Twenty-Three*

HEALTH INSURANCE

Health insurance in the United States has been one of the most discussed of all types of private insurance in existence. Criticisms of the performance of private health insurance have led to many proposals in Congress for a national health insurance program. Much of this criticism has centered upon the high cost of health care, and the high cost and inefficiency of delivery systems. Yet the American people appear to be utilizing private health insurance more extensively than ever before. Private health insurance premiums have shown one of the most rapid rates of increase of any type of insurance. For example, over the period 1950–1973 health insurance premiums increased 13-fold compared to a 4-fold increase in life insurance premiums. The ratio of total health insurance premiums to disposable personal income has risen from .94% to 3.19% over the same period—over a 3-fold increase.[1]

Even with this public acceptance, however, health insurance benefits still account for only about 26% of total expenditures for health care in the United States, the remainder being paid by individuals personally, or directly or indirectly through governmental bodies. (See Table 23–1.) In 1973, insurance plans paid about 35% of all hospital costs and physicians' charges, but only about 7% of the costs of other types of health care.[2]

It is interesting to note that although a majority of persons (over 76%) are covered for hospital and physicians' care,[3] private insurers account for only about 35% of the total expenditures for these expenses. (See Table 23–1.) Private insurers account for only 7.6% of total outlays for dental care and 5.1% for prescribed drugs. These data suggest that private coverage is not complete and private insurers have elected not to cover the entire demand for health care insurance. In view of this, interest in national heath insurance is not surprising. Private health insurers will undoubtedly continue to

[1] *Life Insurance Fact Book 1974* (New York: Institute of Life Insurance, 1974), p. 57, and *Source Book of Health Insurance Data 1974–75* (New York: Health Insurance Institute, 1974), pp. 48–49.

[2] M. S. Mueller, "Private Health Insurance in 1973: A Review of Coverage, Enrollment, and Financial Experience," *Social Security Bulletin* (February, 1975), p. 37.

[3] *Ibid.*

Table 23-1

PRIVATE INSURANCE VS. OTHER METHODS OF PAYING FOR NATIONAL HEALTH CARE EXPENSES, 1973

Type of Expenditure	Total Spent (Billions of Dollars)	Percent of Total	Percentage Distribution by			
			Direct Payments	Private Health Insurance	Government	Philanthropy and Industry
Hospital care	$36.2	45.3	9.9	35.6	53.2	1.3
Physicians' services	18.0	22.5	42.4	35.2	22.4	.1
Dentists' services	5.4	6.7	87.1	7.6	5.3	—
Drugs	8.8	11.0	87.2	5.1	7.6	—
Other	11.6	14.5	39.0	3.2	52.3	5.5
Total	$80.0	100.0	35.1	25.6	37.9	1.4

Source: Barbara S. Cooper, Nancy L. Worthington, and Paula A. Piro, "National Health Expenditures, 1929-1973," *Social Security Bulletin* (March, 1974), p. 13.

offer supplementary coverages, even if national health insurance is ultimately adopted in the United States. For example, nearly 60% of all those persons 65 and over have some type of private hospital insurance, in spite of the fact that Medicare automatically applies to nearly every citizen 65 and over.[4]

WHAT IS HEALTH INSURANCE?

Health insurance may be defined broadly as that type of insurance which provides indemnification for expenditures and loss of income resulting from loss of health. The Committee on Health Insurance Terminology of the American Risk and Insurance Association (ARIA) has recommended the definition for health insurance as "insurance against loss by sickness or accidental bodily injury."[5] The Committee also recommended the use of one term, "medical expense insurance," to embrace other types of health insurance.

Unfortunately there is no sharp distinction among the various contracts as to the type of medical expenses for which indemnity is payable. For example, hospitalization policies usually pay not only for hospital services but also for medicines used in the hospital, physicians' services rendered in the hospital, and other items. In general, however, five types of health insurance benefits may be offered on separate contracts or in combinations in a single contract: hospitalization, surgical, regular medical, major medical, and disabilty income.

Hospitalization

The *hospitalization contract* is intended to indemnify the insured for necessary hospitalization expenses, including room and board in the hospital, laboratory fees, nursing care, use of operating room, and certain medicines and supplies. The agreement may set dollar allowances for the different items or may be on a service basis. Typical contracts offered by insurance companies, for example, may state that the insured will be indemnified "up to $25 a day" for necessary hospitalization, while Blue Cross arrangements may provide for "full hospital service in a semiprivate room."

Surgical

The *surgical contract* provides set allowances for different surgical procedures performed by duly licensed physicians. In general, a schedule of operations is set forth, together with the maximum allowance for each operation. Thus, the $300 schedule may provide $150 for an appendectomy, $25 for a tonsilectomy, $10 for the lancing of a boil, and $300 for a lobotomy. The $300 limit is the maximum allowance and applies to only a few specified surgical procedures.

[4] *Ibid.*

[5] *Bulletin of the Commission on Insurance Terminology*, American Risk and Insurance Association (May, 1965), p. 1.

Regular Medical

The *regular medical contract* refers to that contract of health insurance which covers physicians' services other than surgical procedures and is to be sharply distinguished from the major medical contract. Generally, regular medical insurance provides allowances for physicians' visits, such as $5 or $7.50 per visit, regardless of whether the visits are made in the hospital, at home, or in the doctor's office. Normally, regular medical insurance is written in conjunction with other types of health insurance and is not written as a separate contract.

Major Medical

The *major medical contract*, is designed to meet very large medical bills on a blanket basis with few sublimitations imposed on specific expense items. The contract is issued subject to substantial deductibles of different sorts and with a high maximum limit. A major medical policy might have a $10,000 maximum limit for any one accident or illness, have a $500 deductible for any one illness, and contain an agreement to indemnify the insured for a specified percentage of the bills, such as 80% over and above the amount of the dollar deductible. A few insurers offer a variation of the major medical contract known as *comprehensive*, which reduces the deductible to $25 or $50.

Disability Income

Disability income insurance is a form of health insurance that provides periodic payments when the insured is unable to work as a result of illness, disease, or injury.[6] Usually there is a waiting period before the income payments commence and the disability must be one that prevents the insured from carrying on the usual occupation. Most policies continue payment of the benefits for only a specified maximum number of years, but lifetime benefits are available in some contracts. However, under all loss of income policies, the benefits are terminated as soon as the disability ends.

Expenditures for Health Insurance

Table 23–1 shows that in 1973 Americans spent about $80 billion on health care, of which governmental agencies paid the largest single share, 37.9%. Hospital and doctors' expenses account for about two thirds of these expenditures. Private insurance includes both group and individual plans.

Data collected by the Health Insurance Institute for 1973 indicate the following changes in the number of persons under 65 covered in the United States under the different types of health insurance plans:

[6] *Bulletin of the Commission on Insurance Terminology* (October, 1965), p. 7.

Type of Plan	(Millions of Persons) 1969	1974	Percent Increase 1969/1974
Hospital expense	147.7	160.5	8.6
Surgical expense	140.4	153.3	9.3
Regular medical expense	125.7	143.5	14.2
Major medical expense	72.4	89.6	23.8
Disability Income			
Short-term	57.3	64.6	12.8
Long-term	9.3	17.8	91.8

Source: *Source Book of Health Insurance Data 1975-76,* (New York: Health Insurance Institute, 1975), p. 5.

From these data it may be seen that the most rapidly growing types of private health insurance are long-term disability and major medical. Significantly, each of these constitutes the least numbers of privately covered individuals and are among the most serious causes of health loss. Voluntary health insurance covers most persons in the United States for hospital, surgical, and regular medical expenses, but it is not sold as extensively for other types of health loss. Of course most persons enjoy limited long-term disability coverage under social security.

Group insurance contracts cover many more persons than individual contracts. Although the data for the number of individuals covered are only approximate, it may be said that only one in four people covered by hospitalization and surgical expenses has an individual policy, while one in three having coverage for loss of income has an individual contract. As will be seen later, there are many factors that account for the dominance of the group insurance method of covering health losses.

Insurers of Health Loss

Three main types of private health loss insurers exist in the United States: Blue Cross-Blue Shield plans, commercial insurance plans, and independent (private, clinic, community, or union) plans. Premiums (in billions) under each of these plans were:[7]

	1963	1973	Percent Increase
Blue Cross-Blue Shield	$3.4	$11.1	226
Commercial insurer	4.1	11.7	185
Independent plans	.5	1.8	260
Total	$8.0	$24.6	208

It may be observed that the most dramatic increases in premiums were obtained by independent plans, although these plans enjoy only a tiny market

[7] M. S. Mueller, *op. cit.*, p. 33.

share compared to commercial insurers and Blue Cross-Blue Shield organizations. Enrollment in 1973 as a percentage of civilian population covered was estimated at 76% for hospital and physicians' care, 10% for dental care, 60% for prescribed drugs, and 57% for private nursing care.[8]

COMMON PROVISIONS OF INDIVIDUAL HEALTH INSURANCE CONTRACTS

Because the form of individual health insurance contracts is not standardized, it is impractical to discuss any one given type of policy. Rather, an analysis of the major types of contractual provisions typically found in these contracts will be given. Nearly all states now have adopted a model statute, first proposed by the National Association of Insurance Commissioners in 1950, governing the provisions used by insurers in individual health insurance contracts. This statute, known as the Uniform Individual Accident and Sickness Policy Provisions Law, recommends that certain provisions of health insurance contracts be required, and specifies the wording of other provisions. The purpose of the law is to protect the consumer and to facilitate the settlement of loss claims. The more important of these provisions are discussed below.

Persons Covered

Health insurance may cover only the applicant, or it may cover both the applicant and certain named dependents. Since the health failure of dependents is often as severe in its financial impact as the health loss of the breadwinner, coverage on dependents is considered extremely important. Loss of income coverage, of course, is not written for dependents, but all other types of health contracts generally permit the insured to cover dependents. Sometimes, however, dependents are covered under different schedules of benefits or the dependents may be subject to certain limitations not imposed on the breadwinner.

Defining the Peril

All individual health insurance contracts define, both specifically and by exclusions, what perils are intended to be covered. Two general forms may be found—those insuring accidents and those insuring both illness and accident.

Accident Only Contracts. *Accident only contracts* generally offer quite limited coverage. It is not uncommon to find accidents narrowly defined to include only those injuries caused by *accidental means*. If this wording is used, something abnormal, unusual, and unexpected must have occurred immediately prior to the injury if the insured is to be considered as covered. Because of court decisions, insurers now generally use wording which refers to "accidental injury," which broadens the definition of covered accidents. Accident only

[8] *Ibid.*, p. 22.

policies are commonly issued as, for example, travel accident contracts and vacation policies.

Illness and Accident Contracts. Since over 90% of physical disabilities may be traced to illness rather than to accident, it is not surprising that the greatest demand in health insurance contracts is for the *illness and accident contract.* However, even though a contract covers illness and accident, it will usually narrow the meaning of illness or accident in certain ways. For example, disabilities or expense caused by mental disease, tuberculosis, childbirth or pregnancy, dental treatment, intentionally self-inflicted injuries or attempted suicide (whether sane or insane), preexisting illnesses, cosmetic surgery (unless required after an accident), injuries recoverable through workers' compensation, war injuries, or aviation accidents may be excluded. The main reason for these exclusions is either that recovery can be made from other sources, or that the claim is not insurable because to include it would raise the cost of the contract beyond the means of the average purchaser.

Some health insurance contracts cover only limited types of sicknesses, such as cancer, or other dread diseases such as polio, spinal meningitis, or multiple sclerosis. Usually the coverage is for relatively large amounts, such as $50,000 and the premiums are modest, since the frequency of these diseases is quite low. Often large deductibles apply and the coverage is limited in other ways.

Defining Losses

All individual health insurance contracts carefully define the type of health loss covered. If hospital expenses are to be insured, the contract will set the limit of these expenses as so much per day, for so many days, or subject to a maximum amount. Blue Cross contracts usually set no daily maximum, since the room and board agreement is on a service basis; but they may specify dollar limits on certain hospital services, such as laboratory fees, X-rays, blood plasma, and special nursing.

If the policy offers medical or surgical coverage, it will contain specific limitations on the extent to which doctor bills will be paid. An "operation" is defined as certain surgical procedures, such as cutting, suturing, treatment of fracture, taping, giving injection treatment, electrocauterization, and artificial pneumothorax. If two surgical procedures are performed in one operation, the policy is limited to indemnification for the more serious of the two.

Recurring Losses. The policy must define when one loss ends and when another begins. For example, suppose the maximum hospital expense benefit period is 90 days and the insured is hospitalized for 60 days. The insured is discharged and five days later must reenter the hospital because of a relapse. Has a new loss begun, entitling the insured to 90 additional days' benefits, or is the second loss a resumption of the old, with only 30 additional days of indemnification payable? Under a *recurrent disability clause,* the contract will specify that the reentry must either be from an entirely new set of causes, or that some period, such as one to six months, must have elapsed between hospitalizations, in order for the second period of disability to be considered a new period of entitlement. This definition is also important in ascertaining the application of a deductible or a waiting-period provision. In group contracts this provision is quite liberal in that the test is "Did the insured return to work?" If the insured did return to work, and was later hospitalized, a new period of entitlement began.

In order to specify what losses are to be paid, the contract will generally provide definitions of eligible hospitals. A hospital may be defined as an institution operated pursuant to the law for the care and treatment of sick and injured persons, with organized facilities for major surgery and 24-hour nursing service. Bed confinement to a private clinic during the course of one day is thus probably not a day of hospital confinement. Likewise, nursing homes, sanitariums, rest homes, and similar institutions are not hospitals.

In addition, the policy covers only bills of "legally qualified physicians." Professional fees of optometrists, clinical psychologists, etc., may not be covered.

Disability Income. In disability income policies, two classes of disabilities are usually recognized—total and partial.

Total Disability. For a disability to be considered *total,* a contract may specify that a fairly liberal definition applies for the first one or two years, and thereafter a much stricter definition applies. For example, the contract may state that during the first 24 months of disability, the insured must be able to perform none of the *regular* occupational duties. Thereafter, the insured must be able to perform none of the duties of *any* occupation. Sometimes the contract will reflect court decisions and further define what is meant by *any* occupation. One contract states:

1. For the purpose of determining the commencement of total disability and thereafter for the first 24 months that the Monthly Income Benefit may be payable during any continuous period of such disability, total disability means only such complete incapacity of the Insured that he is able to perform none of the duties of his occupation, business or employment, and
2. for the remainder of any such period of continuous disability, total disability means only such complete incapacity of the Insured that he is able to perform none of the duties of any occupation, business, or employment; provided, however, that in no event shall total disability exist for any purpose of this policy during any period in which the insured is engaged in his or any occupation, business or employment for remuneration or profit.

Partial Disability. *Partial disability* refers to the continuous inability of the insured, because of accidental bodily injury, to engage in one or more of the important occupational duties. For example, an insured has a loss of income policy that pays lifetime benefits of $200 each month in the event of disability by illness. The insured suffers a heart attack and is unable to work for six months, after which work is resumed but in another capacity requiring less strenuous activity and at a much lower salary. Assuming that the contract has no waiting period, the insured will recover only six months' indemnity. Because the insured is not disabled with regard to *any* occupation, disability income may not be drawn, even though the employment is on a much lower level. On the other hand, if the only job the insured could get is selling pencils on the street, in all likelihood the insured may continue to draw disability income because the contract does not require work in a position for which the insured is not reasonably fitted by education, training, or experience.

In order to reduce controversies over whether a disability is really permanent, the contract states that the disability will be *presumed* permanent after the lapse of a given time period. The waiting period may sometimes vary according to the wishes of the insured at the time the contract is issued. For example, a reduced premium may be granted if the insured specifies a waiting period longer than the ordinary time period. Sometimes the indemnity is retroactive to the date the disability began. However, disability income riders on life insurance policies stipulate a four or six months' waiting period which is usually not retroactive. This means that the insured will not collect for the initial period of disability, even if the disability exceeds the waiting period.

Sometimes a disability policy contains what is known as an *aggregate clause*, which places an upper limit of total liability on the amount of income benefits payable. Thus, a policy might promise a weekly income benefit of $25, but the aggregate limit might be $500. Obviously such a limit places a 20-week maximum for total disability during the income period, a factor which might escape the notice of the purchaser.

Deductibles and Elimination Periods

Health insurance policies present serious problems to underwriters because of the difficulties in controlling both moral and morale hazards. It is often difficult to determine whether the loss has actually occurred, because illness is a subjective matter that does not always lend itself to definite medical diagnosis. The same disease may cause severe illness in one person but may not even disable the next. There are no standard charges for medical care, especially for physicians' costs, since the fees are commonly adjusted according to the patient's ability to pay rather than according to the nature of the illness. For these reasons underwriters not only must place definite maximum limitations on losses payable, but also generally require the insured to bear a portion of the loss in the form of a deductible of some type.

Deductibles in health insurance are of two general types: dollar or percentage deductibles from the amount of the loss, and waiting periods or elimination periods. As an example of a contract containing dollar and percentage deductibles, we shall consider the major medical contract.

Major Medical Contract. One of the distinguishing features of the major medical contract, which has enjoyed a rapid growth since its introduction after World War II, is the large limitation of loss which characterizes it and the absence of limitations on expenses within this maximum. The policy may be written with a maximum of $10,000 or $15,000 for any one disability. Policies with higher maximum limits, such as $100,000 or $250,000, are sometimes offered. There is usually no limitation as to how much of this amount may be accounted for by doctor bills, hospital bills, private nursing, medicines, and other expenses stemming from a single physical disability, so long as the expenses are reasonable and necessary. The policy contains exclusions for certain types of care, but theoretically, if an item is not excluded, the entire bill could consist of, say, doctors' fees and be eligible for payment if the charge were reasonable.

To control the losses payable under major medical contracts, it is common to provide a large dollar deductible, such as $300 to $750. The dollar deductible is used to eliminate claims which are presumably covered by other health policies or are assumed by the insured himself. It is the intent of the major medical contract to cover only catastrophic expenses which the ordinary person cannot assume. To prevent the insured from incurring extravagant medical expenses once the dollar deductible amount has been expended, the contract agrees to pay for only a certain proportion of the expenses over the deductible, commonly 80%. This provision is known as *percentage participation* or *coinsurance*. Since the insured is required to share the cost of every medical bill, the inclination to incur unnecessary medical expenses is less.

Suppose the insured is in a severe automobile accident and requires specialized medical care over a period of two years for such things as skin grafts, cosmetic surgery, and artificial limbs. The cost of physicians' services, private nursing, and special hospitalization might easily reach $50,000. Under the $100,000 major medical policy with a $500 deductible and an 80% coinsurance clause, the insured would recover 80% of all amounts over the deductible, or $39,600. The insured must bear $10,400 of the costs, although some contracts eliminate the deduction of the coinsurance percentage on amounts exceeding a given level, thus placing a smaller burden on the insured. Without the deductible and the coinsurance clause there is an inevitable tendency for both the patient and the doctor to be less conservative in the expenditure of amounts needed to purchase the required medical services. In all good conscience the doctor might be able to justify a larger fee if it is known that the charge is covered by insurance, and the patient might order a more costly hospital service than otherwise.

Elimination Periods. A contract may contain two types of waiting periods. There may be a waiting period after the contract is in force before any benefits are payable for certain perils. This is often called a probationary, or *elimination, period*. For example, the contract may specify that no benefits will be payable during the first month, or first three months, of the contract for physical conditions or illnesses which the insured had at the time the policy went into effect. This provision permits a policy to be issued even if the insured was ill at the time application was made for coverage. After the elimination period has elapsed, full coverage is provided.

A second type of waiting-period clause, found in loss of income policies, specifies that no benefits will be paid until the disability, once it has occurred, has lasted a certain length of time. The waiting period of this clause may vary from one week to three or four months, at the option of the insured. If the insured feels that in the event of illness or accident the employer will continue the salary, say for one month, the insured may select a waiting period of one month and thus effect considerable savings in the premium. It is common to require a minimum of a seven-day waiting period to eliminate small claims which are uneconomical to insure.

Substantial rate credits are given by insurers for waiting periods up to about 90 days. For example, one insurer quotes the following annual rates for a disability income policy on a male age 25 paying $400 per month up to age 65 for either sickness or accident on a noncancellable, guaranteed renewable basis:

7-day waiting period	$192.40
30-day waiting period	$154.80
90-day waiting period	$132.80

Thus the insured saves 20% of the annual premium by accepting a 30-day waiting period, and about 32% for a 90-day waiting period on the policy. Reflecting the fact that most disabilities are shorter than 90 days, the reductions in premium for longer waiting periods are modest; for example, about a 15% reduction is given for increasing the waiting period from 90 to 180 days, and a 7% reduction for increasing it from 180 to 365 days.

Cancellation and Renewability

Unlike a life insurance contract, the health insurance contract is sometimes cancellable by the insured or the insurer during the policy term. Also, unlike most life insurance policies, the health insurance contract may not be renewable unless the insurer is agreeable. It is important to observe the difference between cancellability and renewability. A health insurance policy may not be cancellable within the policy term, but the insurer can fail to renew the policy if the insured's experience has been bad; or the insurer may renew the policy subject to exclusions for certain diseases on which the insured may have had a claim.

Guaranteed Renewable Provision. The safest type of health insurance contract is one which is both noncancellable and guaranteed renewable at a constant premium. In this case the insured has the option of whether or not to renew, and may, if desired, renew the contract indefinitely, or until a certain maximum age, usually 64, is reached. The importance of renewability from the viewpoint of the insured should be emphasized. Suppose *G* has a disability income contract which is noncancellable within the policy period but is renewable "at the option of the company only." *G* carries this policy for 15 years against a serious disability. *G* has a slight stroke, makes a claim for disability, and receives income payments for six weeks. At the end of the year the insurer has the privilege of failing to renew this policy or renewing it subject to an exclusion for all future claims arising out of "diseases of the nervous system." If the insured retains this coverage at all, coverage on the very difficulty which is most likely to cause future disabilities will probably be excluded. The insurer may, of course, be generous and renew as before, but this means that other policyholders are being asked to bear claims not contemplated when the original rates were formulated. Certainly the insured cannot assume such generosity. The obvious solution is to purchase noncancellable, guaranteed renewable coverage if possible. If the risk of physical disability is worth insuring at all, it is worth insuring on a permanent basis if such a contract is available and can be afforded.

A word of caution is necessary at this point in interpreting "guaranteed renewable." Some insurers issue a contract which is called guaranteed renewable, but the *rate* is subject to change. The insurer may charge whatever rate it deems correct for the age group and class of risk concerned. Thus, this form has the disadvantage that while the insured knows that the insurance can always be maintained, the premium may become prohibitive.

A fixed-premium, noncancellable, and guaranteed renewable policy costs more money than a cancellable commercial policy or one which does not guarantee the premium rate at which it is renewable. The main reason for this is that reserves must be accumulated to meet the higher morbidity costs which characterize older age groups, just as a higher rate is charged for a permanent life insurance contract. The premium will depend not only on the age of the insured when the contract is issued, but also upon the occupation of the insured, the period during which income is guaranteed (if it is an income policy), and the character of the medical or hospital benefits. Typical rates are:

Renewal Provision	Annual Premium Per $10 Monthly Income
Cancellable (Renewable at the option of the company only)	$3.35
Guaranteed renewable, but with the premium subject to change upon renewal at a higher age	3.86
Noncancellable, and guaranteed renewable at the same rate (Rate can be increased only if all rates in a given class are raised)	6.00

If a policy is guaranteed renewable at a fixed premium, there are certain other clauses that are generally included. These are the waiver of premium clause and the incontestability clause. The *waiver of premium clause* is generally included because it would be incongruous as well as difficult for the insured to be receiving benefits and yet be required to maintain premiums on the contract. The *incontestability clause* has a purpose in health insurance similar to its purpose in life insurance, but the clause is worded in such a way that its effect on underwriting is not so strict. This clause is analyzed below.

Not Guaranteed Renewable Provision. If a policy is not guaranteed renewable, the renewal clause states that the coverage terminates at the expiration of the period for which premiums have been paid, unless within some stated period prior to the expiration of the policy, ranging from 5 to 30 days, the insurer has mailed a notice of intention not to renew. If this notice is not sent, the insured may renew the contract for another year. Such policies never have a period beyond one year.

Most health insurance policies state that if the insured fails to remit the premium, generally there will be a grace period of 30 or 31 days in which to pay during which coverage remains in force. The typical health insurance contract contains a reinstatement clause under which the policy may be reinstated after it has lapsed simply by acceptance of the premium by the agent. In such cases the policy does not cover illness for the first 10 days after reinstatement, although it will cover accidents. If the applicant is in poor health when reapplying for the policy, the agent does not have authority to accept the premium unless requirement is made for an application for reinstatement and a conditional receipt for the premium is given. The effect of this requirement is that the policy is not reinstated unless officials in the insurer's home office approve it. The reinstatement clause provides that if these officials fail to act on the application within 45 days, the policy is automatically reinstated. The intent of the reinstatement clause is to give the insured an opportunity to put the coverage back in force with protection against unreasonable action by the insurer to prevent effective reinstatement or to cast doubt as to the validity of such reinstatement.

Incontestability

Most health insurance contracts contain an incontestable clause which is sometimes found under the heading "Time Limit on Certain Defenses." This clause is as follows:

> *Time Limit on Certain Defenses*—(a) After two years from the date of issue of this policy no misstatements, except fraudulent misstatements, made by the applicant in the application for such policy shall be used to void the policy or to deny a claim for loss incurred or disability (as defined) commencing after the expiration of such two-year period.
>
> (b) No claim for loss incurred or disability (as defined) commencing after two years from the date of issue of this policy shall be reduced or denied on the ground that a disease or physical condition had existed prior to the effective date of coverage under this policy unless, effective on the date of loss, such diseases or physical condition was excluded from coverage by name or specific description.

It will be seen that *fraudulent misstatements*, but not other misstatements, can be used to void the policy. In no event can misstatements about a preexisting disease or physical condition be used to deny or reduce benefits unless such condition is specifically excluded from coverage. It will be recalled that in life insurance, *no* misstatements can be used as a defense by the insurer against paying the claim once the period of incontestability clause has expired. Suppose an applicant is asked whether a claim has been made under another health insurance policy within a period of five years and the answer is "no." Three years later upon receiving a claim, the insurer discovers that the insured had made several claims under other policies, and had this information been known, the contract would never have been issued. The insurer denies liability and the question arises as to whether or not the insured's false answer is a fraudulent misstatement. In all likelihood it would be so considered, if it could be shown that the statement was made deliberately to deceive the insurer, and that the latter relied on this statement to its detriment. Therefore, the insurer could deny liability for any claim and could cancel the contract, even though the two-year period had passed. This applies no matter whether the policy was guaranteed renewable or not. In a life insurance policy the insurer undoubtedly would have to honor the claim even though the insured's misstatement was held to be fraudulent.

Prorating of Benefits

The health insurance policy generally contains no clause that strictly limits the amount that can be collected by an insured in the event that more than one policy is in effect covering the same loss, if they are issued on a valued basis. It is common for the policy to exclude benefits for expenses recoverable under workers' compensation or for services rendered in a government hospital. But if the insured has two private hospitalization policies, there is nothing to prevent a profit being made on a hospitalization for which the insured collects twice or more. The insured is generally required to reveal the existence of other health insurance policies when making application for coverage, and thus the underwriter has some check on this type of moral hazard.[9]

On income loss policies it is the usual procedure to include some sort of restriction on the indemnity payable to the insured in case the total coverage exceeds all or some proportion of average past earnings. Such provisions are often referred to as *coordination of benefits clauses*. A typical clause provides that if, at the time the insured makes a claim, other policies are held which also pay a disability income and the total disability income benefits exceed average earnings in some time period, the amount payable will be reduced. The amount payable is obtained by taking that proportion of the disability income promised which the actual average income bears to the total disability income insurance payable. For example, assume that an insured has a policy with Company S paying \$300 each month and one in Company T paying \$200 each month. Both policies contain the average earning clause. At the time of a disability, the average income over the past two years is only \$400 each month. The insured would collect only 4/5 × \$300, or \$240 each month from Company S, and 4/5 × \$200, or \$160, each month from Company T. In this way at least the insured does not collect *more* than the actual average income. If the insured were permitted to collect more, there would be even less inducement to overcome the illness and return to work. As a matter of fact, a considerable moral hazard can exist in the field of income loss coverage because not all contracts contain the average

[9] It is becoming more common to insert an "other insurance" clause in health insurance contracts. This clause limits the total indemnity payable in case of other insurance covering the same loss.

earnings clause. In this example, if Company T's policy did not contain the clause, it would pay the full $200 and the insured would be recovering $440 each month, tax free, whereas before this disability, earnings were $400 and were subject to taxes and other deductions.

Misstatement of Age

For reasons similar to the situation in life insurance, the loss of income health contract provides that if the insured has made a misstatement of age, the benefits are reduced to that level which would have been purchased by the premium actually paid had the true age been given. Such a clause is particularly important in contracts that provide lifetime income benefits. If the insured makes a misstatement of age, this misrepresentation, even if it is discovered after the period of incontestability, alters the promised benefits but does not deny the insured all benefits.

GROUP HEALTH INSURANCE

As was indicated before, far more people are covered under group insurance than are covered under individual contracts. About 73% of all premiums earned by insurers were under group contracts in 1973. Hospital-medical premiums accounted for most of the group premiums.

Similarly, in terms of benefits paid out, group insurance has been growing steadily at the expense of individual coverage. For example, in 1950, group policies accounted for 58% of total health benefits paid by life insurance companies in the United States. This percentage had grown to 77% in 1960, and 84% by 1973.[10]

Health Maintenance Organizations (HMO's)

Group insurance has been stimulated further by passage of the Health Maintenance Organization Act of 1973 in which the U.S. Congress attempted to encourage the growth of health maintenance organizations (HMO's). HMO's have as one of their central purposes the goal of decreasing the amount of health losses through preventive activity. HMO's include private group clinics of physicians which entitle members to regular medical and hospital care on a prepaid basis.[11] In 1975 there were about 181 HMO's operating with about 5.7 million members.[12] Certain employers offering a health benefit plan to their workers are required to offer employees an optional opportunity to enroll in an HMO, if one is available in the community. HMO's are often sponsored by private insurance companies, which provide financial support, organizational effort, consultation, marketing effort, reinsurance, and other services.

[10] *Source Book of Health Insurance Data 1974-75* (New York: Health Insurance Institute, 1974), p. 38.

[11] The Kaiser Foundation Health Plan is considered a prototype for the HMO.

[12] *Source Book of Health Insurance Data 1975-76* (New York: Health Insurance Institute, 1975), p. 16.

Some of the basic reasons for the growth of private group health insurance plans are:

1. Group insurance is available at lower cost.
2. Group contracts usually provide more generous benefits than do individual contracts.
3. Group contracts have been actively promoted by organized groups such as labor unions and hospital associations.
4. Group insurance has received much publicity as a result of various social insurance programs and legislative discussions about socialized medicine.

Cost Advantages of Group Health Insurance

The sources of savings in group health insurance stem from the same factors as in group life insurance.

Freedom from Adverse Selection. Group health contracts enjoy relative freedom from adverse selection because the covered group exists for some reason other than to obtain insurance. In view of the high moral and morale hazards which characterize the field of health insurance, the element of adverse selection in individual policies is especially severe, requiring higher relative premiums than in group insurance.

Lower Administrative Costs. Administrative costs in group health insurance plans are lower than those for individual policyholders. Employers frequently perform the premium collection function by withholding from each employee's paycheck the correct contribution to the plan. Employers also generally screen claims, help the employee fill out the form properly, answer employee questions, and perform other duties of this nature which would otherwise absorb the attention of a sizeable claims staff employed by the insurer. The fact that the employer has a vested interest in getting the employee back to work is a further check on unreal or exaggerated claims or on unduly prolonged disabilities.

Lower Acquisition Costs. Acquisition costs are generally much lower for group insurance than for individual insurance. An individual salesperson must be paid a substantial share of the first annual premium as compensation for the time taken in selling the policy. A group representative of the insurer and a small staff may in a week's time sell and install a plan involving thousands of dollars of annual premium. Naturally, the percentage acquisition cost will be a small fraction of the total cost of individual selling.

Exemption from Taxes and Economy in Purchase of Services. Some group plans, being nonprofit in nature, are exempt from taxes, and may obtain medical and hospital services at wholesale prices. This advantage characterizes Blue Cross, community-sponsored and industrial-sponsored group clinics, and other plans. To a lesser extent this advantage also characterizes mutual insurer organizations which pay some taxes, but at a lower level than that paid by stock insurers. Hospital associations such as Blue Cross do not compensate the individual insured for expenses, but instead purchase services directly from hospitals, often at lower cost than is obtainable by an individual patient.

Tax Advantage for Employee. The federal government, in effect, subsidizes group health insurance by granting a tax exemption to the individual employee in a group plan for the value of health insurance paid for by the employer. Since the employer often contributes half or more of the total cost, there is a substantial advantage in arranging group coverage over individual coverage.

Group Contracts Versus Individual Contracts

The contractual provisions of group insurance are in many respects similar to those of individual contracts. There are, however, certain differences which reflect the fact that the group contract is a contract between the employer and the insurer, with individual employees being third party beneficiaries, as in group life insurance. There is a master contract which spells out such matters as when the employee may be covered; who is eligible for coverage; termination of coverage; benefit schedules; and cancellation, renewal, and premium provisions.

In some respects the provisions of the group contract that affect the employee are more favorable than under individual contracts, but less flexibility is permitted. For example, the group contract, as far as the individual employee is concerned, is guaranteed renewable and noncancellable. As long as the employee remains in the group, the coverage cannot be changed unless the entire group contract is changed or abandoned. Of course, there is an element of inflexibility attached to a group contract in that provisions cannot be tailored to meet one person's exact needs. Furthermore, if the employee changes jobs, the new employer may not have a group policy. Except in unusual circumstances the employee does not have the option of converting group coverage to an individual contract, an option possible in group life insurance.[13] However, no matter how poor the state of health, the employee may continue to be protected as long as the master contract is in force and as long as this employee is a member of the group.

Another liberalization concerns the definition of disability, which is expressed in terms of whether or not the employee can perform any and every duty pertaining to his or her occupation. An employee who is too ill to report for work, is probably considered disabled. Under individual policies it must generally be shown that the employee is unable to perform a job for which the employee is reasonably fitted by training and education. The liberal definition of disability in the group contract admittedly is a result of the fact that the benefit period for income loss is not long—usually less than six months.

A third advantage of a group contract is the tendency on the part of the insurer to be more liberal in claims settlement than on individual policies. The insurer has to consider that an entire plan involving a large annual premium may be lost by a miserly claims policy. The employee thus receives the benefit of any doubt when filing a claim.

In spite of its advantages, group health insurance is not a complete solution to the problem of obtaining insurance protection against health losses. Group

[13] Blue Cross offers an individual contract, but it is not the same as the group policy coverage.

insurance does not replace individual coverage but supplements it. For example, benefit levels under group insurance are often quite limited and require supplementation from other sources. Income loss contracts in particular are usually limited to short periods and do not at all meet the problem of long-term disability. Hospitalization policies usually do not meet the entire burden, particularly if the illness is long lived or falls under one of the excluded categories, such as mental illness. If an employee falls ill and is no longer able to work, this employee and dependents must be dropped from the group and coverage for future disabilities is lost. Adequate health insurance for retired workers below age 65 (after age 65 they become eligible for Medicare under OASDHI) is not yet available on a group basis, except in isolated instances. Finally, by no means do all employers have group disability insurance, and the group contract is not available to just any group formed for the purpose of obtaining coverage.

MAJOR PROBLEMS IN HEALTH INSURANCE

While all types of insurance have their problems, perhaps no field has been subject to so much criticism and controversy as the health insurance field. Dissatisfaction with the general health of the nation has caused some to push for a general plan of compulsory health insurance similar to Great Britian's plan of socialized medicine. Among private agencies competing for health insurance business, several issues have arisen, which will be briefly analyzed as an illustration of the major problems in the field. These issues revolve around the general problem as to how best to meet, through insurance, the problem of economic loss through health failure. More specifically, the issues center on how best to provide health insurance for everyone needing it, at the lowest cost consistent with adequate coverage, and without the wastes associated with excessive moral and morale hazards.

Problem 1—Rising Costs

What can be done to prevent the existence of insurance from causing a rise in medical costs that otherwise would not take place? Over the period 1948–1973, personal expenditures for medical care have nearly doubled as a percentage of total expenditures, from 4.3% to 7.6%. There is a tendency for doctors to charge more when the ability to pay, as evidenced by insurance or income level, increases. There may also be a tendency for hospitalization costs to rise because, through insurance, the ability of patients to pay for hospital services is enlarged. This comes about because hospital associations such as Blue Cross are often controlled by the hospitals themselves. It becomes easier to incur higher costs and to pass these costs on because the insurer is in the position of determining both the costs and how much the insured shall pay. This is not to criticize doctors or hospital managements for inefficiency and conspiracy to raise medical charges, but rather to point out that there are few, if any, built-in checks to ever-rising medical costs. In a similar way, Blue Shield plans are controlled by physicians. In fields of insurance such as property, those who remedy the loss are subject to competitive pricing and differ from those organizations, the insurance companies, that pay the bills. In health insurance it is usually not feasible for the insured to shop around for the lowest cost service, nor for the insured to require bids and to accept the lowest bid for medical services.

Insurance organizations have attempted to control losses by placing limitations of recovery in their contracts and by the use of deductibles. However, this is no actual solution since the burden is only transferred to the insured and there is little hope that the insured can somehow personally reduce these bills substantially. The first step in any real progress toward solution of the problem must come through the action of physicians to agree on some system of pricing their services in a predictable manner so that their costs can be successfully met through insurance. Further progress must come through increased cooperation between insurers, insureds, hospital administrators, physicians, and others to seek methods of increasing the efficiency of group health insurance plans, and of controlling the costs of medical care, and the administrative and acquisition costs of insurance.

An important cause of rising costs of medical care is the generally inadequate supply of medical care facilities and services and a maldistribution of those facilities and services that are available. For example, many rural areas suffer from lack of doctors and hospitals, thus increasing the charges that can be levied by those facilities and services which are in short supply. Persons in rural areas may have to incur extra transportation and associated costs to reach metropolitan centers for the care they need. Still another contributor to rising costs is the increasing prevalence of malpractice suits against both doctors and hospitals. Until some way is found to control rising medical costs, it may be expected that the cost of health insurance will rise correspondingly, and in many cases, this cost will rise beyond the reach of persons who need coverage.

Problem 2—Overutilization

Closely related to the preceding problem is that of controlling the overutilization of hospital and medical services by the insured. There is an unfortunate tendency for individuals to feel that they have not received any value from their health insurance policy unless they have been ill and collected a claim from the insurer. Pressure is applied on physicians to yield to this desire. Ridiculous as such an attitude may appear to an impartial observer, it leads to the exaggeration of insurance claims and a consequent increase in premiums. Furthermore, insurers have little ability to withstand overutilization as long as physicians certify that care is needed and that there is no satisfactory substitute for it.

On the other side of this question is the fact that what may appear to be overutilization to some is certainly not so to others. A patient may have a pain that could be a symptom of a very serious condition requiring extensive medical examinations and hospitalization to diagnose. The pain could also be an indication of an entirely different and nonserious condition. Should the physician decide not to risk the patient's health and order hospitalization, or should the physician suggest that the patient wait a few days to see what happens? A physician may be charged with contributing to the problem of overutilization, or if not, with malpractice. Clearly there is no simple solution to this problem.

Problem 3—Inadequacy

How can health insurance be made generally more adequate? The provisions of health insurance contracts are somewhat restrictive because of the underwriting problems involved. A relatively small part, 25.6%, of the total medical costs are being met through insurance. While there is no doubt that insurance is not an appropriate method of paying for 100% of all medical bills, there is also no doubt that it can be expanded and that provisions can gradually be liberalized so that more illnesses can be covered, larger limits of liability can be provided, more classes of people can be made eligible for insurance, income benefit periods can be lengthened, and claims settlement can be treated less technically.

The slowness of private insurers to respond to pressures for more adequate health insurance has resulted in governmental entry into the field. The Medicare bill of 1965 provides compulsory hospital care insurance and voluntary physicians' services coverage for persons past age 65. The social security program provides relatively modest disability income coverage, and it seems likely that unless private firms make substantial progress in this area there will be expanded social security coverage in this area as well.

Problem 4—Overinsurance

Strange as it may appear following a discussion of the inadequacy of health insurance benefits, overinsurance is a problem and it is one of the causes of inadequacy of benefits.[14] Overinsurance has two forms: insuring the "first dollar" of claims instead of the "last dollar," and purchasing multiple policies in the hope of making money out of an illness or an accident. Insuring the first dollar of benefits is using insurance premiums in an uneconomical manner. This practice is especially uneconomical if small, frequent claims are likely. Funds that could be used to pay for the severe and catastrophic losses are being used to pay for the small losses which could be more economically paid by the individual. Thus, the demand for major medical policies is less than for contracts which promise to pay the entire bill and which contain no deductibles.

Purchasing multiple policies in order to profit from an illness or an accident may be done consciously or unconsciously. It may result from too much sales pressure, for example. Desire on the part of underwriters to obtain more business on the books or to introduce new insurance contracts may contribute to the lowering of underwriting standards. Advertisements stating that "this policy pays you its benefits in addition to any other insurance you may have" are

[14] William H. Wandel, "Overinsurance in Health Insurance," *Journal of Risk and Insurance* (September, 1965), p. 433.

common in the field. In some states, clauses similar to the pro rata liability clause in fire insurance contracts are not permitted in health insurance, thus making it more difficult to control the problem of overinsurance. Multiple policies result when working wives are covered both as workers and as dependents under a group plan purchased by their husbands. Multiple protection also results when a worker converts a group plan to an individual plan upon terminating connection with the group and obtains coverage in another group upon reemployment.

NATIONAL HEALTH INSURANCE PROPOSALS

Because of dissatisfaction with the way private insurance is operating, the United States Congress has been actively considering national health insurance proposals. In 1974 no less than 17 national health insurance bills were introduced in the 93rd Congress. The provisions of these bills were analyzed in an extensive report prepared by the Social Security Administration.[15] Eight of the 17 bills were classified in this report as mixed public and private.[16] Two bills were classed as mainly public,[17] two as tax credit acts,[18] and five as catastrophic protection bills.[19] Most of the bills provide for participation by private health insurers.

Mixed Public-Private Bills

An important characteristic of these bills is that they would utilize private insurance company services in carrying out their provisions. In the Mills-Schneebeli-Packwood Bill, for example, all employers would be required to provide health insurance for their employees. Coverage would be restricted to members of the labor force and their dependents. Public agencies are utilized for providing health services to certain groups, such as low income families or aged persons. Thus, the present Medicare program and certain parts of Medicaid would be continued. Financing of these bills is usually joint between employer and employee premiums, with some federal subsidies.

[15] *National Health Insurance Proposals*, DHEW Publication No. 11920 (Washington: Social Security Administration, 1974).

[16] Comprehensive Health Insurance Act of 1974 (Mills-Schneebeli-Packwood Bill, H.R. 1268 and S. 2970); National Health Care Services Reorganization and Financing Act (Ullman, H.R. 1); National Health Insurance Partnership Act of 1971 (Railsback, H.R. 2618); National Health Care Act of 1973 (Burleson, H.R. 5200); National Health Care Act of 1973 (Fuqua, H.R. 559); National Health Insurance and Health Services Improvement Act of 1973 (Javits, S. 915); National Comprehensive Health Benefits Act of 1973 (Staggers, H.R. 11345); and Health Benefits and Health Services Distribution and Education Act of 1973 (Pell-Mondale, S. 2796).

[17] Health Security Act (Griffiths-Kennedy, H.R. 22 and S. 3), National Health Insurance Act (Dingell, H.R. 33).

[18] The Health Care Insurance Act of 1973 (Fulton-Broyhill, H.R. 2222), Health Care Insurance Act of 1973 (Ashbrook, H.R. 288).

[19] National Catastrophic Illness Protection Act of 1973 (Roe-Beall, H.R. 1054 and S. 587); National Health Care Program (Saylor, H.R. 1916); Catastrophic Health Insurance and Medical Assistance Reform Act (Long-Ribicoff, S. 2513); Catastrophic Illness Insurance Act (Stanton-Long, H.R. 8380, S. 1416); and Health Rights Act of 1973 (Scott-Percy, S. 2756).

Mainly Public Bills

The two bills of this type would cover all United States residents, be financed by a tax on wages and self-employment income, and would be administered by an agency of the federal government. Benefits would be unlimited, with a few exceptions. Doctors and hospitals would be reimbursed for their services according to a schedule of reasonable costs. The Griffiths-Kennedy bill, which is supported by organized labor, would eliminate Medicare. In effect, the federal government would become the national health insurance company, taking over most of the markets now served by private insurers.

Tax Credit Bills

Two tax credit bills would utilize the services of private insurers, cover all United States residents (except those covered by Medicare) on a voluntary basis, and would grant income tax credits for premiums paid for qualified health insurance contracts. Under the Fulton-Broyhill bill, for example, these credits would range from 10% to 100% of premium, depending on the total tax liability of the consumer. Low income families would receive 100% credit; families receiving incomes above a specified amount would get no credit. A qualified policy would have to cover catastrophic illness, be guaranteed renewable, cover preexisting conditions, and cover certain dental care. A family's annual payment under deductible or coinsurance provisions would be limited to $100 annually for doctors, and an equal amount for each for hospital and dental care.

The tax credit bills, generally endorsed by the American Medical Association, would involve relatively little federal interference with the operations of private insurers or the health care delivery system. State insurance departments would continue present regulation, and private insurers would be required to participate in assigned risk pools operated at the state level under state supervision.

Catastrophic Protection Bills

The approach of these bills is to provide voluntary coverage of medical bills only when they exceed a certain level. The services of private insurers are utilized. The Long-Ribicoff bill, for example, had the following provisions: physicians' bills would be paid after a family had incurred expenses of $2,000 in a year. Expenses covered under the other private or government health plans would count toward the $2,000 expense limit. Payment would be subject to a 20% coinsurance deductible. Any hospital costs for more than 60 days confinement would be covered. A patient's total deductible cost per year could not exceed $1,000. The program would be financed by a tax on wages now subject to social security taxes. The Long-Ribicoff bill also provided for medical assistance for low income persons administered through Medicare, but provided for greater benefits. Private health insurers would voluntarily submit health insurance policies to the Department of Health, Education, and Welfare for certification. The bill specified what provisions would be necessary for certification, including the insurer's minimum benefit/premium ratio.

Future Role of Private Insurers

It seems quite possible that Congress will eventually approve some type of national health insurance. It is difficult to predict which combination of provisions contained in the four types of bills discussed above will be finally adopted. It is significant that only 2 of the 17 bills now before Congress contain provisions to exclude private insurers entirely. In view of this, it seems likely that private insurers will have a role to play in any national health insurance act. They would have the greatest role to play in tax credit and catastrophic protection bills, and they would have an important role in the mixed public-private bills.

How well private insurers cooperate and how skillfully they play any assigned role under this legislation may well dictate their future place in the health insurance market. The somewhat precarious public image of private insurers underscores this point. For example, it is significant that consumer support for national health insurance seems to be growing and confidence in private insurance for this function declining. According to surveys by Opinion Research Corporation, 66% of the people polled in 1972 (versus 56% in 1971) believed that we need a new nationwide federal health insurance program and 38% (versus 45% in 1971) favored a private company as a source for hospital and medical insurance if they had a choice between a private company or a government company.[20] Apparently, little public outcry would exist if private companies were excluded entirely from national health insurance participation. However, even if private companies were excluded from national health insurance participation, there is no reason why private insurers could not still continue as participants in some marginal areas not fully insured publicly.

SUMMARY

1. Health insurance, as a private approach to the problem of disability and loss of income through illness and accidents, has shown a more rapid rate of growth than almost any other line of insurance since World War II.
2. Measured by the expenditures, insurance against hospitalization expense is larger than any other single type of health insurance, constituting approximately 45% of all expenditures in 1973. Benefits under surgical, medical expense, and disability income insurance contracts followed in that order. Studies reveal that most families have some type of health insurance, but that only about 25% of the total health losses are paid through the medium of insurance. Chief among the reasons for this are the relative newness of coverage, the difficulty of underwriting health losses, and the high cost of medical care.
3. Contractual provisions of private health insurance contracts, both group and individual, are complex and relatively little understood. There is often a wide discrepancy between the insurance meaning and the meaning commonly attributed to insurance terms by the

[20] Hugh C. Hoffman, "The Public Challenge to American Business," in *Perspective 1974: Attitudes, Issues, The International Scene,* Proceedings of the Insurance Information Institute, January 24, 1974 (New York: Insurance Information Institute, 1974), pp. 29-30.

layperson. Assiduous reading of policy provisions is a prerequisite to an understanding of what the benefits are, the limitation of benefits, definitions of the peril and the loss, operation of deductibles, and other important matters.

4. One of the major difficulties with an individual health insurance contract, from the viewpoint of the insured, stems from the fact that the insurer generally reserves the right to reunderwrite the policy annually, to raise the premium, to eliminate coverage on certain named perils, or to cancel the contract altogether. The only sure protection against this is to purchase noncancellable and guaranteed renewable coverage, at a substantially higher premium. Until the nature of morbidity statistics improves, major advances in offering a level-premium lifetime contract in the field of health insurance, such as exists in life insurance, will likely be slow in coming.
5. Deductibles and waiting periods of various types are a necessary adjuncts to keeping the costs of health insurance within the reach of most insureds. These deductibles serve the purpose of eliminating small claims, which are costly to administer, as well as placing restrictions on large claims, which are at least partially within the control of the insured.
6. Insurers are only gradually using contractual provisions which prevent the insured from collecting more than the actual medical expenses or loss of income. Overinsurance and overutilization of health insurance benefit rights are major underwriting problems.
7. Because of several major factors, chiefly less cost and easier administration, group coverages have been very popular in the field of health insurance. Group plans in hospitalization and surgical insurance cover about 75% of all wage and salary workers.
8. One of the basic unsolved problems in the field of health insurance is how to prevent the existence of insurance from causing an uncontrollable rise in the cost of the peril against which it is directed. Until this problem and other related problems are solved, it will be difficult to accomplish such objectives as raising the level of adequacy of benefits and extending benefits to more classes of insureds.
9. Private health insurance is not likely to be replaced entirely by national health insurance, since most of the proposals which have been considered by the United States Congress so far would utilize the services of private companies. Of course, national health insurance would importantly influence private insurance by imposing various types of restrictions, including controls over coverage, benefits, and premiums.

QUESTIONS FOR REVIEW AND DISCUSSION

1. A writer stated, "Even with strict limits on the amount of insurance and strict underwriting control in general, it seems that disability benefits for life cannot be promised for two reasons." Suggest two reasons as to why the author felt that disability income benefits for life cannot be promised.
2. The following suggestions have been put forth as possible methods to control the tendency for costs under major medical insurance to rise to prohibitive levels:

   (a) Require a higher coinsurance deductible for insureds with higher income levels.

   (b) Exclude payment for costs covered under other policies or from other sources.

   (c) Require a subrogation clause.

(d) Limit psychiatric care to, say, 50 visits per year, with 50% coinsurance applying.
(e) Place an extra deductible on drugs.
State what you believe is the purpose of each of these proposals, and evaluate the probable effectiveness of each.

3. The opinion has been expressed concerning the need for longer disability income contracts, ". . . even more alarming is the assurance that 'today things are different.' For this new circle of insured persons, insurers generally dispense with medical selection and inspection reports; they leave out the average earnings clause and otherwise underwrite very much as they do cancellable risks. . . . It does not follow that a limited sickness benefit for the new clientele will be an adequate control when jobs are scarce and wages are down." Do you agree?

4. It has been said that because most workers are covered by workers' compensation and by social security for income loss, and because many private income loss contracts contain no average earnings clause, or none with exclusions for social insurance income, a potential moral hazard might still exist in this area.
(a) Explain why the conclusion follows in the statement given.
(b) Does the average earnings clause have a purpose similar to the coinsurance clause in fire insurance? Why? If not, to what fire insurance clause is it similar? Explain.

5. Of the four general classes of proposals for national health insurance, Paul favors mixed public and private, because "everyone would be covered," while Barbara believes a purely public bill would be better, for the same reason. In your opinion, who has the strongest argument? From the standpoint of private health insurance, which type of bill would be preferred? Which would be the least costly?

6. In general, individuals covered for hospital expenses recover a larger proportion of their health bills if they are hospitalized than do individuals covered for regular or major medical expenses. Basic trends also indicate that more patients are being hospitalized, but that the duration of their stay is being greatly shortened through improved postoperative treatment, early ambulation, use of antibiotic drugs, etc.
(a) With reference to policy provisions, indicate why it is more likely that a hospitalized insured would recover a larger portion of the bill than a nonhospitalized patient, assuming insurance exists for both patients.
(b) Is there any connection between the existence of insurance and the fact that more and more patients are being hospitalized? Discuss.

7. It is estimated that about 20% of the patients in a hospital are very ill and need intensive medical care, such as constant nursing, oxygen, fluids, and blood transfusions. About 60% require much less help than this, and 20% need very little help, being able to walk to a hospital restaurant to eat meals, to give themselves personal care, etc. What are the implications of these facts for the cost of health insurance?

8. A writer stated, "Overinsurance is the carrying of insurance for speculative purposes rather than for the indemnification against loss."
(a) Does this definition coincide with the explanation in the text? If so, give any qualifications you would make. If not, explain.
(b) Compare overinsurance with overutilization.

9. (a) What are the major factors accounting for the dominance of group health insurance over individual forms?

(b) Which of these factors are likely to become more important as time goes on?

10. An insured, a laborer, has a life insurance policy on which is attached a loss-of-income rider that pays $10 a month in case the insured becomes totally and permanently disabled. Because of diabetes, the insured made a claim for total disability. The physician stated that the diabetes was fairly well controlled and that the insured could do light work. The insurer refused payment. In your opinion should the insured be considered sufficiently disabled to receive benefits? Why or why not?

11. A surgeon suffered an infection in his fingers and hands and had to cease practice. The surgeon made claim for disability benefits under the health insurance provisions of his life insurance policy but was denied benefits. In the resulting trial the insurer brought evidence that the insured frequently washed automobiles, using a hose and rags, and drove the cars. Furthermore, it was shown that the insured had made no effort to enter a gainful occupation. Should disability income benefits be paid in this case? Why or why not?

12. In an application for hospitalization insurance, the insured stated no other hospital insurance, when in actuality there were a number of similar policies that provided about $44 a day if the insured should become hospitalized. The insurer, in denying a claim under the contract, stated that if the answer had been truthful, the company would not have issued its policy. A trial court held the answer to be false, but not material to the risk, since it did not contribute to the event which matured the claim, and the insurer appealed to a higher court. Decide the results of this case, with reasons.

13. *C*, an insured, has a major medical policy with a $10,000 limit, $300 deductible, and 75% coinsurance. *C* has a covered claim amounting to $14,000 plus lost wages of $7,000. The benefit clause reads: "The Company will pay benefits equal to 75% of the covered expenses in excess of the deductible amount which are incurred on behalf of a covered person as a result of an accident or sickness." *C* claims 75% of $13,700, or $10,275, but the agent states that *C* cannot recover more than 75% of $9,700, or $7,275.

(a) Who is right? Why?

(b) What does this example illustrate with regard to the possible abuse of major medical contracts? Explain.

14. A certain newspaper advertises a health insurance policy that will pay $25 a week in the event of disability for certain accidents. There is a lump-sum benefit of $1,000 in case of accidental death by certain causes. The annual premium is $1.50. What further questions would you have before purchasing this policy?

15. A certain policy is advertised as noncancellable, but when it is examined, bold type across the front states "This policy is renewable at the option of the company only." Are these two provisions inconsistent?

16. Differentiate between a waiting period and an elimination period in a health insurance policy. What purpose is served by these clauses?

17. Why, in a group health insurance contract, is there the requirement that an employee's benefit level be determined by some factor such as income level, job status, or length of service?

18. "In some respects the provisions affecting the employee in group insurance are more favorable than under individual contracts, but less flexibility is permitted." Explain this statement and give several examples.

CHAPTER *Twenty-Four*

SOCIAL INSURANCE

So far we have been concerned primarily with private approaches to the problem of economic insecurity. Public agencies also concern themselves with the problems of premature death, health loss, old-age dependency, and unemployment, the four major perils which threaten personal financial security. Public bodies use several methods to handle these problems, but this chapter will explain the insurance method.

There is an implicit assumption that the insurance institution accumulates an advance fund for payment of losses. Not all government plans to meet personal security problems meet the requirements of this assumption; the state simply meets costs as they occur out of general tax revenues. On the other hand, a state plan to finance unemployment benefits by charging each employer a premium which bears some relationship to the risk involved generally falls within the definition of social insurance. However, certain distinctions characterize social insurance as opposed to private insurance. The types of social insurance to be analyzed in this chapter include: old-age, survivors, disability, and health insurance (OASDHI), including Medicare; workers' compensation insurance; unemployment insurance; and temporary disability insurance.

SOCIAL INSURANCE DEFINED

In deciding whether or not a given plan is social insurance, it is helpful to examine the definition of social insurance offered by the Committee on Social Insurance Terminology[1] as "a device for the pooling of risks by their transfer to an organization, usually governmental, that is required by law to provide pecuniary or service benefits to or on behalf of covered persons upon the occurrence of certain predesignated losses under all of the following conditions." The definition goes on to list certain conditions such as compulsion, absence of a needs test as a condition of receiving benefits primarily

[1] Committee on Social Insurance Terminology, *Bulletin,* Commission on Insurance Terminology, American Risk and Insurance Association (May, 1965), p. 2.

out of contributions by covered persons or their employers and the involvement of government in the plan.

The Committee suggests that under its definition certain plans would not qualify as social insurance that are sometimes so considered. For example, the British National Health Service would not qualify as social insurance because it is paid for primarily by taxes on the general public and not by covered persons or their employers, and because eligibility for benefits is not based on contributions by covered persons. National Service Life Insurance and Federal Crop Insurance operated by the United States government are not plans of social insurance because, among other things, they are not compulsory.

THEORY OF SOCIAL INSURANCE

Social insurance plans tend to be introduced when a social problem exists which requires governmental action for solution and where the insurance method is deemed most appropriate as a solution. A social problem is a social condition or set of circumstances that society as a whole finds undesirable, and for which the solution is generally beyond the control of the individual. Examples are the problems of crime, poverty, unemployment, mental disease, ill health, dependency of children or aged persons, drug addiction, industrial accidents, divorce, and economic privation of a certain class, such as agricultural workers. Insurance is not an appropriate method of solution for many of these problems since the peril is not accidental, fortuitous, or predictable. In other instances insurance is perhaps feasible, but due to the catastrophic nature of the event (as in unemployment), private insurers cannot undertake the underwriting task because of lack of financial capacity. This means that if the insurance method is to be used as a solution for certain problems, governmental agencies must either administer or finance the insurance plan.

The justification for social insurance, then, lies in the fact that some insurance tasks either cannot be or are not accomplished by private insurers without assistance from a government. These tasks concern social problems which are deemed too important to ignore. The economic problems involved in social insurance are such that governmental action is necessary to solve legal difficulties, to supplement financing, to introduce compulsion, to give organization, or to supply other ingredients in a successful insurance formula.

The United States, slow to get started in the field of social insurance,[2] has developed the field rapidly since the passage of federal social security legislation in 1935. As revealed in Table 5–1, the premium income of all governmental insurers is already almost 87% of the level of the premium income from all

[2] For example, Germany passed the first modern workers' compensation statute in 1884 under the sponsorship of Bismarck. It was reviewed as a method of counteracting the growing strength of the Socialist Party in Germany. Britain followed suit in 1897. It is interesting that today in the United States many observers look upon social insurance legislation as the forerunner, not a countermeasure, to socialism. Most Western nations of the world have adopted various forms of social insurance, many of which are more complete than those in the United States.

private insurers. From another viewpoint, the importance of social insurance can be seen by the fact that in 1975 under OASDHI there were nearly 20 million retirement, nearly 4 million disability, and about 2.7 million unemployment insurance beneficiaries.[3] Approximately five out of six aged individuals are receiving benefits under OASDHI.

Table 24–1 reveals the relative growth of expenditures for social insurance and public welfare during the 84-year period ending in 1974. Several conclusions may be inferred from examination of Table 24–1. First, there has been a steady growth in the relative amounts of gross national product devoted to social insurance and welfare payments in the United States. This amount now constitutes 18% of the GNP. Although the United States cannot be termed a welfare state, there seems to be some tendency in that direction. Second, there is an apparent tendency for the method of social insurance to be preferred to other methods as a device for transferring payments from taxpayers as a whole to certain elements of the population. In 1929 social insurance accounted for only .3% of GNP, compared with 7.3% in 1974. Other items of public welfare have not shown the same relative growth.

EXPENDITURES UNDER PUBLIC PROGRAMS FOR SOCIAL WELFARE, 1890-1974

Table 24-1

Year	Total Per Capita	As a Percentage of Gross National Product				
		Total	Social Insurance	Public Aid	Health and Medical Programs	Other*
1890	—	2.4	—	.3	.1	2.0
1913	—	2.5	—	.3	.4	1.8
1929	$ 32	3.9	.3	.1	.3	3.2
1940	66	9.2	1.3	3.8	.6	3.5
1950	153	8.9	1.9	.9	.8	5.3
1960	286	10.6	3.9	.8	.9	4.9
1970	702	15.3	5.7	1.7	1.0	6.6
1974**	1126	18.0	7.3	2.5	1.0	6.9

Source: A. M. Skolnik and S. R. Dales, "Social Welfare Expenditures, Fiscal Year 1974," *Social Security Bulletin* (January, 1975), pp. 10-12.
* Includes veterans programs and education.
** Preliminary estimates.

Third, without the relative growth of social insurance programs, which provide formal ways for society to meet certain social costs, other techniques such as public aid would have been substituted. It is a tribute to the insurance device that its use is preferred. The certainty of benefits may be viewed by the majority as outweighing the costs of administration of the insurance system. Without social insurance, society would still seek to prevent or alleviate social hardships through private or public charity or through placing the burden on the

[3] *Social Security Bulletin* (May, 1975), p. 40. Latest data are published monthly.

relatives of those affected. Society has elected to bear these burdens through the more formal insurance system.

Thus, social insurance has a basic purpose of providing protection against risks which tend to be beyond the control of the individual or a group of individuals organized by a private insurance company. In an industrialized economy, such problems as old-age dependency, ill health, and unemployment are essentially beyond the power of any individual to solve. It is no longer accepted reasoning, for example, that individuals are solely to blame for their unemployment and should personally bear the entire cost. It also may be beyond the power of the individual to provide completely for old age because of the nature of the economy.

International Programs

Social insurance has been accepted throughout the world as a universally adaptable device to meet various economic and social problems particularly in industrialized societies. The following tabulation, reported by the U.S. Social Security Administration, reveals the major types of programs around the world and their growth during the past 30 years. Programs to meet the cost of work injuries are the most widely adopted and programs of unemployment insurance the least adopted. As of 1973, 127 nations reported one or more programs, the total number of which has more than doubled in the past 33 years.

	Number of Countries			Percent Increase
Type of Program	1940	1958	1973	1958/1973
Any type	57	80	127	59
Old-age, invalid and survivor	33	58	105	81
Sickness and maternity	24	59	70	19
Work injury	57	77	125	62
Unemployment	21	26	37	42
Family allowance	7	38	65	71

Source: U.S. Social Security Administration, *Social Security Throughout the World, 1973* (Washington: U.S. Government Printing Office, 1973). Percentages calculated.

Some of the highlights from the compilation gathered by the Social Security Administration report are:

1. Old-age programs are growing faster than any other type. Three general types of old-age pension programs are employed: means-tested systems, universal, and employment-related. Most countries do not have a means test. (Exceptions are Belgium, France, New Zealand, Australia, and the United Kingdom.) Under a universal system, all of the population qualify for some minimum level of benefit for old age, disability, and survivors. Usually eligibility restrictions are imposed. For example, in Sweden a universal pension of about $1,400 annually (with supplements) is paid, but Swedish citizenship and residence of at least six years

is required. By far, the most general system is an employment-related system with benefits based on earned wages, as in the United States.

2. Most systems provide for retirement between ages 60 and 65, although retirement age is as low as 50 and as high as 70 in some countries. There is considerable pressure, however, for earlier retirement ages, with seven countries reducing their retirement age in the four years prior to the current survey.
3. There is a tendency to eliminate or modify the retirement test as a requirement for drawing old-age benefits. In Eastern Europe, many pensioners continue to work and still receive a full pension. In the USSR, all jobs in less desirable areas such as Siberia or the Urals qualify for exemption from the retirement test.
4. A growing number of countries provide for automatic cost-of-living adjustment in pensions. In 14 countries adjustments are based on wage changes, 10 take consumer price changes into account, and 2 countries use both. Many countries make *ad hoc* adjustments as the need arises.
5. Most countries grant disability incomes on the same basis as old-age pensions. Some countries, such as The Netherlands, give the same disability income regardless of whether the disability is work-connected or nonoccupational. In Sweden, housewives who are incapacitated may receive cash benefits even though they were not gainfully employed at the time of their illness.
6. National health programs for sickness and maternity exist in 68 countries to provide cash benefits and medical services.
7. Programs to provide allowances to families with children have shown spectacular growth, mostly since World War II. Most of the programs continue the allowance until the child is 15 or 18 years old, but in the USSR the allowance terminates when the child reaches 5 years.
8. Most unemployment insurance programs were established prior to World War II and few have been established since that time. In general, this is attributable to the generally high level of employment in the world, and the relatively slow industrial development of newer countries. Agricultural workers are usually excluded.

Social Insurance Versus Private Insurance

An understanding of social insurance coverages can be facilitated by an appreciation of the basic differences between these and privately sponsored insurance devices.

Compulsion. Most social insurance plans are characterized by an element of compulsion. Because social insurance plans are designated to solve some social problem, it is necessary that everyone involved cooperate. Thus, if an employer qualifies under the law, this employer and all employees must be covered by workers' compensation or unemployment insurance.

Set Level of Benefits. In social insurance plans, little if any choice is usually given as to what level of benefits are provided. Thus, even if so desired, an employee cannot purchase more or less unemployment insurance than is offered under the plan. All persons covered under the plan are subject to the same benefit schedules, which may vary according to the amount of the average wage, length of service, or job status. In private insurance, of course, one may usually buy any amount of coverage desired.

Floor of Protection Concept. A basic principle of social insurance in a system of private enterprise is that it aims to provide a minimum level of economic security against perils which may interrupt income. This principle, known as the *floor of protection concept*, is not always strictly observed, but it is still a fundamental theme of most social insurance coverages in the United States. In workers' compensation insurance, for example, an injured worker is usually given complete medical care; but under most state laws less than half of the former income during the time of disability is received. Under the 1972 provisions of social security, a worker with average annual earnings of $7,800 may not receive, upon retirement, more than $331 per month, or if there is a dependent spouse, not more than $496.60 per month. The worker is expected to have made other arrangements through private insurance plans if a more adequate level of benefits than that provided under social security is needed. The purpose of social insurance plans is to give all qualified persons a certain minimum protection with the idea that more adequate protection can and should be provided through individual initiative. The incentive to help oneself, a vital element of the free-enterprise system, is thus preserved.

Subsidy Concept. All insurance devices have an element of subsidy in that the losses of the unfortunate few are shared with the fortunate many who escape loss. In social insurance it is anticipated that an insured group may not pay its own way but will be subsidized either by other insured groups or by the taxpayers generally. Thus, when retirement benefits were introduced into social security legislation, many individuals who worked only a minimum of one and one-half years were able to draw a lifetime pension which had a value far in excess of the premiums paid by them and their employers. The younger workers, of course, were subsidizing the old, and still are. Most social insurance plans have access to general tax revenues if the contributions from covered workers are inadequate.

Unpredictability of Loss. For several reasons the cost of benefits under social insurance cannot usually be predicted with great accuracy. Therefore, the cost of social insurance is unstable. For example, in a general depression unemployment may rise to unusual heights, causing tremendous outlays in unemployment benefits which may threaten the solvency of the unemployment compensation fund. Old-age benefits under social security depend on such unpredictable matters as future fertility rates in the population; the general level of employment opportunities for the aged; the proportion of widows who will elect to work rather than receive benefits at age 62; and the average wage level of the worker over the earning years.

Attaching conditions to the right to receive payments is not a feature of private insurance, as it is in social insurance. In a life insurance contract, the worker may elect to use cash values at retirement to purchase a life annuity of a definite promised amount, regardless of employment status or whether the worker meets a retirement test. In a private loss-of-income contract, a worker receives a definite benefit in the event of disability; but in workers' compensation, the benefit may depend on what the worker's average earnings were, number of dependents, or whether permission is given to bring legal action against a third party who was the cause of the loss.

One might argue that it is wrong to attach conditions upon recovery in social insurance under the theory that one should receive benefits as a matter of right. However, an insured worker has no particular inalienable right except the right given by the social insurance law under which the worker is protected. The employee's right can and probably should be conditional. To have it otherwise would mean that some would be receiving payments not really needed, and either costs would rise or others would be deprived of income which is their sole source of support. One of the basic advantages of social insurance is this very flexibility which permits those most in need to receive a greater relative share of income payments than others whose economic status is such that they do not require as much.

Contributions Required. In order to qualify as social insurance a public program should require a contribution, directly or indirectly, from the person covered or the employer or both. Thus, social insurance does not include public assistance programs wherein the needy person receives outright gifts and must generally prove the inability to personally pay for the costs involved. This does not mean that the beneficiary in social insurance must pay *all* of the costs, but the beneficiary must make some contribution or the program is not really an insurance program, but rather a form of public charity. For example, welfare payments to dependent children under the Social Security Act would not be seen as a form of social insurance, as the term is normally understood, although such payments are undoubtedly made to solve a social problem which could have been met by insurance.

Attachment to Labor Force. While it is not a necessary principle of social insurance, most social insurance plans cover only groups that are or have been attached to the labor force. Private insurance contracts, of course, are issued to individuals regardless of their employment status. The basic reason for this feature of social insurance is that nearly all governmental insurance plans are directed at those perils which interrupt income.

The requirement of attachment to the labor force has been a subject of frequent criticism by those who want a greater expansion of social insurance. Among the questions asked are: What about the family man who is unemployed but is not eligible for unemployment insurance benefits because he has not worked long enough, or has not worked in covered employment? What about the unemployed person who is injured while looking for a job and is not eligible for workers' compensation because of the existing unemployment status and hence did not receive a work-inflicted injury? These represent problem areas which so far have not been answered by social insurance, but may be handled by other means, either private or public in nature.

OLD-AGE, SURVIVORS, DISABILITY, AND HEALTH INSURANCE

The Old-Age, Survivors, Disability, and Health Insurance program (OASDHI) is the only major plan of social insurance which is federally financed and administered.[4] OASDHI is one of the basic parts of the Social Security Act originally passed in 1935. The other programs are: (1) grant-in-aid plan to states for assistance to dependent children and the poor (Medicaid), (2) grant-in-aid plan to states for services provided for maternal and child welfare, (3) grant-in-aid plan to states for administration of state unemployment compensation funds, (4) hospital and medical insurance, and (5) income for needy aged, blind, or disabled. The first two grant-in-aid plans mentioned are usually referred to as *public welfare plans,* the third, as simply the *unemployment insurance program,* the fourth as Medicare, and the fifth as Supplemental Security Income (SSI).

OASDHI Benefits

While the level and type of benefits have changed frequently under OASDHI, it is instructive to examine the main features of current benefit provisions as a basis for understanding the law itself. The following discussion is based on the Social Security Act as amended in 1974.

Retirement Benefits. The basis on which all OASDHI benefits are paid is the primary insurance amount of an insured worker. The monthly benefit, based on the worker's average monthly wage, is subject to a minimum of $93.80 and a maximum of $484.00. (The actual benefit is determined from the statutory table.) The formula used in calculating the monthly benefit gives about three times as much weight to the first $110 of average monthly wages as it does to the remaining earnings. Thus, the low-income earner is treated more favorably than the high-income earner. Table 24–2 presents illustrative monthly retirement benefits for different combinations of family groups. Increases in benefits after 1972 are tied to a cost-of-living formula.

Before one may receive a retirement benefit, it is necessary to meet a retirement test. This test is expressed in terms of income earned in any employment or from self-employment after retirement. One is permitted to earn income up to $3,000 each year and receive all benefits for the year. If earnings exceed this exempt amount, benefits are reduced. The sum of $1 in benefits is withheld for each $2 earned. However, no deductions may be imposed for months in which one neither earns over $210 in wages nor renders substantial services in self-employment. The retirement test does not apply after an individual reaches age 72.

[4] Unemployment insurance is federally financed, in part, but is state administered. Workers' compensation and temporary disability insurance are both state financed and administered plans. Health insurance for the aged is administered by private insurers under government contract.

ILLUSTRATIVE BENEFITS UNDER OASDHI — Table 24-2

Average Yearly Earnings after 1950	$923 or less	$3,000	$4,000	$5,000	$6,000	$8,000**	$10,000**
Retired worker at 65	$107.90*	$223.20	$262.60	$304.50	$344.10	$427.80	$474.00
Worker under 65 and disabled	107.90	223.20	262.60	304.50	344.10	427.80	474.00
Retired worker at 62	86.40	178.60	210.10	243.60	275.30	342.30	379.20
Wife or dependent husband at 65	54.00	111.60	131.30	152.30	172.10	213.90	237.00
Wife or dependent husband at 62	40.50	83.70	98.50	114.30	129.10	160.50	177.80
Wife under 65 and one child in her care	54.00	118.00	186.20	257.40	287.20	321.00	355.60
Widow or dependent widower at 65 (if worker never received reduced benefits)	107.90	223.20	262.60	304.50	344.10	427.80	474.00
Widow or dependent widower at 60 (if sole survivor)	77.20	159.60	187.80	217.80	246.10	305.90	339.00
Widow or dependent widower at 50 and disabled (if sole survivor)	56.80	111.70	131.40	152.40	172.20	214.00	237.10
Widow or widower caring for one child	161.90	334.80	394.00	456.80	516.20	641.80	711.00
Maximum family payment	161.90	341.20	448.80	561.90	631.30	748.70	829.50

Source: U.S. Social Security Administration.

* Effective June, 1976. Since social security rates and benefits change frequently, the Social Security Administration should be consulted if exact current rates are desired.

** Maximum earnings covered by social security were lower in past years and must be included in figuring average earnings. The average determines the payment amount. Because of this, amounts shown in the last two columns generally won't be payable until future years. The maximum retirement benefit generally payable to a worker who is 65 in 1976 is $387.30.

Disability Benefits. In 1956 Congress amended the Social Security Act to provide disability income to an insured worker who became disabled between the ages of 50 and 64. Dependents of the disabled worker became eligible for benefits in 1958. In 1960, Congress amended the act to provide for the payment of disability benefits to workers regardless of age and to their eligible dependents. The disability income is equal to the individual's primary insurance amount, and the benefits are increased if the worker has dependents. The dependents each receive one half of the primary benefit, subject to a family maximum.

In order to prove disability there must be medical evidence that the insured is unable to engage in substantial gainful activity. There is a waiting period of 5 months, and the impairment must be such that it is expected to continue at least 12 months. Thus, an illness that is disabling for a period longer than 5 months, but which is not expected to be disabling as long as twelve months, is not compensable under the law. This illustrates the fact that social insurance does not replace private insurance, but merely supplements it. A disability which is fully compensable under a commercial disability income policy may not be compensable at all under OASDHI because of a different definition of disability or a different standard of claims adjustment.

Survivors Benefits. OASDHI provides for substantial amounts of life insurance under the survivors provisions.

The value of the life insurance benefits provided under OASDHI is substantial, although it cannot be determined with certainty because of the conditional nature of these benefits. Table 24–2 shows, for example, that a widow and one child of a worker whose average annual wage was only $3,000 would be entitled to a monthly benefit of $334.80. This benefit is payable until the child is 18, and the widow is entitled to retirement benefits of $159.60 when she reaches age 60. However, if the average yearly earnings were $6,000 the benefit increases greatly. Suppose that when the husband dies the wife is age 40 with one child age 10. Their benefit would be $516.20 per month for eight years. At age 60, some 12 years later, the widow would be entitled to a widow's retirement benefit of $246.10 for life.

The survivorship and retirement benefit programs of OASDHI compete directly with programs offered by private life insurers. In 1973 OASDHI paid out about $51.4 billion in lump sum and monthly amounts to nearly 30 million persons. That year all life insurers combined paid out $20.3 billion[5] to about 3 million beneficiaries. The OASDHI program has obviously grown to the point where it overshadows the private life insurance business. It can be seen that OASDHI and private insurers together are now covering fairly adequately, at least in the aggregate, much of the need for life insurance. Together in 1973 OASDHI and private life insurers paid out about $71.7 billion to the

[5] *Life Insurance Fact Book 1974* (Washington: U.S. Government Printing Office, 1974), p. 46. Payments are made up of $8.6 billion in death benefits, $1 billion in matured endowments, $2.5 billion in annuities, $3.4 billion in surrender values, $.3 billion in disability payments, and $4.4 billion in dividends.

public, compared to $904 billion in disposable personal income—about 8% of disposable income.

Health Insurance for the Aged. Under the 1965 amendments to the Social Security Act, Congress took a far-reaching step in expanding the scope of the social insurance system in the United States. For the first time a program designed to meet the growing needs for health insurance on persons past age 65 was created. Two basic plans were created: a compulsory hospital plan and a voluntary medical plan.

Hospital Insurance. The hospital insurance plan provides the following benefits for persons age 65 and over: (1) Inpatient hospital services for a maximum of 90 days for each benefit period. The patient must bear a deductible of $124 for the first 60 days, and must pay $31 a day for each day in the hospital between the 60th and 90th day of care. (2) Extended care for a maximum of 100 days in a qualified institution. After 20 days of such care the patient will pay $15.50 a day for the remaining 80 days. (3) Posthospital home health services for as many as 100 visits after discharge from a hospital or an extended care facility. (4) An extra 60 days of hospital coverage, known as reserve days, available only once, subject to cost sharing by the patient of $62 a day. A benefit period is considered to begin when the individual enters a hospital and to end when the individual has not been an inpatient of a hospital or extended care facility for 60 consecutive days. The deductible amounts applying to the above coverages are geared to hospital costs and will be increased if hospital costs rise.

Financing of the new hospital insurance program is accomplished by contribution of employers and employees, based on annual earnings of up to $16,500, increasing periodically from .60% of earnings in 1972 to 1.45% of earnings by 1986.

Medical Insurance. The medical insurance plan covers physicians' services, home health services, and several other medical and health services in and out of medical institutions. Coverage is voluntary, with each person age 65 and over being eligible to enroll during a seven-month period, beginning three months before reaching age 65. The premium is $7.20 a month, an amount which is matched by the federal government from general funds. The plan pays 80% of the patient's medical bills above a $60 annual deductible amount. Covered expenses include office and home calls, diagnostic X-ray and laboratory tests, ambulance service, surgical dressings and splints, rental of medical equipment, and prosthetic devices. Coverage on mental or psychiatric treatment is limited to $250 or 50% of the expense in any calendar year, whichever is smaller. As of July, 1972, Medicare protection is available to persons who have been disabled (and are receiving OASDHI benefits) for 24 or more consecutive months.

Administration of the medical insurance plan is carried out by private insurers under government contract. The administering bodies are charged with determining that medical charges are reasonable.

Expenses not covered under the new plans of medical and hospital insurance for the aged include the following: routine physical checkups, eyeglasses, hearing aids, private duty nurses, custodial care, extras such as telephone or television service in a hospital room, and drugs which are not administered by a physician. It can be seen that the combination of hospital and medical insurance under the new program eliminates much of the need for private insurance on the losses due to ill health of aged persons.

Supplemental Security Income. In January, 1974, the Social Security Administration began to administer the public assistance programs, formerly operated by states, for the blind, needy, aged, or disabled persons. Under this program, called Supplementary Security Income (SSI), cash benefits are paid to eligible persons without the requirement that these benefits be earned by that person's having been attached to the labor force or paying taxes. Financing is by general revenues of the federal government. SSI appears to be a step in the direction of ultimate takeover by the federal government of public welfare programs administered by states. It may also be a forerunner of a move to finance, partially, all social security programs from general revenues as well as from payroll taxes.

To be eligible for SSI, the individual or couple must be over 65, or blind, or disabled under the same definition currently used for OASDHI recipients. An individual must also be in need, with less than $168 a month in countable income and less than $1,500 in countable resources. (A couple must have income of less than $252 a month and less than $2,250 in resources.) In determining resources, a person need not count a home, car of reasonable value, personal effects, or life insurance of $1,500 face value or less. Countable income excludes earned income of a child attending school, $20 a month of earned or unearned income, irregular or infrequent income less than specified amounts, and other given types of income, such as food stamps.

Insured Status

The benefit provisions apply only if the worker is fully insured or currently insured under the law. A worker becomes fully insured upon meeting certain tests, and once this status is reached, the worker and all dependents are entitled to certain benefits. If a deceased worker fails to meet the test of being fully insured but meets the test of being currently insured, monthly benefits may be payable to the minor children and the widow or widower for as long as the survivor is caring for the minor children.

A person becomes *fully insured* after meeting either of two tests:

1. Having worked in covered employment for 40 quarters (10 years), or
2. Subject to a minimum of six calendar quarters, the person having worked in covered employment at least one-fourth the number of calendar quarters elapsing from the starting date until the time retirement age is attained, or disability or death occurs, whichever happens first.

Generally, workers are credited with a quarter of coverage if they are paid at least $50 in any calendar quarter. (Different tests apply to self-employed persons and to agricultural laborers.) Thus, if the workers' starting date is January 1, 1967, they become fully insured under OASDHI if they work continuously in covered employment for at least one fourth of the elapsed quarters until death or retirement. Once they have worked 10 years they are fully insured no matter how much longer they work. It should be observed that being insured has nothing to do with the calculation of benefits. Insured status is simply a prerequisite to being eligible for *any* benefits.

Workers are *currently insured* if they have worked in covered employment at least six of the last 13 quarters including the quarter in which death occurs or in which they become entitled to benefits. Thus, workers could enter the covered labor market 30 years after their starting date, work for six quarters, and if death occurs, they are currently insured and have certain rights under the law.

Financing the OASDHI Program

OASDHI is financed by a tax on the employee and the employer in equal amounts. At first, an employee paid a 1% tax on the first $3,000 of annual income earned in covered employment, but this base has been gradually increased until the 1976 amendment raises it to $16,500 effective in 1977, and automatically thereafter as earnings levels rise. The tax rate on covered wages has also been raised so that by 1973 it reached 5.85% for employees and 7.9% for the self-employed. The actuarial soundness of the OASDHI program is analyzed by an Advisory Council on Social Security Financing appointed by Congress.

As noted above, under existing law future beneficiaries are scheduled to receive higher benefits based not only upon expected increases in wages, but also upon expected increases in the cost of living. Payroll taxes, however, are not expected to rise as fast as benefits because in inflationary periods, consumer prices tend to rise faster than wages. As a result, income was expected to fall short of outlays by $4 billion in 1976,[6] unless Congress acted either to levy higher revenues or to reduce benefits, or both. In 1974 the Advisory Council on Social Security stated that the program faced a serious, long-term actuarial deficit over a 75-year valuation period.

The Council recommended that increases in the cost of hospital benefits of the Medicare Program be met from general revenues instead of from payroll taxes, a recommendation not favored by President Ford.[7] The Council also recommended (a) changing the benefit formula so that future benefits would maintain a more consistent relationship to past earnings and would not be so vulnerable to changes in the economy, (b) easing the retirement test so that aged persons would have greater incentive to work without losing social security benefits, (c) changing the self-employed person's tax rate to 1.5 times the employee tax rate, (d) consideration by Congress of the wisdom of increasing the retirement age above 65, (e) extending social security to eliminate present

[6] James B. Cardwell, Commissioner of Social Security, remarks delivered at Region II Media Seminar, New York, N.Y. March 12, 1975.

[7] Statement by the President, Office of White House Press Secretary, March 7, 1975.

gaps in coverage so that 100% of the workers would be covered, (f) making certain other reforms to equalize benefits between men and women and to eliminate windfalls. The Council reiterated its support of basic financial principles of the OASDHI program, namely that the benefits be based on earnings without a needs test, that benefits be supported by a tax on covered workers and employers, and that there be universal compulsory coverage.

At the time of this writing it seems that some basic adjustment in OASDHI will be necessary to assure long-run solvency of the program. Not only will inflationary trends undermine the program, unless changes are made, but the slowing down of population growth will also cause serious long-run difficulties. This is true because as the rate of increase in population growth slackens, the ratio of aged to active workers will rise, increasing the relative tax burden on workers. Other influences raising this ratio are the increasing difficulties experienced by older workers in finding employment and the tendency to elect early retirement by many older persons. To some extent this increased burden can be eased if worker productivity rises sufficiently. According to Rejda and Shepler, however, it seems unlikely that productivity will rise sufficiently to prevent OASDHI from becoming an increasing burden on the active worker. As a result they recommend that increasing reliance be placed on general revenue financing of OASDHI, since otherwise the costs of the program will tend increasingly to fall on the working poor.[8] As noted above, however, there is some resistance to general revenue financing. It seems likely that in spite of how these conflicts are resolved, Congress will act to keep the program in actuarial balance.

This standard of actuarial solvency is of course not the same as that for a private life insurance company, which must have on hand at all times reserves to meet all future obligations even if future premium payments are entirely cut off. The OASDHI trust funds are intended to meet only short-term contingencies, not all future promised pensions. The Advisory Council concluded that it would be inappropriate to require a full reserve by private pension standards, since the social insurance plan can reasonably be expected to continue indefinitely. Furthermore, if Congress wishes to change benefits or if future fluctuations in employment reduced or increased collections, the plan would be in continual trouble under full-reserve methods because the reserve would constantly tend to be either too large or too small.

It may now be seen why OASDHI appears to be such a bargain as compared with private pensions. The premium for the private pension must be large enough to permit the insurer to accumulate a full reserve. The private insurer must pay the pension under definite contractual agreements and must collect a given premium. In social insurance neither of these variables is fixed. The income of the social insurer may increase or decrease, and not all workers will be paid a pension even if they have contributed all of their lives. For example, a worker may have paid taxes during the working years and die at age 64 with no dependents. This worker is paid little or nothing under OASDHI, with personal

[8] George E. Rejda and Richard J. Shepler, "The Impact of Zero Population Growth on the OASDHI Program," *Journal of Risk and Insurance,* Vol. 40, No. 3 (September, 1973), p. 313.

contributions and those of the employer going to the benefit of others. The surviving widow may remarry, thus cutting off social insurance benefits. A retired worker may continue to work part-time, failing to meet the retirement test, therefore losing all benefits, even though taxes have been paid throughout a lifetime. Because of these and other factors, the promised benefits under OASDHI appear large in relation to private plans. However, as noted, there are good reasons why this is true, and it is not because the plan is actuarially unsound, unless one wants to argue about the definition of actuarial unsoundness. Rather, the above result follows from the basic nature of a social insurance plan under which individual benefits are not necessarily closely related to the amount of individual premiums paid.

WORKERS' COMPENSATION INSURANCE

Workers' compensation was the first type of social insurance legislation adopted in the United States. It is the only type of social insurance underwritten primarily by commercial insurers with only very general supervision by state governmental units. It is also unique since in a few states it is not strictly compulsory. Furthermore, the standard workers' compensation policy combines two types of insurance in one—employers' common-law liability and workers' disability benefits for injured employees who suffer on-the-job injuries or occupational diseases. Thus, workers' compensation insurance represents a merging of private and social insurance.

The social problem which gave rise to workers' compensation was that of uncompensated victims of industrial accidents. In the latter half of the 1880's, it became evident that the system of employers' common-law liability for injuries to workers resulted in many hardships. First, the development of mass-production techniques and the accompanying factory system increased the number of job injuries to significant levels. Second, an injured employee seeking redress had no alternative except to sue the employer for damages at common law for presumed employer negligence. Third, such suits, if they were successful at all, resulted in awards which were inadequate and long delayed.

Structural Changes in Compensation

The first workers' compensation legislation attempting to embody the principle of liability without fault was declared unconstitutional on the grounds that it was wrong and inconsistent with the common law that anyone, employers included, could be held liable for something for which they were not to blame.[9] These constitutional objections were finally overcome, but as a result of the uncertainty which they brought, about half the states enacted compensation laws which were elective to the employer. Since 1965 most of these states have

[9] For example, see *Ives* v. *South Buffalo Railway Co.*, 201 NY2 71 (1911), in which New York's first workers' compensation law was held unconstitutional as a deprivation of liberty and property without due process of law. Maryland is credited with the first law, passed in 1902, which was declared unconstitutional two years later.

made their laws compulsory. Even in the few states where workers' compensation is not compulsory, an employer who rejects coverage may lose the common-law defenses, a factor which makes it somewhat easier for a successful employee lawsuit. This gives the employer a strong incentive to purchase coverage. In the remaining states, employee suits are generally prohibited (except under certain conditions).[10] The employee is expected to take as the sole remedy the benefits provided under a schedule embodied in the law. However, increasingly the injured employee is bringing legal action anyway, thus weakening the original idea of workers' compensation that litigation was unsatisfactory as a device to provide a remedy in these cases. For example, in California it is estimated that about 7% of all claims for benefits are litigated; litigation increased more than 20% in 1974 alone.[11]

Because of various weaknesses observed in workers' compensation, a commission, The National Commission on State Workmen's Compensation Laws, was created under the authority of the Occupational Safety and Health Act of 1970 to determine the extent to which state laws provided adequate, prompt, and equitable compensation to injured workers. About 40 studies were commissioned which were published in three volumes.[12] The Commission made a final report with many recommendations for change. In general the studies raised doubts about the effectiveness of workers' compensation as it operated in the United States at the time the studies were made. Since the studies were published and the 1972 final report of the Commission rendered, state legislatures have passed numerous reforms to comply with some 19 "essential" recommendations of the Commission. These recommendations included objectives calling for (a) full coverage for medical care and rehabilitation, (b) adequate income replacement, (c) coverage of all workers, (d) cost-of-living adjustments, and (e) improved data systems.

Examples of some of the changes made so far are cited below. Between 1965 and 1972, 6 states made coverage compulsory; between 1972 and 1974, 6 more states followed suit, making a total of 48 jurisdictions with compulsory workers' compensation coverage. Some 19 states reduced the number of employees permitted for an employer to be exempt from compulsory workers' compensation; 13 states eliminated numerical exemptions entirely, increasing the number of states with no exemptions to 37. About 12 states added farm workers to those required to be covered by workers' compensation, increasing the number of states covering agricultural labor to 27.[13] In 1974 alone, 42 states increased benefit levels, so that the maximum weekly benefit equals or exceeds

[10] An example of when an employee can sue an employer who is covered under workers' compensation arises when the employer injures an employee, when an employer fails to pay the compensation insurance premiums, or when an employer violates certain provisions of the compensation statute.

[11] *Litigation in Workers' Compensation, A Report to the Industry* (San Francisco, California: California Workmen's Compensation Institute, 1975), p. 2.

[12] National Commission of State Workmen's Compensation Laws, *Vol. I, Principles of Workmen's Compensation; Vol. II, Income Maintenance Objective; Vol. III, The Safety Objective* (Washington: U.S. Government Printing Office, 1973).

[13] A. M. Skolnik and D. N. Price, "Workmen's Compensation Under Scrutiny," *Social Security Bulletin,* October, 1974.

two thirds of the average weekly wage for temporary total disability cases in 33 states, and equals 100% in 9 states.[14]

Insurance Methods

There are three methods by which an employer can provide the coverage required by law for employees:

1. Purchase a workers' compensation and employers' liability policy from a private commercial insurer.
2. Purchase insurance through a state fund or a federal agency set up for this purpose.
3. Self-insure.

All states require selection of one of these methods by employers subject to the law.

Private Insurance. The standard workers' compensation and employers' liability policy has two major insuring agreements. These are: (1) Coverage A to pay all claims required under the workers' compensation law in the state where the injury occurred, including occupational disease benefits, penalties assessable to the employer under the law, and other obligations, and (2) Coverage B to defend all employee suits against the employer and pay any judgments resulting from these suits. Coverage B is separate and distinct from Coverage A. While it is not anticipated that there will be many employee suits, such claims are surprisingly frequent because methods are constantly being found to bring an action against the employer in spite of the intention of the statutes to discourage such suits. Under Coverage B there is a basic limit of liability per accident of $25,000, an amount which may be increased by appropriate endorsement. Coverage B is similar to that given in general liability policies. There is no specific limitation for Coverage A; any limits are outlined by the state compensation law.

While the private insurance method involves a contract between the employer and the insurer, the insurer deals directly with the employee and is primarily responsible to the employee for benefits. Thus, even if the employer goes out of business, the injured employee's security is not jeopardized. Private insurers paid out about 54% of all workers' compensation benefits in 1972.

State Funds and Federal Agencies. In 12 states[15] an employer has the choice of using a private insurer or a state fund as the insurer of workers' compensation. In six states[16] the employer does not have this choice, but must insure in

[14] *Analysis of Workmen's Compensation Laws, 1975 Ed.*, (Chamber of Commerce of the U.S., 1975), p. 4.

[15] Arizona, California, Colorado, Idaho, Maryland, Michigan, Montana, New York, Oklahoma, Oregon, Pennsylvania, and Utah.

[16] Nevada, North Dakota, Ohio, Washington, West Virginia, and Wyoming. In Nevada, Oregon, and West Virginia, the laws are elective so that under certain conditions the employer may purchase voluntary compensation from a private insurer, the employer may not insure, or the employer may purchase employers' liability insurance for protection against possible employee suits.

an exclusive state fund, or, in two of the states, may self-insure. Five of the compulsory state funds were established during the period 1913–1915 when compensation laws were new and the success of private insurers in handling the business was uncertain. Most of the Canadian provinces established exclusive state funds. Oregon had an exclusive state fund until 1966 when the law of the state was amended to permit self-insurance and private insurance as alternatives to the state fund.

In addition to state funds, federal agencies provide for workers' compensation coverage. For example, the federal Longshoremen's and Harbor Workers Compensation Act provides for coverage for certain classes of dock and maritime workers. In 1969 the federal government created an agency to provide coverage for coal miners afflicted with black lung disease. Since 1908 the federal government has operated a workers' compensation system for its civilian employees. It also operates a system for all employees in Washington, D.C.

State funds and federal programs of workers' compensation disbursed about 34% of all workers' compensation in 1972.

Self-Insurance. In most states, under specified conditions an employer is permitted to self-insure the workers' compensation coverage.[17] Self-insurance is generally not permitted in Canada. Self-insurers must generally be large concerns with adequate diversification of risks in order to qualify under the law. Self-insurers disbursed about 12.4% of all compensation benefits in 1972.

Evaluation of Insurance Methods. Data from the Social Security Administration covering the period 1939–1972 reveal the following trends in total losses paid under each of the insuring methods above.[18] Losses paid by private insurers increased from 52% to 54% of the total; losses paid by state and federal funds increased from 29% to 34% of the total; and losses paid by qualified self-insurers decreased from 19% to 12.4% of the total. Most of the increase in the share paid by state funds and federal agencies was accounted for by the addition of black lung benefits by the federal government. Actually, the share of private insurers increased from 52% to about 63% over the period 1939–1969 and would have remained at approximately 63% in 1972 had it not been for the increased payments under the black lung program. It seems clear that private insurers are still preferred by most employers in states where they are permitted to operate. Some of the major reasons for this appear to be:

1. Private insurers offer the employer an opportunity to insure in one contract all the liability likely for damages arising out of work-connected injuries, whether these damages stem from employee suits, statutory benefit requirements, or other sources.
2. Private insurers offer more certainty in handling out-of-state risks. Most compensation laws are extraterritorial and there are many complexities to consider in making sure of coverage if the employer has widespread interests. Most state funds do not automatically cover such risks.

[17] Self-insurers must usually post bond.

[18] A. M. Skolnik and D. N. Price, "Another Look at Workmen's Compensation," *Social Security Bulletin* (October, 1970), pp. 3-25.

3. While the expenses of state funds, at least exclusive state funds, are somewhat lower than those of private insurers, this difference is not so great as rough comparisons often lead one to believe. After adjustment for differences in the quantity and the quality of services rendered, many would argue that the supposed cost advantage of exclusive state funds is of insufficient size to warrant giving up the convenience and certainty involved in the private contract, including the ready availability of agents who provide services not usually supplied by the state fund.
4. Self-insurance has the handicap that it is necessary for the insured to enter into the insurance business, which is essentially unrelated to the insured's main operations. Contributions to a self-insurance fund are not generally tax deductible, a factor which may add materially to the cost and risk involved in self-insurance.
5. Experience rating and retrospective rate plans enable the large firm to use a private insurer's facilities in transferring as much of or as little of the risk as is desired, at a very modest cost.

Major Features of State Laws

The provisions of workers' compensation laws are subject to constant change, but a pattern exists even though details of the provisions may vary with each meeting of the state legislature.[19] Those features necessary for general understanding of the coverage provided by these laws are described in the following paragraphs.

Employment Covered. One of the shortcomings of compensation laws is that they still do not cover all workers. For example, domestic labor and often farm labor and public employees are excluded. Employers with just a few employees are excluded even under compulsory laws, and under elective laws there is no guarantee that the employee will be covered. It is estimated that as a result of various exclusions, only about 85% of all workers are covered.[20] One result of this unfortunate condition is that liability suits are necessary if an excluded worker is to recover anything, even though a basic purpose of compensation legislation was to eliminate this condition as a prerequisite for employee recoveries. It is the small employer who is excluded from compensation laws and who is most likely to be the object of such suits. This smallness often could mean that either (1) a successful suit will bankrupt the employer, or (2) if the employer is more or less judgment-proof, the injured worker will recover nothing.

Income Provisions. Compensation laws recognize four types of disability for which income benefits may be paid. These are permanent and temporary total disability, and permanent and temporary partial disability. The laws generally limit payments by specifying the maximum duration of benefits and the maximum weekly and aggregate amounts payable.

For permanent total disability benefits, about half the states permit lifetime payments to the injured worker who is unable to perform the duties of any

[19] The Chamber of Commerce of the United States prepares annually an *Analysis of Workmen's Compensation Laws* outlining the details of the law in each state.

[20] A. M. Skolnik and D. N. Price, *op. cit.*, p. 5.

suitable occupation. In the remaining states a typical limitation is between 400 and 500 weeks of payments, and there is also usually a limitation on the aggregate amount payable, ranging from $21,000 in Mississippi to $50,000 in Kansas. There is a common limitation that income benefits cannot exceed about two thirds of the worker's average weekly wage or some dollar amount. A few states make extra allowances for dependents. Because average weekly wages have risen faster than legislative adjustments, the limiting factor is usually the dollar maximum, and it is estimated that workers' compensation typically restores less than one half of a worker's wage. For example, in 1973 a single worker with three weeks of disability received on the average only 45.6% of wages, up from 37.3% in 1961.[21] Before cash benefits begin, there is a waiting period of between 2 and 7 days, most commonly 7 days. Only a few jurisdictions provide for automatic adjustments in benefits without special statutory changes.

Weekly benefits for temporary total disability are usually the same as for permanent total disability, except that often there is a lower maximum aggregate limitation and a lower time duration for such payments.

In addition to income benefits, most workers' compensation laws specify that lump sums may be paid to a worker as *liquidating damages* for a disability, such as the loss of a leg or an eye, that is permanent but which does not totally incapacitate the worker. The worker may usually draw income benefits during the time that the permanent partial disability prevents the worker from doing anything, and then the worker may receive a lump sum which varies with the seriousness of the injury. There is little consistency among the states on the size of permanent partial disability benefits. For example, indemnity for loss of a hand ranges from $5,250 in Massachusetts, to $126,692 under the Federal Employees Compensation Act. Indemnity for loss of the first finger in Wyoming is $400, but $8,550 in Pennsylvania. A worker would receive more for the loss of a thumb in the District of Columbia ($23,400) than for the loss of an arm at the shoulder in nearby Virginia ($18,200). Furthermore, the laws give no recognition to the relative seriousness of the injury. For example, the loss of an eye to one worker might not prevent returning to the old job as before, but would force another worker into a totally different job at lower pay. Yet, each worker would receive the same settlement. The only solution, if any, to the gross inconsistencies in permanent partial benefit schedules seems to be the adoption of a uniform national scale of benefits by all states.

Survivor Benefits. In case of fatal injuries, the widow or widower and children of the worker are entitled to funeral and income benefits, subject to various limitations. About 40% of the states place a maximum duration of between 300 and 500 weeks on income payments. The remaining states do not specify time limitations. The maximum benefits to the widow or widower alone are generally less than they would have been to the disabled worker, but if the survivor has children, these benefits are comparable to what the worker would have received for permanent total disability.

[21] *Ibid.*, p. 13.

Medical Benefits. Most workers' compensation laws provide relatively complete medical services to an injured worker, including allowances for certain occupational diseases. In 49 jurisdictions there is unlimited medical care for accidental work injuries, and broad coverage on occupational disease is provided, with only three states (Louisiana, Oklahoma, and Wyoming) retaining a schedule of covered diseases. About 40% of the states have some type of limitation on medical benefits for occupational diseases, expressed as a time or dollar limitation or both, and 60% have no statutory limitations on medical benefits. Most states which have medical limitations, however, provide that extensions in time or amount may be granted where circumstances warrant.

Rehabilitation. Benefits for rehabilitation, both physical and occupational, are provided by most states, but it is generally recognized that the quantity and quality of these services are subject to wide variation. Some states still provide no automatic rehabilitation benefits. For example, Georgia and Maryland provide for vocational rehabilitation, but no physical rehabilitation, which is apparently considered a part of the worker's medical benefits. Absence of or restrictions on maintenance benefits during rehabilitation are especially common. The general area of rehabilitation of the injured worker is one which needs much closer attention than it has received in the past. Examples of the potential saving in medical costs, community aid, and in the resultant lowering of compensation premiums made possible through rehabilitation demonstrate that from an economic standpoint alone, the effort is extremely worthwhile. For example, a study in New York of 40 patients who were referred to a community rehabilitation service showed that the state fund saved an average of $4,250 in compensation costs per case.[22]

Costs. In 1972 the cost as a percentage of payroll averaged 1.12%, compared to .96% in 1962 and .89% in 1959.[23] Thus, the relative costs are rising but are still relatively modest overall. Except in a few states, employees are exempt from sharing workers' compensation premiums. For individual employers the premium ranges widely, depending on the hazards attached to the line of business. The rate for clerical help, for example, may be .1% of payroll, and that for metal bridge painters, 24.5%. The rate also varies by geographical area. Then, too, costs depend on the type of insurer chosen, type of rating plan used, and other factors. For example, expense ratios of stock insurers average 30%; mutuals, 25%; and state funds, 13%. These ratios are adjusted for differences in services provided by the respective insurers.[24] In 1972 total medical and hospital benefits in the United States were $1.2 billion and total income benefits were $2.8 billion, for a total of $4 billion, or about .35% of gross national product in that year, up from .26% of GNP in 1962.[25]

[22] W. Scott Allan, *Rehabilitation, A Community Challenge* (New York: John Wiley & Sons, Inc., 1958), p. 169. This book presents an excellent critique of nationwide rehabilitation efforts.

[23] A. M. Skolnik and D. N. Price, *op. cit.*, p. 20.

[24] *Ibid.*

[25] *Ibid.*

THE UNEMPLOYMENT PROBLEM AND INSURANCE

The problem of unemployment is perhaps the most serious single economic problem faced by modern industrial societies under the free-enterprise system. The economic reasons for unemployment in a capitalistic society and the proposed solutions have occupied the attention of economists for many centuries. In the United States a typical peacetime year finds from 3% to 5% of the civilian labor force unemployed, and during depression years this figure is often much higher, reaching nearly 25% in 1933. In 1974–75 unemployment began to rise above 5%, reaching 8.7% by March, 1975, when nearly 8 million persons were out of work.[26] The problem is considered so serious that, in the Full Employment Act of 1946, Congress expressed its intention to do whatever possible to prevent unemployment.

Unemployment insurance is designed to alleviate certain types of unemployment, but not all unemployment. Unemployment problems are more serious for some industries, occupations, and age and racial groups than for others, but unemployment insurance makes no distinction between them. In keeping with the basic purpose of a social coverage, unemployment insurance tends to offer only a floor of protection for everyone, leaving the remaining areas of coverage to be handled by private solutions. To do otherwise might tend to reduce initiative, to remove incentive for personal saving, to cause unwarranted work stoppages, to discourage efforts on the part of private industry to stabilize employment, and to have other undesirable economic side effects.

Employment Covered

The unemployment insurance laws of all states, conforming to minimum federal requirements, cover firms employing four or more workers. Twenty-one state laws cover employers with one or more workers. Most states also specify that the worker must have been with the employer for some minimum period, often 20 weeks, before the employer must pay a tax on the worker's wages. The laws do not cover all types of employments. Among employments usually excluded are railroad workers (covered under a separate federal law), agricultural labor, domestic service in private homes or in fraternity and sorority houses, service rendered by a child under 21 for a parent, employees of nonprofit organizations, state and local government employees (although many states provide some form of coverage for their own workers), commissioned agents, maritime workers, and self-employed persons. In most states, employers may elect, on a voluntary basis, coverage of services which are excluded from the definition of employment under their laws. The effect of these exclusions and other limitations is that about two thirds of the total unemployment is insured.[27] For example, in February, 1975, about 5.1 million

[26] *Monthly Labor Review* (May, 1975), pp. 84-99.

[27] See current issues of *Labor Market and Employment Security* for up-to-date data on insured employment.

persons were drawing unemployment insurance, which represented about 64% of those unemployed.[28]

Benefits

The various states have developed somewhat complicated and diverse formulas for defining the benefits under their unemployment insurance acts. There is general agreement on the main features, but it is necessary to examine the law of a particular state to determine the rights of an insured worker.

In most states the worker must have worked for some minimum period during a base year, as defined, or have earned some minimum amount of wages, such as $400, or both. Most states also require some waiting period, usually one week of total or partial unemployment, before benefit payments begin. The amount of benefit is some fraction of the wages earned during the base year or during some part of the base year. The base year is usually defined as the year preceding the date that claim is filed, with some lag ranging from a week to six months. Once a claim is filed and the weekly income payments begin, a benefit year commences and payments typically continue for a period not to exceed 26 weeks. However, a few states have extended this period to as many as 39 weeks, and benefits beyond these limits have been authorized under federal legislation. The benefit formula is so arranged that if a worker has been fully employed during the base period, the worker may, subject to a minimum and maximum amount, expect to receive benefits equal to about one half of the normal wage. In many states the worker may receive up to two thirds of the average weekly covered wage within the state.

The worker will receive nothing if there were no earnings during the base year. If the worker was employed only part-time or earned very little, the benefits are reduced accordingly, subject to a minimum weekly amount ranging from $5 in Hawaii to $25 in California, but averaging about $10 or $15 per week. As of 1973, the maximum weekly benefits ranged from $55 to $138, with a typical figure lying between $60 and $70 per week. In a number of states the amount of the benefit is enlarged if the worker has dependents. State laws usually permit some unemployment benefits if the worker is not totally unemployed but is able to earn something, say through odd jobs, which is less than the worker's usual wage. In most states the amount of the benefit is the regular benefit less actual earnings or other payments. If actual earnings are less than some allowances, say one half or one third of the weekly benefit, there is no reduction in payment. These provisions reduce the temptation for a worker to cease all attempts at earning something for fear of losing the unemployment check. In some states, workers' compensation benefits disqualify the worker.

Eligibility Requirements

In order to receive benefits, unemployed workers must usually demonstrate not only that they are unemployed but also that they are actively seeking work,

[28] *Ibid.*

that they are able and willing to work, that they are not out of work because they voluntarily quit their jobs without good cause or were discharged for misconduct, and that they have not refused suitable work nor are disqualified for other causes. The enforcement of these conditions is different in each state, not only because of legal provisions but because the administrative agency may choose to enforce them differently.

Ability to Work. All states require that a claimant be able to work if work is offered. Except in a few states, physical illness would therefore cause a worker to be ineligible for benefits. A worker can usually satisfy the ability-to-work requirement by registering for work at a public employment office. Six jurisdictions have enacted special legislation to care for workers who are unemployed and unable to work because of physical disability. About half the states deny benefits to pregnant women, although there is a tendency for the number of these states to decline.

Eleven states have added a provision in their laws that illness or disability will not disqualify an unemployed worker for benefits under the ability-to-work requirements if this disability is the only reason for refusing to accept a job which is offered.

Available for Work. While each state law specifies that the worker must be available (and in most states, actively looking) for work if offered as a condition for drawing benefits, the enforcement of these provisions varies widely. In seven states the law says that the worker need only be available for suitable or usual work or work for which the applicant is reasonably fitted by training or experience. In other states it is suspected that administrative officials enforce the available-for-work provisions with some latitude. Often the law may make an exception of certain types of workers; thus, in Connecticut and New Hampshire, workers are not required to be available for work between the hours of one a.m. and six a.m.; in Alaska a worker does not lose a benefit check when hunting or fishing for survival (and hence not available), providing no suitable work is offered.

Disqualification. The unemployment insurance laws of all states have provisions under which a worker may be disqualified for benefits. Having been disqualified, the worker loses the benefit for some specified number of weeks (often three to eight weeks), for the duration of the unemployment, or suffers a reduction in benefit, depending on the nature of disqualification. Certain penalties may or may not be attached to leaving work voluntarily without good cause (as determined in each jurisdiction); different penalties may be attached for being discharged for minor misconduct or gross misconduct.

Major reasons for disqualification are voluntarily quitting a job without good cause; discharge for misconduct connected with the work; refusal, without good cause, to apply for or accept suitable work; and unemployment due to a labor dispute. If a worker leaves a job for good cause, such as illness or accepting a better job, there may not be disqualification. Usually, (but not in all states) disqualification is terminated by subsequent bona fide employment. Thus, if a worker quits a job without good cause, takes another job, and then is laid off from this second job, benefits may usually be drawn based on the employment with the first employer as well as with the second employer. In most states the definition of good cause is general, permitting a worker to leave a job for personal as well as employment-related reasons.

Refusing suitable work is another major reason for disqualification from unemployment insurance benefits. Suitability is defined either by specific provision in the law or by administrative rulings. If a worker refuses a job offer because the wages, hours, or other conditions of work are substantially less favorable than those prevailing for similar work in the locality, there would be no general disqualification. There is an increasing tendency to view fringe benefits as a condition which should be considered in the definition of suitable work.[29] Other factors considered are distance from the worker's home; the worker's experience and training; the extent of hazards in the new job affecting the claimant's health, safety, and morals; and restraining activity engaged in by the claimant.

Under certain conditions in many states, workers unemployed because of a labor dispute with their employer are disqualified for benefits. A labor dispute is defined under the laws in different ways. Nine states, for example, exclude lockouts from these provisions on the grounds that a worker should not be denied benefits because the employer refused to permit the workers to enter the premises. A few states do not deny benefits to workers who are unemployed because a labor dispute has closed a plant when the dispute does not involve them directly. There are similar escape clauses which permit benefits to be paid to certain classes of workers during strikes.

Claimants are disqualified for fraudulent misrepresentations in order to obtain benefits and, furthermore, must repay the amounts paid to them as a result of such misrepresentations. Usually the recipient is allowed to make restitution in cash or have the overpayments offset against future benefits. Only four states (California, Minnesota, Tennessee, and Virginia) provide punishment under criminal statutes for this offense.

Supplemental Unemployment Benefits (SUB). A supplemental unemployment benefit plan is a system under which a worker may receive an income during layoffs in addition to unemployment insurance benefits. SUB is financed by the employer through a trust fund. The question has arisen as to whether the worker is really unemployed when receiving income from an employer indirectly through this SUB trust fund. All jurisdictions except New Hampshire, New Mexico, South Carolina, South Dakota, and Puerto Rico have taken action on this question; and in all cases except Virginia the worker is permitted to receive SUB in addition to unemployment insurance.

Financing

All states receive grants from the federal government to administer unemployment insurance systems. Federal law provides that the state law must

[29] Mark R. Greene, *The Role of Employee Benefit Structures in Manufacturing Industry* (Eugene, Oregon: University of Oregon, 1964), Chapter 6.

meet certain requirements to receive this grant or to receive what is called a tax offset. The tax offset is 90% of the federal tax. A federal tax of 3.2% is levied on payrolls up to $4,200, but employers receive up to a 2.7% credit against this tax to the extent they pay the states under the existing state law. All tax collections must be deposited with the United States Treasury. Each state has an account and may borrow additional sums to pay benefits, if needed.

Several states have a maximum rate, ranging up to 8.5% (Texas). Furthermore, in several states the amount of the annual wage taxable is greater than $4,200. Due to experience rating, however, which can operate to reduce the tax to an employer who meets given conditions (including having three years' experience or more), the actual tax rate applicable to a typical employer is much lower than 3.2%. It averaged 1.8% of taxable wages in 1971. In Alabama, Alaska, and New Jersey, employees must also pay a tax.

Data are kept on the reserve fund ratio for each employer—i.e., the ratio of funds in each employer's account to the total amount of benefits paid to the workers of this employer. Generally, if the aggregate reserve fund ratio is less than 1.5 times the highest ratio since 1958, it is considered inadequate. In 1973, 31 states had inadequate reserves by this test. Three states had to borrow from the Federal Unemployment Trust Fund to pay benefits. As a result, several states have taken steps to increase their reserves, such as increasing the maximum tax and enlarging the taxable payroll base.[30]

Criticisms of Unemployment Insurance

How well does unemployment insurance work? Labor groups criticize it because of the tight administrative standards which, they claim, are unduly restrictive. Management groups complain that the taxes are too high, benefits are too loosely administered, and financing is unstable. While no attempt will be made to resolve the various issues raised by these criticisms, a listing of the major arguments surrounding the operation of the unemployment compensation system may be helpful in pointing out the main areas which deserve further study.[31]

1. A realistic set of objectives, priorities, and goals for unemployment insurance has never really been established. For example, is unemployment insurance supposed to cover only those who are permanently attached to the labor force? Is it supposed to cover longer-term unemployment? (and how long is longer-term?) What should disqualify a worker for benefits? Until some guiding philosophy is agreed upon, it seems doubtful that unemployment insurance can ever satisfy its critics.
2. As of November, 1974, the average weekly payment under unemployment insurance was $65.49. It is doubtful if these benefits representing the proportion of wage

[30] Joseph A. Hickey, "State Unemployment Insurance Changes in 1974," *Monthly Labor Review* (January, 1975), p. 39.

[31] There have been many studies of unemployment compensation systems, both on a state and a national level. See William Haber and M. G. Murray, *Unemployment Insurance in the American Economy* (Homewood, Ill.: Richard D. Irwin, 1966), and George E. Rejda, "Unemployment Insurance as an Automatic Stabilizer," *Journal of Risk and Insurance* (June, 1966), pp. 195-208.

restoration that the original framers of the legislation had in mind, since an average payment of $65 represented only about 40% of average weekly wages of $158.

3. It has been urged that unemployment insurance could afford to pay larger benefits if eligibility standards were tightened. Currently, individuals who are secondary wage earners and are not really permanently attached to the labor force (temporary workers such as seasonal help and students) may draw benefits even though they may not actually wish to obtain another job. At the same time many groups of workers permanently attached to the labor force are not covered.
4. Because of the operation of minimum and maximum benefits, higher-paid workers are undercompensated and lower-paid workers may be overcompensated during their unemployment. It has been urged that a system of expressing benefits as a proportion of previous wages be instituted.[32]
5. The experience rating system is subject to many criticisms.
6. Many inequities arise because the worker is treated differently in each state, even though the conditions preceding unemployment may have been identical. It has been suggested that a federal program would help to eliminate many of these difficulties and, in addition, would help equalize the tax burden among states. Under present conditions, employers in states with unstable employment due to the nature of their industry are penalized in relation to competing employers in other states.
7. In most unemployment insurance laws no provision is made for a worker who is unemployed because of physical disability. Such a worker is not able or available to work and is therefore usually disqualified. The worker generally has no disability protection under OASDHI unless the disability is expected to last longer than one year. Unless the disability was caused by accident, the worker receives nothing under workers' compensation.
8. An inordinate number of unemployed workers exhaust their benefits and presumably are still unable to find work by the time they receive their last unemployment insurance check. Certainly it can be argued that some program to handle the longer-term unemployment (longer than six months) is needed, whether it be through extended benefits in unemployment insurance programs or through separate programs to deal with the peculiar problems of the long-term unemployed.[33]
9. It has been claimed that unemployment benefits fail to stabilize income during recessions and recoveries, and employer taxes are actually destabilizing because they increase during recessions and are reduced during recoveries. In an extensive study, George E. Rejda showed, however, that unemployment benefits have reacted quickly to downswings. During three out of four post-World War II downswings, 24% to 28% of the decline in national income was offset by an increase in unemployment benefits. Benefits were relatively ineffective as offsets to rising incomes during upswings, however, due chiefly to high unemployment levels that prevailed after each downswing in the period under study. Employer taxes tended actually to increase during prosperities and to decline during recessions, and thus were behaving desirably in a contracyclical manner.[34] Therefore, it cannot be concluded that unemployment insurance exerts an undesirable effect in destabilizing the business cycle—unemployment insurance has demonstrated its effectiveness in offsetting increases and decreases in national income during the cycle.

[32] William Papier, "What's Wrong with Unemployment Insurance?," *Journal of Risk and Insurance* (March, 1970), pp. 65-74.

[33] Haber and Murray, *op. cit.*, Chapters 12-13.

[34] Rejda, *op. cit.*, p. 208.

TEMPORARY DISABILITY LAWS

Temporary disability laws, sometimes called nonoccupational disability laws, grew out of the fact that unemployment compensation statutes usually deny benefits to employees who are not able and available for work; in other words, the statutes cover only healthy unemployed persons. Ten states[35] amended their unemployment insurance laws so that unemployed workers would not be denied benefits simply because they became disabled. Five states and Puerto Rico went further than this and passed separate temporary disability laws under which employees could draw income benefits if they became disabled, regardless of whether they were employed or unemployed at the time their disabilities began. Railroad workers also have a program. In California, Puerto Rico, and Rhode Island there is one program of benefits to workers without regard to whether they are employed, unemployed, or in noncovered employment when their disability begins. In Hawaii, New Jersey, and New York, there are two separate systems of benefits, one for persons who become disabled during their employment or shortly thereafter, and another for those who become disabled while unemployed. Provisions in the six jurisdictions attempt to restrict benefits to those who have had some permanent attachment to the labor force in the past.

Temporary disability laws provide for benefits regardless of whether the disability is caused by illness or accident. Since workers' compensation is intended to cover most job-connected injuries and occupational illnesses, temporary disability laws may be properly described as essentially *nonoccupational*; although, in a strict sense of the word, this distinction is not always made. In Rhode Island, for example, a worker may receive both workers' compensation and temporary disability benefits under certain conditions, not to exceed 85% of weekly wages or $58 per week, whichever is smaller.

In all jurisdictions except New York, temporary disability laws were generally patterned after unemployment laws and provide very similar benefits. The laws are administered by the employment security agency. The financing of the laws in these states comes from employee contributions that were formerly made to unemployment insurance funds.

In New York, it was felt that payment of disability income was more logically a function of the state's workers' compensation board, which was more experienced in the problems of disability insurance than an employment security agency. Furthermore, in New York, separate financing was necessary since employees made no contribution to unemployment insurance. In New York a state fund was established to operate on a fully competitive basis with private insurers. In California, New Jersey, and Puerto Rico employers are automatically covered by a state fund unless they elect private coverage which has met the standards established under the law. Approved self-insurance is also permitted in these jurisdictions. In Rhode Island, however, all employers must cover their workers in an exclusive state fund.

[35] Alaska, Delaware, Hawaii, Idaho, Maryland, Massachusetts, Montana, Nevada, Tennessee, and Vermont.

To be eligible for benefits, a worker must generally show inability to perform regular or customary work because of physical or mental disability. Disabilities due to pregnancy and intentional self-inflicted injuries are limited or excluded. However, two states and the railroad program provide maternity benefits. The employee's contribution is generally considered the main source of financing, although the employer contributes to some extent. A claimant must have been attached to the labor force at one time or another, earning some minimum amount of wages, in order to qualify. The amount of the benefit is low, conforming to the floor of protection concept, and the duration is limited generally to 26 weeks. In general, if a worker is disqualified for unemployment benefits, there will also be disqualification for disability benefits. The benefit formulas are similar to those for unemployment insurance, except in New York. The laws are all compulsory except that individuals who depend on prayer or spiritual means for healing may elect out of the coverage.

In conclusion, it appears that temporary disability legislation is aimed at a real need, one which may be filled by either public or private insurance methods. Unlike unemployment insurance, however, there seems to be no real reason why private insurers could not handle this particular need without assistance since the peril is fully insurable and there are no insurmountable administrative problems. The growth of private insurance plans has probably been a factor in the failure of any further successful action by states to follow the example of those states which have adopted temporary disability laws. It is also likely that extensive discussion of these laws in many state legislatures has stimulated private insurers to promote appropriate disability income policies. In 1973 over 60 million persons (two thirds of the labor force) in the United States enjoyed short-term disability protection.[36]

SUMMARY

1. Social insurance, which is defined to include all insurance plans operated by or financed by governmental agencies, is to be distinguished from public assistance plans under which governments make gratuitous payments to individuals in need who have no resources of their own. The chief types of social insurance are: (a) old-age, survivors, and disability insurance and Medicare; (b) workers' compensation insurance; (c) unemployment insurance and (d) temporary disability insurance.

2. Social insurance is generally introduced when it is impossible or impractical for private insurers to solve a social problem which lends itself to solution by the insurance method. Social insurance in the United States has grown from a negligible amount in 1935, when the Social Security Act was passed, to a point where, in 1974, expenditures equalled about 7.3% of gross national product. Trends suggest that the insurance method is gaining fast as the preferred way to meet social problems that cause an interruption of income.

[36] *Source Book of Health Insurance Data 1974-1975* (New York: Health Insurance Institute, 1975), p. 20.

3. The basic distinctions between social and private insurance are that social insurance, in contrast to private contracts: (a) is compulsory, (b) does not allow individual choice in selecting the amount of benefit, (c) provides only a minimum level of benefit, (d) is subsidized by groups other than the insured group, (e) has a total cost which is basically unpredictable, and (f) covers only individuals who have been attached to the labor force and meet certain minimum requirements.
4. Measured by benefit payments, OASDHI and public retirement plans are three times as large as unemployment insurance, and about seven times as large as workers' compensation and temporary disability insurance combined. OASDHI, which is operated by the federal government, provides three basic types of income payments to qualified beneficiaries: (a) retirement income to the worker and dependents, (b) income to dependents in case of the worker's death, and (c) income to the worker and dependents in case of permanent disability. The size of these benefits depends on the amount of earnings and the length of time the worker has contributed taxes.
5. In common with all plans of social insurance, OASDHI benefits are conditional on many factors. One of the basic reasons why the size of the promised pension can be so large in relation to the total taxes paid is that a certain proportion of those who pay taxes will not qualify for benefits. For example, many persons will not actually retire, and thus will not collect pensions. Many will die with no dependents, and their contributions will be made available to others.
6. In 1956, disability benefits were introduced under OASDHI. Even though at present they are a relatively small part of the total benefits, they represent the first attempt to meet the problem of long-term disability through social insurance and will undoubtedly become more important as time goes on and as qualification standards for benefits are liberalized.
7. The oldest example of social insurance in the United States is workers' compensation insurance. It is the only type of social insurance in which private insurers, under governmental requirements, underwrite a major share of the total volume.
8. The basic purposes of workers' compensation insurance is to replace the negligence system as a method of meeting the costs of occupational injuries. All states now have workers' compensation laws, under which benefits include lifetime payments if necessary for permanent disabilities, income benefits for dependents, death benefits, lump-sum benefits for permanent partial disabilities, and medical and rehabilitation benefits.
9. Unemployment insurance was designed to relieve only certain types of losses, namely those arising from short-term, involuntary unemployment. Long-term, voluntary unemployment is not covered. Unemployment insurance, administered by the states, had its origin in 1935 with passage of the Social Security Act. All states have these acts, which must meet certain minimum federal standards.
10. Benefits under unemployment insurance depend on the amount of wages an employee is able to accumulate during a given base period. Benefits generally may not continue longer than six months and may restore up to one half of the worker's wages during the benefit period. The worker must be able to and available for work at all times. Refusing suitable work, as defined, is a cause for stopping the payments.
11. Among the weaknesses of unemployment insurance is the fact

that under most laws a worker who is physically unable to return to work cannot qualify for unemployment benefits because of the inability to accept employment. To overcome this weakness, six jurisdictions have passed temporary disability laws under which a worker may draw benefits if generally qualified for unemployment benefits had there been no disability, regardless of whether it was an accident or sickness which caused the disability and regardless of whether this disability was suffered on or off the job.

QUESTIONS FOR REVIEW AND DISCUSSION

1. (a) Distinguish between social welfare plans and social insurance plans.
(b) Which, if either, of these types of plans is inclusive of the other?

2. If a social problem is subject to solution by the insurance method, why have not private insurers supplied the insurance facilities to meet certain problems? In other words, why has it been necessary for governmental insurers?

3. What evidence (see Table 24–1) do you find for the position that (a) welfare expenditures are increasing at an alarming rate and should be curtailed, and (b) welfare expenditures, particularly social insurance expenditures, are not an unreasonable burden and could be expanded?

4. It has been said that there is a double subsidy in social insurance plans. Explain.

5. In your opinion, has the floor of protection principle in social insurance been violated? Explain.

6. It has been argued that it is not fair for some workers to receive OASDHI benefits and for others who have paid in an equal amount of taxes to be denied benefits because they failed to meet the requirement test. Rather, it is claimed, all workers should be paid as a matter of right. Analyze this argument and state what results would follow if the situation were "corrected."

7. Those who have urged the adoption of socialized medicine point out that a system of national compulsory health insurance would not provide coverage for everyone needing it, but would meet only some part of the need for coverage. Referring to the basic differences between social insurance and private insurance outlined in the text, draw a conclusion as to the correctness or incorrectness of this position.

8. Suppose Congress passed a law which said that the OASDHI trust fund should be increased immediately to meet the standards of actuarial solvency required of a private insurer. Assess the economic implications of such a law for the coming year.

9. Suppose Levy dies while he is fully insured under OASDHI and leaves a widow with six children under 18. The family is entitled to maximum family benefits each month.
(a) How much will the family receive and how long will they receive this benefit?
(b) What conditions could reduce or stop the benefits?

10. Calhoun has retired at age 65 under OASDHI, but he becomes restless after one year and opens a real estate office. Prior to the time he opened this office, he and his wife were receiving $150 each month from OASDHI. He operated this business for seven months, but it was unsuccessful. Although he devoted full time to the business, he made only one sale, clearing $500 in the fourth month. The next year Calhoun rented a resort property and operated it for three months during the summer, earning $3,000. The rest of that year he did nothing. How many social security pension checks did Calhoun lose (a) during the year he engaged in the real estate business? (b) during the year he operated the resort? Explain why in each case. (c) Is the OASDHI retirement test fair? Discuss.

11. Life insurance agents sometimes object that their sales are hampered by the fact that individuals feel their life insurance needs are fully cared for by OASDHI. Do you think this fear has any justification? Discuss.

12. How is it determined under OASDHI whether or not a worker is considered as having been attached to the labor force to an extent sufficient to entitle the worker to coverage? Explain.

13. In what respects is workers' compensation insurance unique as a type of social insurance?

14. (a) Why is the loss of the common-law defenses a strong stimulus for the employer to purchase workers' compensation insurance?
(b) Does this loss mean that any employee lawsuit is practically certain to be successful? Why?

15. What basic types of protection are offered under Medicare?

16. Offer at least one reason for the fact that one plan under Medicare is compulsory and the other is voluntary. Why should not both plans be compulsory if Medicare is to be classified as social insurance?

17. What exclusions are there in Medicare? Should any of these be eliminated? Why?

18. In a certain year, published ratios of expenses to premiums earned in workers' compensation insurance for nonparticipating stock and mutual insurers were about 31% and 25%, respectively. During the same period the comparable figure for 18 state funds was about 13%.
(a) Suggest explanations for the substantial differences noted.
(b) Is it likely that most of the difference is a result of greater efficiency of one type of insurer?
(c) Are some insurers performing needless and unwanted services? Explain.

19. In a recent year workers' compensation costs amounted to 1.12% of payrolls, while unemployment insurance costs were about .8% of total payroll (1.8% of covered payroll). Hilda Lamas argues that since unemployment is a more serious social problem than the problem of industrial injuries, employers should be paying more for unemployment insurance than for workers' compensation insurance. Do you agree? Why or why not?

20. Assume that the disability period for an average case of temporary total disability resulting from occupational injury is 18 days. It can be seen that because of a one-week waiting period under a typical workers' compensation law, a worker might collect only $75 in income benefits for a disability, assuming the collection of a typical maximum benefit. Estimate what proportion of an average worker's wage loss is restored.

21. An employer in a state with an exclusive workers' compensation fund elects not to come under the state law. The law prohibits purchase of private workers' compensation insurance and the employer does not wish to assume the risk. What alternatives, if any, to insuring in the state fund are available?

22. Why is unemployment insurance generally considered too perilous to write for a private insurer?

23. One of the dangers of unemployment insurance is that it will fail to provide incentives for the employee to return to work. What measures have been taken to combat this tendency?

24. Technically, unemployment insurance is financed by a federal tax of 3.2% on certain payrolls. Yet, state unemployment insurance laws are passed and state agencies administer them. How is the operation of state laws financed?

CHAPTER *Twenty-Five*

GOVERNMENT REGULATION AND COMPETITION IN INSURANCE

Government has commonly laid down rules governing the conduct of business, and insurance is no exception. In the case of insurance, however, special attention has been given by the government, which has actively engaged itself in the business directly. The insurance industry has been challenged and stimulated by the government to do a better job. Some of the reasons for this will be clarified in this chapter.

WHY INSURANCE IS REGULATED

There are characteristics of insurance which set it apart from tangible-goods industries and which account for the special interest in government regulation. First, insurance is a commodity which people pay for in advance and whose benefits are reaped in the future, sometimes in the far distant future, often by someone entirely different from the insured and who is not present to protect self-interest when the contract is made. Second, insurance is effected by a complex agreement which few laypeople understand and by which the initiating party could achieve a great and unfair advantage if disposed to do so. Third, insurance costs are unknown at the time the premium is agreed upon, and there exists a temptation for unregulated insurers to charge too little or too much. Charging too little results, in the long run, in removing the very security which the insured thought was being purchased, and charging too much results in unwarranted profits to the insurer. Finally, insurance is regulated to control abuses in the business.

Future Performance

The insurer is, in effect, the manager of policyholders' funds. The management of other people's money, particularly when it has grown to be one of the largest industries in the nation, immediately suggests itself as a likely candidate for regulation because of the temptation for the unscrupulous to use these funds for their own ends instead of for the ends of those to whom the funds belong. The fact that one party to the contract (the insurer) receives payment currently but the ultimate performance is contingent upon the occurrence of some event which may not happen for many years raises the question of how the insured can obtain a guarantee that the insurer's performance will be forthcoming, and how justice can be obtained in case of failure by the insurer.

Complexity

We have learned that the insurance contract is not particularly simple. There are many instances in which even if the layperson understands the implications of every legal clause in a contract, the rights of the person are vitally affected by the operation of certain legal principles or industry customs to which no reference exists in the written contract. The legal battles which have been fought over the interpretation of the contractual wording of a policy bear testimony to the proposition that misunderstandings can arise over the meaning of provisions even after the best legal minds have attempted to make the intent of the insurer clear. If misunderstandings can arise when they are unintended, it is easy to see that in the absence of any restraint, an insurer would find no difficulty in framing a contract which looks appealing on the surface but under which it is possible for the insurer to avoid any payment at all. (See Chapter 9 for a discussion of the insurance contract.)

Unknown Costs

The price which the insurer must charge for service must be set far in advance of the actual performance of this service. The cost of this service depends on many unknown factors, such as the random fluctuations in loss frequency and unexpected changes in the cost of repairing property. In order to increase business, an insurer may consciously or unconsciously underestimate future costs in order to justify a lower premium and thus attract customers. If the insurer refuses to accept business except at a very high premium, consciously or unconsciously overestimating future costs, those who pay may be overcharged, and those who cannot pay will go without a vital service. Inability to obtain insurance may even prevent potential insureds from engaging in business because of inability to obtain credit or offer surety. Some outside control over pricing in insurance is desirable for both insured and insurer.

Abuses

As in any line of business, abuses of power and violations of public trust occur in insurance. These include failure by the insurer to live up to contract provisions, drawing up contracts which are misleading and which seem to offer benefits which they really do not cover, refusal to pay legitimate claims, improper investments of policyholders' funds, false advertising, and many others.

Some insurance departments maintain offices to handle customer complaints against insurers and their agents and to effect settlements of disputes without formal legal or court actions. In a case in Maryland,[1] an insurer was fined $50,000 for having engaged in a general plan to compel insurance claimants either to accept less than the amounts due them under their policies or to sue the insurer. Most insureds do not find it practical to sue under insurance contracts unless the sums involved are relatively large. In this case the defendant insurer's instructions to its claim adjustors prohibited them from using the customary practice of settling an automobile damage claim as a result of a conference between a repair shop and the insurer's appraiser. Instead, the appraiser would lower the estimate presented by the insured by 10% or 15% and send a check for the reduced amount without explanation. The insured could either accept the reduced amount, attempt to find a garage which would accept the reduced amount, or bring legal action against the insurer.

Abuses in insurance have been such that major investigations of the insurance business have taken place, many of which resulted in reform legislation which currently is reflected in the regulatory environment. For example, in 1906 the Armstrong investigation in New York uncovered many abuses in life insurance and resulted in the mutualization of many stock insurers. An investigation of health insurance in 1910 in New York resulted in the adoption of uniform standard health insurance provisions. The Meritt Committee Investigation in New York in 1910 resulted in outlawing combinations to fix rates in insurance and in antirebating laws. In 1939 the Temporary National Economic Committee investigated insurance and uncovered abuses in industrial insurance, but the occurrence of World War II interrupted any significant reform legislation that might have resulted. The Federal Trade Commission investigated false advertising practices in insurance after 1950, resulting in reforms in the field of mail order health insurance business. The United States Senate Committee on the Judiciary has continued to investigate practices in insurance since 1958 and has been critical of state regulation of the business. Finally, a massive investigation into auto insurance sponsored by the U.S. Department of Transportation in 1970 resulted in pressure on states to pass reforms in the field of automobile insurance establishing the no-fault principle in about half the states. (See Chapter 16.)

THE LEGAL BACKGROUND OF REGULATION

Insurance traditionally has been regulated by the states. In each state there is an insurance department and an insurance commissioner or superintendent who has several specific duties. This was not always so. Prior to 1850, insurance was operated as a private business with no more regulation than any other business enterprise. There was a lack of any financial guarantee that losses would be paid when due; little control was exercised over the investment of funds collected as premiums; and, in general, the doctrine of *caveat emptor* was the rule.

[1] *Maryland Insurance Commissioner* v. *Liberty Mutual Insurance Company,* Hearing 804. Closed January 8, 1975.

As a result of the early abuses of insurance, with their resulting ill effects on the consuming public and upon the insurers alike, the need for regulation became apparent. Although many states by 1850 had passed statutes affecting insurance, no state established special enforcement agencies until 1850, when New Hampshire appointed an insurance commissioner. Massachusetts, California, Connecticut, Indiana, Missouri, New York, and Vermont followed this example shortly afterward, and by 1871 nearly all states had some type of control or supervision.

In 1868 an important United States Supreme Court decision, *Paul* v. *Virginia*,[2] established the right of states to regulate insurance by holding that insurance was *not commerce,* but was in the nature of a personal contract between two local parties. Since insurance was held not to be commerce, the federal government would have no direct regulatory power through its right to govern interstate commerce as given under the commerce clause of the Constitution. This decision was upheld repeatedly until reversed in 1944 by the famous decision, the *South-Eastern Underwriters Association* case.[3]

In 1871, three years after the *Paul* v. *Virginia* decision, an organization which has had far-reaching effect on regulation was formed. This organization, later named the National Association of Insurance Commissioners, was a group of state insurance commissioners through whose efforts a considerable measure of uniformity in regulation has been achieved. One of its first tasks was to introduce some uniformity into regulations governing the type of reports which insurance companies were required to make. Another task was to agree on a system of exchange of information as to the solvency of insurers, so that an insurer did not have to prove solvency to the satisfaction of each state in which it operated. Still another job was to agree on uniform systems for valuation of legal reserves of life insurers.

The *South-Eastern Underwriters Association (S.E.U.A.)* case overturned by a vote of four to three the *Paul* v. *Virginia* ruling that insurance was not commerce. The court held that insurance was commerce and that when conducted across state lines, it was interstate commerce. The impact of this decision was to make insurance subject to federal regulation, and, of course, to all federal laws regulating trade practices in interstate commerce. Laws which were to apply included the Sherman Act, the Clayton Act, the Federal Trade Commission Act, and the Robinson-Patman Act, dealing with the control of business activities in restraint of trade, particularly price-fixing, unfair trade practices, false advertising, and the like. The *S.E.U.A.* case overruled many Supreme Court decisions that exempted the insurance industry and caused great uncertainty as to the future status of regulation.

THE McCARRAN-FERGUSON ACT

The S.E.U.A. decision made it clear that some insurance associations had influence extending considerably beyond that of cooperative rate-making.

[2] 8 Wall. 168, 183 (1868).
[3] 322 U.S. 533.

Certainly it was not the intent of state regulatory laws that boycotts and coercion should be a result of permission to form cooperative rates. Yet, the complete abandonment of state regulation of insurance in favor of federal regulation was not desired by either the insurance industry or state insurance commissioners. Accordingly, the National Association of Insurance Commissioners proposed a bill which later became known as the McCarran-Ferguson Act. This bill, also known as Public Law 15, became law on March 9, 1945. It declared that:

1. It was the intent of Congress that state regulation of insurance should continue, and that no state law relating to insurance should be affected by any federal law unless such law is directed specifically at the business of insurance.
2. The Sherman Act, Clayton Act, Robinson-Patman Act, and the Federal Trade Commission Act, shall, after a three-year delay, be fully applicable to insurance but only "to the extent that the individual states do not regulate insurance."
3. That part of the Sherman Act relating to boycotts, coercion, and intimidation shall henceforth remain fully applicable to insurance.

Except to the extent indicated by the provisions of the McCarran-Ferguson Act, the insurance business continues to be regulated by the states. However, the law does not exempt the insurance business from federal regulation and in fact provides for a limited applicability of certain federal laws to insurance. For example, a recent decision indicates the intent of the Federal Trade Commission (FTC) to limit conglomerate mergers of insurers.[4] The Clayton Act of 1914 prohibits mergers where the effect may be to substantially lessen competition or tend to create a monopoly. In 1972 the FTC claimed jurisdiction in the case of the American Insurance Company acquisition in 1969 of the Fidelity and Deposit Company of Maryland. Both Maryland and Texas had approved the merger, but the FTC claimed that federal jurisdiction holds when the effect of a merger may be national in scope and may lessen competition. Regardless of the outcome of this case, which is still undecided, it seems clear that federal regulation of insurance activity is a continuing force.[5]

Following the passage of the McCarran-Ferguson Act, the National Association of Insurance Commissioners formed a model bill which was designed to accomplish at the state level what the Sherman, Clayton, FTC, and Robinson-Patman Acts accomplish as applied to business generally. This model bill (known as the All-Industry Rating Bill), which was adopted in whole or in part by most states, contained many recommendations. In general, the philosophy of the legislation emerging from these recommendations is that rate-making cooperation is *neither required nor prohibited*, except to the extent necessary to meet the general requirement that rates be adequate, not excessive, and nondiscriminatory. Machinery is provided whereby an insurer may file a lower or "deviated" rate upon showing that the rate meets these requirements. Membership in a rate-making organization is not required.

[4] Roland W. Johnson, "Section of the Clayton Act as a Tool to Curtail Conglomerate Acquisitions of Insurance Companies," *Washington Law Review,* Vol. 46 (May, 1971), pp. 497-539.

[5] David Kamerschen, "Are Conglomerate Insurance Mergers *Sui Generis*?" *Journal of Risk and Insurance,* Vol. 41, No. 3 (September, 1974), p. 481. See also the *Wall Street Journal,* Midwest Ed. (December 14, 1972), p. 3 for a summary of the FTC case.

In summary, the regulatory philosophy has undergone great swings, starting with one which encouraged unrestricted competition (before 1910), especially in rate-making, to one which discouraged any competition in rate-making (1910-1944), and back toward the direction of encouraging more competition (1944 to date). It remains to be seen how far the present trend will continue before it turns back, if ever.

FEDERAL VERSUS STATE REGULATION

For many years the argument as to whether or not federal regulation would be superior to the present system of state regulation of the insurance industry has been of considerable concern to parties both within and without the insurance business. Federal regulation is a continuing possibility since the *S.E.U.A.* case opened the door, a door which was not entirely closed by the McCarran-Ferguson Act. The chief arguments for federal regulation, many of which amount to criticisms of state control, are:

1. State regulation is not uniform and in spite of certain accomplishments toward this end by the National Association of Insurance Commissioners is not likely to become so. Insurers are subjected to different requirements in each state, a result which is expensive and raises the cost of insurance more than need be.
2. State regulation is relatively ineffective. It is not a suitable mechanism to regulate or control the activities of an insurer which is nationwide in its operation. If a given state prohibits a certain activity as being dangerous or unlawful, this of course does not affect the operation in another state, and so the objectionable practice continues elsewhere. If the particular practice is really dangerous, its continuation may affect the insurer's operation in the particular state, even though the practice is not carried on in that state.

   This complaint gave rise in the state of New York to a law known as the Appleton Rule, whereby an insurer admitted to do business in New York must adhere to New York's requirements not only in New York, but in *all other states* where the insurer is doing business.[6] Thus, if New York prohibits an insurer from issuing a certain type of policy in that state, the insurer, as a condition of continued operation there, would have to forego its right to issue the policy in any other state where it is doing business. The Appleton Rule had the effect of greatly extending the influence of New York's insurance underwriting requirements in other states because of the great size of the insurance market and the desire of insurers to operate there. However, many insurers do not operate in New York and are not subject to the Appleton Rule.
3. Federal regulation would be more effective and less costly for insurers than state regulation. Many ill-advised statutes have been enacted by various states which presumably would be avoided under federal control because of the greater political insulation from local pressures enjoyed by national legislators. Federal legislators are full-time representatives, whereas state legislators usually work only part-time. Federal legislators would therefore, it is argued, have more time to devote to the specialized problems of the insurance industry and could give them more thorough attention. The result should be a higher quality of administration and regulation.

[6] The Appleton Rule has been upheld by the courts. See *Firemen's Insurance Co. of Newark, N. J.* v. *Beha*, 30 F.2d 539 (1928).

Opposing these arguments are those who favor continued state regulation. In general, state insurance commissioners and representatives of the insurance industry, particularly those representatives engaged in the marketing of insurance, are opposed to federal regulation. The major arguments in favor of state regulation are:

1. State supervision and regulation of insurance is reasonably satisfactory and there is therefore no overpowering reason why federal regulation should be necessary. The burden of proof that a change is necessary should fall upon those who seek the change, and such proof is yet to be forthcoming.
2. Most of the arguments of those who favor federal control rest upon dubious claims of inefficiency and upon unproved claims that federal control would necessarily be more efficient. There is reason to believe that federal control would actually be less efficient because of isolation from local conditions and inability to deal with these problems from afar.
3. While lack of uniformity is admitted, the really important needs for uniformity have been achieved, or are being achieved through the voluntary cooperation of state insurance commissioners.
4. State regulation is much more flexible than federal regulation would be. State regulation can relate to local needs. It can encourage experimentation and development in insurance procedures and contracts.
5. Those who favor continued state regulation point out that if federal regulation were imposed, the result might be two systems of regulation instead of one. The operations of a very large number of insurance companies are confined entirely within the boundaries of a single state. Presumably the states would continue to regulate these activities as intrastate commerce. Hence, state insurance departments would have to continue their existence and the federal system would be superimposed on a state system, which would result in more wasteful overlapping, confusion, and duplication than now exist.

We will probably continue to have some type of federal influence on state regulation, but outright federal control is unlikely, at least in the foreseeable future. Increasing federal influence in insurance will likely be felt by direct government competition in insurance. This competition has already been established in the field of life insurance for many years, and to a lesser extent, in the field of property insurance through crop, crime, and flood insurance and Fair Access to Insurance Requirements (FAIR) plans.

RESPONSIBILITIES OF THE STATE INSURANCE DEPARTMENT

We can classify the responsibilities of the state insurance department in four categories:

1. Enforcement of minimum standards of financial solvency.
2. Regulation of rates and expenses.
3. Control of business-acquisition practices.
4. Control over contractual provisions and their effect on the consumer.

Financial Solvency

It is the primary responsibility of the insurance department to see that insurers operating within the boundaries of the state are financially responsible. In order to accomplish this task, the insurance commissioner enforces the state's laws regarding the admission of an insurer to do business, the formation of new insurers, and the liquidation of insurers who become insolvent. The commissioner must see that adequate reserves are maintained for each line of insurance written and that the investments of the insurer are sound and comply with the state requirements.

Minimum Capital. To do business in a state an insurer must first be *licensed.* Licenses are granted according to the type of insurance business to be conducted. Different capital standards are applied to each type. Minimum financial standards are set forth in each state and they vary considerably from state to state and by type of insurer. The minimum capital and surplus standards for New York, as an example, are set forth in Table 25–1.

Table 25–1 shows that for some types of insurance greater financial requirements exist than for others. Thus, while only $100,000 of capital must be provided to write boiler and machinery insurance, three times this amount is necessary to write personal injury liability insurance. The reason for this difference lies, of course, in the much greater exposure to loss for liability insurers than for boiler and machinery insurers. In many states no distinction is made in capital requirements according to the type of insurance written, but a blanket amount is required for insurers writing any of a long list of contracts. No consistent pattern seems to emerge as to financial standards among the different states regarding the financial requirements for life insurance in relation to property-liability insurance, or in minimum dollar levels.

There is evidence that minimum legal capital requirements for some types of insurers have not been set at adequate levels. The turnover among insurers has been substantial. One of the important reasons for termination of an insurer is financial difficulties which might well have been avoided with greater financial resources. For example, one of the important reasons for termination of a new young life insurer is lack of adequate capital to meet heavy initial expenses and to write new insurance.[7]

Investments. The assets of an insurer may not be invested in just any type of securities . If no regulation were imposed on the investment of assets, it is clear that there would be little point in requiring the existence of so much capital as a condition of doing business. Accordingly, all states impose investment limitations. In general, the philosophy behind these limitations is to require that funds which have been paid in as an advance payment of premiums be invested conservatively in bonds, mortgages, and other fixed-income securities. The objective is to maintain safety and to give sufficient liquidity to enable insurers to pay claims when due, if necessary, by selling assets. Often the law will

[7] E. J. Leverett, Jr., "Paid-in Surplus and Capital Requirements of a New Life Insurance Company," *Journal of Risk and Insurance,* Vol. 38, No. 1 (March, 1971), p. 27.

EXAMPLES OF MINIMUM CAPITAL AND SURPLUS REQUIREMENTS FOR STOCK AND MUTUAL INSURERS IN NEW YORK

Table 25-1

Kind of Business	Stock Insurers		Mutual Insurers	
	Capital	Surplus	Initial Surplus	Minimum Surplus
Life	$ 500,000	$250,000	$ 150,000	$100,000
Annuities			50,000	50,000
Accident and health				
Excluding noncancellable	100,000		150,000	100,000
Including noncancellable	150,000		200,000	150,000
Boiler and machinery	100,000		150,000	100,000
Burglary and theft	200,000		50,000	100,000
Personal injury liability	300,000		250,000	200,000
Fire	250,000		150,000	100,000
Ocean marine	250,000		500,000	250,000
Multiple-line				
On acquisition of multiple-line powers	1,800,000	900,000	1,925,000	
To be maintained	1,800,000		1,575,000	

Source: *McKinney's Consolidated Laws of New York*, Vol. 27, 1966. In addition, a $250,000 deposit must be made with the Superintendent of Insurance.

Note: These requirements apply to each type of insurance separately. If an insurer writes more than one type, it must possess the capital requirements indicated for each type. Thus, a multiple-line insurer, writing fire, marine, and casualty line, organized since 1940, must possess total capital and surplus of $3,550,000. Slightly lower requirements exist for insurers organized prior to 1940.

specify that each bond or mortgage meet certain minimum standards of asset protection, interest coverage, etc. The law also specifies the manner in which each asset is to be valued; bonds are valued on an amortized basis and stocks at cost or market, whichever is lower.

Furthermore, certain types of assets are not recognized or admitted for purposes of state regulation. Nonadmitted assets typically include office furniture, overdue balances from agents, and other assets not normally subject to liquidation for meeting obligations due policyholders.

Liquidation. The insurance commissioner is charged with the responsibility of liquidating an insolvent insurer. When this happens, an equitable treatment of policyholders and other creditors is essential. Some types of insurers subject their policyholders to additional assessments in the event of financial inability to pay claims, and the insurance commissioner must see that these obligations are paid.

Security Deposits. Most states require that each insurer licensed to do business within state boundaries make a deposit of securities with the insurance commissioner to guarantee that policyholders will be paid claims due them. These laws have been unpopular for several reasons. The size of the deposit is generally too small in proportion to the volume of business carried on to be of any real protection to the insured. The state should logically depend upon the quality of its examinations and other procedures to see that the insurer is solvent. The size of the deposit required generally bears little or no relationship to the size of required amounts of capital and surplus or reserves. It is common for one state to waive the requirements for insurers operating within its boundaries if other states do likewise for insurers chartered in that state. Thus, the security deposits may give little added protection to policyholders while complicating insurance regulation.

There has been some recent evidence that states may begin to tighten up on security deposit requirements for insurers. In Illinois, for example, a bill was passed in 1971 requiring that the security deposit be equal to 50% of the gross written premium for the preceding year, less return premiums, subject to a maximum of $10 million.

Regulation of Rates and Expenses

The insurance department is responsible for regulating the rates and expenses of insurance companies. If inadequate rates are charged, insolvency becomes a threat. If excessive or discriminatory rates are allowed, the insurance department must handle public complaints.

Business Acquisition Practices

The agent has been a dominant figure in the insurance industry almost from the beginning, and for most consumers the agent is the only contact with the insurer. Since insurance is a complex business, it is vital that the agent be well trained and possess a requisite degree of business responsibility. Most states require any insurance representative to be licensed and, as a condition of licensing, to pass an examination covering insurance and the details of the state's insurance law.

Part of the reason for the failure of insurers to insist upon higher standards is traceable to the fact that agents are generally paid on a commission basis and the insurer assumes that since nothing is paid out unless the agent produces business, the easiest way to obtain more business is to hire more agents. In such an atmosphere, of course, the insurer is not likely to insist that its agents be exceptionally well trained. However, standards of licensing and training are steadily improving. It is being recognized that a poor agent may cost the insurer dearly in terms of public ill will and lawsuits, not to mention the cost of furnishing the agent with service, training materials, and the like.

Most state laws prohibit such practices as twisting, rebating, and misrepresentation in the sale of insurance. *Twisting* occurs when an agent persuades an insured to drop an existing insurance policy by misrepresenting the true facts for the purpose of obtaining an insured's business. *Rebating* occurs when an agent agrees to return part of the commission to an insured as an inducement to secure business. An example of *misrepresentation* is making misleading statements about the cost of life insurance. For example, New York has specifically prohibited the use of the traditional net cost method of determining the cost of life insurance by representing that this cost equals the difference between the premiums paid and the sum of dividends and ending cash values.[8] An agent's license can be revoked for any one of these offenses.

The insurance industry has in recent years expanded its offerings to include various types of equity products such as variable life insurance and mutual funds. Since variable annuities are subject to federal as well as state regulation, the Securities Act of 1933, the Securities Exchange Act of 1934, and the Investment Company Act of 1940 affect the insurance business directly. Both the product itself and its distribution are carefully regulated. The 1933 Act requires full disclosure to the buyer of all pertinent data regarding an issue of common stock. The 1934 Act regulates trading and the operations of the securities markets to prevent fraud and manipulation. The 1940 Act gave the Securities and Exchange Commission, which has the responsibility of administering the various securities laws, the power to regulate the type of sales literature, selling behavior, and sales compensation for selling variable annuities and other equity products of insurers.

As a result of these laws, an insurance sales agent of equity products must pass an examination covering the securities market and variable annuities before selling equity products. These examinations are prepared by such agencies as the National Association of Securities Dealers (NASD), the Securities and Exchange Commission (SEC), and the National Association of Insurance Commissioners (NAIC). In addition, the agent must satisfy any state licensing requirements.

Regulation of Contract Provisions

We have seen that the provisions of many insurance contracts are determined by statute. New policy forms must be approved in most states before they are offered to the public.

The insurance department of the state handles complaints of the insuring public which arise over the interpretation of policy provisions. Misunderstandings often arise, even over provisions which are considered standard. In 1967, for example, the insurance department in New York State processed 12,520 complaints involving loss settlements or policy provisions.[9] About half of these involved automobile insurance, and 2,481 involved accident and health insurance. It is interesting but not suprising that only half of these complaints were upheld, indicating the extent of misunderstanding by members of the insurance-buying public as well as the considerable necessity of exerting some regulatory control over the insurance product.

MISCELLANEOUS INSURANCE LAWS

A description of some other government regulations regarding insurance will illustrate the extent of government interest in this field.

[8] Regulation 74, New York Insurance Department, effective January 1, 1975.
[9] New York Insurance Department, *109th Annual Report* (New York, 1967), pp. 83-84.

Service-of-Process Statutes

When a legal action is brought against an insurer, it is necessary to deliver a court summons to the insurer's representative. For insurers admitted to do business within a given state, the insurance commissioner is generally the individual who is authorized to receive such a summons, under what is called a *service-of-process statute*. Formerly a problem arose as to how best to serve an insurer which did not operate within a given state. An insured may have obtained a policy by dealing with the insurer by mail, or the insured may have obtained a policy in one state but subsequently moved to another state wherein the insurer was not admitted to do business. Through the National Association of Insurance Commissioners, most states have now passed statutes known as the *unauthorized insurers service-of-process acts*. Under these statutes it is no longer necessary for an insured to resort to distant courts in order to bring suit on contracts written by such unauthorized insurers. It is only necessary to serve summons on the insurance commissioner or upon someone representing the out-of-state insurer.

Retaliatory Laws

Most states have on their books laws requiring that if an insurer chartered in one state is subjected to some burden such as an increased tax or license fee on business it does in another state, then the one state will automatically impose a like burden on all of the insurers of the second state which are operating in the first state. Such laws are known as *retaliatory laws*, and about three fourths of all states have them. The effect of these laws is to discourage each state from passing any unusual taxes on foreign insurers operating within its borders for fear that the same burden shall immediately apply to its own insurers operating in other states. Only those states without any domestic companies can ignore retaliatory laws; and there is a tendency, therefore, for states with the most domestic insurers to have the lowest insurance taxes. The constitutionality of these laws has been attacked on the ground that they cause one state to surrender its taxing authority to another state, but it has been established that the laws are constitutional.[10]

Anticancellation Laws

A majority of states have passed laws restricting the right of insurers of automobiles to cancel policies without good reason. Laws are not uniform as to the type of vehicles covered but in general only private passenger autos are subject to the restrictions. A few states limit the application of the laws to liability coverages, but in a majority of states they apply to all coverages, both liability and physical damage. Insurers are also required under these laws to give ample advance notice of intent not to renew when the policy is approaching its expiration date.

[10] *American Indemnity Company* v. *Hobbs*, 328 U.S. 822 (1946).

Most of the laws state that unless an insurer cancels a newly-issued policy within 60 days after its effective date, it may cancel after that only for certain specified reasons which may include nonpayment of premiums, insurance obtained through fraudulent misrepresentation, violation by the insured of any term or condition of the policy, suspension of the driver's operator license, existence of heart attacks or epilepsy of the insured, existence of an accident or conviction record, and habitual use of alcoholic beverages or narcotics to excess. The list of permissible reasons for cancellation is so long and is phrased so broadly that it appears to give the insurer broad discretion in the matter of cancellation and would actually impose few limitations or give much protection to an insured whose policy is cancelled capriciously.

Reciprocal Laws

In contrast to a retaliatory law, a *reciprocal law* provides that if one state does something for another, that state shall do the same thing for the first. For example, it is common for state financial responsibility laws to provide that if under the laws of another state an insured motorist would be disqualified from driving, this motorist shall also be prohibited from driving in the first state. Under uniform insurers liquidation acts, it is possible for a claimant of an insolvent insurer in another state to make a claim locally and have it honored, avoiding the necessity of traveling to the other state. In workers' compensation insurance, if an employee is temporarily employed outside a state and if the other state will excuse the employer from complying with that state's compensation law, the first state will do likewise. In this way state legislation is made to work much more smoothly than it otherwise would.

Anticoercion Laws

Anticoercion statutes are aimed against the former practice of some lending agencies to require, as a condition of granting a loan, the placing of insurance with the agency. Thus, the purchaser of a home might be prevented from placing property insurance with a personally chosen insurer. The borrower had to pay premiums which were not necessarily the lowest obtainable. Such tie-in practices were held to be in restraint of trade and illegal under one or more federal antimonopoly laws.[11] As a result, anticoercion laws were passed in many states.

Insolvency Funds

Forty-seven states and the District of Columbia (all states except Alabama, Arkansas, and Oklahoma) have enacted some type of legislation covering the insolvency of property-liability insurers. Much of this legislation is patterned after but not identical to the model bill proposed by the National Association of Insurance Commissioners (NAIC) in 1969. The purpose of the bills, as phrased by the NAIC model, is

[11] See *United States* v. *Investors Diversified Services*, Civil No. 3713, D.C. Minn. (1954).

to provide a mechanism for the payment of covered claims under certain insurance policies, to avoid excessive delay in payment, and to avoid financial loss to claimants or policyholders because of the insolvency of an insurer, to assist in the detection and prevention of insurer insolvencies, and to provide an association to assess the cost of such protection among insurers.

The model bill[12] contains the following major features:

1. An association of insurers admitted to each state is formed on a nonprofit basis to share obligations created by insolvent insurers. Membership in the association is compulsory.
2. The association is governed by a board of nine directors selected by member insurers and approved by the Insurance Commissioner.
3. The association will pay claims up to $300,000 with a $100 deductible. Workers' compensation claims are paid in full. In no case will claims against the association exceed those obligations of the insolvent insurer.
4. Members of the association are assessed for claims in proportion to the net premiums written by each member, but not to exceed 2% of their net premiums written in the preceding year. Any unpaid obligations in a given year will be held over to a subsequent year. The association may benefit from any reinsurance available to the insolvent insurer.
5. The association has the power to settle claims, borrow funds, sue or be sued, contract with others to carry out its functions, and in other ways act as an independent body. Being nonprofit, it is exempt, however, from state taxes.
6. The association has the right to join other creditors of the insolvent insurer in claiming recoveries resulting from bankruptcy proceedings.
7. The association has the duty to notify the Insurance Commissioner of any information which indicates a financially hazardous condition of any insurer operating in the state.

It is estimated that the 2% maximum assessment on member insurers would provide a financial capacity of $500 million to back up insolvent insurers.

Individual state laws specify which types of insurance would be covered by the new guaranty plan. Although it is too early to make an evaluation of the success of the new guaranty associations, it appears that they represent another example of private action to forestall the creation of any new federal government control over insurance. The associations are controlled by the private insurance industry under state supervision. The programs are consistent with state laws governing insolvency procedures and certainly appear to strengthen these procedures.

TAXATION OF INSURANCE

Insurance companies represent a relatively substantial source of revenue to states. In 1973, for example, insurance taxes amounted to $1.6 billion, about 3% of total state tax collections. Insurance company taxes are greater than tax collections from public utilities, from death and gift taxes, and from corporate licenses. They are almost as large as taxes on alcoholic beverages.

[12] *NAIC Proceedings*, 1970, Vol. 1, pp. 253-262.

In each state these revenues are raised mainly from a tax on gross premiums. Premium taxes vary from 1% to 4%, with the most typical amount being 2%, plus an additional .25% or .50% for the support of the state fire marshall's office. Many states have, in addition, special taxes or assessments in connection with different lines of insurance, such as workers' compensation.

Insurance companies are also subject to federal income taxation. Stock property insurers pay taxes on underwriting and investment income at regular corporate rates. Mutual property insurers are treated differently. If a mutual or a reciprocal insurer has a net income of less than $75,000, it is exempt from taxation.[13] It is estimated that about 3% of the total mutual premium volume is written by tax-exempt companies. For larger mutuals, the tax is the larger of 1% of gross income (net premiums written less policyholder dividends, plus net investment income) or that tax which would be collected by applying regular corporate rates to investment income only, as defined.[14]

Life insurers are subject to a special formula for federal income taxation. They pay taxes on that portion of net investment income which exceeds the amount necessary to maintain legal reserves, plus a portion of net underwriting gain. Until 1959 life insurers were exempt from taxes on underwriting profits and enjoyed a favorable formula for the taxation of net investment income. The new federal taxation formula approximately doubled the taxes levied on life insurers.

GOVERNMENT COMPETITION IN INSURANCE

Not only has the insurance industry been subject to government regulation, but it has also had to meet government competition in offering insurance to the public. As shown in Table 5–1, nearly half (46.4%) of all insurance premiums collected in the United States are accounted for by governmental bodies and the percentage has been increasing steadily. Data in Table 5–1 show mainly programs of the federal government (including social insurance coverages) and do not count state government programs, on which data are not readily available.

Governmental Insurance Programs

Government in insurance has a lengthy history, both as an insurer and as a reinsurer. First major evidence of this was in workers' compensation, when both state and the federal governments entered the field (e.g., through 18 state funds and through federal agencies administering such acts as the Longshoremen's and Harbor Workers Compensation Act). During both World War I and World War II, the federal government organized agencies to distribute life insurance to service personnel. The Social Security Act, passed in 1935, originally passed with a modest life insurance program for widows of

[13] Section 501(15) Internal Revenue Code (1954).
[14] Sections 821, 822, 823 Internal Revenue Code (1954).

covered workers and was expanded to encompass a floor of protection for retirement for almost everyone, disability income, and health insurance for the aged. The federal government has entered the field of loan insurance on deposits and housing mortgage loans to the extent that it dominates the whole market for this coverage. In recent years the federal government has also entered the field of property and liability insurance via reinsurance of the FAIR plans, flood insurance, and export credit insurance programs. It became a primary insurer in crime, crop, marine vessel war risk, and other insurance programs.

State governments have also entered the insurance business but not nearly on the scale of the federal government. The 18 state funds (6 of them exclusive funds) in workers' compensation have been mentioned above. One state, Wisconsin, entered the life insurance business through the Wisconsin Life Fund. In 1973 Maryland entered automobile insurance business through the Maryland State Automobile Insurance Fund. A few states (Maryland, New Jersey, and North Dakota) operate unsatisfied judgment funds for automobile drivers unable to collect judgments resulting from uninsured motorists. Some states have established state self-insurance funds for state-owned property. State-owned insured pension programs for state employees are also quite common. Hail insurance funds have been set up in a few states (North Dakota, Montana, and Colorado). Land title insurance state funds are operated in four states, (Massachusetts, Ohio, California, and North Carolina) and in a few other areas title insurance funds are operated at the county level. Five states have adopted compulsory temporary disability benefit plans covering nonoccupational disability (California, Rhode Island, New Jersey, New York, and Hawaii). Private insurers may compete with state funds in all of these states except Rhode Island. Finally, all states under federal supervision have set up unemployment insurance plans.

Rationale of Government Insurance

Why has the government participated directly in the insurance field in an economy dedicated to free enterprise? For example, why has it apparently been necessary to establish OASDHI when private life insurance and private pension plans are available? At least five basic factors seem to explain governmental activity in insurance: (1) incomplete or absent offerings by private insurance in areas of social need for coverage, (2) need to supply the element of compulsion for certain types of coverage, (3) greater operating efficiency, (4) need to achieve some collateral social purpose, and (5) convenience.

The OASDHI program may be used as an illustration of these factors. Before social security was established in 1935 it became clear that private life insurance had been unable to fill all of the public need for survivors' and retirement security. OASDHI could be made compulsory, thus covering most people, a condition not possible for private insurers to meet. Because OASDHI is compulsory, no sales commissions need be paid. Operating expenses could be reduced, also, because other governmental agencies could cooperate in collecting premiums. Thus, direct operating costs of OASDHI are far less than would be possible if private insurers operated the program. Furthermore, since the program is compulsory, many would object to private agencies operating it except on a nonprofit basis, which is not feasible for most private insurers. OASDHI achieved the collateral social purpose of helping to prevent poverty among dependent persons, such as widows, children, and the aged. Finally, the factor of convenience helped explain the use of a governmental agency to handle the social security program, since private insurers are not sufficiently well organized to act cooperatively to meet the extensive operations of this program on a permanent and continuing basis.

Types of Competition

Governments tend to occupy one or more of three basic types of relationships with private insurers: as a partner, as a competitor, and as an exclusive agent. Examples of partnerships are the FAIR and flood reinsurance programs under which private insurers offer coverage but the federal government offers reinsurance of losses above a given level. Examples of the competitor relationship would be the OASDHI program and state government workers' compensation funds. Examples of the exclusive agent position are the federal loan guaranty programs, unemployment insurance, federal war risk insurance for aviation and marine vessels, and federal all-risk crop insurance.

FAIR Plans

Fair Access to Insurance Requirements (FAIR) plans originated as a riot reinsurance plan established under the U.S. Housing and Urban Development Act of 1968 after riots in major cities made property insurance difficult to obtain through normal channels in certain urban areas. In affected areas, property insurance, if it was available at all, was priced several times higher than had been true before the riots. In a survey of 3,000 urban core homeowners and business persons in six cities, it was disclosed that 40% of the business persons and 30% of homeowners had serious difficulties in obtaining property insurance.[15]

FAIR plans are operated in each state by private insurers who cooperate as a pool or syndicate to make property insurance available to customers who are unable to obtain coverage in the regular manner. As of 1975, FAIR plans existed in 28 states, Puerto Rico, and the District of Columbia. Agents and brokers assist property owners by applying for coverage, delivering policies, collecting premiums, and submitting claims. Insurers licensed in a state participate in the pooled experience for losses and expenses in proportion to their share of certain property insurance premiums collected in their state. To induce private insurers to participate, the federal government provides reinsurance against excessive losses resulting from riots or civil disorders.

[15] Staford G. Ross, "Federal Reinsurance," *Best's Review*, (July, 1968), p. 25.

Insurers participating in the riot reinsurance program are required to reinsure losses stemming from fire or extended coverage perils, burglary and theft, and certain multiple-peril contract perils. Optionally, insurers may obtain coverage for riot losses under inland and ocean marine, boiler and machinery, glass, and aircraft policies.

The insured under a FAIR plan pays the standard premium for insurance unless the insured property falls below certain minimum underwriting standards, in which case an excess premium may be levied.[16] The insured is entitled to have the property inspected and to receive a statement of what is necessary to bring it up to given standards. In some cases the insured may receive a grant from the federal government to make the necessary repairs. This insured's application may not be turned down because the property is located in riot-prone areas or for other environmental hazards.

FAIR plan riot reinsurance is funded in several layers. Each layer must be exhausted before the next layer is liable. As of 1971, the original insurer paid .15% of property insurance premium income in the state for its reinsurance coverage. (Originally the reinsurance premium was 1.25%.) In the event of losses due to riot, the following parties are liable in the order listed:

1. The primary insurer for up to 2.5% of premiums written in the state.
2. The Department of Housing and Urban Development (HUD) out of the reinsurance fund.
3. All property insurers in the state for an assessment equal to 2% of premiums collected within the state, divided among insurers in proportion to their premiums in that state.
4. The state government for an amount equal to 5% of all property insurance premiums collected within the state in the preceding year.
5. HUD, which may borrow up to $250 million from the United States Treasury.

FAIR plans appear to have helped in meeting the crisis of discontinuous markets for property insurance in some urban areas. In one study it was reported that FAIR plans represented 21.2% of the total fire and extended coverage market in Washinton, D.C.; 11.9% in New York; 4% in Illinois; and 3.8% in Massachusetts.[17] After 1971, however, the volume of business written under FAIR plans declined. For example, in New York, whose plan writes about a third of the total FAIR premiums, premiums in 1974 were about $26 million, compared to $31 million in 1973, and $66 million in 1971.[18] Furthermore, the FAIR plans have experienced through 1974 underwriting losses of about $175 million since the program began.[19] However, as of

[16] In a study covering the operation of the Minnesota FAIR plan, about 20% of the dwellings and apartment houses were charged standard fire and extended coverage rates, while the most common extra charge was 51% of standard rate. For all the dwellings the average charge was 65%, and for apartments, 76%. Andrew F. Whitman and C. Arthur Williams, Jr., "Fair Plan and Excess Rate Plan Rates in Minnesota," *Journal of Risk and Insurance*, Vol. 38, No. 1 (March, 1971), p. 46.

[17] George K. Bernstein, "Critical Evaluation of FAIR Plans," *Journal of Risk and Insurance*, Vol. 38, No. 2 (June, 1971), p. 273.

[18] *National Underwriter* (May 9, 1975), p. 1.

[19] *Ibid.*

1973 over $17 billion of FAIR plan coverage and $2 billion of beach and windstorm plans in seven Atlantic seaboard states were in force. In 1973 there were over 730,000 new or renewal applications for coverage, attesting to the continuing demand for FAIR plans.[20]

Flood Insurance

Flood insurance has not generally been available from private insurers, who would tend to suffer adverse selection. The only source of income to insurers would be those most likely to suffer the loss, making it difficult for insurers to get a sufficient spread of risk and to avoid catastrophic claims. Furthermore, it would be difficult to solve the problem of adverse selection by providing flood coverage in package policies, because the loading necessary for the additional coverage might be substantial.

A national flood insurance program was enacted in 1968[21] established on (1) land management and other control measures to help prevent losses due to flood; (2) federal subsidies to enable the sale of flood insurance to those most likely to be affected; and (3) cooperation with the private insurance industry and state governments to distribute flood coverage and to control losses. Accordingly, for a community to become eligible for flood insurance, it must agree to adopt loss-prevention measures, and individual property owners must certify the existence of certain loss-prevention devices. It is expected that after land management and use measures have become well established and have reduced flood loss potential, and when actuarial rate levels have been developed and tested, the private insurance market will be able to operate this plan without federal subsidies.

Political subdivisions within states may apply for flood coverage eligibility by establishing programs including measures such as adopting land use regulations which reserve areas subject to frequent flooding for open-space types of use (playgrounds, parks, agriculture); requiring that new building in areas subject to occasional flooding have minimum first floor elevations; and requiring that certain minimum floodproofing treatment be administered to existing buildings.

Flood insurance is distributed through existing agents and brokers in qualified communities. A pool of about 100 private insurers, known as the National Flood Insurers Association (NFIA) has been formed to underwrite the new coverage. Eligible properties include one- to four-family dwellings, properties principally occupied by small business firms,[22] and their contents. During the initial phase of the program, "emergency" rates and coverage are in effect on a subsidized basis. Coverage is limited to $17,500 for a single-family dwelling,

[20] *Insurance Facts 1974* (New York: Insurance Information Institute, 1974), p. 25.

[21] Public Law 90-448, August 1, 1968, 42 U.S.C. 4001-4127. An earlier law was passed in 1956, but was never funded by Congress.

[22] A small business is defined as one which does not have assets in excess of $5 million, does not have a net worth in excess of $2.5 million, and does not have a net income after federal income taxes for the preceding two fiscal years in excess of $250,000.

$30,000 for a multiple-dwelling house, $5,000 on contents, and $30,000 for small business structures. Premiums per $100 in 1971 were $.40 on the building and $.50 for contents. In 1972, rates were reduced to $.25 per $100 of valuation to encourage greater use of flood insurance.[23] Undoubtedly, further rate changes will be made as actuarial studies are made.

The policy is written with a deductible amount of $200 or 2% of the amount of insurance, whichever is greater. The policy covers flood and mudslide. Flood is defined as the inundation of normally dry land areas from the overflow of inland or tidal water, or unusual and rapid accumulation or runoff of surface waters from any source. It does not cover water damage from causes within the insured's control or from conditions that do not cause general flooding in the area.

The program is administered by the Federal Insurance Administration (FIA) which has negotiated a reinsurance agreement with the NFIA for insuring excess losses under the program. Under this agreement, the losses of insurers participating in the program are limited to 125% of the annual premiums collected. Furthermore, HUD pays 90% of all losses incurred during the emergency period before the completion of actuarial studies which form the basis of the permanent rate structure.

Strong impetus for flood insurance was provided when Congress required that flood insurance be taken in flood-prone areas as a condition of receiving loans from ant federally-regulated or insured lending institution, or under any federal assistance program. As of May 31, 1975, 8,382 communities out of an estimated 21,785 flood-prone areas in all states were qualified for flood insurance. Over 424,000 dwellings and 86,000 businesses had coverage amounting to over $12 billion, up from $7.5 billion in the previous year.[24]

If the flood insurance program is successful, as it gives every appearance of being, considerable expansion and improvement are possible.[25] The perils covered might be expanded to include earthquake, rental value, flood business interruption, flood demolition, and replacement cost. Rules could be changed to allow coverage of property owners other than small business owners or owners of private residences. Studies are also needed to answer such questions as the effect of flood insurance on property tax revenues, mortgage lending on property in flood zones, and building codes.

Crime Insurance

Urban blight and other factors similar to those which caused the creation of the FAIR plans also resulted in federally-sponsored crime insurance. In May, 1971, FIA made a formal announcement of the regulations proposed for a new program of federally-operated crime coverage to begin on August 1, 1971. This

[23] Federal Register (July 1, 1972), p. 12062.

[24] *Insurance Facts 1975* (New York: Insurance Information Institute, 1975), pp. 25, 26.

[25] Robert S. Felton, William K. Ghee, and John E. Stinton, "A Mid-1970 Report on the National Flood Insurance Program," *Journal of Risk and Insurance*, Vol. 38, No. 1 (March, 1971), p. 12.

program, authorized under the Housing and Urban Development Act of 1970, permits the federal government to offer crime coverage (mainly burglary, robbery, and theft other than fidelity or auto theft) directly or through private insurers in any state in which it is determined that there is a critical shortage of crime insurance offered at affordable rates. An FIA survey determined that in 1971 there were 18 states and territories in which such a critical shortage existed. (The coverage was actually offered in 11 of these states when the program was started in 1971.) Nine other states were listed as likely to require the sale of federal crime insurance. The list of states affected is amended periodically to reflect changes in the private insurance market or creation of state crime insurance programs. As of 1975, nearly 15,000 residential and 5,000 commercial policies were in force in 15 states. (See Chapter 17 for a description of these coverages.)

The program is operated through private insurers who are service agencies for the federal government. The risk, however, is assumed by the FIA as the insurer. Regular agents or brokers distribute the coverage along with other lines. The federal act provides that the new program will be exempt from any form of federal or state taxation or regulation.[26] Furthermore, no agent or broker will be subjected to any state tax or insurance law or regulation with respect to actions that the agent or broker takes under the law establishing the new coverage. Agents and brokers are not authorized to offer insurance on any terms other than those established by the FIA for the program. Thus, the new program establishes the precedent of taking certain taxation authority and other authority over the operation of insurance away from states, which have traditionally enjoyed freedom in this regard.

The federal program of crime coverage represents a new venture for the federal government in that for the first time a field traditionally reserved for private domestic insurers has been entered on the basis of direct insurance instead of reinsurance. The subsidy involved in the program appears to be substantial. For example, the annual rates per $1,000 for the FIA coverage are substantially lower than comparable commercial insurance, which might or might not be available. Some observers have commented that when the required protective devices are met, private industry is often able to offer the coverage at affordable rates. However, the law requires the FIA to terminate federal coverage if crime insurance becomes generally available through the normal insurance market at affordable rates.[27] Presumably, private insurers will continue to concentrate on the better classes of risk, leaving the poorer classes to be insured through the FIA program.

Although federal crime insurance has not absorbed a large portion of the crime insurance market so far, it seems likely that this insurance will be continued, at least in the foreseeable future. The rate subsidy and noncancellable feature will attract customers, in spite of somewhat strict requirements as to loss-prevention measures. The program is aimed at the substandard market

[26] Section 1250 of the Act (12 U.S.C. 1749bbb-20).
[27] Subchapter C, Federal Crime Insurance Program, p. 18.

which has difficulty in securing private coverage; hence demand is expected to continue in a modest way. Current authority for the program expires in 1977.[28]

Crop Insurance

Crop insurance is of two basic types: crop hail contracts and federal all-risk crop insurance. The former plan is written by private insurers and coverage is generally confined to the perils of fire and hail which cause damage in excess of 5% of the value of the crop. Crop hail insurance has been written since the early 1930's and expanded steadily until 1973 when it reached a volume of $192 million of premium income. The major types of crops insured are wheat, corn, tobacco, soybeans, and cotton. Coverage is based on an estimate of the value of the harvested crop, and indemnities are intended to reimburse the farmer for the costs and anticipated profit.

All-risk crop insurance differs from crop hail coverage in the following ways:

1. All-risk crop insurance is intended to reimburse the farmer only for loss of the actual investment in the crop, not anticipated profit.
2. All-risk crop insurance must be purchased at planting time, while crop hail insurance may be purchased any time up through harvest.
3. All-risk crop insurance must cover the entire crop, while crop hail insurance can be placed on selected acres.
4. In all-risk crop insurance, indemnities are based on the differences between a guaranteed crop size and the actual crop. If the crop falls below a minimum level, the farmer is reimbursed for the production expenses. The coverage cannot exceed 75% of the farm's average yield.

Federal all-risk crop insurance was first made available in 1938. By 1973 the total premium volume approached $42 million and the value of insured crops was nearly $1 billion. Operating expenses of the program are met out of general tax revenues. In 1969 farmers received $4.8 million more in indemnities than were paid in premiums.

Compared to the total value of farm output, estimated at about $48 billion in 1968,[29] the total amount of crop insurance of both types is modest, amounting to approximately 10% of the total value of farm output. In one study, 41% of a sample of farms in 1967 had crop insurance of any type and 13% had federal all-risk crop insurance.[30] In 1968 about 12% of all eligible acres for federal crop insurance were actually insured.

There are several possible explanations for the limited development of crop coverage. First, farmers are not compensated for crop losses resulting from poor farm management or inadequate husbandry, but only for losses from unavoidable causes as determined by a board of the federal crop authorities.

[28] "Government Extends Crime Insurance Despite Less-Than-Spectacular Sales," *Business Insurance* (May 5, 1975), p. 17.

[29] U.S. Department of Agriculture, *Statistical Abstract of the United States* (1969), p. 609.

[30] Warren R. Bailey and Lawrence A. Jones, *Economic Considerations in Crop Insurance* (U.S.D.A. Research Service, August, 1970), p. 36.

Second, there exists a certain degree of adverse selection in crop insurance, since many farmers wait until late in the season to determine if there will be a good crop before purchasing crop hail coverage. This practice is prevented in the case of all-risk coverage. Third, since insurance coverage is only on production expenses and since production expenses vary from about 30% of the value of a wheat crop to 60% of the value of a crop of soybeans, cotton, or tobacco, the total value of all-risk crop insurance is likely to be far less than the estimated total value of farm output. Fourth, not all crops are eligible for federal all-risk crop insurance. Currently the Department of Agriculture lists about 25 eligible crops in about half the counties of the United States.

Considering its limitations, the acceptance of crop insurance has been reasonable. As more experience with this type of insurance is obtained, underwriting may be liberalized. There appears to be no reason why private insurers would not operate successfully under given conditions. One of these conditions would be the absence of competing subsidized federal crop insurance or the granting of similar operating subsidies to private insurers. It seems that all-risk coverage against crop loss, instead of coverage limited to production expenses, could be offered in a manner similar to that which already exists for the crop hail coverage. Potentially, crop insurance is a valuable risk management tool for farmers and it could play an increasingly important future role in successful farm operations if cooperation were developed among government and private insurers.

SUMMARY

1. Insurance is regulated because of several characteristics which set it apart from tangible-goods industries. These include the complexity of insurance, its importance to the financial security of millions of people, the public nature of its many activities, and the necessity for some control over its pricing policies.
2. Insurance is regulated by states, but the federal government, by virtue of the 1944 decision in the case of the *South-Eastern Underwriters Association* and the McCarran-Ferguson Act, also has certain regulatory authority, chiefly in the area of competitive trade practices.
3. For many years a debate has existed over the relative merits of federal versus state regulation of insurance. In spite of some possible advantages of federal regulation, it appears unlikely that the present system of state rule will give way completely unless more convincing proof of the superiority of federal regulation is forthcoming. However it seems likely that increased federal regulation in specific areas of insurance, such as supervision of alien insurers, will occur.
4. The chief areas of regulation have to do mainly with rate supervision, standards of financial condition, business acquisition methods, and policy provisions. An insurer must be formally admitted to do business in a given state, must give evidence of its financial ability to meet all claims, and must subject almost every phase of its operations to the supervision of the insurance commissioner.
5. In general, regulation of insurance has had a beneficial effect upon

the institution by maintaining public confidence, securing desirable uniformity, and preventing destructive practices arising from unrestricted competition within the industry.

6. Government competition in insurance has been significant in the field of life insurance and shows increasing signs of life in the area of property insurance. New government programs of property insurance under the Department of Housing and Urban Development include FAIR plans, flood insurance, and crime insurance. The federal government has operated in the field of all-risk crop insurance for many years. Its operations in personal insurance under OASDHI have been expanded considerably since the inauguration of this program in 1935. It appears likely that these programs will continue to expand, both in property and in life and health insurance, particularly where private insurance fails to meet demand.

QUESTIONS FOR REVIEW AND DISCUSSION

1. A writer stated: "The current probability estimate of long-run socialization of large segments of the insurance business must be placed quite high. Several segments of the business are now waging battles against acute threats of socialization."
(a) Which types of insurance is the author probably referring to? Why?
(b) Indicate the chief characteristics of insurance which place it in jeopardy of being socialized.
2. A representative of an association of insurance agencies stated, "The very nature of our business requires the most rigid adherence to sound methods of operation and therefore there are few who will argue its need for regulation. . . ." Why is it concluded that insurance requires regulation when such an argument would usually be opposed in tangible-goods industries as an interference with the right of free enterprise? Comment.
3. A representative of a group of agents stated, "Because we are small, we do fear federal regulation; while it is difficult enough for the average insurance agent to participate in regulatory problems at the state level, it would be a virtual impossibility for most of us to take our problems to Washington . . . ." What relationship does this argument have to the general case against federal regulation of insurance? Do you agree with it? Explain.
4. Barbara says that if an insurer has adequate reinsurance (see Chapter 7) it will not need the insurer insolvency plans now in force in most states. Do you agree? Why or why not?
5. An insurance commissioner of a large state wrote, "The commissioner's position is not a particularly happy one today. He is . . . criticized for increases in rates, for a lack of insurance markets, for the insolvency of some companies, for maintaining too high a degree of uniformity in rates or coverage, or for being much too soft in the regulation of the industry. On the other hand, the commissioner is sometimes criticized by people in the insurance industry for a lack of uniformity and for regulating too severely . . . strangulation of the business instead of . . . regulation." In your opinion, is it the task of the insurance commissioner to deal with each of the questions listed above? If so, give an example of the type of activity falling under each category.
6. Justice William O. Douglas was quoted as follows on the subject of dual regulation, "Dual

regulation—both by state and federal laws—may be logically permissible but practically unsound. Dual regulation may be inherently so disruptive of the policy of the federal law that the purpose of Congress to foreclose state action may be implied."
(a) Explain the meaning of this statement.
(b) From this comment do you think Justice Douglas is for or against federal regulation of insurance?

7. (a) Why are interlocking directorates looked upon as an undesirable business practice?
(b) Why are interlocking directorates an especially important practice in the insurance industry? Do you think that there is any special justification for them in insurance? Why?

8. Should the federal government supervise insurance company mergers, as it is attempting to do through the Federal Trade Commission in the *American General-Fidelity and Deposit* case? Suggest examples of how such a merger might lessen competition.

9. It has been suggested that under federal regulation of insurance local conditions could be handled through a system of district offices similar to that which exists in the case of the Federal Reserve System. Each of these offices could be given certain degrees of autonomy to adjust to localized conditions. In this way all the advantages of national uniformity could be achieved without any of the disadvantages of rigid supervision by distant authorities. Evaluate this plan, pointing out advantages and disadvantages.

10. In your opinion does real competition exist in the field of insurance? If so, give specific examples.

11. In addition to meeting the organization requirements applicable to a stock insurer, a mutual insurer must meet such requirements as having a minimum number of applications for insurance, a minimum number of risks, and a minimum amount of premiums from these risks. For example, in New York, a mutual insurer desiring a license for personal injury liability insurance must have applications from at least 100 members for insurance on at least 500 separate risks, of which not more than five shall be risks of any one member, with an annual premium cost of at least $50,000 annually. If this is true, how is it practicable for a mutual insurer ever to get started?

12. You are approached by an insurance agent who promises to return 20% of the commission to you if you will give this agent your business. Is this acceptable business practice? Comment.

13. Many professional insurance agents object strongly to the use of part-time agents and are generally in favor of much stricter licensing requirements than most states presently have. Why are part-time agents objected to more than full-time agents?

14. *H* buys an insurance policy from a mail-order insurer and following a loss is unable to secure payment. In fact, the insurer does not even answer *H*'s letter in which the loss was reported. A local agent informs *H* that this particular insurer is not "admitted" in his state and has no representatives there. Is it necessary for *H* to go to the state in which this insurer is chartered in order to bring legal action? Why?

15. A legislator in your state urges that a good way to raise additional state revenue would be to increase the premium tax on all insurers operating within the state. What point should you investigate first, before recommending that this tax be passed?

16. Differentiate between a retaliatory law and a reciprocal law.

17. You have applied to a mortgage company for a loan on your new home. The representative of the company indicates that your application will be approved if you agree to purchase fire insurance through him. You inform your insurance agent that although you would prefer to deal with him, he will have to forego this business because you need the loan. What action should the insurance agent take if he wants to retain your business? Why?

18. Which of the five basic factors used to justify government entrance in the insurance business do you think has the most validity? Can you suggest any additional reasons, justified or not, which may explain why governments enter insurance? Discuss.

19. An official of HUD reported that only half of all eligible communities had qualified for participation in the new federal flood insurance program. Suggest possible reasons for the limited acceptance of flood insurance especially in areas subject to flooding. Are these reasons valid? Discuss.

20. As a way to persuade people to buy flood insurance, Congress provided that anyone in a community which had qualified for flood insurance who had not purchased coverage would be ineligible for federal disaster assistance. This provision was later abandoned. in favor of a requirement that flood insurance be a prerequisite to any federally-assisted mortgage lending activity in areas eligible for flood insurance. In your opinion, which is preferable as a way of handling disaster relief—outright gifts from the government or disaster coverage such as is provided by flood insurance? What are the advantages and disadvantages of each plan?

21. In your opinion why is it possible for the federal government to offer a program of flood insurance whereas private industry cannot seem to do so? What essential ingredient is there to a successful flood insurance program that private insurance cannot control?

22. Are the same problems discouraging private offering of flood insurance (such as adverse selection) also present in the case of earthquake insurance? If so, do you think that the government should expand the flood insurance program to include earthquake? Discuss.

23. When flood insurance was first offered in 1968, relatively few, even those in flood-prone areas, bought it. In 1972, when Hurricane Agnes struck the eastern seaboard, only $98 million was paid under flood policies, out of $3 billion of losses to property generally qualified for flood coverage.
(a) Suggest possible reasons for public inertia on flood insurance.
(b) What measures were taken to cause a near doubling of coverage in 1973?

24. Do you believe that the rates specified for the FIA business crime insurance policy are affordable? Consider the case of a firm with $500,000 of sales, paying $1,225 for $15,000 of protection.

25. Assess the argument that the FIA is likely to be selected against in its crime insurance, with the better risks being taken by private insurers and the poorer risks being assigned to the federal government for insurance.

26. Gilbert states that he can obtain a private crime insurance policy at a rate equal to or below that offered by the government crime insurance plan in his territory. Mike answers this statement with an uncomplimentary remark about Gilbert's veracity. Why should Mike question Gilbert's statement? Explain.

Chapter *Twenty-Six*

PROBLEMS IN INSURANCE PRICING

The cost of insurance is one of the most important factors in a sound analysis of risk. The insured wishes to understand why the premium is as high (or low) as it is, and the insurer wishes to set the premium high enough to cover all future costs, yet low enough to meet competition. Both are interested in a rate that is fair so that each insured group is charged its proportionate share of the total loss and expense burdens. This chapter attempts to throw light on how some of these problems in insurance pricing may be analyzed.

MAKEUP OF THE PREMIUM

The insurance *rate* is the total number of dollars charged per unit of exposure. The insurance *premium* is the product of the insurance rate and the number of units of exposure. Thus, in life insurance, if the rate is $20 per $1,000 of face amount for ordinary life issued at age 30, the premium will be $200 for a $10,000 policy. In the discussion to follow, we shall be primarily interested in the insurance *rate*.

The insurance rate may be split into two parts: that portion intended to cover the pure loss cost per unit of exposure (or pure premium) and that portion, called *loading*, intended to cover the sales expense, overhead, and profit of the insurer. In automobile collision insurance, for example, the pure loss cost might be $30 per low-priced standard car, plus $10 for loss adjustment and claim costs, bringing the pure premium to $40. The loading is usually expressed as a percentage of the final premium. The loading is composed of selling agents' commissions, taxes, underwriting expenses, administrative overhead, and expected profit. The insured's premium therefore includes allowances for two main types of expenditures—those expenditures returned to the insured group as a whole for loss and loss adjustment expenses, and those expenditures necessary for the insurance service.

The relative size of loading in insurance premiums often surprises the uninitiated. The first reaction is "Why must the expenses of distribution be as much as 40% of the total premium?" There is the feeling that somehow the insured group is not getting any value from the expenditures for administration in connection with the insurance plan, whereas it gets back that part of the premium devoted to payment of pure losses. There are several answers to this, including the following:

1. The insured usually is getting more direct value than the statistics reveal. For example, the expenses for loss-prevention efforts, the costs of paying a claim, and even the expenses later returned to the insured as a dividend are often buried in general expenses, thus making them appear greater than they are.
2. It is a mistake to assume that the insured is getting no benefit from general insurer administration, for without these expenses there could be no insurance mechanism. The costs of administering and distributing insurance are no more, for example, than the costs of marketing many of the tangible commodities we consume each day.
3. In a free economy, unnecessary expenses may be expected to be eliminated by a process of squeezing out the marginal producer through the effects of competition. As we have seen, governmental regulation in insurance is an additional factor which attempts to prevent expenses from exceeding reasonable bounds.

CRITERIA FOR SOUND RATE-MAKING

Any plan of rate-making should incorporate certain criteria, some of which are laid down by state regulation, and most of which are not mutually exclusive. The rate:

1. Should be adequate to meet loss burdens, yet not excessive.
2. Should allocate cost burden among insureds on a fair basis.
3. Should be revised reasonably often to reflect as current a degree of loss experience as is feasible.
4. Should encourage loss-prevention efforts among insureds, if possible.

While these criteria seem simple enough upon casual review, they raise many difficult problems in their application. Some of these problems, many of which will probably never be completely solved either by insurers or by regulatory authorities, are described in the following paragraphs.

Adequacy of the Rate

If a rate is to be adequate and yet not excessive, how wide a margin for error should these limits impose? From one standpoint, an underwriter may reason that to have an adequate premium it is necessary to collect an amount sufficient for all unknown contingencies, while another underwriter may have a much different view of the size of these possible contingencies. This problem arises from the fact that the insurance rate must be set *before* all the costs are known. In many lines of business the entrepreneur may ascertain all or nearly all costs before setting a price. If costs cannot be determined, the entrepreneur usually will insist that the contract of sale be subject to later adjustment to reflect the actual costs or will insist on a "cost plus" type of contract. In insurance, however, a definite estimate must often be made in advance with no possibility of a later renegotiation if the estimate of loss was incorrect. Frequently an estimate is inaccurate because the underwriter uses past experience to estimate the future, while the insurance contract may involve a substantial future period during which the original conditions on which rates were based change drastically. It is easy to see that opinions as to the future of insurance costs can vary widely.

The problem of preventing rates from becoming excessive has been the subject of much legislation. Anticompact laws were generally abandoned because of the recognition that cooperation in rate-making (pooling of loss data) is an essential part of sound rating, and that unrestricted competition often leads to rates that are too low for the long-run solvency of the insurance fund. Having rates too low is just as undesirable as, if not worse than, having them too high. Above all, the insured is seeking assurance that personal losses will be paid if and when they occur.

Fair Allocation of Cost Burden

Just how far should the underwriter go in developing a rate that completely reflects the true quality of the individual hazard, thus making the rate fair? Theoretically, it might be argued that, for life insurance purposes, there should be an attempt to set individual premiums on the basis of occupation, income, marital status, drugs or alcohol consumption, automobile accident record, years during which cigarettes have been smoked, and longevity of parents. In practice, none of these factors affects the premium individually, since age and sex are almost the sole discriminants. If the criteria of fairness are carried to an extreme, it might be said that each person should receive a slightly different rate to reflect that person's particular situation. This, of course, would be impossible to administer and would make the rate-making task hopelessly complex. However, a decision must be made concerning where to draw the line and what criteria of fairness to use.

Another class of problems arising out of the criteria of fairness deals with the determination of the exposure unit to which the rate is applied. Automobile rates, for example, apply to the individual car; workers' compensation rates, to each $100 of payroll; fire insurance rates, to each $100 of building value; and life insurance rates, to each $1,000 of policy amount on an insured life. Consider workers' compensation insurance. There are two employers in the same rating class, one paying 300 workers $4 per hour, on the average, and the other paying 400 workers $3 per hour, on the average. Assuming that each has an hourly payroll of $1,200, each would pay the same workers' compensation premiums, but the first employer has an exposure of 300 workers, while the second has 400 workers. Should each employer pay the same premium? It could be argued persuasively that the first employer, aside from having fewer workers exposed to accident, probably hires a better class of people who might have fewer accidents than the more poorly paid workers. However, no one has yet invented a superior, yet practical, base for workers' compensation insurance.

Frequent Revision to Reflect Loss Experience

Insurance rates are generally revised slowly. Often it is many years before rates can be altered to reflect higher or lower costs. Consider automobile insurance, for example. Suppose it is desired to collect all loss experience data for a given year, *X*. Since policies are issued continuously throughout year *X* and have a one-year term, the rate-maker must wait until the *end* of year *X* plus one month before starting to collect loss data. It may take an additional six months to gather and interpret all data and obtain approval for a rate change. The new rate promulgated for the coming year is, on the average, one year and three months old (one half of the period dating from the beginning of year *X* to the time *X* plus one and a half). The lag is much greater for policies issued for terms longer than one year. In life insurance new mortality tables are adopted only after periods of several years and any errors in rate-making assumptions must be corrected, if at all, through changes in dividend schedules. Because of the lags noted, certain allowances are made by the rate-maker for observable trends. Errors in these allowances necessarily affect the criteria of adequacy and reasonableness. However, if a method could be found to incorporate loss data into the rates structure immediately as the losses are experienced, it would probably be undesirable to do so since insurance is a commodity which does not lend itself to daily changes in price. Again, some reasonable compromise between the extremes of immediate adjustment and prolonged delay must be found, even at the expense of some uncertainty and error in future rates.

Encouragement of Loss-Prevention Efforts

While ideally the insurance rate should encourage loss prevention on the part of the insured, it is difficult to achieve this objective. This may be understood when it is recalled that most insurable perils occur outside the control of the insured. In some lines of insurance, such as fire, rate credits are given for measures which tend to reduce the severity of the losses once the peril occurs, but there is great difficulty in defending the size of these credits, since any decision as to how much a safety device is worth in reducing losses is largely an arbitrary judgment. This problem is usually handled by some form of merit rating, discussed below.

RATE-MAKING METHODS

One of the most difficult problems in insurance is that of developing rate-making methods that meet the criteria which were analyzed previously. The methods employed very often can meet these criteria only imperfectly; and underwriting judgment, unsupported by statistical evidence, often plays a major role in rate-making. Even when statistical evidence is available, judgment plays a major role in rate-making in the interpretation of the statistical data, leading perhaps to rates which appear entirely arbitrary. Actuarial formulas themselves represent judgments as to which data will be weighed and how much weight will be accorded each type. Mathematics plays an important role in seeing that rate-making has a degree of consistency so that all members of an insured group who fall into predetermined categories are treated alike. However, as will be demonstrated, the calculation of an insurance rate is in no sense absolute or completely scientific in nature. As in most areas of the social sciences, the scientific method in insurance makes its greatest contribution in narrowing the area within which executive judgment must operate.

The basic approaches to rate-making are:

1. The manual, or class rating (pure), method.
2. Individual, or merit rating, method.
3. Some combination of the first two methods.

Manual, or Class Rating (Pure), Method

The *manual,* or *class rating, method* sets rates that apply uniformly to each exposure unit falling within some predetermined class or group. These groups are usually set up in such a manner that loss data may be collected and organized in some logical fashion. Everyone falling within a given class is charged the same rate. Any differences in hazard attributable to individual risks are considered unmeasurable or relatively small.

The major areas of insurance that emphasize use of the manual rate-making method are life, workers' compensation, liability, automobile, surety, health, and residential fire. For example, in life insurance the central classifications are by age and sex. In workers' compensation insurance, a national rate-making body collects loss experience data of more than 600 industrial groups, and these data are broken down territorially by state. In automobile insurance, the loss data are broken down territorially by type of automobile, by age of driver, and by major use of the automobile. In each case it is necessary only to find the appropriate page in a manual to find out what the insurance rate is to be, hence the term ''manual rate-making.''

Pure Premium. The central technique in manual rate-making is the *pure premium method.* This involves collecting all loss data falling into each class which is to be rated, dividing by the number of exposure units, and arriving at a pure premium. For automobile insurance, as an example, suppose the pure premium in collision insurance ($50 deductible) for low-priced passenger cars in five counties of a certain state, class 1A drivers (no male operator less than 25 years of age, and car not used in business nor to drive to and from work) is $65 for a certain time period. This means that *on the average* the insurer had to pay $65 per car for collision losses falling into the classification named. The rate-maker must then allow for loading. Since loading is usually expressed as a percentage of the final gross premium, the pure premium is divided by 1 minus the loading percentage. In the case above, loading may be 35% of the final premium. The gross premium is found by dividing $65 by .65, thereby obtaining a figure of $100. Although methods are more refined in practice, this formula is the basis of the method.

Loss Ratio Method. In some cases it may be impractical to employ the pure premium method in developing a rate because of the existence of too many classifications and subclassifications in the manual. In other words, there may be so many categories involved that losses on only a small number of exposures occur in a given time period. This small exposure may be deemed insufficient on which to base decisions from a statistical point of view. As a consequence, the new rate is developed by comparing the *actual* loss ratios, A, of combined groups with the *expected* loss ratios, E, and using the formula A/E = Percent change indicated. For example, suppose that the actual loss ratio is .70 while only .60 was expected when the old rate was promulgated. In this example, $A = .70$, $E = .60$, and the formula yields .7/.6. The new rate would be 7/6 times the old, or nearly 17% higher. The loss ratio method is actually a rate-revision method rather than a rate-making method.

Before we can analyze the individual, or merit rating, method of rate-making, it is necessary to pause and define the concept "credible rate."

Credibility. A concept of basic importance in insurance rate-making is credibility. In general terms, *credibility* refers to the degree to which the rate-maker can rely on the accuracy of loss experience observed in any given area. For example, assume that the rate-maker is faced with the task of revising a rate for a certain type of policy issued by the company in a given geographical area. There are 50 policies outstanding and the loss ratio on these policies indicates that losses have been considerably higher than anticipated. Should future rates be based on the experience of these 50 policies, or is there a considerable likelihood that the last year under consideration produced higher-than-average losses only by random chance? The rate-maker wishes to know how many policies there would have to be before the loss experience observed should be given 100%, 90%, 80%, 50%, or 10% weight in preparing the rate revisions.

If upon the next renewal the rate-maker raised the insurance premium of everyone who had suffered a loss, the purpose of loss-spreading, which is inherent in the insurance mechanism, would be largely lost. If each small group were "required to pay for its own losses," it is clear that the idea of risk transfer would not be achieved. It would not do to raise the fire rates of a small community which had a disastrous fire in only one year, because the experience for such a small class for only one year is certainly not credible. Yet the insurer, in the interest of fairness, must make reasonable classifications of insureds and perils and charge an appropriate rate for large groups falling within these classifications. It is not fair for one group to subsidize another group if each group is large enough to develop loss experience that is reasonably credible.

The Credibility Formula. The concept of credibility may be stated succinctly by a formula:

$$PP = PPi\,(Z) + PPp\,(1 - Z)$$

where

PP = pure premium to be developed for a given insured, i,
PPi = pure premium based on the insured's *past* experience,

PPp = pure premium based on the past experience of the *larger population* to which the insured belongs, and
Z = the weight (credibility factor) to be applied to the insured's past experience. Z is a number ranging from 0 to 1.

As Z increases, more weight will be applied to the insured's past experience; and if Z equals 1, the pure premium to be charged is based entirely on the individual insured's past experience. This would be the case if the insured has a very large number of homogeneous exposure units at risk and is in effect large enough to be self-rating. It should be noted, furthermore, that as Z increases, the term $1 - Z$ decreases and with it the weight given to the loss experience of the population.

For convenience the values given to Z are expressed as percentages. The rate-maker generally develops a scale of credibility for different lines of insurance running from 0 to 100%. As an example in applying the formula, let us assume that a given employer's workers' compensation policy is found to produce a loss ratio of .70, compared with an expected loss ratio of .60 for employers in this occupational group. However, the number of exposures on which the .70 loss ratio was calculated was of such size and type that only 60% credibility can be attached to it. In the formula, $Z = .6$, $PPi = .7$, and $PPp = .6$. The pure premium for the employer in the forthcoming period would be based on a loss ratio of .66 rather than .7 ($PP = .7\,(.6) + .6\,(1 - .6) = .42 + .24 = .66$) Because the employer's experience is not fully credible, the rate would be increased only 10% (.66/.60) rather than 16.7% (.70/.60).

The value given to Z in a given problem depends on both mathematical and subjective factors. Essentially, the mathematical problem is one of statistical inference.[1] Losses are assumed to fall randomly according to some underlying mathematical distribution. If this be true, we can determine the number of trials in a sample necessary to produce, with some predetermined degree of accuracy, a loss ratio which falls within some stated error range of the expected loss ratio. For example, it can be determined mathematically under assumptions of the normal distribution that if the probability of a temporary disability per year in a given territory is .06, and it is desired to find what number of employees must be considered before a pure premium can be developed which is within .006 of the expected loss frequency of .06 (i.e., within 10% of expected loss frequency), the rate-maker must observe the loss experience of about 4,170 employees in order to know with 90% probability that the loss experience will be as assumed.[2] The rate-maker may not assign full weight to the pure premium so developed if fewer experiences than this are observed.

[1] For an interesting application of Bayesian statistics to the problem of credibility, see David B. Houston, "Risk, Insurance, and Sampling," *Journal of Risk and Insurance* (December, 1964), pp. 535-538.

[2] Based on the formula given in Chapter 2, $N = S^2 p\,(1-p)\,/e^2$, where $S = 1.645$ (1.645 standard deviations on either side of the mean of a normal distribution include 90% of the area under the curve, so the results have a 90% confidence interval.); $e = .006$, the standard of accuracy; $p = .06$, and $(1-p) = .94$.

Individual, or Merit Rating, Method

The *individual,* or *merit rating, method* differs from the manual rating method in that ways are developed to recognize the individual features of a specific risk and to give this risk a rate which more or less reflects its particular hazard. A variety of merit rating plans are used to give recognition to the fact that some groups of insureds, and some individual insureds, have loss records which are sufficiently credible to warrant reductions (or increases) in their rate from that of the class to which they belong.

Special Rating Classes. One generally-used device is for the underwriter to set up *special rating classes* to which discounts from the manual rate are made, either beforehand in the form of a direct *deviation,* as it is called, or as a dividend payable at the end of the period. Presumably, only those insureds meeting certain requirements are eligible for the special rate. Sometimes insurers restrict their business in such a manner that the entire policyholder group is meant to be that of the general public and therefore qualifies for a lower rate than that charged by insurers dealing with all types of risks. For example, some direct writing companies, such as factory mutuals, severely restrict the classes of risk they underwrite, and, if warranted, pay substantial dividends as a reward for loss-prevention efforts. In the field of life insurance, mutual insurers pay dividends that differ in amount according to the type of policy. Life insurers also grant rate deviations for special classes of insured groups, known as preferred risks, and charge extra premiums on other groups, called substandard risks. Automobile insurers have experimented with this method by distinguishing among applicants on the basis of their automobile and traffic violation records. In workers' compensation, certain groups are entitled to a premium discount which varies according to the size of the annual premium.

Schedule Rating. Another widely-used plan of individual rating is *schedule rating.* The best example of this is in the field of commercial fire insurance, where each individual building is considered separately and a rate established for it. The physical features of the structure are analyzed for factors that presumably affect the probability of loss, and credits in the rate are given for good features. These credits are in the form of a listing, or a schedule. In effect, the insured is rewarded in advance for features which it is hoped will yield a lower loss cost for all similar structures as a group. Schedule rating is also used in burglary insurance, with the insured being given rate credits for loss-prevention devices such as burglar alarms and burglar-proof safes.

Experience Rating. A third way in which an individual risk may receive special consideration by the rate-maker is through *experience rating.* Experience rating is permitted in cases where the hazards affecting the insured's operation are sufficiently within the insured's control so that it is reasonable to expect a reduction of losses through special effort. If this is done, the insured is permitted a lower insurance rate for the coming period. The experience rating plan applies to insureds with a relatively large exposure so that the experience which is developed has some chance to be credible. Thus, experience rating formulas generally apply to business firms with large and diversified types of operations and where the loss ratio is at least partially within the control of the insured. Unlike schedule rating, which grants a discount for safe features, experience rating requires that the insured *prove* the ability to keep loss ratios down before being qualified for a loss reduction. Most experience rating formulas also impose a rate *increase* in case the loss ratios become higher than expected. Experience rating plans are used in workers' compensation, general liability, group health, unemployment, and other lines of insurance. Examples of these plans are analyzed below.

Retrospective Rating. A final way in which attention is given to the problem of recognizing individual differences in risk is through *retrospective rating*. In contrast to experience rating, under which rate adjustments apply only to the future period, retrospective rating permits an adjustment in rates for the period just ended. The premium is determined, in whole or in part, by the actual record of losses suffered by the insured during the policy year. The contract is renegotiated, so to speak, after all the facts have been determined. Employers become partial self-insurers, but they use the commercial insurer to limit their losses.

Combination Method

In many lines of insurance a *combination* of manual and merit rating is used in different degrees. The rate-maker may develop a manual rate and then proceed to set up a system whereby individual members of a group may qualify for reductions from the manual rate if certain requirements are met or be subjected to rates higher than the manual rate under certain conditions.

EXAMPLES OF MERIT RATING PLANS

To appreciate some of the problems in individual risk rating, or merit rating, five examples of merit rating plans will be presented:

1. The safe driver and assigned risk plans in auto insurance.
2. Experience rating in workers' compensation.
3. Experience rating in unemployment insurance.
4. Retrospective rating in workers' compensation.
5. Schedule rating in fire insurance on commercial property.

Safe Driver and Assigned Risk Plans

In the field of automobile insurance, various merit rating plans have proved successful. Such plans have been used in England for many years. Actuaries in Sweden and Canada have reported success with the plans. A few insurers in the United States attempted merit rating plans in 1929 but dropped them shortly thereafter during the depression of the 1930's. Since 1952, New York and North Carolina have used a demerit plan which penalizes unsafe drivers. In 1959, following a study in California that associated claims frequency with traffic law violations, several insurance companies in certain states initiated what has become known as the *safe driver plan*.

Safe Driver Plan. The safe driver plan is built around the automobile rating classification system as revised effective January 1, 1970. There are already a large number of basic factors determining the rate charged for automobile insurance. The safe driver plan adds one more dimension to the rating system; i.e., the number of points charged against the car for unsafe driving.

Under the safe driver plan, points are assessed against the owner-operator of the car for different types of driving faults. Driving faults are measured by certain types of convictions or accidents arising during a three-year experience period prior to the time the application for insurance or for renewal is being made. For example, three points may be assessed against the driver for drunken driving, failure to stop at the scene of an accident, or driving with a suspended driver's license. One point is charged for any accident involving damages of $100 or more in a violation resulting in a financial responsibility law filing.

The driver is penalized in rate according to the number of points assessed. As of 1971, the penalty schedule for a standard car in a single-car family, for example, increases in premium: 1 point, 40%; 2 points, 90%; 3 points, 150%; and 4 or more points, 220%.

If the driver has no penalty points there will be no discount for a standard car, but the driver receives a 15% discount if two or more cars are owned. Even though families have several cars, the schedule of penalties applies to a maximum of two cars.

It can be seen that the effect of the safe driver plan on rates is substantial indeed. Even one accident might result in an increase in premium of 40%, while more serious driving offenses could more than triple one's premium. The youthful (under age 25) unmarried male who is a principal operator of a car already pays about 2.5 to 3 times the basic rate applicable to drivers over the age of 25. If a youthful male driver receives the maximum penalty under a safe driving plan, his automobile insurance may become a prohibitive cost to him. If this high cost results in the youthful driver driving without insurance, the objectives of the safe driver plan may be defeated.

Safe driver plans have the laudable objective of rewarding loss-prevention efforts as measured by actual accomplishments rather than by classification factors that are supposed to distinguish safe and unsafe drivers. Thus, the plans help meet two of the important criteria of rate-making: making a proper distinction between types of risk, and rewarding loss prevention. There are several practical difficulties in these plans, however, such as the difficulty in obtaining accurate information about a driver's traffic violations or accident record, inequities in the penalty scale, arguments over assessing points against the driver in a given accident, and the administrative burden of handling the plan.

A recent modification of merit rating in automobile insurance is the good student discount plan. Under this plan a male student under age 25 who maintains a grade average of B or better, ranks in the upper 20% of the class, or in other ways enjoys distinguished scholastic reputation (such as by being on the Dean's list) receives a discount on auto insurance. Such a student may also be eligible for other discounts, such as a discount for taking driver training courses. The amount of the discount given for being a good student may be as much as 25%. The justification for the discount appears to be mainly statistical. It has been found that accident costs are lower for good students than others. The reasons may include greater intelligence, better driving attitudes, or simply that the student is spending more time in studying and less time driving the family automobile.

Assigned Risk Plans. The question arises, "What happens to the driver who is not acceptable for insurance from any insurer to whom application is made?" To provide insurance for such drivers, private insurance companies have established assigned risk plans. Under such plans, the risk of insuring those previously rejected is shared equally among the participating companies.

As might be expected, loss experience is often unfavorable in spite of the considerably higher premiums which are charged individuals who must use these facilities. For example, the bodily injury liability loss ratio under the assigned risk plan in 1966 in New York was 123%, and the property damage liability loss ratio was 111%.[3] In some areas a substantial proportion of all private passenger cars insured in the area are under assigned risk. In 1968 in New York state, for example, 8.9% of all cars were in assigned risk; and in North and South Carolina, 17%.[4]

In effect the assigned risk plans constitute another rating class for private passenger car insurance, a catchall category for persons who do not fit into any other established rating class. If a person is not acceptable even to assigned risk underwriters (and there is a possibility of rejection here), the person must seek coverage through the surplus line (i.e., alien insurers) market often at very high rates or do without coverage. Undoubtedly, a major reason for assigned risk plans lies in the desire of private insurers to avoid the necessity of creating governmental insurers to take the risk. This is done even though assigned risk business is far from profitable.

Government Auto Insurance. In spite of efforts of private insurers to fill needs for auto insurance, at least one state, Maryland, set up its own auto insurance fund in 1973. This fund is available to any resident who has been turned down for auto insurance by at least two commercial insurers. An important factor leading to the establishment of the fund was the belief that too large a proportion of Maryland drivers had been placed in assigned risk at higher rates than normal. It is too soon to tell whether or not other states will follow Maryland's lead, but similar proposals have already been considered elsewhere, indicating the significance attached by the public to the problem of automobile insurance pricing.

[3] Dennis F. Reinmuth and Gary K. Stone, *A Study of Assigned Risk Plans* (Washington: U.S. Department of Transportation, 1970), p. 38.

[4] *Ibid.*, p. 35.

Experience Rating in Workers' Compensation

Experience rating plans are widely used in workers' compensation insurance. The general theory is that an employer has some control over loss ratio and is entitled to a credit for a good loss-prevention record, or, on the other hand, should pay a higher rate if the loss record is poorer than the average.

In the experience rating plan adopted by private insurers and administered by the National Council on Compensation Insurance, a national rate-making agency, each employer must have some minimum premium such as $1,500 which would be payable if standard manual rates were charged. The details of the plan are quite involved, but the general procedure is to determine for each occupational class some expected loss ratio against which is compared the insured's actual loss ratio. If the actual loss ratio is 90% of the expected loss ratio, the insured's rate for the coming year is 90% of the manual rate. If the actual loss ratio is 130% of the expected loss ratio, the insured must pay 130% of the manual rate during the coming year.

Under experience rating plans not all losses suffered by an insured are counted. The plan involves a stabilizing factor so that unusually large losses cannot operate to increase unreasonably the small employer's rate. However, for the large employer, larger losses receive increasing weight so that if in Massachusetts, for example, an employer's standard premium is $380,000 or more, all losses are considered, no matter how large. The effect is that the very large employer is more or less self-rating, while the medium-sized and small employers, in those years following a period of low losses, receive a credit which is not as large as it would be if they were self-rating. In those years following a period of high losses, the medium-sized and small employers pay a penalty which is not as large as it would be if they were self-rating. Over a period of years if the loss experience in a given category of industry is consistently bad, the manual rate and expected losses for that class will be adjusted so that in any given period a certain rating class of risks will tend to bear its total loss burden. But experience rating deals with rate adjustments for individual insureds within a given class on a year-to-year basis.

Experience rating in workers' compensation gives employers an incentive to do whatever is within their control to prevent accidents, a very desirable objective of any rating system. It rewards the safety efforts of employers by the test of "what effect did it have," not "what effect should it have had," as is the practice in fire insurance. Employers may spend a great deal of money on safety efforts, but if these efforts fail, no rate credit will be forthcoming.

Experience Rating in Unemployment Insurance

Under the general theory that an employer can control the rate of employment in the firm, all states except Alaska have laws which provide that if the employer has a favorable record of losses, the firm's unemployment insurance tax may be reduced. An employer's rate can be reduced to 0 in 15 states, but in 13 states it cannot fall below .1% of covered payrolls. On the other hand, this rate cannot be increased above 4% to 4.5% in about half the states, and in no case can the tax be raised beyond 6.6%.[5]

Although there are several different formulas of experience rating in use, each formula has the basic purpose of providing an incentive to the employer to stabilize employment and to allocate the cost of unemployment as nearly as feasible to those who are considered mainly responsible for it. In about half the states an employer must have three or more years of experience with unemployment claims before claiming eligibility for a reduction from the standard 2.7% rate. In the remaining states the law may permit a reduction based on as little as one year's experience for a new employer. If during this period unemployment insurance benefits paid to workers who were laid off were less than the contributions paid in, a reserve is established for the employer's account. If the ratio of this reserve to the firm's total payroll rises above a certain point, the employer is entitled to a reduced tax rate for the future. The following table shows excerpts from the most favorable experience rating schedule as of January 1, 1965, in California and Missouri. As seen from the excerpts, in California an employer may not obtain a rate lower than 3.5% of payroll until the ratio of reserve to taxable payrolls reaches seven. In California the reserve ratio is calculated by dividing total reserves accumulated in all past years to the average payroll in the preceding three years. In California the employer's contribution rate never is reduced below 2.2%, no matter how high the reserve ratio becomes. In Missouri an employer's effective tax rate can be reduced to zero, once the reserve ratio equals 15 or above. The reserve ratio type of experience rating formula is used in 32 states, but no two schedules are alike. Presumably, these differences arise because of differing conditions of unemployment, different benefit formulas, and other factors. Because of experience rating, unemployment taxes in the past have averaged about 1.2% of covered payroll.[6]

Reserve Ratio	Employer Contribution Rate	
	California	Missouri
Minus balance	3.5%	3.6%
.5	3.5	2.7
2.5	3.5	2.5
5.0	3.5	2.0
7.0	3.2	1.6
10.0	2.9	.8
Above 15	—	0
Above 17	2.2	0

Most state laws contain provisions which seek to excuse the employer from penalties in experience rating for conditions over which the employer has little

[5] U.S. Department of Labor, *Comparison of State Unemployment Insurance Laws as of January 1, 1970* (1971), TT1.

[6] See *Labor Market and Economic Security* for current estimates on this figure.

or no control. Thus, it is common to find that there is a maximum limit which can be placed on the amount charged any one employer, where more than one employer has hired a worker during the base period. Often no employer is charged for certain types of unemployment benefits paid, such as those paid when the period of employment was of short duration.

Experience rating permits an individual employer to earn lower unemployment compensation taxes, but it is possible that a state may find itself in an embarrassing position if the combined tax collections are insufficient to meet all claims. For this reason, a majority of the states provide that the total fund must be of a certain size before any employer is entitled to an experience rate. In 17 states the fund must be equal to some percentage of total payrolls (as defined) in that state before any experience rate can be permitted.

Administrative arrangements have been worked out so that a worker may file a claim in a state other than that in which the employment occurred. Thus, the worker may collect benefits in the new state, but the former state is charged with the claim and must reimburse the state of new residence. In this way, labor mobility is not reduced, and employers in the new state are not required to bear the burden of a new worker's unemployment benefit payments.

Experience rating in unemployment compensation insurance has been criticized on several grounds. The main element of the criticism is that the fundamental basis of experience rating is invalid for this type of insurance. Experience rating presupposes that the insureds, particularly if they are large employers, can to a large extent control their own losses. Through experience rating the insured is given a financial incentive to take measures to accomplish this end. In unemployment insurance, however, employers frequently are subject to market forces over which they have no control and therefore cannot help the unemployment situation except in certain cases. The employer has some control over technological changes within the plant or malfunctions in production scheduling which cause unemployment. On the other hand, there exists little control over the buying habits of the customers.

Another criticism is that experience rating has a destabilizing effect on unemployment. This is caused by the fact that the employer's contributions increase during depression time when they are least affordable, and decrease during good times when the employer can most afford to lay aside funds for future obligations. Experience rating is therefore said to impose penalties on employers for conditions over which they have no control and to reward them for reducing unemployment when individually they had little to do with the economic recovery which gave rise to lowered unemployment.

Retrospective Rating in Workers' Compensation

In workers' compensation insurance, experience rating is applied automatically, but retrospective rating is entirely a voluntary agreement between the insured and the insurer. If the employer's payroll is such that a standard premium of $1,000 or more is entailed, it is considered that the firm is large enough to develop experience that is partially credible. (A *standard premium* is defined as what the employer would have paid at manual rates after adjustment for experience rating, but before any adjustment for retrospective rating.) In practice, an employer likely to use retrospective rating would generally be considerably larger than this, since a standard premium of only \$1,000 means that the payroll approximates \$100,000 and the number of employees is therefore only about 12 (assuming an average wage of \$8,000 a year). Even one accident could easily cause a loss in excess of \$1,000. This might cause a very substantial increase in the employer's retrospective premium, depending on the nature of the plan selected.

There are various plans of retrospective rating and the employer must make a choice among them. Assuming that the employer is large enough and that both parties are agreeable to retrospective rating, which plan should the employer use? Essentially, this question reduces to one of how much risk the employer is willing to assume, i.e., how great a loss the employer is willing to accept if the experience turns out to be bad in return for a reduced premium if the experience is good.

The basic retrospective rating formula is given by the expression: [7]

$$R = [BP + (L)(LCF)]TM$$

where R = Retrospective premium payable for the year in question.

BP = A basic premium (in dollars) designed to cover fixed costs of the insurer in handling the business.

L = Losses (in dollars) actually suffered by the employer.

LCF = Loss conversion factor, a multiplying factor designed to cover the variable costs of the insurer (such as claim adjustment expenses).

TM = Tax multiplier, a factor designed to reflect the premium tax levied by the state on the insurer's business.

The basic premium declines as the size of the employer increases, and differs with the type of plan used. The loss conversion factor is a constant percentage, as is the tax multiplier, regardless of the size of the employer. The formula is subject to the operation of certain minimums and maximums, both of which decline as the size of the employer increases, except for the plan in which the maximum amount paid by the employer is the standard premium.

The operation of the formula is such that the larger the employer, the less risk there is associated with the use of retrospective rating (the maximum and minimum premium declines). Yet, a relatively small employer who is accepted for retrospective rating has an opportunity to lower the premium if the losses can be kept within bounds, and still obtain protection against paying more than would be the case in the absence of the retrospective plan.

To illustrate the operation of retrospective rating, consider the case of employer McGuire, whose standard premium is \$10,000. Two of the choices open in retrospective rating are charted in Figure 26–1. If McGuire takes Plan A, the premium is guaranteed never to exceed \$10,000, but on the other hand,

[7] There are other elements in retrospective rating formulas such as adjustments for individual loss limitations, but for simplicity they will be ignored in the present discussion.

OPERATION OF A RETROSPECTIVE RATING FORMULA **Figure 26-1**

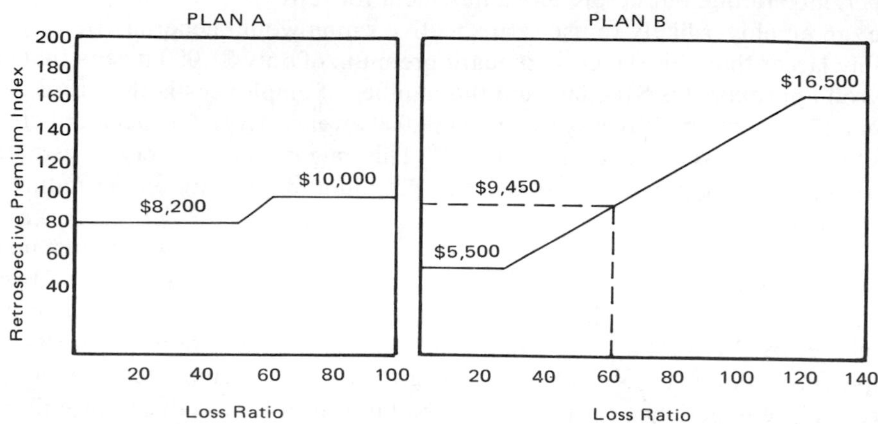

Note: It is assumed that the employer has a payroll such that the standard premium is $10,000. A standard premium is that which the insured would have paid in the absence of a retrospective rating plan. "Loss ratio" represents the ratio of actual losses suffered to the standard premium. "Retrospective premium index" is the ratio of the employer's finally determined retrospective premium to the standard premium. This index is converted to dollars and shown on the graph for an employer with a $10,000 standard premium.

there is the opportunity to reduce the premium modestly to $8,200, which is the minimum for an employer of McGuire's size. For example, if McGuire has losses of $5,000, the retrospective premium would be calculated according to the formula, as follows:[8]

$$R = [\$2,800 + (\$5,000)\ (1.14)]\ 1.026 = \$8,721$$

Since the retrospective premium is higher than the minimum of $8,200 but lower than the maximum of $10,000, McGuire's workers' compensation premium for the year is $8,721. If McGuire has losses less than $4,555 no further credit on the premium is received, due to the operation of the minimum. On the other hand, if losses are approximately $6,100 or more, McGuire pays the maximum premium of $10,000.[9]

One might wonder why every employer would not seek to use Plan A. It would seem that there would be nothing to lose and yet there would be a possibility of gain. The answer is that not every employer may be acceptable to the insurer for retrospective rating, particularly if the employer pays little attention to safety procedures. Furthermore, the employer may wish to have the opportunity of reducing the premium by a greater amount than is possible through Plan A.

[8] The LCF of 1.14; the TM of 1.026; the minimum premium, $8,200; and the basic premium, $2,800; are those applying to employers of this size class in Massachusetts in 1960.

[9] The student should verify this by substituting each figure in the basic retrospective rating formula.

Under Plan B, McGuire may reduce the premium to as low as $5,500, but the maximum possible premium now rises to $16,500, 165% of the standard premium. Under Plan B, McGuire trades the possibility of additional premium savings for the possibility of larger losses. Figure 26–1 shows what McGuire's retrospective premium would be for any loss ratio under the two plans. For example, if McGuire has a loss ratio of 60% (i.e., $6,000 in compensation losses during the year), a total premium of $9,450 will be paid by McGuire under Plan B, which is less than would have been paid under Plan A with the same loss ratio. This is due to the fact that the basic premium is less under Plan B than under Plan A for an employer of McGuire's size. Actually, the majority of the total premium volume in workers' compensation which is subject to retrospective rating is under another plan (Plan D) which permits greater flexibility in selecting the precise limits of liability which the insured may wish to assume. Thus, the insured may select the maximum and the minimum loss ratio to be assumed and may also incorporate within the plan not only workers' compensation exposure but also general liability exposure subject to certain limits.

An employer might not know the results of a retrospective rating plan until several years after the expiration of the policy year, as it may take a long time to reach a final determination of the actual amount of the loss that a given job injury has caused. Furthermore, the retrospective rating plan may be written to encompass a three-year period, a factor which delays the final result even further. Nevertheless, statistics over the past years suggest that an employer may expect to pay, on the average, about 80% of what would have been paid under a standard premium plan.[10] This result does not seem to vary materially, no matter which type of retrospective rating plan is being used.

Schedule Rating in Fire Insurance on Commercial Property

Fire insurance rating systems employ two basic methods: schedule rating for commercial buildings and manual rating for dwellings.

The main objective of schedule rating in the fire insurance field is to provide an incentive for loss prevention and to achieve fairness by recognizing basic differences in fire hazards among insured property. It would obviously be unfair to assign a farm building the same rate as a building directly across from a fire station, or to give a small retail store building the same rate as a factory building. Therefore, an elaborate method has been developed to provide equity in fire insurance rating.

It is not practical to reward the owner of a "safe" building by the techniques of experience or retrospective rating. Losses occur so infrequently that an insurer would be in a position of granting a very large discount annually to almost every insured. If a loss did occur, the insured's premium for the year in

[10] Based on data supplied by the National Council of Compensation Insurance, for three-year plans beginning in 1953. There were 476 accounts with standard premiums of $51,554,176 on which the retrospective premium was $41,099,131, or 79.7% The data represented experience for insureds with both stock and nonstock insurers.

question would certainly be increased, but it is inconceivable that it could be increased enough to compensate for all the years during which very low premiums were paid. Therefore, a system of rewarding the insured for adopting safety features which are judged to reduce the fire hazard has been adopted. Since every commercial building is unique in this respect, rating organizations are set up in each state to inspect and rate each building. Through mutual agreement, most insurers adhere to the rate so promulgated.

Details on fire insurance rating methods vary from state to state. There are, however, two basic systems of rate-making for commercial buildings—the Dean analytic system[11] and the Universal Mercantile Schedule (UMS). Under each system an arbitrary (basic) rate is assigned to a building of a certain type. Each building to be rated is subjected to a schedule of debits and credits from this arbitrary rate to determine the existence or absence of certain safety features. Hence, the term ''schedule'' arises. Under the Dean system, the debits and credits are in percentages; under the UMS the charges are in absolute amounts, while the credits are in percentages. The advantage of the use of percentage lies in the fact that an insured receives proportionate credit for all safety features included in the building (or proportionate charges for lack of them) when the basic rate changes, as might occur when the city is reclassified by the National Board of Fire Underwriters for insurance purposes.

The debits and credits are more or less arbitrary and are not changed frequently. For example, a schedule may add 5% to the basic premium for the absence of fire extinguishers or certain fire walls in the building. Credits of 20% or more may be allowed for an approved sprinkler system. The amount of charge or credit is not based on statistics but on engineering judgment as to how much a particular feature affects the probability of loss. The basic premiums or starting points are also more or less arbitrary. As its starting point, the Dean system might use a one-story brick building of average construction in a city with relatively poor fire protection. (Other tables used in the Dean system might employ a different starting point.) A basic rate of $1 per $100 may be assigned. The arbitrary rate is assumed to cover the unanalyzed hazards facing the building. The debits and credits to the basic rate are then computed and are intended to reflect those hazards which can be analyzed. Since the rate for such a building is assumed to be high, most of the schedule changes grant credits according to how much better than this is the building being rated. Under the UMS, the starting point is a much higher class building and therefore there are more frequent uses of charges against the basic rate.

The basic rate and the debits and credits in both systems are affected by four major underwriting factors: the fire protection class of the city of location, the type of construction, the class of occupancy of the building, and the degree to which the building is exposed to losses originating outside the building confines.

Fire Protection Class. The National Board of Fire Underwriters has established 10 classes of cities of more than 25,000 population, according to such factors as

[11] Named after its originator, A. F. Dean, who introduced it in 1901.

water supply, fire department, fire alarm systems, building laws, police protection, and structural conditions in the city. A Class 10 city is one with very little fire protection and a Class 1 city has fewer than 500 deficiency points. Basic rates might vary from $1 per $100 of building value in Class 10 cities to about $.50 per $100 for Class 1 cities, depending on the height of the structure and its occupancy. Such a system obviously provides a loss-prevention incentive for the community as a whole.

Type of Construction. There are four basic types of construction recognized in fire insurance rating: A, B, C, and D. A Class A building is one with walls, floors, and roof of masonry or concrete, and with all load walls supported by an independent steel frame. A Class B structure is similar to Class A except that interior walls and floors are not constructed of masonry or concrete. A Class C building does not meet all the specific requirements of Class B. For example, a Class C structure may have a frame structure on the roof, or it may have one or more exterior walls of hollow tile. Class D buildings are generally frame structures and include most private residences.

Class of Occupancy. Occupancy is an important factor in schedule rating, since some tenants of commercial buildings, such as hat shops, lumberyards, and explosives manufacturers, obviously present a more serious fire hazard than hardware stores or grocery stores. Consideration is given to susceptibility of stock to loss, speed with which fire may spread, and other factors.

Exposure to Losses Outside the Building. Exposure to other structures will affect the fire insurance rate on commercial buildings. For example, charges are made when other buildings are located too close to the building being rated.

One may ask, "Why are fire insurance rates not based on statistics gathered for each type of building to justify the rate charged?" The answer lies in the fact that because commercial structures are so different with respect to each of the four basic rating factors, it would be extremely difficult to gather credible data for each factor. Since fires are relatively infrequent, many years must pass before a sufficient record of losses could be accumulated to lend credence to a rate so charged. By the time sufficient losses would have been recorded, the management, protection class, exposure, and even type of construction may have changed so much that an entirely different classification would have to be made. The rate-maker cannot wait for all this to happen, but must develop some type of rate, according to the best methods available.

RATE-MAKING IN LIFE INSURANCE

In life insurance the pure premium method is the basis of what is essentially manual rate-making. There are two basic factors that affect the pure premium—the costs of mortality and the interest rates earned by the insurer of funds deposited with it. These funds exist because of the practice of requiring payment in advance for life insurance protection, and because of the practice of issuing policies on a level premium basis. We shall see precisely how these two factors affect the calculation of the pure premium. Once the pure premium has been determined, a loading formula is applied, and the final gross premium to the policyholder is determined.

Net Single Premium

The *net single premium* is the amount the insurer must collect in advance to meet all the claims arising during the policy period. To illustrate the general method of calculating the net single premium, we shall assume that a given insurer wishes to determine the premium for a one-year term insurance contract with a face amount of $1,000 for a group of entrants, age 20. Reference to the CSO 1958 table of mortality reveals that the probability of death at age 20 is .00179. This means that out of 100,000 persons living at the beginning of the year, 179 will die during the year. The rate-maker in life insurance makes two assumptions in calculating the necessary premium:

1. All premiums will be collected at the *beginning* of the year and hence it will be possible to earn interest on the advance payment for a full year.
2. Death claims are not paid until the *end* of the year in question. In practice, of course, death claims are paid whenever death occurs. Thus, the assumptions of the rate-maker are inaccurate, for on the average, one half of a year's interest will be lost on the sums so paid. However, an adjustment for this loss of interest is made in the loading formula, to be discussed later.

Calculation of the premium under these assumptions is simplified since the insurer knows that if a $1,000 policy is issued to each of the 100,000 entrants, death claims of $179,000 will be payable at the end of the year. The problem then is one of discounting the sum for one year at some assumed rate of interest. Thus, if the insurer is to guarantee earnings of 2.5%, $.9756 must be on hand now in order to have $1 at the end of one year.[12] Therefore, to find the present value of $179,000 at the end of one year, this amount is multiplied by .9756, obtaining $174,632. The proportionate share of this obligation attached to each entrant is $174,632/100,000, or $1.75. If each entrant pays $1.75, the insurer will have sufficient funds on hand to pay for death costs under the policy. The $1.75 is known as the *net single premium*.

The net single premium for a $1,000 term policy of, say, three years is calculated in a similar manner, except that the calculation is carried out over a three-year period instead of one. The following tabulation illustrates the method.

Number Assumed To Be Living At		Number Dying	Amount of Death Claims	Present Value of $1 at 2½% Interest	Present Value of Death Claim
Age 20	100,000	179	$179,000	.9756	$174,632
Age 21	99,821	183	183,000	.9518	174,179
Age 22	99,638	186	186,000	.9286	172,720
					$521,531

[12] See Appendix C for an explanation of the calculation of this figure.

$$\frac{\$521,531}{100,000} = \$5.22, \text{ Net single premium}$$

It will be observed that each person must pay *in advance* the sum of $5.22 for three years of protection.

While the calculation above is a simple one, it illustrates the basic method of premium calculation in life insurance. The net single premium for a whole life policy, for example, is figured in exactly the same manner as the example above, except that the calculations are made for each year from the starting age to the end of the mortality table.

Net Level Premium

It would be impractical to attempt to collect a net single premium from each member of an insured group. Few people would have the necessary funds for an advance payment of all future obligations. Therefore, actuaries must calculate an annual premium. At first consideration, it might be assumed that the annual premium would be found by dividing the net single premium by the number of years in the premium-paying period. Such a calculation would produce a net annual premium of $1.74 (5.22/3) in the preceding example for a three-year term policy. However, such a calculation would be erroneous for two reasons: (1) since the insurer will not have the entire amount of the net single premium on hand at the beginning of the period, it will not earn the amount of interest assumed in the calculation of the net single premium, and (2) the individuals who die will, of course, not be able to make their annual premium payments. In calculating the net single premium, it is assumed that members of the insured group will contribute their share of total claims at the beginning of the policy period.

Actuaries find the net level premium by dividing the net single premium by an amount known technically as the *present value of an annuity due,* which provides for an appropriate adjustment of the two factors described above. The present value of an annuity due of $1 a year for three years is the present value of a series of payments of $1 each year, the first payment due immediately, adjusted for the probability of survival each year. The calculation may be shown as follows:

Age	Present Value of $1, First Payment Due Immediately, at 2½% Interest	Number of Entrant Group Still Living	Discounted Value of Each Payment
20	$1.00	100,000	$100,000
21	.9756	99,821	97,385
22	.9518	99,638	94,835
			$292,220

$$\frac{\$292,220}{100,000} = \$2.92, \text{ Value per entrant}$$

The present value of an annuity due may be interpreted as follows: What is the present value of a promise of a large group of people to pay a sum of $1 each year for three years? Since the first payment is due immediately (corresponding to the fact that life insurance premiums are collected in advance), its present value is $1. The second payment is due one year from now. If everyone lived to pay his or her share, the present value of the second payment would be $.9756. Since not everyone will live, however, the $.9756 must be reduced to reflect this fact. The amount is therefore reduced by a factor which specifies how many may be expected to live to pay their share (i.e., the amount is multiplied by the probability of survival of the original group of entrants). This process is continued, and we find that the present value of the promise is $2.92. If the sum is divided into the present value of the total death claims (i.e., the net single premium), the insurer knows how much must be collected annually from a specified group of insureds in order to have a sum which will enable the insurer to pay all obligations. The net level premium for the three-year term policy is, thus, $5.22/$2.92 = $1.79, which is, of course, greater than the quantity $5.22/3 = $1.74, determined by a division of the net single premium by the premium-paying period.

Gross Annual Premium

The net level premium for life insurance represents the pure premium which is unadjusted for the expenses of doing business. The pure premium is actually the contribution that each insured makes to the aggregate insurance fund each year for the payment of both death and living benefits. Various formulas are used to load the pure premiums to allow for the necessary expenses of the insurer. In general, an attempt is made to separate all costs into two categories: (1) fixed overhead cost per policy, representing a portion of those costs which continue regardless of the volume of business being conducted, and (2) variable cost per policy, reflecting those expenses made necessary by issuance of a particular contract. Variable costs are further subdivided into those which depend primarily on the amount of the premium per policy and those which depend on other factors, such as face amount, type of contract, and special underwriting considerations.

Examples of fixed overhead loading would be the proration of expenses such as home office clerical costs, executive salaries, rent, and other expenses which continue at the same rate regardless of current business volume. Each policy may be assigned a flat dollar amount as its pro rata share of these costs.

Examples of variable costs depending on the amount of premium per policy include agent's commissions, premium taxes, and loss of interest because premiums are not always collected in full at the beginning of a policy year but may be collected in installments. Acquisition costs are large by comparison with the annual premium, often amounting to more than the annual premium. To eliminate an extra charge in the first year, these costs are usually spread out over the premium-paying period. A further loading factor must be added to offset the fact that due to lapses, a certain portion of these costs will not be collected.

Examples of variable costs depending on factors other than premium size include the following:

1. The physician's medical examination fee.
2. Loss of interest due to the fact that death claims are paid immediately rather than at the end of the policy year.
3. Higher mortality costs resulting from the fact that certain types of contracts, especially those with a large term element, have an element of adverse selection. (Thus, those persons with term policies who suffer poor health are more likely to convert them to permanent contracts than those persons whose health remains sound.)
4. Additional costs of service since certain contracts require more service than others, e.g., industrial insurance policies in which premiums are collected at the insured's residence.
5. Contingency costs. Life insurance contracts are written for long periods and are predicated on forecasts of mortality, interest, and loading factors, all of which may vary from those values on which the contract is based. Therefore, each contract is loaded to provide a margin for these fluctuations. In participating policies, any excess amounts are returned to the policyholders in the form of dividends.

Loading formulas which reflect these elements in the premium may sometimes be quite complicated in practice. Furthermore, there is little uniformity in specific methods of loading. For competitive reasons, a nonparticipating insurer must calculate its loading costs more carefully than a participating insurer, since there is no possibility for the former to return any excess collections through dividends.

Effect of Other Factors

In recent years, many insurers have taken into consideration factors other than age, such as sex, policy amount, and general health status, in calculating their life insurance rates. For example, while it has been long known that women outlive men on an average of six or seven years, still not all insurers grant women a lower life insurance rate, although they universally charge them a higher rate for annuities. Among insurers granting a lower rate to women, the typical practice is to charge women the rate that applies to a man three years younger.

Many insurers now offer ''specials'' at lower rates than standard, reflecting a variety of cost-reducing factors achieved through savings inherent in issuing larger policy amounts, by reduction of agents' commissions, or by inserting less liberal settlement options. The rates on these ''specials'' are usually accounted for in the loading formulas.

Most life insurers will accept an applicant with a medical or physical handicap at a substandard (higher) rate, depending on the nature of the handicap. Extra premiums for substandard physical risks are promulgated largely on the basis of underwriting judgment, supported by some statistical evidence on the longevity of these classes.

Critique of Life Insurance Rate-Making

Although life insurance rate-making is based on statistical procedures and is supposed to be quite scientific in nature, there are still wide variations in rates for which no really adequate explanation exists, other than variations in the degree of subjective risk as perceived by actuaries. Subjective risk tends to be a significant factor in life insurance rate-making for several reasons. Once a life insurance premium is promulgated for a given insured, it cannot be increased during the life of the policy. In the case of whole life policies, the insurer must guarantee the same rate for a period which may range up to 100 years (in case of a policy issued on an infant). Under settlement options, the obligations of the insurer under a single contract may exceed this period. Therefore, it is common for life insurers to charge premiums that are loaded for contingencies and which may turn out to be excessive. For example, the mortality table itself contains a built-in safety factor since the actual death rates are overstated by a certain amount. Insurers guarantee only a minimum rate of interest which is almost invariably much lower than the amount they expected to earn on investments. If death rates are lower than those anticipated, the insurer has charged more than necessary. In the case of mutual insurers, dividends represent the return of the excessive premiums and may be looked upon as a method of achieving necessary adjustments in the premium rate as costs vary over the years. Stock insurers who issue nonparticipating policies attempt to meet the competition of mutuals by issuing a rate which is lower than the mutual rate by approximately the amount of the anticipated dividend.

Life insurance rate-making gives no specific recognition to the criterion of loss prevention, other than perhaps the suicide clause, since it is assumed that each insured already has a strong incentive to continue living and no further stimulus is required. Of course, life insurers themselves are among the strongest supporters of campaigns to reduce death claims and to maintain health standards.

Interest-Adjusted Rates

Traditionally, the cost of life insurance (the net cost method) is determined by subtracting the sum of the dividends paid and the cash value at the end of the period in question from the premiums paid. Because this method ignores the time value of money, a newer method of pricing, called the *interest-adjusted method*, has been developed. Under this method, one first accumulates the annual premiums at some stated interest rate, say 4%, for a given period, say 20 years. Next, dividends, if any, are accumulated at the same interest rate for the same period. Then one subtracts the accumulated dividends and the cash value at the end of the period from the accumulated premiums. The result is then reduced to a common denominator by dividing through by the accumulation of $1 per year at 4% for 20 years.

The interest-adjusted method may be compared to the traditional method as follows. Suppose on a given policy of $1,000 there is an annual premium of $25, with anticipated dividends of 20%, or $5. Suppose the 20-year cash surrender value is $350. Assume money is worth 4% and the calculating period is 20 years. The cost of life insurance under the net cost method would be: 20 years of premium, $500, less dividends of $100, less terminal cash value of $350, equals $50 for 20 years, or $2.50 per year. Under the interest-adjusted cost method, the cost would be:

1. 20 years of premium accumulated at 4% (30.969 × $25)	$774.23
2. Subtract 20 years of dividends accumulated at 4% (30.969 × $5)	−154.85
	$619.38
3. Subtract cash surrender value in 20 years	−350.00
	$269.38
4. Interest-adjusted cost: Divide by accumulation of $1 a year for 20 years at 4% ($269.38/30.969)	$ 8.70

Note that, when adjusted for interest, the cost is much larger than without such an adjustment.

In studies by Joseph M. Belth, wide variations were found in life insurance rates, whether the rate was expressed as a gross premium, net premium (after dividends), or an interest-adjusted rate.[13]

Belth compared prices and premiums quoted on ordinary life policies, standard rates, age 35, in 1962 for 88 participating and 60 nonparticipating companies. A summary of his results follows.

	Participating Insurers	*Nonparticipating Insurers*
Premium Rate Comparison		
Approximate range of premium rates per $1,000 of face amount	$21—$29	$17—$22
Mean	$24.11	$19.32
Standard deviation	$ 1.22	$ .63
Coefficient of variation[14]	5.1%	3.3%
Price Comparison[15]		
Approximate range of prices per $1,000 of protection	$ 4—$14	$ 7—$11
Mean	$ 7.55	$ 8.80
Standard deviation	$ 1.52	$ .71
Coefficient of variation	20.1%	8.1%

[13] Joseph M. Belth, "Price Competition in Life Insurance," *Journal of Risk and Insurance*, Vol. 33, No. 3 (September, 1966), pp. 365-379. See also Belth's works, *The Retail Price Structures in American Life Insurance* (Bloomington, Indiana University, 1966), and *Life Insurance—A Consumer's Handbook* (Bloomington: Indiana University, 1973).

[14] The coefficient of variation is the standard deviation divided by the mean.

[15] Prices shown are 20-year level prices per $1,000 of protection, using 3% interest and certain specified mortality and lapse assumptions.

It may be observed that the relative variation in both premiums and interest-adjusted prices is greater for dividend-paying insurers than for those not paying dividends. The amount of variation in interest-adjusted rates is three or four times as great as that which exists in premiums alone.[16] These results were confirmed in another study of 81 insurers, covering a 20-year period.[17] It was found that the average interest-adjusted cost per $1,000 of ordinary life insurance issued to a male age 35 in 1972, and using projected dividend scales, varied as follows:

	Average Cost	*Standard Deviation*
Mutual (paying dividends)	$5.84	$1.15
Stock	6.30	.87
All insurers	6.01	1.07

In both studies, nondividend-paying insurers had a higher interest-adjusted cost, but with smaller variation, than dividend-paying companies. Specifically, stock insurer policies cost on the average 8% more than mutuals, but the relative variation was 24% lower. Significantly, for all insurers considered, the range of costs was such that the price charged by the lowest-ranking insurer was nearly 2.4 times that of the highest-ranking insurer.

These studies show the need for careful shopping by the life insurance buyer. They also reveal the heavy influence of subjective elements in life insurance rate-making. Hopefully, careful price comparisons by more life insurance consumers will help to reduce the large variations in existing rates.

RATE-MAKING IN OTHER LINES OF INSURANCE

Rate-making practices in residential fire, multiple-line, and marine insurance follow their own methods. A brief description of each follows.

Fire Insurance on Residences

Manual rating on residences is justified on the grounds that the exposure units are fairly homogeneous in character and it is neither necessary nor practical to make an inspection of each building for particular fire hazards. Manual classifications are therefore made with the following rating factors: type of roof, nearness to fire hydrants, and type of fire protection district in which the residence is located. Generally, the rate for contents, in both residential and commercial property, is higher than the rate applicable to the building because of their greater susceptibility to loss. This follows because total losses are relatively rare and often a majority of the damage is done to the contents instead of the building itself.

[16] For a book-length treatment of this subject, see Joseph M. Belth, *Life Insurance: A Consumer's Handbook* (Bloomington: Indiana University Press, 1973).

[17] Robert C. Hutchins and Charles E. Quenneville, "Rate of Return Versus Interest-Adjusted Cost," *Journal of Risk and Insurance,* Vol. 42, No. 1 (March, 1975), pp. 69-79.

Multiple-Line Rate-Making

A multiple-line policy, one covering many different types of perils under one contract, is mainly distinguished from other property liability contracts in that a separate rate is devised for a given class of insureds which is indivisible. A year-end audit determines the final premium. Under this approach, known as *composite rating,* a single rate is promulgated for an entire group of exposures regardless of location, type, special hazards in given areas, or other underwriting factors. Special rating organizations collect loss data and promulgate rates for multiple-line contracts. Usually these plans involve experience rating.

In certain multiple-line contracts, such as homeowners policies, indivisible rates are made up for contracts which cover both liability and physical damage perils. Rate-making in multiple-line contracts generally is in an experimental stage and there is little agreement upon the methods which should ultimately be adopted.

Marine Insurance

In marine insurance, both inland and ocean, underwriting judgment plays an even greater role than in commercial and residential insurance because of the great diversity of exposures. For example, because of changed conditions of weather, cargo, political conditions, nationality of the vessel, and other factors, the rate quoted for a given ocean passage might be different for each voyage. Two identical ships might be assigned a different rate depending on the type of operation in which each is engaged. In inland marine insurance, a given contractor's rate for an equipment floater will depend on the type of equipment used, record of losses, conditions under which the work is being done, etc. Statistics are of little help in formulating insurance rates for such diverse exposures. The underwriter must exercise judgment as to the value of the risk and act accordingly.

SUMMARY

1. The insurance premium is designed to cover two general types of costs: (a) the costs of loss claims under the contract, and (b) the costs of administering the insurance mechanism. The former cost is usually referred to as the pure or net premium, while the total charge is called the gross premium.
2. Criteria for sound rate-making specify that a rate should be adequate, but not excessive, and should distinguish risks fairly according to the degree of hazard. These criteria are usually specified in state regulations, but there is no general agreement on just how the criteria shall be applied to each type of insurance. Additional criteria for sound rate-making are that rates should be kept current and should encourage loss prevention.
3. Although statistics form the basis of many rate-making methods, in other instances it appears that the rates are more or less arbitrarily or subjectively determined. In all cases, underwriting judgment

plays an important part in determining the final rate.

4. There are two basic types of rates: the manual, or class, rate and the individual, or merit, rate. For the manual rate, it is assumed that homogeneous classes of insureds can be distinguished and each risk in the group is charged the same premium, representing its fair share of the total losses. For the merit rate, it is assumed that individual risks are sufficiently different that recognition can be given to particular hazards attaching to each risk.
5. A concept of great importance in rate-making is credibility, the degree to which the observed loss experience can be relied upon in formulating or revising a rate. Merit rating plans are based on this concept, which in turn rests upon the basic assumptions of the law of large numbers.
6. Individual, or merit rating, plans are of four general types: (a) Those where special recognition is given to particular subclasses of insureds beforehand in the form of manual rate deviations or afterward in the form of dividends for meritorious loss experience. (b) Those plans using *schedule* rating, where the particular hazards of an insured's operation are recognized by special charges or credits from some base rate. (c) Those plans involving *experience* rating. (d) Those plans involving *retrospective* rating.
7. Experience rating affects the individual rate of an insured after an actual loss experience in a given period has been analyzed. The revisions, if any, affect the future premium rate. Retrospective rating allows the insured to determine the premium, in whole or in part, for the period under consideration; i.e., the final premium for a period is determined by the loss experience of that period.
8. Although rate-making in life insurance is supposed to be among the more scientific applications of rate-making in insurance, nevertheless large differentials exist in premiums and price structures which cannot be easily explained except in terms of subjective factors in rate-making. A pure premium is determined by reference to a table of mortality and a consideration of minimum assumed interest rates. The gross premium is determined by somewhat refined loading formulas.

QUESTIONS FOR REVIEW AND DISCUSSION

1. (a) What is the main distinction between a rate and a premium?
   (b) In this connection, why is reference usually made to a retrospective premium rather than to a retrospective rate?
2. Judgment in insurance rate-making enters in at least two major respects. It is common to mention the role of judgment in arriving at rates on new coverages or unique exposures where no adequate statistics are present. What is the second way in which judgment affects rate-making? Discuss.
3. In what way does judgment enter into life insurance rate-making, even though objective factors such as mortality rates, interest, and expense margins are reasonably well known? What evidence is there that judgment plays a significant part in life insurance rate-making?
4. A witness at a Senate hearing on insurance stated, "An insurance rate is the price charged for insurance. The price should bring enough money into the insurer's pockets so that the insurer will be able to pay claims when and as claims are made. That principle is the law and the prophet; all else is commentary. Everything else . . .

must take second place to this elementary point that if the insurer does not get enough money to pay claims as they mature, then he is not an insurer but a fraud."
(a) Which of the criteria for sound rate-making is being emphasized?
(b) Do you agree that this criterion is of greater importance than any other?
(c) What fundamental characteristic of insurance rate-making differentiates it from pricing in other lines? Does this characteristic explain the emphasis in the above comments? How?

5. An underwriter is reviewing a body of loss experience to decide what rate to promulgate in the next year. The dwelling experience for fire losses is based on $1,650,000 of earned premiums, and the mercantile contents experience is based on $3,150,000 of earned premium. The loss ratio used in promulgating the old rate was .50 in both cases, but the loss ratio developed during the period under review was .30 for dwellings and .70 for mercantile contents. The dwelling experience is 80% credible and the mercantile experience is 30% credible.
(a) Using the credibility formula in the text, develop the rate increase or decrease, as a percentage, for the forthcoming year. Show all your calculations.
(b) Why is the credibility factor assigned to the dwellings larger than the factor assigned to the mercantile contents, in spite of the fact that the dollar value of the earned premiums for the mercantile contents is twice the earned premium developed on the dwellings?

6. In the field of credit insurance a critic charged that under the experience rating system used, if an insured has a large loss in a given year, the premium is increased the following year. The result is that the insured pays for personal losses in the higher premiums that are charged. The critic reaches the conclusion, therefore, that if an insured must pay for these losses in any event, the insurance contract is of little value, except perhaps as a device to smooth out fluctuations in bad debt loss experience. Criticize the above conclusions.

7. Carver notices in the paper a report that national fire losses are 10% above the previous year's level. Carver asks your advice as to whether or not fire insurance rates can be expected to rise correspondingly in the area. What would you tell Carver?

8. A financial publication reported, "For most people, insurance is second only to the car itself among the costs of owning an automobile . . . . Yet the cost of auto liability insurance, which has been climbing steadily . . . seems sure to go higher still . . . and many motorists will find it increasingly difficult to buy insurance at all . . . . This year underwriting losses probably will total some $300 million. . . . The size of the coming rate increases will vary widely from area to area."
(a) What factors are likely to be dominant explanations of the increase in automobile rates?
(b) What general method of rate-making is used in automobile insurance, as suggested by the reference to area differences.

9. Why is cooperation among insurers regarding certain rate-making procedures looked upon as desirable and even essential when there are strict prohibitions against collusion in price-fixing among sellers of tangible commodities? Explain.

10. Following the San Francisco earthquake of 1906, many insurers failed to liquidate all their claims and went into insolvency. Suggest a fundamental rule of rate-making which may have been violated by those insurers.

11. It has been suggested that the practice of rating automobiles on the basis of the number of exposed vehicles introduces an element of unfairness into automobile rating structures. The claim is that one car may be driven by several drivers and another car may be driven only by one driver. Yet both cars would be assigned the same rate, other things being equal. Is there any justification in this argument?

12. You are given certain data (simplified) below:

Age	Number Living	Number Dying	Present Value of $1 at 2%	
			Year	Factor
25	1,000	10	1	.98
26	990	12	2	.96
27	978	13	3	.94

(a) Calculate the net single premium for a two-year term insurance policy of $1,000 issued at age 25.
(b) Calculate the net level premium for the same policy.
(c) What premium will the insured actually pay?
(d) Why cannot the level premium for the policy be properly computed by dividing the net single premium by two? Explain.

13. "Empirical studies reveal wide variations in life insurance rates." To what extent does the evidence referred to justify the conclusion (a) that price competition is ineffective in the life insurance field because otherwise less efficient producers would be eliminated and (b) that it is cheaper to buy life insurance, on the average, from a nonparticipating insurer than from a participating insurer?

14. State what modifications you would make in the calculations in Question 12 if the problem were to find the answer for (a) a whole life policy, and (b) a 30-year endowment policy.

15. Using the fictitious data in Table 26–1, calculate the net single premium and the net level premium at age 110, at 3% interest, for a face amount of $1,000 for: (a) an ordinary life policy, (b) a three-year pay whole life policy, and (c) a two-year endowment policy. (d) Suggest why life insurance is seldom purchased by the aged.

16. In life insurance the probability of death per 1,000 persons born was such that 25% of the group would die by age 5 in 1850, by age 25 in 1901, by age 48 in 1930, and by age 63 in 1959. This remarkable decline in mortality has not been accompanied by proportionate decreases in life insurance premiums. For example, an advertisement by Mutual Life of New York in the *Boston Daily Advertiser* dated February 28, 1843, quoted insurance rates "for life" for a person age 35 as $27.60 annually. Seven-year term insurance for age 35 was $15.30 and one-year term insurance, $13.60. Today term insurance rates are about one-half those levels, and ordinary life rates are only four fifths of those quoted. Suggest possible reasons why rates are not even lower today in spite of the great decline in mortality rates.

17. Concerning unemployment insurance a writer stated, "Experience

DATA FOR QUESTION 15

Table 26-1

Age	Number Living	Number Dying	Number of Years	Discount Factor
110	50	10	1	.97
111	40	10	2	.94
112	30	10	3	.92
113	20	15	4	.88
114	5	5	5	.85
115	0	..	..	..

rating may in part tend to be self-defeating. Employers, in attempting to secure more favorable tax rates, are likely to engage in a variety of practices (some ethically defensible, others not so) that may increase employment stability for a small core of employees, but which will greatly increase the instability for another group." Explain how this might be possible.

18. What is the basic distinction between experience rating and retrospective rating? What is the basic similarity?

19. Employer *X* and *X*'s insurer agree to retrospective rating for the workers' compensation risk, but *X* is undecided as to which of the two plans, A or B, is better. *X*'s standard premium would be $10,000 if no plan were selected. *X* believes that due to an unusually effective effort of the safety engineer in operating a loss-prevention campaign the loss record will be very low. Advise *X*, pointing out the advantages and disadvantages of your recommendation.

20. It has been argued that retrospective rating eliminates the need for self-insurance in the lines of insurance where it is used. Do you agree? Why or why not?

21. A cement manufacturer, *M*, in Connecticut has a payroll that generates a standard workers' compensation premium of $85,000. *M* is considering four retrospective rating plans, which, assuming annual compensation losses of $35,000, would produce premiums as follow: Plan A, $75,500; Plan B, $67,449; Plan C, $69,893; and Plan J, $70,900. *M*'s agent presents the information in Table 26–2. Which plan should *M* accept? What assumptions underly your answer? Explain.

22. (a) What are the chief factors affecting the fire insurance rate in commercial structures?
(b) Are the rating systems that reflect these factors based on statistics? Why or why not?

23. A trade publication reported in 1971 that a newly-installed payroll deduction plan for employees offering them property and liability insurance at a reduced rate was selling well. The plan covered auto, homeowners, and personal excess liability insurance at rates "about 15% lower than the insurance rating board figures."
(a) What type of justification might there be for a 15% reduction in rates for this coverage below that normally sold to individuals?
(b) Besides lower rates, what other advantages might group property and liability insurance have for an individual? Are there any disadvantages? Discuss.

24. Irma's employer complained that the price of unemployment insurance is too high. Irma brought certain data to the employer's attention: In 1974 nearly $7 billion was paid out in unemployment insurance benefits to approximately 2.6 million persons. In that year covered employment was over 70 million persons and total disposable personal income in the United States was $980 billion.
(a) Judging from Irma's data, do you think that the economic impact in 1974 of unemployment insurance was great?
(b) What additional data should be analyzed in order to answer the employer's objection more fully?

DATA FOR QUESTION 21 **Table 26-2**

	A	B	C	J
Maximum premium	$85,000	$109,820	$109,820	$97,410
Minimum premium	54,995	45,390	none	46,070
Basic premium	23,630	16,065	18,360	19,380

Chapter *Twenty-Seven*

FINANCIAL ANALYSIS OF INSURERS

There are several features of financial statements of insurance companies which require special interpretation and explanation. Of special importance are the reserves, or liabilities, of insurers. These reserves may be calculated in several different ways and the final result depends on what methods are used and the particular problems involved. The size of the estimates for reserves is a vital element in assessing the degree of financial security given to the insured. Also, an understanding of how the reserves are developed is necessary before an intelligent judgment can be made as to the net worth of the insurer, from the viewpoint of the investor or insurer management. The relative size of reserves is a reflection of the adequacy or inadequacy of rate-making practices, and so a careful analysis of how reserves are developed throws light on this question.

In Chapter 6 we discussed a general approach to the analysis of financial statements of insurers, under the assumption that the amounts on a financial statement could be accepted as given. As we shall see, this assumption is not always justified and the results of our financial statement analysis must sometimes be modified.

THE BALANCE SHEET

The balance sheet of any corporation provides a picture of the financial standing of the corporation. The balance sheet shows the assets, the liabilities, and the net worth. The assets of an insurance corporation are made up primarily of marketable stocks and bonds, the composition and natures of which are carefully regulated by law. The liabilities of an insurer are somewhat different from the liabilities found on the balance sheet of an industrial corporation. First, there is seldom any long-term debt on an insurer's balance sheet. The reason for this is that there is seldom any reason to float a long-term debt since the insurer has no great need for tangible assets. Second, most of the liabilities are estimated and appear as reserves instead of accounts payable, as is true on the balance sheet of an industrial corporation. It will become clear later why insurers show liabilities in this manner.

BALANCE SHEETS OF TWO PROPERTY-LIABILITY INSURERS

Table 27-1

	Insurer A (Millions of Dollars)	Insurer B (Millions of Dollars)
Assets:		
Bonds (amortized value)	$ 5.5	$11.8
Stocks	6.4	8.2
Cash, premium balances, etc.	1.8	3.6
	$13.7	$23.6
Liabilities and surplus:		
Loss reserve	.9	10.2
Unearned premium reserve	6.7	6.4
Miscellaneous liabilities	.4	.5
Total liabilities	$ 8.0	$17.1
Paid-up capital	1.0	1.0
Policyholders' surplus	4.7	5.5
	$13.7	$23.6

We shall devote our major attention to the nature of an insurer's liabilities and its net worth. Table 27–1 shows the balance sheets of two small stock insurers: Insurer *A*, writing primarily fire and allied lines, and Insurer *B*, whose business is largely workers' compensation and liability insurance. What is the capital structure of these insurers, and what accounts for the differences observed? By *capital structure* is meant the composition of liabilities and net worth, that is, in what manner the corporation has raised its funds. A corporation's liabilities may be looked upon as a description of the manner and extent to which creditors of various types have loaned money to the firm. Liabilities, then, are a source of funds, in the same manner that stockholders' contributions, capital, and surplus are for the insurance firm.

Insurer *A*'s capital structure may be described as follows: creditors have furnished $8 million of the firm's assets, and stockholders, the balance of $5.7 million. For each dollar of assets contributed by stockholders, creditors (who are policyholders) have furnished $1.40. In Insurer *B*, for each dollar of assets contributed by stockholders, the policyholders have contributed approximately $2.60. The question arises, what accounts for these relationships? What set of conditions operated to create these particular results? What are the financial problems involved? What are the various factors affecting an insurer's surplus? Is it desirable for an insurer to have as large a surplus as possible? These and other questions are discussed in the following paragraphs.

Capital and Surplus

The capital of the insurance firm is represented by two items, capital stock and surplus. *Capital stock* represents the value of the original contributions of stockholders, and *surplus* represents a combination of the original paid-in capital and the accumulated profits. On the balance sheet of an insurer, the surplus is commonly called policyholders' surplus instead of stockholders' surplus, which it really is. The surplus, representing the claims of stockholders on existing assets, is a cushion against the decline in value of assets for the protection of creditors, who in the case of an insurance company are policyholders.

Danger of Inadequate Surplus

An insurer with inadequate surplus, or with excessive amounts of liabilities relative to surplus, is subject to unstable financial operations. This instability may hamper underwriting, damage profitability, create difficulties in raising new capital, and have other negative results for management.

Suppose Insurer *A* from Table 27–1 is writing an annual premium volume of $5.7 million, while Insurer *B* is writing $19.5 million. In Insurer *A* the ratio of premiums to policyholders' surplus is 1:1, while in Insurer *B* the ratio is 3:1. Assume that, in a year of adverse underwriting experience, each insurer suffers an underwriting loss of 10% of the premiums written. In Insurer *A* this loss is equivalent to 10% of its surplus, while in Insurer *B* the loss is equivalent to 30% of its surplus. The loss is three times as serious to Insurer *B* as it is to Insurer *A* because of the higher ratio of premiums written to policyholders' surplus.

Insurer *B* could achieve the same stability as Insurer *A* by either reducing the volume of premiums it is accepting, or by tripling the amount of its surplus. Neither alternative may be easy to achieve. Insurer *B* could raise underwriting standards, but this step may discourage its agents and permanently damage its market position. It could raise premium rates, but with somewhat the same effect unless other competitors did likewise. It could attempt to increase its surplus by selling new stock at a premium. Unless something is done, however, it would take only three years of such losses to endanger the solvency of the company. Once losses start to mount, raising new capital may be difficult because investors are unlikely to be attracted to an unprofitable insurer which seems to be heading for financial trouble.

Types of Reserves

The reserve is the major type of liability on the balance sheet of an insurer. Oftentimes a reserve is referred to as though it were a fund of some sort, out of which policyholders or others can be paid. Of course, the reserve is not a fund, but merely tells the purpose for which a fund is accumulated.

The two main types of reserves are loss reserves and unearned premium reserves. The *loss reserve* is set up to estimate losses, loss adjustment expenses, and other related items. Since often the exact losses are not known at the time the balance sheet is prepared, the insurer sets up a reserve or an estimate designed to approximate the insurer's eventual liability. The *unearned premium reserve,* on the other hand, arises because policyholders pay for insurance in advance. These collections, which are returnable to the policyholder in whole or in part in the event of cancellation of the contract, must be closely accounted for and give rise to the liability to policyholders, which is called the unearned premium reserve.

In Table 27–1, the loss reserves are relatively small for Insurer *A* but relatively large for Insurer *B*. The unearned premium reserve is by far the most important liability of Insurer *A*, and is an important liability of Insurer *B*. One of the reasons for this lies in the nature of business done by each insurer. In Insurer *A*, when a fire or a windstorm strikes, the loss can usually be quickly determined and paid. Therefore, there is little need to carry a large reserve for the payment of future claims.

On the other hand, the unearned premium reserve is generally large in a fire insurer because of the practice of writing business for a three- or a five-year term. The advance premium is relatively large and a reserve must be set up showing this liability to policyholders, who, as we have seen, have a right to cancel their insurance and obtain a return of premium if desired.

In Insurer *B* the situation is reversed. Loss reserves are relatively large because in liability and workers' compensation insurance, it is usually impossible to determine the extent of loss immediately following an accident which gives rise to the claim. A liability suit may be unsettled for months or even years. In workers' compensation the insurer may be required to set aside a large fund to pay a lifetime pension to an injured worker. On the other hand, unearned premium reserves are considerably lower than loss reserves because in casualty lines it is not common for the policyholder to pay premiums for more than one year in advance. Sometimes premiums are not paid in advance at all, but are paid monthly. In workers' compensation insurance, it is common to require a relatively small deposit premium, with the final premium liability determined by audit of the insured's payroll at the end of the year. For these reasons, the unearned premium reserve in Insurer *B* is smaller than the loss reserve.

PROBLEMS ARISING FROM THE UNEARNED PREMIUM RESERVE

It would appear entirely equitable to require an insurer to set up a liability for advance premium payments by its policyholders in the form of an unearned premium reserve. However, there are many important financial problems caused by the manner in which this is done. The following accounting transactions illustrate how the unearned premium reserve arises and the financial effects of these transactions.

Transaction 1

On January 1 the ABC Insurance Company is authorized under its state law to begin business as an underwriter of fire and allied lines. Its initial capital is $100,000 and its surplus is $50,000. The $150,000 capital and surplus was obtained by selling 1,000 shares of $100 par value common stock at $150. The reason for selling stock "at a premium" will become apparent later. Ignoring any investment in office equipment, organization expenses, and the like, the balance sheet at the start of business would appear as:

ABC Insurance Company
Balance Sheet
January 1, 19—

Assets		Liabilities and Surplus	
Cash	$150,000	Capital Stock	$100,000
		Surplus	50,000
		Reserves	—0—
Total assets	$150,000	Total liabilities & surplus	$150,000

Transaction 2

During the first month of business, local agents submit 400 three-year term fire insurance policies on residences for a total premium of $30,000. This $30,000 represents advance payment by policyholders for fire insurance protection during the coming three-year period. The law requires the insurer to set up a reserve for unearned premiums, representing the liability to policyholders. Before any expenses are paid, the balance sheet appears as follows:

ABC Insurance Company
Balance Sheet
January 31, 19—

Assets		Liabilities and Surplus	
Cash	$150,000	Unearned premium reserve	$ 30,000
Cash collections	30,000	Capital stock	100,000
		Surplus	50,000
Total assets	$180,000	Total liabilities & surplus	$180,000

Transaction 3

Property and liability insurance companies, in contrast to most other business firms, are required to keep their accounts on a cash basis, instead of on an accrual basis. In other words, all the expenses in connection with issuing a policy are written off at the time the advance premium is collected instead of being prorated over the life of the policy. The expenses might be as follows:

Agents' commissions (25%)	$ 7,500
Premium taxes (2.5%)	750
Miscellaneous (15%)	4,500
Total (42.5%)	$12,750

After paying these expenses, the balance sheet appears as:

ABC Insurance Company
Balance Sheet
February 1, 19—

Assets		Liabilities and Surplus	
Cash	$167,250	Unearned premium reserve	$ 30,000
		Capital stock	100,000
		Surplus..................	37,250
Total assets	$167,250	Total liabilities & surplus ..	$167,250

Payment of the expenses reduced cash and surplus by $12,750. None of this amount may be paid from the assets represented by the unearned premium reserve. In other words, our new insurer must have a surplus to begin with, or it would not be allowed to write any business. (This explains why the initial stock was sold at a premium of $50 per share.) This fact is of vital importance in understanding the balance sheet of an insurer and cannot be overemphasized. The amount of the surplus determines the ability of the insurer to expand its business and, in effect, is a measure of its *underwriting capacity*.

The unearned premium reserve is sometimes called the *reinsurance reserve*. This name arises because if our insurer had decided to go out of business as of February 1 and to request some other insurer to assume the liabilities in connection with the fire insurance on the books, the reinsurer would demand a payment about equal to the unearned premium reserve, less an allowance for the expenses already paid. On the assumption that the $12,750 of first-year expenses represents approximately 95% of all expenses which will be paid under the policies during their three-year life, the reinsurer knows that if it collects about $18,750, it will have enough funds to pay any remaining expenses which might be incurred, plus expected losses and profits, as follows:

Remaining expenses (5%)	$ 1,500
Expected losses (52.5%)	15,750
Profit (5%)	1,500
	$18,750

The implication of all this is that because of the cash basis of accounting, there is a hidden equity in the unearned premium reserve, represented approximately by the advance payment of expenses on insurance premiums. This equity is normally recovered as the policies run their term. In Transaction 3, the amount borrowed from surplus to pay these expenses was $12,750. We saw that a reinsurer might be willing to assume all the liabilities under the policies for a payment of $18,750. This leaves $11,250 for the ABC Insurance Company and, in effect, allows it to recover all but $1,500 of its outlay in putting the business on the books. This sum, $11,250, actually belongs to the insurer's stockholders, thus the use of the term "equity in the unearned premium reserve."

For fire insurers the equity in the increase in the unearned premium reserve from year to year is often approximated at 40%. For various lines of property-liability insurance, this estimate varies, depending on the size of the advance premium payment and upon the advance expenses. The larger the advance premium payment and expense allowance, the larger the equity in the unearned premium reserve. A figure of 35% is often used to estimate this equity for property-liability insurers.

Recovery of the Equity in the Unearned Premium Reserve

The equity in the unearned premium is usually returned to surplus gradually as the policies run their term. Continuing with the case a bit further, assume that one year has passed and the ABC Insurance Company submits a balance sheet as of December 31. Assume also that no other insurance business has been transacted, and that losses have been exactly as planned for in the premium structure, 52.5%, or $5,250. (The premiums for the first year would be $10,000 since the $30,000 represented three-year term policies.) Assume that no further expenses have been incurred. The cash account is reduced by $5,250, representing the loss payments. Since one third of the time has elapsed, the insurer is permitted to reduce the unearned premium reserve by one third of its initial amount; that is, the insurer is allowed to recognize one third of its advance collections as being earned. Thus, $10,000 is transferred from the unearned premium reserve to surplus. Surplus, in turn, is reduced by $5,250, representing the loss payments. The balance sheet would then appear as follows:

ABC Insurance Company
Balance Sheet
December 31, 19—(End of First Year)

Assets		Liabilities and Surplus	
Cash	$162,000	Unearned premium reserve	$ 20,000
		Capital stock	100,000
		Surplus	42,000
Total assets	$162,000	Total liabilities & surplus ..	$162,000

By comparing the December 31 balance sheet with that of February 1, one can observe that there has been only one change in the cash account, that of reducing it by the amount of the loss payments. The unearned premium reserve is two thirds of its former level and the surplus has increased by the net difference between the reduction in the unearned premium reserve and the loss payments. Part of the equity in the unearned premium reserve has been recovered.

What happens now to the company's financial position during the second year of operation? For simplification, let us assume that no further insurance is sold and again the losses are exactly as planned. The identical change that we noted above occurs. Cash is reduced by $5,250, and surplus is increased by $10,000 minus $5,250, or $4,750. The same thing happens again in the third year. At the end of the third year, the unearned premium reserve has been completely eliminated because the insurer has no further liability, the contracts having run their full term. The balance sheet then appears:

ABC Insurance Company
Balance Sheet
December 31, 19—(End of Third Year)

Assets		Liabilities and Surplus	
Cash	$151,500	Unearned premium reserve	—0—
		Capital	$100,000
		Surplus	51,500
Total assets	$151,500	Total liabilities & surplus	$151,500

We may summarize the results of the insurer's operations in the three years as follows:

Premiums collected		$30,000
Less:		
Losses (52.5%)	$15,750	
Expenses (42.5%)[1]	12,750	28,500
Profit (5%)		$ 1,500

As we expect, the insurer's balance sheet at the end of the period, under the simplified assumptions made, ends with cash and surplus increased by a net amount of $1,500, the planned profit. In the meantime, however, surplus has fallen as low as $37,250. Without an initial surplus, the insurer would never have been able to accept the business offered it by its agents, since under legal requirements it would have started out with a deficit and would have been legally insolvent. This result stems from the cash basis of accounting. The cash basis of accounting, in turn, stems from the desire of public regulatory authorities to provide protection for the advance premiums of the insuring public.

A rapidly growing young insurance company often has the appearance of losing money, in comparison to the older, more mature company. Observe, for example, the results of the first year of the ABC Insurance Company. At the end of the first year on December 31, the income statement would be reported to the insurance commissioner as follows:

Premiums written		$30,000
Increase in the unearned premium reserve		20,000
Premiums earned		$10,000
Less: Losses	$ 5,250	
Expenses	12,750	18,000
Statutory underwriting loss		$ 8,000

Although the insurer has had exactly the experience which was anticipated in the rating structure, it shows a loss because of the way of keeping books

[1] Assuming that there were no further general expenses incurred.

required by law. Hence, the underwriting results reported to the insurance commissioner are known as a *statutory underwriting profit or loss* to distinguish them from the real underwriting results. To obtain the actual underwriting results, the statutory underwriting loss must be adjusted by adding back the equity in the net increase of the unearned premium reserve in the first year of $20,000. In the case above, this equity amounted to 42.5% of $20,000, or $8,500. Thus, the real underwriting results produce a profit of $500, which is 5% of earned premiums, as expected.

Once an insurer reaches a point where its business is stabilized (it no longer is increasing its new premium writings), the recoveries from unearned premium reserves of past business will offset new requirements imposed by new business. The statutory underwriting profit will, assuming that loss experience has been as predicted, be equal to the anticipated underwriting profit. There will be no net increase in the unearned premium reserve and hence no need to adjust profit for this factor. By similar reasoning, it follows that if an insurer is reducing its premium volume and hence its unearned premium volume by some absolute amount, it will show a statutory underwriting profit which is greater than its underwriting profit in the period under consideration.

Unless the above considerations are understood, it is likely that the analyst would incorrectly interpret the financial results of an insurer. The analyst would suppose that the new rapidly growing insurer is destined for bankruptcy because of statutory underwriting losses and would erroneously conclude that the insurer which had reduced its business and had a rising statutory underwriting profit is the healthier of the two.

Financial Effects of the Unearned Premium Reserve

The important financial conclusion to draw from the preceding analysis is that, because the unearned premium reserve is redundant, an artificial restriction on insurance underwriting capacity is introduced. The unearned premium reserve is redundant for several reasons, two of the most obvious of which are: (1) Not all the amounts required to be set aside are actually paid out irrevocably. Agents' commissions on the unearned part of a premium must be returned if a policy is cancelled. Thus, if an insurer collects $100 in advance premiums and pays an agent $25 and the policy is cancelled by the insurer after the contract has run half its course, the agent must return $12.50 of this amount. This sum becomes available to the insurer to be returned to the policyholder. (2) If the insured cancels a policy, the insured does not receive a full pro rata return, but a short-rate return. In the case above, the insured who cancelled after the contract had run half its term would receive not $50, but closer to $40 in return of premium. Yet the unearned premium reserve requirement would be $50. Thus, in extremely few cases would the entire premium reserve be necessary if all policyholders cancelled their policies and demanded a return of premium.

Because of the necessity of drawing on surplus to meet unearned premium reserve requirements and because the size of surplus is not an unlimited quantity, there is an artificial restriction on the ability of the insurer to accept new business, that is, on the insurance underwriting capacity. This is particularly true of the small and growing insurer. It is precisely among such insurers that new equity funds might be attracted into the insurance field. With the limitation on growth imposed by unearned premium reserve requirements, the anticipated profit to potential investors in insurance is necessarily limited too. As a result, there has been a problem of attracting sufficient new equity capital to insurance in the market. Another result is that underwriting tends to become unduly strict during certain periods.

One of the important ways in which property and liability insurers have attempted to avoid setting up redundant unearned premium reserves is to write policies for shorter terms. Thus, insurers introduced automobile policies running for six months instead of one full year. Fire insurance policies have been written on an installment basis, whereby the insured pays one third of a three-year premium each year. Such techniques greatly reduce the amount of surplus an insurer is required to have in order to write business. The unearned premium reserve requirement on a $200 annual automobile insurance policy would average $100, but the requirement on the same policy collected in two installments of $100 paid six months apart would average only $50. Even with such methods, however, there has been a general shortage of insurance capacity.[2]

Calculation of Unearned Premium Reserves

In actual practice, an insurer does not keep separate records of required unearned premium reserves on every policy written, but uses an averaging process to obtain a reasonable estimate. Under the half-year method, for example, it is assumed that business is written evenly throughout the year and that therefore on the average, the unearned premium reserve will equal six months' premiums. The insurer would accordingly set up in the unearned premium reserve one half of all one-year premiums, one fourth of all two-year premiums, and one sixth of all three-year premiums. This method is permitted by most states. For its own guidance, however, an insurer generally uses a more exact, semi-monthly method.

In recent years it has become common for insurers to allow payment of an advance premium on the installment plan. For example, the insured may pay a full annual premium the first year and for the successive four years, 78% of the annual premium. The amount which should be set up as the unearned premium reserve depends on the amount which is returnable to the insured in case of cancellation prior to the expiration of the policy term.

LOSS RESERVES

A *loss reserve* is an amount set aside for the payment of claims not settled up to the date of the balance sheet. This amount is, of course, an estimate of a

[2] See Otto Ingolf, "Capacity," *Journal of Risk and Insurance* (March, 1961), pp. 53-70.

liability. If the exact liability were known, it probably would not be called a reserve, but merely accrued claims payable.

Estimating Loss Reserves

Two problems in estimating loss reserves are: (1) estimating the amount of reserves which should be set up on claims known to have occurred, but where the amount of the claim is uncertain, and (2) estimating the amount of reserves on claims not known to have occurred, but which past experience indicates most probably have occurred. A claim might have occurred on December 28, but notice of the accident has not reached the insurer at the time it estimates its reserves for the balance sheet as of December 31.

There are several methods of estimating reserves. For claims known to have occurred, very often the underwriter or adjuster makes an individual estimate of the final loss for each case. This method, known as the *individual case estimate*, is widely used. Where the average amount of the claim is small, or not subject to much variation, the underwriter may assign an *average value* to each claim notice received. When the amount of the claim is dependent on such factors as length of life, probability of remarriage, or average duration of total disability, tables are consulted which are similar in nature to life insurance mortality tables. This method is called the *tabular value* basis of eliminating claims.

For certain lines of insurance, such as workers' compensation and liability, the loss reserve is estimated on a formula basis set up by statute. In New York, for example, the law in workers' compensation requires an insurer to set up 65% of the earned premium as a loss reserve, (60% in liability insurance) less any losses and expenses paid at the date of the annual statement. This reserve must be maintained for three years. The law provides that if the insurer's individual case estimates of reserves exceed the amount required by the 65% formula, the individual estimates will become the required reserve. For long-term claims (those running three years or longer), the law requires that the loss reserve shall be the estimated present value, at 3.5% interest, of all future payments.

Adequacy of Loss Reserves

It is difficult to assess the adequacy of loss reserves in a given insurer except by the test of past results. There are no reliable rules of thumb which can be used to make comparisons among various insurers because of the important differences in operating conditions giving rise to different reserves. While the composition of coverages written by an insurer is primarily responsible for the relative size of its reserves, there are other factors which should be considered; namely, territory of operation, age of the insurer, and rate of growth.[3]

[3] These are undoubtedly many other factors which affect reserves. For example, some insurers set up contingency reserves for large losses. Reinsurance arrangements also affect the size of reserves, as do the proportion of claims going to court.

Territory of Operation. The territory of operation affects the size of reserves because losses vary by territory. In one territory the law may provide far larger benefits for workers' compensation than in other territories. An insurer operating in a high-benefit territory must set up larger estimates for losses than an insurer operating in a low-benefit territory. In the field of fire insurance, certain areas may be subject to more severe wind losses than others, and hence larger reserves must be set up in these areas. In some areas courts may have a tendency to be more liberal with personal injury awards than in other areas. Insurers must maintain appropriate reserves.

Age of the Insurer. The age of the insurer is an important factor in assessing the size of loss reserves. An insurer which has been in business for many years has had an opportunity to obtain a diversified number of risks with expectation that losses will follow a predictable pattern. A new company has less experience on which to base its estimates of reserves. Therefore, the loss reserves of the new insurer may not be at all typical of what might be found if the company had been in business for a longer period of time.

Rate of Growth. The faster an insurer is gaining in premium volume, the more rapid, generally speaking, will be the rate of growth of its loss reserves (as well as its unearned premium reserves). Loss reserves are often larger than normal because of the uncertainties involved in accepting new insureds. An insurer which has stabilized or has a slow rate of growth has loss reserves based on known experience with old risks. Its loss reserves will probably be relatively smaller because it has had an opportunity to weed out the bad risks and is not taking on new ones.

Implications for Financial Analysis

The difficulties and dangers of conventional balance sheet analysis in assessing the relative strength of two insurers are now apparent. For example, in Table 27–1, the ratio of net worth to liabilities for Insurer *A* is 5.7:8, or 71%, and for Insurer *B*, 6.5:17.1, or 38%. Does this mean that Insurer *A* is a stronger company than Insurer *B*, because of greater relative protection for its policyholders against declines in the value of assets? On the surface it would appear so. However, this conclusion rests on an analysis of the accuracy of the loss reserves. Also, Insurer *B* has about 50% of its assets invested in bonds, while Insurer *A* has only about 40% so invested. Hence, there is an element of safety in Insurer *B*, which offsets in part the lower ratio of net worth to liabilities. Until more facts are known, there is little we can say as to the relative financial strength of these two insurers, which are operating in entirely different lines of business, have different financial problems, may be operating in entirely different territories, and may be subject to different philosophies of underwriting.

Determination of Profit

The amount of profit shown on the insurer's income statement depends upon the adequacy of its reserve liabilities, more particularly its loss reserves.

An adjustment must be made to reflect the equity in the unearned premium reserves. The profit shown in a single year is somewhat unreliable as an indicator of the true profits since only over a period of time can it be determined whether or not the loss reserves have been adequate. Some insurers publish income statements on the basis of *policy year* statistics rather than *calendar year* statistics in order to overcome this difficulty. Under policy year statistics, all losses attributable to the policies issued in a given year are accumulated and charged back to the premiums collected on those policies. Obviously it will be two or more years before complete policy year data are available, and by that time the analyst may have little use of them. Therefore, calendar year data are normally used and estimates must be made, on the basis of past experience, of the reliability of the loss estimates.

Assuming that all reserves are fairly and adequately estimated, it is possible to obtain an estimate of the final net profit of a property and liability insurance company by considering two major sources of gain—underwriting profit and investment profit. The statutory underwriting profit must be adjusted for the equity in the unearned premium reserve, if any. For an insurer of fire and allied lines, this is done by adding to the statutory underwriting profit or loss approximately 40% of the *increase* in the unearned premium reserve during the prior period. A figure of 35% is often used for an underwriter of liability, compensation, automobile, and other casualty lines. For greater accuracy the analyst may use the actual expense ratio of the insurer to estimate the equity in the unearned premium reserve.

Level and Stability of Profits in Insurance

The level and stability of profits in nonlife insurance have been of considerable public interest because of the implications of profits and their measurement to the regulatory process. Regulators have been concerned with the rising consumer costs of insurance, particularly automobile insurance, and have been under pressure to give more weight to insurers' investment profits as well as to underwriting profits. It is claimed by some that industry profits have been reported at unrealistically low levels in order to justify higher insurance rates, and that if investment profits were considered, the returns in insurance would be most adequate and would permit reductions. Regulators have also been concerned with such questions as the relative monopolistic position of insurers and with economies of scale in insurance. For example, if large insurers operate more efficiently than small insurers, would the consumers' interest be served by regulations that encourage greater industry concentration?

Richard Norgaard and George Schick studied a sample of 110 nonlife insurers and concluded that, when compared to 622 industrial corporations, risk-return position of insurance over the period 1953–1967 was at least on par with industrial firms. They found that there are economies of scale in insurance based not only on size of insurer, but also upon the degree to which the insurer specializes in one line of insurance.[4]

[4] Richard Norgaard and George Schick, "Profitability in the Property and Liability Insurance Industry," *Journal of Risk and Insurance,* Vol. 37, No. 4 (December, 1970), pp. 579-587.

However, other researchers, using somewhat different methods, came to different conclusions. In these studies profitability in nonlife insurance has been found to be generally unsatisfactory. In 1967 was published perhaps the best known of these studies by Arthur D. Little, Inc., supervised by Irving H. Plotkin.[5] Covering the period 1955–1966, the Plotkin study revealed that the average rate of return on total assets, as defined for the whole industry, was 4.2%. Risk, measured by the average of the yearly intercompany dispersions, was much greater for insurance than for other industries with comparable returns. Plotkin cited industry studies by the First National City Bank of New York, revealing fire and casualty companies to be earning 4.5% on net worth over the period 1955–1965, compared to banks, earning 9.2%, and sales finance companies, earning 13.3%. Plotkin's risk and return measures were criticized by others, but subsequent studies did not contradict the basic findings.

In a study of 82 stock insurers randomly selected over the period 1955–1967 and using different measures of total return and risk, Stephen Forbes drew conclusions similar to those of Plotkin. In Forbes' study, the measure most comparable to the measure employed by Plotkin showed a nonlife industry return of 3.87% (or 4.58%, if data are weighted by earnings bases) with a coefficient of variation of 66% (84% using a weighted earnings base). Comparing nonlife insurance returns with those in other industries, Forbes concluded that an investor could have earned a greater return in such risk-free securities as government bonds. Nearly 40% of the insurers in his sample earned less than 5% on their average capital and surplus and 76% of them earned less than 10%. Forbes also discovered that large insurers exhibited greater stability of earnings than smaller insurers, but their average returns were not significantly larger, thus casting doubt on the advantages of economies of scale in the nonlife industry.[6]

In a study of risk-adjusted rates of return among 40 large insurers, 40 medium-sized insurers, and 40 small insurers, James S. Trieschmann came to several interesting conclusions.[7] In this study, risk-adjusted return was defined as the rate of return (defined in several different ways) divided by the standard deviation of these returns (defined in two separate ways).[8] It was discovered that over the period 1955–1968 the average risk-adjusted rate of return in property-liability insurance was significantly lower than comparable measures in other industries, regardless of the method of measuring risk. Trieschmann's

[5] *Prices and Profits in the Property and Liability Insurance Industry, Summary Report* (Cambridge, Mass.: Arthur D. Little, Inc., November, 1967). See also, Irving H. Plotkin, "Rates of Return in the Property and Liability Insurance Industry: A Comparative Analysis," *Journal of Risk and Insurance,* Vol. 36, No. 3 (June, 1969), pp. 173-200.

[6] Stephen W. Forbes, "Rates of Return in the Nonlife Insurance Industry," *Journal of Risk and Insurance,* Vol. 38, No. 3 (September, 1971), pp. 409-422.

[7] James S. Trieschmann, "Property-Liability Profits: A Comparative Study," *Journal of Risk and Insurance,* Vol. 38, No. 3 (September, 1971), pp. 437-453.

[8] The two ways of measuring risk were spatial and temporal. Spatial risk measures variation in rates of return among a group of companies each year and the separate measures are then averaged for the number of years studied. Temporal risk is the variation of a single firm's rate of return throughout the time period to be studied. The industry temporal risk is the weighted average of the average risk-adjusted rates of return for all firms comprising the industry.

data showed that rates of return in nonlife insurance, as defined, were not generally below those of other industries if the data are unadjusted for risk, but once risk is taken into consideration, the returns are relatively unattractive to the investor.

This study also revealed that large-sized firms had lower unadjusted rates of return than medium- or small-sized firms, but if the returns were adjusted for risk, they were larger than either medium- or small-sized firms. This finding confirmed the conclusion by Forbes that large firms are not necessarily more profitable than smaller firms in insurance unless the risk factor is considered. Large firms have been able to reduce their risk considerably through diversification techniques. However, Trieschmann believes that large firms do not enjoy monopoly positions or their unadjusted rates of return would be much higher than they are.

It may be concluded that in general, profitability in insurance has left something to be desired. In the field of property and liability insurance, investment income is a major source of profit. Not only are investment income and capital gains usually larger than underwriting gains, they are also generally more stable. In a tabulation by Best covering the period 1913–1970, for example, in all but 13 years investment results were superior to underwriting results for a group of stock insurers whose assets in 1970 totalled $43 billion.

As shown in Table 27–2, in the period 1961–1973 for this group of insurers, investment profits were earned in all but four of the years, compared to underwriting losses in six of the years. Over that period investment profits totalled $19 billion, compared to a total underwriting gain of $.52 billion. It seems clear that investment profits have been the mainstay of leading property and liability insurers and that had it not been for these profits, most insurers could not have continued in business.

Table 27–2 reveals that in the 13-year period ending in 1973 major stock property and liability insurers earned an average of 10% on their net worth. They earned 4% on total assets. The fluctuation in earnings was very great, however, ranging from a loss of about 7% in 1969 to a gain of about 26% in 1972, indicating considerable investment risk in the property and liability insurance business. Since investment earnings constitute such a large share of total earnings, property and liability insurers actually owe more of their financial results to fluctuation in the stock market than to fluctuations in underwriting results.

Summary. From the above analysis it may be concluded that (a) evidence is lacking that nonlife insurance profits are excessive or that they are even equal to noninsurance company profits, particularly if the stability of these profits is considered; (b) without investment profits insurers could not continue in business without substantial increases in insurance rates; (c) although there is a fairly high level of economic concentration in the insurance business, small and medium-sized insurers tend to have profit levels that are superior to those of larger insurers, although the stability of profits of smaller insurers is somewhat less. Thus, there is a limit to the economies of scale in insurance.

There is an increasing tendency for insurance commissioners to require that investment income be considered formally or informally in the rating methods

EARNINGS RATES IN STOCK PROPERTY AND LIABILITY INSURANCE COMPANIES, 1961-1973 (Billions of Dollars)

Table 27-2

Year	Assets	Net Worth (Policy-holders' Surplus)	Under-writing Gain (Loss)*	Invest-ment Profit (Loss)*	Total Earnings	Percent Earnings/ Net Worth
1973	$ 62.2	$ 20.1	$ .23	$— 1.40	$— 1.17	— 5.82
1972	58.5	21.4	.91	4.70	5.61	26.21
1971	49.3	17.3	.68	3.40	4.08	23.58
1970	42.6	14.0	—.15	1.25	1.10	7.86
1969	38.0	12.7	—.40	— .50	— .90	— 7.09
1968	37.7	14.9	—.20	2.28	2.08	13.96
1967	34.2	13.6	.01	2.30	2.31	16.99
1966	31.0	12.0	.10	— .55	— .45	— 3.75
1965	31.3	13.7	—.42	1.47	1.05	7.66
1964	30.1	13.7	—.35	1.82	1.47	10.73
1963	27.9	12.7	—.22	2.02	1.80	14.17
1962	25.8	11.1	.03	— .23	— .20	— 1.80
1961	25.6	11.7	.30	2.52	2.82	24.10
Totals	$494.2	$188.9	$ .52	$ 19.08	$ 19.60	
13-Year Averages	$ 38.0	$ 14.5	$ .04	$ 1.47	$ 1.51	10.39

Source: *Best's Aggregates and Averages, 1974* (Morristown, New Jersey: A. M. Best Co., 1974), p. 30.

* Underwriting gains and losses are from annual statements and reflect statutory results; hence they are unadjusted for equity in the unearned premium reserve. Investment profits and losses are also statutory results and reflect net investment income plus capital gains, based on market prices of common stocks and amortized values of bonds.

used in nonlife insurance. (Interest assumptions are made in calculating life insurance rates; thus, investment income is already being formally considered in the field of life insurance rate-making.) Insurance commissioners in 21 states hold that some part of investment income of nonlife insurers must be reflected mathematically in insurance rates.[9] If it becomes the general practice to consider investment income in nonlife insurance rates, on some formal basis, it is likely that profits will become even less stable than heretofore because of uncertainties introduced by the new dimension.

Causes. Although there are undoubtedly many causes of the low level and great instability of profits in insurance, the major ones appear to be (1) fluctuations in the stock market, (2) accounting practices in reporting underwriting gains, (3) the rate-cost lag produced by inflation, (4) failure of the rating system to reflect properly the risk to which the insurer is exposed, and (5) inefficiencies in the distribution of insurance.

Major gains and losses are often caused by increases or reductions in asset values due to stock market changes (see Table 27–2). We have seen, for example,

[9] George B. Flanigan, "Investment Income in Rate-Making and Managerial Investment Attitudes," *Journal of Risk and Insurance*, Vol. 41, No. 2 (June, 1974), p. 230.

why accounting practices that require uneven charging of expenses over the life of the policy will produce statutory losses, when the actual result might have been profitable. Inflation tends to increase losses to which property and liability insurers are exposed at the time claims are paid. Such increases may not be planned for completely when the rates were formulated, since rate increases tend to lag behind cost increases. The rating system itself may not reflect the true loss-producing event. Car insurance rates, for example, are more sensitive to the characteristics of the driver than to the automobile; and yet it may be the fragile nature of the automobile that accounts for more of the loss than the driver's age or accident record.

The distribution of insurance generally has not been efficient, mainly because most insurers have tended to rely on long channels of distribution over which it is difficult to exercise cost control. Agents are paid by commissions which provide windfalls to the agent when rates or premiums rise due to factors such as inflation. The agent is paid more when premiums rise, regardless of cause, although often no additional work is performed. This has tended to produce benefits to the agent at the expense of the insurer. Enlarged volumes of business thus may produce few if any economies of scale as far as the insurer is concerned.

Conclusion. The level and stability of profits in the property and liability insurance industry has been relatively low. This poor profitability has had several unfortunate results, among them the following:

1. Managements have tried to tighten underwriting requirements and raise insurance rates to stem losses. This has caused some discontinuity in insurance markets, and as a result the government has entered the insurance business to supply coverage.
2. It has been difficult for the insurance industry to attract new capital. Most growth is internally financed. This makes it difficult for the industry to meet the needs of a growing economy.
3. It is more difficult for the industry to attract professionally trained personnel because of relatively low salaries. Such personnel could conceivably bring sufficient expertise to improve profitability.

It is anomalous that an industry whose purpose is to reduce risk has been unable to achieve a level of profits which is considered adequate and stable. There are, however, several sources of potential improvement. The wave of mergers in the industry is expected to increase diversification among insurance companies with an improvement in the stability and level of profits. Increased attention to expense control, particularly in the distribution of insurance through greater use of group plans, may help. Greater attention to the causes and prevention of losses could also have a major beneficial effect. Adoption of no-fault automobile bodily injury and property damage insurance could greatly reduce insurance costs with resulting improvement in profitability. Finally, computer technology may be of major assistance to underwriters in the development of more sensitive and accurate rating systems by predicting losses more accurately.

RESERVES IN LIFE INSURANCE

Reserve liabilities are much greater in life insurance than in property insurance because of the practice of issuing life insurance contracts on a level-premium basis for long periods. This results in the collection by an insurer of amounts in excess of current mortality costs. These reserves are held in trust for the insured until such time as the policy matures or is terminated, when the fund is returned to the insured. Thus, the reserve in life insurance may be looked upon as an unearned premium reserve, although its official name is "policy reserve," of which there are many different classes.

Loss reserves are not of great size in a life insurer because of the speed with which losses are paid and because there is usually no difficulty in determining the amount of a loss. Hence, at the date of the balance sheet the loss reserve is minimal.

Determination of Reserves

The policy reserve must be large enough so that if the insurer ceased doing business, it would have sufficient funds on hand to pay all claims on existing contracts outstanding. The reserve in life insurance may be looked upon in two ways, retrospectively and prospectively.

Retrospectively, the reserve is the excess of accumulated net premiums over outlays. More precisely, it represents the sum of all net premiums collected by the insurer, plus guaranteed interest assumed by the contracts, less tabular death claims. The reserve deals with total funds, not the funds assigned to an individual policy. We speak, therefore, of *aggregate reserves,* not individual reserves. Furthermore, the reserve calculation is based on net premiums, not the gross premium. Also, the amount of the reserve is determined by certain authorized assumptions as to mortality and interest, and not in terms of actual results. In other words, the reserve is expressed as a legal requirement, and hence is a *legal reserve*. This expression is used in describing an insurer as a *legal reserve life insurance company*. The insurer must have actual assets equal to its required legal reserves, or it is said to be insolvent. Normally, the actuarial assumptions involved in making up rates are so conservative that the insurer will have no difficulty in meeting these legal requirements. The insurer will guarantee a lower rate of interest than it actually earns and will use a mortality table that overstates actual mortality by some extent.

Looked upon prospectively, the reserve in life insurance represents the amount an insurer must have on hand now in order to meet all future claims. The prospective reserve must be equal to the present value of future benefits, less the present value of future premiums to be collected. When a life insurance policy is issued, the present value of future premiums equals the present value of future benefits. Indeed, this is the way the net single premium is calculated. However, as time goes on, the present value of future benefits rises because the time is nearer when claims must be paid, and the present value of future premiums declines since fewer premiums remain to be paid. Hence, the insurer

THE RESERVE LOOKED UPON PROSPECTIVELY RESERVE = PV FUTURE BENEFITS − PV FUTURE PREMIUMS **Figure 27-1**

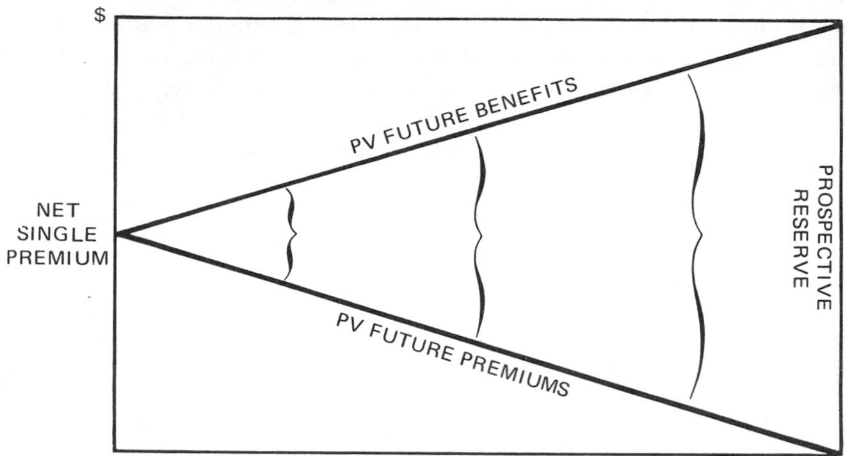

must have a reserve equal to this difference. Schematically this result is shown in Figure 27–1.

Figure 27–1 demonstrates that at the date of maturity of any contract, the reserve must equal the face amount of the policy. At the date of issue, the present value of future benefits equals the present value of future premiums, but a difference begins to appear immediately and gradually widens until the policy matures. The reserve is, of course, the same no matter whether it is looked upon retrospectively or prospectively. In general, it is easier to see the true nature of a reserve by looking at it prospectively.

Factors Affecting the Size of the Reserve

The reserve in life insurance is affected by several important factors, the most significant of which are: interest assumed, mortality rate assumed, and reserve basis.

Interest Assumed. The higher the interest assumed, the lower the amount of the reserve, and vice versa. The truth of this relationship can be seen by going back to the basic formula: Reserve = Present Value of Future Benefits − Present Value of Future Premiums. The higher the interest, the less is the present value of future premiums. Remember that the present value of future premiums represents the present worth to the insurer of a stream of income to come to it in the future. This quantity may be looked upon as a sum of money which, at the interest rate assumed, will produce, together with liquidation of principal, the promised income. The greater the interest to be earned, the less this sum has to be. Hence, the higher the interest, the lower is the present value of future premiums.

Mortality Rate Assumed. The greater the rate of mortality assumed, the greater must be the reserve. It is not the level of mortality at each age that matters, but the rate of change in mortality from year to year. If the rate of mortality were constant, as is the rate of loss (as a general rule) in property insurance, there would be no necessity for a reserve. Of course, the higher the level of mortality, the higher the premium must be. But if there were no change from year to year in the rate of loss, there would be no necessity to accumulate a fund for the payment of excess rates of loss in later years. The steeper the rate of change in loss from year to year, the more that must be accumulated to meet these future liabilities.

Reserve Basis. The *reserve basis* in life insurance deals with the question of whether the reserve is to be valued on a net level premium basis or on some modified reserve basis. The problem in life insurance is similar to that which exists in property insurance. First-year expenses are heavy, often exceeding the first-year premium. Unless some arrangement is made to prevent heavy first-year expenses, they will constitute a drain on surplus. In life insurance if an insurer keeps its reserves on a net level premium basis, all the first-year expenses are charged off against surplus (to the extent necessary) and a full reserve is set up the first year. Of course, this is the most conservative way of stating a reserve liability. Large insurers with generous surpluses often use this basis of valuing their reserves.

For a new or small insurer with a relatively small surplus, it would be very difficult for substantial growth to take place if the reserve liabilities had to be maintained on a full net level premium basis. Hence, under most state laws a modified reserve valuation method is permitted. The most common of these bases is known as the Commissioners' Standard Valuation (CSV) method. Under this method the policies are divided into two classes: (1) those for which the premium is less than that of a 20-pay life policy issued at the same age for a like amount, and (2) those where the premium exceeds this amount.

For the first group of policies, the insurer may use the *full preliminary term* method of valuation. Under this method the law allows the insurer to view the policy as though the first year of the policy period were represented by a term insurance contract, and the remaining years as a whole life contract for one year less than usual. Thus, a 30-pay life policy would be viewed as a combined one-year term policy plus a 29-pay life policy. Since the term policy has no reserve requirement, there would be no reserve liability during the first year and the entire first-year premium would be available for payment of the heavy first-year expenses. The reserve liability for later years builds up at a slightly higher rate than would be true if the insurer used the full net level premium reserve method.

For the second group of policies, those whose premium exceeds that of a 20-pay life policy, use of the full preliminary term method would leave an inordinate amount of the first-year premium for expenses. Since this might constitute an inducement for management to make reckless and competitive expenditures to acquire new business, the law states that for policies falling into this classification, a partial reserve is required the first year. The formula for calculation of this reserve becomes quite complicated, but the intent is to require that by the end of the policy term the reserve equals the amount which would be available under the net level premium reserve basis.

The *modified reserve basis* is a slightly less conservative method of calculating reserves than the full net level premium basis. However, it is actually more logical in many ways than the net level premium basis, since it recognizes that acquisition expense in the first year is a nonrecurring expense and should not have to be written off all at once. To do so understates the true earnings of the life insurer for that year. If the insurer wishes to use more conservative assumptions than those dictated by the Commissioners' Standard Valuation method, it may do so. For example, in most states the CSV method permits the use of a 3.5% interest assumption. If the insurer wishes to use a lower interest rate, thus increasing its required reserves, it may do so. Also, the insurer may put aside voluntary reserves for various types of contingencies, such as a reserve for dividends and a reserve for group life contingencies. In most states there is a limitation on the size of the voluntary reserves, usually 10% of the legal reserves, to prevent an unreasonable accumulation of funds and to encourage a quicker return of redundant premium collections to policyholders.

Nonforfeiture Values

Calculation of the cash values and other nonforfeiture values on a life insurance contract is entirely separate from the calculation of a reserve. In determining a schedule of cash values, the insurer considers not only mortality and interest, but also expenses. These assumptions may be different from those used in calculating the reserve, although the law specifies some minimum basis for calculation. The nonforfeiture values are a matter of contract and cannot be changed, although the reserve basis of the contract can be changed at any time.

The standard nonforfeiture valuation legislation (also known as the Guertin laws) places a limitation of 40% of the adjusted premium (or 4% of the face amount of the policy) as the maximum allowable expense. The adjusted premium differs from the net premium in that it includes the initial expenses on the contract. The calculation allows the insurer to recover the heavy first-year expenses during the premium-paying period of the policy. If the policy lapses before these expenses are recovered, the insurer loses that much money. To offset this loss, additional loading is charged on all policies.

Factors Affecting Surplus

Many life insurers, particularly new companies with limited surplus, employ those reserve methods which will minimize surplus drain as new policies are written. The modified preliminary term method minimizes first-year surplus drain, but the reserve liability must be made up in later years. The net level premium reserve basis creates the most initial surplus drain, but minimizes the drain in later years. The Commissioners' Valuation Method lies between these two.

Many other factors also influence surplus position, such as expense allowances, lapse rates, mortality experience, and differences between interest earnings and interest assumptions. Because of these factors it is not uncommon for an insurer to incur costs in excess of the first-year premium in order to accept new business. If the company is growing rapidly, surplus drain from new business can be severe. In one study of life insurer capital requirements an assumption was made that first-year outlays would be 103% of the first year's premium plus $87 for an average expense pattern; a higher expense pattern called for 150% of the first year's premium to be used for expenses.[10]

On top of expense requirements would come whatever reserve liabilities were indicated by the particular reserve valuation method employed. Because of the surplus drain imposed by first-year expenses, it can be appreciated why most new life insurers will employ the modified preliminary term method of reserve valuation when it is permitted. Surplus positions of life insurers, traditionally small, have been judged to be inadequate, particularly for new insurers just entering the business.[11] The relative size of surplus is small in life insurance (approximating 7% or 8% of the total assets in mutual and 15% of the assets in stocks).[12]

Surplus tends to be understated or overstated in an insurance company because of the accounting conventions that have been adopted in the valuation of assets. For example, an insurer will have certain assets, such as furniture and fixtures, which are not shown on the balance sheet because they are nonadmitted under state regulatory conditions. Premium balances (accounts due from agents after a certain span of time) are also in this category, even though in the normal course of business the premium balances will either be collected or the liabilities on business which they represent will be cancelled. An insurance company may be very prone to understate the true value of its home office or real estate, particularly that real estate which has been acquired by foreclosure. To the extent that an insurer actually has valuable assets which it has not shown or has undervalued, its surplus, the balancing item on a balance sheet, is also understated.

Surplus may be overstated or understated because of methods adopted in valuing stocks and bonds. Common stocks are valued at market value, but bonds are valued at cost. If market rates of interest rise, the price of these bonds falls, but the insurer's books do not reflect the reduced market values. On the other hand, if interest rates fall and the price of bonds in the portfolio rises, the increased value is not reflected in surplus position either. In recent years, interest rates have risen considerably and the surplus position of many life insurers is probably overstated. The financial effect of this situation is to lock in lower-priced, long-term bonds in the insurer's portfolio so that the losses which would be incurred upon their sale will not have to be recognized,

[10] E. J. Leverett, Jr., "Paid-In Surplus and Capital Requirement," *Journal of Risk and Insurance,* Vol. 38, No. 1 (March, 1971), pp. 15–28.

[11] *Ibid.*

[12] Donald S. Cody, "Financial Management of Mutual Life Companies," *Transactions Society of Actuaries,* Vol. 26 (1974), p. D283.

thus protecting the surplus position. This condition reduces investment flexibility which would otherwise exist, particularly since long-term bonds are a fairly substantial investment for most life insurers.

Profitability and GAAP Accounting

The same factors which make it difficult to evaluate assets and the proper value of reserve liabilities in life insurance also make it difficult to assess the level and stability of profits. Since life insurers charge off most of the costs of writing new business during the first year, they understate profits, especially for a rapidly expanding company. Accounting for fluctuations in asset values is also a complicating factor. Securities of a subsidiary insurer are carried at book value on the statement of the subsidiary, without adjustment for unrealized gains or losses. The law requires that profits be charged with a mandatory securities valuation reserve which is not directly related to asset values but is determined by a somewhat arbitrary formula.

The net effect of these adjustments is generally to understate true profits for a life insurer, particularly a fast growing insurer writing large amounts of new insurance. However, when profits are related to net worth, some of the understatement noted above is reversed, since net worth is also understated due to conservative accounting practices which tend to overstate actual liabilities. In 1969 the Association of Insurance Financial Analysts proposed a uniform method for adjusting life insurance company earnings for the factors listed above. Known as GAAP accounting[13] (Generally Accepted Accounting Principles), this method began to be reflected in published statements of life insurers after 1973 along with those issued on the traditional statutory basis. GAAP accounting will undoubtedly facilitate comparison of the profitability of life insurers and permit a more penetrating economic analysis of the industry. GAAP accounting will also affect management policies such as pricing, agents' compensation, reported earnings per share, and public communications.[14] As yet, however, no extensive studies of life insurance profitability have been published which are comparable to those in property-liability insurance which were cited previously.

It may be concluded that although the life insurance companies generally operate on a financially sound basis, it is not always easy to demonstrate this fact because of the complexities and uniqueness of life insurance accounting. A greater degree of uniformity in accounting under GAAP will likely improve this situation.

SUMMARY

1. The relative security of the insured, the adequacy of rate-making, and the value of an insurance company from the viewpoint

[13] Robert S. Posnak, "Perspectives on Life Insurance Financial Reporting," *Journal of Risk and Insurance,* Vol. 40, No. 1 (March, 1973), pp. 7-22.

[14] "Consequences of Adjusted Earnings," *Transactions Society of Actuaries,* Vol. 26 (1974), pp. D293-D321.

of an investor are among the important questions affected by reserve valuation methods of insurance companies.

2. Two major reserves on the balance sheet of an insurer are unearned premium reserves (which in a life insurer are called policy reserves) and loss reserves. Unearned premium reserves represent the liability of the insurer for advance premium payments made by the insured, while loss revenues represent estimates of the amount of losses and loss expenses attributable to losses that the insurer has incurred. Loss reserves are generally relatively large in property and liability insurers, while unearned premium reserves are dominant in fire and allied lines and in life insurers.
3. The accounting requirements in connection with the unearned premium reserve cause several financial problems for the property and liability insurer, chief among which are the drain on surplus for an expanding insurer and the resulting limitations on its potential growth. Insurance capacity is reduced and underwriting standards are tightened as a consequence. Recognition of these accounting requirements is vital in an interpretation of the financial statements of property and liability insurers.
4. In interpreting the loss reserves of an insurer, attention must be given to the type of insurance written, the territory of operation, the trend of premium growth, and the age and experience of the insurer in a given line of business.
5. As a result of accounting systems for reserve liabilities and other factors, the level of stability of profits in property and liability insurance has not been considered generally adequate. Problems which result include reduced underwriting capacity, inability to attract new capital, and difficulty in attracting qualified personnel.
6. Policy reserves (unearned premium reserves) in life insurance are by far the most important liability. They are large because of the practice of issuing life insurance on a net level premium basis over a long period of time. Loss reserves are minimal.
7. Policy reserves must be at such a level that if the insurer ceased doing business, all existing obligations on contracts could be met. Looked at prospectively, the reserve is defined as the present value of future claims less the present value of future premiums. Looked at retrospectively, the reserve represents the net difference between premiums collected, plus interest, and death claims assumed to have occurred.

QUESTIONS FOR REVIEW AND DISCUSSION

1. An insurance firm writes $100,000 of new premiums in a certain year on fire insurance policies with a term of two years.
   (a) How much liability should be shown in the unearned premium reserve at the end of the first year, assuming that the business is written evenly throughout the year? Explain.
   (b) What would the unearned premium reserve be if the policies had been for a five-year term?
2. Why is a new insurer likely to show a statutory underwriting loss for the first few years after it begins business, even though its underwriting experience may be considered profitable?
3. The chief auditor of the New York State Insurance Department wrote as follows: "Theoretically, the unearned premium reserve in the fire and casualty statement is the amount that will discharge all obligations of the company that can

possibly occur in the unexpired terms of all policies in force as of the statement date. Actually, it is greater, since it is computed on the premium charged, which is gross as to commissions, and, therefore, represents a liability carried by the company in excess of the actual amount necessary to discharge all obligations that may be incurred during the periods the policies have yet to run."

(a) Is it true that the unearned premium reserve represents an amount which will discharge all obligations of the company that can *possibly* occur on the unexpired policies in force? Explain.

(b) Do you agree that the unearned premium reserve is excessive?

(c) What financial problems are introduced by the requirements that the unearned premium reserve be excessive?

4. In establishing loss reserves, how can an insured set up a reserve for losses which have been incurred but are unreported at the time the statement is prepared?

5. A state insurance department auditor said, "If during a period of mounting claim costs on certain casualty lines, a company's reserves on them did not reflect the trend, a question as to the adequacy of its claim reserves would arise. If on a line of business on which past experience was credible the company's reserve seemed unreasonable when compared with previous statement figures, the liability carried would be questioned." Judging from these criteria employed by an insurance examiner, would you say that an audited statement of reserve liabilities can be relied upon? Why?

6. Table 27–3 is an abbreviated set of financial statements for the Actual Fire and Casualty Company, for the two years, (1) and (2).

ABBREVIATED FINANCIAL STATEMENT

Table 27-3

Balance Sheet, December 31 (000,000's Omitted)

	(2)	(1)
Admitted Assets:		
Bonds	$5.6	$5.3
Stocks	.8	.9
Real estate	.4	.4
Cash	.3	.3
Premium balances	.3	.6
Other	.6	.1
	$8.0	$7.6
Liabilities:		
Loss and expense reserve	$2.3	$2.0
Unearned premium reserve	2.6	2.2
Other	.1	.3
Total liabilities	$5.0	$4.5
Paid-up capital	1.0	1.0
Net surplus	2.0	2.1
Total liabilities & surplus	$8.0	$7.6

Income Statement For Year Ended December 31 (000,000's Omitted)

	(2)	(1)
Premiums written	$ 5.4	$4.7
Premiums earned	5.0	4.6
Expenses (35%)	1.9	1.6
Losses	3.3	2.8
Underwriting profit (statutory)	—.2	.2
Investment profit	.1	.1
Total	$—.1	$ .3

Distribution of Premium Writings in Year (2):

Fire and allied lines	$ .1
Auto liability	2.2
Auto physical damage	2.0
Miscellaneous	1.1
Total premiums written	$5.4

(a) In your opinion, what is a more accurate estimate of year (2) underwriting results than the one shown? Explain.
(b) In your opinion, what is the true net worth of this company?
(c) Explain the difference between premiums written and premiums earned. What is the probable reason why the difference between these two quantities was greater in year (2) than in year (1)?
(d) Comment on the investments of the company. Would you say they are more or less conservative than need be? Why?
(e) If you did not know the distribution of premium writings of this insurer, what evidence is there that it is not primarily a fire insurer?

7. Several studies of property-liability insurance profitability cited in the text show that profits in the industry have been relatively low compared with other industries and the risk higher.
(a) Suggest possible reasons why an industry supposedly aimed at reducing other people's risk cannot itself earn a competitive profit and experiences considerable instability in the profit it does make.
(b) Is there an underwriting cycle of profits and losses in the industry? Explain.

8. A witness testifying before a congressional hearing on regulation and rate-making in the insurance industry stated, "The industry needs a better measure of its future liabilities and a more useful and accurate treatment of its income statements in any event, but if a better measure of future liabilities can be found, one which is not tied directly to the rate level, as the unearned premium reserve is . . . then fire and casualty insurers' solvency can be watched and preserved while the rates charged to the customers are left free to fluctuate . . . according to individual companies' needs, opportunities, and markets."
(a) In what sense is the unearned premium reserve tied to the rate level?
(b) Will it be generally true that a company with low rates will have a relative advantage, surplus-wise, over a company with high rates because of unearned premium reserve requirements? Why? If so, does this mean that the unearned premium reserve requirements result in rates higher than those which would otherwise exist?
(c) Suggest some way of estimating an insurer's liability to policyholders other than the method currently used and represented by the unearned premium reserve.

9. (a) Why are life insurance companies often identified as legal reserve life insurers?
(b) What aspects of life insurer reserves are subject to law?

10. The formula for the prospective reserve in life insurance is calculated as the present value of future benefits less the present value of future premiums. After a policy has been in force for a few years, why is it that the present value of future benefits exceeds the present value of future premiums, thus necessitating a reserve?

11. Why is it that the reserve on an individual ordinary life policy increases continually until at maturity it is equal to the face amount, whereas the *aggregate* reserve of the insurer for all ordinary life policies declines, until at the maturity of all policies it is exhausted? (See Figure 27–1.)

12. It may be said that the life insurance reserve for any particular policy year is obtained by adding the net level premium for that year to the terminal reserve of the preceding year, increasing this sum by the minimum rate of interest guaranteed by the insurer, and deducting the cost of insurance for the current year. What method of calculating the reserve is thus described?

13. (a) Calculate the required reserve on a 20-payment life policy issued at age 30 for a level premium of $27.04 by the time the insured is age 45. The present value of future claims at age 45 is $551.37. The present value of one dollar due from all survivors age 45 for five years is $4.68. What reserve calculation method is illustrated here?
(b) How would you proceed in calculating the $551.37?

14. Explain why the higher the interest assumed, the lower is the required reserve in life insurance.

15. A life insurance agent stated, "When the new (1958) mortality table was adopted, premium rates, and hence the reserve requirements, went down." Is this statement wholly true, wholly false, or partly true and partly false?

16. It has been stated that life insurers are permitted to reduce their reserve requirements by the amount of the heavy first-year expenses involved in putting a policy on the books, but a property insurer is not so permitted. Is this true, and if so, can you think of some reason for it?

17. In calculating life insurance policy reserves, which is the more conservative, the net level premium method or the Commissioners' Standard Valuation method? Why?

18. (a) What is the preliminary term method of valuation?
(b) In what way is this method related to the Commissioners' Standard Valuation method?

19. A writer stated, ". . . in most life insurance companies there is probably some understatement of surplus as a result of valuing assets low and liabilities high . . . this relation probably varies considerably from company to company."
(a) Suggest specific ways in which liabilities might be overstated and asset values understated in a life insurance company.
(b) How should this information be considered in judging the relative safety of a given insurer? Explain.

20. One of the larger life insurers in the U.S., The Equity Funding Company, went into receivership in 1974 after it was revealed that assets and insurance in force had been greatly overstated, and liabilities understated. This was due to the creation of fictitious life insurance policies which were then sold to reinsurers who paid Equity Funding more than the first year's premium for each policy. In order to obtain funds to pay continuing premiums on these reinsured policies, Equity Funding created more new fictitious policies and sold them in satisfaction of the premium obligations. The scheme was revealed when a former employee informed the securities market authorities.
(a) Why would a reinsurer be willing to pay the primary insurer more than the first year's premium in order to own the policy?
(b) What does this case illustrate about regulation of legal reserve requirements of life insurers?

21. GAAP accounting is supposed to have the effect of increasing the earnings per share of many rapidly growing new life insurance companies. Explain why this might be true.

Chapter *Twenty-Eight*

INTERNATIONAL INSURANCE PROBLEMS

In recent years it has become increasingly important for the student of risk and insurance to recognize the importance of the international dimension. Although basic principles of risk and insurance are applicable without reference to international boundaries, the application of these principles abroad is often quite different from at home. This chapter is devoted to a consideration of some of these differences. Emphasis is on the contrasts between United States and foreign insurance practices and environments. The treatment here should be considered illustrative rather than comprehensive in nature.

GROWTH OF WORLD TRADE

Tables 28–1 and 28–2 demonstrate the tremendous growth of world trade and international investments during the past 18 years. With this expansion an enlarged world market for insurance was created. Insurance is especially significant because operations outside one's own country are usually considered riskier than domestic operations, and if insurance had not been available it is unlikely that the pace of expansion could have been as great as it has. Over the period the compound rate of growth in exports approximated 9% annually.

Table 28–2 shows that large sums of money have been invested abroad by United States corporations. The rate of growth in this investment has exceeded the rate of growth of exports. Over the period 1955–1973, United States private long-term investments increased nearly 5-fold, compared to a 4.6-fold increase in exports. Similarly, foreigners have been increasing their investments in the United States, but at an even faster pace.

The implications for insurance of this growth in world commerce are significant. For example, there has been the development of the multinational corporation, which views the world as its market and attempts to locate its manufacturing operations in the country with the greatest economic advantages. The multinational corporation also seeks insurance coverage on a worldwide basis and has presented a challenge to the world's insurance industry. Ways must be found to protect investments in foreign locations against

U.S. EXPORTS OF MERCHANDISE, 1955 AND 1973

Table 28-1

Trading Area	Exports		
	(Billions of Dollars)		Percent Increase
	1955	1973	
Developed countries	$ 9.8	$47.2	382
Developing countries	5.8	21.0	261
Communist areas	—	2.5	—
Total Western Hemisphere	6.9	25.0	262
Western Europe	5.1	21.4	320
Asia	2.6	18.4	607
Australia and Oceania	.3	1.7	466
Africa	.6	2.3	283
Canada	3.4	15.0	341
20 Latin American nations	3.3	8.9	169
Total	15.5	71.3	360

Source: U.S. Department of Commerce as compiled and reported in *Statistical Abstract of the U.S., 1974,* pp. 792-795. Percentages calculated.

INTERNATIONAL INVESTMENTS OF THE U.S., 1955 AND 1973

Table 28-2

Investment	(Billions of Dollars)		Percent Increase
	1955	1973	
Total U.S. assets abroad	$65.1	$226.1	247
Private long-term investments*	29.1	143.5	393
Foreign investments in the U.S.	27.8	163.1	486
Net international investment position of the U.S.	37.2	63.0	69

Source: U.S. Department of Commerce, *1975 Economic Report of the President,* p. 357.
*Direct investments in plant and equipment, as well as portfolio holdings.

insurable hazards on some basis acceptable to investors; otherwise, an important deterrent to increased trade and investments exists. The insurance industry must expand its financial ability and create administrative arrangements for protecting increased values exposed to loss abroad. Worldwide networks of agents and claims service offices are being developed. Reinsurance facilities must be continually expanded.

Insurance and Economic Development

Analysis of the world markets and economic development reveals the consistent link between economic development and the growth of insurance. Without answering the question of whether or not insurance is indispensable to economic development, it would appear that the two are highly correlated. The economic facts shown in Table 28–3 illustrate the importance of population,

Table 28-3

POPULATION, G.N.P., INVESTMENT, AND INSURANCE PREMIUMS, MAJOR WORLD AREAS, 1972

Area	Percent of World Total			
	Population	GNP	Investments by Insurers	Insurance Premiums
North America	9.33	40.88	61.59	57.24
Western Europe	15.14	33.27	26.14	27.77
Japan	4.32	9.63	7.05	9.46
Asia (Except Japan)	43.78	5.91	1.18	1.19
Africa	14.78	2.57	1.05	.95
Latin America	12.00	5.94	.68	1.32
Australasia	.65	1.80	2.31	2.07
Total	100.00	100.00	100.00	100.00

Source: Swiss Reinsurance Company, *Sigma,* No. 10, (October, 1974).

gross national product, investment activity, and insurance premiums collected in major areas of the world. It may be seen that industrialized areas such as Western Europe and North America have relatively small proportions of population, but dominant shares of total production, investment, and insurance activity. The converse is true in less developed areas of Asia, Africa, and Latin America. The major economic fact of life is that insurance development tends to accompany economic development, wherever it occurs.

As might be expected, there is a particularly close relationship between insurance premiums and investment activity by insurers, revealed in the last two columns of Table 28–3. Some of the reasons for the relationships shown may be understood by a review of the contributions of insurance toward economic development. Insurance tends to increase the supply of investable capital through creation of reserves for losses, both present and future. This tends to create a more favorable investment climate and reduces the drain on government resources. Through insurance, credit is expanded by reducing the subjective risk experienced by lenders. Insurance contributes to the incentives to preserve and improve property through loss-prevention effort.

The problem of insuring personnel, including expatriates, against personal risk must be solved, since investment activity necessarily involves extensive use of many types of trained people for foreign assignments. Loss-prevention engineering is often difficult in strange settings. Countless other problems must be solved by insurers in meeting the demands of worldwide trade and business expansion.

INTERNATIONAL INSURANCE INSTITUTIONS

It is estimated that 10,479 domestic insurers and 3,200 foreign branches exist in 76 major countries of the world (see Table 28–4). Over 83% of these insurers are located in North America and Europe. The number of insurers for

THE WORLD INSURANCE MARKET, 1972 (76 COUNTRIES)

Table 28-4

Area	Number of Insurers	Percent of Total	Insurance Density *
Europe	3,932	37.5	14.60
North America	4,783	45.7	22.14
Latin America	805	7.7	4.71
Africa	202	1.9	2.42
Asia	369	3.5	.98
Australasia	388	3.7	3.09
World Total	10,479	100.0	6.41

Source: *Sigma* (Swiss Reinsurance Company, October, 1972).
* Number of companies per 1,000,000 population.

each million of population varies greatly, averaging about 22 in North America and 15 in Europe. Insurance is not well developed in emerging nations of the world. It is estimated that in 1900 there were only about 1,300 insurance companies in the world. Today, the United States is by far the most important insurance country in the world, with about 4,700 insurers. In terms of the number of domestic insurers, the following countries ranked below the United States: Germany, 729; Spain, 614; Great Britain, 584; The Netherlands, 372; Denmark, 304; Sweden, 301; France, 284; and Argentina, 244.[1]

United States insurers operate abroad fairly extensively. It is estimated that there are 45 principal foreign underwriting company groups operating in nonlife coverages overseas with admitted assets of $13 billion. These insurers operate in over 150 jurisdictions through 360 overseas branch offices, employing nearly 10,000 local nationals. They are represented in addition through more than 10,000 foreign agencies. In life insurance, United States insurers and their subsidiaries have a premium income of over $100 million with reserves of over $300 million invested in local markets.[2]

Not only do American insurers operate abroad fairly extensively, but foreign insurers operate in the United States. For example, in 1970, it is estimated that the assets employed by alien nonlife insurers to underwrite risks in the United States amounted to about $2.5 billion, or approximately 5% of the assets devoted to property and liability insurance in the country. There are about 30 alien insurers whose business in the United States exceeds $1 million in premium volume annually. This volume represented about 3.6% of the total premiums written in property and liability insurance in the United States in 1970.

The relative importance of insurance in major world countries is shown in Table 28–5, giving estimated total premiums in life and nonlife insurance in 1973 for 34 nations. It is seen that the leading insurance countries of the world are the United States, West Germany, Japan, Great Britain, and France, in that

[1] "The World Insurance Market," *Sigma* (Zurich: Swiss Reinsurance Company, October, 1972).

[2] U.S. Chamber of Commerce, *Position Paper on International Insurance and Reinsurance,* (Washington: Chamber of Commerce of the United States, 1972), p. 11.

INSURANCE PREMIUMS WRITTEN, SELECTED COUNTRIES, 1973

Table 28-5

Rank	Country	Premiums (Millions of U.S. Dollars)	Percent of World Total
1	U.S.A.	88,672	51.55
2	West Germany	15,909	9.25
3	Japan	15,842	9.21
4	Great Britain	9,884	5.75
5	France	8,007	4.66
6	Canada	5,722	3.33
7	Australia	3,530	2.05
8	Italy	3,306	1.92
9	The Netherlands	2,922	1.70
10	Switzerland	1,919	1.12
11	Sweden	1,666	0.97
12	Spain	1,539	0.89
13	Belgium	1,519	0.88
14	South Africa	1,300	0.76
15	Denmark	976	0.57
16	Austria	926	0.54
17	India	772	0.45
18	Brazil	737	0.43
19	Finland	709	0.41
20	Norway	676	0.39
21	Argentina	598	0.35
22	New Zealand	574	0.33
23	Mexico	424	0.25
24	Portugal	285	0.17
25	Israel	280	0.16
26	Ireland	279	0.16
27	Venezuela	253	0.15
28	South Korea	196	0.11
29	Philippines	159	0.09
30	Greece	144	0.08
31	Peru	133	0.08
32	Iran	123	0.07
33	Taiwan	121	0.07
34	Malaysia	112	0.06

Source: Swiss Reinsurance Company, *Sigma,* No. 5 (May, 1975).

order. These five countries account for over 80% of the world premium volume, with the United States dominating all other countries combined. Interestingly enough, all of the countries shown without exception increased the proportion of gross national product spent on insurance over the period 1963–1973. The United States, Great Britain, Australia, New Zealand, and The Netherlands had the largest increase in the proportion of GNP spent on insurance.[3]

[3] Swiss Reinsurance Company, *Sigma*, No. 5 (May, 1975).

Reinsurance

In 1968 a significant change occurred in the trend of United States reinsurance transactions. Before this date, during the period 1950–1968 there was a tendency for the United States to purchase more reinsurance abroad than it sold to foreigners. After 1968, premiums received from foreign insurers increased at a faster rate than premiums paid for cessions abroad. As shown in Table 28–6, in 1968 the United States sold $170 million of reinsurance abroad, a figure which grew to $471 million by 1973, an increase of 177%. In contrast, reinsurance purchased abroad increased from $408 million in 1968 to $607 million in 1973, an advance of only 49%.

After adjustments for losses paid and collected on foreign reinsurance, reinsurance premiums had relatively little effect on the United States balance of payments. The net effect of reinsurance was −$80 million in 1973, contrasted to −$97.6 million in 1968. In the period 1965–1973 the negative balance did not exceed $106.4 million, a figure reached in 1971. These amounts are minor when related to the $10.7 billion of adverse balance of payments (current account and long-term capital) suffered in 1974.

An analysis of reinsurance transactions reflects the growth of world trading partners of the United States and the importance of insurance in facilitating world trade and investment. Unfortunately, political and economic pressures have existed in developing countries to limit the importation of insurance, in the desire to conserve foreign exchange and to reduce the negative effect which this has upon the balance of payments. Careful examination of the world balance of payments data reveals, however, that most countries (even the United States) import insurance and that there are two major exporting nations, the United Kingdom and Switzerland.[4] These countries are specialists in world reinsurance. Efforts to limit the purchase of reinsurance from abroad may be counterproductive, since without foreign reinsurance, capital must be employed locally for this purpose. Often, local markets are small and the use of local capital for insurance on a small scale may be inefficient. As Professor Launie has stated,[5]

> There is no question that the development of a large, sophisticated domestic insurance industry is an important step in the development of a modern economic system. But at an early stage in the development cycle, when domestic savings are typically low, this type of financial intermediary may be an expensive luxury that the economy might more wisely forego.

The International Insurance Market

Multinational corporations usually deal with two major classes of international insurers: American-based insurers operating at home and in foreign countries, and foreign-based insurers operating both in the United States and abroad. Brokers and agents will often be necessary as intermediaries.

[4] See *Balance of Payments Yearbook,* International Monetary Fund, published annually.

[5] J. J. Launie, "The Balance of Payments Implications of Reinsurance for Emerging Nations," *Best's Review* (April, 1973), p. 94.

INTERNATIONAL REINSURANCE TRANSACTIONS OF THE U.S. (Millions of Dollars)

Table 28-6

	1973p*	1970	1968
1. Net premium paid for foreign reinsurance	$607.3	$447.7	$408.1
2. Less: Losses recovered from abroad	361.7	287.8	291.2
3. Net outflow on foreign purchases	$245.6	$159.9	$116.9
4. Premium received on reinsurance sold abroad	$470.9	$251.4	$170.7
5. Less: Losses paid abroad	305.3	174.2	151.7
6. Net inflow from foreign sales	$165.6	$ 77.2	$ 19.0
7. Net balance on U.S. reinsurance transactions abroad (3)–(6)	$–80.0	$–82.7	$–97.6

* p: Preliminary

Source: "Commerce Reports 1973 Reinsurance Transactions," DIBA 74-125. (News release of U.S. Department of Commerce by James F. Rourke, December 3, 1974).

International Insurance Brokers. According to estimates by *Business Insurance* the largest international brokerage offices are:

Company	Gross Revenue 1974 (Millions of Dollars)	Number of Employees 1974
Marsh & McClennan	$204.9	7,235
Johnson & Higgins	125.0*	3,500*
Alexander & Alexander	100.5	3,400
Frank B. Hall	85.8	2,850
Reed Shaw Osler	75.2	3,600
Fred S. James	63.3	2,004

* Estimates. Johnson & Higgins does not publish official figures.

Source: *Business Insurance* (July 28, 1975), p. 7.

Most brokers operating in international markets establish local offices in foreign countries to service the needs of the corporations operating there. In many cases these offices take the form of foreign correspondents, local insurance agencies given a license to represent the international broker in its dealings with local clients. In other cases the international broker actually sets up a subsidiary office for handling local business.

American Insurers. United States insurers have organized in different ways to offer coverage of multinational companies operating abroad. Some companies operate individually and others operate through associations. Current examples of major international insurers operating individually are Insurance Company of North America, Commercial Union, Royal Globe, and Continental National American. In the life insurance field, John Hancock, American International

Life, Combined Insurance Companies, and Aetna Insurance Company are overseas leaders.

Some U.S. insurers prefer to operate through groups or pools. There are three major examples of these pools: AFIA (American Foreign Insurance Association), AIG (American International Group), and the factory mutuals.

AFIA. Currently operating in about 80 foreign countries, AFIA began business in 1917 in China. A number of insurers had been operating independently in China and maintained separate offices. The idea for a central organization rose out of the need for coordinating these operations, maintaining some degree of uniformity, and obtaining some expense reduction. Currently there are about nine United States insurers who are members of the AFIA, which operates as a management pool. AFIA members are entered individually into the countries in which AFIA operates. AFIA is an unincorporated association. Each member submits to AFIA a book of limits, which states maximum amounts for which AFIA may bind them in each country. Each year a profit is distributed to local members or each member is asked to make up a deficit, which last happened in 1928 following a major fire in Ecuador.

More than 50% of the total premium income of AFIA stems from indigenous business; that is, from customers operating entirely within a foreign country. The remaining premium income is from firms operating as foreign subsidiaries of United States parent corporations.

American International Group. American International Group, in contrast to AFIA, is an incorporated company. AIG is a holding company whose subsidiaries engage in property, liability, and life insurance business in more than 135 countries. Its principal subsidiaries include the American Home Assurance, National Union Fire Insurance, New Hampshire Group, American International Underwriters Corporation, American International Life Insurance, and the American International Underwriters Overseas. AIG operates as a pool similar to AFIA except that AIG has greater control over the insurers whose capacity it commits on foreign risks. There is a predetermined percentage of premiums and losses applicable to each of the member companies. As with AFIA, a majority of AIG's business is indigenous in nature, with approximately two thirds being collected from customers whose total business exists in foreign countries.

Factory Mutuals. Factory mutuals are also engaged in writing international insurance. Two major systems exist, the Factory Insurance Association (FIA), made up of 81 stock companies which share in a pool, and the Factory Mutual Association (FMA). The FIA as an entity does the underwriting, and its members get a predetermined share of each premium and pay a predetermined share of all losses. The FMA, on the other hand, is composed of four companies which compete until one is awarded the business. The winning company is the sponsoring company and must convince the others to go along with the risk.

Factory mutuals offer engineering service to clients. Actually, both FIA and the FMA usually accept only risks which stress loss-prevention activities, i.e., the high protection risk (HPR) business.

Private International Insurance Organizations

In addition to private companies or associations of companies, there may exist many international organizations which affect insurance practices abroad. A few of these organizations are described here.

Le Comité d'Action pour la Productivité dans l'Assurance (CAPA). CAPA, an organization to encourage management efficiency in the field of insurance, operates in all of Europe from its headquarters in Paris. Its members are 125 insurance companies and associations in France and 105 similar organizations in 15 other nations in Western Europe. CAPA carries on research which assists its member groups and distributes publications based on this work. Typical of its activities are the coordination of insurance with government administrative agencies, development of uniform insurance accounting practices, and sponsorship of international conferences. Its work is carried out by about 15 standing committees whose leaders are European insurance executives. CAPA works closely with groups such the Life Insurance Agency Management Association and the Institute of Life Insurance in the United States, and with the British Insurance Association.

International Union of Marine Insurance (IUMI). The IUMI, founded in 1874, is one of the oldest existing international insurance organizations. It comprises 48 marine associations from 46 countries. Its major activities involve annual conferences on marine insurance, promotion of the interests of world marine insurance markets, adoption of uniform policy provisions in marine policies throughout the world, exchange of information, and loss prevention.

International Union of Aviation Insurance (IUAI). Founded in 1934, the IUAI comprises over 500 private aviation insurers operating in 25 countries. This organization generally performs for the field of aviation insurance what the IUMI does for the field of marine insurance.

International Credit Insurance Association (ICIA). The ICIA, founded in 1946, consists of about 18 insurance companies in 17 nations. Its major function is to study domestic and export credit insurance and to promote uniformity of coverage in the field of export credit insurance.

Bureau International de Producteurs d'Assurances et de Reassurances (BIPAR). BIPAR is an organization of insurance agents and brokers in 12 countries. Over 16 professional associations are represented. In general, the organization attempts to advance the interests of agents and brokers. Under its auspices the European Center for Insurance Education and Training in St. Gall, Switzerland, was established. In 1971 this center cooperated in publishing an insurance dictionary showing about 1,200 equivalent terms in four languages.[6]

The Permanent Committee of International Congresses of Actuaries. This committee, established in 1889, aims to link actuaries and actuarial associations of various countries. It helped organize the International Congress of

[6] Dr. H. L. Muller-Lutz (ed.), *Insurance Dictionary* (Madrid: MAPFRE, 1971). This book shows insurance terms in German, French, English, and Spanish.

Actuaries, which sponsors an annual conference for the advancement of actuarial science. Thirty-four nations are represented in the permanent committee. An important work of the committee was to publish the international insurance dictionary in 1970, published in 11 languages and containing 1,800 terms.

International Insurance Seminars, Inc. Founded in 1964 by Professor John S. Bickley of the University of Alabama, the International Insurance Seminars, Inc., sponsors an annual management conference for insurance executives in different countries around the world.

Insurance Hall of Fame. The Insurance Hall of Fame, sponsored by the Griffith Foundation for Insurance Education, The Ohio State University, honors outstanding individuals in the world who have made exceptional contributions to insurance. Approximately 60 persons have been selected for membership, and each year 5 to 7 additional individuals are so honored.

INTERNATIONAL LEGAL ENVIRONMENT

One of the important problems facing the international business person is that of adjusting to the different legal climate which characterizes overseas operations. Some of the legal variations which affect insurance operations are: rules governing admitted versus unadmitted insurance, the Napoleonic code, the Treaty of Rome provisions, and the operation of tax laws.

Admitted Versus Unadmitted Insurance

A problem which must be faced by a business firm seeking insurance on international risks concerns the use of domestic insurers who issue so-called unadmitted insurance. *Unadmitted insurance* is that coverage on risks within a given country by insurers not admitted to do business in that country. Some countries permit unadmitted insurance, but others impose penalties for it ranging from fines to confiscation and imprisonment. Yet, use of the unadmitted market may be necessary in order to obtain adequate coverage, and it is used in apparent violation of the spirit, if not the letter, of the law in some countries.

Admitted insurance is that insurance which is written by insurance companies or branches admitted to do business in the country where the exposure is located and which is governed by the laws of the country concerned. Usually, the policy is written in the local language, and rates and indemnities are payable in local currency. Unadmitted insurance usually is written outside the country concerned, with premiums and losses payable in dollars. The unadmitted contract is normally written in English, with terms similar to those in the United States market.

In countries which do not prohibit unadmitted insurance, the insured may still have to use admitted coverage for compulsory insurance such as workers' compensation or automobile liability. There are several advantages in the use of unadmitted coverage: it is easier to control, it usually carries lower rates, it is exempt from foreign sales taxes, and it generally offers more flexibility. Still, because many countries require the use of local insurers, most multinational firms employ a combination of admitted and unadmitted insurance. Countries which prohibit unadmitted insurance or severely restrict its use include most South American countries, Portugal, Spain, Italy, Mexico, France, Ireland, and Japan. Unadmitted insurance is generally allowed (except for compulsory coverages) in the United Kingdom, Australia, New Zealand, Belgium, Denmark, West Germany, The Netherlands, Switzerland, Malaysia, Thailand, Korea, Hong Kong, and the Philippines.

If a multinational firm is operating in a country which prohibits unadmitted insurance and yet it cannot secure the coverage it desires, it may often employ what is called a *difference in conditions* (DIC) *policy* to fill in the gaps left by the policy issued in the country. Under this policy, which is unadmitted, the home office of the firm pays the premiums and collects any losses, usually in dollars, if there is a loss under the policy.

Unadmitted insurance is often used in such areas as general liability or products liability. A product may be assembled in one country, use parts manufactured in another, and be sold in several countries. Products liability which is insured locally in one country may not be available to meet claims which arise in another country. Hence a general worldwide policy is needed. Unadmitted insurance is also used to cover machinery in some cases because replacing machinery often requires importing it and paying for replacement in dollars. Local policies may not respond in dollars and may not be suitable.

The Napoleonic Code

Besides unadmitted insurance, international insurance operations are affected by the basic legal system under which the country operates. For example, the Napoleonic code affects insurance contracts in France, Belgium, Egypt, Greece, Italy, Lebanon, Spain, Turkey, and various African (formerly French) countries. The code of Napoleon of 1810 is the basic foundation of current French law. An example of its effect on insurance is the system of passing responsibility for fire losses on to third parties. For example, if a fire originates on a person's property and through this person's negligence (known as *faute lourde*) spreads to a neighbor's property, causing the neighbor loss, liability exists. This doctrine is called *recours des voisins*. However, it is up to the neighbor to prove that the liability exists. Since this may not be easy to do, the situation is not serious for the owner. Nevertheless, the potential liability is generally insured in a comprehensive general liability policy. In some cases the liability may be covered by attaching an endorsement to the fire policy or through providing a separate fire policy. This latter solution is generally used in France, Belgium, and Italy, since public liability policies in these countries exclude the *faute lourde* exposure.

The Treaty of Rome Provisions on Insurance

Free markets for insurance are important to support business activity because of the implications they have for adequate capacity at reasonable rates. In the European Economic Community (EEC), where a majority of United

States investment is located, the 1957 Treaty of Rome attempted to achieve free markets by providing in Article 61 as follows: "The liberalization of banking and insurance services connected with the movement of capital shall be effected in harmony with the progressive liberalization of the movement of capital." This process became known as "harmonization."

Harmonization of insurance for each of the members of the EEC was to be accomplished in two main stages: freedom of establishment phase and freedom of service phase. Freedom of establishment means that an insurance company in one common market country is free to set up business in another common market country. The freedom of service phase implies freedom for the insurance company to operate in any common market country on the authority it holds in the country of origin within the common market. The freedom of establishment phase was completed by 1965, while the freedom of service phase, which involves considerably more adjustment, is still not completed. The reason for the delay may be summed up by listing the practical difficulties of licensing insurers in countries where the insurance laws vary markedly:

1. Reconciliation of insurance control laws, including registration requirements and compulsory deposit.
2. Establishment of uniform laws covering the terms of contracts.
3. Achievement of uniformity of legal concepts such as those affecting liability of third parties.
4. Simplification of formalities for the execution of judgments.
5. Standardization of premium tariffs and policy taxes.

Significant progress in completing the freedom of service stage was accomplished when the EEC Council of Ministers accepted two directives in July, 1973, to abolish limitations imposed on the freedom of movement and to effect the necessary coordination of provisions concerning the commencement and practice of direct nonlife insurance. The nine EEC countries were given 18 months to alter their national laws to conform to the new directives.

Once the freedom of service phase has been completed, the market for insurance in the European Economic Community should expand greatly. Insurance purchases in the EEC are comparatively far below the United States equivalents. Part of this difference lies with the concern in other countries of rapid depreciation of the currency (hindering the growth of life insurance) and with the fact that workers' compensation premiums and other social insurance coverages may be paid largely to the state as an additional tax. Furthermore, there are fewer registered automobiles in the EEC than in the United States, as well as generally lower property values. However, this situation is rapidly changing; and the growth of insurance in the EEC, may be expected to approach that of the United States since the populations of the two regions are roughly equal.

For example, the ratio of life insurance in force to national income in major industrial countries over the period 1960–1972 was as follows:[7]

[7] *Life Insurance Fact Book 1975* (New York: Institute of Life Insurance, 1975), p. 98, and previous editions.

	1960	1965	1970	1973
France	23%	34%	44%	52%*
West Germany	29	37	45	45
Italy	14	14	16	14
United Kingdom	70	86	113	101*
United States	141	159	176	150
Japan	59	95	131	161

* Data are for 1972.

The major members of the EEC, while far behind the United States in insuring lives, are increasing their acceptance of life insurance at a more rapid rate than the United States. In Japan the relative growth of life insurance has been especially rapid. Although data are not available, similar trends may be expected in the case of property and liability insurance.

Tax Laws

Tax legislation abroad affects insurance in many ways. For example, taxes on insurance premiums in foreign countries are often much higher than in the United States, making insurance costs considerably higher in some countries. Premium taxes can be as high as 30% to 40% (as is true in Argentina) compared to between 2% and 3% in the United States. The existence of wide variations in tax rates obviously favors the use of unadmitted insurance, where possible, in countries with high premium taxes.

Because of the operation of income tax laws abroad, the foreign subsidiary of a firm headquartered in another country may not be allowed to deduct the cost of unadmitted insurance for income taxes. This is true even if the subsidiary purchases admitted insurance to the fullest extent possible and then seeks unadmitted insurance to fill in some of the coverage gaps unavailable on the local market. Obviously some care is required in arranging foreign coverage most advantageously with respect to tax legislation.

It is common in several foreign countries to allow income tax deductions for the purchase of life insurance, a condition not yet applicable to United States residents. In Great Britain, a direct credit against the income tax is allowed. The tax relief is equal to one-half the income tax rate times the premium. Tax relief is not applicable to premiums greater than one sixth of one's income. Thus, in Britain, the government subsidizes the life insurance industry directly.

CONTRASTS IN INSURANCE CONDITIONS ABROAD

There are many variations in insurance policy provisions, insurer practices, and government regulations in foreign countries. Examples of these follow.

Underwriting Conditions

Many differences with regard to underwriting conditions in international insurance can be listed.

1. Insurance policies are usually written in the language of the country, not necessarily in English. Official translations are in many cases not available, but must be made individually. This requires special effort to achieve effective communications between headquarters and foreign branches on insurance programs.
2. In the field of fire insurance, United States firms are accustomed to coverage which does not restrict the definition of fire. Abroad, fire following explosion, windstorm, volcanic eruption, strikes or riot, earthquake, etc., is often not covered in primary policies. Coverage may be provided by endorsement.
3. In foreign countries it is not uncommon for the customer to be appointed as the licensed insurance agent to whom a commission is due. In this role as agent, the customer then receives a "kickback" in the premium equal to the amount of the commission. Known as rebates, these kickbacks are illegal in almost all states of the United States. In some countries, however, the agent is in a more secure position than would be true in the United States. In Argentina, for example, insurance law prohibits circumventing the agent and dealing directly with the insured. Thus, a place for the intermediary has been formally established by law. Agency commissions are also considerably higher in many lines than is true in the United States. For example, workers' compensation commissions in Brazil are 25%, auto liability commissions are between 20% and 30%, and fire insurance commissions are 35%. Typical commissions in the United States might be 10%, 15%, and 20%, respectively, for these lines.
4. Insurance policies generally are stricter regarding duties of an insured to disclose essential information, including notice of loss and filing a proof of loss, and advising the company of changes which affect the risk.
5. Blanket insurance covering buildings, machinery, and stock in one undivided amount, and blanket insurance for covering a number of separate risks, whether at the same location or not, are usually not permitted abroad.
6. Insurance on inventory based on the selling price value of the inventory calls for special approval and is not readily available from foreign insurers.
7. Fire insurance in other countries is usually written subject to 100% coinsurance requirements. In some areas subject to rampant inflation, such as in South America, reduced coinsurance percentages are sometimes available; but usually coinsurance below 80% is not permitted and even then is restricted to building and machinery values.
8. Policy periods vary considerably. For example, in the United Kingdom the standard fire policy is written for one year with no cancellation provision. Sometimes it may be extended for three years upon the exchange of letters of agreement. In the case of fire insurance on commercial properties, the contract period may be as long as 10 years, with premiums payable annually and cancellation allowed only under specific conditions, such as fire loss, transfer of the property, disposal of stock, or by mutual agreement.
9. Policies which are usually compulsory in the United States are not compulsory in many foreign countries. On the other hand, many policies that are not compulsory in the United States are compulsory elsewhere. For example, workers' compensation insurance is not required in Argentina, Hong Kong, or Jamaica, and applies only to employers with 200 or more employees in Korea. Life insurance is required on employees in Peru who have had four years of service with an employer. Automobile liability insurance, usually not compulsory in the United States, is required in many foreign countries, including New Zealand, Singapore, Malaysia, Hong Kong, Korea, and most of South America. Fire and transportation insurance is required in Brazil if values exceed a certain level. Travel accident liability insurance is required in Mexico.

As a further complication, some insurance which is not legally required in a foreign country may be, in a sense, required by virtue of custom, breach of which may not be advisable for American companies operating abroad. It is not uncommon that a joint venture agreement, for example, will provide that insurance shall be purchased "in accordance with the customs" of the country. Under these customs, some coverages would not be purchased in a foreign country whereas they would be required in the United States. An example is fidelity bonds, which might offend a foreign partner. Some coverages which the United States partner might think of as required or highly indicated, such as earthquake insurance in Japan, are not usually purchased as part of the customary protection.

10. Occasionally standard coverages available from foreign insurers vary markedly from their United States equivalents.[8] For example, in Japan the automobile insurance policy covers only three fourths of the insured's liability and the insured must adjust any claims. Underinsurance is not unusual in the field of fire insurance, where buildings might be insured for only 50% of their value.

Most policies in Western Europe cannot be cancelled by the insurer or the insured during their term. Furthermore, in many countries (excluding the United Kingdom) 90 or 180 days' notice must be given by either party if renewal is not desired.

11. Under United States policies, negligence of the insured is generally not a bar to recovery. In other countries, however, the law may alter this result. In Japan, for example, the law requires that if there is heavy negligence on the part of a tenant or the employees of the tenant, the tenant must pay fire damages.

12. Special hazards often exist in foreign countries. Some areas are particularly subject to earthquakes, tidal waves, or typhoons. Because incomes are often lower in foreign countries than in the United States, the problem of embezzlement is compounded. Many insurance experts feel that fidelity coverage is mandatory because of this problem.

13. The financial strength of foreign insurers is often far below the norms expected in the United States. For example, Spanish insurers tend to write about twice as much business for each dollar of surplus as is true of the typical insurer in the United States. Some insurers in Spain, writing restricted lines of business in a small territory, may be organized under the law for as little as $30 of capital.[9] Also, under the laws of many foreign countries it is legal and common for insurers to invest rather heavily in equities such as real estate, which may further restrict the insurer's liquidity and could hamper the payment of claims under some conditions.

14. There is a tendency for greater secrecy in private business abroad than exists in the United States. Premiums and terms of insurance coverage are most often negotiated and usually are not subject to the degree of governmental regulation that exists in the United States. As a result, some common United States insurance practices, such as a year-end audit to determine the premium due in workers' compensation, liability, and physical damage coverages on inventories, are not practical. The deposit premium tends to become final.

[8] Some interesting examples of the results of these differences are reported by Philip J. Brown, Jr., "The Role of the U.S. Broker in Europe," *International Insurance and Employee Benefit and Pension Management* (New York: American Management Association, 1966), pp. 6-11. For example, many foreign automobile insurance policies exclude coverage when the driver is drunk, under the influence of drugs, or without a proper license. Sometimes policies exclude damage caused by bad repairs or negligent operation.

[9] Mark R. Greene, "The Spanish Insurance Industry—An Analysis," *Journal of Risk and Insurance,* Vol. 39, No. 2 (June, 1972).

Difference in Conditions (DIC) Policies

Because of wide variations in contracts and underwriting conditions throughout the world, the multinational firm seeking uniform protection of properties in different locations is facing some difficulty. The instrument through which the problem is often solved is the *difference in conditions,* or excess, *policy*. This policy is written to cover many losses that would normally be covered under policies issued locally around the world. DIC policies are written to cover certain perils causing physical loss to property, as well as liability risks. In the field of physical losses the most common causes of DIC claims are collapse of building, water damage, and burglary. Flood is also insured under specific conditions. In liability coverage, the DIC is written as excess coverage over primary insurance. The insuring clause of one DIC policy in liability insurance reads:

> The underwriters hereby agree, subject to the limitations, terms, and conditions hereinafter mentioned, to indemnify the insured for all sums which the insured shall be obligated to pay by reason of the liability (a) imposed upon the insured by law, and (b) assumed under contract or agreement by the named insured and/or any officer, director, or stockholder, partner, or employee in the named insured while acting in his capacity as such for all damages, direct or consequential, and expenses all more fully defined by the term ultimate loss on account of (1) personal injuries including death at any time resulting therefrom, (2) property damage, (3) advertising liability caused by or arising out of each occurrence happening anywhere in the world.
>
> The underwriters hereon shall only be liable for the ultimate net loss the excess of either (a) the limits of the underlying insurance as set out in the attached schedule with respect to each occurrence covered by said underlying insurances, or (b) $25,000 ultimate net loss in respect of each occurrence not covered by said underlying insurances.

This policy provides coverage in the event that the primary insurance is inadequate or, subject to a limit of $25,000, does not cover the particular source of loss which would have otherwise been covered by the broad insuring clause mentioned.

One common requirement of DIC policies is that the primary policies be maintained in full effect during the term of the DIC policy, except for any reduction of aggregate limits caused by the payment of claims under the primary policies. If, for example, the insured allows a basic fire insurance policy to expire, the excess policy will not pay the first $10,000 of loss. Furthermore, before the DIC policy will pay, it requires that insurers of the underlying policies admit liability or that a final judgment against them be rendered.

Ultimate net loss is the amount payable in settlement of a liability of an insured after deductions for all recoveries and for other valid and collectible insurance (other than the coverage provided by the underlying primary and excess insurers) and excludes expenses and costs.

Premiums for DIC policies are usually figured as percentages of the underlying premium; for the DIC policy quoted, this amounts to 15%.

Foreign subsidiaries of American corporations generally purchase admitted insurance to the fullest extent possible. The parent company in the United

States then purchases the DIC policy for any losses which would otherwise not be covered.

EMPLOYEE BENEFIT PLANNING ABROAD

Another problem in international insurance management is that of administering employee benefit programs for nationals working in foreign countries and for employees who are citizens of those countries. Among the decisions which must be made are:

1. Should the firm attempt to extend the pattern of benefits applicable to domestic employees for foreign employees or should a different plan be developed for each country?
2. Should the potential cost of employee benefits be given consideration in the foreign investment decision?
3. What is the importance of union organization abroad in setting the patterns and levels of employee benefits?
4. How should the employee benefit structure be integrated with the social security system of the foreign country?

There are no quick answers to these questions and relatively little published information on the subject exists. This author conducted a study in 1967 of 236 American firms operating in 13 foreign countries, from which a few observations may be made.[10] This study surveyed the ways in which foreign subsidiaries handled employee benefits. It was found that about half of the firms maintained private retirement plans supplementing the social security benefits of the country concerned. This compares with about 70% of a sample of domestic firms in the Portland, Oregon metropolitan area.[11] About half of the industrial workers in the United States are covered by private retirement plans.[12] Since large firms are more likely to provide retirement benefits and to operate abroad than small firms, one would have expected a greater use of retirement plans abroad than the 1967 study indicated.

The 1967 study revealed that the following percentages of multinational firms operating abroad were offering the benefits listed:

Insurance	
Hospital expense	35.9%
Doctor bill	36.7
Major medical	15.2
Disability income	35.9
Group life	46.4
Accidental death and dismemberment	61.2
Retirement	51.5

[10] Mark R. Greene, "International Levels of Employee Benefits," *Journal of Risk and Insurance,* Vol. 35, No. 1 (March, 1968).

[11] Mark R. Greene, *The Role of Employee Benefit Structures in Manufacturing Industry* (Eugene: The University of Oregon, 1964), p. 20.

[12] Walter W. Kolodrubetz, "Trends in Employee-Benefit Plans in the Sixties," *Social Security Bulletin* (April, 1971), p. 24.

Noninsurance	
Paid sick leave	44.2
Paid holidays	87.8
Profit-sharing plan	18.1

In general, the incidence of these plans was less frequent than the incidence of plans applicable to purely domestic firms. One may make a tentative conclusion that although most of the American-type employee benefits are offered to foreign employees, the development is not as extensive as is true domestically, partly because of more extensive social insurance plans abroad.

The study revealed that fewer than 20% of the firms differentiated retirement benefits for United States nationals and foreign nationals working abroad, and it is likely that they did not differentiate other benefits either. Only in about a sixth of the firms were employee benefits subject to collective bargaining. This was the case even though two thirds of the firms were organized. There is some indication that firms attempt to keep their employee benefits equal or superior to local standards.

Asked whether or not the cost of employee benefits should enter into the foreign investment decision, about 29% of the 236 respondents indicated that these costs were of great importance; about half thought the costs were of moderate importance; only about 20% felt that employee benefit costs were of little or no importance in the foreign investment decision. Those firms not offering a pension plan tended to feel that the costs were of minor importance in the foreign investment decision.

The 1967 study revealed large variations in the incidence of benefits of different types, and between foreign countries. In coordinating company plans it would seem desirable for each country to be considered individually from the viewpoint of its social security benefits. In countries with large social security retirement benefits (e.g., Germany, Sweden, France, and Italy), it would appear unnecessary for the employer to provide substantial contributions to supplementary retirement plans.

Other features of social insurance plans may require special attention. In Mexico, for example, the law requires the payment of a severance allowance amounting to three months' wages, plus 20 days' wages for each year of service. Another law requires an average of about 10% of after-tax profit to be distributed to employees. If a person quits voluntarily, the severance allowance is forfeited; however, retirement does not cause loss of severance allowance. An employer in Mexico can provide a generous pension benefit (in relation to the wage level) for less than the amount which would otherwise be spent on the severance allowance. A common procedure there is to ask the employee to resign voluntarily, thus forfeiting the severance allowance, in return for a tax-free pension of an amount equal to or larger than the after-tax severance allowance. The cost of the pension plan is funded out of the severance allowance with money to spare for additional benefits to the workers.

In Japan, a worker is often attached to a single employer for a lifetime. Obviously one of the major reasons for employee benefits, namely the attraction and retention of good employees, is not nearly so crucial in Japan as it is in other countries. Furthermore, it has been the custom in Japan to pay retirement benefits in a lump sum; and since early retirement is the general rule there (age 55 is common), the pension benefit will generally be inadequate for the employee to live on for the remainder of his or her life. As a result of these factors, multinational companies have had to make special arrangements for supplementary pensions payable during retirement and for special emphasis on company welfare plans.

Some multinational companies, recognizing the wide variations that occur among constantly changing social security benefits in the world, have adopted a type of excess plan under which a worldwide standard of employee benefits is applied. For example, a firm may establish that a retirement benefit of 50% of wages will be provided workers with 30 years' service. To the extent that the local social security benefits do not meet the goal, the firm contributes the balance needed. This plan also helps solve the problem of retirees who are citizens of one country, working in another country for an employer whose corporate headquarters are in a third country. Expatriates may be totally or partially ineligible for social security in their own countries. Nevertheless, they are protected under the plan providing uniform benefits. Needless to say, the existence of such a plan is likely to be a powerful incentive to attract a skilled worker from a third country. The excess plan greatly reduces barriers to international operations.

INSURANCE FOR EXPORTS AND FOREIGN INVESTMENTS

Export credit insurance was initiated in the United States in 1961 by the Trade Expansion Act, which directed the Export-Import Bank of the United States (Eximbank) to offer insurance against losses from credit and political risks. The purpose of this program was to place United States exporters on an equal basis with foreign competitors and to promote exporting among private financial institutions. Export credit insurance is also used in most leading countries in Europe and elsewhere.[13]

In the United States, export credit insurance is underwritten jointly by Eximbank and an association of about 50 major stock and mutual insurance companies known as the Foreign Credit Insurance Association (FCIA).

FCIA insures credit term sales by United States exporters to responsible buyers in all free-world markets. The risks covered are: (1) commercial credit, i.e., insolvency or deliberate payment default, and (2) political, i.e., exchange transfer delay, war, revolution, expropriation, and other causes of loss arising principally from government action and beyond the control of the buyer or seller.

In 1974, $4.3 billion of exports were covered by credit insurance, nearly 6% of total United States exports in that year. Business in 1974 increased 133%

[13] Mark R. Greene, "Export Credit Insurance—Its Role in Expanding World Trade," *Journal of Risk and Insurance,* Vol. 32, No. 2 (June, 1965).

over 1973. About $2.5 million in claims payment were made in 1974. Most export credit insurance is issued on five major types of products listed in order of importance as follows: machinery, food and kindred products, electrical and electronic equipment and supplies, chemicals, and transportation equipment. Insured shipments were made to over 140 different countries covering approximately 2,000 exporters.[14]

The Foreign Credit Risk

Many factors contribute to the foreign credit risk. These may be divided into hazards and perils.

Hazards. Hazards of credit losses abroad include:

1. Language barriers and differences in accounting make it difficult to interpret financial information on the buyer.
2. Credit reports on foreign buyers often involve delays.
3. Reduced tariffs (e.g., among EEC countries) have opened huge new markets to relatively efficient producers, causing insolvencies among less efficient producers operating in previously protected territory. Insolvency figures attest to the dangers involved.
4. Increased world trade has put financial pressures on firms whose capital has not been able to expand sufficiently fast to accommodate the rising volume of trade.
5. In many countries the supply of trained and experienced managers has not been adequate for the rising volume of business.
6. In certain developing countries, unsound fiscal controls have existed, resulting in shortages of international currencies with which to pay debts. (Brazil is a leading current example.) Developing countries often run trade deficits for long periods. This problem tends to become more severe as rising debt repayments put a strain on a nation's ability to retire new debt commitments on schedule. Demand for longer credit terms greatly increases the credit hazards and the chances for occurrence of unknown perils.

Perils. What specific events can produce a bad debt loss to the exporter? In addition to entering formal bankruptcy, the debtor may delay payment indefinitely, refuse to accept goods, or cancel orders during the manufacturing period. The costs of bringing suit in a foreign country may be prohibitive to the seller. Even if buyers wish to pay, they may be prevented from doing so by acts of their government. These include war, revolution, blocked or delayed transfer of currency, changes in the rate of exchange, blockage in the conversion of money from local to contract currency, and withdrawal or cancellation of licenses.

Available Coverage

Two basic forms of export credit insurance are written: short- and medium-term. Short-term comprehensive covers commercial credit risks (normally to 90%) and political risks (to 95%) on sales of any product sold on payment terms up to 180 days. Medium-term covers both commercial and

[14] Foreign Credit Insurance Association, *Report of Operations, 1974.*

U.S. EXPORT CREDIT INSURANCE IN FORCE, 1974 Table 28-7

By Geographical Area	(Millions of Dollars) Face Amount of Coverage	Percent of Total
Africa	$ 138.4	5
Asia	239.4	9
Canada	50.4	2
Europe	784.2	31
Latin America	1,057.6	43
Middle East	156.1	6
Oceana	108.9	4
	$2,535.0	100
By Type of Policy		
Short-term	$1,650.5	65
Medium-term	220.3	9
Combined short-term and medium-term	187.4	7
Master policies	476.8	19
	$2,535.0	100

Source: Foreign Credit Insurance Association, *Report of Operations, 1974.*

political risks on terms of from six months to five years and is mostly for financing the sale of capital equipment on individual policy applications. In 1970 a new master comprehensive policy was introduced. This policy offers 90% coverage of accounts, both short- and medium-term, covering political and commercial risks, subject to a deductible. Coverage longer than five years (long-term) is not usually available.

Short-Term Insurance. Short-term comprehensive insurance is the dominant form of export credit insurance. As shown in Table 28–7, it accounted for about two thirds of the coverage in 1974. The policy is issued to the exporter, who may insure against political or commercial risks or both under a comprehensive policy.

In obtaining this insurance, the exporter may be permitted to select individual accounts for coverage providing that a sufficient number of accounts are covered to constitute a fair spread of risk. However, the FCIA may permit exclusion of sales to certain major buyers or countries, or allow coverage to be confined to sales of certain product lines. These controls are necessary to prevent adverse selection against the insurer and to obtain a suitable spread of risk.

The premium varies directly with the length of terms extended and inversely with the financial stability of the market to which the merchandise is being shipped.

For the short-term comprehensive policy, for example, the average premium rate might be 50 cents per $100 of gross invoice value. Special coverage limitations apply to high-risk markets.

Medium-Term Insurance. Medium-term insurance, which usually covers credit terms up to five years, insures 90% of the loss (98% for certain agricultural commodities). It accounts for 9% of all export credit insurance coverage (see Table 28–7). Unlike the short-term policy, it is written on a case-by-case basis. It protects exporters against nonpayment of installments and interest due on credit sales (up to 6%) of capital goods or durable consumer goods where longer payment terms are the usual custom of the trade. Normally these policies are comprehensive, including commercial and political risks. Preshipment coverage is available. This coverage protects the seller against loss from cancellation of orders before they are shipped. These losses may stem, for example, from scrapping partly finished orders which cannot be sold elsewhere.

Medium-term policies require that the buyer make an initial cash payment of about 10% of the invoice value. It is also expected that the exporter will personally retain for the risk throughout the life of the credit at least 10% of the financed portion.

Master Comprehensive Combined Risk Policies. The master comprehensive policy provides blanket coverage (usually 90%) of political and commercial credit risks for short-term and medium-term sales. A feature of this policy is the primary loss deductible, which is an aggregate amount applying in one fiscal year which represents the normal credit losses of the exporter. The deductible applies only to commercial risks, not political risks. If the exporter agrees to a primary loss deductible larger than the normal loss expectancy, a commensurate reduction in the rate is received as is a speeding up of the time it takes to approve credit risks; furthermore, the exporter will receive a larger discretionary credit limit under which automatic approval of insurance is granted for credit shipments without special advance approval by the FCIA.

An alternative form of the master policy is one which offers 70% coverage on political risks only. The exporter is required to cover all or a reasonable spread of all accounts and may not select individual accounts for coverage.

Another form of the comprehensive policy is one designed for small business persons who are just getting started in exporting. The policy is offered to those whose average annual export volume in the preceding three years did not exceed $200,000 and it may remain in effect not over two years or until a total of $500,000 in export credit sales have been made. It offers 90% coverage on all credit sales, either short- or medium-term. A deductible may be offered or required. The exporter is expected to obtain credit information on buyers or request the FCIA to do so.

Medium-Term Guarantees to Commercial Banks. As an alternative to the FCIA medium-term insurance policy, an exporter may obtain assistance for credit sales abroad of terms from 180 days to 5 years through guarantees issued by Eximbank to United States commercial banks. Eximbank offers this protection only when banks agree to finance medium-term export sales without recourse to the exporter. This program serves the same purpose as FCIA medium-term comprehensive insurance, but commercial banks initiate the coverage and deal directly with the Eximbank in administering the policy.

Costs. Costs of short-term commercial export credit insurance policies vary according to the country of designation, terms of payment, the exporter's credit loss record, and other factors. Costs vary from about .1% to 2% of gross invoice value. These rates are not annual interest but rather flat rates applying to the full term of the insurance or guarantee. Charges for preshipment coverage and advance commitments are additional.

Investment Guarantee Program

Since 1948 the United States government has sought to increase direct investment by United States private enterprises in the economies of friendly, less developed countries by protecting investors against certain risks. Under sections 221–224 of the Foreign Assistance Act of 1961 as amended, Congress has authorized three investment guarantee programs:

1. Specific political risk guarantees against inconvertibility of foreign currency; loss by expropriation or confiscation; and loss due to war, revolution, or insurrection.
2. Extended risk guarantees covering up to 75% of political and general business risks.
3. Extended business guarantees covering up to 100% of losses on certain housing projects.

Definition of Perils. Expropriation and war are defined in the guarantee contract as follows:

Expropriation occurs when the foreign enterprise is prohibited from exercising: (1) effective control over a substantial portion of its property, (2) fundamental rights acquired by reason of ownership, or (3) the receipt of declared dividends. The definition of expropriation may in some circumstances include a breach by the foreign government of a concession agreement which it has made with the foreign enterprise.

The definition of *war, revolution,* or *insurrection* does not require that there be a formal declaration of war. Hostile acts of any national or international organized force are covered, as are hostile acts of organized revolutionary or insurrectionary forces, including acts of sabotage. The guarantee does not cover injury to the physical property of the enterprise that is caused directly by civil strife of a lesser degree than revolution or insurrection.

Specific Risk Investment Guarantees. Before guarantees can be issued for investments in a particular country, its government must have agreed to institute a guarantee program. Under the agreement, the project in which the investment is being made must be approved by the foreign government. Guarantees are issued to the investor in the form of a contract between the investor and the Overseas Private Investor Corporation (OPIC), a United States government agency.[15] This guarantee is backed by the full faith and credit of the United States government. Eligible entries include corporations, partnerships, and

[15] OPIC was formed in 1970 to take over the investment guarantee program, which was formerly administered by the Agency for International Development (AID). Eventually, it is expected that OPIC will become a private corporation.

other associations created under the laws of the United States and substantially owned by citizens of the United States. The investor may be a foreign entity, such as a branch of a United States company wholly owned or substantially owned by the United States company.

The form of the investment may be buildings, plants, cash, materials or equipment, patents, processes or techniques, engineering or management services, loan guarantees made to foreign banks or corporations, or money advanced to long-term suppliers under certain conditions. The investment must further the economic development or productivity of an economically less developed country. There is no restriction on the amount of the investment, which has been written for as little as $1,000. Contracts may be written for a maximum term of 20 years for equity investments or for the term of a loan in the case of debt investments.

Cost. Annual premiums for coverage on debt investments are as follows, expressed as a percent of the value of the investment: .3% for the lack of convertibility peril; .6% for expropriation peril; and .6% for war, revolution, or insurrection perils. These premiums are the same in all countries. Premiums for coverage on equity investments may be varied somewhat from the premiums applicable to debt investments.

The Extended Risk Guarantee. Broader coverage than is possible under the specific risk program is now available under the extended risk guarantee program. The contract is issued on an all-risk basis (except fraud or misconduct of the investor) up to 75% of an investment of private foreign enterprise. Both loan and equity investments are eligible. If the investor wishes, the remaining 25% of the investment can be insured against the risks of nonconvertibility, expropriation, war, revolution, or insurrection.

A loan made by a United States institutional lender to a foreign enterprise is eligible for this insurance under specified conditions. Such loans must be part of a sound financial plan in support of an eligible project, be made and repayable in dollars, be amortized over a reasonable period, and carry an appropriate rate of interest.

In general, such loans must be made for procuring United States goods and services. Loan insurance is not generally issued if the company is able to obtain private financing on reasonable terms without the guarantee.

If the investment is to be made on an equity basis, normally the extended risk guarantee will not exceed 50% of the original amount of the investment. Equity investments must generally be in projects which contribute to improved food supply or otherwise are of relative importance to the economic and social development of the project country. Annual premiums are 1.75% on that portion of the investment covered by the extended risk guarantee.

Housing Investments. The OPIC has authority to guarantee coverage up to 100% on investments in certain housing projects. The program is aimed at countries in which long-term financing is not normally available. Practically all loan guarantees for housing have been in Latin America and East Asia. Specific conditions must be met for housing guarantees. The annual premium ranges from .5% to 2% of the monthly outstanding balance of the guaranteed investment, depending on the availability and type of local guarantee. In general, housing projects require that local sources provide 25% of the financing.[16]

Effectiveness and Acceptance. Increasing nationalism, exchange controls, foreign takeovers, and worldwide inflation have increased the need for some type of protection for foreign investors. It is estimated that about a third of all new United States investment (two thirds if oil investments are excluded from the total) in less developed nations is now insured by OPIC against political risk. As of 1974, investment guarantees in force totalled $3.2 billion against inconvertibility in 77 countries, $3 billion against war in 57 countries, and $3.5 billion against expropriation in 71 countries.[17] Revenues under the program grew from less than $10 million in 1967 to over $40 million in 1974.

In 1974, legislation establishing OPIC was extended through 1977. The legislation encourages OPIC to involve the private insurance industry with the objective that OPIC would be acting ultimately only as a reinsurer. In 1975 a partnership of 13 private insurers called the Overseas Investment Insurance Group (OIIG) was formed to accomplish this purpose. The OIIG cooperates with OPIC, which reinsures OIIG coverage on convertibility and expropriation loss above certain limits. Currently, OPIC manages OIIG operations.

Considerable controversy about OPIC was generated in 1974 when OPIC denied several claims arising from the political disturbances in Chile. Some claims went to arbitration, among them a claim for $95 million by the International Telephone and Telegraph Co. (ITT). OPIC denied ITT's claim on the grounds that ITT plotted to interfere in Chile's elections, thus bringing on its own loss. However, the arbitration board ruled in favor of ITT and OPIC settled the claim. Two surveys of OPIC policyholders generally upheld the fairness of OPIC's claims procedures and most users reported that investment insurance is essential or desirable.[18]

One limitation of OPIC's coverage is that it may not be issued on existing investments, only new investments. Furthermore, even if an investment is covered initially, the coverage may not be increased as its value is enhanced through inflation. Another restriction is that OPIC generally limits coverage to 75% of an equity investment, and 90% of a debt investment. A new plan to augment coverage is now offered through the European Economic Community's Council of Ministers, the Office of Private Investment Guarantees (OPIG), to cover 100% of the original equity for loss due to war, nationalization, expropriation, confiscation, transfer of profits and capital, inconvertibility, and foreign exchange controls. It would apply to existing investments and could be increased to cover a maximum 8% annual growth of the initial net worth due to reinvested earnings or new capital contributions.

[16] U.S. Department of State, Agency for International Development, *Aids to Business (Overseas Investment)* (Washington: U.S. Government Printing Office, 1966).

[17] Overseas Private Investment Corporation, Annual Report, 1974.

[18] *Hearings* before the Subcommittee on Foreign Economic Policy of the Committee on Foreign Affairs, House of Representatives, 93rd Congress, 1st session, p. 99.

SUMMARY

1. The rapid increase in world trade and investments in recent years has brought about a new world environment for insurance: increased risk, enlarged markets, new drains on financial capacity to underwrite business, and the necessity for developing new techniques to meet the needs of the multinational corporation.
2. The insurance institution will probably continue to expand to meet the challenges of rising world economic development. United States-based insurers and brokers are attempting improved coordination and cooperation to increase their international effectiveness.
3. In many respects the legal environment for international insurance differs considerably from the domestic United States environment. Among the differences are laws regulating admitted versus unadmitted insurance, the operation of the Napoleonic code, the harmonization principles of the EEC, and the effect of tax laws applying to insurance.
4. There are many interesting contrasts in insurance conditions throughout the world which require special attention by multinational business firms. These include differences in policy conditions, differences in unwritten customs affecting the interpretation of policies, and differences in regulations, insurer financial strength, agency practices, and claims settlement practices. In many countries certain types of insurance are compulsory and special policy provisions, such as 100% coinsurance on fire coverage, prevail. One way the insurance industry has responded to these variations is the development of the difference in conditions (DIC) policy, which offers the multinational corporation relatively uniform protection throughout its worldwide operations.
5. Among the important problems in insurance facing the multinational firm is that of coordinating an employee benefit structure in different countries. Special attention must be given to differences in social insurance benefits, union organization and influence, community standards, and creating a benefit structure that is fair for all employees.
6. Export credit insurance and investment guarantees have been developed as a partnership between business and government in many countries to facilitate export credit and investment in fixed plant and equipment abroad, particularly in developing countries. These programs are relatively new in the United States, but their potential appears substantial.

QUESTIONS FOR REVIEW AND DISCUSSION

1. Among the problems in international insurance is the shortage of insurance capacity. Explain the factors which may contribute to this shortage and which are traceable to differences which exist on the international level as distinguished from the purely domestic level in the United States.
2. Explain possible reasons for the fact that relatively few United States-based insurers have undertaken international operations.
3. How can unadmitted insurance lawfully exist in countries which have laws prohibiting it?
4. Why is the difference in conditions (DIC) policy so popular among multinational enterprises?

5. A United States firm was exporting its products to a Latin American nation. A products liability suit was initiated in that country against the firm. The firm's product liability insurance provided that the insurer was only obligated to defend legal actions brought in the United States. The Latin American plaintiff could not afford to come to the United States to prosecute the case, and complained to his government. As a result, the firm's foreign assets were confiscated and an embargo placed on further imports of its product line. How should the problem have been handled to avoid the disastrous consequences which resulted?
6. What value is there in studying differences in foreign insurance conditions as they might affect conditions in other countries such as the United States? Give examples.
7. The Foster Wheeler Corporation carried an investment guarantee plan for its investment in Turkey. It suffered a loss of $183,947 due to inconvertibility. The government paid the loss and then salvaged practically the entire amount. Explain what an inconvertibility loss is. Why was the government able to recover its loss later through salvage?
8. An FCIA release stated, "Dresser Industries, which has nearly doubled its foreign sales over the past five years, has taken an FCIA Comprehensive Master Policy to further expands its export sales.... Approximately one quarter of Dresser's international revenues are U.S. exports." What might have encouraged Dresser to purchase export credit insurance when it apparently was able to expand easily without such insurance in the previous five years?
9. In 1974 the FCIA sent a message to its policyholders as follows: "During the last fiscal year . . . approximately $13 billion of export sales were supported by FCIA and Eximbank, which translates into over 750,000 full-time jobs . . . and a $4.2 billion favorable impact on the U.S. balance of payments, which helped to strengthen the U.S. dollar both here and abroad. . . ." At the same time, the United States Congress reduced the authority of the Eximbank to grant foreign loans and insurance. Suggest possible reasons why Congress would wish to restrict the Eximbank when an important goal has also been to encourage exports.
10. A new service of the FCIA is a computerized credit rating system enabling quick references to the credit ratings of 88,000 foreign buyers, permitting faster service to the clients. Credit ratings may be updated as quickly as every 24 hours. Why is such a service of importance to the users of credit insurance?
11. In 1973 OPIC's total reserves for losses rose from $217 million to $261 million. It is estimated that total potential liabilities approximate $10 billion. Does this imply that OPIC may be unable to pay its claims in the event of a large increase in world conflict resulting in investment losses?
12. OPIC reported that in 1974 it had agreed with the new government of Chile to accept payments of about $37 million including interest over an 8-year period arising from debts paid by OPIC on two claims in Chile arising from the expropriation of assets of United States investors. One of these claims was that of the ITT for about $95 million in total. Suggest possible reasons why the government of Chile did not agree to reimburse the entire loss, in view of the fact that it had signed an agreement on expropriations with the United States government, an agreement required before OPIC coverage is granted.

Appendix *A*

BEST'S RATINGS OF PROPERTY AND LIABILITY INSURERS

The following explanation of Best's Ratings of property and liability insurers is based on *Best's Insurance Reports,* published annually.

Companies and associations are assigned two ratings: a Policyholders' Rating and a Financial Rating. If an insurer is not rated, it may be for one of the following reasons: necessary information was refused or furnished too late for use; a company disputes the application of the rating system or disputes the construction of items appearing in the annual statements; the insurer writes primarily life insurance; or four years' operating experience is not available.

POLICYHOLDERS' RATINGS

Six policyholders' rating classifications are used: A+ and A (Excellent), B+ (Very good), B (Good), C+ (Fairly good), and C (Fair), to reflect Best's opinion of the relative position of each institution in comparison with others, based upon averages within the insurance industry. Companies classified as Excellent are considered outstanding on a comparative basis, whether rated A or A+. Only nominal variances from industry standards generally exist among A companies, with the most common difference being in underwriting results. For other ratings the variances or median points widen at each level.

Five main factors determine policyholders' ratings: quality of underwriting, economy of management, adequacy of reserves, adequacy of resources to absorb unusual shock, and soundness of investments.

In 1975, after a large underwriting loss in 1974, Best reduced its ratings of about a fourth of all insurers. Still, 71% of all listed insurers carried ratings of A+ or A, 19% had B+ or B ratings, 4% had C+ or C. The remainder of the insurers were either not rated or had deferred ratings.[1]

Quality of Underwriting

A comparison of incurred losses and claim adjustment expenses with premiums earned is made. Premiums earned reflect the increase or decrease of the equity in the unearned premiums, an important underwriting factor. Expenses incurred are compared with premiums written. This procedure gives an

[1] *Wall Street Journal* (August 11, 1975), p. 8.

underwriting profit or loss ratio which takes into account the increase or decrease of the equity in unearned premium reserve.

The amount of the underwriting profit or loss so calculated is then compared with the earned premiums, as a measure of the underwriting ability of the management. The underwriting profit or loss is also compared with the net safety factor, for the reason that the same amount of profit or loss might be of negligible importance to one company having large net resources but of great importance to one having small net resources.

Economy of Management

This factor is measured by the ratio of expenses incurred (excluding claim expenses, which are added to losses) to premiums written.

Adequacy of Reserves

Unearned premiums are calculated in accordance with laws so clear and uniform that there is little or no possibility for honest error, and this item is accepted as it appears in the statements, except in those infrequent instances where the customary formula is not used by the insurer under review. The reserves for pending loss claims are set up on a formula basis in connection with liability and workers' compensation business. On most other lines, loss reserves represent the opinion of the management of the ultimate cost of each pending claim. Various schedules comparing the final cost of claims with the reserves originally set up against them are available, and are very carefully analyzed. If these data indicate that the claim reserves set up in the current statement are inadequate (even though they may be in accord with statutory provisions), such an apparent deficiency is considered in testing the adequacy of the surplus to policyholders. Similarly, if reserves are more than adequate, any indicated equity in such reserves is taken into account.

Adequacy of Net Resources

Surplus is a safety factor used to absorb increases above normal in loss and expense requirements. An insurance company may be doing too great a volume of business in proportion to its net resources, just as any other kind of business may be overextended; and this is a very dangerous practice which is prejudicial to the safety of policyholders. This question does not hinge wholly upon the volume of premiums written; a company which has a high average profit may safely write a larger volume of business in proportion to net resources than another which operates with less favorable results. Again, some companies operate on a basis which requires the setting up of little or no unearned premium liability, as, to illustrate, companies writing only accident and health business on the weekly or monthly premium plan. Such companies have only their capital and surplus to absorb the shocks of unfavorable operating results, while other companies collecting premiums in advance, and setting up the statutory unearned premium liability, have an equity in that item which can be realized if an emergency makes necessary the reinsurance of the business. The character of assets and the maintenance of proper claim reserves are of great importance. These and many other variations, including diversification and spread of underwriting commitments, are taken into account in measuring the adequacy of net resources.

Soundness of Investments

Best's rating as to investments is based upon soundness, diversification, and liquidity. The standards used are not arbitrary, but, as in other sections of the rating schedule, are based primarily upon current averages of all companies. It is possible for an insurance company to show an apparently adequate safety factor—that is, excess of assets and equities over present and potential liabilities—and yet be in an unsafe position so far as policyholders are concerned. Assets may be of such character that they cannot readily be converted into cash for the purpose of either reinsuring the business and liquidating other liabilities or of meeting any unusual demand for cash, such as might arise through an abnormal loss ratio or because of an increase in the cost of liquidating claims now pending over the amount of the reserves set up against them. Various other matters of importance are considered, particularly where some condition exists which is dangerous to policyholders.

Effect of Size of Insurer

A small insurer can be just as safe as a large insurer. Many small insurers writing specialized lines are carefully and efficiently managed, and are sound in proportion to liabilities assumed. The policy of a small specialty fire insurance company which writes only moderate lines and conscientiously avoids writing in any congested area more than it could afford to pay in the event of a conflagration or a catastrophe may be more desirable than that of a much larger concern operating in less conservative lines.

FINANCIAL RATINGS

The financial rating indicates Best's estimate of the net safety factor of each company and is based upon the surplus to policyholders, plus equities, less indicated shortages in reserves, if any. Policyholders' surplus is the sum of capital and surplus funds in stock companies, and surplus funds as regards mutual companies, Lloyds organizations, and reciprocal exchanges, including guaranty or permanent funds, if any; contingent resources are not considered.

Ratings of foreign companies are based upon their home office balance sheets which include the assets and liabilities of the United States branches.

Foreign companies keep in trust, for the exclusive benefit of U.S. branch policyholders and creditors as required by law, funds to cover all liabilities and statutory deposit requirements. Furthermore, all assets, whether trusteed or not, are subject to withdrawal only with the consent of the State Insurance

Department of qualified entry. In addition to resources in this country, all of a company's free funds, capital and surplus, are liable for losses wherever they are incurred.

To prevent confusion of these ratings with general policyholders' ratings, the financial ratings in all cases consist of at least two letters. The letters used to indicate net safety factors are as follows:

Financial Rating	Net Safety Factor
AAAAA	$25,000,000 or more
AAAA+	20,000,000 to $25,000,000
AAAA	15,000,000 to 20,000,000
AAA+	12,500,000 to 15,000,000
AAA	10,000,000 to 12,500,000
AA+	7,500,000 to 10,000,000
AA	5,000,000 to 7,500,000
BBBB+	3,750,000 to 5,000,000
BBBB	2,500,000 to 3,750,000
BBB+	1,500,000 to 2,500,000
BBB	1,000,000 to 1,500,000
BB+	750,000 to 1,000,000
BB	500,000 to 750,000
CCC	250,000 to 500,000
CC	250,000 or less

Appendix *B*

BEST'S RATINGS OF LIFE INSURERS

Best's reports on life insurers cover such items as the history of a company, a description of the management and operations, a list of officers and directors, territory of operations, investment data and yields, quality of assets, and efficiency of operations.

Of special interest are Best's comments on an insurer's operations. Reports are not made on all life insurers—only those which are large enough and which have been in business a sufficient length of time for reasonable evaluation. The following criteria are used:

1. Net yield on investments.
2. Required interest earnings to cover the interest assumed in rate calculations.
3. Renewal expenses.
4. Mortality experience.
5. Lapse rate.
6. Net cost.
7. Overall margins for contingencies.

Each of these items is studied and compared to those typical of other insurers, and a ranking is made of the insurer over seven to ten categories, ranging from "good" to "poor" or "high" to "low." The ranking for renewal expenses, for example, is one of the following: remarkably low, very low, low, fairly low, moderate, fairly moderate, fairly high, high, very high, and excessive. Similar terms are employed for the other criteria.

The items "net cost" and "overall margins for contingencies" summarize Best's opinion of the particular insurer. Net cost is assigned on the basis of the current guaranteed cost or net scale cost and is based on the analysis of $10,000 whole life and 20-payment life plans. The net cost, the difference between gross premiums and the sum of guaranteed cash values and expected dividends, is based on current scales and not past histories.

The overall margin for contingencies is based upon a consideration of assets and surplus position, the profit or loss margin in current operations, and other items such as net yield, expenses, and lapses. Thus, this measure reflects factors other than solely surplus position. The final ranking is one of the following: most substantial, very substantial, substantial, or considerable. The user of these ratings should realize that according to this ranking system an insurer rated as substantial or considerable has the lowest rating assigned by Best, and the results should be interpreted accordingly. This is not to imply that such an insurer is not sound, however. If an insurer is thought to be unsound, presumably Best would not recommend it at all.

Appendix C

INTEREST TABLES

Problems in the use of life insurance and annuities may often be solved more easily by the use of interest tables than by laborious hand calculations or even by use of a computer. Examples of the use of these tables follow.

COMPOUND INTEREST

If $1,000 is left with an insurance company at interest as savings and the insurer pays 3% compound interest, what will the value of the savings be in 20 years?

Referring to Table C–1, we see that $1 left at 3% compound interest for 20 years amounts to $1.806. Therefore, the value of the savings would be $1,806.

PRESENT VALUE

If an insured wishes to have the sum of $1,000 in a savings account 20 years from now, how much must be deposited at compound interest if the insured receives interest at the rate of 3%? At 6%?

Referring to Table C–2, we see that at 3% interest, the present value of $1 is $.55367. Therefore, the sum of $553.67 must be deposited at 3% in order to accumulate $1,000 in 20 years. At 6%, we see that $311.80 must be deposited.

AMOUNT OF AN ANNUITY

If an estate planner saves $1,000 a year, to what sum will this savings accumulate if it is earning 4% interest? If it is earning 5% interest? How much more will this savings be if it earns 5% instead of 4% after 20 years? After 40 years?

According to Table C–3, $1 per year accumulates to $29.778 in 20 years at 4% interest. Therefore, the saver would have an account worth $29,778. At 5%, the saver would have $33,066. Due to the operation of compound interest, after 20 years the saver has about 11% more money in the account at 5% than with 4%. After 40 years, the saver would have about 27% more in the account at 5% than at 4% ($120,799/$95,025 = 1.27).

PRESENT VALUE OF AN ANNUITY

1. If a person wishes to be paid the sum of $1,000 annually over a period of 20 years, how much money must the person pay, assuming the funds earn 4%

interest? How much must be paid if the person wishes to receive $1,000 a year for 15 years?

From Table C–4 we see that at 4% interest the present value of $1 annually for 20 years is $13.5903. Therefore, the annuitant must pay $13,590 in order to receive $1,000 a year for 20 years. For 15 years, the annuitant must pay $11,118.

2. If an insured has $25,000 of insurance proceeds available, how much of an annual income will be paid by the insurer in an equal amount over 20 years if the insurer earns 4% interest?

According to Table C–4, the present value of $1 a year for 20 years is $13.5903. Dividing this amount into $25,000, we obtain an annual equal payment of $1,839.54.

LIFE ANNUITIES

If an insured age 65 has $25,000 of proceeds, how much guaranteed life income per month can he leave his wife, who is the same age, under a 10-year certain, 20-year certain, and joint and last survivorship option?

Referring to Table C–5, we see that for each $1,000 of proceeds, the insured wife age 65 may obtain $5.63 monthly under the 10-year certain, $5.02 under the 20-year certain, and $5.23 under the joint and last survivorship option. Multiplying these sums by 25, we obtain $140.75, $125.50, and $130.75, respectively.

AMOUNT AT COMPOUND INTEREST $(1 + i)^n$ Table C-1

Periods	Rate *i*				
n	.03 (3%)	.04 (4%)	.05 (5%)	.06 (6%)	.07 (7%)
1	1.0300 0000	1.0400 0000	1.0500 0000	1.0600 0000	1.0700 0000
2	1.0609 0000	1.0816 0000	1.1025 0000	1.1236 0000	1.1449 0000
3	1.0927 2700	1.1248 6400	1.1576 2500	1.1910 1600	1.2250 4300
4	1.1255 0881	1.1698 5856	1.2155 0625	1.2624 7696	1.3107 9601
5	1.1592 7407	1.2166 5290	1.2762 8156	1.3382 2558	1.4025 5173
6	1.1940 5230	1.2653 1902	1.3400 9564	1.4185 1911	1.5007 3035
7	1.2298 7387	1.3159 3178	1.4071 0042	1.5036 3026	1.6057 8148
8	1.2667 7008	1.3685 6905	1.4774 5544	1.5938 4807	1.7181 8618
9	1.3047 7318	1.4233 1181	1.5513 2822	1.6894 7896	1.8384 5921
10	1.3439 1638	1.4802 4428	1.6288 9463	1.7908 4770	1.9671 5136
11	1.3842 3387	1.5394 5406	1.7103 3936	1.8982 9856	2.1048 5195
12	1.4257 6089	1.6010 3222	1.7958 5633	2.0121 9647	2.2521 9159
13	1.4685 3371	1.6650 7351	1.8856 4914	2.1329 2826	2.4098 4500
14	1.5125 8972	1.7316 7645	1.9799 3160	2.2609 0396	2.5785 3415
15	1.5579 6742	1.8009 4351	2.0789 2818	2.3965 5819	2.7590 3154
16	1.6047 0644	1.8729 8125	2.1828 7459	2.5403 5168	2.9521 6375
17	1.6528 4763	1.9479 0050	2.2920 1832	2.6927 7279	3.1588 1521
18	1.7024 3306	2.0258 1652	2.4066 1923	2.8543 3915	3.3799 3228
19	1.7535 0605	2.1068 4918	2.5269 5020	3.0255 9950	3.6165 2754
20	1.8061 1123	2.1911 2314	2.6532 9771	3.2071 3547	3.8696 8446
21	1.8602 9457	2.2787 6807	2.7859 6259	3.3995 6360	4.1405 6237
22	1.9161 0341	2.3699 1879	2.9252 6072	3.6035 3742	4.4304 0174
23	1.9735 8651	2.4647 1554	3.0715 2376	3.8197 4966	4.7405 2986
24	2.0327 9411	2.5633 0416	3.2250 9994	4.0489 3464	5.0723 6695
25	2.0937 7793	2.6658 3633	3.3863 5494	4.2918 7072	5.4274 3264
26	2.1565 9127	2.7724 6978	3.5556 7269	4.5493 8296	5.8073 5292
27	2.2212 8901	2.8833 6858	3.7334 5632	4.8223 4594	6.2138 6763
28	2.2879 2768	2.9987 0332	3.9201 2914	5.1116 8670	6.6488 3836
29	2.3565 6551	3.1186 5145	4.1161 3560	5.4183 8790	7.1142 5705
30	2.4272 6247	3.2433 9751	4.3219 4238	5.7434 9117	7.6122 5504
31	2.5000 8035	3.3731 3341	4.5380 3949	6.0881 0064	8.1451 1290
32	2.5750 8276	3.5080 5875	4.7649 4147	6.4533 8668	8.7152 7080
33	2.6523 3524	3.6483 8110	5.0031 8854	6.8405 8988	9.3253 3975
34	2.7319 0530	3.7943 1634	5.2533 4797	7.2510 2528	9.9781 1354
35	2.8138 6245	3.9460 8899	5.5160 1537	7.6860 8679	10.6765 8148
36	2.8982 7833	4.1039 3255	5.7918 1614	8.1472 5200	11.4239 4219
37	2.9852 2668	4.2680 8986	6.0814 0694	8.6360 8712	12.2236 1814
38	3.0747 8348	4.4388 1345	6.3854 7729	9.1542 5235	13.0792 7141
39	3.1670 2698	4.6163 6599	6.7047 5115	9.7035 0749	13.9948 2041
40	3.2620 3779	4.8010 2063	7.0399 8871	10.2857 1794	14.9744 5784
41	3.3598 9893	4.9930 6145	7.3919 8815	10.9028 6101	16.0226 6989
42	3.4606 9589	5.1927 8391	7.7615 8756	11.5570 3267	17.1442 5678
43	3.5645 1677	5.4004 9527	8.1496 6693	12.2504 5463	18.3443 5475
44	3.6714 5227	5.6165 1508	8.5571 5028	12.9854 8191	19.6284 5959
45	3.7815 9584	5.8411 7568	8.9850 0779	13.7646 1083	21.0024 5176
46	3.8950 4372	6.0748 2271	9.4342 5818	14.5904 8748	22.4726 2338
47	4.0118 9503	6.3178 1562	9.9059 7109	15.4659 1673	24.0457 0702
48	4.1322 5188	6.5705 2824	10.4012 6965	16.3938 7173	25.7289 0651
49	4.2562 1944	6.8333 4937	10.9213 3313	17.3775 0403	27.5299 2997
50	4.3839 0602	7.1066 8335	11.4673 9979	18.4201 5427	29.4570 2506

PRESENT VALUE OF $1/(1+i)^n$ **Table C-2**

Periods	Rate i				
n	.03 (3%)	.04 (4%)	.05 (5%)	.06 (6%)	.07 (7%)
1	.9708 7379	.9615 3846	.9523 8095	.9433 9623	.9345 7944
2	.9425 9591	.9245 5621	.9070 2948	.8899 9644	.8734 3873
3	.9151 4166	.8889 9636	.8638 3760	.8396 1928	.8162 9788
4	.8884 8705	.8548 0419	.8227 0247	.7920 9366	.7628 9521
5	.8626 0878	.8219 2711	.7835 2617	.7472 5817	.7129 8618
6	.8374 8426	.7903 1453	.7462 1540	.7049 6054	.6663 4222
7	.8130 9151	.7599 1781	.7106 8133	.6650 5711	.6227 4974
8	.7894 0923	.7306 9021	.6768 3936	.6274 1237	.5820 0910
9	.7664 1673	.7025 8674	.6446 0892	.5918 9846	.5439 3374
10	.7440 9391	.6755 6417	.6139 1325	.5583 9478	.5083 4929
11	.7224 2128	.6495 8093	.5846 7929	.5267 8753	.4750 9280
12	.7013 7988	.6245 9705	.5568 3742	.4969 6936	.4440 1196
13	.6809 5134	.6005 7409	.5303 2135	.4688 3902	.4149 6445
14	.6611 1781	.5774 7508	.5050 6795	.4423 0096	.3878 1724
15	.6418 6195	.5552 6450	.4810 1710	.4172 6506	.3624 4602
16	.6231 6694	.5339 0818	.4581 1152	.3936 4628	.3387 3460
17	.6050 1645	.5133 7325	.4362 9669	.3713 6442	.3165 7439
18	.5873 9461	.4936 2812	.4155 2065	.3503 4379	.2958 6392
19	.5702 8603	.4746 4242	.3957 3396	.3305 1301	.2765 0833
20	.5536 7575	.4563 8695	.3768 8948	.3118 0473	.2584 1900
21	.5375 4928	.4388 3360	.3589 4236	.2941 5540	.2415 1309
22	.5218 9250	.4219 5539	.3418 4987	.2775 0510	.2257 1317
23	.5066 9175	.4057 2633	.3255 7131	.2617 9726	.2109 4688
24	.4919 3374	.3901 2147	.3100 6791	.2469 7855	.1971 4662
25	.4776 0557	.3751 1680	.2953 0277	.2329 9863	.1842 4918
26	.4636 9473	.3606 8923	.2812 4073	.2198 1003	.1721 9549
27	.4501 8906	.3468 1657	.2678 4832	.2073 6795	.1609 3037
28	.4370 7675	.3334 7747	.2550 9364	.1956 3014	.1504 0221
29	.4243 4636	.3206 5141	.2429 4632	.1845 5674	.1405 6282
30	.4119 8676	.3083 1867	.2313 7745	.1741 1013	.1313 6712
31	.3999 8715	.2964 6026	.2203 5947	.1642 5484	.1227 7301
32	.3883 3703	.2850 5794	.2098 6617	.1549 5740	.1147 4113
33	.3770 2625	.2740 9417	.1998 7254	.1461 8622	.1072 3470
34	.3660 4490	.2635 5209	.1903 5480	.1379 1153	.1002 1934
35	.3553 8340	.2534 1547	.1812 9029	.1301 0522	.0936 6294
36	.3450 3243	.2436 6872	.1726 5741	.1227 4077	.0875 3546
37	.3349 8294	.2342 9685	.1644 3563	.1157 9318	.0818 0884
38	.3252 2615	.2252 8543	.1566 0536	.1092 3885	.0764 5686
39	.3157 5355	.2166 2061	.1491 4797	.1030 5552	.0714 5501
40	.3065 5684	.2082 8904	.1420 4568	.0972 2219	.0667 8038
41	.2976 2800	.2002 7793	.1352 8160	.0917 1905	.0624 1157
42	.2889 5922	.1925 7493	.1288 3962	.0865 2740	.0583 2857
43	.2805 4294	.1851 6820	.1227 0440	.0816 2962	.0545 1268
44	.2723 7178	.1780 4635	.1168 6133	.0770 0908	.0509 4643
45	.2644 3862	.1711 9841	.1112 9651	.0726 5007	.0476 1349
46	.2567 3653	.1646 1386	.1059 9668	.0685 3781	.0444 9859
47	.2492 5876	.1582 8256	.1009 4921	.0646 5831	.0415 8747
48	.2419 9880	.1521 9476	.0961 4211	.0609 9840	.0388 6679
49	.2349 5029	.1463 4112	.0915 6391	.0575 4566	.0363 2410
50	.2281 0708	.1407 1262	.0872 0373	.0542 8836	.0339 4776

AMOUNT OF ANNUITY $[(1+i)^n - 1]/i$ Table C-3

Periods	Rate i				
n	.03 (3%)	.04 (4%)	.05 (5%)	.06 (6%)	.07 (7%)
1	1.0000 0000	1.0000 000	1.0000 000	1.0000 000	1.0000 000
2	2.0300 0000	2.0400 000	2.0500 000	2.0600 000	2.0700 000
3	3.0909 0000	3.1216 000	3.1525 000	3.1836 000	3.2149 000
4	4.1836 2700	4.2464 640	4.3101 250	4.3746 160	4.4399 430
5	5.3091 3581	5.4163 226	5.5256 313	5.6370 930	5.7507 390
6	6.4684 0988	6.6329 755	6.8019 128	6.9753 185	7.1532 907
7	7.6624 6218	7.8982 945	8.1420 085	8.3938 376	8.6540 211
8	8.8923 3605	9.2142 263	9.5491 089	9.8974 679	10.2598 026
9	10.1591 0613	10.5827 953	11.0265 643	11.4913 160	11.9779 887
10	11.4638 7931	12.0061 071	12.5778 925	13.1807 949	13.8164 480
11	12.8077 9569	13.4863 514	14.2067 872	14.9716 426	15.7835 993
12	14.1920 2956	15.0258 055	15.9171 265	16.8699 412	17.8884 513
13	15.6177 9045	16.6268 377	17.7129 828	18.8821 377	20.1406 429
14	17.0863 2416	18.2919 112	19.5986 320	21.0150 659	22.5504 879
15	18.5989 1389	20.0235 876	21.5785 636	23.2759 699	25.1290 220
16	20.1568 8130	21.8245 311	23.6574 918	25.6725 281	27.8880 536
17	21.7615 8774	23.6975 124	25.8403 664	28.2128 798	30.8402 173
18	23.4144 3537	25.6454 129	28.1323 847	30.9056 525	33.9990 325
19	25.1168 6844	27.6712 294	30.5390 039	33.7599 917	37.3789 648
20	26.8703 7449	29.7780 786	33.0659 541	36.7855 912	40.9954 923
21	28.6764 8572	31.9692 017	35.7192 518	39.9927 267	44.8651 768
22	30.5367 8030	34.2479 698	38.5052 144	43.3922 903	49.0057 392
23	32.4528 8370	36.6178 886	41.4304 751	46.9958 277	53.4361 409
24	34.4264 7022	39.0826 041	44.5019 989	50.8155 744	58.1766 708
25	36.4592 6432	41.6459 083	47.7270 988	54.8645 120	63.2490 377
26	38.5530 4225	44.3117 446	51.1134 538	59.1563 827	68.6764 704
27	40.7096 3352	47.0842 144	54.6691 264	63.7057 657	74.4838 233
28	42.9309 2252	49.9675 830	58.4025 828	68.5281 116	80.6976 909
29	45.2188 5020	52.9662 863	62.3227 119	73.6397 983	87.3465 293
30	47.5754 1571	56.0849 378	66.4388 475	79.0581 862	94.4607 863
31	50.0026 7818	59.3283 353	70.7607 899	84.8016 774	102.0730 414
32	52.5027 5852	62.7014 687	75.2988 294	90.8897 780	110.2181 543
33	55.0778 4128	66.2095 274	80.0637 708	97.3431 647	118.9334 251
34	57.7301 7652	69.8579 085	85.0669 594	104.1837 546	128.2587 648
35	60.4620 8181	73.6522 249	90.3203 074	111.4347 799	138.2368 784
36	63.2759 4427	77.5983 138	95.8363 227	119.1208 667	148.9134 598
37	66.1742 2259	81.7022 464	101.6281 389	127.2681 187	160.3374 020
38	69.1594 4927	85.9703 363	107.7095 458	135.9042 058	172.5610 202
39	72.2342 3275	90.4091 497	114.0950 231	145.0584 581	185.6402 916
40	75.4012 5973	95.0255 157	120.7997 742	154.7619 656	199.6351 120
41	78.6632 9753	99.8265 363	127.8397 630	165.0476 836	214.6095 698
42	82.0231 9645	104.8195 978	135.2317 511	175.9505 446	230.6322 397
43	85.4838 9234	110.0123 817	142.9933 387	187.5075 772	247.7764 965
44	89.0484 0911	115.4128 770	151.1430 056	199.7580 319	266.1208 513
45	92.7198 6139	121.0293 920	159.7001 559	212.7435 138	285.7493 108
46	96.5014 5723	126.8705 677	168.6851 637	226.5081 246	306.7517 626
47	100.3965 0095	132.9453 904	178.1194 218	241.0986 121	329.2243 860
48	104.4083 9598	139.2632 060	188.0253 929	256.5645 288	353.2700 930
49	108.5406 4785	145.8337 343	198.4266 626	272.9584 006	378.9989 995
50	112.7968 6729	152.6670 837	209.3479 957	290.3359 046	406.5289 295

PRESENT VALUE OF ANNUITY $[1 - (1 + i)^{-n}] / i$ Table C-4

Periods	Rate i				
n	.03 (3%)	.04 (4%)	.05 (5%)	.06 (6%)	.07 (7%)
1	0.9708 7379	0.9615 3846	0.9523 8095	0.9433 9623	0.9345 7944
2	1.9134 6970	1.8860 9467	1.8594 1043	1.8333 9267	1.8080 1817
3	2.8286 1135	2.7750 9103	2.7232 4803	2.6730 1195	2.6243 1604
4	3.7170 9840	3.6298 9522	3.5459 5050	3.4651 0561	3.3872 1126
5	4.5797 0719	4.4518 2233	4.3294 7667	4.2123 6379	4.1001 9744
6	5.4171 9144	5.2421 3686	5.0756 9207	4.9173 2433	4.7665 3966
7	6.2302 8296	6.0020 5467	5.7863 7340	5.5823 8144	5.3892 8940
8	7.0196 9219	6.7327 4487	6.4632 1276	6.2097 9381	5.9712 9851
9	7.7861 0892	7.4353 3161	7.1078 2168	6.8016 9227	6.5152 3225
10	8.5302 0284	8.1108 9578	7.7217 3493	7.3600 8705	7.0235 8154
11	9.2526 2411	8.7604 7671	8.3064 1422	7.8868 7458	7.4986 7434
12	9.9540 0399	9.3850 7376	8.8632 5164	8.3838 4394	7.9426 8630
13	10.6349 5533	9.9856 4785	9.3935 7299	8.8526 8296	8.3576 5074
14	11.2960 7314	10.5631 2293	9.8986 4094	9.2949 8393	8.7454 6799
15	11.9379 3509	11.1183 8743	10.3796 5804	9.7122 4899	9.1079 1401
16	12.5611 0203	11.6522 9561	10.8377 6956	10.1058 9527	9.4466 4860
17	13.1661 1847	12.1656 6885	11.2740 6625	10.4772 5969	9.7632 2299
18	13.7535 1308	12.6592 9697	11.6895 8690	10.8276 0348	10.0590 8691
19	14.3237 9911	13.1339 3940	12.0853 2086	11.1581 1649	10.3355 9524
20	14.8774 7486	13.5903 2634	12.4622 1034	11.4699 2122	10.5940 1425
21	15.4150 2414	14.0291 5995	12.8211 5271	11.7640 7662	10.8355 2733
22	15.9369 1664	14.4511 1533	13.1630 0258	12.0415 8172	11.0612 4050
23	16.4436 0839	14.8568 4167	13.4885 7388	12.3033 7898	11.2721 8738
24	16.9355 4212	15.2469 6314	13.7986 4179	12.5503 5753	11.4693 3400
25	17.4131 4769	15.6220 7994	14.0939 4457	12.7833 5616	11.6535 8318
26	17.8768 4242	15.9827 6918	14.3751 8530	13.0031 6619	11.8257 7867
27	18.3270 3147	16.3295 8575	14.6430 3362	13.2105 3414	11.9867 0904
28	18.7641 0823	16.6630 6322	14.8981 2726	13.4061 6428	12.1371 1125
29	19.1884 5459	16.9837 1463	15.1410 7358	13.5907 2102	12.2776 7407
30	19.6004 4135	17.2920 3330	15.3724 5103	13.7648 3115	12.4090 4118
31	20.0004 2849	17.5884 9356	15.5928 1050	13.9290 8599	12.5318 1419
32	20.3887 6553	17.8735 5150	15.8026 7667	14.0840 4339	12.6465 5532
33	20.7657 9178	18.1476 4567	16.0025 4921	14.2302 2961	12.7537 9002
34	21.1318 3668	18.4111 9776	16.1929 0401	14.3681 4114	12.8540 0936
35	21.4872 2007	18.6646 1323	16.3741 9429	14.4982 4636	12.9476 7230
36	21.8322 5250	18.9082 8195	16.5468 5171	14.6209 8713	13.0352 0776
37	22.1672 3544	19.1425 7880	16.7112 8734	14.7367 8031	13.1170 1660
38	22.4924 6159	19.3678 6423	16.8678 9271	14.8460 1916	13.1934 7345
39	22.8082 1513	19.5844 8484	17.0170 4067	14.9490 7468	13.2649 2846
40	23.1147 7197	19.7927 7388	17.1590 8635	15.0462 9687	13.3317 0884
41	23.4123 9997	19.9930 5181	17.2943 6796	15.1380 1592	13.3941 2041
42	23.7013 5920	20.1856 2674	17.4232 0758	15.2245 4332	13.4524 4898
43	23.9819 0213	20.3707 9494	17.5459 1198	15.3061 7294	13.5069 6167
44	24.2542 7392	20.5488 4129	17.6627 7331	15.3831 8202	13.5579 0810
45	24.5187 1254	20.7200 3970	17.7740 6982	15.4558 3209	13.6055 2159
46	24.7754 4907	20.8846 5356	17.8800 6650	15.5243 6990	13.6500 2018
47	25.0247 0783	21.0429 3612	17.9810 1571	15.5890 2821	13.6916 0764
48	25.2667 0664	21.1951 3088	18.0771 5782	15.6500 2661	13.7304 7443
49	25.5016 5693	21.3414 7200	18.1687 2173	15.7075 7227	13.7667 9853
50	25.7297 6401	21.4821 8462	18.2559 2546	15.7618 6064	13.8007 4629

MONTHLY LIFE INCOME PER $1,000 PROCEEDS (3% INTEREST ASSUMPTION)

Table C-5

Age	Men 10 Years Cert.	Men 20 Years Cert.	Women 10 Years Cert.	Women 20 Years Cert.	Joint and Last Survivor [2]
15	2.96	2.96	2.88	2.88	—
20	3.05	3.05	2.96	2.96	—
25	3.17	3.16	3.06	3.05	—
30	3.31	3.30	3.17	3.17	—
35	3.49	3.46	3.32	3.31	3.20
40	3.72	3.67	3.50	3.48	3.35
45	4.00	3.91	3.73	3.69	3.55
46	4.07	3.97	3.78	3.74	3.59
47	4.14	4.02	3.84	3.79	3.64
48	4.21	4.08	3.90	3.85	3.69
49	4.28	4.14	3.96	3.90	3.75
50	4.36	4.20	4.03	3.96	3.80
51	4.44	4.26	4.10	4.02	3.86
52	4.53	4.32	4.17	4.08	3.93
53	4.62	4.39	4.25	4.14	3.99
54	4.71	4.46	4.33	4.21	4.06
55	4.81	4.52	4.42	4.28	4.14
56	4.92	4.59	4.51	4.35	4.22
57	5.03	4.66	4.61	4.42	4.30
58	5.15	4.73	4.71	4.50	4.39
59	5.27	4.80	4.82	4.57	4.49
60	5.40	4.87	4.94	4.65	4.59
61	5.53	4.94	5.06	4.72	4.70
62	5.68	5.00	5.19	4.80	4.82
63	5.83	5.07	5.33	4.88	4.95
64	5.98	5.13	5.47	4.95	5.08
65	6.15	5.18	5.63	5.02	5.23
66	6.32	5.24	5.79	5.09	5.39
67	6.50	5.28	5.96	5.15	5.56
68	6.68	5.33	6.14	5.21	5.74
69	6.88	5.36	6.33	5.27	5.94
70	7.07	5.40	6.53	5.32	6.15
71	7.27	5.42	6.73	5.36	6.38
72	7.48	5.45	6.94	5.40	6.63
73	7.68	5.46	7.16	5.43	6.91
74	7.88	5.48	7.38	5.45	7.21
75	8.08	5.49	7.60	5.47	7.53
80	8.94	5.51	8.64	5.51	—
85	9.42	5.51	9.32	5.51	—

[1] Participating during period certain. Since cost assumptions vary among insurers, these data should be considered as illustrative only.

[2] Man and woman of equal age, life only.

Appendix *D*

BIBLIOGRAPHY

PART I
THE NATURE OF RISK AND RISK BEARING

Books

Binford, Charles, Cecil Fleming, and Z. A. Prust. *Loss Control in the OSHA Era*. New York: McGraw-Hill Book Company, 1975.

Edelstein, Robert H. *The Theory of Insurance Reconsidered for Urban Analysis: An Expected Utility Approach*. Philadelphia: The Wharton School of Finance and Commerce, University of Pennsylvania, 1975.

Faulkner, E. J. (ed.). *Man's Quest for Security*. Freeport, N.Y.: Books for Libraries, Inc., 1966.

Greene, Mark R. *Risk Aversion, Insurance, and the Future*. Bloomington: Indiana University Press, 1971.

____________. *Risk and Insurance Management*, 2d ed. Washington: U.S. Government Printing Office, Small Business Administration, SBMS No. 30, 1970.

Hardy, C. O. *Risk and Risk-Bearing*. Chicago: University of Chicago Press, 1931.

Hoffman, Fredrick Ludwig. *Insurance Science and Economics*. Chicago: The Spectator Co., 1911.

Knight, Frank H. *Risk, Uncertainty, and Profit*. Clifton, N.J.: Kelley, 1921.

Kogan, N., and M. A. Wallach. *Risk Taking—A Study in Cognition and Personality*. New York: Holt, Rinehart & Winston, Inc., 1964.

MacDonald, Donald L. *Corporate Risk Control*. New York: The Ronald Press Company, 1966.

Mehr, Robert I., and Robert A. Hedges. *Risk Management—Concepts and Applications*. Homewood, Ill.: Richard D. Irwin, Inc., 1974.

Municipal Risk Management: A Risk Management and Insurance Handbook. Cincinnati: Society of Chartered Property and Casualty Underwriters, 1971.

Petersen, Daniel C. *Techniques of Safety Management*. New York: McGraw-Hill Book Company, 1971.

Pfeffer, Irving. *Insurance and Economic Theory*. Homewood, Ill.: Richard D. Irwin, Inc., 1956.

Rosenbloom, Jerry S. *A Case Study in Risk Management*. New York: Appleton-Century-Crofts, 1972.

Watson, Donald, and D. Homan. *Insurance and Risk Management for Small Business*. Washington: Small Business Administration, 1963.

Werbel, B. G. *General Insurance Guide*. New York: Werbel Publishing Company, annually, and supplements.

Willett, A. H. *Economic Theory of Risk and Insurance*. Homewood, Ill.: Richard D. Irwin, Inc., 1951.

Williams, C. Arthur, Jr., and Richard M. Heins. *Risk Management and Insurance*, 3d ed. New York: McGraw-Hill Book Company, 1976.

Periodicals

Allen, Tom C., and Richard M. Duvall. "A Theoretical and Practical Approach to Risk Management—An Overview of the Risk Management Function." *Risk Management,* Vol. 17, No. 8 (October, 1970), pp. 12-20.

Clark, J. B. "Insurance and Business Profit." *The Quarterly Journal of Economics,* Vol. VII (October, 1892), pp. 40-54.

Clark, Russell D., III. "Group-Induced Shift Toward Risk: A Critical Appraisal." *Psychological Bulletin,* Vol. 76, No. 4 (December, 1971), pp. 251-270.

__________. "Risk Taking in Groups: A Social Psychological Analysis." *The Journal of Risk and Insurance,* Vol. XLI, No. 1 (March, 1974), pp. 75-92.

Close, Darwin B. "An Organization Behavior Approach to Risk Management." *The Journal of Risk and Insurance,* Vol. XLI, No. 3 (September, 1974), pp. 435-450.

Coombs, C. H., and S. S. Kormorita. "Measuring Utility of Money Through Decision." *American Journal of Psychology,* Vol. 71 (1958), pp. 383-389.

Crowe, Robert M., and Ronald C. Horn. "The Meaning of Risk." *The Journal of Risk and Insurance,* Vol. XXXIV, No. 3 (September, 1967), pp. 459-474.

Frenkel-Brunswik, Else. "Intolerance of Ambiguity as an Emotional and Perceptual Personality Variable." *Journal of Personality,* Vol. 18 (1949), pp. 108-143.

Friedman, M., and L. J. Savage. "The Utility Analysis of Choices Involving Risk." *Journal of Political Economy,* Vol. LVI (1948).

Greene, Mark R. "Attitudes Toward Risk and a Theory of Insurance Consumption." *The Journal of Insurance,* Vol. XXX, No. 2 (June, 1963).

__________. " 'Insurance Mindedness'—Implications for Insurance Theory." *The Journal of Risk and Insurance,* Vol. XXXI, No. 1 (March, 1964).

__________. "Marketing Research as an Aid to Insurance Management." *The Journal of Insurance,* Vol. XXIV, No. 3 (December, 1957).

__________. "Applications of Mathematics to Insurance and Risk Management." *The Journal of Insurance,* Vol. XXVIII, No. 1 (March, 1961).

__________. "Pitfalls in Insurance Management." *Professional Management Bulletins,* Administrative Management Society (February, 1970), pp. 1-6.

__________. "How to Rationalize Your Marketing Risks." *Harvard Business Review,* (May-June, 1969), pp. 114-123.

Hawley, F. B. "The Risk Theory of Profit." *The Quarterly Journal of Economics,* Vol. VII (July, 1893), pp. 459-479.

Head, George L. "Property Insurance Deductibles, A Theoretical Model for the Corporate Buyer." *The Journal of Risk and Insurance,* Vol. XXXII, No. 3 (September, 1965).

__________. "An Alternative to Defining Risk as Uncertainty." *The Journal of Risk and Insurance,* Vol. XXXIV, No. 2 (June, 1967), pp. 205-214.

Hodges, J. Frank, Jr. "Effect of Fire Loss and Loss Adjustments on Consumer Attitudes Toward Insurnace." *The Journal of Risk and Insurance,* Vol. XLI, No. 2 (June, 1974), pp. 267-285.

Hofflander, Alfred E., and Lawrence L. Schkade. "A Rule for Least Cost Selection of Collision Deductibles." *The Annals of the Society of Chartered Property and Casualty Underwriters,* Vol. 20, No. 1 (March, 1967), pp. 5-17.

Houston, David B. "Risk, Insurance, and Sampling." *The Journal of Risk and Insurance,* Vol. XXXI, No. 4 (December, 1964).

__________. "Risk Theory." *The Journal of Insurance,* Vol. XXVII, No. 1 (March, 1960).

Komorita, S. S. "Factors Which Influence Subjective Probability." *Journal of Experimental Psychology,* Vol. 58 (November, 1959), pp. 386-389.

McCahill, F. X., Jr. "Avoid Losses Through Risk Management." *Harvard Business Review,* Vol. 2, No. 3 (May, 1971), pp. 57-65.

McRell, Robert J. "Advantages of a Self-Insurance Program." *Risk Management,* Vol. 17, No. 8 (October, 1970), pp. 23ff.

Mehr, Robert I., and Stephen W. Forbes. "The Risk Management Decision in the Total Business Setting." *The Journal of Risk and Insurance,* Vol. XL, No. 3 (September, 1973), pp. 389-401.

Mosteller, R., and P. Nogee. "An Experimental Measurement of Utility." *Journal of Political Economy,* Vol. 59 (1951), pp. 371-404.

Preston, M. D., and P. Baratta. "An Experimental Study of the Auction-Value of an Uncertain Income." *American Journal of Psychology,* Vol. 61 (1948), pp. 183-193.

Rabel, W. H. "Increasing Knowledge as a Technique for Treating Risk." *The Journal of Risk and Insurance,* Vol. XXXVI, No. 2 (June, 1969), pp. 296-299.

Reavis, Marshall W. "The Corporate Risk Manager's Contribution to Profit." *The Journal of Risk and Insurance,* Vol. XXXVI, No. 3 (September, 1969), pp. 473-479.

Rim, Y. "Social Attitudes and Risk-Taking." *Human Relations,* Vol. 17, No. 3 (1964), pp. 259-265.

Seldow, Leona. "Inter-Relationship of Economics and Insurance." *The Annals of the Society of Chartered Property and Casualty Underwriters,* Vol. XI, No. 1 (February, 1959).

Swadener, Paul. "Gambling and Insurance Distinguished." *The Journal of Risk and Insurance,* Vol. XXXI, No. 3 (September, 1964).

Trowbridge, C. L. "Insurance as a Transfer Mechanism." *The Journal of Risk and Insurance,* Vol. XLII, No. 1 (March, 1975), pp. 1-15.

Williams, C. Arthur, Jr. "Attitudes Toward Speculative Risks as an Indicator of Attitudes Toward Pure Risks." *The Journal of Risk and Insurance,* Vol. XXXIII, No. 4 (December, 1966), pp. 577-586.

__________, and O. D. Dickerson. "Game Theory and Insurance Consumption." *The Journal of Risk and Insurance,* Vol. XXXIII, No. 3 (September, 1966).

PART II
THE INSURANCE INSTITUTION

Books

Athearn, James L. *General Insurance Agency Management.* Homewood, Ill.: Richard D. Irwin, Inc., 1965.

Attitudes Towards Group Automobile Insurance. Washington: *U.S. News & World Report,* 1974.

Best, A. M. *Fire and Casualty Aggregates and Averages.* New York: A. M. Best Company, annually.

Bickelhaupt, David L. *General Insurance,* 9th ed. Homewood, Ill. Richard D. Irwin, Inc., 1974.

Goshay, Robert C. *Corporate Self-Insurance and Risk Retention Plans.* Homewood, Ill.: Richard D. Irwin, Inc., 1964.

Gregg, Davis W., and Vane B. Lucas (eds.). *Life and Health Insurance Handbook,* 3d ed. Homewood, Ill.: Dow-Jones-Irwin, Inc., 1973.

Heinrich, H. W. *Industrial Accident Prevention,* 4th ed. New York: McGraw-Hill Book Co., 1959.

Huebner, S. S., and Kenneth Black, Jr. (eds.). *Life Insurance,* 8th ed. New York: Appleton-Century-Crofts, 1972.

Kenney, Roger. *Fundamentals of Fire and Casualty Strength.* Dedham, Mass.: Roger Kenney, 1957.

Marshall, Robert A. *Life Insurance Company Mergers and Consolidations.* Homewood, Ill.: Richard D. Irwin, Inc., 1972.

Mehr, Robert I., and Seev Neumann. *Inflation, Technology and Growth: Possible Long Range Implications for Insurance.* Bloomington, Ind.: Division of Research, Graduate School of Business, Indiana University, 1972.

Mehr, Robert L., and Emerson Cammack. *Principles of Insurance,* 5th ed. Homewood, Ill.: Richard D. Irwin, 1972.

Michelbacher, G. F., and Nestor Roos. *Multiple-Line Insurers: Their Nature and Operation,* 2d ed. New York: McGraw-Hill Book Co., 1970.

Olson, Douglas. *Insolvencies Among Automobile Insurers.* Washington: U.S. Government Printing Office, 1970.

Orren, Karen. *Corporate Power and Social Change: The Politics of the Life Insurance Industry.* Baltimore: Johns Hopkins University Press, 1974.

The Regulation of Mass Marketing in Property and Liability Insurance. Milwaukee: National Association of Insurance Commissioners, 1971.

Periodicals

Belth, Joseph M. "Deceptive Sales Practices in the Life Insurance Business." *The Journal of Risk and Insurance,* Vol. XLI, No. 2 (June, 1974), pp. 305-326.

Fitzgerald, John F., Jr. "Demutualization of Mutual Property and Liability Insurers." *The Journal of Risk and Insurance,* Vol. XL, No. 4 (December, 1973), pp. 575-584.

Goddard, Russell P. "Property and Liability Insurance Companies as Investing Institutions." *The Annals of the Society of Chartered Property and Casualty Underwriters,* Vol. 24, No. 3 (September, 1971), pp. 197-216.

Greene, Mark R. "The Effect of Insurance Settlements in a Disaster." *The Journal of Risk and Insurance,* Vol. XXXI, No. 3 (September, 1964).

___________. "Research Problems for Insurance in the 1970's." *The Annals of the Society of Chartered Property and Casualty Underwriters* (December, 1971), pp. 293-312.

King, Alan L. "The Market Performance of Diversified and Non-Diversified Organizations Within the P-L Insurance Industry." *The Journal of Risk and Insurance,* Vol. XLII, No. 3 (September, 1975), pp. 471-493.

Kunreuther, Howard. "Disaster Insurance: A Tool for Hazard Mitigation." *The Journal of Risk and Insurance,* Vol. XLI, No. 2 (June, 1974), pp. 287-303.

Long, John D. "Mutual Property-Liability Insurers: Low Ceiling on Growth?" *The Insurance Law Journal* (August, 1970), pp. 472-491.

Main, Jeremy. "Why Nobody Likes the Insurers." *Fortune,* Vol. LXXXII, No. 6 (December, 1970), pp. 83-87.

Mehr, Robert I. "The Effect of Mass Merchandising on the Agency System." *The Journal of Risk and Insurance,* Vol. XXXVII, No. 1 (March, 1970), pp. 142-147.

Pritchett, S. Travis. "Operating Expenses of Life Insurers, 1961-70." *The Journal of Risk and Insurance,* Vol. XL, No. 2 (June, 1973), pp. 157-165.

Rodda, William H. "Insolvency Funds: A Desirable Security or a Needless Expense for the Policyholder?" *Business Insurance* (February 2, 1970), pp. 21-22.

Stone, James M. "A Theory of Capacity and the Insurance of Catastrophe Risks (Part I)." *The Journal of Risk and Insurance,* Vol. XL, No. 2 (June, 1973), pp. 231-243.

———. "A Theory of Capacity and the Insurance of Catastrophe Risks (Part II). *The Journal of Risk and Insurance,* Vol. XL, No. 3 (September, 1973), pp. 339-355.

Trieschmann, James S., K. Roscoe Davis, and E. J. Leverett, Jr. "A Probabilistic Valuation Model for a Property-Liability Insurance Agency." *The Journal of Risk and Insurance,* Vol. XLII, No. 2 (June, 1975), pp. 289-302.

———, and George E. Pinches. "A Multivariate Model for Predicting Financially Distressed P-L Insurers." *The Journal of Risk and Insurance,* Vol. XL, No. 3 (September, 1973), pp. 327-338.

Webb, Bernard L. "The Framework for Insurance Marketing Changes." *The Journal of Risk and Insurance,* Vol. XLI, No. 2 (June, 1974), pp. 239-248.

Winklevoss, Howard E., and Robert A. Zelten. "An Empirical Analysis of Mutual Life Insurance Company Surplus." *The Journal of Risk and Insurance,* Vol. XL, No. 3 (September, 1973), pp. 403-425.

PART III

FUNDAMENTALS OF INSURANCE CONTRACTS

Books

Freedman, Warren. *Richards on the Law of Insurance.* New York: Baker Voorhis and Company, 1952.

Greider, Janice E., and William T. Beadles, *Law and the Life Insurance Contract,* 3d ed. Homewood, Ill.: Richard D. Irwin, Inc., 1974.

Head, George L. *Insurance to Value.* Homewood, Ill.: Richard D. Irwin, Inc., 1971.

Horn, Harold M., and D. Bruce Mansfield. *The Life Insurance Contract.* New York: Life Office Management Association, 1948.

Horn, Ronald C. *Subrogation in Insurance Theory and Practice.* Homewood, Ill.: Richard D. Irwin, Inc., 1964.

Keeton, Robert E. *Insurance Law: Basic Text.* St. Paul: West Publishing Company, 1971.

McGill, Dan M. *Legal Aspects of Life Insurance.* Homewood, Ill.: Richard D. Irwin, Inc., 1959.

Patterson, Edwin W. *Essentials of Insurance Law.* New York: McGraw-Hill Book Company, Inc., 1957.

Schwartzschild, Stuart. *Rights of Creditors in Life Insurance Policies.* Homewood, Ill.: Richard D. Irwin, Inc., 1963.

Vance, William R. *Handbook on the Law of Insurance,* 3d ed., edited by Buist M. Anderson. St. Paul: West Publishing Company, 1951.

Periodicals

Denenberg, Herbert S. "Insurance Regulation: The Search for Countervesting Powers and Consumer Protection." *The Insurance Law Journal,* No. 566 (May, 1969).

———. "The Legal Definition of Insurance." *The Journal of Insurance,* Vol. XXX, No. 3 (September, 1963).

Duesenberg, Richard W. "Recent Developments in Insurance Law." *The Insurance Law Journal,* No. 511 (August, 1965).

Gorman, John P. "Cancellation of the Fire Insurance Policy." *The Insurance Law Journal* (April, 1966), pp. 220-228.

Hinkle, B. David, "The Meaning of 'Actual Cash Value'." *The Insurance Law Journal,* Vol. 1967, No. 539 (December, 1967), pp. 711-723.

Jackson, Don M. "Wrestling with Strict Liability." *The Insurance Law Journal,* Vol. 1966, No. 518 (March, 1966), pp. 133-139.

Levit, Victor B. "The Legal Climate for Insurance in the 1970's." *The Insurance Law Journal,* No. 574 (November, 1970).

Salzman, Gary. "The Law of Insurable Interest in Property Insurance." *The Insurance Law Journal,* Vol. 1966, No. 522 (July, 1966), pp. 394-405.

Watson, Jack L. "The 'Other Insurance' Dilemma." *Illinois Bar Journal* (March, 1966), pp. 151-159.

PART IV

MAJOR PROPERTY AND LIABILITY INSURANCE CONTRACTS

Books

Bickelhaupt, David L. *General Insurance,* 9th ed. Homewood Ill.: Richard D. Irwin, Inc., 1974.

Black, Kenneth, Jr., and Robert S. Cline (eds.). *Property and Liability Insurance,* 2d. ed. Englewood Cliffs, N.J.: Prentice-Hall, Inc., 1976.

Elliott, Curtis M., and Emmett J. Vaughan. *Fundamentals of Risk and Insurance.* New York: John Wiley & Sons, Inc., 1972.

Existing and Proposed Auto Insurance Systems, revised Fall, 1971. New York: Insurance Information Institute, 1971.

Fire, Casualty, and Surety Bulletins, 3 volumes. Cincinnati: National Underwriter Company.

Gordis, Philip. *Property and Casualty Insurance.* Indianapolis: Rough Notes Company, annually.

Keeton, Robert E., and Jeffrey O'Connell. *Basic Protection for the Traffic Victim.* Boston: Little, Brown and Company, 1965.

Long, John D., and Davis W. Gregg (eds). *Property and Liability Insurance Handbook.* Homewood, Ill.: Richard D. Irwin, Inc., 1965.

Magee, John H., and Oscar Serbein. *Property and Liability Insurance,* 4th ed. Homewood, Ill.: Richard D. Irwin, Inc., 1967.

Mehr, Robert I., and Emerson Cammack. *Principles of Insurance,* 5th ed. Homewood, Ill.: Richard D. Irwin, Inc., 1972.

No-Fault Motor Vehicle Insurance. Hearings before the Subcommittee on Commerce and Finance of the Committee on Interstate and Foreign Commerce, House of Representatives, Ninety-Second Congress.

O'Connell, Jeffrey. *The Injury Industry and the Remedy of No-Fault Insurance.* Urbana, Ill.: University of Illinois Press, 1971.

————, and Rita James Simon. *Payment for Pain & Suffering: Who Wants What, When & Why?* Santa Monica: Insurors Press, Inc., 1972.

Rodda, William H. *Marine Insurance: Ocean and Inland,* 3d ed. Englewood Cliffs, N.J.: Prentice-Hall, Inc., 1970.

—————. *Property and Liability Insurance*. Englewood Cliffs, N. J.: Prentice-Hall, Inc., 1966.

Rokes, Willis Park. *No-Fault Insurance*. Santa Monica: Insurors Press, Inc.,1971.

Tuan, Kalin, ed. *Modern Insurance Theory and Education*. Orange, N.J.: Varsity Press, 1972.

Periodicals

Brainard, Calvin H. "Massachusetts Loss Experience Under No-Fault in 1971: Analysis and Implications." *The Journal of Risk and Insurance,* Vol. XL, No. 1 (March, 1973), pp. 95-101.

Bromwich, G. R. E. "Pollution and Insurance." *Risk Management* (April, 1971), pp. 14-19.

Keeton, Robert E. "Beyond Current Reforms in Automobile Reparations." *The Journal of Risk and Insurance,* Vol. XXXVII, No. 1 (March, 1970), pp. 31-37.

Kelly, Ambrose B. "Business Interruption Insurance." *Spectator,* Vol. XVI, No. 4 (July-August, 1969), pp. 32-36.

—————. "Insurance and Inflation." *Risk Management,* Vol. 17, No. 1 (January, 1970), pp. 32-40.

Knepper, William E. "Some Observations on the Personal Liability of Professionals, Insurance Agents, Corporate Directors, and Officers for Misconduct and Malpractice." *Insurance Counsel Journal,* Vol. 38, No. 1 (January, 1971), pp. 39-48.

Kunreuther, Howard. "Disaster Insurance: A Tool for Hazard Mitigation." *The Journal of Risk and Insurance,* Vol. XLI, No. 2 (June, 1974), pp. 287-303.

Levit, Victor B. "California Superior Court Holds Insurer Guilty of Bad Faith, But Denies Punitive Damages." *The Insurance Law Journal* (June, 1974), pp. 321-326.

Mehr, Robert I., and Gary W. Eldred. "Should the 'No-Fault' Concept be Applied to Automobile Property Damage?" *The Journal of Risk and Insurance,* Vol. XLII, No. 1 (March, 1975), pp. 17-33.

Mehr, Robert I., and Mack H. Shumate. "Primacy in Automobile Bodily Injury Coverage." *The Journal of Risk and Insurance,* Vol. XLII, No. 2 (June, 1975), pp. 201-225.

O'Connell, Jeffrey. "An Elective No-Fault Liability Statute." *The Insurance Law Journal,* No. 628 (May, 1975), pp. 261-293.

Pawlak, Ronald R. "Manufacturer's Design Liability: The Expanding Frontiers of the Law." *Risk Management,* Vol. XVII, No. 10 (December, 1970), pp. 8-13.

Rosenbloom, Jerry S., and J. Finley Lee. "Economic Consequences of Automobile Accident Injuries." *The Annals of the Society of Chartered Property and Casualty Underwriters,* Vol. 24, No. 2 (June, 1971), pp. 129-142.

Ross, H. Laurence. "Social Problems of the Automobile." *The Annals of the Society of Chartered Property and Casualty Underwriters,* Vol. 21, No. 3 (September, 1968), pp. 227-234.

Rottman, Dick L. "History of Perpetual Fire Insurance." *The Annals of the Society of Chartered Property and Casualty Underwriters,* Vol. XXIII, No. 1 (March, 1970), pp. 25-41.

Thompson, A. Edward. "Products Liability: Loss Control Key to Continued Coverage." *Risk Management* (February, 1971), pp. 13-19.

Wise, Paul S., and Senator Philip A. Hart. "The Case For/Against No-Fault Insurance." *Popular Science,* Vol. 198, No. 1 (January, 1971), pp. 56, 120.

PART V
LIFE AND HEALTH INSURANCE

Books

Belth, Joseph M. *Life Insurance: A Consumer's Handbook.* Bloomington, Ind.: Indiana University Press, 1973.

Bowe, William J. *Estate Planning and Taxation,* 3d ed. Homewood, Ill.: Richard D. Irwin, Inc., 1972.

Cummins, J. David. *Development of Life Insurance Surrender Values in the United States,* Monograph No. 2, S. S. Huebner Foundation for Insurance Education, Wharton School. Homewood, Ill.: Richard D. Irwin, Inc., 1973.

Dickerson, O. D. *Health Insurance,* 3d ed. Homewood, Ill.: Richard D. Irwin, Inc., 1968.

Eilers, Robert D., and Robert M. Crowe (eds.). *Group Insurance Handbook.* Homewood, Ill.: Dow Jones-Irwin, Inc., 1965.

___________, and Sue S. Moyerman (eds.). *National Health Insurance.* Homewood, Ill.: Richard D. Irwin, Inc., 1971.

Employee Benefits 1970. Washington: Chamber of Commerce of the United States, 1971.

Flitcraft Compend. Morristown: A. M. Best Co., annually.

Gagliardo, D. *American Social Insurance,* rev. ed. New York: Harper & Brothers, 1955.

Greene, Mark R. *The Role of Employee Benefit Structures in Manufacturing Industry.* Eugene, Ore.: University of Oregon, 1964.

Greenough, William C., and Francis P. King. *Benefit Plans in American Colleges.* New York: Columbia University Press, 1969.

Gregg, Davis W., and Vane B. Lucas (eds.). *Life and Health Insurance Handbook,* 3d ed. Homewood, Ill.: Dow Jones-Irwin, Inc., 1973.

Hamilton, James A., and Dorrance C. Bronson. *Pensions.* New York: McGraw-Hill Book Company, Inc., 1958.

Huebner, S. S., and Kenneth Black, Jr. (eds.). *Life Insurance,* 8th ed. New York: Appleton-Century-Crofts, Inc., 1973.

Life Insurance Fact Book. New York: Institute of Life Insurance, annually.

Marshall, Robert A. *Life Insurance Company Mergers and Consolidations.* Homewood, Ill.: Richard D. Irwin, Inc., 1972.

McGill, Dan M. *Fulfilling Pension Expectations.* Homewood, Ill.: Richard D. Irwin, Inc., 1962.

___________. *Fundamentals of Private Pensions,* 3d ed. Homewood, Ill.: Richard D. Irwin, Inc., 1975.

___________. *Guaranty Fund for Private Pension Obligations.* Homewood, Ill.: Richard D. Irwin, Inc., 1970.

___________. *Life Insurance,* rev. ed. Homewood, Ill.: Richard D. Irwin, Inc., 1967.

Mehr, Robert I. *Life Insurance: Theory and Practice.* Austin: Business Publications, Inc., 1970.

Melone, Joseph J., and E. T. Allen, Jr. *Pension Planning: Pensions, Profit Sharing, and Other Deferred Compensation Plans,* rev. ed. Homewood, Ill.: Richard D. Irwin, Inc., 1972.

Meyers, Robert J. *Social Security.* Homewood, Ill.: Richard D. Irwin, Inc., 1975.

Olson, Douglas G., and Howard E. Winklevoss (eds.). *Variable Life Insurance: Current Issues and Developments.* Philadelphia: University of Pennsylvania Insurance Department, 1971.

Reed, Louis S., Evelyn S. Myers, and Patricia L. Scheidemandel. *Health Insurance and Psychiatric Care: Utilization and Cost*. Washington: The American Psychiatric Association, 1972.

Shopper's Guide to Pennsylvania Automobile Insurance: Some Key Premium Comparisons for Beginning Your Search for the Best Automobile Insurance Bargain, rev. ed. Harrisburg, Pa.: Pennsylvania Insurance Department, 1972.

Social Security Administration. *Social Security Programs Throughout the World, 1973*, Research Report No. 44. Washington: U.S. Government Printing Office, 1973.

Source Book of Health Insurance Data. New York: Health Insurance Institute, annually.

Stephenson, Gilbert T., and Norman A. Wiggins. *Estates and Trusts*, 5th ed. New York: Appleton-Century-Crofts, 1973.

1975 Study of Industrial Retirement Plans, including Analysis of Complete Programs Recently Adopted or Revised. New York: Bankers Trust Company, 1975.

Turnbull, John G., Jr., *et al. Economic and Social Security*, 4th ed. New York: The Ronald Press Company, 1973.

White, Edwin H., and Herbert Chasman. *Business Insurance*, 4th Edition. Englewood Cliffs, N.J.: Prentice-Hall, Inc., 1974.

Periodicals

Anderson, Dan R., and John R. Nevin. "Determinants of Young Marrieds' Life Insurance Purchasing Behavior: An Empirical Investigation." *The Journal of Risk and Insurance*, Vol. XLII, No. 3 (September, 1975), pp. 375-387.

Antliff, John C., and William C. Freund. "Some Basic Research into Historical Results Under Pension Plans with Benefits Based on Common Stock Performance." *The Journal of Finance*, Vol. 22, No. 2 (May, 1967).

Belth, Joseph M. "Insurance Markets in a Decade of 'Naderism'." *Best's Review*, Vol. 71, No. 7 (November, 1970), pp. 30ff.

———. "A Note on the Interest Adjusted Method." *The Journal of the American Society of Chartered Underwriters*, Vol. 25, No. 4 (October, 1971), pp. 74-75.

———. "Price Competition in Life Insurance." *The Journal of Risk and Insurance*, Vol. XXXIII, No. 3 (September, 1966).

Bragg, John M. "Life Insurance with Guaranteed Purchasing Power." *Best's Review*, Vol. 72, No. 4 (August, 1971), pp. 10-12.

Chastain, James J. "The A, B, C's of Life Insurance Rate and Reserve Computation." *The Journal of Insurance*, Vol. XXVII, No. 4 (December, 1960).

Davis, Harry E. "Negotiated Retirement Plans." *Monthly Labor Review*, Vol. LXXXXII, No. 5 (May, 1969), pp. 11-15.

Gordon, T. J., and R. E. LeBelu. "Employee Benefits, 1970-1985." *Harvard Business Review*, Vol. 48, No. 1 (January-February, 1970), pp. 93-107.

Greene, Mark R. "Federal Income Taxes and the Variable Annuitant." *The Journal of Insurance*, Vol. XXV, No. 4 (February, 1959).

———. "Fringe Benefits or Salary?" *Journal of Marketing*. Vol. 27, No. 4 (October, 1963), pp. 63-68.

———. "Life Insurance Buying in Inflation." Proceedings of the 18th Annual Meeting, *Journal of the American Association of University Teachers of Insurance*. Vol. XXI, No. 1 (March, 1954).

———. "Should Variable Policy Loan Interest Rates Be Adopted?" *The Journal of Risk and Insurance*, Vol. XL, No. 4 (December, 1973), pp. 585-597.

———. "Inflation and Life Insurance." No. 4 in the Ben F. Hadley Distinguished Manuscript Series (1974), 34 pages.

__________, and J. Paul Copeland. "Factors in Selecting Tax-Deferred Annuities." *C.L.U. Journal,* Vol. XXIX, No. 4 (October, 1975), pp. 34-46.

Hamwi, Iskandar S. "Cash Value: An Examination of Company Practices." *The Journal of Risk and Insurance,* Vol. XLII, No. 1 (March, 1975), pp. 35-49.

Heffner, Robert W. "Tomorrow's Fringe Benefits; Predictions for 1980, a 30-hour Week, Two-month Vacations, 15 Paid Holidays." *Best's Fire and Casualty News,* (June, 1966), pp. 44-50.

Hickey, Joseph A. "A Report on State Unemployment Insurance Laws." *Monthly Labor Review,* Vol. 95, No. 1 (January, 1972), pp. 40-50.

Hutchins, Robert C., and Charles E. Quenneville. "Rate of Return Versus Interest-Adjusted Cost." *The Journal of Risk and Insurance,* Vol. XLII, No. 1 (March, 1975), pp. 69-79.

Kensicki, Peter R. "Consumer Valuation of Life Insurance—A Capital Budgeting Approach." *The Journal of Risk and Insurance,* Vol. XLI, No. 4 (December, 1974), pp. 655-665.

Kittner, Dorothy R. "Changes in Health and Insurance Plans for Salaried Employees." *Monthly Labor Review,* Vol. LXXXXII, No. 2 (February, 1970), pp. 32-39.

Lin, Cheyeh. "Investment Experience and the Price of Life Insurance." *The Journal of Risk and Insurance,* Vol. XLII, No. 3 (September, 1975), pp. 461-469.

McLean, Ephriam R. "An Appraisal of Computerized Life Insurance Estate Planning." *The Journal of Risk and Insurance,* Vol. XLI, No. 3 (September, 1974), pp. 497-509.

Mehr, Robert I. "The Concept of the Level-Premium Whole Life Insurance Policy—Reexamined." *The Journal of Risk and Insurance,* Vol. XLII, No. 3 (September, 1975), pp. 419-431.

__________, and Seev Neumann. "Life and Health Insurance—The Year 2000." *The Journal of the American Society of Chartered Life Underwriters,* Vol. 25, No. 4 (October, 1971).

Nelli, Humbert O. "A New Look at the History of Personal Insurance." *The Journal of the American Society of Chartered Life Underwriters,* Vol. 23, No. 3 (July, 1969), pp. 45-57.

Olson, Douglas G., and Howard E. Winklevoss. "Equity Based Variable Life Insurance." *Wharton Quarterly,* (Summer, 1971), pp. 26-40.

Papier, William. "What's Wrong with Unemployment Insurance?" *The Journal of Risk and Insurance,* Vol. XXXVII, No. 1 (March, 1970), pp. 63-74.

Pettengill, Daniel W. "Writing the Prescription for Health Care." *Harvard Business Review,* Vol. XLIX, No. 6 (November-December, 1971), pp. 37-43.

Severiens, Jacobus T., and Mark R. Greene. "Variable Life Insurance in The Netherlands—A Case Study." *The Journal of Risk and Insurance,* Vol. XLI, No. 3 (September, 1974), pp. 511-521.

Wood, Glenn L., and J. Finley Lee. "Mutual Funds and Variable Annuities: Consumer Purchase Decisions." *The Journal of the American Society of Chartered Life Underwriters.* Vol. 23, No. 1 (January, 1969), pp. 8-15.

PART VI
GOVERNMENT REGULATION OF INSURANCE

Books

Blair, Franklin B. *Interpreting Life Insurance Company Annual Reports.* Bryn Mawr, Pa.: American College of Life Underwriters, 1960.

Center, Charles C., and Richard M. Heins (eds.). *Insurance and Government*. New York: McGraw-Hill Book Company, Inc., 1962.

Cooper, Robert W. *Investment Return and Property-Liability Insurance Ratemaking*. Homewood, Ill.: Richard D. Irwin, Inc., 1974.

Denney, Richard L., *et. al. Federal Income Taxation of Insurance Companies*, 2d ed. New York: The Ronald Press Company, 1966.

Greene, Mark R. *Government and Private Insurance*. Des Plaines, Ill.: National Association of Independent Insurers, 1975.

Hensley, Roy J. *Competition, Regulation, and the Public Interest in Non-life Insurance*. Berkeley: University of California Press, 1962.

Kimball, Spencer L., and Herbert S. Denenberg. *Insurance, Government, and Social Policy*. Homewood, Ill.: Richard D. Irwin, Inc., 1973.

Loss and Expense Ratios–Insurance Expense Exhibits. Albany: New York Insurance Department, annually.

Nelson, Daniel. *Unemployment Insurance: The American Experience, 1915-1935*. Madison: University of Wisconsin Press, 1969.

O'Connell, Jeffery. *The Injury Industry and the Remedy of No-Fault Insurance*. Urbana, Ill.: University of Illinois Press, 1971.

Orren, Karen. *Corporate Power and Social Change: The Politics of the Life Insurance Industry*. Baltimore: The Johns Hopkins University Press, 1973.

Spiegelman, M. *Significant Mortality and Morbidity Trends in the United States Since 1900*. Bryn Mawr, Pa.: American College of Life Underwriters, 1962.

Stalson, J. O. *Marketing Life Insurance*. Homewood, Ill.: Richard D. Irwin, Inc., 1971.

Williams, C. A. *Price Discrimination in Property and Liability Insurance*. Studies in Economics and Business No. 19. Minneapolis: University of Minnesota Press, 1959.

Periodicals

Allen, Tom C., and Richard M. Duvall. "Determinants of Property Loss Ratios in the Retail Industry." *The Journal of Risk and Insurance*, Vol. XL, No. 2 (June, 1973), pp. 181-190.

Anderson, Dan R. "The National Flood Insurance Program—Problems and Potential." *The Journal of Risk and Insurance*, Vol. XLI, No. 4 (December, 1974), pp. 579-599.

Anderson, John J. "Alternative Methods of Accounting for Equity Investments in the Stock P-L Insurance Industry." *The Journal of Risk and Insurance*, Vol. XLII, No. 2 (June, 1975), pp. 263-275.

Brainard, Calvin H. "Economic and Actuarial Explanations of Life Insurance Premium Computations." *The Journal of Insurance*, Vol. XXX, No. 2 (June, 1963).

————, and John F. Fitzgerald. "First-Year Cost Results Under No-Fault Automobile Insurance: A Comparison of the Florida and Massachusetts Experience." *The Journal of Risk and Insurance*, Vol. XLI, No. 1 (March, 1974), pp. 25-39.

Cummins, J. David, and Douglas G. Olson. "An Analysis of the Black Lung Compensation Program." *The Journal of Risk and Insurance*, Vol. XLI, No. 4 (December, 1974), pp. 633-653.

DuBois, Frederic M. "Where Do We Go From Here with F.A.I.R. Plans?" *The Annals of the Society of Chartered Property and Casualty Underwriters*, Vol. 24, No. 4 (December, 1971), pp. 355-369.

Fitzgerald, John F., Jr. "Demutualization of Mutual Property and Liability Insurers." *The Journal of Risk and Insurance*, Vol. XL, No. 4 (December, 1973), pp. 575-584.

Forbes, Stephen W. "Rates of Return in the Non-Life Insurance Industry." *The Journal of Risk and Insurance*, Vol. XXXVIII, No. 3 (September, 1971), pp. 409-422.

Goodman, Oscar. "Misstatement of Age Clause in Life Insurance Contracts." *The Journal of Risk and Insurance,* Vol. XXXVIII, No. 1 (March, 1971), pp. 147-152.

"Insurance: The Mutuals vs. the Stock Companies." *Forbes,* Vol. CIX, No. 3 (February 1, 1972), pp. 41-42.

Kahane, Yehuda, and Haim Levy. "Regulation in the Insurance Industry: Determination of Premiums in Automobile Insurance." *The Journal of Risk and Insurance,* Vol. XLII, No. 1 (March, 1975), pp. 117-132.

Kamerschen, David R. "Are Conglomerate Insurance Mergers *Sui Generis*?" *The Journal of Risk and Insurance,* Vol. XLI, No. 3 (September, 1974), pp. 463-482.

Kelly, A. B. "How Factory Mutual Rates are Established." *National Insurance Buyer,* (November, 1957).

Kleiler, Frank M. "Regulation of Private Pension Plans in Europe." *Monthly Labor Review,* Vol. LXXXXIV, No. 4 (April, 1971), pp. 33-39.

Lange, J. T."General Insurance Liability Ratemaking." *Proceedings of the Casualty Actuarial Society* (May, 1966), pp. 26-60.

Leverett, E. J., Jr. "Paid-in Surplus and Capital Requirements of a New Life Insurance Company." *The Journal of Risk and Insurance,* Vol. XXXVIII, No. 1 (March, 1971), pp. 15-28.

McCormick, Roy C. "Federal Crime Insurance Examined." *Rough Notes,* Vol. CXIV, No. 8 (August, 1971), pp. 18, 60-64.

Pinches, George E., and James S. Trieschmann. "The Efficiency of Alternative Models for Solvency Surveillance in the Insurance Industry." *The Journal of Risk and Insurance,* Vol. XLI, No. 4 (December, 1974), pp. 563-577.

Stern, H. R. "The McCarran Act 20 Years After." *The Insurance Law Journal* (October, 1966), pp. 605-614.

Stern, Philipp K. "Current Rate Making Procedures for Automobile Liability Insurance." *Proceedings of the Casualty Actuarial Society,* Vols. XLIII, LXXIX, and LXXX (1956).

Stewart, Richard E. "Ritual and Reality in Insurance Regulation." *The Insurance Law Journal,* No. 553 (February, 1969), pp. 85-92.

Trieschmann, James S. "Property-Liability Profits: A Comparative Study." *The Journal of Risk and Insurance,* Vol. XXXVIII, No. 3 (September, 1971), pp. 437-453.

Williams, C. Arthur, Jr. "Insurance Rate Regulation—A New Era?" *The Annals of the Society of Chartered Property and Casualty Underwriters,* Vol. 22, No. 3 (September, 1969), pp. 203-219.

___________, and Andrew F. Whitman. "Open Competition Rating Laws and Price Competition." *The Journal of Risk and Insurance,* Vol. XL, No. 4 (December, 1973), pp. 483-496.

Witt, Robert Charles. "Pricing Problems in Automobile Insurance: An Economic Analysis." *The Journal of Risk and Insurance,* Vol. XL, No. 1 (March, 1973), pp. 75-93.

___________. "Credibility Standards and Pricing in Automobile Insurance." *The Journal of Risk and Insurance,* Vol. XLI, No. 3 (September, 1974), pp. 375-396.

PART VII
INTERNATIONAL INSURANCE

Books

AFIA Guide Europe. New York: American Foreign Insurance Association, 1968.

AFIA Guide Latin America. New York: American Foreign Insurance Association, 1968.

AFIA Guide Pacific. New York: American Foreign Insurance Association, 1967.

Baglini, Norman A. *Risk Management in International Corporations*. New York: The Risk Studies Foundation, 1976.

Clayton, G. *British Insurance*. London: Elek Books Ltd., 1971.

Supervision of Private Insurance in Europe. Paris, France: Organization for Economic Co-operation and Development Publications, 1963.

Weese, Samuel H. *Non-Admitted Insurance in the United States*. Homewood, Ill.: Richard D. Irwin, Inc., 1971.

Periodicals

Aldrich, C. Frank. "The World Insurance Industry as a Single Market." *Best's Review*, Vol. LXXI, No. 2 (June-July, 1970).

Boylan, Francis X. "Fundamentals of Export Credit Insurance." *Risk Management*, Vol. 18, No. 8 (October, 1971), pp. 38-41.

Carter, R. L., and N. A. Doherty. "Tariff Control & The Public Interest: Report on British Fire Insurance." *The Journal of Risk and Insurance*, Vol. XLI, No. 3 (September, 1974), pp. 483-495.

"The Ceylon Oil Expropriations." *American Journal of International Law* (April, 1964), pp. 445-449.

Davis, James S. "Protection for Overseas Construction Risks." *The Annals of the Society of Chartered Property and Casualty Underwriters*, Vol. 23, No. 3 (September, 1970), pp. 223-234.

Dickinson, Gerard M. "Classification of Foreign Capital Flows of Insurance Companies." *The Journal of Risk and Insurance*, Vol. XXXVIII, No. 1 (March, 1971), pp. 93-98.

Greene, Mark R. "The Spanish Insurance Industry—An Analysis." *The Journal of Risk and Insurance*, Vol. XXXIX, No. 2 (June, 1972), pp. 221-243.

————. "Export Credit Insurance—Its Role in Expanding World Trade." *The Journal of Risk and Insurance*, Vol. XXXII, No. 2 (June, 1965), pp. 177-193.

————. "International Levels of Employee Benefit." *The Journal of Risk and Insurance*, Vol. XXXV, No. 1 (March, 1968), pp. 1-15.

————. "The Insurance Environment in Foreign Countries." *Risk Management* (February, 1973), pp. 17-20.

————. "The Management of Political Risk." *Best's Review (Property/Liability Insurance Edition)*, Vol. 75, No. 3 (July, 1974), pp. 71-74.

————. "Insurance in Colombia." *Best's Review (Property/Liability Insurance Edition)*, Vol. 75, No. 12 (April, 1975), pp. 49-53.

Hanrahan, I. Michael. "International Levels of Employee Benefits—An Exploratory Study: Comment." *The Journal of Risk and Insurance*, Vol. XXXVIII, No. 1 (March, 1971), pp. 143-144.

Herrick, Kenneth W. "Auto Accidents and Alcohol in Great Britain—An Analysis." *The Journal of Risk and Insurance*, Vol. XL, No. 1 (March, 1973), pp. 55-73.

Hofflander, Alfred E. "International Insurance: Some Needs and Developments." *The Insurance Law Journal* (April, 1970), pp. 197-204.

Holmes, R. A. "British Columbia's Need for No Fault Automobile Insurance." *The Journal of Risk and Insurance*, Vol. XXXVII, No. 4 (December, 1970), pp. 609-619.

Jackson, E. S. "A Canadian View of Life Insurance." *The Journal of Risk and Insurance,* Vol. XXXVIII, No. 4 (December, 1971), pp. 515-520.

Keir, Jack C. "Nationalization of Insurance in Developing Countries." *Best's Review* (June, 1975), pp. 50-52.

Kelly, Ambrose B. "Inflation and Insurance." *Risk Management.* (January, 1970), pp. 32-40.

Kimball, S. L. "Comparative Study of American and European Insurance Regulation." *The Journal of Risk and Insurance,* Vol. XXXII, No. 2 (June, 1965), pp. 195-210.

Lusztig, Peter A. "Rate Control and Government Competition in Australian Non-Life Insurance: Comment." *The Journal of Risk and Insurance,* Vol. XXXVII, No. 2 (June, 1970), pp. 310-311.

Matheson, G. Lloyd. "No Fault Auto Insurance in Canada." *The Journal of Risk and Insurance,* Vol. XXXIX, No. 1 (March, 1972), pp. 27-29.

McClelland, R. B. "A Comparison of U.S. Business Interruption and British Profits Insurance." *The Annals of the Society of Chartered Property and Casualty Underwriters,* Vol. 20, No. 1 (March, 1967), pp. 19-32.

Meyers, R. J. "Voluntary Insurance in the U.S.S.R." *The Eastern Underwriter* (May 22, 1959).

Morone, James A. "The Argentinian Insurance Market." *The National Insurance Buyer* (September, 1965).

Munich Reinsurance Co. "The Influence of Inflation on Insurance." *Best's Review (Property/Liability Insurance Edition),* Vol. 72, No. 9 (January, 1972), pp. 14-16+.

Neave, J. A. S. "Current Problems of the International Reinsurance Market." *Best's Review (Property/Liability Insurance Edition),* Vol. 71 (April, 1971), pp. 18-20+.

"OPIC Insurance—$2.4 Billion of Political Risk Coverage." *Best's Review,* Vol. 72, No. 11 (March, 1972), pp. 24-30.

Owens, B. D. "Legal Aspects of International Life Insurance." *The Journal of Risk and Insurance,* Vol. XXXI, No. 2 (June, 1964).

Pfeffer, Irving. "Residual Risks in Europe." *The Journal of Risk and Insurance,* Vol. XLI, No. 1 (March, 1974), pp. 41-56.

Radcliffe, Julian. "Political Risk Insurance Market Expands." *Risk Management* (April, 1974), pp. 8-13.

Rodgers, William W. "Insurance in All Languages." *Columbia Journal of World Business,* Vol. VII, No. 5 (September/October, 1972), p. 87.

Rodgers, Paul P. "The Structure of Soviet Insurance." *The Journal of Risk and Insurance,* Vol. XXXII, No. 2 (June, 1965).

__________. "The 1967 Insurance Law of Yugoslavia." *The Journal of Risk and Insurance,* Vol. XXXVII, No. 2 (June, 1970), pp. 326-329.

Root, Franklin. "The Expropriation Experience of 38 American Companies." *Business Horizons* (April, 1968), pp. 69-79.

Shulman, R. B. "Are Foreign Exchange Risks Measurable." *Columbia Journal of World Business* (May/June, 1970), p. 55.

Terrell, Harry. "The New British Investment Guarantee Scheme." *The Banker* (1971), p. 376.

Vaughan, Emmett J. "Social Insurance in Yugoslavia." *The Journal of Risk and Insurance,* Vol. XXXII, No. 3 (September, 1965), pp. 385-393.

Yuan, Tsungwei. "A Review Article: A Brief on Chinese Insurance Literature." *The Journal of Risk and Insurance,* Vol. XXXV, No. 4 (December, 1968), pp. 639-640.

INDEX

A

B

C

D

E

I

N

O

P

Q

R

S

T

U

V

W

Y